The Gospel
According to Matthew

By
G. CAMPBELL MORGAN, D.D.

Fleming H. Revell Company
OLD TAPPAN, NEW JERSEY

Printed in the United States of America

Foreword

AS in the case of my volume on *The Acts of the Apostles,* and that on *Mark,* in this volume we have stenographically reported sermons. They consist of seventy-three such.

From this method they suffer, and gain. They suffer the loss of literary finish possible to the Writer; but they gain from the very roughness and directness associated with the word extemporaneously uttered, as to the form of sentences.

They proceed, from first to last, on the assumption that it was the intention of the writer of this Gospel to set forth the Person of our Lord in relation to His Kingly office.

From the mystic account of His advent in human history, through the record of the authority of His ethical enunciation, the mercifulness of His method, the majesty of His Death, and the glory of His Resurrection, to the ringing claim of "all authority," and clarion command to "disciple the nations," we are ever in the presence of the King.

With happy memories of the days when they were prepared and spoken, and profound gratitude to God for His acceptance of them then, manifested in the blessing they were to many, I now commit them to the wider ministry of the printed page, praying that they may still be helpful, in some measure, in showing forth some of the glories of Him Who was attested of God in the words, "This is My beloved Son, in Whom I am well pleased;" and thus the Son, to Whom He gives the nations for His inheritance, and the uttermost parts of the earth for His possession.

G. C. M.

Glendale,
California.

THE GOSPEL
ACCORDING TO MATTHEW

MATTHEW I. 1-17

THE first verse of this chapter gives the title to the section under consideration; while the last verse of that section summarizes its content. The first is undoubtedly the title of the genealogy of Jesus as it appeared in the Jewish records. The last is Matthew's summary of the content thereof.

It is not my purpose to dwell at any length upon the matter of the difference between this genealogy and that which we have in the gospel according to Luke. There are, however, one or two matters that it may be well for us to note by way of introduction.

The first is that to which I have already twice drawn attention. The opening words, "The book of the generation of Jesus Christ, the son of David, the son of Abraham," do not constitute the title to the gospel according to Matthew, but the title of the genealogy of Jesus Christ as it is here given. We shall take it for granted that this genealogy was taken from the legal records by Matthew in order to preface the gospel in which he was about to present the One Whom he had come to know as the long-looked-for Messiah-King of his people.

My personal conviction is that this genealogy does not appear in our gospel exactly as Matthew found it in the records. His concluding summary, in which he declares that these generations from Abraham to the Messiah fall into three cycles of fourteen, makes this improbable for the simple reason that there are conspicuous omissions. In the eighth verse between Joram and Uzziah the names of Ahaziah, Joash, and Amaziah are omitted, and in verse eleven Jehoiakim is omitted between Josiah and Jehoniah. I am inclined to believe that the former omissions were deliberately made for spiritual reasons.

It is noticeable that the evangelist says, "All the generations from Abraham unto David are fourteen generations," and in that section there are no omissions. But with regard to the subsequent divisions he says, "from David unto the carrying away to Babylon fourteen generations, and from the carrying away to Babylon unto the Christ fourteen generations;" not that they are all, but that he has named those chosen to complete the chain. When it is remembered that those omitted first were the immediate descendants of the daughter of Ahab and Jezebel, we may have a clue to the principle of Matthew's selection. In all likelihood the omission of Jehoiakim was due to the work of a copyist, because that omission makes it necessary, in order to the three fourteens, to use the name Jechoniah at the end of the second and at the beginning of the third.

It should finally be noticed that this genealogy does not say that Jesus was the son of Joseph. It is the genealogy of Jesus only because of His mother's marriage with Joseph, and in the Jewish records He appears as one born to Mary whose husband was Joseph.

I propose to glance briefly at the genealogy itself as given in the paragraph commencing with the second verse and ending with the sixteenth verse; and then to examine more carefully the title as given in the first verse, and the summary as given in the seventeenth verse.

These intervening verses are interesting for several reasons. The first is that while they are entirely Jewish in outlook, they do nevertheless overleap the boundary of the Hebrew nation in a most remarkable way in the inclusion of Rahab; and they violate the prejudice of Judaism in the introduction of women. This violation is the more remarkable when we remember the character of the women whose names are introduced. The first is that of Tamar, a notorious sinner. The second is that of Rahab, a foreigner and a sinner. The third is that of Ruth, a foreigner, although received into the nation. The fourth is that of Bathsheba, through whose sin with David the shadow of shame for ever rests upon the royal line. The fifth is that of Mary the mother of the Lord. Thus in this genealogy, consciously or unconsciously, there are signs and portents of the grace which is being brought to all men through the coming King.

Another point of interest is that of the closing declaration of the genealogy proper; " Jacob begat Joseph, the husband of Mary, of whom was born Jesus," which is entirely out of harmony with the method of obtaining all through until that point. It marks a separation to be explained by the story of the birth of Jesus which immediately follows. It emphasises the fact that He was not the son of Joseph. Thus on the first page of the gospel Jesus is presented as connected with a race which nevertheless could not produce Him. He came into it, was of it; and yet was distinct from it. As we have said, the mystery is not explained here, but waits for the unveiling of the subsequent story.

Turning to the examination of the first verse, which constitutes the title of the genealogy, we are at once arrested by the fact that it emphasises a relation between Jesus Christ and the two outstanding men in Hebrew history, namely Abraham and David. In each case the relationship is distinctly affirmed to be that of sonship. He is the son of David, and the son of Abraham. Thus His connection with the Hebrew people is royal and racial. He is of the kingly line, and He is from the father and founder of the people. It may be as well at this point to draw attention to the fact that the genealogy given in Matthew corresponds exactly with that given in Luke between Abraham and David. The differences are found in the portion of the genealogy from David to Jesus. The genealogy in Luke gives His lineal descent through Mary, and He was through her, son of David. Matthew therefore speaks of Him as son of David, and not as son of any of those who are in the genealogy of Joseph subsequent to that point.

The remarkable fact of this title is that it speaks of Jesus as son of David and son of Abraham. Now the peculiar promise of God to each of these men, according to Old Testament history, was that of a son; and the immediate fulfilment in each case was in many senses disappointing. Therefore the son of Abraham, who came for the fulfilment of the ideals for which he stood in obedience to faith; and the son of David, who came for the fulfilment of the ideals for which he stood in obedience to faith; was neither Isaac, nor Solomon, but Jesus.

This fact is worthy of a somewhat closer examination in each case. Let us take them in the order of statement in the verse.

The son of David to whom he looked for the fulfilment of his purpose of the establishment of the kingdom around the temple of Jehovah was Solomon. His name, Solomon, the peaceful, suggested the principle of the kingdom. His greatest endowment was that of wisdom. His specific work was that of the building of the temple. His reign was characterised by peace and prosperity. Nevertheless the story of Solomon is one of disastrous failure. In spite of the gifts of wisdom from on high he lived a life of unutterable and appalling folly. Even though he built the temple, he so contradicted all that for which it stood as to make it a centre of form without power; and even though, through the goodness of God to him, for the sake of his father, the kingdom was maintained in peace and prosperity during the period of his life, he had sown it with seeds of disruption which bore harvest immediately after his death. Thus was David disappointed in his son after the flesh.

Jesus Christ, the Son of David after the flesh, but the Son of God as the resurrection finally attested, came for the overcoming of all the failure which characterised the life and reign of Solo mon. With an infinite wisdom He proceeded to the building of the temple which cannot be destroyed; and laid the foundation for the establishment of the Kingdom in peace and prosperity from which all that offends will finally be cast forth.

The son of Abraham to whom he looked for the fulfilment of the promise of God, that from him there should spring a nation which should be the medium of blessing to all the nations, was Isaac. His name, Isaac, laughter, was to Abraham for evermore a witness of the merging of the human and the Divine, in that he was born because " Sarah received power to conceive seed when she was past age." Through him there was given to Abraham that seed which consisted of sons who, to his vision, were destined to carry forward the enterprises of God. The one influence which he exerted was that of the power, which he retained by faith, of blessing his sons after him.

Nevertheless the story of Isaac is one of disappointment, both in the weakness of his own character, and in the appalling failure of his sons through the long succession of the ages; and in the fact that they failed to enter into the true meaning and value of the blessing he pronounced. Thus was Abraham disappointed in his son after the flesh.

Jesus, the son of Abraham after the flesh, but in the mystery of His Person able to say, " Before Abraham was I am," came to realise and fulfil all the purpose which had failed through Isaac and his seed after him. He was the true son of Abraham both human and Divine, and there sprang from Him " so many as the stars of heaven in multitude, and as the sand, which is by the seashore, innumerable," to carry out the purposes of God.

Thus Jesus Christ, the Son of David and Son of Abraham, came in the fulness of the times to overcome the failure of Solomon the son of David and Isaac the son of Abraham; and to establish the throne and to perfect the nation.

In the summary with which the section ends three crises in the history of the people are mentioned. The first is that original movement connected with the call of Abraham; his obedience and consequent founding of the new race on the principle of faith. The second is connected with David, the king after God's own heart; whose appointment was nevertheless the outcome of national failure in that they clamoured for " a king like unto the nations." The last is that of the carrying away into captivity to Babylon of the people whose very existence in the economy of God was intended to be a force antagonistic to everything of which Babylon was the embodiment.

The three cycles culminate in Christ, and that fact suggests His relation to all. As we think of them and of Him, we are impressed by the threefold fact of relationship in each case which may be described as identity of principle, superiority of realisation, and correction of failure.

The relationship between Abraham and Christ is first that of identity of principle. The principle on which Abraham acted when he left Ur of the Chaldees, and throughout the whole of his life, in so far as it was in accord with the Divine will, was that of faith. The whole life and ministry of Jesus, on the plane of His humanity, was true to the selfsame principle; and as it has often been pointed out, the writer of the letter to the Hebrews gives Him precedence of Abraham in this matter, as he declares Him to be the Author, or Fileleader of faith.

The difference is at once seen in the absolute superiority of His realisation of this principle of faith. In the life of Abraham we have accounts of deflections issuing in disgrace, and almost in disaster. In the life of Jesus there was no doubt, and consequently no deviation from the path of obedience.

Moreover, and principally, the relation between Christ and Abraham is that of His correction of the failure. In His case the city of God is not only looked for, but built; the glory of God is not only sought, but manifested.

The relationship between David and Christ is first that of identity of principle in the matter of kingship. David's loyalty to Jehovah was the condition of his royalty. It was because of his fidelity to Him in circumstances of difficulty that he came at last to full and glorious crowning. In the case of Jesus all that was imperfectly foreshadowed in the experience of David was absolutely fulfilled. Loyalty to the will of God was the master passion of His life, and created the majesty and might of His regal authority.

The superiority of realisation is even more marked in this case than in the former. David's deflections from loyalty not only tarnished the escutcheon of his royalty, but limited the extent of his authority. The absolute abandonment of Jesus to the acceptable will of His Father created the lustre of His crown, and ensured that limitlessness of empire which enabled Him to say, " All authority hath been given unto Me in heaven and on earth."

The final and gracious fact of relationship between Christ and David is that of His assured establishment of the Kingdom, and the vindication of the glory of God.

The relationship between the carrying away into captivity and Christ is again that of identity of principle. These people passed under the yoke of a nation full of pride and rebellious against God's government. Christ was born under the yoke of Rome, amid His people, in days when their independence was lost. The very surroundings of His birth were created by the fact that His mother with Joseph her husband were travelling in obedience to the edict of the Emperor that all the world should be enrolled.

His infinite superiority is seen in the quiet dignity of His submission through all the days of His earthly life, as He rendered to Cæsar the things that belonged to Cæsar; and in that fine triumph over the outward yoke of Cæsar, as He rendered to God the things that belong unto God.

The final fact of relationship between Christ and the captivity is that of His breaking of all the bonds resulting from sin, and leading the exodus of all such as trust Him.

Thus in this genealogical paragraph humanity's aspirations and incompetencies are represented in these generations; and aspirations and incompetencies alike look wistfully to Him. The founder and the king look to Him as Son for the fulfilment of purpose. Faith, which by comparison with sight has seemed feeble through the passing of the centuries, waits His vindication. Government which has perpetually failed waits His administration. Captivity which has sighed and sobbed in its agony waits His emancipation. What can He do? We will pursue the story presently, and in the meantime crown Him in hope;

" Hail to the Lord's anointed:
  Great David's greater Son!
Hail, in the time appointed,
  His reign on earth begun!
He comes to break oppression,
  To set the captive free,
To take away transgression,
  And rule in equity."

MATTHEW I. 18-23

WE have considered the genealogy of Jesus as recorded in the first seventeen verses. Now we commence the study of the story of His birth.

Dr. Horton once ended a singularly beautiful sermon on the Virgin Birth of Jesus in words which are well worth reading as a preliminary to this study. After treating the story as constituting one of the idylls of the infancy and life —dealing with it in a most reverent way, as being one of those sweet and sacred things that never could have been known unless told by Joseph, or

Mary, or both—he said, " I believe, my dear friends, that you can do a great service to-day; you can relieve the minds and consciences of thousands of people if you can simply pass on the thought: I believe in the Divinity of Jesus Christ my Lord, on the grounds that St. Paul and St. John have given; and then, I believe in the stories of the infancy because I believe in the Divinity of the Lord, and I have found in them a beautiful illustration of what Christ meant when He said, ' I am from above; I am not of this world.' "

10

That position one is fully prepared to accept. Our belief in the truth of this sacred story is based upon the facts of the Person and purposes of Jesus as unfolded in the writings of the Apostles, which writings are in turn demonstrated true in our own personal experience.

The very position indicated makes it impossible to agree with Dr. Horton in a statement immediately preceding this. Speaking of the Virgin Birth of Jesus, he said, " Never give anyone the impression that the faith of Jesus depends upon it, or that a man cannot believe in our Lord because he does not believe in the idylls of the infancy."

While recognizing the spirit of patience and toleration which such a statement breathes, it is impossible to accept it as logical. If belief in the teaching of Paul and John necessarily leads to belief in the truth of this story of Matthew, then it necessarily follows that to reject this story of Matthew is finally to reject the teaching of Paul and John, and so not to believe in the Deity of the Lord Jesus Christ.

All our future studies will be from the standpoint of belief in the Deity of Jesus as taught in the subsequent writings of the New Testament, and therefore as accepting this story, as presenting in idyllic form, the sublime, mysterious, and infinite truth—" that which is conceived in her is of the Holy Spirit."

From this whole idyll we select the words which chronicle two prophecies. The angelic prophecy is in the words—

" She shall bring forth a Son; and thou shalt call His name JESUS; for it is He that shall save His people from their sins."

The angel's quotation is from the prophecy of Isaiah, and follows immediately.

" Now all this is come to pass, that it might be fulfilled which was spoken by the Lord through the prophet, saying,
" Behold, the Virgin shall be with child, and shall bring forth a son,
" And they shall call his name Immanuel."

Eliminating the words which speak of the method of His coming—words which are so severely plain as to demand simple acceptance or equally simple rejection—because we accept them, for the reasons already stated, we shall take the two prophetic words concerning Him—

" Thou shalt call His name Jesus, for it is He that shall save His people from their sins,"

and,

" They shall call His name Immanuel, which is, being interpreted, God with us."

The second is a prophecy of the past, expressing the hope of the people. The past looked on, and looked up, and looked out, and sighed for " Immanuel —God with us." The first is the prophecy which tells us how that hope has been realised. The angel declares that all that longing is to be answered, for Jesus is to be born, Who is to save His people from their sins. Observe carefully the angelic message. He is to fulfil the prophecy of the past, " Immanuel—God with us."

While in the text the prophecies are placed in the order, first of realisation, and then of the statement of the hope, in this study we will take them in the other order, which is that of their real occurrence in the Divine Library.

We will consider, then, first, the hope —" They shall call His name Immanuel, which is, being interpreted, God with us;" and secondly, the realisation —" Thou shalt call His name Jesus, for it is He that shall save His people from their sins."

I. This old-time prophecy quoted by the angel, is from the seventh chapter of the prophecy of Isaiah. Look very carefully at its setting therein. It reads thus : " Therefore the Lord Himself will give you a sign; behold, a virgin shall conceive, and bear a son, and shall call His name Immanuel. Butter and honey shall He eat, when He knoweth to refuse the evil, and choose the good. For before the Child shall know to refuse the evil, and choose the good, the land whose two kings thou abhorrest shall be forsaken." (Ch. vii. 14-16.)

To take the quotation in this way is at once to be brought into the presence of something that increasingly seems to have, as the history is examined, no connection with this great subject of the Birth of Jesus. If the whole chapter be read, it will be found that the prophet Isaiah was talking to king Ahaz who was in peril, because Rezin, king of Syria, and Pekah, king of Israel, were coming up against Jerusalem. The prophet told Ahaz to be quiet; that there need be no panic in his heart.

Comparing the prophecy of Isaiah with the historical books, we discover that Ahaz was bent upon seeking aid from some other power. The prophet appealed to him to do nothing of the kind. and said. "Ask thee a sign of Jehovah thy God; ask it either in the depth, or in the height above." Ahaz replied that he would not ask a sign of God. Then said the prophet, "Therefore the Lord Himself will give thee a sign; behold the virgin shall conceive." "For before the child shall know to refuse the evil, and choose the good, the land whose two kings thou abhorrest shall be forsaken." He then proceeded to say that not only should the enemies be defeated, but that his own nation should be broken because of their lack of faith.

That prophecy was perhaps partially fulfilled in the birth of a child to Isaiah. In the story in the following chapter there was a child born who was named Maher-shalal-hash-baz, the meaning of which is, *the spoil speedeth, the prey hasteth.* For all local fulfilment this was the child referred to. The phrase, "Immanuel, God with us," had never occurred before. It occurs twice in Isaiah—once here, and once in the following chapter—and never again until the angel whispered it to Joseph, as chronicled in the story in Matthew. We can hardly understand the value of this in a study of the mere text. The whole context must be taken. For an interpretation of this prophecy chapters six to nine should be studied. The reference to Immanuel in chapter seven is incidental—not accidental—but preparatory, a gleam of light flashing on a purely local circumstance.

Let us epitomise chapters *six* to *nine* in order to see the setting.

In chapter six the death of Uzziah is recorded, also the story of that marvellous vision, as a result of which Isaiah was anointed and consecrated for his work.

Then, immediately we pass into changed circumstances. Ahaz was on the throne. The two kings Rezin and Pekah had come up against Jerusalem, and Ahaz wanted to call in aid from without. The prophet besought him not to do this, but to trust in God; and told him that a son should be given.

Notice what is here stated concerning Immanuel, for the prophecy merges into something larger than the local setting, as prophecies always do.

It is impossible to study the prophecies of the Old Testament without discovering that the prophets looked down the vista of years, and sometimes described something quite close at hand; then saw how its lines ran out into the coming ages; and omitting intervening ages, described the final issue. So here Isaiah's prophecy merges into something larger. He said that when Immanuel came He should eat "curds and honey," which signifies that He would come into the midst of circumstances of poverty and trouble.

Turn to chapter eight. A son was born to Isaiah, and the prophet announced the coming of Assyria in verse eight—"It shall sweep onward into Judah; it shall overflow and pass through; it shall reach even to the neck; and the stretching out of its wings shall fill the breadth of thy land, O Immanuel."

There was a person in the mind of the prophet, not yet focussed or revealed, as he spoke of the Virgin's Child, *Immanuel.* As he saw desolation coming to the land of the ancient people he spoke of it as the land of Immanuel. He evidently contemplated the incoming foes and spoke of them, and said, "Make an uproar, O ye peoples, and be broken in pieces. . . . Take counsel together, and it shall be brought to nought; speak the word, and it shall not stand; for *Immanuel,* God is with us."

The name is mentioned in the local prophecy, but thus it merges into a larger application when the prophet speaks of the land as "Immanuel's land." It includes a still larger outlook when the prophet declares that the foes coming against the land will be defeated because Immanuel will be with Israel.

The Messianic quality gradually grows as we read through the prophecy. Who is Immanuel? What is He to be? He is to be a sanctuary, and a rock of offence.

The Person Immanuel, incidentally mentioned in local connection, in chapter *seven*, blazes out into splendid light in the ninth chapter as the prophet wrote, "For unto us a Child is born, unto us a Son is given; and the government shall be upon His shoulder: and His name shall be called Wonderful Counsellor, Mighty God, Everlasting Father, Prince of Peace. Of the increase of His government and of peace there shall be no end, upon the throne of David, and upon His kingdom, to establish it."

Long centuries passed, and an angel came in a dream to a man and told him that the ultimate fulfilment of that prophecy was at hand. While the words of Isaiah had local applications, they had vaster values than such applications could contain. So the birth of Jesus was for the fulfilment of those vaster values that lay within the old-time prophecy. This hope must be interpreted in its local setting, and yet with that more spacious intention which it evidently contains.

From this examination of Isaiah's prophecy we make general deductions. Take the first and the last of these verses. The first (ch. vii. 14)—"A Virgin shall conceive, and bear a Son, and shall call His name Immanuel;" the last (ch. ix. 6)—"Unto us a Child is born, unto us a Son is given." This one great prophecy, beginning in such a simple circumstance and growing to such a sublime declaration, expressed the hope that God would presence Himself in actual human life through a human birth; that by some mysterious method which could not be expressed fully in human language, God would come and manifest Himself in a fourfold character.

The Bible may be divided around that description of manifestation. "Wonderful Counsellor;" so man first knew Him. "Mighty God;" so was He revealed through all the processes of the history of the Hebrew nation. "Everlasting Father;" so is He known in this dispensation. "Prince of Peace;" so shall He be revealed in the established Kingdom. All that was focussed in this Child.

Thus the immediate teaching of Isaiah's prophecy flashed its light forward. Immanuel shall come into the midst of His people's degradation and share it. Immanuel shall become a sanctuary and a stone of stumbling. Immanuel shall finally conquer all His enemies. At last the God-inspired hope of His people, expressed through prophecy, is declared to be realised in the birth of the Child of Mary. Joseph heard it and believed it. Mary heard it and sang the Magnificat. Early disciples heard it, and hearing it believed it, and proclaimed it. It is far easier for us to believe it than it was for any of these to do so, because we see the programme carried out into the centuries. As we read carefully and ponder it, we discover the whole programme of events, from the time Isaiah spoke until now, and beyond it, gathered round the word Immanuel. It was a great hope, and all that we see fulfilling the prophecy, is the result of His birth.

II. Now let us go back to the first prophecy, made directly by the angel to the man Joseph—"She shall bring forth a Son; and thou shalt call His name JESUS; for it is He that shall save His people from their sins."

Take the local setting. This story is beautiful in its simplicity. Joseph was a just man, "a righteous man." One hardly knows which word is best to use. We talk to-day of a just man; and we may think of a man hard and cold. We talk of a righteous man, and we have said, "Scarcely for a righteous man will one die; for peradventure for the good man some one would even dare to die." The good man is the man of the simple heart. A blunt translation would be Joseph was a straight man, a true man. Not that he was severe and harshly just; not coldly and cynically righteous; but he was a true man, the carpenter, the village builder.

Mary was his betrothed, and according to the old and beautiful Hebrew custom was bound to Joseph, the betrothal ceremony being as sacred as the marriage rite, after which the bridegroom took his bride home, with songs and rejoicing, and accompaniment of music. They were simple village folk of royal lineage, for when the angel spoke to Joseph he did not call Jesus his son, but Son of David. A straight strong man, and a simple, sweet maid.

There is no love story quite as sweet as the love story of mountain, hill and village. All the conventional arrangements of marriages are of hell. Love that is a dream, breaking in upon the soul, is always beautiful.

In the midst of that period of betrothal came that awe-inspiring and Holy Mystery, that sacred Mystery that we meditate in solemn silence; the Holy Mystery—the touch of God upon the simple life that made it for ever sublime. A thing not to be repeated; unique, and alone in the history of the race. The word of God is not void but powerful; and the maiden was possessed with the Holy Mystery.

Then the angel visitor came, and announced the name, " Thou shalt call His name Jesus." It was just an ordinary Jewish name about as common in Judæa as John is common amongst us. The name had not the significance that we understand to-day. Thank God it has gathered so much beauty and fragrance about it, that we can never dare call our children by that Name, and we are right. It was a beautiful, Jewish boy's name, a common name of the common people. But here, as everywhere in the great spiritual movement, God took hold of the commonplace to show that there was something infinitely more than the common. Jesus is a Greek form of the Hebrew Joshua, meaning Saviour. Other men had borne that name. Many a mother called her boy Joshua, in the hope that he would be a saviour, and break oppression, and set the people free. Now the angel said: Give that name to this Boy; " It is He that shall save His people from their sins." Take the human name, sweetest of them all, and give it to the Child of the Holy Mystery; the Child Who is not of Joseph, but of God. Tell His sweet

mother Mary to give Him the name Jesus. Moreover, the name means " Jehovah Salvation."

Mark the intention of it. They are " His people." Give Him the name as one of His people; calling Him by the ordinary name of His people; He is coming to identification with them. They are under a yoke, eating curds and honey; He is coming to eat curds and honey with them, as the prophet said. They are an oppressed and a devastated people; He is coming to identification with them; give Him the name signifying identification in all its deepest meaning. He is coming to suffer.

Then mark how the angel told heaven's secret in heaven's language. What the people thought they wanted was a Joshua who could reveal himself to this material Jerusalem as King, break the power of Rome, and set up an earthly Kingdom. The angel said the deeper trouble was not that of the Roman yoke; or that they had been beaten in battle; the trouble with them was that they were sinners—" He shall save His people from their sins." He will not come to battle with externalities, but to grip sin at its heart.

We look on as the angel speaks, and we see the Cross, the way by which " He shall save His people from their sins." The name is a prohecy. Joseph was commanded to give it to Jesus, and when Joseph gave it to Him, it was prophecy only—" Call His name Jesus, for it is He that shall save His people from their sins."

A generation passed away, three score years, and, at the close of the period, the story was recorded by the evangelists. At last the Apostle of the Gentiles told it also. Jesus, " existing in the form of God, counted not the being on an equality with God a thing to be grasped, but emptied Himself, taking the form of a Servant, being made in the likeness of men." He did not abhor the virgin's womb, but came in " the likeness of men." That is the apostles' story of the incarnation.

Now follow the story. " Becoming obedient even unto death, yea, the death of the Cross. Wherefore also God highly exalted Him, and gave unto

Him the name." What name is this? Joseph called Him Jesus because the angel said that He was to be named so. It was a prophecy; but it was fulfilled by His birth, His Cross, and His Resurrection.

God gave Him the name when He ascended. What name was it? "That in the name of *Jesus* every knee should bow." It was prophecy at His birth. It is an evangel on the Ascension morning. It was an indication of purpose when He was born. It is a declaration of accomplishment when He ascended on high.

> "Jesus, name of sweetness,
> Jesus, sound of love;
> Cheering exiles onward,
> To their rest above.

> "Jesus, oh the magic!
> Of the sweet love sound,
> How it thrills and trembles
> To creation's bound."

Never was there so much music as there is in that Name.

So came the King. Standing back to-day, and looking over the centuries, we see the merging of the Hope Immanuel, into realisation in Jesus. God is born of a virgin into human life. God is born into the midst of the degradation of man. God moves in this Man to the Throne of imperial and unending Government. God through this Man saves from sins, and establishes and upholds a Kingdom for ever. God performs all this in His own zeal through Jesus Christ.

> "O little town of Bethlehem,
> How still we see thee lie!
> Above thy deep and dreamless sleep
> The silent stars go by;
> Yet in thy dark streets shineth
> The everlasting Light;
> The hopes and fears of all the years
> Are met in thee to-night!

> "For Christ is born of Mary;
> And gathered all above,
> While mortals sleep the angels keep
> Their watch of wondering love;
> O morning stars! together
> Proclaim the holy birth,
> And praises sing to God the King,
> And peace to men on earth.

> "How silently, how silently
> The wondrous gift is given!
> So God imparts to human hearts
> The blessings of His heaven;
> No ear may hear His coming;
> But in this world of sin,
> Where meek souls will receive Him still,
> The dear Christ enters in.

> "O holy Child of Bethlehem,
> Descend to us, we pray;
> Cast out our sin, and enter in—
> Be born in us to-day!
> We hear the Christmas angels
> The great glad tidings tell—
> Oh, come to us, abide with us,
> Our Lord Emmanuel!"

MATTHEW II. 5, 15, 17, 23

THIS second chapter of the Gospel is at once historic and prophetic.

All the stories gather round four prophecies, and indicate the fulfilment of their deepest intention in history.

The first prophecy is from Micah: "But thou, Bethlehem Ephrathah, which art little to be among the thousands of Judah, out of thee shall One come forth unto Me that is to be Ruler in Israel."

The second is from Hosea: "I . . . called my Son out of Egypt."

The third is from Jeremiah: "A voice is heard in Ramah; lamentation, and bitter weeping, Rachel weeping for her children; she refuseth to be comforted for her children, because they are not."

The fourth is a truth uttered by many of the prophets in some form: "That He should be called a Nazarene."

Thus the chapter shows us that the coming of the King was the fulfilment of the prophecies of the past.

But that is only one of the values that we find in this chapter. It becomes in itself a prophecy not directly or intentionally, but incidentally, and yet by no means less powerfully. The whole chapter is a prophecy indicating the line of the new history revealing as in a flash the condition of things which will obtain around this King through all the period following His first advent, until His second advent. It is a microcosm of the Christian age, revealing principles that abide unto this hour.

First, then, we will consider the fulfilment of the prophecies of the past in the coming of Jesus; and secondly we will attempt to notice how a new prophecy is articulated in these stories.

Now the Bible student, finding in the New Testament a reference to the Old, must always take time to turn to such a reference. If we take these prophecies simply as they are uttered here, we cannot appreciate all their value. We must see them in their relation to context.

Turn first to the prophecy of Micah. In ch. v. 2, we find this prophecy which Matthew first quotes: "But thou, Bethlehem Ephrathah, which art little to be among the thousands of Judah, out of thee shall One come forth unto Me that is to be Ruler in Israel; Whose goings forth are from of old, from everlasting."

Let us consider the circumstances under which these words were uttered; and remember the great burden of this prophecy. It centres round the subject of authority. Every one of these old prophets had a burden and a message. They had many burdens, and yet in every single prophecy you will find that the many burdens are included in some one great conception of truth. Micah's is the message of authority. He thundered denunciations against the false rulers of his own time, and looking on down the centuries, saw the revelation of the coming of the true King. It is the voice of the prophet of order, of authority; the voice of the prophet who uttered the sob of the nation for the King, and fore-announced His coming.

Now we go back to our story. Jesus, Child of the virgin, is born, not at Nazareth, but at Bethlehem; born there through the decree of the Roman Emperor, under whose yoke the chosen people are serving at the moment; born there because His parents were going up to the taxing which had been ordered by the Imperial decree. For that reason the people of Nazareth were in Bethlehem, and out of Bethlehem Jesus comes—little Bethlehem, from which no one would look for a governor or a ruler, or expect a great man to arise. Thou art little to be among the thousands of Judah, but out of thee shall come a Governor, a Ruler. And Matthew, who by this time has learned the character of Jesus, takes liberties with the text of the old prophecy, and says more than Micah said; adds to the prophecy of Micah a tender touch which explains the character of the Ruler. Matthew has seen a little more deeply into the nature of the Ruler, and says that He shall be a Shepherd.

Now notice the actual facts surrounding that prophecy which was here fulfilled. Two forces are represented. Homage is rendered to the Ruler as to kings; hatred is manifested against Him. Standing in opposition and contrast to each other, are the Wise Men with their gold, frankincense, and myrrh; and Herod with the hatred of his lust and blood-thirstiness. So, as out of Bethlehem there comes the Ruler, the Shepherd, the Governor, the King, Who is yet to occupy the throne and hold the sceptre, there are those who welcome Him, and those who hate Him. There are those who take the long journey, following the guiding star, to lay at the feet of the new King— even though He came in lowliness in little Bethlehem—their gold and frankincense and myrrh; and there are those who are stupid, blind, and untouched, and moved wholly to destroy Him. So He comes; and concerning the coming of the King the prophet spoke long before. Homage and hatred are revealed side by side.

Pass to the second of these prophecies. Again we must go back to the prophecy of Hosea. In ch. xi. 1 are the words from which Matthew is quoting —"When Israel was a child, then I loved him, and called my son out of Egypt." It is perfectly evident that the reference here is to Israel as a nation.

Let us see the whole scope of this prophecy of Hosea. The message of Hosea is one concerning the decadence and failure of Israel to fulfil its first intention. The subject-matter of Hosea's

16

prophecy is that of spiritual harlotry as the worst of all sin. Hosea spoke of the condition of affairs, the worst that ever existed in the history of the nation, and he spoke to the people out of the strangest and most tragic of circumstances; experiences in his domestic life through which God had brought him into sympathy with Himself. When Hosea's heart was broken; when he had seen the fair ideal of his dreams wrecked before his eyes; when he had suffered that worst agony that ever comes to the human heart, the agony that follows upon the infidelity of husband or wife; then God said to him in effect: Now, Hosea, you know what I am feeling about Israel, for Israel has played the harlot against Me. Around that tragic training of the prophet lies the great message he bore.

There are three cycles in the prophecy of Hosea. In the first cycle, the prophet dealt with pollution and its cause; in the second cycle, with pollution and its punishment; at the beginning of the third cycle the prophet sang the love song of Jehovah.

Take the whole love song and analyse it, and there are again three great movements: first the prophet sang the song of the present condition of the people in the light of God's past love; then he sang the song of the present condition of the people in the light of God's present love; finally he sang the song of the present condition of the people in the light of the love of God which is yet to come.

In ch. xi. 1-4 God is singing, through the prophet, of the way He loved Israel as of old: " When Israel was a child, then I loved him, and called my son out of Egypt. . . ." Out of the midst of that love song, Matthew made a quotation, applying it to Jesus Christ; and at first it appears almost strange. " Out of Egypt did I call My Son." What does it mean? When God is telling the story of His love to Israel, He says to them: I loved you, and brought you out of Egypt. Egypt to you was a place of oppression, the place of slavery; but I brought you out. There was a great exodus, and I led the exodus out of Egypt. What has happened to these people? They have been scattered.

The message of Hosea was heard for a little, and then forgotten. The movement of degeneration went on until Jeremiah thundered denunciations against the nation; until finally the last prophet, Malachi, spoke. Then no prophetic voice sounded for four hundred years.

Now, four hundred years after the voice of prophecy and the last vision, a Child is born, the Child upon Whom all the hopes of God should rest, and therefore the hopes of men. The Child immediately shares the result of the sin of His own people. The man who occupied the throne when the Child was born was not an Israelite but an Edomite. Herod was outside the Covenant, and he was on the throne. The sin of Israel was that of making alliances with outside powers. By His coming, the true worship, and the worship of the false, are brought to light. Herod, the corrupt in his degradation, sat upon the throne, expressing in the very fact of his kingship everything that was unlike the purpose of God. He drove the chosen King down into Egypt, the place of oppression and sin. But the chosen King was not to stay in Egypt—" Out of Egypt did I call My Son."

It was a statement having historic value when Hosea sang it, but it had a prophetic value also; and now that at last the fruition of Israel, the fruitage of Hebraism, is to be found in the Person of this One, we see this historic Child, driven by the corruption of Israel into Egypt. As of old God loved Israel when a child, the child nation, and brought it out of Egypt; so His love centres still upon the King Who is yet to build a city and establish a nation; and as He also shall come out of Egypt, and coming out shall lead the exodus, so, with others following, a great ideal shall be realised. It is a simple historical fact. Herod was mad with rage, and the angel warned Joseph and Mary, and they took the little Child and hurried into Egypt. But heaven watched and saw all Israel driven into Egypt in the Person of that little Child. Matthew says that He was to come back again. He had only gone there that He might be afflicted in all their affliction, that He might enter into their sorrows. And as of old it was written, "Out of Egypt did I call my son," so again shall the King come out of Egypt; only a little Child, but leading a great and glorious exodus.

Take the next prophecy, Jeremiah xxxi. 15: "Thus saith the Lord; A voice is heard in Ramah; lamentation and bitter weeping, Rachel weeping for her children; she refuseth to be comforted for her children, because they are not." Such is the part of Jeremiah's prophecy that Matthew quoted. What were the circumstances under which Jeremiah uttered his prophecy? We will go over its content that we may see the connection between it and the birth of the King. The prophesying of Jeremiah was in some senses the most tragic of all. Jeremiah uttered the doom of a dying nation, and as every man of God does when he utters a doom, uttered it in tears. Presently Another shall come greater than Jeremiah; One Who will say everything in more fiery words; Who shall stand upon the slopes of Olivet, and look at the city smitten with the glow and glory of the setting sun; and as He sees it He shall say, "O Jerusalem, Jerusalem, that killeth the prophets, and stoneth them that are sent unto her! how often would I have gathered thy children together, even as a hen gathereth her chickens under her wings, and ye would not! Behold, your house is left unto you desolate." And as He shall say it, the very tears of God will rain down His cheeks. Jeremiah was the forerunner of Jesus, centuries before in this matter. It is a terrible and awful story, that of his prophesying, and suffering, and tears. But in Jeremiah, as in every other prophecy, there was a gleam of the glory of hope. How great were these Hebrew prophets—so cloudy, so rough, so stormy; but on every storm-cloud there is a rainbow, and the promise of deliverance. Reading the prophecy of Jeremiah, we find that, beginning with chapter xxx. and ending with chapter xxxiii., there are four chapters in the heart of the book, full of consolation, full of comfort, full of joy; and these are the chapters in which Jeremiah went a little higher than the cloud-land in which he spoke,

and saw the dawning of another morning far off, the coming of the Branch, and the Deliverer.

Now the prophecy that Matthew quotes is in the Book of consolation, but we seldom read it as though it had consolation in it. Rachel was weeping for her children and would not be comforted because they are not. Surely this should not be in the book of consolation! Let us read the context of the passage in Jeremiah. We have heard the plaintive wailing, the weeping of Rachel, the mother, because her children were gone; but "Thus saith Jehovah: Refrain thy voice from weeping and thine eyes from tears: for thy work shall be rewarded, saith Jehovah; and they shall come again from the land of the enemy. And there is hope for thy latter end, saith Jehovah; and thy children shall come again to their own border."

Now we begin to understand why this prophecy is so placed, when we see the sequence of it all. Yes, there was weeping when Jesus was driven out. How many suffered death in Bethlehem, we do not know; but there were mothers weeping, and Matthew heard of it, and said, It is the wail of the Mother Rachel, Mother of us all. Then, said Matthew, was fulfilled the old prophecy of Jeremiah. Matthew did not quote the entire prophecy, but only that part dealing with the weeping. Surely, though, he meant to refer us to the context of the quotation.

The first prophecy quoted in the second chapter mentioned the Coming of the King. The second prophecy concerned His leading of an Exodus from Egypt. The third prophecy was that Rachel should have her tears dried and her weeping should cease. The King has come, as Micah foretold; the Exodus has come, as Hosea prophesied; and Rachel's weeping shall cease, as Jeremiah foretold.

There is a triumphant march and a great sequence through this collection of the prophetic words, which leads us to the last of these prophecies, the general word—"That He should be called a Nazarene."

What is the meaning here of this

word Nazarene? It is a term of contempt. We must first get back into the historic setting, and understand the story as Matthew wrote it, and as the men of the day understood it. To have lived then, and to have said that a man was a Nazarene, would have been to use a term of contempt. Nothing decisive can be said as to the root origin or real meaning of the word Nazareth. There are two interpretations—one meaning *a sprout, a branch;* the other meaning *a protectress,* or *a guard.* Probably the name Nazareth came from the old Hebrew "Nêtzer," which means *a sprout,* and so was something to be held in contempt. A tree is cut off, hewn down and left. One morning the passer-by sees just one green sprout coming up from the stump; "nêtzer." It is of no use. The tree is gone. And so this little town, high up off the main roads at the foot of the mountains; along which the great merchants of Greece came; along which Roman legions marched, and the priests passed; was held in contempt. There were great movements down in the valley, but Nazareth was so much out of reach as never to be affected by them. And there is that thought in the quotation, "He shall be called a Nazarene;" a Man belonging to the city that is not worth naming; a Man off the highways of life, knowing nothing of the great movements of the world; a Nazarene.

In Isa. xi. 1 we read, "And there shall come forth a shoot out of the stock of Jesse, and a *Branch* out of his roots." It is the Hebrew word "nêtzer," the same word as that from which Nazareth is probably derived. The figure is that of a green tree cut down. Isaiah has foretold this cutting down, the destruction of the nation, of the country, of its city; but he says there shall come forth a shoot, just a little sprout that nobody will think to be of value; something that everyone will despise: and " The Spirit of Jehovah shall rest upon Him, the Spirit of wisdom and understanding, the Spirit of counsel and might, the Spirit of knowledge, and of the fear of Jehovah." The prophecy declared that when Messiah comes He shall be despised, counted nothing worth, just a branch, a sprout.

Go on through the prophecy and you will find out more about the Branch.

Then in the prophecy of Jeremiah, xxxiii. 15, we read: "In those days, and at that time, will I cause a Branch of righteousness to grow up unto David; and He shall execute justice and righteousness in the land." The branch, the sprout, the thing held in contempt, shall count; a thing despised shall have dominion. When will the world learn its lessons? When will the world come to see that though He is the Nazarene of men, counted nothing worth, He is God's Imperial One in the race?

Micah said the King should come through Bethlehem; and He came. Hosea said through Egypt He should come, living through all oppression; and from Egypt He came. Jeremiah said Rachel should weep, but that He should Himself stop her weeping, for her captives would be brought back. And finally the prophets said He would be a Nazarene, a sprout; He would dwell in Nazareth. But the Sprout became a Branch, Spirit-clothed, and flaming with the majesty of God.

The whole chapter is microcosmic. It is a picture for all time, until He come again. It indicates the treatment Christ will receive at the hands of the world through the centuries, until He come the second time. Through every century the critics of that chapter have been manifest. Take these four prophecies, and what have you?

Homage and Hatred.

Exile and Exodus.

Sorrow and Song.

Meanness and Majesty.

Where is the King to-day? Hated. But, thank God we bring our gold, frankincense, and myrrh, to lay at His blessed feet.

Where is the King? Exiled from hearts and homes and lives; but, thank God, He is leading an exodus of men and women.

What is the result of His presence in this world? Sorrow. Rachel still weeps for her children; the suffering saints are all here; but there is a song that rises high above the dirge of sorrow.

How is He accounted of men to-day?

19

Men are still saying, "Can any good thing come out of Nazareth?" only they are now talking in past tenses and saying Christianity is worn out; it has had its day. But that is not all. We are crowning Him, we are lifting high above the conflict the song that tells He is King of kings, and Lord of lords.

MATTHEW III. 1-12

AT the commencement of this passage we read, "In those days," but the reference is not necessarily one of immediate time. Matthew takes the story up after thirty years have elapsed, and gives us no details of the happenings of that period. A generation has passed away since we saw Jesus carried to Nazareth as He returned from Egypt. The time of the showing of the King is approaching; the hour at which He must be manifested to His people; the hour at which He is coming forth from privacy to publicity. He will cease to tread the lowly, patient pathway of a subject merely, and will begin to exercise His authority by declaring His manifesto, by exhibiting the benefits of His kingdom, and by finally moving to His Cross and Throne. But before His manifestation, His herald is seen, and it is with the herald that we have to do in this passage.

Let us, then, look at the herald himself. Let us consider the ministry he exercised among the Hebrew people. Let us finally consider his Christian ministry—that is, the ministry by which he linked the old economy to the new; culminating one dispensation, and uttering the word which indicated the commencement of the new movement.

In the first four verses the man himself is presented to our view. The keynote of his ministry is struck; but we are principally occupied with the man.

Let us look at the man first according to the old-time prophecy (ver. 3). Secondly let us see the man as he appeared to his day and generation (ver. 4). Finally let us listen to the key-note of his ministry (ver. 2).

First, then, the man, according to prophecy. Here again the Hebrew evangelist, writing specifically from the Hebrew standpoint, linked the coming of John with the prophecies of the past. Turn to the prophecy of Isaiah (ch. xl. 3): 'The voice of one that crieth, Prepare ye in the wilderness the way of Jehovah, make level in the desert a highway for our God." Let us endeavour to keep in view the whole sweep of the prophecy of Isaiah, for we can only grasp individual verses by great outlooks. We shall only see where this quotation fits into the ministry of Jesus Christ, as we attempt to fasten upon our minds what this prophecy teaches.

Leaving any discussion of the unity of the authorship of Isaiah, but remembering that it is a unified message, there will be manifest a very distinct method. The book falls naturally into three great divisions. There are first thirty-five chapters, constituting a great movement; of judgment pronounced, shot through again and again, as all the Hebrew prophecies are, with the light of mercy, and the gleaming glory of infinite grace, that for evermore enwraps the judgment of God. The great subject of this first division is judgment. The prophet first of all utters an impeachment of the nation, with strange, alarming, and terrible denunciation of the condition of God's ancient people. Then moving on, he tells the story of how he was called and commissioned to his work. In those chapters are two movements of judgment: first, the judgment of the chosen people on account of their failure; secondly, the judgment of the nations.

Then there is a small division in the heart of the prophecy, chapters xxxvi.-xxxix., four chapters only, which may be called historic; corresponding with the story in some of the historic books of the Bible. In these the prophet describes the condition of affairs in his own time, and so explains the great burden of judgment that he has been compelled to utter.

Then at chapter xl. commences the supreme message of the Book of Isaiah, that for which all the rest has been necessarily preparatory. In Isaiah, as in every Hebrew prophecy, judgment is not the final word, and the prophet breaks out, "Comfort ye, comfort ye My people, saith your God." Then, as if he were listening to something that was not to come for centuries after—for an inspired man has not only keen vision, but acute hearing—he says, without naming the man, "The voice of one that crieth, Prepare ye in the wilderness the way of Jehovah, Make level in the desert a highway for our God." The prophet has heard the cry afar off before any one else has heard it. It is a voice in the desert; but he understands it, he knows what it means, and in a moment he begins, "Every valley shall be exalted, and every mountain and hill shall be made low; and the uneven shall be made level, and the rough places a plain;" and the majestic description of issues moves on through chapters xl. and xli., and everything moves forward to chapter xlii. "Behold My Servant, Whom I uphold; My Chosen in Whom My soul delighteth." From that moment the prophecy centres in, and proceeds through, that Servant of Jehovah.

We shall find presently in Matthew's Gospel that he quotes this prophecy of the Servant of Jehovah. We stand back from this old prophecy, and turn over to ch. iii. of the Gospel and read, "And in those days cometh John the Baptist, preaching in the wilderness of Judæa, saying, Repent ye; for the Kingdom of heaven is at hand. For this is he that was spoken of through Isaiah the prophet saying,

The voice of one crying in the wilderness,

Make ye ready the way of the Lord,

Make His paths straight."

The King is coming; the Servant of God that Isaiah described in all the remaining portion of his great book. John is preaching, and the voice that Isaiah heard with keen, quick hearing, centuries before, is singing in the wilderness, sounding over the Jordan, through the region round Jerusalem, through Judæa, penetrating to the heart of the metropolis Jerusalem. It is the voice that foretells the advent of the Kingdom of heaven, when "Every valley shall be exalted, and every mountain and hill shall be made low." The voice announces the new age, the new movement; a new age and movement not sentimentally, but personally governed. The Kingdom is at the doors, and the fulfilling of the ancient prophecy, the ministry of John the Baptist commences.

Secondly, let us look at the man as he appeared to his people (ver. 4). "Now John himself had his raiment of camel's hair, and a leathern girdle about his loins, and his food was locusts and wild honey." That is all. It is one of those pictures that has very little light and shade from without. There are no fine outlines merging into the shadows and coming up into great light. There was nothing of this in John the Baptist. He was a man severe, ascetic; one burdened with a sense of the sin of his times.

The story of John is a wonderful one. He was born in the priesthood, and therefore for the priesthood. As to how far he and the Boy Jesus knew each other there has been much speculation. This boy John was born in remarkable circumstances. He grew up, coming to young manhood, when he should have taken upon him the vows of the priesthood according to Divine and human arrangements. But elections of the past are set aside, and suddenly the young man, cared for, prayed for, and nurtured in the home of his father, turned his back upon home, and upon the priesthood; and went, for preparation for his work, into the wilderness, and dwelt there until the hour of his manifestation. There he may have brooded over the story of the past; brooded over the strange conviction within him that told of day-dawn at hand; brooded, if he had known the Boy Jesus, over what he had seen in Him, perchance of simplicity which had astonished him; brooded almost certainly over his mother's story of his own birth, and the birth at the same time of this Boy Jesus. He thought long and in loneliness. It is quite true that if a man would know something of the sin of his own age, he must live in the midst of his age. But no man has ever spoken against the sin of his age with the authoritative voice of God, who has only lived in the midst of his age. He must also see it from the distance. This man went into the wilderness, and suddenly, without warning, he broke upon the whole nation; a great voice, ringing over the mountains and plains.

Thirdly, what was his message? "Repent"—Change your minds. This word, Repent, was the key-note of Jesus' teaching. This is radical, revolutionary. A man comes out of the wilderness, and looks into the faces of the village-folk, of the suburban people, of the metropolitan people, and he says: Repent; you are all wrong; wrong at the heart and core of things; wrong in your seeing, and therefore in your doing.

But the reason is, that the "Kingdom of heaven is at hand." The "Kingdom of heaven" was a current phrase of Jewish speech, which is almost peculiar to the Gospel of Matthew, representing a perpetual consciousness in Jewish thinking. "The Kingdom of Heaven" —the theocracy, the Divine government, the heavenly Order. In earthly life the authority of God exercised among men. Now, said this strange ascetic preacher as he came, This Kingdom is at hand. The ideal your fathers have cherished is about to be realised in your midst, and you are not ready for it. "Repent," change your minds. It was a great word and a great message, delivered with no tone of tenderness judging from the records which, while meagre, are yet sufficient. There was never a tone of tenderness about John until he saw Jesus; and then the stern ascetic became full of tenderness as he used the greatest phrase of the spirit of tenderness: "Behold, the Lamb of God, that taketh away the sin of the world." But until the great Sin-bearer came, John was the sin-bearer in his own consciousness; the sin of the nation was on his heart. He was the most magnificent in many ways of all the long line of prophets, with an awful monotony in his message—"Repent ye, for the Kingdom of heaven is at hand."

Yet his message to the Hebrew people is given a little more fully. We have only so far looked at the key-note. Now look at ver. 5. "Then went out unto him Jerusalem, and all Judæa, and all the region round about the Jordan, and they were baptized of him in the river Jordan, confessing their sins. But when he saw many of the Pharisees and Sadducees coming to his baptism, he said unto them, Ye generation of vipers"—offspring, genus, kin—"who warned you to flee from the wrath to come?" And yet he did not turn them back. He did not say they could not flee. He did not say their repentance was not genuine; but he told them what to do. "Bring forth, therefore, fruit worthy of repentance: and think not to say within yourselves, We have Abraham to our father: for I say unto you, that God is able of these stones to raise up children unto Abraham."

Such is the brief analysis of the Hebrew ministry of John; and there are three qualities in it. First, it was attractive—"Then went out unto him Jerusalem, and all Judæa, and all the region round about the Jordan;" secondly, it was convictive—"They were baptized of him in the river Jordan, confessing their sins;" finally, it was invective. Against the men who constituted the fountain-head of all Israel's trouble—Pharisees, Sadducees— he flung himself in passionate protest.

We sometimes imagine that there is nothing attractive in our ministry, except the winning, wooing note. But there are times when we seem to need again the voice of the herald; and when God finds a John the Baptist and sends him out, his message is full of attractiveness. This is a great picture of attractiveness, of a man with a note of conviction in his message and authority in the way that he deals with sin. He came with no theology; he came with no philosophy to discuss; he came with no new cult to introduce; he did not come to ask men to consider a position which they could accept or reject as they pleased; he came with the thundering voice of a great inspiration —"Repent;" and the message of God's authority stirred every place, and every one. Thank God it is true to-day. We do not need one Gospel for the city, and another for the suburbs, and another for the country. Jerusalem, and all Judæa, and all the villages need the same message. Before Jesus come, John Baptist must come to the city, and suburbs, and country; and as his message is heard there will be attractiveness in it.

Then notice, his message was convictive. At least men acknowledged the truth externally, and submitted to the baptism which was a symbol of their repentance. Of course it all fell short there. It can never be any more than that. John Baptist can never communicate life. Coming after him is the Sinbearer, the great tender-hearted King of men, Who does not only produce repentance, but gives life. If we are convinced of sin, thank God for it, but it is not enough. The crowds that thronged the banks of the Jordan, and went down into its waters of baptism, which was a baptism of repentance, were very sincere; but to accept Jesus there must be something more than this.

Once again, notice the invective note in his preaching. Now the leaders were responsible—Pharisees and Sadducees. The Pharisee was a ritualist; the Sadducee a rationalist. The Pharisee believed in all supernatural things, but imagined that they could be expressed in external things, and that is always the story of ritualism. The Sadducees did not believe in angel, spirit, or resurrection. They were rationalists, cold and hard. These are the forces that damn a people, that blight a nation. John saw them coming; the ritualists and the rationalists, who with their splendid observance of externalities and their inward corruptness of life, had blighted the whole nation. And John said with roughness, "Who warned you to flee from the wrath to come," ye kin of vipers? And then, as if he had said: You have come, and you say you repent; but by you, more than by all others, must be manifested the reality of your repentance. "Bring forth therefore fruit worthy of repentance;" trust no longer in your physical relationship to Abraham—"God is able of these stones to raise up children unto Abraham."

What a message it was! It must have burned and scorched these men. The more one studies it the more glad one is that Jesus' ministry of renewing

followed. Thank God that the message to-day is that of this blessed King!

Notice what John said about the King, for after all it is the supreme matter. "And even now the axe lieth at the root of the trees; every tree therefore that bringeth not forth good fruit is hewn down, and cast into the fire." It is a wonderful message! God help us to catch its notes.

The first thing that John testifies, is to the coming One, and he says two things of Him—first, He is supreme in His Person; secondly, He is supreme in His work. There is a humility about this; there is a touch of modesty in it; and the difference between a real humility and a mock humility, we all know. Real humility never knows it is humble; mock humility is proud of its humility. "He that cometh after me is mightier than I, Whose shoes I am not worthy to bear." John was quite right. We will take Another's estimate of John: "Verily I say unto you, Among them that are born of women, there hath not arisen a greater than John the Baptist." This is what the King said of him, and this is true also. And yet, greatest of women born, said the King, he was not worthy to bear the shoes of the King. This is quite true.

There is a supreme difference in their work. We need not describe the difference between the two men—the rugged and rough prophet, and the magnificent and majestic King, Whose very gentleness is mightier than the hurricane of His herald. "Thy gentleness hath made me great." The contrast is not only in the persons; it is in their work. "I indeed baptize you with water unto repentance, but He that cometh after me is mightier than I— He shall baptise you in the Holy Spirit and in fire"—I lead you to the external symbol of your repentance; He shall whelm you in the fire-whelming of the Holy Ghost, that burns your sin out of you, and re-makes you. I have to do, said John, with the external thing— water, that which can only touch the surface of things; He shall work with fire, that which shall go through everything.

That is the difference between Jesus and John to-day. If we listen to the message of John only, we shall be busy with water-baptism and washing. But if we listen to the message of Jesus, the fire will burn, and burn to purity, and burn to realisation, and burn to crowning. The work of Jesus is superior to the work of John.

Listen to what John says about His methods. This is to be a strange and wonderful King Who is coming. He is to be destructive and constructive in His method; and His victories are to be destructive and constructive.

His methods of destruction are, " the axe," " the fan," and " the fire." " The axe lieth at the root of the trees," said John. It is ready. He is coming, and His " fan is in His hand," the fan that winnows. And the fire will burn.

But His methods are constructive. He shall baptize you with fire; He shall cleanse the threshing-floor, not destroy it, and " He will gather His wheat into the garner." Mark the contrast. The axe at the root of the trees for destruction—for the cutting off of the fruitless; the fan for scattering the chaff; the fire for immediately devouring the chaff. But mark the constructive work. The fire is for cleansing and energy; the cleansing of the threshing-floor, that perfect work may go forward, and the garnering and the gathering in of the wheat. It is the same thing, and the same instrument that does two opposite things. The fan drives away the chaff, leaving the wheat. The fire burns up the thing that cannot stand its fierce flame; and perfects that which can bear the flame. And so the King Who comes is to be destructive and constructive—destructive, for the fruitless tree is to be hewn down; the chaff is to be driven away and burnt,—constructive, for the threshing-floor is to be cleansed; the wheat is to be gathered and garnered, and men are to be fire-baptized.

Nineteen centuries have gone since this rugged prophet heralded the coming of the King. The work of Jesus has proceeded in human history for nineteen centuries on exactly the lines he laid down. Jesus Christ has always been the King of destruction and construction. Glance back; think of the centuries, and think of the influence of Jesus in the centuries. What has He done? Oh! the things He has burnt up. Oh! the things He has built. Always fanning, and chaff is flung before it; always a gatherer, and the wheat is being garnered. It is so to-day. The axe of Jesus lies at the root of the tree that is fruitless. The winnowing fan of Christ is at work; the chaff must go. Do you imagine that after all the chaff is going to submerge the wheat, and fruitless trees crowd out the fruit-bearing vines of God? Then you do not know the King. His fan is in His hand, and if we live on the mountains of God, we shall feel the wind of God which blows and scatters things which must go.

The question of importance for us, for our work in the little day God allows us to live, is this: Am I chaff, or wheat? Is the work I am doing chaff or wheat? If I am chaff, His wind will blow me to the unquenchable fire; but if I am wheat, He will gather me, and garner me. So with my work, and with everything.

MATTHEW III. 13-17

THESE few verses reveal the relation of the King to heaven, as they tell the story of His attestation and anointing.

The paragraph commences with the word " then," which connects it with what has preceded, and reminds us that these events took place in a time of general consciousness of sin, and of that great moral movement throughout the whole region consequent upon the ministry of John the Baptist. *Then,* the King came out of seclusion to manifest Himself to men. The voice had cried in the wilderness, and the way of the Lord was thus made ready, and His paths made straight. At the set time, the King came from privacy into publicity. From the quiet seclusion of the years spent in Nazareth, He came to inaugurate His work and assume His office.

24

In these few verses there are three matters for our consideration: the baptism of the King; His anointing; and the Divine word concerning Him.

Notice that it is carefully stated that He came " to be baptized." His coming was of set purpose and for a special reason. Considering the note of John's message, and the meaning of his ministry, this action on the part of Jesus at once arrests attention and arouses inquiry. John had been preaching repentance, and his baptism was the baptism of repentance. All men had crowded to him—the men of the city, of Judæa, of the wayside, and of the whole region of Jordan. Among the rest, Jesus of Nazareth set His face towards the place where the prophet's voice was heard and the prophet's baptism was being administered. He set His face, moreover, not as one of a curious multitude going to listen and observe, but for the special purpose of being baptized. We ask with wonder and amazement, Why should He be baptized with the baptism of repentance? That is the question to which we are to attempt to find an answer.

I. In looking at the baptism let us first notice its place in the life of Jesus. Forgetting His office, which is the supreme matter in this Gospel; turning our attention from the fact that He is King, anointed of God from eternity for this work, we will simply look at Him as the Man as He has appeared before us in the story of His genealogy and birth. The life of Jesus was absolutely sinless. If He were not sinless, then we have no Gospel. All the value of His dying depends upon the virtue of His living. Why, then, did the Sinless submit to a baptism of repentance? John looked into the face of this one Man, among all other men coming to his baptism; and with the keen, quick insight of the truly inspired seer, he saw the difference. He had been baptizing many men as they had pressed to him, and as he looked upon their faces he had seen in all of them the evidences of anxiety for repentance. But when this Man came to him, One among a crowd, so like them that the crowd did not distinguish Him, there was yet a difference. John said, " In

the midst of you standeth One Whom ye know not." And then John looked at Him and said, " I have need to be baptized of Thee, and comest Thou to me ? "

John, looking into His face, became conscious of the absolute perfection and sinless spotlessness of this Man. He was amazed and arrested; he felt as if he dare not lay his hands upon that Man to immerse Him in the waters of the Jordan.

So far as the human life of Jesus is concerned, John was perfectly right in that feeling. There was no place for John's baptism in the life of Jesus; He had nothing to repent of, no sin to be put away, the putting away of which was symbolised in this ablution in water. If Jesus was simply living out a human life to consummation, which would henceforth be pattern and ideal only, then that baptism was out of place, having neither value nor meaning.

Then we must go further if we are to understand the meaning of the baptism of Jesus. If it did not occupy a place in the life of Jesus, did it occupy a place in the mission of the King?

The question suggests the answer. When John was reluctant, and felt he could not lay his hands upon Jesus to baptize Him, Jesus looked at him and said, " Suffer it now; for thus it becometh *us* "—that was John and Himself—" Thus it becometh *us* to fulfil all righteousness "—thus it becometh you to act with Me, and Me to act with you for the fulfilment of righteousness.

In that statement we find the meaning. The supreme element in the baptism of Jesus was the identification of the Sinless with the sinner. He Who had no sin to repent of, took His place among those who had sin to repent of. He Who was sinless, went down into the baptism that was the portion of the sinner.

In Isaiah liii. we read, " He . . . was numbered with the transgressors." There, in baptism as in incarnation and birth, and finally and for consummation, in the mystery of His Passion, we see the King identifying Himself with the people over whom He is to reign, in the fact of their deepest need, and direst failure. This chapter of Isaiah

25

is the one in which the picture of the Servant of God finds its culminating glory. The prophecy of the forerunner, which was fulfilled in the ministry of John, is found in chapter xl. In chapter xlii. is recorded the beginning of the new movement, "Behold My Servant," and from there onwards, the Servant of the Lord is presented. In chapter liii. we see the Servant of the Lord rejected, bruised, cast out; the suffering Messiah, the King that men will not have. Towards its close we have the story of His Person, and of His ultimate victory, and in verse 11 we find these words, "He shall see of the travail of His soul, and shall be satisfied. By the knowledge of Himself shall my righteous Servant justify many; and He shall bear their iniquities."

These words, "My righteous Servant shall justify many," are the explanation of the meaning of Jesus when He said to John, "Thus it becometh us to fulfil all righteousness." By identification with them in sin and suffering "He bare the sin of many." He identified Himself with them in their sins, and "was numbered with the transgressors;" and therefore "by the knowledge of Himself shall My righteous Servant justify many." His knowledge of Himself is His first-hand knowledge (see John ii. 24, 25), and so is knowledge of the need, knowledge of the remedy, and consent to all such knowledge is involved. "He shall bear their iniquities." The King was facing the problem of obtaining His Kingdom, and He faced first the sin of man. He submitted to the baptism of John, indicating by this symbolic action His identification of Himself with His people in their sin, in order that He may put that sin away, and build and establish the Kingdom of God, and so fulfil all righteousness.

His going down into the waters of baptism was a consent and a prophecy. It was a consent to the only method by which the King could save from sin; and it uttered the prophecy of that final baptism towards which His face was set through all the days of public ministry—the baptism of His Passion. Jesus referred to personal baptism only

twice subsequently. Both Matthew and Mark tell the story of some office-seeking disciples who asked to sit one on the right hand, and the other on the left in His Kingdom. And He looked at them and said, "Are ye able to drink the cup that I drink? or to be *baptized* with the *baptism* that I am *baptized* with?" Perhaps they thought He was speaking of that past baptism in water, for they said, "We are able." We know He was looking on to that other baptism of which the first baptism was the foreshadowing and the prophecy— the Passion Baptism. That was His great baptism.

Only on one other occasion did He make reference to His own personal baptism. In that wonderful soliloquy of His recorded by Luke, when, surrounded by His own disciples and oppressed, He broke out into these words, "I came to cast fire upon the earth; and what will I? Oh that it were already kindled! But I have a *baptism* to be *baptized* with; and how am I straitened till it be accomplished?" John baptized in water. Jesus came to baptize with fire; but He could not baptize with fire, until He Himself had been baptized in the whelming waters of death.

Thus the King is seen commencing His public ministry. There lie behind Him the quiet years of seclusion and preparation, the years in which He has done the Will of God in the commonplace. Now the great crisis has come. He will presently enunciate the laws of His Kingdom, personally exhibit the benefits of that Kingdom; and enforce the claims of His Kingship. He knows that the culminating work will be the Cross; that these multitudes, baptized of John, will reject Him. He knows that He cannot win them by His example and by preaching, but only by the way of His dying. He knows the issue of sin. These sinners on the banks of the Jordan are making necessary His death—death in its profoundest sense; and as He watches them going down to those waters, He goes with them, and in that whelming in the Jordan He typifies and prophesies that death-whelming through which He, the Innocent, will presently pass in order to fulfil all righteousness, to cancel sin, to banish it, to make it not to be; that He may build His Kingdom on the foundations of righteousness, and "bring forth the topstone with shoutings of Grace." By His knowledge—as Isaiah said long before—by His knowledge of the need, and of the real meaning of sin; by His knowledge of the way by which men may be redeemed, His soul consents to an identification that shall issue in death, the supreme character of which shall be expressed by the terrible words, "The pains of Sheol gat hold upon Me." And as He goes down into these waters of baptism He consents to that mission, and formally commits Himself to the cause of man, for man's saving.

This baptism of Jesus has no application to us. We rob this passage of all its significance when we say that as Jesus was baptized, therefore we ought to be baptized. Let us not take hold of this great and marvellous passage, and use it in a small and unworthy way. We have something to do with this baptism of Jesus, but it is a baptism that we cannot be baptized with save by identification through His grace. "The cup that I drink ye shall drink; and with the baptism that I am baptized withal shall ye be baptized." That was a word of infinite love.

There are two applications of the great baptism—that of judgment and of death, and that of life and of fire. We share only in that of life and fire. That, He can only bestow upon us by the way of judgment and of death; by the mystery of His Cross. Thus He fulfilled all righteousness. By His baptism He committed Himself to men, and to the purposes of God; consented at the beginning of His public ministry to God's method for the saving of men.

II. Now let us turn to that which immediately followed the baptism. "And Jesus, when He was baptized, went up straightway from the water; and lo, the heavens were opened unto Him, and He saw the Spirit of God descending as a dove, and coming upon Him; and lo, a Voice out of the heavens, saying, This is My beloved Son, in Whom I am well pleased." There is little doubt that none saw this descent of the Spirit save Jesus and John. What was the meaning of this anointing, in the life of Jesus? Jesus did not now for the first time receive the Holy Spirit. There was a permanent relation between Jesus and the Spirit of God. He was, in a sense in which none other ever has been or can be, born of the Holy Ghost; His development had been under the control of the Spirit of God. When He came to baptism, He was a Man of the Spirit of God, as all men might have been, had there been no sin. Jesus was a natural Man; not as Paul uses the word, not in the theological sense, but in the simpler sense that lies behind the theological sense. We are told that the natural man is the sinner, and there are present senses in which that is true; but God's ideal for a man is that he should live in perpetual communion with the Spirit of God. That is truly natural life. The natural life of the ideal man is supernatural. The whole life of Jesus was dominated by the Spirit of God. He willed, and thought, and lived under the Spirit's power, and illumination, and impulse.

Therefore without question this was a special anointing of Jesus as He entered upon His public ministry. The Spirit of God never appears under the figure of a dove anywhere save here. The Spirit of God never manifested Himself in this form before. We have no right to pray that the Spirit may descend on us as a dove. It descended on Him in this outward, and visible, and symbolic fashion, and on Him alone.

It has been said by Puritan writers that the dove is among the birds what the lamb is among the beasts—a symbol of great gentleness and sweetness. Jesus used the figure of a dove in that application in those remarkable words when He said to His disciples that they were to be "wise as serpents, and harmless as doves." The dove and the lamb are gentle and harmless in their character; and they are therefore also types of sacrifice. Jesus was led "as a lamb . . . to the slaughter, and as a sheep that before its shearers is dumb" so was He.

The Spirit therefore came upon Him as a dove. The Book of Leviticus depicts this strange yet wonderful rite of

Hebraism which typified and shadowed sacrifice. In the great sin-offerings men brought offerings graded, as to value, according to their social position. A man who could afford it brought a bullock, another would offer a lamb, and the poorest brought a dove. It is interesting to remember that when Mary brought Jesus up to the Temple, her offering was a dove. The dove therefore is the bird that signifies patience, gentleness, harmlessness; and is the type of sacrifice possible to the lowliest of the people.

We must put ourselves back into Hebrew thinking to understand these things, and their spiritual significances. Matthew wrote his Gospel specifically for the Jew. When the Hebrew heard of a dove, or of a lamb, he always thought of a sacrifice for sin. The coming of the Spirit as a bird of sacrifice for sin for the lowliest was the equipment of Jesus for the carrying out of the deepest purpose of sacrifice. He had just consented to death in His whelming in the waters, and the Spirit of God fell upon Him as a dove. The bird of sacrifice for sin in the ancient economy rested in holy gentleness upon Him, Who is God's one, perfect, final Sacrifice for sin. The dove is the emblem of weakness; but the Spirit of God in the form of a dove is an emblem of power in gentleness—Deity submissive to sacrifice for the salvation of men. This was an anointing for death, for atonement. It was not simply an anointing for preaching, but for living in order to dying. He had consented to death; and Heaven crowned Him with power for that death. "Christ . . . through the eternal Spirit, offered Himself without blemish unto God;" and when the Spirit came as a dove, it was for that crowning and that purpose. The King as a man is energised by God for dealing with that which is fundamentally wrong in the Kingdom, and setting it right. God clothes Himself with man that He may proceed to the redemption of the lost race; and the Son is enwrapped in the power of the Spirit's anointing, and crowned with the dove-like form. So the King faces the conflict, already conquering in the glory of the victory that is to be.

III. Finally we listen to the attestation. The Voice is heard saying: "This is My Beloved Son, in Whom I am well pleased." We must interpret that Divine affirmation by the second Psalm, in which we see the anointing of the Son, and the King, "upon His holy hill of Zion." Therein we hear the decree of God:

" Jehovah said unto Me, Thou art
    My Son;
This day have I begotten Thee."

That is one of the most glorious references to the Son of God as the reigning King that the Old Testament Scriptures contain. God's King is to ask for the nations, and possess them with the heathen, and hold them for an inheritance. "Thou art My Son." The thought of the Scriptures that He was a Son runs through the old Hebrew prophecies, and ritual, and thinking. Now at last, on the banks of the Jordan, God says, "This is My . . . Son." This is the Son of man, but He is "My . . . Son," Whose advent the prophets foretold. Men have been waiting and looking for His appearing; calling to the watchers on the mountains, and asking, "What of the night?" They have wondered at the delay of His coming, and have cried out through the days, Come quickly! "This is My . . . Son." So God marks out the King.

But God declares another thing concerning Him. "In Whom I am well pleased." This declaration flashes its light back on those hidden years of Nazareth. We have no chronicle of those years. There is an almost complete silence from the time He was twelve years of age to His thirtieth year. It is now at thirty years of age we see Him on the banks of the Jordan, spotless, and sinless, and ready for sacrifice. One's mind goes necessarily back to the old economy, and we see the priest examining the sacrifice, which must be without blemish. Is this Man without blemish? God says "I am well pleased." He sets the seal of perfection upon the hidden years. We want to know no more. We ask for no details; it is enough.

In Nazareth He has pleased God as a Man; He has done what no other did, or could do, since man fell by sin. And so the light is flashed upon the past, and shows its perfection.

But there is a further value. Said Jesus, "Therefore doth the Father love Me, because I lay down My life." And when God said, "I am well pleased," it was a declaration of the Divine complacency with the act of baptism, which indicated perfect union with God in the purpose of salvation, even by the way of the Cross of death.

There was the most perfect unity of purpose and of spirit between the Father and the Son through all the process of redemption. Smitten? Yes. Afflicted? Yes. Bruised? Yes. Because of righteousness and holiness? Yes. But, "In all their affliction"—even in the affliction of the Cross—"He was afflicted," not merely as Man, but One with God Himself working for

salvation. "Therefore doth the Father love Me"—because of this accomplishment. And as He sets His face toward the Cross, in perfect union with the Will of God, God breaks the silence and says, "I am well pleased."

Thus in baptism He assumed responsibility for sinning men; by the anointing of the Spirit He was crowned and empowered; and by the Divine Voice He was attested God's King, set upon the holy hill of Zion.

Let us close with the words of the Psalmist:

' Now therefore be wise, O ye kings:
Be instructed, ye judges of the earth.
Serve Jehovah with fear,
And rejoice with trembling.
Kiss the Son, lest He be angry, and ye perish in the way,
For His wrath will soon be kindled.
Blessed are all they that put their trust in Him."

MATTHEW IV. 1-11

WE have now to consider the King in His relation to the great under-world of evil, and to its god, "the prince of the power of the air." The King has come, not merely to reign. There is an initial work devolving upon Him—that of subduing the Kingdom to Himself. He does not enter into a Kingdom waiting for Him, responsive to His claim. He comes to a Kingdom characterised by anarchy and rebellion. In God's economy of the Kingdom, a Man is to be King. But this Man, if indeed He is to receive the Kingdom, and reign over it, must be demonstrated as personally victorious over these forces of antagonism, by victory over the master foe. The King has been attested as being in perfect harmony with the order and beauty of the heavens, in the word that God spoke at His baptism, "This is My beloved Son, in Whom I am well pleased." But He is now to face the disorder and the ugliness of the abyss. Goodness at its highest He knows, and is. Evil at its lowest He must face, and overcome.

The subject reveals Him to us in three ways: first, as perfect Man; secondly, as Man demonstrated perfect

through testing; and finally, as Man victorious, and therefore fitted for supremacy.

I. In this story of the temptation, the King is revealed as perfect Man. Turning our attention for a moment from the enemy and his method, and fixing it upon the Person of Jesus, we see in the background, not distinctly described, but most evidently present, God's ideal of humanity. This is brought out in the threefold movement of temptation.

This temptation is an orderly temptation, if we may use such a word in speaking of any method of hell; it is utterly disorderly in the profounder sense; but it is a scientific and systematic attack upon a Man. It is this we need to see. These temptations are not the swift, sudden, subtle, insidious temptations that sweep upon men. Our Lord faced such also; but these constitute an organised and systematic attack upon a man in every department of his life.

Mark in one brief glance the order of the temptations. First, an appeal to the physical nature—bread; secondly, an appeal to the spiritual nature—trust in God; finally an appeal to the vocational purpose—Here are the Kingdoms of the world for which Thou hast come, take them from me.

In that glance there stands revealed in all the sombre shade, and yet the vivid light of the wilderness, God's Man. What is man? Physical and spiritual in being; yet existing, not merely for the sake of existence, but for a purpose. Material, spiritual, vocational. In this order Matthew records the temptations.

We see Jesus in this first temptation as of the earth. He is of the material order, consciously realising all the facts of the material life, its limitations and its necessities. He depends upon the material for the sustenance of the material side of His nature; He is a Man Who fasts for a long time, but afterwards becomes conscious of His hunger. Superior, in His material nature, to all the material order; able for a period not to eat; yet needing to eat eventually in order to the sustenance of His life. That is the first fact about man, any man. There are differences between this Man and other men, because others are not perfect men; they are members of a ruined and fallen race. This Man is a perfect Man according to the Divine pattern, but in the essential facts of being He is our Kinsman. We are children of the earth, and the first thing we come into contact with, if we meet each other, is the material. We do not know the spiritual fact of the man we meet in the street. We must get nearer to him before we can know that. Here in the wilderness is Jesus of Nazareth—of the dust, but crowned and glorified; yet, dust as every man is. Man on his physical side is the highest and final fact in God's material creation, superior to everything else; rising over every form of life, master of the rest, regnant in the midst of a magnificent creation, of which he is the consummation and culmination. The physical side is temporal, transient; but it is essential to this strange and marvellous thing which we speak of as human nature.

In the second of these temptations we see Jesus, no longer of the earth, material; but of the infinite, spiritual. In that spiritual nature He is conscious of God, seeks to know the will of God, is submissive to the spiritual order, yields to the law of God.

On the material side He is of the earth, and something of the earth is needed to sustain Him—bread. On the spiritual side He is of the infinite, and something of the infinite is needed to sustain Him. Thus here we see a Man, physical and spiritual, but the spiritual is the deepest fact in His life, as it is the deepest fact in every life. The physical is temporary, transient, and passing; the spiritual is the abiding and the supreme.

Then once again, in the third temptation, Jesus is seen as existing for a purpose. He was born to serve. He was equipped in His being for service. He knew that service could only be rendered as He worshipped God. " Thou shalt worship the Lord thy God, and Him only shalt thou serve."

Here, then, is revealed the Man Whom God ordained to be King—God's archetypal Man, the perfect Man—and as we look at Him we see that the supreme end of life is vocation; that the essence of life is spiritual; that the present expression of the spiritual fact and vocation is physical. Temptation commences in the external, which is physical; passes to the internal, which is spiritual; attacks finally the vocational, which is the supreme thing in the life of every man. This is the picture of human life, according to the purpose of God.

The government of such beings is placed by God in the authority of One of them; but the King must be unimpaired in realisation of the Divine Ideal. A man who has failed at any point cannot govern men. He cannot govern those who have not failed, and he certainly cannot redeem those who have failed. A man who has prostituted his physical nature to base uses; a man who has silenced and stifled and dwarfed his spiritual nature; a man who has failed to realise his vocation, cannot be king. An imperfect being cannot demand our loyalty; we cannot be loyal to inferiority; we cannot bow the knee and worship in the presence of anything other than perfection. That is only one side of the great story.

See it from the other side, and in view of the fact with which we commenced this study—that the King has first to subdue to Himself a Kingdom full of anarchy and rebellion. He cannot do it if there be anarchy in His own personality. If there be failure in His own life, His arm is paralysed, His heart lacks courage, and He cannot redeem. There must be the perfection of humanity in order to reign over humanity.

II. Therefore, in order to reign, the perfect One must be demonstrated perfect through testing.

Here we touch the deepest mystery and majesty of human nature. The awful and yet magnificent responsibility of choice is imposed upon every individual. Man stands in his probation between two possibilities. He can use his whole nature in response to evil, or to good, both in the material and spiritual realms, for evil and good assault and woo him.

Again we are bound to pause and make a distinction between the perfect Man and ourselves. It is still true that we are called to choose between evil and good, but we start in life, and find that when the choice is presented to us we would do the good, but evil is present with us; and that perpetually in our life, we want to choose the good, and would choose it, but the force and passion of evil and the feebleness resulting therefrom are in us, and we cannot. Some man says, That is exactly the truth. That is what I want explained in my case. What am I to do? In answer—" Where sin abounded, grace did abound more exceedingly," and while in our own unaided strength, the strength of the nature into which we were born, we cannot do good; in the strength and victory that this Man won, and the work He did, we can choose and do the good if we will, and there is no reason why any man should continue in sin.

But let us get back to Jesus in the wilderness. He stood alone. There were no forces burning within Him which He could not overcome. He occupied the position which was occupied by the first Adam before he failed.

Standing there, with a perfect Manhood in the presence of temptation, He must be tested, and make His choice between the good and the evil.

The first purpose of the enemy is the spoiling of the instrument of expression. He appeals to the physical, he appeals to the material, he appeals to that external fact in the Person of Jesus, through which impressions are received by the spirit, and through which the spirit for a while is to express itself. The occasion of the testing is the proper desire for sustenance. This Man felt the clamant cry of the physical, for material sustenance. Here was His infirmity.

What is an infirmity? We are told by the writer of the letter to the Hebrews that " we have not a high priest that cannot be touched with the feeling of our infirmities." What are these infirmities? A man with an atrociously bad temper says, That is my infirmity. That is not so; that uncontrolled temper is sin. A man with some evil habit, for which he blames his father, says, That is my infirmity. It is not; it is sin. An infirmity is a weakened power that requires strengthening. You go forth to toil and work, and presently there comes to you the sense of hunger. That is an infirmity. Oh, you say, I always thought hunger was a sign of strength. No, it is a sign of weakened strength, a beneficent, beautiful sign, a sign that you are in health, a sign that God is still governing your life, at least on the physical side. Your hunger is the voice that says, Supply sustenance, and the thing that makes you need sustenance is that the physical part of you is weakened for the moment. That is your infirmity. That weakening is the avenue through which temptation comes; it presents itself to the clamant cry of a weakened power, properly weakened through exercise. And a man who never weakens his powers is wasting his life; a man who never takes the force that is in him and uses it until it grows a little flaccid and nerves give way, is wasting his life. Yet that weakened power is the opportunity of temptation.

Now, what is the testing? It is as though the enemy had said: There is an inter-relation between the two sides of Thy nature. The physical is hungry; but Thou art the Son of God, Thou art offspring of God, Thou art kin of God; there is in Thee this spiritual entity. Turn Thy spiritual nature into a means of satisfying Thy material need without reference to the will of God. If Thou art the Son of God, if Thou hast a spiritual nature. use that power in order to turn stones into bread, and satisfy Thy physical need. Act for Thyself, prove Thy Sonship by Thy independence.

The perfection of the Man Jesus is demonstrated in His refusal. Hunger was not wrong; bread was not an improper thing; but Jesus stands for evermore in the isolated splendour of the wilderness saying to man; It is better to be hungry than to be fed without reference to the will of God. I cannot, He says, take hold of a spiritual capacity, and use it for the supply of a proper physical need, without reference to the will of My Father. I cannot act in independence as a Son; the essence of Sonship is obedience; and if for the moment the circumstances into which the Spirit has led Me necessitate My hunger, then I will do nothing to alter the Divine condition and surrounding. I do not live only by bread; man lives also by the word of God—that which conditions His life. And so in the first temptation against the physical He is victorious.

Next came the test of the spiritual. What is the purpose here? If, in the first, it was the spoliation of the instrument, here it is the ruin of the essential.

The occasion of the test of the spiritual is the strain which has just been put upon the spiritual relationship by the choice made to suffer hunger by faith in God. The material victory was a spiritual victory. And in the moment of that victory what happened? A Man feeling all the pangs of hunger, all the weariness of weakness, said; I choose the hunger, and choose the weakness, because, essentially, I am not material, but spiritual. And the hunger continues, and there is a strain put upon relationship; and as the strain is put upon relationship the tempter comes

again, and says, "If Thou art the Son of God."

The suggestion is that He should make improper use of the relation between the spiritual essence, and the physical mode of expression; that He should take the instrument, and venture something heroic in demonstration of the perfection of His spiritual nature. It is as though the enemy had said to the perfect Man, You have declared your allegiance in response to my first temptation; you have declared your trust in God; very well; if you do trust Him, venture something on your trust; do something heroic; do something splendid; show how much you trust in God by flinging yourself from the pinnacle of the temple.

The moment a man begins to tempt God, to prove trust; he proves that he does not trust. The moment a man begins to do something heroic to demonstrate trust, he gives evidence that trust is lacking. Perfect trust is quiet, and waits. Trust trembling, wants to do something heroic to make it steady. Jesus said, No, My trust is so perfect that I need to do nothing heroic to prove it. "Thou shalt not tempt." The spiritual nature retained its dignity; He refused to do anything spectacular.

Finally, the temptation moved into the last realm. Its purpose was the prevention of the accomplishment of the work of the King. Its occasion was the consciousness of victory already won, and the consequent new flaming of the supreme passion to serve. The moment you have won a great victory, in the power of the victory won, you want to be doing. Jesus had won a victory in the physical realm, and had won a victory in the spiritual realm. Now the enemy came again and said: Well, you have won, you have not failed as an instrument; now here is your work; here are the kingdoms of the world; you have come for them; give me one moment's homage, and I will abdicate. What a lie it was!

Did he imagine for a moment that he could deceive Immaculate Purity this way? He was a liar from the beginning, and he never lied more directly— I will give Thee the kingdoms! Never would he have done so. That was the tempting bait. Jesus saw the kingdoms, and their glory, but He saw all the permeating influence of evil and destruction, and He knew—had He not consented to it in baptism?—that these kingdoms could only be won by blood and suffering, and death. And with the voice of quiet authority, He said, " Get thee hence, Satan: for it is written, Thou shalt worship the Lord thy God and Him only shalt thou serve," which is to say, My vocational power is assured under the Divine Government, and I abide there. I will take these kingdoms from God, in God's way. In His answer there is a prophecy, a flaming prophecy. " Get thee hence." Thou dost offer Me the kingdoms if I will give thee homage ; I will take the kingdoms by turning thee out: " Get thee hence, Satan ! " Thus the King is demonstrated perfect by victory.

III. The great value of all this is discovered as it is remembered that the victory was won wholly within the sphere of human life. To every assault of evil He has answered wholly as Man. There is no obtrusion of Deity into the conflict. The law He quoted was man's law, and in human obedience to that law, He has won.

But His victory was the victory of a Man with God. Every man by original design and creation is offspring of God, and has certain claims on God. Man can urge his claim on God if he fulfils the law of God. Jesus fulfilled the law, and urged His claim, and in communion with God, He won His victory.

And yet, thank God, His victory was won not only as Man, and as Man with God, but for men. To defeat the victor is to save the vanquished, and one reads that one brief sentence at the close, that makes one's soul thrill with music —" the devil leaveth Him."

Thus the great personal conflict is over. There are other battles to be fought and won, but they will be in more direct sense representative and redeeming. Never again will the foe directly attack Him, and in the open. The attack was made against every vulnerable point—hunger, trust, and responsibility—and when these are held, there remains no other avenue through which the foe can assault the citadel of the human will. The need of material sustenance, the spirit's confidence in God, and the carrying out of a Divine commission in a Divine way, these are all the avenues. The King has held every one. His defeated foe now leaves Him, and the King in personal life, and character, and victory, holds the field.

MATTHEW IV. 12-25

IT is quite plain that between verses 11 and 12 there is a gap in the chronology. It is interesting and remarkable, that the three evangelists whom we describe as synoptists, omit a section of the public ministry of Jesus, covering twelve months. There can be no doubt that such a period of time elapsed between verses 11 and 12, in this fourth chapter of Matthew. We read, " Then the devil leaveth Him ; and behold, angels came and ministered unto Him ;" and immediately following, " Now when He heard that John was delivered up "—that is, when John was arrested and imprisoned—" He withdrew into Galilee."

Although we are studying the Gospel of Matthew, it will not be out of place, and certainly not lacking in interest, if we attempt to fill up the gap, in order that we may know what happened in the ministry of Jesus.

Coming back from the wilderness, and from His temptation, Jesus seems to have lingered in the neighbourhood of John's ministry for at least three days. On the first day, He stood amongst the crowd unrecognized by them, but discovered by John. On that first day John said, " In the midst of you standeth One Whom ye know not." On the second day, for some purpose, Jesus moved through the crowd towards John himself, and John saw Him coming to him, and then made his great pronouncement, " Behold, the Lamb of God, that taketh away the sin of the world ! " On the third day, Jesus was again seen by John, but walking away ;

and as He went, John cried out, "Behold the Lamb of God," and immediately two at least of John's disciples left him, and followed Jesus. On the first day, John spoke of the perfect Person—"In the midst of you standeth One Whom ye know not, even He that cometh after me, the latchet of Whose shoe I am not worthy to unloose." On the second day he spoke of the perfect Propitiation—"The Lamb of God, that taketh away the sin of the world!" On the last day he spoke of the perfect Pattern—"The Lamb of God."

Immediately following this, Jesus turned to John's disciples who came after Him, and said, "What seek ye?" One of them replied by asking, "Rabbi, where abidest Thou?" And He said, "Come and ye shall see." And they followed Him. One of them was Andrew. The other is not named. Andrew immediately found Simon his brother, and brought him to Jesus. And Jesus "findeth Philip." Whether He knew him before or not, we cannot tell, but He sought him and found him. And "Philip findeth Nathanael." That group constituted the first nucleus of disciples.

But we are not yet at the point in the history which Matthew records. The disciples and Jesus went to Cana of Galilee. Jesus went as a guest. It was a purely social function. He tarried for two or three days down in Capernaum, and then went on to Jerusalem; presented Himself in the Temple; and cleansed it. This was His official presentation to the rulers of His people. Then we have an account of His conversation with Nicodemus, after which He left the metropolis and came into Judæa. John was still pursuing his ministry, and "baptizing in Ænon near to Salim, because there was much water there." Jesus preached in Judæa, and baptized (though He did not baptize personally, but His disciples for Him).

Thus He did not commence to exercise His definitely official ministry as King until John's ministry ended, through his arrest. These things that John records for us are of value, but they have a peculiar relation to the message of John.

In this Gospel of Matthew all these matters are omitted. Matthew, writing the Gospel of the Kingdom, after having presented the person of the King, takes up the story at the point where, the message of the herald having been silenced by his arrest and imprisonment, Jesus began His official work as King, proclaiming His Kingdom prior to enunciating its laws and exhibiting its benefits.

In this paragraph we have the account of the initial work in the proclamation of the Kingdom; the propaganda of the King commences.

There are three movements to notice in this brief passage. First, Jesus came down into Capernaum, and took up His residence there, and began to utter the fundamental note of His Kingly ministry—"Repent ye, for the Kingdom of heaven is at hand."

Then Jesus gathered a nucleus of men, for purposes of co-operation with Him.

The rest of the paragraph is occupied with a very brief and yet beautiful statement of the remarkable success attending the initial ministry of the King.

His residence in Capernaum is in itself remarkable, demanding attention. Why did Jesus come to Capernaum of all other places? Matthew, who is perpetually tracing the connection between the ministry of Jesus and the great prophecies of the past, distinctly says that "He came and dwelt in Capernaum, which is by the sea, in the borders of Zebulun and Naphtali: that it might be fulfilled which was spoken by Isaiah the prophet, saying,

> The land of Zebulun and the land of Naphtali,
> Toward the sea, beyond the Jordan,
> Galilee of the Gentiles,
> The people that sat in darkness
> Saw a great light,
> And to them which sat in the region and shadow of death,
> To them did light spring up."

Now let us go back to the prophecy of Isaiah. In ch. ix. 1 we read:

"But there shall be no gloom to her that was in anguish. In the former time He brought into contempt the land of Zebulun and the land of Naphtali, but in the latter time hath He made it glorious, by the way of the sea, beyond the Jordan. Galilee of the nations. The people that walked in darkness have seen a great light: they that dwelt in the land of the shadow of death, upon them hath the light shined."

In the consideration of the beginning of our Gospel we saw how Matthew quoted from Isaiah with regard to the virgin birth of our Lord; "The virgin shall be with child, and shall bring forth a son." The prophecy begins with the promise of the virgin conception and ends here with the Child born, and the government placed upon His shoulders; and constitutes a complete unveiling of the Divine purpose. The prophet Isaiah, standing on that mountain peak, and looking out over the mist and the darkness of his own time, saw the coming of Immanuel, God with us. He saw Immanuel go down to Zebulun and Naphtali, the lands that suffered most from the Assyrians, to the place and peoples most degraded as the result of their presence. This is not merely a geographical prophecy—it is that in a secondary sense—but it is a prophecy based upon a principle. When God visits His people for redemption, He comes where the darkness is greatest; where the peoples sit in the shadow of death. Geographically, and according to principle, He did that very thing. Capernaum was in the despised region of the country of the chosen people known as "Galilee of the Gentiles."

And you must be a Hebrew to understand that, or at least must feel with the heart of a Hebrew. It was "a portion of the country which had been overrun more than any other by the foreign invader, and therefore known as 'the region and shadow of death.'"

That was Capernaum; and Jesus began His public ministry there. He went down and dwelt in Capernaum. There was the first Christian settlement. Jesus did not go down to teach them how to obtain better social conditions, but to bring them to God. The difference is fundamental. His first word was "Repent." He did not commence where people were least likely to need it. Capernaum was His basis; His centre; the point from which He moved out to begin His preaching. The people which sat in darkness saw light; the people which sat in the

region of the shadow of death saw the great light; He began His initial, Kingly ministry, in Capernaum, on the fringe of things.

If we would be partakers with Christ in work, we must go to Capernaum; to the fringe of things; to the despised countries, to the helpless districts; to the regions wrapped in the pall of a great death, and a great darkness. It was not accidentally that Christ went and dwelt in Capernaum.

But what did His coming to Capernaum mean? When He came it was a great day for Capernaum, if Capernaum had only understood it. "The people that sat in darkness saw a great light. And to them that sat in the region and shadow of death, to them did light spring up." Think of it, that for a little at least, there dwelt in Capernaum the very Light of Life, the very Light of Love, the very Light of Truth. They became familiar with His form and the tones of His voice; for everywhere they crowded to Him from all the district, bringing unfit people in crowds. He was the prophet Who had lived in Nazareth through long years; now He made Capernaum His base of operations, that neglected city living under the shadow of death. When He came, men saw Life at its highest, and its best, according to a Divine Ideal; the Light of Love flashed over their sorrows and their sins; the Light of Truth illuminated the dark corners, and revealed evil things. There, in the midst of the darkness and in the midst of the need, He struck the key-note of His ministry.

That key-note was the proclamation of a great fact, and the uttering of a great call! The fact—"the Kingdom of heaven is at hand;" the call—"Repent ye." Jesus came into Capernaum, and men woke from their stupor, slumber, and degradation, and asked the meaning of the light.

He said, "the Kingdom of heaven is at hand." And while they heard Him say "the Kingdom of heaven is at hand," His own heavenly, Kingly life revealed it. Then they heard Him say, "repent," change your minds. They heard Him say, You are wrong in your surroundings because you are wrong in your heart. The darkness is on you because the darkness is in you. The Kingdom of heaven is come to you, and the Light is on you. Admit it by repentance. There was much more to say, much unveiling, much exposition, much illumination, but that was the key-note of all the message.

Then there came the necessity for something more; and we find Him calling to Himself these four men. Let us notice first, the call of the four men; secondly, the purpose for which He called them; and finally, their answer to Him.

Simon and Andrew were already personal disciples, as we see by reference to John's Gospel.

Andrew was one of John's disciples. On that third day, when Jesus had moved away and left John in order to proceed to His own work, Andrew had followed Him, and having come to the Messiah, had called Simon. In this picture in Matthew they are all fishing. This call was not to discipleship; it was the call to fellowship in service. He saw them there at their work, and looking at them while they handled the net, He said, " Come ye after Me, and I will make you fishers of men." It was the call to new work; to the abandonment of everything, in order to devote themselves to Him and His work.

This is not a call that comes to every man. Every man was not called, even in the days of our Lord's earthly ministry. All men are not called now. These men were thus specially called. For a year they had been personal disciples; now He called them to quit their fishing, to lay aside their nets, to go with Him for a new vocation and work. He illustrated their new work by using the figure of their old occupation—" I will make you fishers of men."

James and John were in their father's boat mending nets, and doing the work of their daily calling. It may be they had been called into personal fellowship before, but this was the call to service and work.

The King was about to enunciate His great propaganda of the Kingdom. In order to do so it was necessary that He should have a few men gathered around Him, who were loyal to His kingship.

He desired to utter the laws of His Kingdom, but He could only do so to men who were in His Kingdom.

When our Lord calls men away from their daily vocation into a new vocation, He calls them with infinite simplicity, and great sublimity, by suggesting to them that all that they have been using for themselves they can now use for Him. " I will make you fishers of men."

The principle here is not that Jesus is going to make us all fishers of men. He is going to make us all workers, and turn any capacity we have into account. Jesus found me at my desk with boys about me, teaching them, and He passed me one day and said, Come with Me, and I will make you a teacher of men. He took hold of that which I could do, and said, Do it for Me. If He had said "fishers," He never would have won me. He took fishermen, and He said, Fish. He will take soldiers if they will hear, and He will say to them, Fight for Me. He will take the teacher and say to Him, Teach for Me. What He wants, is men who will give Him the capacity they have, and let Him lift it into a higher realm, and He will use it, never mind what it is. He said to these men, Come with Me and I will make you fishers of men; I will take the training you have, and use it on higher levels.

And how beautiful is the answer! It is the same in each case. " Straightway " for Andrew and Simon; and " Straightway " for James and John. Straightway they dropped their nets and went out after Him. They left their nets and their father, and went out after Him to follow Him. At His command for service, they abandoned their daily calling. They did not do this until He ordered them to. The vast multitude of Christian people are not called to leave their fishing-nets. They are called to abide in their calling with God; which is quite as honourable as leaving it. The honourable thing is to obey Christ, and the despicable thing is to disobey. What He wants is men who can keep hold of the things of the daily calling, until He calls. Has He called you? If He has called you to the ministry, drop the things in your hands straightway; the Kingdom waits for violent hands. If He has not called you, keep hold of the fishing-nets, and you will find when the glory breaks upon your vision by and by, that the fishing-nets, and the fishing, were parts of God's work for winning the world. He called them, and they went straightway.

That last paragraph which tells of the initial success of this ministry of the King is very beautiful. He went everywhere, teaching, preaching, and healing. "The report of Him went forth into all Syria, and they brought unto Him all that were sick, holden with divers diseases and torments, possessed with devils and epileptic, and palsied." Was there ever such a crowd as that? The picture is hardly fascinating at first. Look at the crowd. Look at the fit, who are bringing all the unfit people of the district to Him. Yet it is the most beautiful picture. They brought the sick, the diseased, and the devil-possessed to Him, and He healed them. He is doing it to-day wherever He comes and exercises His ministry, though His word be stern as the flash of Heaven's own word—"Repent." They came after Him with diseased people, and broken people—those physically and spiritually afflicted. They are still gathering to-day, notwithstanding the fact that people criticise certain men and methods. Some come out of idle curiosity, but deep down underneath is the hunger to find some one Who will heal. This is a great picture! —Oh, it is a fearfully sad picture! One is always thankful as one reads it, though it seems a strange thing to say, to remember that the Master was not deceived by the multitudes. He knew perfectly well those thronging multitudes. He took accurate measure of the depth of their conviction, and its shallowness. He knew that within a short year or two, some of these very people would hound Him to His death. He knew they would kill Him, and He stayed with them, and loved them, and died for them. Oh! matchless King! Let us crown Him anew. Let us put upon His brow some other wreath, some other chaplet!

MATTHEW V. 1, 2

IT is important that we should intelligently understand the place of this Manifesto in the work of Jesus. We will therefore consider its occasion, its method, and its nature as revealed in these words; "And seeing the multitudes He went up into the mountain; and when He had sat down, His disciples came unto Him; and He opened His mouth and taught them." Its occasion was Christ's vision of the multitudes. Its method was that of the enunciation of the laws of His Kingdom, not to the multitudes, but to His own disciples. Its nature was that of revealing to them the first value of the Kingdom as being spiritual, and its ultimate expression as being material.

The occasion—"Seeing the multitudes." This is a very familiar phrase. Jesus had commenced His ministry. The days of privacy were for ever over. He had emerged from the quietness and seclusion of Nazareth, and had commenced to tread the pathway upon which there beats a fiercer light than ever falls upon a throne—the pathway of the public teacher. As He began there was a strange and wonderful attractiveness in Him, and the multitudes gathered round Him. The unfit people of all the countryside were attracted to Him. Probably the people in that district had no idea how many unfit and incompetent people there were in their midst until Jesus, moving through the towns and villages, drew them round Himself. We cannot too often read these words or too solemnly consider them and catch their meaning—"They brought unto Him all that were sick, holden with divers diseases and torments, possessed with devils, and epileptic, and palsied, and He healed them." What a gathering of unfit people! But not merely such. They crowded after Him, from Decapolis, from Galilee, from Jerusalem, from Judæa and beyond Jordan.

The people attracted by Jesus were

not a people of one class or of one caste. He attracted to Himself all sorts and conditions of men; and as the King passed through that region, all kinds of people came out after Him, crowded after Him; many of them to see His works,—the curious crowd, always attracted by something out of the ordinary, the weakest part of the crowd, always the most difficult to deal with. Other men were attracted to Him not so much by His works as by His words. But whatever the motive, they came, all sorts and conditions of men. People jostled each other who had never done so before; Pharisees side by side with publicans; ritualists side by side with harlots, and sinners; men of light and leading, and the scholarly men of the age, side by side with the illiterate, the degraded, the depraved. The presence of Jesus meant the massing of humanity without any reference whatever to the mere accidentals of birth, and caste, and position. Pharisees dropped their quibbling for a little to listen. Publicans quitted their seats of custom to hear Him. Men forgot everything about their divisions. Caste never lives for five minutes in the presence of Jesus Christ. He burns it up with His coming. He is never attracted to a man because of the breadth of his phylactery, or the enlargement of the border of his garment. He is never repelled from a man—blessed be God! —by his rags. Underneath the rags and the phylactery He sees the man, and He is after the man, not his clothes. And men know it, and they are always attracted by a man who is after them; so they gather to Him. That, then, was the occasion—"Seeing the multitudes, He went up into the mountain"—leaving the multitudes in the valley.

They did not stay there; they followed Him, and there is no doubt they heard a great deal of this Manifesto. But He did not address it to them; the Manifesto was not for the mixed multitude. It is not for the mixed multitude to-day. "Seeing the multitudes, He went up into the mountain, and when He had sat down His disciples came unto Him, and He opened His mouth and taught them—the disciples, not the multitudes. You ask; Do you mean to say Jesus did not intend this enunciation of laws for the multitude? Do you mean to say He left the multitude, abandoned the multitude, had no care for the multitude, and gave His teaching to a handful? Yes; but He left the multitude in order that He might get back to the multitude. He left the multitude in order that He might equip the men who would obey His law, and then show the multitude what that law really meant in life. He left the multitude in order that He might begin the training of that company of men who should return to the multitude and bless the multitude.

The method of Jesus is manifested in this. The multitude cannot appreciate this law; cannot obey it; will not be attracted by it; will rather be affrighted by it. He must give the law to some souls who can appreciate it, obey it, and then manifest it. He must give His law, not to the promiscuous mob, which is curious merely, but to the selected souls who are loyal. That is the principle. Do not forget that the multitude is in His vision and in His heart. It is that He may get back to them, that He leaves them, and enunciates the ethic of His Kingdom to the few. He saw the multitudes. How think you, He saw them? He saw them as they were, and He saw them as they might have been. Christ's vision of the crowd is a vision of the crowd as it is, in comparison with the crowd as it might be. He saw their ruin, but He saw the possibility lying behind the ruin. He saw God's order. He was God's King. He knew what God's Kingdom meant in an individual life, for He was living therein Himself. He knew what God's government meant in a social order. He knew that if God's Kingdom were established among the multitudes, there would be none of the class bitterness and caste distinction driving man from man, brother from brother. He knew that if God's Kingdom were established among the multitudes there would follow the true social order; that humanity in the Kingdom of God would not be an aggregation of individuals fighting for individual existence, but a great community of men, in which every man

38

should make his contribution to the commonwealth. He saw the possibility of a great communism. Do not be afraid of great words because they have been abused. Jesus Christ's was the real socialism, the communism of humanity, the great brotherhood of men. He knew these things could only be realised as men were related to the throne of God. He knew that socialism is not anarchy. First there must be the relation of all men to the throne of God, and then their necessary and consequent interrelation among each other. And as Jesus Christ looked out over the multitudes He saw them scattered as sheep without a shepherd; no one to fold them, no one to feed them, no one to lead them, no one to govern them. And seeing the multitudes, and knowing that they needed supremely the Kingdom of God set up, He left them and took a few men with Him, and unfolded to them the laws of the Kingdom, and began the work of coming back to the multitude with the revelation of that Kingdom.

He saw the multitudes. One loves to read those words, for here we see the King, God's King, our King, the King of the whole world, looking at the disorderly multitudes, the disorganised multitudes, and we see burning in His heart the primal passion of a King. God's kings are always shepherds, and shepherds feed the flock, rather than are fed by the flock. Shepherds fold the flock, rather than expect the flock to fold them. And the primal passion of the King is burning here. Here are the people, spoiled, disorganised, because they have lost their relation to the throne of God; and seeing them, seeing the multitudes, the great heart of the King yearning over His people, He went up into the mountain.

That leads us by a necessary sequence to the second matter—the method of the Master as He sets Himself toward reaching the multitudes with the Kingdom of God. "His disciples came unto Him, and He opened His mouth and taught them." Here we must pause carefully, for an understanding of that principle, and this method will help us through the study of this Manifesto.

Who are these men to whom He is speaking? Souls loyal to His Kingdom. Jesus never gives the law of His Kingdom to any save to those in His Kingdom. No man can have the benefits of this Kingdom until he has kissed the sceptre of the King. When a man has bowed to the King then he has an obligation to the King and must obey the law of the King.

The late Archbishop Magee once said that it was impossible to conduct the affairs of the English nation on the basis of the Sermon on the Mount, and there was a great commotion among the religious and irreligious papers, and he was criticised from Dan to Beersheba. But Archbishop Magee was quite right. You cannot govern the English nation on the basis of the Sermon on the Mount—because the nation is not loyal to the King. If you have any doubt, all you have to do in these interesting days is to get a seat in the legislative chambers and endeavour to introduce half a dozen principles from the Sermon on the Mount in a short bill, and see if you can get them carried. You will find that to be the surest test of the accuracy of what the Archbishop said. You cannot do it, because you are not dealing with a people prepared to obey.

Let not this be misunderstood for a single moment. Has a Christian man nothing to do with Government? He has everything to do with it, or ought to have. We are to dictate the terms of righteousness to every Government. The Church of God needs to shake herself free from all complicity with every political party in the State, and then she will be able to dictate the terms of righteousness on behalf of humanity and God. That is her business.

It is quite impossible to take the Sermon on the Mount and try to get men to obey it until they are themselves obedient to the King. Think of some of the things He said: " Ye are the salt of the earth. . . . Ye are the light of the world." Do you suppose He meant the mixed multitude when He said that? And every benefit that He speaks of is a benefit belonging to the man who is in the Kingdom, and not to the man outside. A man comes and asks if we will not treat him as Jesus has taught us to do in the Sermon on the Mount. Certainly we will. But when a man in rebellion against the laws of Jesus asks us to give him our coat, we decline. Let him enter the Kingdom, and as God shall help us we will try and help him, suffer with him, rejoice with him. We have no right to take these benefits of the Kingdom and scatter them before a people who are still rebelling against the King. He begins by enunciating the law to the disciples.

The nature of this Manifesto is revealed in the words, " He taught them." Now the need of a Kingdom was common consciousness in the days of Jesus Christ. The very crowd who crucified Him were sighing after the setting up of a Kingdom. There was no question in the mind as to the value which would have accrued if this Kingdom could have been set up in some way. That is true to-day. Men are everywhere acknowledging the need of some new social order. Jesus had to teach in order to show that the ideal of the Kingdom in their mind was a degraded ideal. The ideal of the Kingdom, popular in the days of Jesus, was that of a Kingdom material in its conception and exclusive in its application.

We need not follow the subject further than to say that we have only to watch the disciples themselves to see how degraded their ideal was. Notwithstanding the teaching, it was a long time before the vision of the Kingdom broke upon them ! After His resurrection they came back with the same old question : " Lord, dost Thou at this time restore the kingdom to Israel ? " It was purely a material question. They expected a king with an earthly policy, an earthly government, an earthly army and retainers, setting up a kingdom of the earth. That is what men were looking for. Even men outside the circle of His followers had hoped that Jesus Christ had come to break the power of Rome, to be the divider amongst them as to property. And Christ had to teach these men that He was not proposing to begin His government thus. The Christ does not begin in the material realm ; He came to teach men that character is before conduct. He came

to teach them that the spiritual relation underlies the material manifestation. He came to teach them, as we shall see, that He does not say a word about policy, not a word about the government of property, not a single word about any of these things ; but He gets down under the surface, and He corrects man in the realm of his character. He says " Blessed," but never a single blessing does He pronounce upon having anything or doing anything ; every blessing is pronounced upon *being*.

When Jesus came to set up a Kingdom, the first thing He said was ; It is not a question of what you have, or what you do, save in a secondary sense ; it is a question of what you are. And that abides until this hour in all national affairs. We are bound to go on legislating in this country, of course. The Legislature must meet and do some good or harm, as the case may be. They must go on. But the true imperialist is the Christian man who recognizes that Jesus was right when He said : Deal with men as to what they are first, then you can touch all the other things. Everybody else who has tried to lift the world has tried to purify a stream. He passes back to the fountain source and purifies it there. Character is supreme. The spiritual is the fundamental. These things being set right, everything else will be set right. And so Jesus left the world without a political programme uttered, without the constitution of a State given to men in detail. And yet He left having uttered the one and only political programme, the one and only State constitution—He left the world, leaving behind Him the revelation of the fact that *being* is more than *having* or *doing;* that the spiritual fact is the fundamental fact in all life.

The occasion of the Manifesto, then, was Christ's vision of the multitudes, and their need, and His determination to reach them. Retiring from them, He took time to instruct a few loyal souls concerning His Kingdom in order that through them the multitudes might see the breadth and beauty and beneficence of the Kingdom of God.

His method was that of gathering

loyal souls around Him, giving them the law of the Kingdom because they had yielded to the claim of the King.

Finally, the nature of the Manifesto is an unfolding of principle, a teaching of men, which corrects the mistaken notions of national greatness and reveals the things which are supreme.

MATTHEW V. 3-12

IN considering the first two verses of this chapter, we dwelt upon the fact that the ultimate purpose in the mind of the King was that of bringing the multitudes into the Kingdom of God; but that in order to do so it was necessary for Him to gather round Him a nucleus of such as were actually submitted to His Kingship, in order to unfold to them the meaning of that Kingdom by an enunciation of its laws.

Perhaps the best name for this enunciation is that given to it by Dr. Oswald Dykes, " The Manifesto of the King." That exactly expresses the truth concerning the nature of this great utterance of law.

In these opening Beatitudes, the King revealed the truth concerning the essential nature of His Kingdom, as He made plain this one, simple, and all-inclusive fact, that the Kingdom of Heaven has first of all to do with character. How strange these words of Jesus must have sounded in the ears of His disciples, if, peradventure, they were expecting Him to give them a Manifesto of the Kingdom. They had heard the herald say, " The Kingdom of Heaven is at hand. Repent." They had heard Jesus say, " Repent ye, for the Kingdom of Heaven is at hand," but in all probability so far they only looked upon Him as another teacher, preparing the way, and leading them on toward the coming King.

But, supposing for a single moment, that they understood the fact that He was indeed God's anointed King, and supposing that in their submission to Him there was an intelligent submission to the Kingdom of God, focussed, and manifested, and demonstrated in a Person; then if they had climbed that mountain to listen to Him as King, they must have been strangely startled with His first words. There is not a word in these Beatitudes which appears to have anything to do with a kingdom,

according to popular conceptions of what kingdoms are, and in what the greatness of kingdoms consists.

Human ideas of a kingdom gather round thoughts of race power, of military prowess, of material pomp. Even to-day we hear people, largely void of the Christian spirit, boasting of such things, imagining that greatness consists in armaments. Our ideals of a kingdom are still somehow strangely mixed with trust in military prowess. But they are false ideals if we understand the deep meaning of righteousness. We still think of pomp, and glitter, and tinsel, as signs of greatness. Our ideas of a kingdom are still very much what they were in olden days. Slowly, very slowly, there is dawning on the common consciousness of man the conception that national greatness is the greatness of character.

This, however, forms the first stage in the teaching of the Manifesto of God's great King. Both in His Person, and in His teaching, He ignored popular conceptions concerning the ideas of government, and, by ignoring, denied them. When He ascended the mountain it was with no fanfare of trumpets, with no pomp, and no pageantry. This King, sublime in the simplicity of His Manhood, ascended a mountain, gathered around Him a few loyal souls, who did not perfectly understand Him, and taught them that nothing is of greater importance than the making of character. Thus He taught them; and the first things He said were the fundamental things of the Kingdom; but there is not a word about race power, or military prowess, or material pomp, from beginning to end.

Let us, then, consider the words; and in doing so, we will attempt first of all to indicate the general principles; and then we will endeavour to see the particular revelation of character granted.

In looking at the general principles, we notice the first word that fell from the lips of the King when He commenced the enunciation of the laws of the Kingdom—"*Blessed.*"

This word reveals God's will for man, and so reveals the purpose of the King in the establishment of His Kingdom. How strange a thing, and yet how gracious a thing it is! The word in the original is translated in our Authorised Version as "blessed" forty-three times, and as "happy" six times. There is a general consensus of opinion that the word most accurately expressing the meaning here is the word "happy" rather than "blessed." There is no doubt that the finer and fuller word is "blessed," always providing we understand it in its true meaning, as indicating a consciousness and a condition, rather than as referring to bestowment from without. It is true that the blessing is bestowed, but the word "blessed" here, refers to a condition, and therefore to a consciousness. But the word "happy" more easily suggests the simple thought of the Greek word in its common use. "Blessed" is correct if we understand it in the sense in which we use it of God in the phrase —"The glorious Gospel of the blessed God." Yet that may be translated with equal accuracy, and perhaps with a finer sense of its real meaning, "The Gospel of the glory of the happy God." "Blessed" is therefore a condition—such a condition as to create a consciousness, which is the consciousness of a perfect peace, and a perfect joy, and a perfect rest. All these things are included in the condition of Happiness! That is God's will for man. That is the Divine intention for human life. Sorrow and sighing are to flee away; He will wipe away all tears. Happiness and joy are never to flee away; He will never banish merriment and laughter.

"Happy" is the first word of the Manifesto. It is a word full of sunshine, thrilling with music, brimming over with just what man is seeking after in a thousand false ways. The Manifesto is not formal and documentary. It does not begin "Whereas," but "Happy." That was the first word

of the King as He sat upon the mountain, surrounded by His disciples. But ah! His own heart was unhappy, wrung with a great anguish, moved with an infinite compassion. But why His sorrow, why His unhappiness, why the melting, moving, thrilling compassion? Because He saw all the tragedy of human sorrow. From the centre of that sorrow He said, "Happy;" and thus revealed the Divine purpose for men.

Then we notice that happiness is declared by the King to depend, not on doing, not on possessing, but on being. "Blessed *are* the poor." "Blessed *are* they that mourn." "Blessed *are* the meek." "Blessed *are* they that hunger and thirst." "Blessed *are* the merciful." "Blessed *are* the pure in heart." "Blessed *are* the peacemakers." Not a single word about doing or possessing. It is what a man *is* that matters.

An evangelical value runs through these "Blesseds;" for the King declared happiness for such as, through sin, lack true happiness. "The poor in spirit." Apart from the King's Beatitude, this is the description of a condition which popular conception looks upon as unhappy. "Poor" is a word which does not suggest happiness. "Poor" means lack, lack means sorrow; and yet the King said, "Blessed are the poor in spirit." That is the recognition of a lack, but it is also a recognition of something that supplies the lack; and so sounding through the Manifesto we hear the music of the great evangel. There was in the mind of the King the consciousness of a great need, a great provision, and the possibility of a great result.

Once again, notice the peculiar form of the Beatitudes. "Blessed are the poor in spirit; *for* theirs is the Kingdom of Heaven." "Blessed are they that mourn; *for* they shall be comforted," and so throughout. "Blessed are . . . for." Character creates conditions which result in happiness.

Take the first, by way of illustration. Poverty of spirit results in realisation of the Kingdom of God. That is happiness. Jesus does not say that the Kingdom shall be given to the man that is poor in spirit. He does not say that if a man is poor in spirit, He will give him the Kingdom to make him happy. The poor in spirit is happy because he has the Kingdom of God. The happiness of the Kingdom is a natural sequence, not an arbitrary reward. The King does not bestow gifts to make men happy. He creates a condition within the man, which enables him to find happiness everywhere. He does not create happiness by new surroundings. He creates new surroundings by happiness. He takes a man and makes him happy by reason of his character, and then immediately this man puts his hand on everything that lies about him, changing his environment by himself being changed. Happiness begins within the man, never without.

There are thousands of illustrations of this to-day. Some one stands outside certain circumstances of life, saying;—Oh, if only I were in those circumstances I would be happy. The King does not begin there. " Blessed " is a condition consequent upon character. Happiness has its root, not in outward circumstances, but in inward condition of character.

But in order that these things may be more clearly revealed, let us pass to a particular examination of the particular character in the Kingdom which the King revealed. First, let us take the characteristics, remembering that a characteristic is always a smaller matter than a character. Character is the sum and substance of characteristics. It is very difficult to describe a character. Character may defy our perfect analysis. It does not defy the perfect analysis of the King. He thus described the characteristics. Poor in spirit; they that mourn; the meek; they that hunger and thirst; the merciful; the pure in heart; the peacemakers. These are the characteristics that go to make the perfect character, upon which the Kingdom of God is to be based.

There are two sets of characteristics in the seven Beatitudes. The eighth, which is a double Beatitude, has to do with the process and not with the character. But in the first seven you have a set of four which are passive, and a set of three which are active. The poor in spirit : the mourners : the meek ; they that hunger and thirst, these are

the passive characteristics of the character. Merciful ; pure—and pure here means infinitely more than clean, it means undivided, wholehearted—peacemakers ; these are the active qualities in character.

Let us consider the passive characteristics. " Poor in spirit." It means truly subject. The man who is poor in spirit is the man who is willing to be governed. The man who is not poor in spirit is rebellious, troublesome, creating discord within the Kingdom. This is the first thing. It is very simple! It is very sublime! If this life of mine is willing to be ruled, it is ruled. If this life of mine is willing to be governed, it is governed. If I will but take this life of mine and surrender it wholly to the King, the King will take charge of it and administer it, and I shall be in myself, when every one else is excluded, a Kingdom of God ; and I shall be in myself, when all others are included, a part of the Kingdom of God. " Poor in spirit "—theirs is the Kingdom of God. We never know the breadth and beauty and beneficence of God's humanity by looking at it from without. The poor in spirit are those in whom the pride of the will, and the pride of the intellect, and the pride of the heart, are alike bent to the royalty of the King. We obtain the Kingdom when we submit in poverty of spirit to the King.

But again, " They that mourn." And here the evangelistic value is at once manifest. The first matter is initial. The man poor in spirit is so because he has learned his own incompetence, his own unworthiness; because he is conscious of his own failure, conscious that he cannot of himself take hold upon all the ideals that are being represented to him by the King. This man mourns over his own sin, over his own failure. This is the mourning intended. Jesus says, " They shall be comforted." The great word " comforted " is related to the word that Jesus used when He promised the coming of the Holy Spirit. The Comforter disannuls orphanage, takes hold of a man in his sorrow and assuages it, heals it. The poor in spirit, submitting to the Throne, and to the government of the King, is troubled immediately ; he mourns over sin, and incompetence, and failure. That soul is comforted with the comfort of the Holy Spirit, the Paraclete, the very life and soul of the Kingdom.

"Blessed are the meek." The meek are those who are obedient to the rule of the King; meekness is the submissive spirit, the spirit of true humility, which is unconscious of humility; the spirit that rejoices in the Kingdom already established, on account of the comfort already given, and waits for orders, and does not obtrude itself. As we read these words, "Blessed are the meek, for they shall inherit the earth," we seem to hear those other words, "Come unto Me . . . for I am *meek* and lowly in heart; and ye shall find rest unto your souls." The men, poor in spirit, mourning over failure, comforted by the One great Comforter, are meek; and "they shall inherit the earth," for they have partaken of the very spirit of the King Himself.

And yet again. "Blessed are they that hunger and thirst after righteousness." This seems to be a retrogression, a going back. But it is a progression, a going forward. Who is the man that hungers and thirsts after righteousness but the man who himself is meek and possesses the earth, who has mourned and has been comforted, who is poor in spirit and has submitted to rule? What is hunger and thirst after righteousness? It is Divine discontent with everything unlike God. Do not make this a small and narrow personal experience. It is that, but it is infinitely more. It is the passion for the setting up of the Kingdom of God amongst men. It is the thing that makes you—if you are a Christly soul—hot, and restless, and angry, and discontented, in the presence of all the mal-administration of the affairs of men, which results in the ruin and sorrow of men on every hand. "They that hunger and thirst after righteousness . . . shall be filled," they shall be satisfied, there shall come to such all that for which they hunger and thirst. Perchance not to-day, perchance not to-morrow;

"The fog's on the world to-day,
It will be on the world to-morrow;

Not all the strength of the sun
Can drive his bright spears thorough.

"Yesterday and to-day
Have been heavy with care and sorrow;
I should faint if I did not see
The day that is after to-morrow.

"The cause of the peoples I serve
To-day, in impatience and sorrow,
Once more is defeated—but yet,
'Twill be won the day after to-morrow.

"And for me with spirit elate,
The mire and the fog I press thorough;
For heaven shines under the cloud
Of the day that is after to-morrow."

These, then, are the passive characteristics of the character of the Kingdom; poverty of spirit, which submits to government and possesses the Kingdom; mourning over declension, which is comforted with the great comfort of God; meekness which is unconscious humility and willingness to submit, which possesses the earth; hunger and thirst after righteousness—a great passion for the Kingdom of God, which is filled in hope and at last shall be filled in actual realisation.

Then immediately the characteristics pass from the passive into the active. "The merciful." That is, those who give and those who serve. It is the activity of life toward the suffering. "Blessed are the merciful, for they shall obtain mercy."

"Pure in heart." And here, as has been already noticed, we have more than cleanness; we have wholeness, the undivided heart, the heart that is utterly and absolutely loyal. This is the expression toward the King of the mercifulness described. "They shall see God."

And this again merges into yet another description—"The peacemakers." This is the propagative character, the man who, being all the rest, therefore brings peace wherever he comes. And the great word concerning the peacemakers is, "They shall be called sons of God," for in that they manifest the nature of the Father and the likeness of the Father more than in anything else—making peace among the sons of men.

This description of character is a growth. Poverty of spirit issues in mourning for sin, and the twofold primary condition is answered by the Kingdom bestowed, and comfort given.

Then meekness of spirit is submission to the will of God. Hunger and thirst evidence passion for the will of God, and the twofold answer to those who have submitted to His will in meekness is a present contentment. " They shall inherit the earth;" and to those in whom there burns the passion for the final setting up of His Kingdom, and the accomplishment of His will, there is a promise of the ultimate satisfaction—" They shall be filled."

Then upon the basis of that growth there follow the virtues of Christian life. Mercifulness—indicating service; purity of heart—indicating the inward condition; peacemaking—indicating the effect produced on others.

Then crowning all, there is the great Beatitude which illuminates the process of pain, and suffering, and persecution, through which men pass into this great character.

This is not merely a growth, it is a unity. We can take any one of the rewards and use it after any one of the conditions, and find no lack of harmony. We may say, " Blessed are the poor in spirit, for they shall be comforted." It is perfectly true. " Blessed are the merciful, for theirs is the Kingdom of Heaven." That is equally correct. " Blessed are they that hunger and thirst after righteousness, for they shall inherit the earth." That is a great philosophy. " Blessed are the meek, for

they shall be satisfied." That is equally true. We may transpose all these answers of happiness to all these conditions. The King gave us an analysis of one character rather than a description of different characters. All these virtues and values are to be found in the one type of character which lies at the foundation of this Kingdom.

And yet that must not be misunderstood, for there is a great sequence. Experimentally no man enters into any of these, save in the order indicated. First, the poverty of spirit, which ends rebellion, and, submissive to the King, kisses His sceptre; then the mourning that follows; then the meekness that ensues; then the passion that flames; then the service that is merciful; then the purity of heart that enables a man to see God; and then the great, sweet, strong, influence of peace, and man becomes a peacemaker.

The proportion in which men realise this character is the proportion in which they realise happiness. But the realisation of such character in the midst of all the conditions of worldly life which are contradictory to that character, will stir up opposition. How correct a picture of worldly life we have in this passage if before each promise or blessing the word *not* were added! Theirs is not the Kingdom of Heaven; they are not comforted; they shall not inherit the earth; they shall be hungry and thirsty, yet they shall not be filled; their hearts are corrupt, they cannot see God.

MATTHEW V. 13-16

IT is at once evident that these words were addressed, not to the promiscuous multitude, but to the inner circle of disciples. Having declared that the supreme matter in His Kingdom is character, and having described that character in the Beatitudes; the King showed that the purpose of the realisation of character, in the subjects of the Kingdom, is that they may exercise an influence upon those who are outside the Kingdom, and revealed the nature of that influence.

Influence is His ultimate intention in

His present government of, and relation to, His Kingdom. To recognize this is again to be brought face to face with that fundamental truth, that, although He spoke to His own, the multitudes were ever in His sight, and on His heart. The law of the Kingdom is for such as have submitted to the King; but they are to be governed by that law in order that they may become the means of blessing to the multitudes beyond. As the Shepherd King leaves the multitudes, for the saints, that He may instruct them, it is not for their sakes merely. He loves the people, the vast unheeding multitudes; and if He blesses us, it is that we may bless them. If He conditions our life, it is that we may exert among them an influence that shall be for their healing and for their uplifting.

Christ's estimate of the needs of the multitude is revealed by His description of the influence His people are to exert. The influence is to be that of salt and light. Salt is needed where there is corruption. Light is needed where there is darkness. Jesus, looking out over the multitudes of His day, saw the corruption, the disintegration of life at every point—its break-up, its spoliation; and, because of His love of the multitudes, He knew that the thing they needed most was salt in order that the corruption should be arrested. He saw them also wrapped in gloom, sitting in darkness, groping amid mists and fogs. He knew that they needed, above everything else, the irradiation of the pathway, the illumination of all things; that they needed light.

This is Christ's estimate of the need of the multitude of to-day, for His words were not for a day or an age, for a geographical position, a coast limitation, or a national boundary; His words were words for all ages. He did not deal with the accidentals of human life, but with the essentials. As Jesus looks out over the vast multitudes, for whom we are responsible, He knows their need, and that need is still expressed in the two thoughts suggested by the description of influence; they are in circumstances of corruption and darkness.

With these preliminary positions in mind, let us consider the passage before us in three ways. First, the character of the influence which Jesus declares will be exerted by such as are in His Kingdom; secondly, the influence of character; thirdly, the solemn, and earnest, and urgent teaching of Jesus concerning the responsibility of the subjects of the Kingdom with relation to the exertion of such influence.

First, then, the character of the influence which is to be exerted.

According to the teaching of Jesus, the character of the influence is the influence of character. "Ye are salt," "Ye are light;" not, Ye have salt, or, Ye have light. Much less does He say, Ye dispense the salt, or, Ye dispense the light. There is all the difference between a living influence and a dead, official, attempt at influence. If Christ had said, Ye dispense the salt, then we might have looked upon our position as official. There is no such thought. The King began with the fundamental necessity of human nature, and He said, "Ye are." It is only as a man is salt in his character that he can exercise the influence of salt in his age. It is only as a man is light in himself that he can scatter light upon the pathway of others. Jesus always takes hold of human nature as it is according to Divine intention, and bases His whole philosophy of life and influence upon the first Divine thought in the creation of man. The influence you exert is always the influence of what you are. No man exerts upon other people any influence by what he says to them, save only as what he says is the outcome of what he is in the deepest fact of his being.

As the father of a family, the influence you exert upon your boys and girls, is the influence of what you are, and not of what you tell them they ought to be. It is the influence of your own personality in its deepest fibre that is going to make or mar your bairns. There is no escape from this. We may tell our boys to be good; and, if we are bad, by the grace of God they may be good—some other hand may mould them, some other life may win them—but if we are going to win our boys for goodness, we must be good. Our influence comes out of what we are. "Ye are salt," and if you are not salt, you lack the power to exercise the aseptic function.

"Ye are the light of the world," and if we are not light we cannot shine.

As one studies the teaching of our Lord, one is more and more impressed with the fact that He never tarried upon the surface of things, but that He got down to the depths. We shall never exercise the influence of salt, or the influence of light in our family, in our church, or in our city or nation, unless we are right ourselves. One of the most damnable heresies that has ever been foisted upon the thinking of any age is that a man may be pure in public influence if impure in private life. He cannot be. What we are, determines the character of our influence in the world, whether we will or no. Thus the character of the influence to be exerted by those who are in the Kingdom, is the influence of character.

Secondly, what is this influence of character? The Lord made use of two figures, "salt" and "light." Here, again, He was careful with the infinite care of an infinite wisdom, and He made application of each figure in a natural sphere, and not carelessly. He did not say, Ye are the salt of the world. He did not say, Ye are the light of the earth. He said, " Ye are the salt of the earth," " Ye are the light of the world."

We will look in each case at the property described, and at the sphere of its activity.

First, salt and its sphere—the earth; secondly, light and its sphere—the world.

" Ye are the salt of the earth." The one value of salt is aseptic. In the presence of the fact of corruption, it prevents its spread. Salt never changes corruption into incorruption; it has no power to do so, but it prevents it spreading; moreover it reveals soundness, and creates the opportunity for its continuance.

There is not a believing man, woman, or child, who is able to take hold of any corrupt man and make him pure. That is not our work; we are not equal to it. Thank God, the Master is equal to it. Thank God, the King at the wicket-gate of the Kingdom can take hold of the vilest man and make him pure as He is pure. Our influence is of another value. Salt takes hold of that which is not yet corrupt, and prevents its becoming corrupted; it holds back the corrupting forces, and creates the opportunity for the exercise of goodness, and the continuity of soundness. Jesus never made a mistake in His figures. The intellectual supremacy of Jesus is such as to enable us to take the smallest figure He made use of, and

base on it a whole philosophy that is suggested by its use. " Salt " we are to be, men and women, who by our life and presence in the world check the spread of corruption and give goodness its opportunity.

Do not forget that the Beatitudes closed with the affirmation of persecution. Do not be surprised at that. But we want " salt " men and women in the stores, in the offices; we want men and women everywhere, who, by their living, check corruption—young men in whose presence no man dare tell a questionable story; young women to whom other young women in their sin will come, and ask for help and advice, that the good desire that has been hindered by evil power may blossom into beauty.

Now let us notice the sphere in which salt operates. " Ye are the salt of the *earth*." The word which Jesus made use of here marks the distinctly material side of things—the earth, literally the standing place; primarily the soil. It is a purely material word. But, of course, here it is used with reference to the people, the people viewed as of the earth. Men and women are of the earth. It is impossible for us to escape from the material, while we are in the material, and of the material; and we need have no desire to escape from it. But Jesus said you are to be the salt of the earth. You are to live in the midst of men and women who live in earthly conditions, and are material, in order to influence that side of things with an aseptic influence. You are to save men, render possible their salvation by hindering corruption on that side of their nature that is distinctly of the earth.

To go back to the first of the Beatitudes, " Blessed are the poor in spirit, for theirs is the Kingdom of Heaven." Now, look at those people poor in spirit. Theirs is the Kingdom of Heaven. The government of heaven, the touch of heaven, is upon their life, dominating, thrilling, and impulsing. Ye are the people who have the Kingdom of Heaven; ye are the salt of the earth, the medium through which the heavenly government shall operate in material things. The earth divorced from heaven is corrupt. Live in it as heavenly people, and check the spread of the corruption. The earth divorced from heaven has in it unrealised capacities. Realise in it the heavenly order, so that the capacities may be realised.

But again, "Ye are the light of the world." Here our Lord takes another figure, with a different note. The value of light is illumination, and that is at once a positive principle of life, and the condition for intelligent activity. Light is a revelation of how life ought to be lived, and wherever you get a revelation of how life ought to be lived, there is in the revelation that which begins to help men to live it. Example is not enough to save a man, but example is a great force in the growth of the man who is saved. It is a great force also in luring a man toward salvation. We are not called upon in any sense to save men. We are called upon to shine on men, revealing to them the truth concerning human life, the possibilities of human life, the principles that underlie human life, giving them to see what life may be; we are called upon *to be* light.

Now, notice the sphere of its operation—the world. "Ye are the light of the world," not the age, but the world, the cosmos. A great word, which includes not merely the life, but the whole created order. Here Jesus declares that His people are to illuminate other men as to their relation to the whole order, of which they form a part, and as to the necessary laws which govern it. All about us are men and women living not merely on the earth, but having relation to the infinite spaces, having relation to all created things, and therefore having necessary, even if unconfessed, relation to the Christ Himself. The cosmos is a word which speaks of the infinite order, and presupposes the intelligence which caused and controls the infinite order. Every man loyal to the law of Jesus Christ, and living in His Kingdom, is in himself a revelation of the unity of the universe of God, of the perfection of the harmony of all its parts, and of that unity and harmony as consisting in relationship to the Throne of God.

To live on Christian principles is to show men what would result if all the world were obedient to the whisper of

the Throne of the Most High. Every truly Christian life, every life submitted to the King, in loyal surrender, lights up the order of the universe; and from such life light will flash which will help men who are groping in darkness, and trying to find out secrets. The "Riddle of the Universe" will never be solved by examining the protoplasmic germ, or by careful examination of natural phenomena. Men living in the will of God are the light of the world.

But notice two things here. We are not to try to illuminate the universe; we are to live in loyalty to Christ; that is all. It is not by effort after illumination of the problem; but by quiet simple abiding in His will in the world, that character will flash its light abroad.

But, then, do not forget another matter. We hear a great deal about reflected light. We have heard it said that Jesus is the infinite Sun, and that we take the place of the moon. True, the great allegorical passage in the Song of Solomon says "she is fair as a moon," but it also says she is "clear as the sun," and she will only be fair as the silver moon, which kisses the night with softness and beauty, as she is clear as the sun. It is not reflected light merely; it is the light of our own life, communicated to us from the Essential Light. When we received the Essential Light it was not merely that we might reflect it; it was that it might ignite us and burn in us. It is only when Christian men are burning, as well as shining lights, that the world knows they are the light of the world.

Finally, what did Jesus say about the responsibility of the subjects of the Kingdom as to being the salt of the earth? "If the salt have lost its savour, wherewith shall it be salted? It is thenceforth good for nothing but to be cast out and trodden under foot of men." This has nothing to do with the question of a man's ultimate salvation. It has everything to do with the question of a man's present influence. We have no right to take things out of the context and say that Jesus says, if Christian people do not exercise the Christian influence of salt He will cast them out and they will be lost. This is a question of influence. The Master says, "If the salt have lost its savour." It is difficult to find a word that seems to catch and carry the real value of this word "savour." Of course, there is a simpler translation, "If the salt have lost its taste."

In a little pamphlet containing the Gospel of Matthew in broad Scotch, the reading is "The saut o' the yirth are ye, but gin the saut hae tint its tang." Perhaps that gets nearer to it than anything one can find. "Tang" is that quality in taste which is pungent, keen. Have you lost the "tang" of your Christianity? Do men know that you are a Christian? If there is no "tang" then listen to Jesus. He says you are good for nothing except to be cast out and trodden under foot of man. There are thousands of Christian men who have lost their "tang" and men trample them under foot; laugh at them, make fun of their Christianity. It is not enough to recite the Beatitudes. We must live in them, in order that the savour of them may tell among men.

As to the other responsibility for light, the King declared that there is a twofold influence of light—a city, and a lamp. "A city cannot be hid on the top of a mountain lying." Take out the affirmation that it cannot be hidden, and observe the description, "A city on the top of a mountain lying." That is the element of the Church influence of light. No individual Christian can exert that. One may be a beacon on the top of a mountain, but one cannot be a city. By the way of those who are in the Kingdom there will be the illumination of vast expanses. A city on a mountain lying, is seen from all the distant valleys; its flaming glory is caught from peaks far off and near. This is the picture of an influence that the Church has almost entirely lost; it is the picture of the Church's social order flashing its light upon the age. This is no careless figure. A city in which God is the Governor; a city in which there is nothing that defileth, nor worketh an abomination, nor maketh a lie; a city in which all things of beauty, and order, and light, and delight, are gathered; all that, the Church ought to be, and consequently she should guard the gates of entrance against all likely to corrupt and harm her. And when the city is that, when within her borders there is the realisation of the social ideal, so that when one weeps, others weep; and when one laughs, others laugh; when to the poor saint there is given of the world's substance, and to the needy, of spiritual help; and when no man says anything belongs to him, but they have all things common— when that is realised, then the Church is the "city on the top of the mountain lying," flashing her light over far places of the earth.

That is not all. "A lamp." The King passes from the city to the house. "A lamp that shineth unto all that are in the house." If the figure of the city illustrates the light as illuminating vast expanses, the figure of the lamp illustrates the light as irradiating private places. One cannot be a city lying on a mountain, but one can be a lamp in the house. That is the other exercise of the influence, so that all the family order is illumined by the presence of one Christian soul, one lamp burning for Jesus in the house. "Neither do men light a lamp and put it under the bushel, but on the stand, and it shineth unto all that are in the house." Do not forget this negative application. The exposition of Dr. Alexander Maclaren makes others unnecessary. He says, "No man lighteth a lamp and puts it under the bushel; but supposing he does, what will happen? One of two things: Either the bushel will put the lamp out, or the lamp will set fire to the bushel."

Lastly, the King said, "Let your light shine before men that they may . . . glorify your Father." And thus He summarized, employing in the final utterance—the last part of His figure— the whole truth, that in His Kingdom, character counts, because it exerts influence.

MATTHEW V. 17-20

HAVING thus declared the necessity for character; and indicated its issue in influence; the King prefaced His enunciation of laws, by a prologue on the general subject of law.

Let us carefully examine this prologue. Let us first analyse it, that we may discover its revelation of the relation of the King to the law; and the relation of His subjects to the law; and, secondly, let us notice two great principles, which are all-inclusive, and must be understood and remembered as we proceed to consider the law as He enunciated it.

When He said, "Think not that I came to destroy the law or the prophets," what did He mean by "*the law,*" and "*the prophets*"? What did the phrase mean to the men who heard it? If we can put ourselves in their place, and find that out, we shall have the true thought.

They were men born in Hebraism, brought up in the atmosphere of the Hebrew economy; and there can be no doubt that they understood Him to refer to the Scriptures of the Old Testament. These consisted of three sections—the Law, the Prophets, and the Hagiographa, or Writings. These men, therefore, certainly understood Him to say: I have not come to destroy the ethical code under which you have been living; I have not come to minimise morality; I have not come to loosen bonds which are intended to hold you to everything that is high and true and pure and noble; I have not come to destroy the law and the prophets, but to fulfil. These men thought of the law and the prophets as giving the economy which conditioned their life in the minutest particular and detail. They were governed by the law and the prophets; or they knew they ought to be governed by the law and the prophets; and that the measure in which they were sinning men, was the measure in which they were breaking the law, and disobeying the voice of the prophets.

The King ruthlessly swept away all the traditions of the elders; denying, by ignoring, the method of the Pharisee, the tithing of mint and anise and rue and cummin, the constant washing of hands. All this is of no value; the matters of importance are, the law, a Divine conditioning of life; and the prophets, a Divine call to obedience. Thus He brought these men face to face with the ethical requirement, and declared, "Think not that I came to destroy the law or the prophets"—I have not come to minimise morality; within the sphere of My government there will be no license; none of these laws will be destroyed in My Kingdom; nothing will be abrogated by My coming—"I came not to destroy, but to fulfil."

There are various interpretations of the King's meaning when He said He had come to fulfil the law. All of them may be correct, but most of them are partial. In my own study of these wonderful sayings of Jesus, I am more and more impressed that one of the surest methods of true interpretation is to get back and stand with the men who heard them.

Did He mean He had come to establish that great Kingdom wherein the law would be realised and obeyed? Yes, He meant that. But when the men heard Him, what did they understand Him to mean? On the eastern sky, so long grey and dark, the glory of a new morning was flashing. These men who had lived so long in the cold wintertide heard "the voice of the turtle in the land," and felt that springtime was coming whenever He spoke. Their hope was for the coming of the golden age, the dawning of the great day, of which the Psalmist sang, and which the prophets foretold. When He said, "I came not to destroy, but to fulfil," He meant: I have come to realise all that the law attempted to realise. It is not likely that they saw the Cross in His programme; although He knew it to be so. What they understood Him to mean was that He had come to fulfil the law personally, communicatively, universally.

And yet again. This was not merely

the declaration of a personal determination; it was an official proclamation. "For I say unto you, till heaven and earth pass away, one jot or one tittle shall in no wise pass away from the law till all things be accomplished." Here again one is tempted to ask, What did our Lord mean; "Till heaven and earth pass away"? The answer which comes most easily is that this was a figure of speech; that it was an indefinite way of saying that the law can never pass away. But it was not so. It is a most matter-of-fact utterance on the part of Jesus. When He said those words, it is as though He stood at the centre of the cosmos; of Heaven, which was ever the supreme place with Him; of Earth, the things which are patent to the senses; and said: The law cannot fail in the tiniest accent, in the minutest matter; it cannot be set aside, it cannot be abrogated, it cannot be trifled with as non-important while these things last as they are; "*Till* heaven and earth pass away; . . . *till* all be accomplished."

If we interpret the words by the constant law of Scripture we shall find that the words were not carelessly chosen. Is heaven to pass away? Yes, He says so; "Heaven and earth *shall pass away*, but My words shall not pass away." Is the material order in the midst of which the Son of God and Son of Man stood, in the midst of which we live, to pass away? He says so. The law, which is the statement in words of God's ideal, cannot pass, cannot be done away, cannot be abrogated in one jot or tittle, *until heaven and earth pass*. It must last while the cosmos as it is, lasts.

But when heaven and earth pass, does the law pass into non-existence? Until righteousness, the ultimate of law, be realised, law cannot pass; and that will not be till the heaven and earth pass. But beyond the heaven and earth that shall pass away, Peter saw "new heavens and a new earth, wherein dwelleth righteousness" (2 Peter iii. 13). Then righteousness will be unhindered, dynamical, masterful. Then the law will pass. It will not then be destroyed; it will have passed from word into spirit, from the cold letter

which affrights us, into the warm life which energises. That is what we are living for, and working toward. If you want to know how God is getting on, do not look around you to-day. Fight to-day, but look on to the new heavens and the new earth, wherein dwelleth righteousness.

Do not let us read these words of Jesus as though they were merely human rhetoric! I have not come to destroy law. I have not come to destroy the prophets. I am come to fulfil them. The law will abide; the prophets will remain until this sin-scarred earth and sullied heaven pass; and there come the new heavens and the new earth wherein dwelleth righteousness. That is the King's official declaration. Underneath that declaration, and in the presence of that manifesto, we who have seen Him and love Him are to live and fight and serve, God helping us.

Now, what does Jesus say of the relation of His subjects to law? I am not referring to the law of Moses—the ten commandments; but to the underlying principles which the law of Moses and the ten commandments imperfectly portrayed. We need not attempt to discover the relation between the Mosaic economy and that of the King; all that He will presently explain. He will show us how far the law of Moses is binding on us still. It is a deeper, profounder matter with which He was now dealing—"Whosoever shall break one of these least commandments, and shall teach men so, shall be called least in the Kingdom of heaven." This was a word of warning for the men inside the Kingdom. Notice carefully, "break" and "teach." You never find a man teaching that any commandment of God is unimportant, but that behind his teaching is the fact that he himself is breaking that commandment. "Whosoever shall break, and teach men so." That is a close connection, and the issue for that man is that he is to be least in the Kingdom. It is not a question of being cast out of the Kingdom; it is a question of his losing the honours and the rewards; the sense that he is co-operating in the building of the city, and the bringing in of the new heaven and the new earth.

But mark also the other side, in which the same philosophy is manifest —" Whosoever shall do and teach them." The only power of teaching is that of the doing which precedes it. No man ever teaches a commandment with power, if he is breaking it in his own life.

This is the relation of His disciples ιο law. Break the commandment, and teach men so, and you are least in the Kingdom. Do the commandment and teach men so, and you are great in the Kingdom.

Now from this analysis let us gather out the principles revealed.

The summary of all is in this last word of Jesus—" I say unto you, that except your righteousness shall exceed the righteousness of the Scribes and Pharisees, ye shall in no wise enter into the Kingdom of Heaven."

The conflict with the Scribes and Pharisees was beginning. It continued as He exhibited the benefits of the Kingdom; and when He enforced the claims thereof, it became more acute, until there came a day when He stood face to face with Scribes and Pharisees in constant conflict. In order to under-- stand what He says here, we must turn to chapter xxiii., " Then spake Jesus to the multitudes and to His disciples, say-ing, The Scribes and the Pharisees sit on Moses' seat; all things therefore whatsoever they bid you, these do and observe." Have you ever noticed that Jesus said that these men were to obey the teaching of the Scribes and Phari-sees? His quarrel is not with their teaching, in the measure in which it is an interpretation of law. He sweeps ruthlessly aside, as we shall see again and again, their whole teaching, when it becomes traditional merely. In so far as they sat on Moses' seat, men were to do and observe all they told them. " But," He continued, " do not ye after their works; for they say, and do not."

That is the whole story. At last He unmasked them. He warned His dis-ciples, however, at the beginning, that their righteousness must exceed the righteousness of the Scribes and Phari-sees. When at last the time came to expose them, He explained the inner

meaning of their failure. He began His preaching with the manifesto and the eight Beatitudes. He closed it for the public, by hurling eight woes upon the heads of the Pharisees. " They say and do not." That was the trouble with them. " They bind and bear not." " They do to be seen of men." " They love the chief seats . . . and the salu-tations." All the rest is a growth. The root is—" they say and do not." Jesus declared that in His Kingdom the prime necessity is that there must be a right-eousness which exceeds that.

What is the righteousness that ex-ceeds? He that " shall do and teach," the same shall be great. You are to do and say; you are to be and teach; you are to do to be seen of God; you are to be poor and meek and merciful. Briefly, the righteousness of the Pharisees was the righteousness that conditioned ex-ternalities only. The righteousness that the King demands is one that condi-tions the hidden and the internal, and so conditions the externalities. The righteousness of the Pharisees is the righteousness which expresses itself in the correct garment, and the wide phy-lactery on which quotations from law are written; something wholly for the eyes of men.

Here is a point at which to pause, lest we misunderstand. The righteous-ness which exceeds is not the right-eousness which is careless of testimony; but it begins farther back. The Phari-see is careful about the platter and the cup, the tithing of mint and anise and rue and cummin. The righteousness that exceeds is not careless about the platter and the cup; the righteousness that exceeds is not careless about the tithing of the small, the minute; but it does not begin there. The righteous-ness that exceeds is the righteousness that is anxious about righteousness, judgment, mercy, truth, the weightier matters of the law. The ethic of Jesus is far more severe than the ethic of Moses.

One other word. " I came to fulfil." Is not that a stern word? Oh to say it as it ought to be said! He says to these men standing about Him: Do not imagine that I have come to make things easy; I have not; do not imagine that I am going to let you loose from obligation; do not imagine for a single moment that I am going to destroy law or prophetic interpretation of law; I have come to fulfil. These multitudes would give anything to be let loose from obligation to law; I have not come to do that.

It is Christ's word to this hour. There is to be no license for passion. Here in My Kingdom, says Christ, you are not to be permitted the indulgence of sin if you pay pence; you are not to be excused from moral obligation and ethical exactitude, because you have high ideals.

"I came not to destroy . . . but to fulfil," and as the King utters the words, the flaming splendour of the law bursts upon us and the white searchlight of the Divine holiness lays bare our inner sin. Do not imagine that if you give yourself to Christ and crown Him King; He is going to minimise moral obligation. Do not imagine for a single moment that because you trust in this great, wounded, stricken, dying Redeemer; you are going to be allowed to nurse your sin, and refuse to confess it, and go on insulting His holiness. "I am come to fulfil." As He speaks one is affrighted. And yet, oh sinning heart, behold the Man Who speaks. While you see the white light of Divine holiness gleam from His eyes; see also the tender, God-like compassion of those eyes; and know this, that ere He has finished the prophecy of that word, "I came not to destroy but to fulfil,"

He will in some mystery of death and pain have taken hold of paralysis, and replaced it by empowerment. So that the King says; If you are going to follow Me, you must be pure, and you can. I will make you pure. You must fulfil law, and I will enable you to do it; I have come to fulfil. It is a great word; the last cry of the dying agony of the Son of God is in it.

Yet that is not the final thing. The triumphant shout of the risen Christ is in it. From that moment until this, He has taken men who come to Him to fulfil law in them, and so make law unnecessary. We do not want any ten commandments now, because His word is written in our hearts. We want no external standard to show how short we come, for we have the eternal dynamic that shows how great we may become in Jesus Christ.

Thus the King sets forth the value of law. It is a guide to righteousness in the sense of being a text-book revealing its expression. Law is not, nor can it ever be, the dynamic of righteousness. The law is a revelation of righteousness, and as a revelation of requirement cannot become obsolete until the righteousness described is realised. That righteousness exceeds that of Scribes and Pharisees.

The King will next proceed to describe it by example. The prelude may well affright us; it is a flaming sword; but let us follow the King, and we shall find that the great message of law is the evangel of grace.

MATTHEW V. 21-48

I SAY unto you, that except your righteousness shall exceed the righteousness of the Scribes and Pharisees, ye shall in no wise enter into the Kingdom of heaven."

"Ye therefore shall be perfect, as your heavenly Father is perfect."

The first of these verses constitutes the concluding statement in the prologue on law. In that statement the inspirational principle of obedience is declared to be passion for a righteousness which exceeds that of Scribes and Pharisees. In the giving of the laws of

the Kingdom there was neither the abrogation of existing laws, nor the utterance of any which are to replace them. In other words, Jesus lays down no rules for the government of human lives. He rather enunciates principles and communicates a life, which life in itself is at once pattern and power, a revelation of purpose, and a dynamic for the realisation thereof. No soul living in His Kingdom is governed by anything external to himself or to herself. We are not governed by a law of carnal ordinances; we are not governed by anything which Jesus said from without; we are governed by the living Christ Who dwells within, and interprets His will to us by the Holy Spirit. And yet speaking to these men who were to form the nucleus of His Kingdom He illustrated the ethic and illuminated the righteousness which exceeds, by reference to the Mosaic law.

This He did first with regard to human inter-relationships.

He first quoted two illustrative commandments from the decalogue (vv. 21-32).

He then laid down two bases of wider social relationship by quotations from other of the writings of Moses (vv. 33-42).

He finally declared that in His Kingdom the new attitude of men toward all other men, and especially toward enemies, is to be that of a great love (vv. 43-48).

In each case, after making quotations from the old economy, He interpreted their true meaning, and showed that He was not destroying but fulfilling. Making use of words they had been accustomed to, which had been interpreted by Scribes and Pharisees as to external obligation, He showed that these external requirements could only be fulfilled according to the mind of God, as men acted from an inner life which was pure. From the decalogue He selected the words which deal with the foundations of life—the laws of murder and marriage; the organism and its organisation—" Thou shalt not kill," " Thou shalt not commit adultery;" the one conditioning life as to the rights of personal being, the other conditioning that social system into which life is to be built up.

He then made selections from what we have sometimes called the minor laws of Moses, and in doing so He laid two bases of a wider social application, and dealt with the twofold spirit which is to actuate men in their relationship to one another—truth and justice. He conditioned their converse, banishing the oath, and establishing the simplicity of undeviating truth; and then showed them that justice is to be ensured between man and man, not from the centre of personal insistence, upon rights,

but from the new centre of making a man supremely anxious to do something more for his neighbour than his neighbour has any right to expect him to do.

He then rose to the final and supreme word of love. He did not insist upon love among neighbours and friends. That, with a tender and beautiful scorn, He treated as of small value—" If ye love them that love you, what reward have ye? " There is nothing which *exceeds* about that. It is not wrong to love the man that loves you. It is not wrong to love your friend and neighbour, but there is no particular virtue in it; there is none of the righteousness which exceeds. Scribes do it, Pharisees do it, Publicans do it, sinners do it. So He began with the impossible—" Love your enemies."

Here is a threefold process, moving out from the lower to the higher. In the individual man we first have laws conditioning physical life; then laws which condition mental attitudes; and, finally, one law conditioning spiritual being. From the basis of the body, through the superstructure of the mind, we come to the crowning glory of the spirit. Such is the line of development in man. So also in society comes first that which is physical—life and its culture; then that which is mental— the tone, the temper, truth, and justice; and then that which is spiritual— love. Not that the lowest is divorced from the highest, for all the truth concerning life and the marriage relationship is smitten through with the crowning glory of a spiritual love; and the underlying inspiration of truth and justice is the love which He insists upon at last. Into the warm light of the infinite Love—the crowning glory— are lifted all the lower relationships. It is a harmony, a great unity. The Master Lawgiver touches life in every one of its relationships.

Take, first, the illustrative commandments from the decalogue. " Thou shalt not kill," " Thou shalt not commit adultery." These are the foundation laws of social relationship. You cannot build up a new society except as these fundamental facts and requirements are perpetually borne in mind.

First, the sacredness of life, and

therefore the sternest possible dealing with anything which might issue in the destruction of life. "Thou shalt not kill." That is the first law of social life—individual life. Life is so sacred a thing, received from God, that it must not be interfered with or destroyed by any other living being. That is fundamental. There are a thousand ways of killing; you do not merely kill a man when you shoot him or stab him. This word of the Sinaitic requirement is a word which safeguards, as with a flaming sword, every life from harm, wrought by any other life. "Thou shalt not kill."

Then, "Thou shalt not commit adultery." Here is a recognition of the sacredness of marriage, through which the race is to be propagated and trained. God's first circle of society is not the Church, it is the family. Races are to be made or unmade as the family is made or unmade. Nations are to rise to progress, to power; or to pass, to perish, in proportion as they obey or break this Divine law.

Thus with delicate touch the King takes out of the Decalogue the fundamental things when He would illustrate the righteousness which is to exceed.

What does He say about the first? He gives us the picture of Jewish legal proceedings. "In danger of the judgment;" "In danger of the Council," "In danger of Gehenna." These phrases are purely Jewish. There was a court which dealt with minor matters, things of which, if a man were guilty, he was "in danger of the judgment"— the lower court. There were other matters that could not be dealt with in the lower court, things in which it had no jurisdiction; they must be submitted to the Council, the Sanhedrin, the higher court. And finally there was the valley of Hinnom, where the bodies of criminals were thrown, where they cast all the refuse of the city, and the heaps were set on fire for their utter destruction. Jesus, and those whom He addressed, were perfectly familiar with these things. When He said "judgment," nobody understood Him to mean the final day of assize; He meant this first tribunal, which dealt with minor matters. When He said "the Council,"

every one knew He meant the higher court, the Sanhedrin. And when He said "Gehenna," the hell of fire, they knew He meant that rubbish heap outside the city into which all its refuse was poured, and where fires were perpetually burning for its destruction; the rubbish heap on to which they cast the dead bodies of malefactors. Because this is a Jewish figure it does not lose its force. In the figurative the fact is always of greater force than the figure.

Now let us hear the King. He says, If you are angry with your brother, you are "in danger of the judgment." He is not now dealing with the actual Jewish judgment; that is the figure. The fact is His own judgment. You are in danger of having to stand before a tribunal, which is the tribunal of the criminal. Anger in the heart creates the condition of the criminal. This is the law inside the Kingdom. Not if you are angry with your brother "*without a cause*." Mark well the omission. We like these words, we would like to keep them. We can always find *a cause* if we want to be angry with our brother. Practically there is no doubt that the words "without a cause" are an interpolation, and do not occur in the original manuscripts; and their omission by the Revisers is the result of most careful examination, and a correct conclusion. If you are angry with your brother, He does not say you will appear for judgment, but you are in danger of it. You are on the path of peril that may lead you there.

But if you say to your brother, "Raca!" A great deal of time has been spent over this word, as to what it signifies, but this much is perfectly certain, it is a term of contempt. Address your brother with contempt, call him "Raca," and you are "in danger of the Council." The offense is more heinous, it will take a higher court to deal with you, because your sin is subtler, and more pronounced.

But if you shall call your brother, "Thou fool," which is a term of insult, then you are in danger of the ultimate punishment, of the casting out, of being counted fit only for the rubbish heap, which is outside the Kingdom of God, and shares neither its benefits nor its privileges.

When you are angry, when you hold a man in contempt, when you insult him, you are in danger of the Judgment, of the Council, of Gehenna. There is not a word about murder here. And there is not a word about killing here. There is no need. Jesus Christ does not begin to insist upon His penal code when a man has murdered; He arrests him before that. Murder in the making is arrested; and no man was ever murdered yet, whether by cool and calculating forethought, or in the heat of passion, but that at the back of it was the spirit that insults, the spirit of contempt, the spirit that is angry.

So to come back to the first of these, the King says: If you are never angry you will never murder. I will make your anger penal, and thus save you from murder. Life is to be sacred, so sacred that there is not to be the remotest chance of your hurting or harming by killing, because you will never hurt in insult, or despise in contempt, or nurse in your own bosom the anger in which lies the making of the ultimate murder.

Jesus has not yet done with this. He goes still further. He now gives them a law by which they are to govern their own conduct. It is law by illustration rather than by rule—"If therefore thou art offering thy gift at the altar, and there rememberest that thy brother hath aught against thee"—not that thou hast aught against thy brother; that is another thing which the Lord deals with elsewhere—"If therefore thou . . . rememberest that thy brother hath aught against thee," if you have been angry with him, if you have called him Raca, or fool, if you have wronged him, what are you to do? Drop your gifts and leave them. You are first to be reconciled to your brother, "and then come and offer thy gift." So the King safeguards the altar of God from the unholy intrusion upon its steps, or the unholy pouring upon its fires, of gifts by men who have in their hearts something which is harmful to the community. That is the law. Obey it, and there will be no murder. Obey it, and life will become sacred; every man's life will become as sacred to every other man as is his own.

But the King goes further yet. "Agree with thine adversary quickly while thou art with him in the way; lest haply the adversary deliver thee to the judge, and the judge deliver thee to the officer, and thou be cast into prison. Verily I say unto thee, Thou shalt by no means come out thence, till thou hast paid the last farthing." It would seem that Jesus is here passing behind the feeling that may be in a man's heart against his brother, and is dragging the arch-enemy into the light. Probably this term adversary refers here, as everywhere, to Satan. This is a figure of law. The adversary is the antagonist. It is strictly a legal word, and yet it is a curious fact that it occurs only four times in the New Testament, and every time it is used of an antagonist in law in a bad sense, and never in a good. It is the one word Peter uses concerning the great enemy, "Your adversary the devil." And the Greek word very bluntly translated means, "against right." It is the adversary in law, who is not on the side of righteousness.

But you say, Surely Jesus was not advising us to agree with the devil? Yes, exactly that. Let us follow it carefully. Here again in a flash He reveals the relation Satan bears to all such as are in His Kingdom. Satan is not powerful over such as put their trust in God. Jesus said on another occasion, "Satan asked to have you, that he might sift you as wheat." Now He says: If there is evil in your heart toward your brother, if you have wronged your brother, and he has that against you, then the adversary himself has a claim upon you; he can claim you to deliver you to punishment. His claim is established because of your wrongdoing. Haste from the altar, be reconciled to your brother; have the evil put away; agree with your brother; and so have done with the adversary that he may have no complaint. Remember Satan is the accuser of the brethren, the one who charges us with sin. So long as we are living in sin he has right over us, even though we be in God's Kingdom; we give him the right to lead us into the place of ultimate penalty. Thus the King safeguards human life.

Oh this ethic of Jesus, how it scorches! It was so easy a thing to do no murder. Through the accident of birth, or the accident of earlier surroundings we are devoid of a certain kind of animal courage, and so do not murder. But, oh my soul, when He says if I am angry and contemptuous I am in danger of Gehenna, there is only one thing for me to do—hurry to the Cross and its blood and its cleansing; to the Resurrection and its life and its dynamic. This ethic of Jesus, which does not express itself in small rules, but in great principles; not in a decalogue on stone, but in a requirement in the heart, is the severest thing that the world has ever had.

Again, how will He feel with this whole question of the marriage relationship and the first circle of human society? This is one of the things that Jesus, the Infinite Purity, knew must for evermore be handled with a touch of infinite delicacy, and yet with the grip of steel. There are no words wasted. There is no long description, satisfying the morbid curiosity of the unclean. There is one swift, burning, heart-searching flame. "Every one that looketh on a woman to lust after her hath committed adultery." Let no man who begins to undervalue the sacredness of the marriage relationship ever dare to say that he is in any sense a Christian. Here speaks the flaming heart of the Infinite Purity, loving the bairns, taking care of succeeding generations. The sin that curses society is a sin of the heart. Though that which Moses forbade be never committed, if the evil thing is there, the King says that it is sin. Stern words! Surely with love He is thinking of the little children. He is thinking of home, and the family; He is talking in the interests of the boys and the girls, of what they are to be when they touch the larger life. But there is no need to attempt to scent the rose, or to paint the glow of an evening sky, or to add any lustre to Infinite Purity. Read it until it search you and burn you, and know for evermore that this is the ethic of purity in the Kingdom of the great King.

So we pass to the two bases of wider social reform.

First of all, truth. Here we need not tarry, for again the words are so beautifully simple. Jesus says oaths of any kind are unnecessary in His Kingdom. The new character will make the old oath superfluous. You need not swear by heaven or earth, by Jerusalem, or by your hair. You will say, Yea, and it will be yea. You will say, Nay, and it will be nay. Simple truth, profounder far in convincing men than all your laboured oaths. We know full well that an oath is always a revelation of a possibility of deceit. We know perfectly well when a man is talking to us, if he begins to say that he is prepared to take his oath, we begin to think he is a liar. No man ever begins to offer to take an oath to prove a thing, but that one knows, that, even supposing this time he is true, the fact that he needs an oath to make one believe him, shows that at other times he is not true. Jesus says, Do not swear by heaven, for it is God's throne. Do not swear by Jerusalem, for it is His city, the "city of the Great King." Do not swear by your head, for you cannot make one hair white or black. Live in the consciousness of God, and you will not want to swear by things that are less than God. Do not swear by heaven, it is God's throne. Remember that, and you will always tell God's truth. The earth—green, beautiful—is God's earth. Remember that, and on its sward, and on its dust, and on its heaving billows you cannot lie. Remember that you are in the presence of God; that He clothes the earth with green; He is in the city, with its thrill, and throb, and pressure; that He is watching the silver of your hair; and then you will say, No, and every man will know that you mean No; you will say Yes, and the world will believe it; because they have come to know you.

And, secondly, justice. Justice is to have a new centre, a new desire. It is to be secured to others by overplus of love. The old economy proceeded from the centre of personal rights, but the new proceeds from the centre of delight in undeserved and unnecessary generosity. The other cheek! The man who struck the one does not deserve the other. Thy cloak also! No man deserves your cloak if he has made you give your coat up. The second mile! No man deserves that we should go the second mile with him when he has compelled us to go one. Notice, it is not if you go with a man, but if he compel you to go one, you must go the second. You say impracticable for London? Yes, utterly, until London bends at the Cross. You will have truest justice from the man who does more than can be required, for the more always means the inclusion of everything which can be required. When one sees a man cheerfully tramping the second mile, justice is there in the first, but the demonstration of it is in the second. That is Christianity; that is the overplusage. It is more than is required. The Christly soul, the man in the Kingdom is for evermore overfilling the measure, overstepping the necessity, doing that which no man had any right to expect from him. Justice becomes love-lit, and full, when He interprets it.

Finally, He says, love not your friends only, but your enemies. How does it culminate? " Ye therefore shall be perfect." And that is not the end of the Sermon on the Mount. There is a great deal more to be said after that. That commandment does not refer to anything except that which is set in close relation. Love your enemies, and so be like your Father. This is the ethic only, not the dynamic. Presently we shall have to say, Be like your Father, and so love your enemies. For the moment love is the law, the rule, the regulation, the principle of life that crowns everything. Go back over all this chapter, and you will find it is so. If you love you will never be angry, or call your brother Raca, or call him fool. If you love there will be no breaking down of the holy enclosure of marriage relationship, and the family circle. If you really love you will tell the truth, for a liar cannot love. If you love, as we have seen, justice will always be satisfied. Love is everything. And so the whole law is fulfilled in the one word love.

Let us take these requirements of the King one by one, and by them let us test our lives. It is impossible for us to do so without being driven to the conclusion that, unless He does infinitely more for the world than give it a code of ethics, He has but mocked our impotence and revealed our weakness. Thank God that we know Him not only, or first, as Lawgiver; but first as our great Redeemer, blotting out the sin of the past by blood, communicating new power by resurrection, and coming with us through all these human interrelationships, enabling us to fulfil them.

MATTHEW VI. 1-18

WE now pass to that section of the Manifesto which deals with the relation of man to God.

The King first lays down a fundamental principle, negative in form, but positive in intention and result. That principle is expressed in the words, " Take heed that ye do not your righteousness before men to be seen of them." The Authorised Version reads, " Take heed that ye do not your alms before men." The Revised Versions, English and American, substitute the word " righteousness " for " alms." " Righteousness " includes alms, and prayer, and fasting, the three matters subsequently dealt with. When Jesus uttered that first word He said everything, and all that followed was illustrative of the application of this principle to life; three departments being selected which peculiarly reveal human relationship to God in the present and probationary condition.

The principle is first applied in the matter of the giving of alms; secondly in the matter of prayer; and, finally, in the matter of fasting; alms, prayer, and fasting, the three great means of grace; the first stated being the final one in the order of experience. Alms is the last thing; prayer precedes it; and fasting prepares for prayer. The statement moves backward from the external manifestation of Divine relationship, to the internal sources of power. The proof of human relationship to God in the world is the giving of alms. The power that creates the giving of alms is prayer. The condition that makes prayer powerful, is that of fasting. These are the three *great* means of grace. There are others, external and smaller ones, which are merely sacramental symbols of the larger. The means of grace—and let us begin where the King finished—are: first, fasting; secondly, prayer; thirdly, the giving of alms.

First, fasting—the denial of everything that interferes with intimate, direct fellowship between the life and God. We may have our symbol of fasting if we like, in a day in which we eat no food; but that is by no means essential. Fasting is a matter far deeper, far profounder. It is the life suffering the loss even of rights in order that it may come into more strenuous relationship with God. That is the deepest means of grace; and in proportion as we learn what fasting really means, we approach the infinite sources of power.

After that comes prayer; and to the fasting life this is delightful, natural, spontaneous. The highest outreaching of the life is only possible as it is free from sordidness, sensuality, and the dust of to-day; and thus can hold unhindered spiritual communion with God.

The result of such prayer will always be that we hurry from the secret place, to give; to pour out alms! The giving of alms is much more than the giving of money. We may have no money. We may honestly be unable to put anything in a collection plate; and yet we may be giving God the richest gifts, a service of sacrifice—our blood, our life to help our brother.

The first words are fundamental. Let us begin there. "Take heed!" That is a flaming sword, warning men off from holy ground. Do not let us play with fire, do not let us come to these statements imagining that we have found a soft and sentimental teaching. They constitute rather a fierce fire! "Take heed." That is the word of a King. It is the word of in-

carnate Light. It is the word of absolute Purity. "Take heed."

Let us pause upon the threshold. We have been listening to what He said about murder and adultery; about truth, justice, and love. We have listened to the words, "Ye therefore shall be perfect, as your heavenly Father is perfect;" and as we are filled with fear at that requirement, He warns us yet again, "Take heed!" We are bound to listen reverently when Jesus says, "Take heed."

A reason precedes every deed. It may be a very poor one, an utterly false one, but it exists. There was never a deed done, but that it was preceded by a dream; never a victory won, but that it was inspired by a vision. Therefore the King says: Get your right dream, your true vision; that is, see to it that your motive is pure. Motive is everything in the Kingdom. Take heed that ye do not your righteousness before men. If we give alms that men may see us, we fail utterly in the ethic of this Kingdom. If we pray to be heard of men, or seen of men, our prayer is not prayer in this Kingdom. If we fast that men may be impressed with our religious devotion, we have our reward, but we are not in this Kingdom. Thus the King denounces as unworthy all religious acting which is inspired by the opinion of men.

How this scorches and burns! Dare any of us bring our lives to this test? We dare, we must, but it is a terrible ordeal. How much have we prayed before men? How much of our conduct is regulated by the opinion of men, and the thought of men? How much of our lower things, and even of our higher affairs, are under the impulse of what men will think? Probably the vast majority of people are more influenced by what men will say, than by what God Almighty thinks.

But listen again: "Do not your righteousness before men, to be seen of them; else ye have no reward with your Father Who is in Heaven." God has no reward for the man who is living before men. Thus the negative statement of principle becomes positive, in that it teaches us that the one, all-inclusive, all satisfactory motive of life is to be well pleasing to God. That is the ethic of the King.

He now proceeds to make application of the principle. First to alms, begin· ning in the external, with that which reveals to men, our relationship to God. " When therefore thou doest alms, sound not a trumpet before thee." This is a picture of the popular method of the hour in which Jesus lived. It is an actual piece of portraiture. Some Pharisee, intending to distribute gifts, would come to a conspicuous place in the city, and blow a small silver trumpet, at which there would gather round him the maimed, the halt, the blind. Then, with a great show of generosity, he would scatter gifts upon them. We may say that has no interest for us in these days. But it has interest for all time ; for here, as ever, if the Eastern and local colouring has faded from the picture, the great lines of truth stand out. Listen to the sarcasm of Jesus, " Verily I say unto you, They have received their reward ;" they did it to be seen of men ; they have been seen of men ; that is all they need ; they have what they sought. " But when thou doest alms, let not thy left hand know what thy right hand doeth ; that thine alms may be in secret." Nothing is in secret finally—" Thy Father Who seeth in secret shall recompense thee." Your Father has to do with that secret thing. Your Father has to do with the hidden things, the motives, the reasons that lie at the back of life ; and He says that the secret alms, given from secret love, He will reward.

Amos, in scathing sarcasm and de- nunciation of the people of his own age, said, You " proclaim freewill offerings, *and publish them.*" And this age is a continuation of the age of Amos. The King declares that this is not right- eousness before God.

If I left this here, where Jesus did not leave it, it would present a very difficult ideal. Yet it is simple, if mo- tives are right ; and therefore we go beyond this externality, this giving to others ; to that deeper thing that ought to underlie such giving—the prepara- tion of prayer. The order of statement is, first, Divine relationship in its out- ward expression toward men—alms ;

and secondly, Divine relationship in its secret expression toward God—prayer.

Here again we have first an applica- tion of the principle to the communion of man with God. It is to be between the man and God. The popular method, to be seen of men, again meets with the sarcasm of Christ. " They have re- ceived their reward."

Then follow instructions for prayer. First, privacy—go to your inner cham- ber, shut the door. That is the true place of prayer. We call the church building the house of prayer. In a sec- ondary sense it is so, but the true place of prayer, for the man who is in the Kingdom, is in the inner chamber with the door shut. How much do we know of the inner chamber and the shut door ? When a man announces that he is always, at such a time, in the inner chamber, with the door shut, that is a denial of secrecy. The principle is that we go there when no one else knows ; that we escape from human observation to loneliness with God. That is the first principle of prayer.

The next matter is directness. When you find your way into that inner cham- ber and the door is shut, " pray to thy Father." Directness of application and directness of statement are included in this simple phrase. There is a story which strikingly illustrates this prin- ciple of directness in prayer. In a Yorkshire chapel a prayer meeting was being held, and a few people were there who knew what prayer meant. There wandered into that meeting a man from the city, who had very little under- standing of the force and fire and fer- vour of true prayer meetings. He had that most terrible habit of *making pray- ers ;* and he made a prayer in that prayer meeting which consisted of beautiful sentences, in which he gave God all kinds of information which He had long before this man was born. For well nigh twenty minutes he prayed. At last he said, " And now, Lord, what more shall we say unto Thee ? " One old man, who knew his way into the Secret Place, and knew what prayer was, and who was weary and tired of this exhibition, cried out, " Call Him Feyther, mon, and ax for summat." That is the whole philosophy of prayer. "Pray to thy Father."

And then simplicity, "not vain repetitions." Of course this again is local colouring, for these Orientals would take one sentence, and repeat it again and again, imagining that the exhaustion that such repetition produced was a sign of power. Privacy, directness, simplicity, are the notes of true prayer.

He then gave them a pattern. In the opening sentence we have a great doctrine of God—" Our Father Who art in the heavens." The word here is plural, though our translators have not shown it; "Our Father Who art in the heavens." The New Testament speaks at least of three heavens. "The birds of the heaven," where the reference is to the atmosphere encircling the earth. "Wonders in the heaven," where the stellar spaces are intended. "Caught up even to the third heaven," that is, beyond the stellar spaces, to the place of the supreme manifestation of the presence of God.

"Our Father Who art in the heavens"—all of them. That is a doctrine of the transcendence of God; He is far away beyond all that of which we can be conscious. It is also a doctrine of the immanence of God; He is in the very air we breathe, as well as far away, infinitely out beyond the possibility of the mind's comprehension; in all infinite spaces, and in all near details, everywhere. That doctrine of God is the doctrine which enables a man to pray.

Again He is Father. If we understand that, we shall not stay arguing as to the possibility of prayer. We shall pray.

This pattern of prayer also reveals the true order of prayer. It falls naturally into two halves; the first has to do with God's Kingdom; the second with our need. "Our Father Who art in the heavens Hallowed be Thy name. Thy Kingdom come. Thy will be done, as in heaven, so on earth." That is the first concern in prayer. Prayer is not first of all a means by which we get something for ourselves; it is rather a method of helping God to get something for Himself. Thus, as in life, so also in prayer, the same law obtains—" Seek

first His Kingdom, and His righteousness, and all these things shall be added unto you." Apply this pattern of prayer to much of our praying, and we are ashamed! We pray about our need, and our family, and our neighbours, and our Church, and our country; and if we have a few minutes at the end, we pray for the missionaries. Jesus says that this is all wrong, for first must come God's Kingdom, and then our need. There is nothing omitted from that prayer. Our daily sustenance—physical, mental, spiritual—it is all there in "daily bread." Our inter-relationship amongst men—" Forgive us, as we forgive." We cannot expect forgiveness while there is malice in our heart. It is the only petition of which Jesus gives us an exposition. It will not do to say: We will forgive our debtors. We must get our paying done, before we begin our praying. And finally, prayer concerning the conflict with evil. "Bring us not into temptation "—that is the sense of fearfulness; "But deliver us from the evil "—that is the determination that whether through temptation or without it, the supreme matter is that of deliverance from evil.

Yet look at the prayer again. It is the inspirer of work. "Hallowed be Thy name. Thy Kingdom come. Thy will be done." If we are praying that way we must live that way, we must work that way; not merely for ourselves, but for our city, our nation, and the world, that everywhere God's name may be hallowed, God's Kingdom come, God's will be done. We shall work along that line if we pray in that way.

Then, again, it is the prayer of trust. We need sustenance; we tell our Father about it. We need restoration; we go to our Father. We need discipline; we talk to Him about it as we stand upon the threshold of it.

Then observe the socialism, the communism of the prayer. We must use a strong word because it is a strong prayer. Notice the pronouns of the prayer, the pronouns in the first person; "Our—us—our—us—our — we — our—us—us." There is not a pronoun in the first person singular. They are all plural. We cannot pray that prayer alone. There is no room for selfishness there. We are bound to bring somebody else in with us. It is interesting moreover to look at the cases here. There are four possessives, four objectives, and only one nominative. The nominative case is the popular one. We always like to be the subject of the sentence, and use the capital We. There is only one nominative here, and it occurs when we say, "as we also have forgiven our debtors." The only right we have to be the subject of the sentence is the right to forgive the man who has wronged us. That is prayer according to Jesus. It is a great social prayer. We cannot pray it alone, and yet we should go alone and pray it. He says, "Enter into thine inner chamber, and . . . shut thy door," and when nobody is there but yourself, begin to pray as though the whole world were with you. That is Christ's socialism. It is based upon strong individualism; —individually, a man alone with God; socially—the world on the heart, as the prayer is offered. If we learn to pray this way, a great deal of praying will cease, and a great deal of praying will begin.

And now the final matter. "When ye fast." The popular method is a sad countenance, a disfigured face, "that they may be seen of men to fast." What is Christ's instruction? "Anoint thy head, and wash thy face; that thou be not seen of men to fast, but of thy Father Who is in secret; and thy Father, Who seeth in secret, shall recompense thee." That is the true method of restraint and of self-denial.

We are perpetually insisting upon the necessity for self-denial, and we do well to insist upon it. It is at the very heart and centre of Christian life. That is the process by which the life is made strenuous. The athlete denies himself a great many things, in themselves harmless and proper, in order to win. There must be self-denial, there must be restraint, there must be fasting. But the mistake is that we fast in order that men may think how good we are. We get our reward, and there is nothing beyond. But if fasting is for the pur-

pose of finding the stronger, the truer, the nobler; in order to create larger room for the coming and going and sweep of the Spirit—then it is true. But what are to be the outward signs of fasting? The sad countenance and the disfigured face? Rather the washed face and the anointed head. Is it not time that we in the Christian Church talked a little less about self-denial, and lived it more? Have we not by over emphasising in our conventions on the one hand, and on the other, in the new ascetic ideal manifesting itself in scourging, been false to this word of Jesus, "Anoint thy head and wash thy face"? Oh, my life, thou shouldest keep perpetual Lent within the secret chamber of thy being, and everlasting Easter on thy face! The inner life must always be a denial of self, but we must come to the world with a smile and a song, and the anointed head, and the washed face. This is religion, this is life.

These are three great subjects, and they mark the revelation of man to God —alms, and prayer, and fasting. Deny the Divine existence, wholly or in part, and wholly or in part all these will cease. As a man loses his hold upon God, or as a man comes to deny God altogether, these things cease in the inverted order. First, fasting ceases. Then prayer ceases, for a man cannot pray unless he fasts—that inner fasting of the life; if that cease, prayer will cease. And then alms will cease. A man gives less now than when he had less to give, because he has been so very busy getting, that he forgot to pray. He forgot that not in making, but in fasting, is the real strength of life, and there is always degradation and deterioration, when that is forgotten.

These words and these deeds and these activities must be undertaken in actual relationship with Him. Alms must be given in the consciousness of His observation. Prayer must be offered in the place of loneliness with Him. Fasting must be solely a means of helping communion with Him.

MATTHEW VI. 19-24

THE King having declared the laws of human inter-relationship, and having dealt with the principles of Divine relationship, proceeded to the discussion of the attitude of His subjects towards earthly things. The subjects of the Kingdom still have necessary relationships with the earth. They are spiritually minded, but they have to touch material things. However much the inner life may be, and ought to be, in communion with that which is essentially spiritual, we can only continue to live at all as we touch and handle things which are seen and temporal.

The Manifesto of the King proceeds, therefore, to make clear what our relationship ought to be to the material things by which we are surrounded, and with which we have to deal.

Here, as on all former occasions, there is a remarkable absence of rules, but there is the clearest revelation of principle. Not by legal enactments, formulated, tabulated, and learned by heart; but rather by the creation of an atmosphere, and the indication of an attitude, does the King correct and condition our relationship to the things of the present life. Broadly, He teaches that, in all contact of His subjects with earthly things, they must be dominated by a super-earthly consciousness. Men must deal with the wealth of the world, but if their consciousness is conditioned merely within that material wealth, they fail. If all their dealing with wealth is motived by, and conditioned within a spiritual conception, then they will have found the deepest secret of life, and fulfilled the highest purpose of their Master. Men must have food to eat, must have clothes to wear; but if they spend all their days thinking about what they shall eat, or what they shall wear, they are not understanding or realising the ethic of Jesus. If, on the other hand, they recognize their Father's recognition of their need, and trust it; and then seek the Kingdom, in matters of food and in clothing, they are living in the realm of the true morality.

This section consists of two parts, each characterised by warning and instruction. The first is a revelation of the attitude of the subjects of the Kingdom toward wealth—they are to be without covetousness. In the second section, which we shall take for our next study, the attitude of the same subjects toward necessary things is indicated—they are to be without care.

This is the whole of His will for His people. This is not irrational; He proves it to be reasonable. This is not an appeal to credulity; it is a call for faith. This is not fatalism; it is the essence of fidelity, fidelity to the principles afore enunciated, to the purposes perpetually revealed, and to the great Lord and Master to Whom allegiance is owned.

In this first section, in which our Lord deals with the true attitude of His subjects toward wealth, let us first notice His distinct commands: "Lay not up," . . . "Lay up." Here is a negative and a positive—"Lay not up for yourselves treasures upon the earth." "Lay up for yourselves treasures in heaven."

Then let us notice the comparison of values. On the one hand are treasures laid up on earth which moth and rust consume, and thieves break through and steal. On the other are treasures laid up in heaven, to which neither moth, rust, nor thieves have access.

Next we will notice Christ's reason for this injunction, and revelation of attitudes. "Where thy treasure is, there will thy heart be also."

Still further we will look at Christ's exposition of the urgency of His commandments. The single eye necessary to the true illumination of the life.

Finally, we will consider Christ's last word, "No man can serve two masters."

First as to Christ's distinct command, "Lay not up for yourselves treasures upon the earth." The same word occurs twice; in the one case as verb, and in the other as substantive. We come nearer to an appreciation of what He said when we read, "Treasure not up treasures upon the earth, but treasure for yourselves treasure in heaven."

The simple idea of the word treasure is that of placing something somewhere; but it is in striking contrast to other words which also mean to place something somewhere. There is a peculiar quality in the Greek word which is not suggested by our word "treasure." Very literally the idea is to place something *horizontally*. There are other Greek words which mean to place something perpendicularly. Here we have an instance of the figurative element in language.

What was meant by placing horizontally? To place in a passive condition, as the word which indicates to place something perpendicularly means putting it in an active relationship. This word means to lay something aside horizontally—that is, to store something up, to keep it; not to place something perpendicularly, ready for activity and work, but to hoard it. It is the laying of things up, one thing upon another, piece upon piece, horizontally, that we may possess them, take care of them, and accumulate them. Every boy remembers that he has often been told, that the miser says coins are flat that they may rest; and the spendthrift says they are round that they may roll.

Now the King does not say that it is wrong to lay up, for while He says "treasure not up," He also says "treasure up." We need to recognize the positive as well as the negative part of the command. The common capacity to which He is here appealing is that of the passion for possession. There is not a single capacity of human life wrong inherently. The abuse of it, the misuse of it, is wrong. Whenever we see a man passionately desirous of possession we may say: That is all right. It may be made all wrong by his method and motive; by the way in which he attempts to possess, and the purpose for which he desires to possess. It is always the purpose at the back of things which matters. The King does not begin with externalities; He gets back to the deepest thing in a man's life, and deals with that. It is as though He said: You have a passion to possess wealth, you want to be able to place things horizontally; and it is

quite right that you should do so—God made you so. Being, having, doing; that is the story of human life. There is no Beatitude on possessing, but possession may be sanctified.

We want to make our fortunes. We have desires as passionate as those of any man to possess. And the nearer we come to our Lord, and the more we know of the indwelling Spirit, the more powerfully is the passion to possess burning in our heart and life. But the question of importance is as to the principle upon which we seek possession. Passion without principle burns out the life. Principle without passion sterilises it, and makes it hard and cold and stony.

That is a great word in the book of Ezekiel, spoken to the Prince of Tyre: "I have destroyed thee, O covering cherub, from the midst of the stones of fire." What a strange bringing together of contradiction! "Stones of fire." A stone is the last embodiment of principle—hard and cold. Fire is of the essence of passion—warm and energising. Put the two together, and we have stones—principle; fire—passion; principle shot through with passion, passion held by principle. Men have the passion to possess, to treasure up. What principle is going to govern us? That is the matter with which the Master is dealing.

The principle revealed is not that it is wrong to lay up treasures *for ourselves*, for when the Master comes to the positive statement, He distinctly says, "Lay up *for yourselves*." We have not yet discovered the secret.

It is discovered in the phrases, "Treasures upon earth." "Treasures in heaven." Christ says to His subjects, You are to fulfil that passion for possession by making your fortune, not for the present, the perishing, the passing; but for the future, the lasting, and the eternal. You are to remember, with the passion burning within you, that you are not the child of to-day, you are not of the earth, you are more than dust; you are the child of to-morrow, you are of the eternities, you are the offspring of Deity. The measurements of your lives cannot be circumscribed by the point where blue sky kisses green earth. All the fact of your life cannot be encompassed in the one small sphere upon which you live. You belong to the infinite. If you make your fortune on the earth,—poor, sorry, silly soul,—you have made a fortune, and stored it, in a place where you cannot hold it. Make your fortune, but store it where it will greet you in the dawning of the new morning, when old earth passes from you. Make your fortune there. Possess not the things of the now; but the things of the now and the forever.

In dealing with Christ's comparison of values, we must allow for the Eastern colouring. Wealth consisted in those days very largely of fabrics, purple and fine twined linen: and the King says, I will tell you the story of them—moths! That is a fine touch of tender sarcasm. There is no anger in it. There is no thunder in it. It is a fine play of the summer lightning. Moths! Your immortal life cannot be hurt by a moth; do not try to enrich it with stuff which moths eat.

Or, if you will take some other currency, such as metal, store it up, lay it horizontally, pile it up, make it your treasure. The King says, Rust! What is rust? Fire. Present in all things is this *eremacausis*, this slowly burning fire, which eats into, disintegrates your most solid metal, melting it into azure air. The subjects of the King are not to try and make themselves rich with things which the frail moth can ruin, and the silent rust destroy.

And once again, " Where thieves dig through and steal." We need not dwell upon that. That is so modern that it needs no exposition.

What does Jesus say about the storing of the heavenly, about the laying up of treasure in heaven? Nothing positive; it is all negative, but thank God for the negatives of the spiritual world. No moth, no rust, no thief. If we can only store the true riches, as we work and toil, we shall know that no moth can ever eat the garment, or destroying fire touch the fine gold, or marauding thief rob us of that which is our own.

But next, why this urgency? " For where thy treasure is, there will thy heart be also." There is a passion for possession. We must satisfy it. The thing which matters is not so much the possession of the treasure, as the effect the possession of the treasure will have upon us. Here we hear our Lord's deepest heart speaking, and it is as though He said: My child, I know that passion for possession; it is quite right; God made thee so. It must be met and satisfied; but I am seeking, even more than the satisfaction of any desire of thy life, proper as it may be, to teach thee that everything depends upon where thy treasure is as to where thy heart will be; and everything depends upon where thy heart is, as to what thou wilt be, for as a man thinketh in his heart so is he.

If we take our treasures and place them here, our heart will be here, and we shall be here, and we shall become of the earth earthly, sensualised, materialised, degraded, because we have put our treasure here. But if we put our treasure out yonder in the infinite, if we somehow learn the secret of laying up treasure beyond, our heart will be beyond, and our life will be lifted, and all the light of the infinite spaces will be within us, and all the love of the Infinite Heart will dominate us, and all the undying life of the infinite God will be ours, surging, beating, thrilling, throbbing through us.

And then, as though the Lord turned from these things to give an exposition of the meaning and urgency of it all, He says, " The lamp of the body is the eye." The eye is the lamp, not the light. The light is outside it, beating all round about it, but it is the lamp which catches the light, and enables us to see and to realise. " The lamp of the body is the eye: if therefore thine eye be single, thy whole body shall be full of light. But if thine eye be evil, thy whole body shall be full of darkness."

The word " evil " here does not mean wicked, but out of order. Evil is a larger word than sin. Evil includes sorrow, and affliction, and calamity, and fault, as well as definite and positive and wilful sin. " If thine eye be evil " —out of order—" thy whole body shall be full of darkness." Here Jesus seems to say, the thing of utmost importance is that you should have a right view of these things in satisfying the passion for possession. You must have a true view, and that is what He has been attempting to give. The single eye. The evil eye. These are the contrasts. The single eye is the eye that is unified or simple. The evil eye is the eye that is not simple. An oculist will tell you that there is such a thing as astigmatism—a malformation of the lenses, of such a nature that rays of light proceeding from one centre do not converge in one point. The single eye is the eye without astigmatism. It is the eye with the lenses properly adjusted, of such a nature that rays of light proceeding from one centre do converge at one point. Jesus was not using the word here carelessly when He said "single." It is the eye which has no obliquity, which sees everything true, and in proper proportion. If the eye be evil, then how great is the darkness, what misunderstanding of life, what dire and disastrous failure!

In *Modern Painters* John Ruskin says: "Seeing falsely is worse than blindness. A man who is too dim-sighted to discern the road from the ditch may feel which is which; but if the ditch appears manifestly to be the road, and the road to be the ditch, what shall become of him? False seeing is unseeing, or the negative side of blindness."

That is the modern method of saying what Jesus said in far more remarkable language: If your eye is single your body is full of light. If it is evil, suffering from malformation, distorted in its view, then your conceptions will be false. The single eye is the eye that looks always toward the infinite, and answers the passion of the soul to possess, in the light of it. The evil eye is the eye that suffers from astigmatism, or obliquity, and has varying centres, and varying reasons, and no focussed light, and consequently produces a degraded conception of things.

Finally, the King sums up, saying, "No man can serve two masters: for either he will hate the one, and love the other; or else he will hold to one, and despise the other. Ye cannot serve God and Mammon." Here is the deepest thing of all. We want to possess. What shall we do with this passion of our life? We must worship with it, as we must worship with every passion. With it we may worship Mammon. With it we may worship God. We cannot do both. That is the great distinctive principle. No man can become the slave of his treasure and worship it, without thereby proving himself traitor to God. No man can be the bond-slave of God, worshipping and serving Him with all the heart, and all the mind, and all the strength, and be enslaved by Mammon.

"Lay not up for yourselves treasures upon the earth." "Lay up for yourselves treasures in heaven." Does our Lord, then, mean that we are to have nothing to do with the wealth of the earth when He says, "Lay up for yourselves treasures in heaven"? Does He simply mean we are to pray, and strive, and work for the salvation of men? All that we are to do, but that is not what the Lord means here. He is simply speaking of earthly treasure from beginning to end. He is referring to the same class of treasure when He says, "Lay not up treasures upon the earth," as when He says, "Lay up treasure in heaven." He does not mean by this second "Lay up treasure," your toil and prayer and work. He is speaking of the self-same material, earthly wealth. He teaches His people what is the right and wrong use of wealth. He tells them how to deal with a superabundance of wealth. You may say: There is not a man who has a superabundance. There is not a man who has not a superabundance! This is not an attempt to put any measure upon the quantity of it. Do you know what is necessary after all? What God has promised to supply us with in the matter of material things is that which is necessary for our life to-day—bread and water; that is all God has promised. "His bread shall be given him; his water shall be sure." Whatever additions you have had to bread and water, have been superabundance. Think it out in the light of all Christ's habit of teaching, and you will come to the recognition of the fact that we are living in an age which is being spoiled by its softness. We call very many things necessary to-day that our fathers called luxuries.

A man may say, What shall I do? I cannot lay purple up in heaven, ducats up in heaven! Oh, yes, you can! Christ hereby declares that every child of His love, and every subject of His Kingdom, is the steward of all he possesses, and that, beyond the necessities, with which we shall deal in our next study, all the superabundance is to be at the disposal of the King, in the interests of the Kingdom of heaven. On another occasion He said, "Make to yourselves friends by means of the mammon of unrighteousness; that,

when it shall fail"—mark the new rendering of the Revised—"they"—the friends that you have made by means of the mammon—"may receive you into the eternal tabernacles." "Lay not up for yourselves treasures upon the earth." Do not take the mammon and pile it to possess it. So use it as to make friends by its means, that presently they, the friends, shall meet you, and greet you in the everlasting habitations. Let us make such a fortune that when at last we come home we shall be greeted by the friends that we have helped to reach home. Let us rather have our fortune on the other side than on this.

MATTHEW VI. 25-34

IN this section of our Lord's Manifesto; continuing His revelation of the principles which are to govern His people in their relation to the things of this life, He enjoins on them the necessity for a super-earthly consciousness in touching earthly things. Towards superabundance, as we have seen, they are to be without covetousness. We will now consider their attitude towards necessary things, which is, that they are to be without care.

In this connection one injunction is thrice repeated. "Be not anxious." "Therefore I say unto you, Be not anxious" (ver. 25). "Be not therefore anxious" (ver. 31). "Be not therefore anxious" (ver. 34). This is the all-inclusive word. It is illustrated, emphasised, argued, with inimitable skill by the great Master and Teacher Himself. It accurately defines the whole attitude of mind which His disciples should maintain toward necessary things. "Take no thought" was a most unhappy mistranslation, for, as we shall see before we have finished, that is exactly what the King did not mean. All His argument as to our attitude being characterised by freedom from anxiety, is based upon the fact of our ability to take thought. He does not hint for a single moment that we are to be careless or improvident. That against which He charged His disciples, and still charges us, is carking care,

the care which means fretting, worry, restlessness, feverishness; or perhaps, better than all, in the simple terms of the Revision, "Anxiety;" "Be not anxious." There are things of this life which are necessary, which, so far as we know, have no place in the larger life toward which we go. Food, drink, raiment, are necessary things, but are not provided for us by God apart from our own thought, our own endeavour, our own activity. But none of these things is to produce anxiety in the hearts of the subjects of the King.

"Be not anxious." The Lord argues for this injunction by three positions. "Therefore I say unto you, Be not anxious;" the first proposition occupying verses 25-30. "Be not therefore anxious;" the second proposition found in verses 31-33. "Be not therefore anxious;" the third proposition of illustration and enforcement found in verse 34. There are three movements and one message; three methods of emphasis and illustration and enforcement; and one matter of importance. Our Lord not only says, "Be not anxious;" but "Be not *therefore* anxious." Thus, in each new movement of emphasis and illustration He drives us back to something preceding. This is the word of the King.

Let us see how He enforces it. First, He declares anxiety to be unnecessary in the children of such a Father. In the second movement He declares anxiety to be unworthy in the subjects of such a Kingdom. In the third movement He declares anxiety to be unfruitful.

First, then, our Lord teaches us that anxiety is unnecessary. Look at the "therefore." "Therefore I say unto you." We are compelled to ask wherefore? On what is Jesus basing this appeal? You will remember two truths brought before us in the previous section. In showing what our attitude ought to be toward superabundance, He first made the truth about values perfectly clear. He insisted on the necessity for the single eye which sees things properly focussed; sharp, clear, true; in proportion and perspective. The point of view is everything. The evil eye is that which sees things obliquely; its vision is distorted, nothing is sharp, nothing is true, everything is out of proportion and perspective. Christ emphasised the necessity for the single eye, truly focussed; and He told His disciples in effect that they had that single eye when they lived for the glory of God, and that the true view-point of life is that of seeing things in their relation to the Infinite, to the Divine, to God Himself. The eye, single for God's glory, admits true light into the life. Further, we noticed how Jesus declared the unification of life in worship to be necessary. We cannot serve God and Mammon. Whomsoever we worship will demand the whole of our service. Life is unified by the principle of worship which governs it. He takes it for granted that these men have found the unifying principle in the service of God; that because they are serving God they cannot serve Mammon. Now, He says, "Therefore," upon the basis of the true vision of values, upon the basis of the fact that your life has become unified in the service of God; " Therefore be not anxious." Thus He defends the word; charging His own to be free from fret and friction and feverishness; upon the fact that, being in His Kingdom, they have found the true view-point, they have found the true principle, unifying and making life consistent.

From that He proceeds to work out in detail the truth of the love and the care of God. " I say unto you, Be not anxious for your life, what ye shall eat. or what ye shall drink; nor yet for your body, what ye shall put on. Is not the life more than the food, and the body than the raiment?" Declaring the care of the Father for the birds, He asks, "Why are ye anxious concerning raiment? Consider the lilies of the field, how they grow." The lilies to which Jesus pointed were not, of course, our lilies of the valley, but the great huleh lilies of Palestine, the most gorgeous and beautiful of all the flowers growing there. They grow in cultivated districts, or amongst the rankest verdure.

" As a lily among thorns,
So is my love among the daughters."

Of this gorgeous flower the Master said, " Consider the lilies of the field, how they grow." Mark this again: " they toil not, neither do they spin; yet "—even though they do not toil or spin—" yet I say unto you, that even Solomon in all his glory was not arrayed like one of these." The King comes where the children can accompany Him, and among the birds and flowers, in sweetest and tenderest of illustrations, He teaches the sublimest truths for the comfort of the heart of His people.

Let us ponder His teaching, first about the birds. He says in effect: These birds of the air neither sow nor reap nor gather into barns, but your Father feedeth them; you can sow and reap and gather, therefore much more does your Father care for you. The Lord's argument here is not that we are to cease our sowing and reaping and gathering, but that if He takes care of those who cannot do such things, much more will He take care of those who can. These birds of the air are without rational forethought. By comparison with men there can be no toiling, no sowing, no reaping, no gathering. But Jesus says, God has given you the power of rational forethought, and much more will He take care of you. It is not that we are to neglect the use of reason, or forethought, or preparation. It is not that we are to take no thought—unhappy mistranslation—but that we are to take thought for the morrow without anxiety, knowing that, as God cares for the birds, He will more perfectly take care of us.

So also with the flowers. "They toil not, neither do they spin; yet I say unto you that even Solomon in all his glory was not arrayed like one of these." Did you imagine that was figurative, an overstrained metaphor? Take that flower, that huleh lily, gorgeous and beautiful in its colouring, and put it by the side of Solomon in his magnificence, in his robes of gold and silver and jewels and splendour—the lily is more beautifully clothed than Solomon. Take the finest fabric that monarch ever wore, and submit it to microscopic examination, and it is sackcloth. Take the lily and submit its garment of delicate velvet to microscopic examination and investigation, and the more perfect your lens the more exquisite the weaving of the robe of the lily will be seen to be. Christ is not indulging in hyperbole. He is stating cold fact. No garment loomed to the finest and softest texture is anything but rough sackcloth when placed by the side of the drapery with which He clothes the lily. Christ says: Open your eyes, My children, and look at the lilies lying scattered over the valleys and mountains, growing among thorns, and know that when God makes the lily, kings desire and cannot obtain such a robing. Looking at the flower, and seeing all its decking, know this:

"He Who clothes the lilies,
    Will clothe His children too."

There is not a flower and not a petal which, in exquisite finish and delicate perfection, would not put all the robes of a king to shame.

But all this is true not only of those flowers of Palestine. Consider the daisy of the English fields, the sweet and simplest flower which you tread beneath your feet; and a king in all his robes of state is not arrayed like one of these. "But if God doth so clothe the grass of the field, which to-day is, and to-morrow is cast into the oven, shall He not much more clothe you, O ye of little faith?"

The emphatic words are, "much more," and it is important that we grasp their true meaning. The lily cannot toil, it cannot spin. You can do both; and if God takes care of the flowers which He has not gifted with this power of reason to toil and work for self-preservation, how much more the creatures to whom He has given this superabounding gift, and to whom He perpetually gives Himself in immediate and living presence.

Let us now look at the other two arguments briefly. He passes from this first statement, which shows how unnecessary care is if we are the children of such a Father, and He says "Therefore" once again. "Be not therefore anxious, saying, What shall we eat? or, What shall we drink? or, Wherewithal shall we be clothed? For after all these things do the Gentiles *seek;* for your heavenly Father knoweth that ye have need of all these things." Do not be anxious about these lower things, but there is something you ought to be anxious about. Do not always be planning and scheming even to the point of anxiety about food and raiment; "but seek." No life is complete that does not feel upon it some great compulsion, driving it. We want to learn to be loving and patient with all sorts of people, but it is difficult to have patience with some men! Their eye never gleams, they have no passion, no power; they drift. A man that is a real man has something that drives, something that creates enthusiasm. Now, says the Master, I have told you not to be anxious about these things. But there is something you are to be anxious about, something to seek, something to consume you. There is something that ought to drive you, making every nerve tingle and throb, and every artery flow with force. What is it? The Kingdom of God. So the Master would save us from the anxiety of a lower level, which makes force impossible on a higher, in order that He may develop force on the higher. Do not be anxious about the lower things, "But seek ye first His Kingdom, and His righteousness." Seek it in essence. Let it be the underlying passion. Seek it in enterprise. Seek it everywhere.

But is there not an immediate application? Food, drink, raiment. Do not be anxious about them, but seek the Kingdom in them. Dress for the Kingdom of God. Eat for the Kingdom of God. Let the great underlying passion, which is the great principle of the life, find its throbbing way into the extremities of the life. Things about which you are not to be anxious in themselves, and for themselves; you are to be anxious about, in order that through them also the Kingdom of God may come. Seek that in essence, in enterprise, and in individual application. With a touch of fine and beautiful disdain, which is not contempt—if we may make so fine a distinction—the Lord says, " All these things shall be added unto you." " Added unto you." Mark the conception—food, drink, raiment, added. That is, the necessary luggage with which you travel, the added things which are nevertheless impedimenta. Some people are always worrying, when travelling, about their luggage, and that is just what a great many are doing about food and raiment. These things shall be added. Trust them to your Father. Trust them after your toil is over, after your planning is done. After you have sown and reaped and gathered, leave the rest. And if you do not think by your calculation that your doing, and reaping, and gathering is enough for all, then let there be no anxiety. Your Father knows, and here is your blank cheque for necessities— " These things shall be added unto you."

Once again, anxiety is always care about the future. To-morrow, that is it. It is always to-morrow, and so Jesus sums the whole thing up finally, and says: " Be not therefore anxious for the morrow; for the morrow will be anxious for itself," by which we do not understand the Lord to mean that it is a proper function of to-morrow to be anxious about to-morrow, but by which we do understand Him to mean, Do what you will, there will be something in to-morrow to be anxious about. You cannot kill to-morrow's anxiety by being anxious about it to-day. And so He says, " Sufficient unto the day is the evil thereof." Evil does not mean sin.

It means adversity. Every day that comes will have in it evil—adversity— things calculated to make us anxious. To-morrow will be anxious. The evil will come whatever you do. All of which may be stated thus: Live, oh child of thy Father, subject of thy King, live to-day.

" Lord, for to-morrow and its needs
　　I do not pray.
Keep me, O Lord, from stain of sin
　　Just for to-day."

There is no suspicion of asceticism in this section. Our Father knows that His people will be here in the world, and will have to do with earthly things. He does not even say it is wrong to lay up treasure. He only advises us as to how we shall make our investment of treasure. Do not lay it up on earth. Lay it up in heaven. There is nothing ascetic here. There is no warrant for improvidence here. The man who will go out and say, Very well, I will be like the sparrow, I will not sow, or reap, or gather—well, we know the issue, and neither we nor anyone else will pity him. If a man shall say, I will go and be as the flower of the field, I will not toil or spin—well, we see at once the unutterable folly of such an argument. Do not imagine that the King commands us not to think for the future. Do not say, that because God cares, you are not to provide for your wife, and your bairns, in the case of your dying. Let us have no nonsense talked about the evil of insurance. " If any provideth not for his own, and specially his own household, he hath denied the faith, and is worse than an unbeliever," says the apostle; and the whole teaching of Jesus is, not that we are not to reap, sow, gather, toil, spin; but that through our toil and planning we are not to be anxious; through reaping we are to trust; in our gathering we are to sing; as we toil we are to rejoice; as we spin we are to be quiet. It is a call to the life that is frictionless, because by the principle of faith man takes hold upon God, and, submitting, knows what it is to have His power operating through his work, and His life providing for his need.

MATTHEW VII. 1-12

THIS chapter contains the last section of the Manifesto of the King, and may be described as a summary of principles of action. Its light flashes back on the teaching of our Lord, and forward on the obedience of His subjects.

The first twelve verses deal with the attitude of the subjects of the Kingdom to those who are without. In the first six verses the King describes that attitude. In the next five (7-11) He tells His subjects of the power in which they will be able to obey the injunctions given. In verse 12 He returns to the original teaching, linking it, in a crystallised form, with the truth He has declared concerning the power at their disposal.

First the attitude described. It is a twofold attitude—without censoriousness, "Judge not;" but with careful discrimination—Do not cast holy things to dogs.

As there breaks upon us a consciousness of the difficulty of obedience to this description of attitude, it seems as though the Lord, looking at that little group of men listening to Him, the first subjects of the Kingdom, had said to them, Does this appear to be difficult? Do you feel this is an impossible ethic? Is this something far exceeding the righteousness of Scribes and Pharisees? Are you doubtful as to how you will be able to obey? "Ask," "seek," "knock," and everything you need for obedience is at your disposal.

Then, having revealed the dynamic, He continues, and we specially need to notice one word in His next statement, for it is the key to the unity of the whole section. He says, "All things *therefore*," and that "therefore" leans back upon the "ask," "seek," "knock." "Therefore" links the final declaration concerning our attitude to the outside man, with the initial description, through the medium of the promised power.

This paragraph is unified, and its one teaching has to do with our attitudes toward other people. First, a detailed description; secondly, a declaration of the power in which we shall be able to obey so fine and searching an ideal; and finally, a command, which we describe as the golden rule, and often misquote by taking the words out of the context, and by omission of the "therefore," rob of half its force. We have no right to read this verse, "All things whatsoever ye would that men should do unto you, even so do ye also unto them." We have no right to quote it in that way, and to call it the golden rule. We must not omit the "therefore." If we do we cannot obey. If we retain the "therefore," then, amazed and terrified by the tremendous claim, we are driven to ask, to seek, to knock, and to know that the Listener to the asking, to the seeking, to the knocking, is our Father. Then the rule is golden, golden with heaven's own light, flashing with heaven's own fire, possible with heaven's own power—but in no other way.

Now let us turn to a consideration of these three sections. First, our Lord's description of the attitude of His subjects to those who are without. As already indicated, this divides itself into two parts. The first five verses forbid censoriousness; and the sixth verse insists upon a careful discrimination. The one commandment is contained in the first words. Everything that follows explains and argues for obedience to that command—" For with what judgment ye judge ye shall be judged; and with what measure ye mete it shall be measured unto you." That is graphic illustration. The King decrees that whatever measure we use, the other man will use the same. In what measure we mete in that same measure it shall be measured unto us.

A careful understanding of the use of the word "judge" here is very necessary, because in the second section when our Lord says, "Give not that which is holy unto the dogs, neither cast your pearls before the swine," He commands us to judge; and upon another occasion He distinctly said to His disciples, "Judge righteous judgment." So that this command, "Judge not, that ye be not judged," must not be taken superlatively as though we were not to use the reason and the powers of discrimination which are ours within the Kingdom of God. We must therefore understand what our Lord really meant by the word, and how He used it in this particular connection.

The strict meaning of the word " judge " is to distinguish, to decide; and the variety of applications possible to such a word is evidenced by the fact of the variety of ways in which it is translated in our New Testament. In the Authorised Version it is translated in all these ways: Avenge, condemn, decree, esteem, go to law, ordain, sentence to, think, conclude, damn, determine, judge, sue at the law, call in question. There is no value in that grouping save as it reveals the fact that the simplest thought in the word is that of distinguishing decision. Sometimes the decision may be adverse, sometimes it may express itself as a decree determined upon, sometimes it may express itself as a sentence to be carried out. All these varieties are seen in the translations made use of. The simplest thought is that of distinguishing, coming to a decision. Sometimes it runs out into action, sometimes it conditions a passive position. Therefore its particular sense must always be determined by the context. Here, evidently, the Lord did not use the word " judge " in the sense of forbidding us to discriminate, to distinguish, to decide. There can be no doubt whatever that He used it of coming to adverse conclusion in the sense of condemnatory censoriousness. " Judge not," condemn not, come to no final decision, do not usurp the throne of judgment, or pass a sentence, or find a final verdict; " Judge not, that ye be not judged." So He forbids to His subjects, the usurpation of the throne of final judgment about any human being. He tells them that they are not to judge in the sense of condemnation; that there is no power deposited in the individual life that shall enable that individual to find a verdict, and to pass a final sentence; and He warns us off, every one of us, from that spirit of critical censoriousness which decides concerning our brother, as to the rightness or wrongness of his action, because we cannot possibly weigh in the balances all the motives that may lie behind that action.

Our Lord then proceeds to give reasons against such judgment. First, retributive judgment will fall back upon the man who exercises such judgment. Of course there are different interpretations of the meaning of the words, " With what judgment ye judge, ye shall be judged." Does He mean with what judgment we judge our fellow man we shall be judged by God? Some commentators tell us so. We may judge our fellow man falsely; God cannot. We come to wrong conclusions because of the limitations of our being; God cannot come to wrong conclusions. That can hardly therefore be the meaning.

Then He proceeds to say, " With what measure ye mete, it shall be measured unto you." Luke chronicles the uttering of the same words at another time: " Give, and it shall be given unto you; good measure, pressed down, shaken together, running over, shall they give into your bosom. For with what measure ye mete it shall be measured to you again." There is no doubt that the King's purpose is to teach us that we must expect to receive judgment on the same basis as that on which we give it. If we set ourselves up as men finding verdicts and sentences, then we must expect to be so judged; and in the measure in which we mete to men our judgment, in that measure they will mete their judgment to us.

The King immediately rises into what would appear to be a higher realm— " Why beholdest thou the mote that is in thy brother's eye, but considerest not the beam that is in thine own eye? Or how wilt thou say to thy brother, Let me cast out the mote out of thine eye; and lo, the beam is in thine own eye? Thou hypocrite; cast out first the beam out of thine own eye; and then shalt thou see clearly to cast out the mote out of thy brother's eye."

" Beam," " mote." Nowhere else in the New Testament are these words used. Very literally, a beam is just exactly what the word means to us, the branch of a tree, or a massive piece of timber. A mote is hardly what we understand by a mote. It is a dry twig off a branch, a chip from the beam itself. Of course, the proportion is the same. The small thing is the mote; the beam is the great thing that blinds entirely. What is the beam to which the Lord refers? He is speaking to men who exercise a spirit of criticism against other men, who are supposed to be sinners above the measure in which the critic is a sinner. This cannot apply, therefore, to the case of a man who is living in vulgar sin if he criticise the man guilty of a sin less venal. The beam is not what the world calls a vulgar sin, because the man living in open and vulgar sin never does criticise the man guilty of small sin. If the beam be some prominent vulgarity, then there is no point in the illustration at all. The man who says there is something in the other man's life which is not consistent, is the man that says that there is nothing inconsistent in his own life. Yet the King says that there is a beam in his eye; he who professes to have the right to criticise his brother has something greater—a beam in his own eye, and it is that lack of love which expresses itself in censoriousness. When men look for motes, the passion that makes them do so is a beam, more guilty in the sight of heaven than the mote for which they look. We should be far more pitiful, far more gentle and kindly in our judgment, far less anxious to criticise the man with the habit that we have not, had we more love. Christ arrests the man who has no mote, and says, Your search for a mote is evidence of a beam, and you have no power to see the mote in its true relation and proportion; there is a hindrance to the vision because the beam is in your own eye. The slight change in the final word is interesting. " Thou hypocrite, cast out first the beam out of thine own eye; then shalt thou see clearly to cast the mote out of thy brother's eye." He did not say, " Then shalt thou see clearly the mote," but, " Then shalt thou see clearly to cast it out." The man with the beam is the man who is looking for the mote, and beholding it. Notice the question, " Why beholdest thou the mote?" You criticise it, you

attack it, but you cannot move it. Get the beam out of your own eye, get the passion for criticism removed, get the ungodly and unchristlike endeavour to find the mote destroyed; and then you will see clearly, not the mote, but how to remove it. The power for removing the mote to which you object lies, not in the acuteness of your vision, but in the passionate love which makes you desire to remove it. And so with the beam of unchristly censoriousness and criticism gone, you will be able to take the mote out of your brother's eye.

There is nothing more ungodly than a critical spirit; nothing more unchristly than that false righteousness which is always looking for a mote. Once let the beam be removed, then will come the Christlike spirit that knows how, with gentle delicate touch, to remove the mote, that the brother's vision may be clear. So the Lord warns us from usurping the throne of judgment. Do not form a final judgment; do not come to adverse and critical conclusions concerning men.

Then there is a sudden change. " Give not that which is holy unto the dogs, neither cast your pearls before the swine, lest haply they trample them under their feet, and turn and rend you." We are not to be critically censorious, but we must exercise discrimination and discretion. There are characters we must discern and be careful of, for there are things committed to our care which we must safeguard at all costs. This may appear a rough description of the characters, but the King makes use of no vulgar descriptions save when He is describing vulgar things. Who are the " dogs," the " swine "? Let Scripture interpret Scripture. No doubt Peter heard Him say this, and after he had passed through very wonderful experiences he wrote, and used words his Master used. " It has happened to them according to the true proverb, The dog turning to his own vomit again, and the sow that had washed to wallowing in the mire " (2 Peter ii. 22). " It has happened unto them." In the previous chapter we have a remarkable exposition of these words of Jesus. The chapter begins with false prophets. As we go on through the chapter we have the terrible teaching that, though we may be in the place of privilege and blessing, if we turn our back upon it we must be cast out therefrom. It is a terrible and dark description of certain men who resolutely set themselves against holy things, but who come into holy places to traffic with holy things with unholy purposes—dogs, who presently will go back to their vomit; swine, who presently will be back to their wallowing in the mire. Do not judge your fellow man hastily; but when a man has manifested his character do not give holy things to dogs, do not fling pearls before swine. Remember, if out of false charity or pity you allow men of material ideals and worldly wisdom to touch holy things, to handle the pearls of the Kingdom, presently they will turn and rend you. That is the whole history of Christendom's ruin, in the measure in which Christendom is ruined. There is a very clear distinction between the Church of God and Christendom. The Church of God is not a failure—the great holy entity in union with Him—but the outward manifestation is. We gave holy things to dogs. We imagined that when a Roman emperor espoused the cause of Christianity, it was a great thing. We cast the pearls of the Kingdom before swine; and the men who had to do only with the earthly things have turned again, and rent the outward manifestation of unity. If a brother stands out, makes choice against the will of God, and refuses the light, then we are to discriminate. There is a separation made within the borders of Christ's Kingdom, and, while we are to indulge in no censorious criticism and final judgment of our fellow man, if that man, judged by his own action and character, is unworthy, then we are not to give him holy things, we are not to cast our pearls before swine.

Then notice what immediately follows. This fine distinction between censoriousness and discrimination creates a difficulty, in the presence of which we may well be afraid. How shall we know just where to draw the line? What is to be the difference between the thing Christ will not have, and the

thing He commands? How are we to know in this world whether we are to come to a judgment or no? The Lord lays down no rule, but He says, "Ask"—"seek"—"knock." So important are the two injunctions—that we should judge not; that we must discriminate—that we must for evermore maintain our attitude toward our fellow men by maintaining our relationship with God. These great words, "Ask"—"seek"—"knock" may have a far wider application, but this is the application the King made of them in His Manifesto. Christ could say no little thing, and for two smaller matters He applies great principles. We do no wrong to the principles if sometimes we apply them to larger matters; but we do wrong if we miss the fact that He applies them to the smaller things. "Ask" in relation to "these things." If you question this link you have only to go to the repetition in the Golden Rule and remember the word "therefore." The Golden Rule is closely connected with these instructions. It would be perfectly correct to read the first six verses, and then immediately the twelfth. Do not judge men; do not come to hasty decision; discriminate between them; do not give to dogs. "All things therefore whatsoever ye would." Between this final epitome and the clear statement at the beginning, occurs this command to Ask, Seek, Knock. The King drives us back into perpetual and intimate relationship with God in order that our attitude with regard to our fellow men should be what it ought to be.

Let us, then, consider that threefold command.

"Ask." The Lord never used the same words to describe His own prayers as those He employed to describe the prayers of other people. The word "ask" here means as to simplest intention, to beg in the sense of dependence. It is the word of the man who comes with empty hands and says, "I have nothing to buy with." Christ never used that word of His praying; He never asked God as a pauper. When He spoke of His own praying He used words that might be translated: I will inquire of the Father, I will speak with Him concerning this matter —as One upon a perfect equality. But, for us, " ask " is the first thing. We must recognize our dependence upon God.

The next word is " Seek," and in that there is the suggestion of care; it marks the true anxiety. Do not merely ask in dependence, but ask with the urgency of a great desire.

Finally, " Knock." In that word we have the mingling of dependence and effort, suggested by the first two— " ask," " seek." " Ask " when you do not know how to judge. " Seek " which is the effort of the sanctified man after the mind of God. " Knock," perpetually making application. We cannot live one day in office, or shop, or ordinary place of action, and know when to discriminate, and when not to judge, except as we live every day and every hour asking, seeking, knocking. We must live near God if we would live in right relationship with our fellow men. We must live right with our fellow men if we would live right with God.

Again, if these are the words that mark human responsibility, let us mark the words which reveal the Divine attitude.

First, God is willing to bestow, and Jesus bases His argument on the character of God. Notice the suggested contrast: " If ye, then, being evil, know how to give good gifts unto your children, how much more shall your Father Who is in heaven? "—evidently the suggestion is that He is not evil, nor can be evil. The word " evil " does not merely mean sinful; it is a word which includes natural and moral limitation and fault. It takes in frailty, and weakness, and sickness, and sorrow. We are evil, subjects of limitation as well as sin. God is not evil. Time writes no wrinkle upon the Infinite Brow of Deity. He fainteth not neither is weary. He is not limited by observation or bounded by horizons; and if we, with our limitation, know how to give our children good gifts, how much more our heavenly Father?

Are you afraid as you face the demand Christ's law makes upon you? Ask, seek, knock, and know that the Listener is your Father. Learn, says Jesus, how He listens, and how He appeals to the highest thing within yourself,—even though you are evil— your own fatherhood. If your boy asks you for bread you will not give him a stone. The thing is absurd. It is well sometimes to be superlative. We stand among men having to discriminate, never to judge; forbidden the usurpation of a final throne of judgment, and yet forbidden to cast holy things before dogs and swine. How can we do it? " Ask, seek, knock." It is not a servant keeps the door; it is your Father. The King has taken us into the powerhouse of all true living; He has brought us back to the place where wheels are throbbing with infinite energy; but at the centre of the wheels is not an axle, but a heart. All the infinite dynamic of righteousness is born in the compassion of the heart of God. " Ask, seek, knock;" " Your Father."

Finally, " therefore." How that " therefore " flames upon one as one searches one's own soul in the presence of these commands. Do not judge, yet discriminate. How devilish is the critical spirit that sees the mote; and yet how necessary is the discrimination that withholds holy things from dogs and swine. The voice of the infinite Fatherhood says, " My child, for obedience to every command I am here to provide you power," and we are afraid no more. " Therefore " links the necessity with the power—" Ask, seek, knock."

What is this summarising of our duty? Do unto your neighbour what you would that your neighbour should do to you. That is the whole thing. We are told sometimes that this is not peculiar to Jesus Christ. That the Golden Rule is not the peculiar property of Christianity. But you cannot find this rule anywhere else. Hillel, the great Hebrew master, said, " Do not do to thy neighbour what is hateful to thyself." That is very like it. He said that before Jesus came. Socrates, before Christ, wrote these words: " What stirs your anger when done to you by others, that do not to others." That is very much like it Aristotle said, " We should bear ourselves to-ward others as we would desire they should bear themselves toward us." That seems even nearer, but it is not the same. Confucius, the great Chinese teacher, said, " What you do not want done to yourself, do not do to others." These things were said before Christ spoke, and we are told they are the same.

There is this radical difference—these are negative and passive; Christ's command is positive and active. These say to man, Stand still, and do not do what you do not want anyone to do to you; Christ says, Go and do what you would that he should do to you. It is

not merely that you are to refrain from harming him; you are to do him good. It is not that you are not to rob him; you are to give to him. It is not that you are not to murder him; you are to love him. And so the gleams of light which characterise the teaching of Gen-tiles, as well as the revelation which had come to Jews, He took up, and ful-filled and made final. We might, out of a selfish self-respect, decline to harm our neighbour but we cannot do this higher thing without power. We can-not do continuously what we would our neighbour should do to us save as we ask, seek, and knock, and know that our Father is pledged to us in power.

MATTHEW VII. 13-28

THE final words of the King in this Manifesto are full of dignity—in very deed the words of a King. Nay, rather, and more correctly, they are the words of the one and only King of men. They are words of warning; thrilling with the concern of a great love; vibrant with the majesty of His own power.

The passage may be divided into two main parts. In the first section (vv. 13-23) the Lord laid upon those who had been listening to Him a threefold responsibility; while in the second sec-tion, the very last utterance of the Manifesto (vv. 24-27), He laid before them alternative issues.

The Manifesto was introduced by the words; " Seeing the multitudes, He went up into the mountain: and when He had sat down, His disciples came unto Him: and He opened His mouth and taught *them*"—that is, the dis-ciples, not the multitudes. At the end He spoke still to His disciples, for the things He said cannot have their first application to the outside crowd. He desired to set up the Kingdom of God everywhere; therefore He had in-structed those who were already in it, that they were to live it, and teach it, and apply it in all the larger relationships.

Speaking still thus to His own, He laid upon them a threefold responsi-bility, first as to the beginning (vv.

13-14); then as to progress (vv. 15-20); and, finally, as to issues (vv. 21-23).

Notice carefully the sequence of these three. First, responsibility as to the beginning: " Enter ye in by the narrow gate "—that is, get into the true way. Then responsibility as to progress upon the way; " Beware of false prophets "—that is, be true to truth after you have entered the Kingdom. Finally, live in the light of the ultimate day; and re-member that then, no profession of re-lationship or of service will avail, but one thing only—life homed in the will of God.

These, then, are the words which condition responsibility as to the way, as to the truth, as to the life. " Enter ye in by the narrow gate," that you may be in the true way; " Beware of false prophets," that you may live in the sphere of truth; Live in the light of the final day, that your life may be not only progressive, but finally rounded out to that perfection for which God is seeking.

Said Jesus on another occasion to men—and the words flash their light upon this passage—" I am the Way, and the Truth, and the Life." " Enter ye in by the narrow gate," and find the true way, for " I am the Way." " Beware of false prophets, who come to you in sheep's clothing, but inwardly are raven-ing wolves," but listen to the true Prophet, Who is essential Truth, for " I am the Truth;" and walk in comradeship with Him upon the way, having come to Him for entrance to the Kingdom. Do not depend upon what you do, but upon what you are. Do not trust to the fact that you have named the name of Christ, and have rendered Him service. Trust only to the fact that you are in yourself, as He was in Himself—conditioned in the will of God, for "I am the Life."

Now let us examine these one by one. First, He brings us to the wicket gate. He pointed to the wicket gate in the very first words of the Manifesto. "Blessed are the poor in spirit." Poverty of spirit, lowliness, and meekness, constitute the true tone and temper of the mind—that is, submission, allegiance, and obedience. That was the beginning. It is very sweet and tender in its wording; but we know, if we have come to the King, that it is a drastic requirement, which demands the giving up of everything that interferes with a man's quick and ready obedience to the King.

Now He brings us back again to the wicket gate, and shows how men enter. Notice the figures of speech of which He makes use. There are two entrances and two ways. He describes them. There is a narrow gate and a wide gate; a broad way and a straitened way. Yet to leave these things grouped in that way is not to catch the final movement of this suggestive teaching of Jesus. We need to keep the way in each case in relation to the gate. Doing so, we find that in effect the King says; You enter this Kingdom by a very narrow gate; and you walk along a straitened way which for evermore grows broader, until at last it becomes broad in the fulness of eternal life. If you enter through the other gate, it is wide, it is easy to get through; and you walk along a broad way, which is for evermore straitening, until at last it becomes destruction. We generally take these verses, and deal only with the gateways and the pathway immediately beyond the entrances. Never omit the final words in either case; it "leadeth to destruction," it "leadeth unto life." The word "destruction" suggests the narrowing of

things, the limitation of things, the imprisonment of everything. It means a condition of life in which aspiration never realises, in which a man is shut up within the things that are narrow. So that Jesus says: If you refuse My teaching, if you will not have this Kingdom, then you go through the wide gate and find yourself on a broad way, which may be smooth, and even flowery, but it "leadeth to destruction." The man who is only looking at the gate and the road he is tramping to-day is a fool. Lift your eyes and look ahead. The wide gate and the broad way of refusing this King and His ideals, and refusing allegiance to Him "leadeth to destruction;" the way narrows, until the soul is in the prison-house.

But on the other hand—and with this positive element we are now more interested—the way into the Kingdom is by a narrow gate; and the way is a straitened road. But it "leadeth unto life."

What does He mean when at the close of this wonderful unfolding of law He brings us back to the narrowness of the gate, to the straitness of the way? These conditions imply the making of heroic character! For entrance to, and abiding in, this Kingdom there can be no dilettante fooling with the passing hours. If men would pass that gate and walk that way they must enter into strenuous life. If a man should tell you that Christianity is an easy softness, he knows nothing of it. If a man should tell you that for your life there is nothing to do, he is right as to the initiation of it by the act of God, for life is the gift of His grace; but he is wrong as to human responsibility for entering into it. Every man who would enter this Kingdom must come through the narrow gate. Every man who would live in this Kingdom must walk the straitened way.

There is no great kingdom which man desires to possess which does not bring him to a narrow gate and a straitened way. Those who have set their faces, honourably and splendidly, toward proficiency in medical skill know there is the narrow gate and the straitened way of toil—hard, strenuous toil. Those in whom there burn the fires and the passions of the true artist can never expect to succeed by going through a wide gate and treading a broad way. There must be the infinite patience which takes pains. Was ever a true artist born who had not to take pains? These illustrations are on a low level; lift them into the higher. If you would possess the Kingdom that includes all kingdoms; if you would live within the Kingdom in which all values are to be finally perfected and realised, you must get through the narrow gate and the straitened way. No man can be a Christian in all the full senses of the word who is not prepared to get to the wicket, and strip, and tramp the straitened way. These are the words of the King, and He knows! He gained His redemptive authority by submission; He yielded Himself to the supreme authority of His Father, and we read this very startling thing concerning Him in the Scriptures of inspiration. "He . . . learned obedience by the things which He suffered." That does not mean that He learned to be obedient through suffering; but that He learned obedience experimentally through treading the pathway of suffering.

So He brings us back again to the wicket. It is a narrow gate, a straitened way; and with that infinite tenderness, so characteristic of Him, just as He has taken hold of us with a grip of infinite power and charged us to strip, He points us to the ultimate, the infinite life. When Jesus says *life* we have nothing to add.

Secondly; as to progress, He said; "Beware of false prophets, who come to you in sheep's clothing, but inwardly are ravening wolves." Notice very carefully that our Lord is not warning us against heretical views in this passage. He is not warning us against heterodox teaching, so far as heterodoxy means a wrong system of truth; but He is warning us against the prophet who is a wolf, but who wears a sheep's clothing; that is against the orthodox veiling of heterodox life. He is not warning us against a man who does not exactly express truth in the terms with which we are familiar; but He is warning us against the wolf in sheep's clothing; the teacher who

affects the speech of orthodoxy, but lives a false life; not the man who holds a false doctrine, but the false prophet. His prophecy may be perfectly accurate, his preaching may be absolutely orthodox, but the man is false. That is the man who will lead farthest from truth. It is possible to pronounce the shibboleths of the Bible in the most accurate manner, and yet for the heart to be far away from their purpose and intention. Here it is not intellectual heterodoxy; but men who laud the teaching, and deny the spirit; men whose appearance is outward and ostentatious; who appear in sheep's clothing; but whose energy and influence are wolfish.

How are we to know these men? This evil cannot be dealt with by a committee, or conference, or synod, or council. We cannot find out whether a man is orthodox or heterodox in life, by examining him in words. We can only know men by their fruit. We must wait. "By their fruits ye shall know them." Our Lord introduced and closed His statement by that word; but between, He made an appeal as to the accuracy of His position, first by asking the question: "Do men gather grapes of thorns, or figs of thistles?" It is as though He said, This is a true test. Is not fruit the final test of the nature of life? Notice how He immediately proceeded; "Even so." Have you ever tried to connect that "even so"? Have you asked yourself why He said "even so"? He asked them, "Do men gather grapes of thorns, or figs of thistles?" There was the answering, No, on the faces of the men. Perhaps they shook their heads, as though they would say, Of course not. "Even so" shows that He had carried their judgment, that they had agreed with Him; that it is impossible to gather fruitage from any tree save that which is the outcome of its inner life. One of the Puritan Fathers, writing on this passage, said: "It is quite possible to put grapes on thorns. It is quite possible to put figs on thistles, but they cannot *grow* there." It is quite possible for a wolf to wear a sheep's clothing, but it cannot *grow* a sheep's clothing. And when our Lord had asked the question, and gained the assent of the judgment of His hearers, then He made a great positive affirmation; " Even so every good tree bringeth forth good fruit;" and a great negative affirmation, " but the corrupt tree bringeth forth evil fruit;" and then a further negative statement; " A good tree cannot bring forth evil fruit; neither can a corrupt tree bring forth good fruit." It is the repetition of a principle from which we cannot depart. We cannot gather good fruit from a corrupt tree.

We cannot make any appeal against such repetition as this, in which our Lord by affirmation, negation, question, and by renewed affirmation, stating the case from every standpoint, asserted this great truth; that the test of the prophet is the prophet's life. It is a searching word for the prophet, to be spoken quietly, to be thought of seriously; to the testing of which every man who opens his mouth to prophesy, should bring his life every day and every hour.

And once again; as to the issue, the King said, perhaps, some of the most solemn things He ever said. Profession of allegiance is absolutely valueless. We all believe that. To hear the law, and to disobey, is the most terrible kind of profanity of which man can be guilty. This does not need arguing, but simply restating, because of its terrible solemnity and its most searching application. You have perhaps heard somewhere a child of the slum using profane language, and you have said, He is taking the name of God in vain; it is a terrible sin. It is. But when you prayed, " Our Father, Who art in heaven, Hallowed be Thy name. Thy kingdom come, Thy will be done," unless you had let His Kingdom come in your life, your profanity was worse than the profanity of the man on the street, your blasphemy was more terrible than the blasphemy of the child of the slum. Jesus said, " In that day "— the light of which flames over all these days if we have but eyes to see— " In that day " He will say to the man who says, " Lord, Lord," but does not obey Him, " I never knew you." Yes, the blasphemy of the sanctuary is more awful han the blasphemy of the slum.

To pray, " Lord, Lord," and to disobey Him, is of the very essence of villainy. That is what Judas did; kissed Him, and betrayed Him! If these words of Jesus have startled us with their severity; let us know that there is a profound reason for that severity.

Finally as to the issue. This, perhaps, is a more searching word still. " Many will say to Me in that day, Lord, Lord, did we not prophesy by Thy name, and by Thy name cast out demons, and by Thy name do many mighty works? And then will I profess unto them, I never knew you: depart from Me, ye that work iniquity."

Listen to what they say. " We have done." Yes, they had done everything but the Lord's will. They had hoped to make up for disobedience to His will, in personal life, by doing many things for Him in their church, their city, and in the world. Mark well what the King said of the whole of such activity. " Workers of iniquity."

So that if it should be that we who have prophesied in His name, yet disobey Him in the individual and personal matters of our own life; if we should preach about this Manifesto, and yet not submit to the King in all the details of our life; what then? Our preaching is iniquity, our casting out of demons is a sin. All service is rejected, except the service rendered by such as are themselves doing the will of God. Christ will say to such; " I never knew you," which does not mean, I did not know about you, I do not know your name, I did not watch your life; but, " I never knew you;" there was no intimacy, no comradeship, no fellowship between us. You took My name to make your name; you took My name to work your miracles; you took My name for certain self-centred purposes; but you did not know Me, and I did not know you.

Here is the imperial King, in these last utterances of His Manifesto, standing in the light of " that day " which is to be—claiming the throne, claiming that His verdict will be the final one, claiming that the final sentences will fall from His own lips.

What shall we do in the presence of these words? We had better betake ourselves to some lonely secret chamber and read them all again. We had better say, Have we ever come through the strait gate? Have we been misled by some false spirit of prophecy, which says the correct thing, and lives the wrong life? Have we been saying, "Lord, Lord," and failing to do the will?

Do you think this is all hard and harsh? It is the hardness and the harshness of the Infinite love. "Narrow is the gate, straitened is the way—" beware of anything that is false in the prophet, beware of saying, "Lord, Lord." Let the light of "that day" flash; and the thunder of it arrest; and the fire of it affright; yet know that He will save us from the things that harm and blight and curse and spoil. May these words with which He closes the Manifesto come into our life as a new fire, as a new force of purity.

Lastly, notice the second division of the paragraph. There is an alternative of issues. We need specially to remember the majesty of these last words of Christ, the marvellous claim He makes. He says, in effect: You must all build character. This is the day of character building. This is the day in which, in our systems of pedagogy, and of philosophy, we are discussing character building. The King supremely recognizes the importance of it. He says: Every man builds. There is a common quantity in this final illustration—the fact of building. But notice the difference. It is not in the men who build; or in the materials with which they build; but in the foundation on which they build. The foundation is everything. We may build with the same materials, and with the same structural correctness upon sand as upon rock; and all through summer days the buildings both appear to be all right. But summer days do not exhaust the days. There are days of pelting rain, of sweeping winds and hurricanes; and those are the days that will test our buildings. Therefore, it is not so much a matter of the man building, not so much a matter of the material, but of the foundation.

Hear, then, the imperial claim of Christ. He says: Take these sayings of Mine and build on them; and no storm can destroy your building. Hear these sayings of Mine and disobey them—and remember that this has nothing to do with the man who has never heard them; he is not here in view at all; this word is not to the heathen, it is to the man who hears and disobeys, the man who has seen a vision and dreamed a dream, the man who has heard the Infinite music, and will set his instruments to catch the tune—you can go on building, and we may look at the structure and say: What is the use of Christianity? that house is as beautiful as this; this man's character is as beautiful as the other's. But observe it, wait, wait! Presently there will come the storms of sorrow, of bereavement and of temptation, and then presently "that day;" and unless there be rock foundation, the fair superstructure will be spoiled by the sweeping storm. The King stands before all of us as He closes His Manifesto, and says, "These sayings of Mine;" build on them; and no storm can wreck your building.

We know all this to be true. We are not discussing the Person of Christ. We are not discussing the larger question of the work of Christ. We pause now where He ended. "These sayings of Mine." We know perfectly well that if we build on them our character will be such that no storm can wreck it. And if we will not, if we, having heard the sayings, do not obey them, there is no foundation upon which we can build a character that will weather the storm and stand to the very day of destiny.

We thus end our study of the Manifesto, listening first to a sublime claim, that His teaching is such foundation that no storm can disturb it; hearing also a message of hope, that here is stability on which we may build, knowing that our building will abide; and finally impressed by a solemn warning, that mere knowledge is of no value in the day of storm and flood.

When presently men shall rest in perfect peace, it will be within the sacred circle of this unfolding of law.

May God grant that we may be, not hearers only, but doers of the word of the King.

MATTHEW VIII. 1-17

WE now come to the consideration of the section in which the King is seen acting in power in every realm.

In the course of His Manifesto He had presented a great deal of life; but dreams are of no avail unless deeds follow. Men cannot live by merely gazing on a vision. The vision may arrest, may attract; but unless it can be translated into victory, it is of very little use to men. And so, now that the ethic was unfolded, the Manifesto uttered; now that the wondrous words had fallen upon the listening ears of His disciples, and of the crowds, the natural and inevitable question was: What can this Man *accomplish?* Is He equal to doing, as well as dreaming? Is it possible for Him to realise a victory, as well as project a vision?

In this paragraph we see that He began to answer that question by a series of simple and yet sublime manifestations of the fact that the Unfolder of the ethic, is also the Giver of dynamic; that He is not merely a Dreamer come to suggest better ways to men; but a Doer, equal to reaching them in the places of their need, and making them doers also.

In chapters eight and nine of this Gospel, we have nine manifestations of His power; and these arrange themselves naturally into three groups of three each. He gave three illustrations of power; and immediately afterwards we find the effect produced on the people by what they saw. Then three other illustrations of power, and again the effect produced. Finally, three further illustrations of power, and once again the effect produced.

In looking at these two chapters let us be careful not to imagine that Jesus Christ presented Himself to the people, and asked them to observe what He was able to do. There was nothing theatrical in these manifestations of power; they were natural, necessary, and beautiful; but they have been so grouped that, looking back, we may see how, having taught in wondrous words, He now triumphed in equally wondrous works.

The first three illustrations were those of the cleansing of the leper, the healing of the centurion's servant, and the restoration of Peter's wife's mother. Immediately afterwards a man said to him: "Teacher, I will follow Thee whithersoever Thou goest."

Then moving beyond the realm of the physical, He proved Himself Master of the elements, in the stilling of the storm; Master of the great world of spiritual forces, as He cast out the demons; Master of disease and its source of sin, as He cured the palsy and forgave sin. Immediately after these things we read, "They were afraid, and glorified God."

Then we have the third group of three—the raising of the child of Jairus, the healing of the woman who touched Him; and the healing of the blind. Then we read, "The multitudes marvelled."

We have now to deal with the first of the three groups only; the leper, the centurion's servant, and Peter's wife's mother.

Let us first take a general survey of the passage. As Jesus commenced these deeds of His Kingship, we are arrested by the peculiarity of that commencement. Here is God's attested King; gathering first a small nucleus of loyal souls. He had enunciated the ethic of His Kingdom; now the moment had come in which He was about to accomplish something. He did not form a party, formulate a policy, or plan a campaign. There is nothing more remarkable in all His ministry than the fact that He never held consultations with men, or attempted to form a party in our sense of the word, or gave men a programme. He was not restricted by party, policy, or programme.

Glancing over the movement of these seventeen verses we notice, first, that the King began to deal with need at its lowest, in the physical realm; with leprosy, palsy, and fever. This King, in order to set up His Kingdom, did not stay on the summit of the mount; He went down to the depth of the leper's condition. The first call to the

King was the call of the most needy man. We shall come to a higher plane presently, and find Him dealing with spiritual qualities and quantities; but the first exhibition of His power was given in the realm of the most conscious need.

We notice in the second place, as He commenced His work, that He acted in response to appeals, and voluntarily also. First there came the cry of a leper, separated from the crowd, and yet in the vicinity of the crowd, "Lord, if Thou wilt, Thou canst make me clean"—it was a cry of need and He responded to it. In the second place, it was the cry of a man, not for himself, but for another, for his servant—"My servant lieth in the house, sick of the palsy." And Jesus said, "I will come and heal him." In the third place, His action was in response to the appeal of friends (see Luke iv. 38). In the first case He was yet on the mountain; in the second He had entered the city; in the third He had entered into the narrowest circle—the home of Peter.

Then notice, He commenced His work with the unfit in more senses than one. If we had been with Him, and had been Hebrews, as His disciples were, we should have been greatly startled. First, He touched a leper, an outcast, whom no man must dare to touch. Secondly, He healed the servant of a Roman, who was outside the covenant of Israel, and with whom there could properly be no communication. Thirdly, He touched a woman, who, according to Jewish ideas, did not count. He began with the unfit persons for whom there was no provision in the economy of the nation. A great many people have been sorely troubled about this touching of the leper, saying that in doing so He broke the law. But He was not as other men. On another occasion they said, "This Man receiveth sinners, and eateth with them." They meant to say; Pollution is mightier than purity; though He be pure, contact with sinners will produce pollution in Himself. But He was such that He could be a friend of sinners, and suffer no contamination by contact, but rather surcharge them with His purity. We

dare not become friends of sinners save in the power of His redeeming life, or their pollution will be communicated to us. When He touched them, He imparted His purity to them, and the proportion in which Christ actually possesses us and dwells in us, is the proportion in which we can become the friends of sinners. If we touch a leper, we catch the leprosy because our every fibre is weakened through the agency of sin; but the very material life of the Son of God was absolutely strong, and perfect, and pure, and when He touched a man He took no contamination, for there was nothing in Him upon which leprosy could fasten; but rather He communicated the strength and virtue and purity of His Manhood to the leper, and healed him. So also He answered a Roman's prayer; and thus overstepped all narrow and provincial bounds; and the cool, healing hand of the Master touched the hand of a woman, and the fever left her.

At the end of this section we read, "And when even was come, they brought unto Him many possessed with demons; and He cast out the spirits with a word, and healed all that were sick." That reads so easily and seems so simple, but let us continue our reading—"That it might be fulfilled which was spoken through Isaiah the prophet, saying, Himself took our infirmities, and bare our diseases."

Here we need to pause for a moment. When He healed with a word, with a touch, what did He? "Himself took our infirmities, and bare our diseases." It is a very superficial exposition which makes it appear that the King, as He came to touch and heal, took into His own heart, sympathetically only, the feeling of the pain and the weakness. This action of healing was the fulfilment of the prophecy of Isaiah, and we cannot interpret this working of the power of the King save in the light of that prophecy. There is a growing revelation through the teaching of Isaiah until we come to the culminating glory of the great Servant of God suffering to save, and in that sense the fifty-third chapter is the very heart of the prophecy. Here we see that word being fulfilled; "He was wounded for our transgressions, He was bruised for our iniquities; the chastisement of our peace was upon Him." Briefly, it is the chapter of atonement, of vicarious suffering; the chapter in which we see the King dealing, not with the superficial externality of things; but getting down until He touched the deep underlying reason of all suffering and evil in the moral and material realm alike. In order to deal with these He took hold of sin itself; and when He healed the leper, the centurion's servant, Peter's wife's mother, with a word and a touch; and the multitude, halted for a moment with surprise, brought unto Him many possessed with demons, He perfectly understood that all the disabilty He corrected was the outcome of man's sin; that at the back of physical leprosy lay sin, not necessarily in the actual leper, but in the past of the race. When He dealt first with physical need, He knew that His right to work these miracles was the right of the coming Cross in which He should gather into His very heart the sin that lay at the back of all these things. In the Cross was the right by which He distributed His virtues to the impure, and gave of His strength to the sick. Thus the King revealed the fact that His power in dealing with disability was based upon His passion. We shall see this yet more clearly when we come to another group; He said to the sick of the palsy, " Son, be of good cheer, thy sins are forgiven;" and when men criticised Him, He said, "Which is easier, to say, Thy sins are forgiven; or to say, Arise, and walk?" He acted as knowing that physical disability and moral malady are linked, and whenever He healed disease it was in the right of His coming Passion, in which He would deal not merely with these manifestations, but with the root of evil from which they sprang. And so it was in the power of the Cross, ante-dating the historic accomplishment of a Divine purpose, that He healed the leper, and the servant, and the woman sick of the fever.

All this does not mean that immediate physical healing is secured to us in the Atonement. This is not so, any more than immunity from natural dy-

ing is immediately secured. Ultimately freedom from disease and triumph over death are ours through the Cross, but for the period of probation sickness is permitted, always with some value in the Divine purpose, even though at the moment we may not know what that value is.

Notice one other thing about these actions of the King. Not only did He accomplish at cost, He restored to the natural. This is a day in which we are spending a very great deal of time discussing the possibility of the miraculous. As men get to see more clearly, they will understand that a miracle is not a setting aside of law, but that it is rather an operation in a realm of law not yet discovered by men living on a lower plane. We are constantly discovering laws unknown to our fathers, and applying them. Every miracle Jesus wrought, He wrought, not to prove His Deity, not essentially in the power of His Deity, but in the power of a perfectly poised humanity through which God could work. These miracles of Jesus, so far from being violations of law, were restorations of men to the life according to law. Leprosy is unlawful; cleansing is lawful. Fever is due to violation of law; and this Man by a touch restored to law. The King came to restore a lost order.

Finally, as we survey this first of the three groups,we see that the one thing the King was doing was that of drawing attention to Himself. If we said that of any other man, it would be to utter his condemnation; when we say it of Him, we are all conscious of the eminent fitness of the action. This Man, meekest of the meek, proceeded from beginning to end along a line that demanded that men should attend to Him, listen to Him, obey Him. The King Who had uttered words of wisdom that astonished men, now came to do such things that must of necessity make the people look at Him, listen to Him, decide concerning Him. In quiet, kingly attitude, He proceeded through all these miracles of healing in perfect naturalness. "If Thou wilt, Thou canst make me clean," and in a moment came the word of the King, "I will, be thou made clean." "Only say the word, and my servant shall be healed;" and the word was spoken, "Go thy way; as thou hast believed, so be it done unto thee." The touch of the King, and the woman was cured.

Now let us turn from general examination to a more particular one.

Mark how the leper came to Jesus. He came with a known need. "If Thou wilt, Thou canst make me clean." If we are coming to the King, we must know what we want. All the prayers that storm heaven are brief. There is a place for the longer prayer. There is a place for the adoration and the pouring out of the heart; but it is when a man knows what he wants, that he takes hold of God. "Lord, if Thou wilt, Thou canst make me clean." It is hardly a prayer, it is a statement, an affirmation, a cry of need. Next, his attitude was submissive—he worshipped. His cry was an honest cry, "If Thou wilt, Thou canst make me clean." Why question the willingness of Jesus? Because the man was not sure that Jesus would be willing, and he was honest enough to say so. If we look closely we see that this man had learned a lesson, that the will of the King is supreme; "If Thou wilt, Thou canst." He did not question His power. It is not that he questioned His willingness unkindly, but that he recognized that it must be as He willed. It is when a soul gets there that he makes contact with all the power of Jesus Christ. To state it boldly, the Master, Jesus Christ, could not possibly do other than answer this man as He did. This King had come to claim the surrender of the will, and the man yielded. "If Thou wilt." And glorious and Kingly, like the flashing of the sun illuminating the morning, came the answer, "I will, be thou made clean." When the man's will bent to the will of Christ, Christ's will touched the man's will, and through that contact there was communicated to him the power and virtue of the King.

Then He sent him away, telling him not to tell any one of this miracle, to keep silent about it. That is the first intimation that Christ's estimate of the physical is that it is secondary. He always prevented men talking about physical miracles because He did not deal with things on the surface. In the fourteenth chapter of the Book of Leviticus you will find that when a man was healed of leprosy he had to offer sacrifice. Through all the Hebrew economy men were taught that this is the basis of man's approach to God. Clean or unclean, there must be the ceremonial law of sacrifice. Christ's was not accomplished, and until it should be this man must go back to Moses and offer the shadow of sacrifice. The healing that had come to him was at the cost of infinite sacrifice, of which all others were but shadows.

The next case is that of a man coming to Christ, not for himself, but for another; and the first fact to be noticed is, that he stated his need, and Jesus said, "I will come and heal him." When reading the New Testament nothing is more wonderful than the tremendous assumptions of Jesus. The man came to him in trouble. Christ did not say, I will come and see what I can do. He said, "I will come and heal him." There was perfect confidence in Himself. It was the quiet, but dignified voice of a great authority.

The centurion said, "Lord, I am not worthy that Thou shouldest come under my roof: but only say the word, and my servant shall be healed." Notice the centurion's faith, "Speak the word and my servant shall be healed." And then notice his philosophy of authority. "For I also am a man under authority having under myself soldiers; and 1 say to this one, Go, and he goeth; and to another, Come, and he cometh; and to my servant, Do this, and he doeth it." The centurion was not putting himself into contrast with Jesus, but was saying, What is true of me is true of Thee; Thou art also under authority, and because Thou art under authority Thou art able to exercise authority. This is the true philosophy of government. And so, "when Jesus heard it, He marvelled." The word "marvelled" does not mean necessarily that He was surprised, but that He admired his faith, that it startled Him by comparison with the faith of other men. What was it in the faith of the centurion at which Jesus marvelled? Probably the intelligence of it,

We hear a good deal about simple faith. But here is a man whose faith is based upon a true philosophy of life. With the leper it was the consciousness of a great need in himself, a great might in the Master. But when the centurion came, Jesus marvelled at his faith and said, " Verily, I say unto you, I have not found so great faith, no, not in Israel." It was a moment of great joy for Jesus. But with the joy a great shadow came, for He saw the exclusion of the very children of the King, who, disobedient to the King, should be cast out.

In the case of the woman in a fever, the appeal was made by her friends. He touched her, and the fever left her, and she arose and ministered unto them. The Revised Version says, " She arose and ministered unto *Him.*" He touched her, the fever left her, and she responded by becoming His servant.

Then we have that last brief account of the wonderful eventide. It is a great picture—the incapable and suffering gathered to Him, possessed of evil spirits, and all manner of diseases; and the King, by speaking a word, imparting health, and all in fulfilment of prophecy.

In conclusion; as to the King we learn from these first three movements, that the Dreamer is the Doer, that the Teacher is a Man of action, that the Unfolder of the great task is the Giver of a new dynamic; and these facts, first revealed in the physical, are for us to-day true supremely in the spiritual. If not, He has merely revealed a great ideal.

You are a leper and need cleansing; palsied and need healing; fever-stricken and need to feel the touch of His coolness and His balm. Oh, blessed be God, the Teacher is the same, great in words; but to a poor struggling heart, greater yet in works. If there be something in your life, something of moral depravity, something of incapability, some evil desire that prevents your doing the thing you would, come to Him as the leper came, " Lord, if Thou wilt, Thou canst. . . ." Come as the centurion came, " Speak the word only ;" He is close to you, and if you will only look into His face with all the pain of your incompetence, and sigh in trust, He will touch you, and break the power of cancelled sin, and set the prisoner free.

MATTHEW VIII. 18-34

THIS section of the Gospel consists of a brief paragraph, revealing certain effects produced by the works already recorded; and of further illustrations of His power.

" Now when Jesus saw great multitudes about Him, He gave commandment to depart unto the other side." This decision on His part called forth the words which show the effect produced on the minds of some who had seen His works. One man said to Him, " Teacher, I will follow Thee whithersoever Thou goest ;" and another said, " Lord, suffer me first to go and bury my father." These were typical cases, and reveal what, in all probability, was going on in the minds of vast numbers of the people. The King's methods of dealing with these first impressions made by His words and by His works are clearly revealed.

Then follows the account of how the King crossed the sea in the boat with His disciples; and we have a new manifestation of His power operating in a new realm; a manifestation made, not to the multitude, but to His own, who were in the boat with Him. As to actual realisation at the moment the whole Kingdom of God was in that boat—the King and His subjects; and to that inner circle He revealed a new plane upon which He moved with the same quiet, Kingly authority, as that which they already had seen Him exercise upon the plane of physical disease.

Finally, we have the story of the demoniacs; and the King's power is seen exercised in yet another sphere. With quiet dignity and authority, free from all perturbation and feverishness, He approached that strange and mystic realm, of which men have ever been more or less conscious—the spirit-world. This manifestation was to the whole company of people, and not merely to His own.

Let us consider first the effects immediately produced by the words already spoken, and the works already manifest.

We see the multitudes, and we see the action of Jesus because of the multitudes—a somewhat strange action as it appears at first—and then we have these two illustrations of the feelings of probably hundreds of people gathered round about Christ.

The multitudes were growing in number. He had gone up into the mountain, taking with Him a few disciples, and to them He had enunciated the ethic of His Kingdom. As He taught the disciples, the multitudes had climbed the mountain, had come nearer to Him, and heard Him, and by the time the last sentence of that marvellous Manifesto had passed His lips, it is recorded that those outside the little group to whom He was primarily speaking, " were astonished at His teaching, for He taught them as One having authority, and not as their scribes." When He was come down from the mountain these multitudes followed Him, and He entered into Capernaum.

As we have seen, at the beginning of His ministry, " He came and dwelt in Capernaum," in " Galilee of the Gentiles," which was despised because contaminated with Gentile thought and Gentile connection. He now came back into the same city, and the multitudes who had followed Him from the mountain were swelled in number by the city folk. They all knew of the leper cleansed on the way down the mountain; of the servant of the centurion healed from a distance; of the fever-stricken woman restored in the house of His disciple. Attracted first by His words, their interest was deepened by these things. Then, suddenly, as already noticed, when Jesus saw them, " He gave commandment to depart unto the other side."

This was a strange action, one which inevitably arrests our thought. He was attracted by the crowds; the crowds sought Him; and yet, over and over

again, just as the crowds were gathered, just as the moment seemed ripe for proclaiming the Kingdom, asserting His claim, stirring up the populace, beginning the march, He withdrew Himself from them. But He never left them because He did not love them; He left them because He did love them. These people were impressed with material values only, and Jesus withdrew in order that, having fixed and centred attention upon Himself, He might presently return to them for deeper matters, and higher things.

If we study this ministry of Jesus Christ, whether in His propaganda as King, which is specifically brought before us in Matthew, or whether in any of the other phases, as taught in the other gospels, we find this constantly—that our Lord discounted the value of His miracles. That is to say, He never appealed to men by miracle, save as a secondary method. The whole philosophy of this may best be expressed in His own words, when He said to Philip, " Believe Me . . . or else "—if you are not equal to that, if you cannot be persuaded by the supreme credential, by the final argument—" believe Me for the very works' sake." But the " works' sake " is secondary. Jesus did not work miracles in order to convince men; and when men, impressed by works of wonder wrought in the material realm, wanted to see what other thing He could do, He took ship and left them, with a larger intention in His mind.

It was just as our Lord was leaving that the events transpired which constitute our two illustrations. A scribe came to Him and said, " Teacher, I will follow Thee whithersoever Thou goest." And then a disciple said, " Lord, suffer me first to go and bury my father." But we will first take them together. When Luke told the same story, he introduced a third man, who said, " I will follow Thee, Lord; but first suffer me to bid farewell to them that are at my house." Most people imagine that none of these men followed Christ. There is not a word to prove that they did not follow Him. We are not told the sequel, and we have as much right to think that they ultimately followed Him, as that they did not.

Let us look at this first man, the scribe. He was one of the literary men of his time. He had listened to Jesus in all probability, and had watched Him. Just as his interest was becoming deeper, he saw that Jesus was leaving the crowds, and was going towards the boat, and, pressing through the crowds, he said to Him, "Teacher, I will follow Thee whithersoever Thou goest." We call this impulsiveness. Would that there were a great deal more impulsiveness of this kind in the world to-day! May God give us a new baptism of emotion! Here was a man who laid bare his heart to Jesus Christ; and to whom, therefore, Jesus could lay bare His heart. This He did in the unveiling of His poverty. He looked at the man and said, "The foxes have holes, and the birds of the heaven have nests; but the Son of Man hath not where to lay His head." That was heart answering heart. When a man out of his heart said, I am going to follow Thee, Lord, the Lord told that man what He did not tell to every one —the secret of His poverty, the secret of His homelessness. Some one has written about the blessed poverty of Christ. There is no such thing as blessed poverty. Poverty was part of the curse He bore, the curse that rested upon humanity on account of sin. It was part of His sorrow, and He told this man of His sorrow of homelessness.

Yet this is not the deepest note. This scribe, impulsive, daring, had undoubtedly been moved by the physical miracles; and it seems to me that Jesus not merely told of His own personal poverty, but uttered a great word revealing His ideal of life. He called Himself the Son of Man. It was Christ's favourite description of Himself; He seems to have loved it. It is on the lips of Jesus an illuminative word, standing for humanity as true to the ideal. It would seem as though Jesus looked at that scribe, captivated by His words, impressed by His works, and said to him in effect; For what are you coming after Me? Do not forget that the Son of Man is homeless in this world. The ideal Man in the midst of

such conditions as I am in, and as you will be in, if you follow Me, will have no anchorage here. "The foxes have holes, and the birds of heaven have nests, but the Son of Man," the Master of the new order, the King of the new Kingdom, in the midst of present conditions, can have no home. Thus, to the man who bared the deepest thing in his heart, Christ revealed the cross. Not Christ's Cross for the man; that is not revealed here; but the man's cross, if he would come into the Kingdom and into power. To him Christ said, Everything must be lost. You must be homeless if you would be with Me. Every tie that binds you and hinders you and fetters you must be dropped. Men who are coming after Me wherever I go, must come to homelessness, must understand that there is no rest until the Kingdom is built; the Son of Man can only be homed in the very Bosom of God.

Then another man spoke to Him, and Luke tells us that it was in answer to something that Jesus said to him. Jesus said, "Follow Me," and the man replied, "Lord, suffer me first to go and bury my father." Notice that Matthew calls this man a disciple, so that when Jesus called him to "follow," it was not a call to discipleship, but to service, for Luke again introduces something which Matthew omits. Jesus said to him, "Leave the dead to bury their own dead; but go thou and publish abroad the Kingdom of God."

What was the trouble in this man's case? There was in his heart a conflicting affection—that for his father. We have hardly caught the real value of this story; we have treated it as though this man wanted to attend a funeral, and asked time to do so. Dr. George Adam Smith tells of how he was one day trying hard to persuade a young man to go with him as a guide into a district not frequented by travellers. Healthy and robust he stood by his tent, a genuine Arab; and there, sitting in the doorway of the tent, was his father, of patriarchal appearance, but well and healthy. The intended journey would have occupied some months at least, and the young man at last, with peculiar courtesy, said, " Sir, suffer me first to bury my father," thus using the very words of the Bible story, and revealing its true meaning. There was no immediate prospect of the death of the father; but the son said, I cannot leave my father, a most admirable thing, a beautiful thing, examined by all the canons of human conduct; a noble decision on the part of the young Arab, and right, if anybody else called other than the King. But here at once we see the claim of Jesus. He was perpetually setting up these superlative claims for Himself. He had none of the humility of the human teacher. His claim was always the claim of an absolute supremacy. He never admitted that any other tie of affection could be allowed for a moment to interfere with the soul's loyalty to Himself, and He crystalised this fact into one burning sentence when He said, " He that loveth father or mother more than Me, is not worthy of Me." That is the principle He applied when He said, " Leave the dead to bury their own dead."

So far, then, the King having given the first evidences of His power, two men spoke of following Him. To the man who bared his heart, Christ revealed the deepest fact, the necessity for the cross. To the man who had a tie of affection that hindered him, Christ gave rebuke in most stern words. Having thus dealt with these men, He entered into the boat and left the multitude.

The King's power was now exercised on other planes. It operated first in the sphere of the elements, which is peculiarly retained for God; and it operated in the spirit-world, of which man is conscious, and by which he is influenced, but which he never yet has been able to master.

It is a great comfort that even to-day God has kept some things absolutely in His own hands. The winds and the waves are under His command. The King now revealed Himself to that little inner circle of His disciples as Master there also. It was a revelation of Himself made to His own. They saw that day, perhaps as they had never done before, the composure of the King. He could sleep when the storm was

sweeping. They were fishermen used to the sea. He was a landsman. They who were used to the sea were perturbed, but He was fast asleep through it all. They saw His sympathy the moment they roused Him. Then they saw His authority. Standing on the side of the vessel, He looked out on those heaving waters, and said very literally, " Be muzzled." And, like dogs, hounds held by the leash, the waves cowered back, and the sea was calm. They saw His supremacy also, not merely as manifested in His power over wind and water, but in the strange thing He said to them. Before He rebuked the sea, He rebuked them, in the words, " Why are ye fearful, O ye of little faith? " by which He meant that men never ought to be afraid if they are with Him. This again was a superlative claim. We dare not say such a thing to our children, except under certain very restricted circumstances.

When they saw His power they said, " What manner of Man is this that even the winds and the sea obey Him ? "

There is also a revelation here of these men. They were loyal; they went with Him; they sought His aid; but they did not rightly know His power. " Carest Thou not that we perish? " That is what they said when they woke Him. I do not believe it was the cry of personal fear so much as the revelation of their conviction that if that boat went down, all the Kingdom would perish. Sometimes it is better not to wake Jesus when we are troubled. There is a higher faith; a faith that waits for deliverance out of a storm; a faith that says, If He is here, it is all right; let the waves roll, let the waters beat.

" With Christ in the vessel,
　I smile at the storm."

There is here also a revelation of the Kingdom. The perfect King and the imperfect subjects; and the King perfecting the subjects by process. They cannot bear the storm, they are afraid. Then He will hush the storm, and He will answer the prayer of imperfection in order that He may build upon it. Some day they will brave the storm, and will be content to abide it, trusting Him for peace under all circumstances.

When He came out of the boat on the other side, they had a new manifestation of His power. This was a manifestation both to disciples and to the multitudes, in which we touch for the first time in the progress of our study, the fact of demon possession. It is an unfortunate thing that in the English revision the word which should be *demons* is translated *devils*. The American revisers have made the distinction. Demon possession and devil possession are not identical. This is the story of two possessed by demons. As to who these demons were, all kinds of theories have been advanced. Probably they were fallen angels under the control of the arch-enemy of the race, the personal devil, and no doubt there is still a good deal of demon possession in the world. This is a terrible illustration of the power of a demon over a man, first obsessed, and then possessed by the spirit. First there was the temptation to give way to the evil spirit, and the struggle that followed; and then the bringing of the man into subjection by the demon, who obtained entire possession of him. Here were men so fierce that none could tame them; so fierce that men were afraid to pass by their way. In the presence of that awful fact of which men were conscious, but with which they could not deal, the Lord came. His authority was acknowledged by the demons. "What have we to do with Thee, Thou Son of God?" That authority He immediately exercised; and when the demons asked that they might pass out into the herd of swine, He uttered one word, "Go." Thus the King exercised His power beneficently; for the individual, by freeing him of possession; and for the community, by freeing them of their swine, for all traffic in swine was forbidden within the area of the Hebrew economy.

We have a strange ending to the chapter. "And behold, all the city came out to see Jesus; and when they saw Him, they besought Him that He would depart from their borders."

This is our King. The human limitations have passed away. His essential powers are abiding powers. There is no sphere in which He is unable to act. We listen to His teaching; it is superlative teaching. He came down from the mountain top, and the question arose, What can He do? His works gave the answer. In the physical plane He was Master; among the elements He was Master; and in that strange spirit-world, which encompasses us, and of which we know so little, He was Master also.

There is no limit to His power. Yes, there is limitation. His power is limited in us. We may send Him away, as did the Gadarenes. We may limit Him as did the disciples; by the very deliverance they procured, preventing Him working out a more marvellous manifestation. We may love father or mother more, as the man seemed to do when he came to Christ.

Let us rather say to Him, with the scribe, "Teacher, I will follow Thee whithersoever Thou goest." And let us say it though He has shown us the cross, though we know it may mean homelessness in the deepest sense of the word; though we know it must mean sacrificial living, if we are to live for the saving of men.

MATTHEW IX. 1-17

IN this study we have the third illustration in the second group showing the power of the King. It is that of the forgiveness of sins and the healing of the sick of the palsy. This is followed by the account of the call of Matthew; which is thus set in relation to the healing of the palsy and the forgiveness of sins, in a very striking manner. That in turn is followed by a record of criticism and inquiry. Let us mark the lines of analysis before we give more detailed attention to the teaching.

In the first eight verses we have the story of Christ's crossing over into His own city, and His pronouncing forgiveness upon the man and healing him.

Then in verse nine we have the story

of the calling of Matthew; all told in the compass of one verse, and yet thrilling with suggestiveness.

Immediately following, in verses ten to thirteen, we have the first criticism. " Why eateth your Teacher with the publicans and sinners? "

Then in verses fourteen to seventeen we have the inquiry, " Why do we and the Pharisees fast oft, but Thy disciples fast not? " This, then, is the outline of our study.

We commence with the incident of healing, and notice first some of its points of beauty.

"When He saw their faith." That is the statement which first arrests attention on reading the story. Details are not given here, beyond that of the faith with which these men came. One of the other evangelists tells us that they broke up the roof, and let the sick man down into the midst. The fact here standing out is, that " He saw their faith." There has been a good deal of speculation as to whose faith is referred to, but of one thing we may be perfectly sure, it was not only the faith of the men who brought him. " *Their* faith " demands some other interpretation; it demands the faith of the man, as well as the faith of the men who brought him, because Christ said to him, " Thy sins are forgiven." It would appear that our Lord saw that in his heart there was a desire for something deeper than physical healing; and that he was conscious that physical disability was the result of his own sin; and therefore with a great tenderness, in words thrilling with the music of the evangel He had come to create, He said to him, in effect: Be of good cheer—I am able to deal with the deepest matter; *thy sins are forgiven.* That word was a response to faith.

And yet, while we believe there was faith in the heart of the man himself, we must not miss the important fact here that there is such a thing as vicarious faith. It is possible to help a man's faith. " Jesus seeing *their* faith."

Then notice that when they brought him, instead of first dealing with his disability, Jesus at once said to him, "Be of good cheer, thy sins are for-

given." In a moment the suspicion of the crowd was evident, and their criticism was aroused, because He pronounced forgiveness with authority. The men who had been watching with curiosity became angry, and charged Him with blasphemy. It was then that the King for the first time in His process of revelation, defended an action. He looked at these men criticising, and said to them, " Which is easier, to say, Thy sins are forgiven; or to say, Arise, and walk? But that ye may know that the Son of Man hath authority on earth to forgive sins" (He turned to the man), " Arise, and take up thy bed, and go unto thy house." And he arose and left. Then there came upon the people a great sense of fear, and they marvelled. The fear was due to the fact that there was demonstrated to their consciousness the fact that somehow, in that Man, or through that Man, God was very near. They had heard the great word of forgiveness, the word for which the heart of an honest man hungers, more than any other. They had heard this Man say, " Thy sins are forgiven," and they did not believe it; they questioned it; they thought He was blasphemous; they felt that He was saying something easy, a word that was not capable of demonstration, and which therefore they did not accept as truth. And instantly, with a great tenderness, not because the Lord was anxious for His own defence, but that they might believe, He challenged the man to rise up and walk. And so in concrete and evident fashion He demonstrated His power.

But there is more than that in the story. Probably to all intelligent men who watched Him that day there was a clear consciousness of the connection between the man's physical disability and his sin; and that instead of touching the surface, Jesus went right to the root of the matter, when He pronounced forgiveness. The demonstration which the King gave these men in very concrete fashion, is the perpetual demonstration of the fact of forgiveness. With the forgiveness of sin, if it be a true experience, there pass away disabilities, which hold men in bondage while sin remains unforgiven.

90

When Jesus asked these people, "For which is easier to say, Thy sins are forgiven, or to say, Arise, and walk?" He suggested to them the relation between sin and suffering. Again one is driven back to the prophecy of Isaiah. In Matthew viii. 17 we read, "That it might be fulfilled which was spoken by Isaiah the prophet, saying, Himself took our infirmities, and bare our diseases." Thus Matthew claimed that the healing of all those who came to Jesus was in fulfilment of Isaiah's prophecy in chapter liii. 4: "Surely He hath borne our griefs, and carried our sorrows." Let us continue the reading in Isaiah: "Yet we did esteem Him stricken, smitten of God, and afflicted. But He was wounded for our transgressions, He was bruised for our iniquities, the chastisement of our peace was upon Him; and with His stripes we are healed." Thus the prophet looking down through the centuries to the perfect Servant of God, the Great Healer, said of Him, first, "He hath borne our griefs and carried our sorrows." He did not end there; but went on to tell how this One would heal, not in the local cases merely, but in the great issue of all His mission as the Servant of God: "He was wounded for our transgressions." That is to say that by the vicarious suffering of the Servant of God sin would be dealt with. Sin lies at the back of all human disability; and because sin is dealt with all its results can be dealt with. That is the whole mission of the Servant of God. This was so in the case of this man. He had palsy. Sin is the root of palsy. The King pardoned his sin by virtue of the fact that He would presently bear it in His own body on the tree. The Passion was the right and warrant for everything that Jesus did in this realm of healing physical disability. He healed by the mystery of the Cross, by bearing our transgressions and being bruised for our iniquity. In the long outworking of the mission of Jesus, by the way of that Cross, every tear shall be wiped away, all diseases shall be dealt with and cast out, and His ultimate victory in the physical realm, based upon His bearing of sin, the cause of disease, will be the perfect physical salvation of the race that puts its trust in Him. The mission of the Son of Man is that of dealing with sin; and, secondly, that of healing disease; so that here again is manifested the fact that the miracles of Jesus were wrought by the restoration of a lost order, rather than by violation of existing law. Men who had seen Him Master in the realm of the physical; Master of the elements; Master of the surrounding spiritual world; now saw Him King in the moral realm, pronouncing absolution, and giving the evidence of the absolution, in the curing of a physical disability.

Now it is not without suggestiveness that the next thing we read is that Jesus called Matthew. Matthew was a tax-gatherer, and we know how unpopular the Roman tax-gatherer was, and how far more unpopular was the Jew who lent himself to the work of Rome. Matthew was of such, a lower caste of Jew; not necessarily the poor Jew; but the man who, in the opinion of his compatriots, was of blunted moral sense, and of dead national aspiration. The King saw this man, one of a class supremely despised by the people, and as He passed said to him, "Follow Me," and thus immediately included one outcast of the nation, in the inner circle of His Kingdom. He had claimed the power to forgive sins. Here in the eyes of the people was a sinner above all men, and the King called him, and he followed. The way Matthew himself tells the story is full of beauty: "And as Jesus passed by from thence, He saw a man, called Matthew, sitting at the place of toll; and He saith unto him, Follow Me. And he arose and followed Him." "As Jesus passed by from thence He saw"—What did He see? The man. What did they see? The tax-gatherer. The world sees all sorts of things in us—the accidental things. Christ will not see them, although He sees everything. He sees the man. We may be bruised and broken and scarred, and it may be all our own fault; but in each case He sees the man; and He calls us in the same sweet voice that Matthew heard: "Follow Me."

Is not this a new exhibition of the King's power and authority in yet another sphere? Here the King is seen exercising His authority, so far as He can exercise it, in the realm of human will, by expressing the demand of a paramount claim, " Follow Me." Perpetually one is being startled at the Master's method. Only once in the four Gospels can we find any occasion when He asked advice. He once asked Philip what they were to do to feed the crowd. But notice the parenthesis. " This He said to prove him, for He Himself knew what He would do." He always knew what He would do; and He came to this man, sitting there in the midst of custom and toll, and He said to him, " Follow Me." There was no argument, no apology. He did not even suggest to him that it might be well if he first considered His claims. It was a quiet, strong, musical, mystical demand; and everything for that man, depended upon his answer.

But if there is here a note of great authority, mark its limitation. Yes, the King is limited. " Follow Me," He said; but the " I will " of the man was needed to complete the relationship. One stands appalled with the tremendous fact that a man can say, No. These chapters reveal it. He went to the country of the Gadarenes, and they said, Leave us, and He left them. The King is limited by human will. But thank God for the issue of this story, for we want to live in the light of it. " He arose and followed Him." So the despised tax-gatherer became the royal chronicler, and has given us this great Gospel of the Kingdom.

Now let us turn to the paragraph of criticism and inquiry.

The first criticism circles round the question of the Pharisees: " Why eateth your Teacher with the publicans and sinners? " The occasion of the criticism was the action of Jesus in sitting familiarly and eating with publicans and sinners. It was in Matthew's house that He thus sat down; and the occasion was a special one. The first thing Matthew did was to make a great feast for Jesus and invite to it all the publicans and sinners of his acquaintance. That is the way to entertain Jesus. It is very beautiful. Everybody else despised the publican and the sin-

ner. Matthew gathered them together, the people of his own despised class, and Jesus sat down—" reclined " is the word—with them. Now the Pharisees came and said to the disciples, " Why eateth your Teacher with the publicans and sinners? " We have referred to their philosophy on a previous occasion. They objected because they believed if a man sat down among publicans and sinners to eat, he would be contaminated. What they failed to appreciate was the difference between this Man and themselves. His answer was again a vindication of His action: " They that are whole have no need of a physician, but they that are sick. But go ye "— ye Pharisees, ye men of the false philosophy, ye men that do not know God —" Go ye and learn what this meaneth; I desire mercy, and not sacrifice; for I came not to call the righteous, but sinners." It is as though Jesus said: Why do you criticise me? I am a physician, and therefore I must be where the people are who need Me. They that are whole do not need a physician, but they that are sick.

We notice here particularly how the physical and the moral necessarily merge in the thinking of Jesus. He used the figure of the physician, in connection with His presence in the midst of the moral depravity of which the Pharisees were so afraid. The very thing that kept the others away drew Him irresistibly.

There is yet a deeper note: " Go ye and learn what this means: I desire mercy, and not sacrifice." This He quoted from one of their own prophets (Hosea vi. 6). We ought to read the whole prophecy to catch the meaning of it. The prophecy of Hosea deals with spiritual adultery, spiritual harlotry. The great agonising emphasis of the prophetic message is that God is wounded in His love, because of the infidelity of His people to the Covenant. And this is the cry of God, " O Ephraim, what shall I do unto thee? " Then he tells these people that their goodness is as the morning cloud, it vanishes and is gone. You bring Me sacrifices as though I wanted them. Ephraim, Judah, it is not sacrifice that I want from you; it is mercy toward you that I want; and I would fain find a way unto you in love and mercy.

Jesus looked at these men who thought they knew the law and the prophets, and said to them: You do not understand the God Who is revealed in your own writings. He was talking to the teachers, to the men who were interpreting the prophets, and He said, " Go ye and learn what this meaneth, I desire mercy, and not sacrifice." Go and learn what the heart of God is; go and find out, that according to your own writings, God is far more anxious to have mercy than He is to receive any offering that a man brings to Him. When you have learnt this, then you will understand why I sit down with publicans and sinners, why I recline and eat in the midst of them.

After the criticism of the Pharisees came the inquiry of the disciples of John. " Why do we and the Pharisees fast oft, and Thy disciples fast not?" Sometimes this has been treated as though it were a question inspired by the Pharisees, and part of the criticism. But I am inclined to think that this was not so, but that it was a perfectly honest inquiry.

There are really two questions here: " Why do we and the Pharisees fast?" and " Why do Thy disciples fast not?" These men came to Christ; and they said in effect: The religious ideal which we have believed to be true, and which the Pharisees have evidently believed to be true, seems to be utterly different from the religious ideal of Thy disciples; we fast, we mourn, but these men that Thou hast gathered about Thee seem to be pre-eminently happy; they make no place for fasting and mourning.

Christ's answer gives colour to that explanation of the inquiry. He said, " Can the sons of the bridechamber mourn, as long as the Bridegroom is with them?" Christ defended that which puzzled them, by taking a figure that was more full of rejoicing than anything else could be. A wedding ceremony in an Eastern country lasted for seven days. It was a week of unbounded and unceasing rejoicing, of songs and music and mirth. And Jesus said, These men are the sons of the bridechamber, and you must not expect them to fast while the Bridegroom is with them, but, " the days will come, when the Bridegroom shall be taken away from them, and then will they fast."

This is Christ's defence of the right of His people to be merry; and that right to be merry is the fact that He is with them. If that be true, then we have the right to be merry always. What He said about sorrow was fulfilled. He was taken away from them, and they fasted and were sad through those days of darkness; but He came back, and, standing on the slope of Olivet, He said, " Lo, I am with you alway." Then there is no more room for mourning; no more room for the sad face of agony; but there is room for mirth, room for joy, and room for gladness.

Then the Lord uttered the final word of illustration in this connection. You cannot put a piece of undressed cloth upon an old garment. It will pull and tear the old garment to destruction. You must not put new wine into old wine-skins; the old are not strong enough to hold it; it will break them and the wine be wasted. Thus the King said in effect to these questioning men, Do not attempt to measure this new thing by that old thing. The old was right as long as it lasted; but this is new. There are new motives, new forces, new impulses coming into play; and you must not try to place the new within the narrow limits of the old. It is Christ's clear declaration that the new covenant which He had come to initiate, demanded new methods of expression; the purple of royalty, instead of the sackcloth of sorrow; the laughter of triumph, instead of the weeping of defeat; Easter morning instead of the day of Crucifixion.

Yet we can never get to the purple, but by the way of the sackcloth; never triumph save through defeat; never reach Easter morning, but by the way of Good Friday.

The whole genius of Christianity is in this. He went by the way of Good Friday, and He gives us Easter for ever. He wore the sackcloth, and turned it into purple for us. He trod the winepress alone, and we have the cup filled with the new wine of the Kingdom.

There is in this study a great sequence of revelation. Sin is forgiven; a despised man is included in the inner circle; God's heart is revealed, " I will have mercy;" God's answer is affirmed in those figures of the new forces.

What, then, shall we say? Let us trust His heart, let us trust His power, by leaving all and following Him, knowing that in Him we shall find all we need.

MATTHEW IX. 18-34

THIS is the last paragraph in that section of the Gospel which deals with the King's exhibition of the benefits of His Kingdom. Of course, that is not to say that there was no further manifestation of His power, for He continued to work wonders to the very end.

This account is full of life, full of light, full of love, full of colour. Here the King is seen dealing with specific cases as they made application to Him. All sorts and conditions of men mixed together in the multitudes that surrounded Him at this time—publicans and sinners, Scribes and Pharisees, beggars by the highway, wealthy men who watched and listened with great interest, country people who had crowded into the cities, learned people who were deeply interested in His teaching. And yet the people He brought into prominence, upon whom men have continued to look through the long centuries, were all of one class —they were needy people. In those days in which He passed from teaching to doing, He drew to Himself the people who were in trouble, in need, in difficulty.

Of those we are now to observe, some were wealthy and some were poor. Here a wealthy ruler, and there a woman beggared by her illness; and yet again two men who were begging by the highway-side, but who turned to Him because of a great sense of need, and finally a man demon-possessed. Such power was resident in Him that weakness felt its attraction, and out from the great curious, jostling, crowding multitudes, individuals conscious of their need came near to Him. As we look back at the pictures of this chapter we see the crowd generally and indefinitely; but the needy souls particularly and definitely. The King rendered need conspicuous, that He might meet it and cancel it. The cases are drawn out of the crowd one by one, brought into living contact with Christ, and dealt with; and as we look at them, the impression made upon our minds, carrying complete conviction, is that our King is not a Teacher only, but a Worker also; that He does something more than propound a theory, He is ever communicating strength; that He not only holds up before men a great ideal, as He did in the Manifesto, but that He ever touches men in their paralysis, and makes them powerful in the very places of their need with perfect sufficiency.

Let us first survey the cases, noticing their diversity. How different are the people with whom Christ deals in this section! Matthew tells these stories very briefly. In Mark and Luke the details stand out far more conspicuously, but Matthew chronicled the facts simply, in order to reveal the power of the King. In the other Gospels other aspects of the work of Christ are revealed—His perfect service, and His perfect Manhood with its human sympathy; and it may help us to borrow from Mark and Luke in order that we may see more clearly the need that came to the King.

The first picture is that of a father, whose life was shadowed because at home his little daughter, twelve years of age, lay sick. Twelve years of sunshine were threatened with eclipse; twelve years of playfulness were merging towards a tragedy in the heart and life of Jairus. This man came to Jesus, driven towards Him by his sense of awful sorrow. Matthew says, " Behold,

94

there came a ruler, and worshipped Him, saying, My daughter is even now dead," which of course does not mean that Jairus declared that his daughter was actually dead. The "even now dead" is an idiomatic phrase, signifying at the point of death, very nearly dead, or, as we sometimes say in the blind brutality of our overwhelming dread, as good as dead. So Jairus came to Christ, a man driven to the King by the need of his threatened sorrow.

The next picture is that of the woman overwhelmed in weakness and sorrow. Again Matthew tells us very little about her, but quite enough for us to understand her condition. He says, "A woman, who had an issue of blood twelve years, came behind Him." That descriptive phrase must be considered in the light of the age in which she lived, and not in the light of our age. First, by reason of her trouble, she was excommunicated religiously. The Hebrew economy did not permit a woman so suffering to take any part or place in the worship of God. She was shut out from temple and synagogue worship. She was divorced from her husband by the same law. She was ostracized from society. We are not dealing with that law, certainly we have no right to criticise it; but we thank God that it has passed away for ever, and that the spirit of the age is one which desires to take care of the helpless and suffering. This woman had been spending her money perpetually for twelve years to find a remedy; and, as Luke says, could not be cured of any, or, as Mark says, was nothing bettered but rather the worse. Twelve years. Jairus's little girl twelve years of age; this woman, twelve years of suffering. Twelve years of sunshine, twelve years of shadow. A little child full of laughter going out towards death; and a woman who had been in the midst of a living death for twelve years; and they both came into contact with Him.

Then two blind men. They heard, but could not see; they felt, but could not perceive. Two blind men, but they fought their way to Him.

And finally a demon-possessed man, whom the demon held in the thrall of dumbness; for there was a close connection between the dumbness of the man and his possession.

The sorrowing father, a wealthy man, a man of position, but his life overshadowed because his bairn was dying; he came to Jesus. The woman who had lost everything that was worth having, religious privilege, family care, social position, all her wealth; she came to Jesus. Two blind men who, perhaps, as one of the commentators says, did often talk about what other men saw, and perchance did often talk about the Healer Whose fame had gone through all the district, unable to see His face, unable to see their own, unable to see the faces of their loved ones; they found their way to Him. The demon-possessed man, who could not find his way to Jesus, was brought by others. All kinds of need. Thus the King passed into the midst of the multitudes, and He drew to Himself, into the closest circle, the most needy people from among the crowds. And so it is to-day. It is the broken heart, the bereft, the discouraged, the unfit, that He will bring nearer to Himself than any others.

Now notice the method of their coming. Jairus came for his child, and he came asking that Jesus would come and lay His hand upon her. He said, "She is even now dead"—there is practically no hope; indeed, there is no hope apart from God, for that is the meaning of the confession—"but come and lay Thy hand upon her, and she shall live." He asked for the touch of the hand of Christ. That was one method.

The woman came quite differently. While Jairus came and publicly proffered his request, this woman tried to get to Him without anybody knowing. She did not ask Him to touch her; she touched Him. It was quite a different method.

Then came the blind men, crying out —they were clamorous, noisy men— "Have mercy on us, Thou Son of David." In the other evangels we are told that the crowd tried to silence them, and they cried out the more, "Jesus, Thou Son of David, have mercy." They were not only clamorous, they were persistent. They got right into the house where Jesus had gone. It was the method of men determined to get to Him, persisting in spite of opposition.

And then the last case. This man did not come to Him at all; other people brought him; he was too far gone to come. Reason was dethroned. The other people brought him, and there is no word in the story about his faith. There is no single word that indicates that he had anything to do with his own coming. He was past the possibility of realising his need, so that there was not only diversity of need, there was diversity also in the method of approach.

And yet there is a great unity in these illustrations. They all approached Him. They all appealed to Him for force. They all appealed to Him for exactly what they needed. Jairus came to Him with quiet dignity, surcharged with the sorrow of his heart; but he came to Him for just what he needed. The woman came to Him secretly, pressing her way through the crowd, not a surging crowd only, but a moving crowd on the way to Jairus's house. Perhaps a little way in front of all the rest was Jairus himself, for if he could have hurried Christ that day he would. And then next to Jesus and round about Him were the apostles, the most dignified men in the whole company. Through that crowd of jostling and pressing strong men, with perchance here and there a mother, lifting up her little child to look into the face of the great Prophet as He paused, one woman, weak and wan and emaciated and thin, pressed near to Him. In that woman's coming one sees the most wonderful combination of weakness and strength. She forced her way through that crowd until she touched Jesus. It was quite different from Jairus's coming, but it was a coming for what she needed, the claim for power. The blind men came to Him for the same thing, and the dumb demoniac, brought to Him by others, came for the same thing.

What was the issue in every case? The need was met; death vanquished, disease cured, sight granted, and, in the case of the man possessed, freedom from the demon, followed by speech.

"Behold your King" is the word of Matthew from first to last. He vanquishes death for the broken heart of a father; He deals with all the necessity of the excommunicated, divorced, ostracized woman; He opens the eyes of the blind; He looses the silence of the tongue of the dumb as He exorcises the demon that has seized him.

Let us now look at the King more closely. Notice first of all His readiness. When Jairus came it is written, He "arose and followed." He needed no pressure save that of the man's broken heart. That is an argument He never can refuse.

When the woman touched Him she was healed before He spoke, when she grasped the border of His garment. Perhaps it was the fringe of the garment on which she took hold; that in which the Hebrews were commanded to wear a ribbon of blue that they might look upon it, and remember the words of the law to do them. While Jesus Christ was supremely disdainful of all merely Hebrew ritual, He observed the law of Moses to its last tittle. So, probably, He wore the ribbon of blue, and the woman grasped at it with her frail hand. He knew it, and swifter than the lightning's flash, quick as the heartbeat of God, His virtue healed her. There was no persuasion necessary beyond the persuasion of her agony; and the moment she took hold, healing came.

Then the blind men. You may say there is a good deal of persuasion necessary here. No; it is simply that wonderful method by which Jesus Christ did sometimes proceed, of letting people pour out their whole heart, and show their earnestness, before He answered. When they had persistently clamoured for His help, following Him into the house, sight came.

In the healing of the dumb demoniac, which is almost brutal in its bluntness as Matthew tells the story, there is never a word of request, to say nothing of appreciation. "There was brought to Him a dumb man possessed with a demon. And when the demon was cast out, the dumb man spake." That is all. It was the movement of a great readiness. So through all we see the King ready.

But look at the King again, and mark His method. How the method varies! It is a great picture, this of Jesus coming to the house of Jairus. We need the three Gospel stories to see it, it is so exquisite in its beauty. He came in where the child was lying dead, and He said, "She is not dead, but sleepeth." And they laughed Him to scorn. What did He do? He put them all out. Do not imagine that this King is only capable of tenderness; He can do very drastic things. He was justified in His action. When He came in they were wailing; before He had been there two minutes they were laughing; but there are some people who must be put out before Jesus can do anything. "He could there do no mighty work . . . because of their unbelief." A critical, scorning, scoffing crowd must be put out before He can do anything. He Himself was affected by it. Criticism was sterilising in its effect upon Him. Faith was fertilising. Then there is a beautiful touch of tenderness in the Master's method with the maiden. Remember He was also healing the man's heart. He put His hand on the child and said, "Talitha cumi; which is, being interpreted, Damsel, I say unto thee, Arise." Yet that does not interpret it, it hardly translates it. If you translate "Talitha cumi" literally, Jesus really said, Little lamb, I say unto thee, Arise. Oh that sweet touch, that tenderness of tone! Then "He charged them much, that no man should know this; and He commanded that something should be given her to eat." Observe the sweet reasonableness of the Lord! He ordered them to give her, not the catechism, but meat—physical food. Jairus, here is your bairn. Take care of her, give her meat. We talk about the *Man* Jesus, and blessed be His humanity; but this is God, and He robs death of its prey, and thinks about the meal of a little maiden; and springtime comes into the heart of the man, and summer follows it, and all life is different to him.

But on His way to the house of Jairus, in dealing with the woman, the King's method was quite a different one. First, a question was asked, not because He wanted to know, but because it was necessary that this woman should go a good deal further than she had done. "Who touched Me?" said Jesus. You need not be angry with the question the disciples asked, "Thou seest the multitude thronging Thee, and sayest Thou, Who touched Me?" That is precisely what we should have said. Tenderly and reverently, with a touch of amazement in our voice, we would have said, Dear Master, why do you ask that? Many have touched You in the last half-hour. He always knows the difference between the jostle of a curious mob and the touch of a soul in its agony. The soul that touches Him is the soul that will gain the virtue. "Who touched ME?" He differentiates between the curious crowd and the soul in its need. But follow on a little, and see His method, for He has not finished. The woman seeing that everything was known, came in front of Him and told Him all the truth. Then Matthew tells us the most beautiful thing. The King said, "Daughter." We cannot say these things as they ought to be said. Oh for the breath of the Spirit of God to make the music for us! All that came after, "Be of good cheer; thy faith hath made thee whole," was included when He said, "Daughter." She is excommunicated; "Daughter"—she is adopted. She is divorced; "Daughter"—He takes her to His heart. She is ostracized; "Daughter"—and He admits her to heaven's society. In one word He drove the clouds away and showed her the blue sky, with the golden sunshine all about her. By one word the shackles of her pain and impotence fell from her, and she stood in all the light and liberty of conscious relationship with God. But before He could say "Daughter," He had to bring her from secret discipleship into the place of confessed discipleship. She took hold of the border of His garment, and the power came. Then He said in effect, I want you to have more than that. I do not want you to be satisfied with virtue communicated through My garments. Come, and look into My face. He looked down into her face. Behold those eyes! Oh the light and glory o them—the quiet tenderness, the surpassing beauty of them!

Then came the blind men. Here was another method. "Believe ye that I am able to do this?" "Yea, Lord." Then His hands were put upon their eyes. Have you ever thought it would have been worth while to be blind for fifty years to feel those hands touch the eyes, and know the breaking of the light?

In healing the dumb man we have no account of His method; we simply see His quiet majesty. All need appealed to His force. He appealed in every case to faith; and where faith responded, either personally or vicariously—His power was made manifest over death, disease, blindness, demons —power that defies explanation, but arrests because of its abundance.

The thing which is supremely impressive is the ease of His might. There is no struggle, no long mysterious preparation. The need comes; He speaks, He touches; the need is met. And all these are little things that He did not account worth talking about. He said to the men about Him, Do not go and talk about these things; do not go and publish this abroad. This is not the thing I want you to see: "Believe Me that I am in the Father, and the Father in Me; *or else* believe Me for the very works' sake."

The spiritual miracles, the moral remakings, are going on all around us to-day. God help us all to see the King, to touch the King as He passes. The arm of flesh need not be lifted; the sigh of faith is enough. Make it thine by submission, and all the glory of His reign will shine upon you, and the supernatural power resident within Him will be yours.

Oh matchless King! In this exhibition of benefits we have seen the supremacy and the power of the King in every realm. He has demonstrated His power to do as well as to teach. Do not be afraid to let Him tear away the veil behind which thou hast hidden some evil thing in thy life. Let Him reveal it, for He will heal it. This is the method and purpose of the King.

The final word in this section reveals the antagonism of His foe and ours. It expressed itself through the religious leaders of the time. "By the prince of the demons casteth He out demons." A King so marvellous in teaching and power, yet to the prejudiced mind bringing no conviction; and there were men who dared to say that He moved to victory in the power of evil. Let us jealously inquire in what attitude we listen and study, for it is possible for prejudice and pride to blind us to the most solemn and sacred truths. May God grant that instead of the blasphemy which attributes His victories to evil, we may be among the number of those who say, This is our King; we have waited for Him; upon His brow we put the crown, and by God's help we will serve Him.

MATTHEW IX. 35-38

IN reading this passage we notice that it chronicles no definite acts in the work of Jesus. The verses form rather a statement of general facts and general effects. This statement deals with the passing of the King from place to place; with what He saw as He thus passed through cities and villages; with what He felt in the presence of the things He saw; and with the result of that consciousness.

The general statement is that "Jesus went about all the cities and the villages," and, by way of introduction, the one matter to be recognized is that, in so doing, He came into contact with all sorts and conditions of people. The problem of the city, and the problem of the village existed in those days as it does to-day. Jesus went to cities and villages; to the people who lived in crowds, and at the heart of the movements of the day; and to the people far away in the hamlets on the hillside, and in the valley, whose little world was the vineyard and the cornfield. As He went He had a threefold method: that of teaching, preaching, and healing. Thus He prosecuted His Kingly work.

His teaching of the people consisted of interpretations of their own Scriptures and economy. That was the first method of the King; emphasising the truth taught by immediate application. We have no detailed account of this teaching of the general multitudes, but occasional illustrations by the record of what happened at some particular place. Once we are told He went, as His custom was, to the Synagogue, and, finding the book of the Prophet, He read old and perfectly familiar words, giving them new life and meaning, teachíng their deepest intention.

His preaching consisted of the proclamation of the good news of the Kingdom of God; or, to put that into other words, the good tidings of His own work in establishing that Kingdom. He was preaching that prophetically only. He waited for the Cross ere that great evangel could be sent forth in all its fulness; but He went through the cities and the villages preaching the Kingdom of God; saying to men, God is on the Throne; affirming the fact of the Kingship of God.

The ministry of healing was the manifestation of His power to work as well as to preach; and such manifestation was, moreover, a revelation of the order of the Divine government. God is King, and everything that limits the sphere of His control must be subdued to His purpose; and, therefore, He healed disease. We have already seen that the miracles of Jesus were not interferences with law, but restorations of law; and that disease is lawlessness. Therefore to heal is not to interfere with law, but to restore the operation of law. In all the miracles of Jesus, miracles of physical healing, there was a symbolic value, and a spiritual intention. Whenever Jesus healed a sick person, He said in effect to that person, All suffering results from failure to yield to the control of our Father; all these limitations of life, and this destruction of life, result from rebellion against the Kingship of God. Thus, doing this threefold work, He went about all the cities, and all the villages. But now the time had come in the

mission of the King, when it was necessary to appoint fellow-labourers, labourers together with Himself. This passage reveals the reason for such appointment. The work was one in which He needed helpers of a very definite type—*labourers;* and the need for the work was created by compassion in the heart of Jesus, which is the deepest thing in the heart of God; and it is that which this passage reveals to us.

Let us state that again in other words. The time had come in the work of Jesus when He was constrained to appoint other labourers who should help Him. Humanly speaking, He could not overtake His work. He had been preaching, teaching, healing; but there were so many places He could not reach in His human and localised and straitened circumstances; and He must have men to help Him, for the work must be done. *Must,* because Jesus saw the multitudes distressed, scattered as sheep without a shepherd.

O Man of Nazareth, majestic, with eyes all love-lit; strange King of men, enunciating such an ethic that one's soul has been ashamed in its flaming glory, what matter about these people, why not leave them alone? Why must they be cared for? And the answer is, " He was moved with compassion." The necessity for the salvation of men is revealed in that statement. There is no reason in man that God should save; the need is born of His own compassion. No man has any claim upon God. Why, then, should men be cared for? Why should they not become the prey of the ravening wolf, having wandered from the fold? It has been said that the great work of redemption was the outcome of a passion for the righteousness and holiness of God; that Jesus must come and teach and live and suffer and die because God is righteous and holy. I do not so read the story. God could have met every demand of His righteousness and holiness by handing men over to the doom they had brought upon themselves. But deepest in the being of God, holding in its great energising might, both holiness and righteousness, is love and compassion. God said, according to Hosea, " How shall I give thee up,

Ephraim?" It is out of the love which inspired that wail of the Divine heart, that salvation has been provided, and our evangel has come.

"He was moved with compassion." That is just a simple lattice-window made up of crossing human words. Look through it, and you will see the flaming glory of the infinite love of the infinite God. You will see the birth-place of everything that makes for the uplifting of man.

The thoughts of paramount importance in this passage are such as are suggested by two pronouns. "He" and "they." "*He* saw, and was moved with compassion." "*They* were distressed and scattered, as sheep having no shepherd."

Let us look, then, first at the King as here revealed; secondly, at the Kingdom as He saw it waiting to be redeemed and realised; and, finally, at His purpose and His method.

The King of Whom we have already said so much, was moved with compassion. The word compassion has come into our language from the Latin. It is, no doubt, the correct word at this point, spiritually; and yet the Greek word here translated compassion is a very remarkable one. It is a word of the kind which is largely passing out of use to-day, and the passing would not appear to be a loss, but rather a gain. The Greek word is one of those in which emotion is suggested by a physical figure. Very literally the declaration is that "His bowels were moved within Him." By the Greek, the bowels were regarded as the seat of violent passion, such as anger or love. By the Hebrew, they were regarded as the seat of the tender affections. Isaac Watts sang a hymn bearing on this verse, which we have changed in most of our hymn-books, and yet he was but translating from his Greek Testament,

"With joy we meditate the grace
    Of our High Priest above;
His heart is made of tenderness,
    His bowels yearn with love."

If Isaac Watts is a little out of date, he is quite accurate. He translated literally, definitely, and positively, from

this very word here rendered compassion. Then knowing that the translation was insufficient, Isaac Watts moved on, and took another word:

"Touched with a *sympathy* within,
    He knows our feeble frame;
He knows what sore temptations
    mean,
    For He hath *felt* the same."

Thus on the human level, this picture of God is that of a Man Who went into the cities, and into the villages, and looked at the people; and what He saw made His whole inner physical life, as the sacramental symbol of the spiritual, move and burn. We all know some little of this; how in certain circumstances, in some great overwhelming fear, in some sudden sorrow, our very physical life, acting in harmony with the mental, is filled with pain. "He was moved with compassion." He was moved to the agony of the physical by the pain of the spiritual.

But that was only sacramental and symbolic. What lay behind it all? Let us go back to our translation—"He was moved with compassion." What is compassion? Feeling with, pain with, comradeship in sorrow, fellowship in agony; an at-one-ment between this King and those upon whom He looked, culminating in the Cross as to outward expression. It existed in the heart of God long before the material Cross was uplifted; and it expressed itself in the suffering of the Son of God through all the years of His sympathy with man before He went to that actual Cross. He could not see a woman who had suffered twelve years of pain but that He felt her feebleness. He came so intimately into comradeship and sympathy with human life that its pain was His pain. Do not ever think of this word compassion as though it meant pity merely. You can pity people and see them die in misery; but He bare with them; He identified Himself with the very issue of their pain; the very issue of their sin. That is compassion.

Then look at the King again. He wanted to shepherd these distressed ones. That was His main desire. "They were distressed and scattered as sheep not having a shepherd," and

He wanted to shepherd them. Perhaps we cannot quite understand this desire; yet every mother appreciates it in some measure; the mothers who, seeing the neglected children of the slum, yearn to mother them all, understand. That is God's heart. That is how Jesus felt. He wanted to shepherd these people, He wanted to take care of them. He wanted to fold them; He wanted to feed them.

These are the two functions of the King. The real King is always folding and feeding the sheep. In spiritual things the one who folds the sheep is the priest, and the one who feeds the sheep is the prophet. So that in true Kingship there are included the functions of the priest and the prophet; and these were the passions stirred in the heart of Jesus by His vision of the multitudes.

But let us turn our eyes from this wonderful King, moved with compassion, a shepherd by nature, desiring the folding and feeding of all sheep, and look at the Kingdom as He saw it. The people at whom He had been looking were not all of one class. It cannot too often be stated that His view was of *Humanity*. Jesus did not pay special attention to the rulers, neither did He pay special attention to the people of the submerged classes as they came to Him, and appealed to Him. He saw all sorts and conditions of people. He saw the multitudes *as sheep*, not as goats and sheep. The Scriptures never speak of men as goats except once, and it is a very great question as to whether it is not wrong to look upon that as a picture of the judgment of individuals. It is the picture of a national judgment, and the figure applies not to men, but to nations. Jesus saw men as sheep out in the highways. Every man is in God's image. Every human being has, if we can but see it, the hall-mark of the likeness of God, and He saw in the multitudes their natural possibility of realising a Divine purpose. If a man is lost, if a child shall so wander from the pathway as eventually to be lost, it will be by not realising the possibility of their own lives, and so being lost by degeneration and degradation. He saw the multitudes as sheep.

Yes, but He clearly saw their actual condition. Here again the Greek words are graphic words. They were distressed, fleeced, lacerated by the fleecing, scattered, flung, tossed by violence. In these words we have the picture of sheep departed from the fold, into the midst of wolves; they are seen with their fleece torn, half-dead, bleeding from wounds, and fainting. This is how He saw men and women, because they had no shepherd. That is a dread and awe-inspiring passage in Ezekiel about shepherds who fed themselves instead of the sheep, shepherds who came with no healing to the wounded sheep, shepherds who never went to seek lost sheep. That is Ezekiel's picture. That is how the King saw the people; and He had come to do what the shepherds had failed to do. He had come to fold and feed them. He had come to heal them. He had come to seek and save that which was lost. He was the "Good Shepherd," and "The Good Shepherd layeth down His life for the sheep."

Finally, let us notice His purpose and His method. His purpose is to be the Shepherd, to fold the sheep and to feed the sheep. In order to fold the sheep He must come into conflict with the foe, and He accomplished His victory by the purity of His life, and by the infinite passion of His dying. He had also come to feed the sheep, that is to give sustenance to their neglected life.

Now the moment had come when the King, Who is the Shepherd, was about to gather a few more around Himself; when He would avail Himself of the help of others. What did He do with them? He first gave them *His* vision of the multitudes, and then He said, "Pray ye therefore the Lord of the harvest that He send forth labourers." If we are going to do anything that is worth doing we must see as He sees. Let us say: O Shepherd true, open our eyes that we may see as Thou seest. And if we see as He sees we shall hear Him say to us, "Pray thou the Lord of the harvest to thrust forth labourers into His harvest."

In this brief paragraph Jesus makes use of two figures, and here again, as on other occasions, it looks as though

He almost inadvertently confused figures, and mixed metaphors. But He never really did so. First it is the figure of the shepherd and the sheep; and then it is the figure of the harvest and the labourers. But in these two you have the perfect unfolding of two sides of the great question. In the sheep and the shepherd you see man's need met by God. But in the harvest and the labourers you see God's need met by

man. Our Gospel is, "Jehovah is my Shepherd." But the Master says to us, If that is the Gospel, and if My compassion has given you the Gospel; now look, the fields are white unto harvest. That is God's harvest. All those sheaves ought to be garnered for Him. They are sheaves of harvest which God would have gathered and garnered, but He needs labourers to gather His white harvest.

MATTHEW X. 1-23

BETWEEN the final charge of the last chapter, and the action of the King now described, there is a close and a very striking connection. It is first to be carefully noted that the men whom He charged to pray specifically for labourers, were those whom He immediately sent forth to labour. "Pray ye," is the first command; "go ye," is the next. The men who have learnt to look with the eyes of Jesus until they feel with the heart of Jesus; and who, out of such vision and such feeling, begin to pray, are more than half ready for the work of bringing in the harvest. "Pray," that is the first thing; but "go" is the next; and as surely as He says "pray," He says "go." Yet let it be remembered that He never says "go" until He has said "pray."

If that fundamental connection between the compassion of the King, and His commissioning of the twelve is recognized, then we may proceed to the discovery of the main value of this section. That main value lies in the fact that it contains "His commandments." Chapter eleven begins, "And it came to pass, when Jesus had finished commanding His twelve disciples, He departed thence to teach and preach in their cities." Thus it is at once seen that chapter ten consists of the Master's charge to those men whom He was about to send out, in co-operation with Himself, to do the work which lay so heavily upon His heart. In this charge the King Himself reveals the lines of service, the methods to be adopted, and the prayer to be offered.

So far in the propaganda of the King we have considered His enunciation of

ethics; and have observed His exhibition of benefits. Now we see Him about to enter upon the great work of enforcing His claims; and first He sends forth these disciples. Thus they become more than disciples; He constitutes them apostles. This is the first time the word is applied to them. Only once in Matthew is this word, which indicates their relation to Him in specific and well-defined service, made use of. An apostle is a delegate, the first messenger, the one who represents the King, whose only business is to represent the King, who speaks the word of the King, and speaks it with authority because he is sent, delegated, the ambassador of the King.

Let us first make a broad analysis of the whole chapter, that we may follow its movement, and understand to some extent what the King was really doing, as He prepared those twelve men and sent them forth on their mission. The King's outlook was upon the work which those whom He appoints will have to do to the end of the age. Some of the things which He said have no application to us; they were only for the men who were then with Him. Nevertheless there are underlying principles in every part of these charges which are of perpetual application. The changes which would follow in circumstances and conditions were recognized by the King; and in an orderly movement, perfectly balanced, perfectly adjusted, He gave instructions to the apostles for the whole dispensation which He was about to initiate. As the King stood in the midst of the twelve, He looked at them and at the immediate present; but He also looked with those clear, far-seeing eyes into the near decades; and still further He looked down all the centuries; and speaking to the first apostles, He delivered a charge which in its comprehensiveness and finality is applicable to the whole movement of His enterprise, until His second advent. He declared the abiding principles, which must obtain through all the ages; and He described the changing conditions, which would necessitate changing methods.

This charge divided the age into three distinctly-marked epochs. In the first four verses we read of how our Lord called these disciples and named them apostles; and we have the names of the twelve. Then from verse five to the end of verse fifteen we have the first section of the charge. The fifteenth verse reads, "Verily I say unto you, It shall be more tolerable for the land of Sodom and Gomorrah in the day of judgment, than for that city," that is for any city to which these men would come and would be refused; against such a city He charged them to shake the dust from their feet. This is one movement, one division of the discourse.

At verse sixteen it is evident that our Lord lifted His eyes and looked further on, and saw how His apostles, His messengers, these very men, would presently enter upon a new phase in their work, and have to face new difficulties; He said, "Behold I send you forth as sheep in the midst of wolves." That was the description of a new movement, quite different from the one described in verses five to fifteen, as we shall see more clearly presently. It ended with the strange words of verse twenty-three, "But when they persecute you in this city, flee into the next: for verily I say unto you, Ye shall not have gone through the cities of Israel, till the Son of Man be come." There ends the second movement in the great charge.

Then begins the third, which commences with the words, "A disciple is not above his teacher, nor a servant above his lord;" and runs to the end of the chapter.

Thus, in this one discourse, the King

referred to three distinct epochs; the first division, verses five to fifteen, exactly describing the work of the apostles from the day when He ordained them, until the day of His own crucifixion. It had to do with their immediate work. All His instructions in that division were applicable to the men whom He sent forth, while He still lived amongst them, until the day of His crucifixion. With His crucifixion, the order initiated ended, and save in fundamental principles, the commission of those verses has no application to us.

Immediately following these instructions, He continued, "Behold I send you forth as sheep in the midst of wolves." Now, these men knew practically nothing of persecution until after the crucifixion of Jesus. He was rejected, but they were treated with respect, even by the crowds. The crowds argued with them, tried to understand what relation they bore to Jesus, asked them what Christ meant by certain things; but did not persecute them. He kept them to the end, bore the brunt of persecution, gathered it into His own heart, and they knew nothing of it. But when the rough and rugged Cross was revealed, persecution broke upon them from their own nation In view of this He charged them that when they were persecuted in one city they were to flee to another, saying, "Ye shall not have gone through the cities of Israel, till the Son of Man be come." In these words He was evidently referring to His coming in judgment at the fall of Jerusalem, which took place in the year A. D. 70. Thus the second period ended with the fall of Jerusalem. It was then that the Son of Man came in the sense in which He meant here. A very remarkable fact of history throws light upon this; never from the day of Jerusalem's fall until now has a Christian believer been scourged in a Jewish synagogue. From the moment when Jerusalem passed out of human history as a commonwealth, her direct persecution of Christ ended. Alas, and alas, that Christians have persecuted Jews, but the Jew has never persecuted the Christian since the fall of Jerusalem. Thus in the second movement the King was dealing with the new conditions of His apostles' service, following His crucifixion and continuing until the fall of Jerusalem; and again, save in fundamental principles, the instructions are not applicable to us.

Then He saw still further down the centuries, all that would follow the fall of Jerusalem, to the end of the age; and in view of that period He began to talk about the relationship of His servants to Himself, going back to the word disciple, and no longer using the word apostle, thus including in the final movement of His instruction all the company of His children who will be His servants until He come again. "A disciple is not above his teacher;" and so on, in that wonderful passage in which He revealed this supreme truth, that after Israel's nationality ceased, and His Church should become the instrument for the proclaiming of His Gospel, her power would consist in her immediate identification with Himself; and her mission be that of constant co-operation with His purpose.

That is, of course, only a broad survey of these commandments of the King. We shall need to consider them more carefully; but before we do so, let us notice that the change of conditions created by the crucifixion of Jesus, and again by the fall of Jerusalem are self-evident. The position of these men was greatly changed after the crucifixion of Jesus; and it was as greatly changed again when the principal force in persecuting them was broken. It is perfectly clear that the King foresaw these things, and that He understood perfectly the whole movement of the years that stretched before Him. Let us recognize the perfect wisdom and sufficiency of the King. One of the profoundest reasons for trusting Christ to-day in the matter of all Christian service is that here and elsewhere He revealed His perfect knowledge of conditions which no man could forecast, and which yet have transpired exactly as He foretold them.

Now let us go back to a more particular examination of the first two of these movements. We will notice the immediate application of what He said to the men who stood around Him as to their work until His crucifixion; and

then the application of the next words, which He spoke to them concerning the period after His Cross until the destruction of Jerusalem. After considering the immediate application of these things, we will consider two principles of permanent value which bear their message to us.

As to the first period, we first notice the sphere of their operations. They were not to go to the Gentiles, they were not to go to the Samaritans. They were to "Go rather to the lost sheep of the House of Israel." It was a limited sphere. Ere He ascended all this was abrogated, as He said, "Go ye into all the world, and preach the Gospel to the whole creation."

Notice further, that He charged them that came into a city of Israel, being forbidden to go to a Gentile city, or a city of the Samaritan, they were to seek out those who were worthy. If the house were worthy they were to enter; if not, they were not to enter. That is the exact opposite of what we are to do to-day; the messenger to-day seeks the house of the lost and the unworthy. So that the charges He gave to these men, are not the charges He gives to us.

Yet again, notice the message these men were to deliver; that "The Kingdom of Heaven is at hand;" that the Kingdom was close because the King was there; that the King, long looked for, hoped for, waited for, was amongst them; that if they did but turn to Him they would find the Messiah. It was a peculiar message. Not a word about forgiveness of sin, not a word concerning the filling of the Holy Spirit, not a word concerning the things which are our special message and glory. Their message was Messianic, but not fully interpreted, and the proofs they were to give evidenced the divinity of their mission, "Heal the sick, raise the dead, cleanse the lepers, cast out demons." It is because men have lost the sense of the proportion of our Master's orderly speech that, to-day, some imagine that all this is still our work. This is not our work. We have no commission to heal the sick miraculously. If we have a commission to heal the sick miraculously we have also a commission to raise the dead, for the two things are closely connected. Every man who claims that he has a commission to heal the sick, must, in order to convince of his authority, be able to raise the dead also. We are not now discussing the question of divine healing. All healing is divine; the devil never heals. It is possible for God to heal us without medicine, without aid, but we have no warrant for claiming healing at the caprice of our will, but only as we use the means that God has given to us. This commission to heal the sick, and raise the dead, and cleanse the lepers, and cast out demons, was a commission to those early disciples, their credentials of power, because they were preaching the Kingdom of Jesus Christ. The whole was withdrawn when the Spirit came, and made the Church the spiritual messenger of the Spiritual Kingdom, which finally is to unfold and manifest and realise the material also.

Then notice the methods they were to adopt. They were to make no physical provision for themselves. They were to be dependent upon those to whom they came. They were to take no gold nor silver nor brass. That command was definitely set aside by our Lord in the words chronicled by Luke; "When I sent you forth without purse, and wallet, and shoes, lacked ye anything? And they said, Nothing. And He said unto them, But now, he that hath a purse, let him take it, and likewise a wallet: and he that hath none, let him sell his cloak, and buy a sword." The necessity for provision presently became part of the work of these men. In this first commission He was speaking of a local and limited ministry which they were immediately to exercise.

Then the result of their coming was to be that they were to pronounce peace, a message of joy and gladness. But if the house refused, in the dust they cast behind them their curse remained upon that house. All that has changed now.

Has He changed His method because this earlier method failed? No; this is a mistake we all often make. He fulfilled His first intentions by these early methods and then changed them.

In the next section also we find words which were of immediate application. First He said, " Behold I send you forth as sheep in the midst of wolves." There have been other eras of persecution in the Church, but never from the day in which Jerusalem fell has there been a systematic persecution of Christians by Jews. That was a manifestation peculiar to the period immediately following His crucifixion. Another was that of the destruction of family peace. As the evangel came into the families of the Jews, and certain therein believed, strife followed in peculiar form and ferocity, such as had never been known. Then was to come the Spirit's witness under circumstances of trial, the peculiar witness of defence.

Finally they were to haste through the cities of Israel because the coming of the Son of Man was imminent, and unless they hasted they would not have passed through the cities of Israel before He came. Here again is a fact to be carefully noted. Never since the destruction of Jerusalem has Israel had a city anywhere on earth. She has gathered into the cities of the Gentiles and the people have made their power felt, but to-day Israel has no city to call its own. Jerusalem itself, "the city of the great King," whose very dust is precious to the Jew, is the one spot in all the world he would fain possess. It is the one city in all the world that those who possess wish they did not. And yet those who hate it cannot lose it, and those who want it cannot gain it. Here is a problem for the politicians, in the face of which we must take God into account. There are more Jews gathered together in New York than ever were gathered together in Jewish cities in later times, but it is not their city; they are aliens among the nations.

What is meant here by the coming of the Son of Man? Some hold that the Second Advent of Jesus is past; that He actually came in Person at the time of the fall of Jerusalem; and was seen of some few faithful souls. There may be an element of truth in that view, but that does not exhaust the teaching of the New Testament concerning the Second Advent. He had often come before; He had talked with Abraham,

He had spoken to men in the past as the Angel of Jehovah, and who shall say that in His Personal Form He did not guide the Roman legions as they took Jerusalem? It is quite certain there can be no explanation of the coming of the Son of Man in this case except in the sense of judgment. His coming at the fall of Jerusalem, ended the cities of Israel, and this accounted for His urgency and haste in driving His apostles out to tell the story of the King and the Kingdom.

But if these two sections are very largely applicable to the days we have referred to, there are permanent principles in each. In the first section none of the things we have mentioned apply to us. But in the words, " Freely ye received, freely give;" we touch a deep permanent truth which never changes. It was His word to those early disciples who went with the first proclamation of His Messiahship; it was His word to those whom He sent out as sheep among wolves; it is His word to us, " Freely ye received, freely give."

It is the law of Christian service as to its disposition, rather than in its amount. The word " freely " does not mean abundantly. Jesus does not say, " Abundantly ye have received, abundantly give." The word signifies rather, " Gratuitously ye have received, gratuitously give." Our giving in service is to be on the pattern of God's giving to us. We cannot buy anything from God; we are not to expect men to buy anything from us in this sacred service. God is good to us not for gain to Himself, but out of His grace, out of His passion for giving. Now as Jesus said to His workers in that earliest period, so He says to us, " Freely ye received, freely give." Our service is not to be for success or profit, but for the sake of those we serve, expecting nothing in return. This is the law of Christian service. Freely we are to pour out of our best in sacrifice, in order to be in true co-operation with Him.

Then again in the second period, we find a word of immediate application, and of abiding principle; " Be ye therefore wise as serpents, and harmless as doves." " Wise " means sagacious, not sly; it is the quality of the serpent in its wariness for self-defence. " Harmless " means simple, or as Luther almost perfectly translated it, without fault, without flaw, simple and undeviating in life. That is a strange combination, but it is a perfect revelation. It is impossible to be wise as serpents save as we are simple as doves, for the serpent's wisdom ends when it becomes vicious. It is impossible to be harmless as a dove without the wisdom of a serpent, for the dove's simplicity ends when it becomes careless.

But we can have the perfect combination, because He says, " I send you;" and if He send us, He will give us His wisdom, His harmlessness. Let us see to it that we are about His business, ready to do His will, then we can lean back upon all that He is, and appropriate it for our work.

The teaching here for us in these first movements may be simply stated.

Our authority is His; and proceeds out of His compassion for the unfit.

Our service must be like His; gratuitous, free.

Our attitudes are to be worthy of Him; we must be wise with His wisdom, simple with His simplicity.

MATTHEW X. 24-42

IN this section we have words which have direct application to ourselves. Just as in the great intercessory prayer of Jesus, recorded in the seventeenth chapter of John, He included us with those who were then round about Him, so here He included all those who should share in His toil, until the consummation of the age at His second advent.

This, then, is a section of supreme interest to us, and of supreme helpfulness. The area of application widens. This is indicated by the instruction given to those to whom the Lord began to speak when He said, " A disciple is not above his teacher, nor a servant above his lord." Keep these two words in mind—disciple, servant. Then go to the end, and in verse forty-one, where, when dealing with that great subject of identification, He said, "He that receiveth a prophet in the name of a prophet shall receive a prophet's reward; and he that receiveth a righteous man in the name of a righteous man shall receive a righteous man's reward." These are words descriptive of those to whom He speaks in this final section—not apostles exclusively, but disciples also. There cannot be an apostle who is not a disciple, but there may be a disciple who is not an apostle. The apostle is the first messenger of the King. That is the distinct office of the apostle. The apostle always breaks up new ground, flashes light into darkness that has never before received it; and we thank God for those who have been successful in that long succession of apostolic toil.

But the apostles are not the only workers in the orderliness of Christ's Church; they do not exhaust the line of service. "He gave some to be apostles; and some, prophets; and some, evangelists; and some, pastors and teachers." Even these do not exhaust the line of service, for, following the word of that Ephesian declaration we read, He gave these "for the perfecting of the saints, unto the work of ministering." That is to say, the whole Church is in the ministry, and those gifted within the Church are gifted in order that they may perfect the Church for the doing of this work. So not the apostle only, not the prophet only, not the evangelist only, not the pastor and teacher only, is in the ministry, but every disciple, the every servant of Jesus. When any man receives the gift of the apostle, that constitutes him the first messenger of the King; or of the prophet, that sends him like a flame of fire through the land; or of the evangelist, that bids him go forth in wooing tenderness to bring men to Christ; or of the pastor and teacher, that enables him to feed the flock of God, and take the oversight of all sacred and holy work; all are in order to find and equip disciples and servants for ministry

Every disciple is called into fellowship with Jesus in His work; and standing here among these first twelve, who were to be apostles, He spoke to them, and through them, to the whole company of His disciples; and in this wonderful section He teaches us supreme and fundamental lessons about our relationship with Him in service. The work to be done is not described in detail here, but it is inferentially seen. It is that of confessing Christ before men. That is the Church's work. It is all-inclusive. When we have said that, we have said everything we can say about the apostle, the evangelist, the prophet, the pastor and teacher, and the disciple and servant. Whatever our gift may be within the Church, or as a member of the Church, our work is to confess Christ before men. Confession does not mean merely saying, He is mine, and I am His. That is a blessed thing to say, and, if only all disciples would say that to men, multitudes would be born into the Kingdom of God. But by confession we are to reveal Him, to flash His glory, to make Him known. The Church of Jesus Christ is not constituted in order that it may discuss philosophies or indulge in speculations. It is created to confess Christ, and it never ought to rest for one moment, until the last weary, sin-bound soul, in the furthest region of the world, has heard His evangel, has beheld His glory.

The first movement of this chapter had to do with men who were going to be sent away from Jesus, though, of course, identified with Him in sympathy. In the second movement, when they were to go as sheep in the midst of wolves, and yet bound to Him by the Holy Spirit, they were to have no fear when they stood upon their defence. This last movement becomes more gracious and tender, more searching and fiery; and the whole theme is that of the identification of the worker with Jesus, and all that it means to him as he goes forth.

First, our Lord shows what the result of identification with Himself will be in the personal position of the workers (verses 24-28); secondly, what the result of identification with Himself will

107

be, in the matter of the workers' relationship to God (verses 29-33); finally, what the result of the workers' identification with Himself will be in the matter of the workers' relationship to men who are outside, and to whom they are sent (verses 34-42).

Let us take the first of these—the worker in identification with Christ. The Lord first stated the fact of identification. He declared the issue of identification. Next He spoke a word of assurance based upon the fact of identification. Further He uttered the commission which is the outcome of identification. Finally He revealed the one and only fear that need result from identification.

The fact of identification is revealed in the statement, "A disciple is not above his teacher, nor a servant above his lord. It is enough for the disciple that he be (or become) as his teacher, and the servant as his lord." One need hardly say anything here by way of exposition. This statement of the fact that the worker is identified with the Lord, is a wonderful statement, thrilling with grace. We readily bow to the first position, "The disciple is not above his teacher, nor a servant above his master." The word servant here is bond-servant, slave, and means not merely a servant as one who renders service, but a servant as one who is the property of his master, and therefore renders service. That is the word that runs through the New Testament as descriptive of service. Thus our Lord introduces us to the fact of our relationship to Him. We are His disciples, learning. We are His bond-slaves, bound to obey Him. We are therefore not above Him.

If the statement had ended there, we should reverently have bowed the head and worshipped. But He said another thing, a very wonderful thing, a thing no other master ever said, and no other lord ever said, "It is enough for the disciple that he become as his teacher, and the servant as his lord." By this word the King teaches us that, in all our service for Him, He reckons us as identified with Himself, as going in His place, for at the conclusion He said, "He that receiveth you receiveth Me,

and he that receiveth Me receiveth Him that sent Me." We are His disciples, He is our Teacher, and He is above us; but His teaching is to make us become as He is, and all He is, is ours in this matter of service. Thus He brings us into the place of perfect identification with Himself. The bond-servant, bound to obey, because the property of the King, is yet as he goes forth, identified with his Lord, with his Lord's royalty, his Lord's dignity, his Lord's authority, delegated by the King to speak for the King, in the name and nature and the power of the King.

Next we are taught the issue of that identification; "If they have called the master of the house Beelzebub, how much more them of his household!" That is to say, the Master has been misunderstood, the Master has been misinterpreted, and we must not expect any other experience. If the Master has not been able to make clear to certain minds the truths He has been teaching, we must remember that we have to face the same difficulty. No doubt the Lord knew that there lurked in the mind of these twelve men the thoughts that are so often with us— the thought of their inability, the thought of the tremendous work He was sending them forth to do, and they trembled. They were afraid of the forces that were moving against them, and He said in effect; Yes, you will have difficulties, you will be misunderstood, you will be misrepresented, but ever remember this is the necessary issue of identification.

In view of that He uttered the word of assurance, "Fear them not therefore: for there is nothing covered, that shall not be revealed; and hid, that shall not be known." Here our Lord did not mean that the evil secrets of the hearts of evil men were going to be uncovered. That is also true, but here there is another application. It is as though He had said; Do not be afraid of difficulties which are in front of you; men will misunderstand and misinterpret you as they have misunderstood and misinterpreted Me; but do not be afraid; the covered thing you want to make known must be made known sooner or later; the thing that is hidden, that you strive to make real, must be revealed sooner or later. He said to these men and to us in effect; You are going out against terrible odds; I have been called Beelzebub; Men have attributed My works to demons, and My words to satanic agency; You are not going to be understood any better than I have been; but do not be afraid, the truth must triumph; the covered thing that you cannot make men see, must be seen at last; the hidden thing you desire to bring out into the light, must come out into the light at last. It was a great word of assurance.

Now mark the commission—and it is this commission, flinging its light back upon the former consideration, that explains the previous word—"What I tell you in the darkness"—that is the covered thing—"speak ye in the light: and what ye hear in the ear"—whispered—that is the hidden thing—"proclaim upon the house-tops." In other words, the King said; You are to be acquainted with the covered things, and the hidden things, the things not seen by the rulers of this world, the things not discovered by human philosophers, of this or any other age; the things that the wise and prudent never knew; and your work is a twofold work; you are first to listen while I whisper them to you, and then to mount the house-top and proclaim them to men. That is the real order of Christian service. No man has anything to say worth saying to a congregation who has not been alone and waited while the Lord whispered secrets to him. This is our commission, "What I tell you in the darkness, speak ye in the light." Note the change here. He had constantly been telling them not to tell. He told them to tell the vision to no man until the Son of Man should be glorified. They were secret things which He told them in those days of preparation. Such was the attitude of the Lord during the days of His flesh; but the day was coming when they were to tell the secret, to flash the light. That is our work to-day.

Then came the final word here, as to their personal relationship. You have only one thing to fear, said the Lord.

You need not fear these men who do not understand when a hidden thing is revealed, and who, when the light flashes, will become angry. Ignorance will merge into hostility when light rebukes the sin which resulted from ignorance.

And did our King ever say anything more thrilling with dignity than this, "Be not afraid of them which kill the body, but are not able to kill the soul"? There is no utterance more vibrant with victory. If a man kills the body that is the utmost he can do; and the Lord said, that by comparison, that is a small thing. Presently this King went to the Cross without faltering, without flinching, with regal bearing, so that the men who condemned Him look for all time mean and contemptible in His presence. He went to the Cross in the power of that philosophy. Beyond the limits of human power stretch the infinite realities. He said, Do not be afraid, there is a spiritual entity which they cannot touch.

But there is One to fear. By some strange perversion there are those who say that Jesus here meant the devil. Satan has no power to fling soul and body into Gehenna, and we are never told from Genesis to Revelation to fear the devil. We are always told to fear God. Men may destroy the body, but there is One Who can take hold of the body and the spirit, and condemn them to the place of rubbish and ruin. Fear Him!

Then immediately, and by a change as startling as it is sudden, Jesus proceeded to discuss the relation of the worker to God, the outcome of identification with Himself. There is an interesting merging here of the two sections. The last closed by charging the disciples that in service only one fear is necessary or warranted, and that is the fear of God. Now carefully note the sequence. He first tells them the truth about the God Whom they are warned to fear, by giving two very simple illustrations. First, He is always with a sparrow when it dies; secondly, He numbers the hairs of our heads. Always with the sparrow. Yes, do not spoil this quotation by saying that Jesus meant that not one of them shall fall to the ground without the Father's knowledge. He did not say that. A Scotch commentator, usually to be absolutely trusted, in his commentary puts it thus, "Not one of them shall fall on the ground without your Father"—and then he puts in brackets, "That is without His permission," and by that parenthesis spoils his exposition. The King said that God is with the dying sparrow!

And the hairs of your head are numbered. That is a passage out of which some would-be clever men have found great amusement. They have said, Do you suppose that God counts the number of hairs in a man's head? Jesus never said so. He said God *numbers* them. Counting is a human process. Numbering is more than counting. It is attaching a value to every one, almost labelling each; a far more wonderful thing than counting. Jesus was showing that God is in the infinitely little as well as in the infinitely great, and when the tired man at his work passes his hand across his brow to brush away the perspiration and just one hair goes with it, God knows! Do not be afraid, fear God, He is very tender, very gracious, very loving. Our Lord here charges us to fear, in order that we may be fearless; He charges upon us the fearlessness that grows out of fear. Dread Him, and Him alone, Who is able to cast the soul and body into Gehenna. But does He cast soul and body into Gehenna? It depends. The sparrow that fulfils the purpose of its being, He gives a nest in which to die, and the nest is His own soft and infinite Presence. Do not be afraid slavishly, only fear Him because He is right.

"Fear Him, ye saints, and ye will then
Have nothing else to fear."

So God is here revealed in all His tenderness, and our relationship to Him is made plain.

Then notice what follows in close connection. "Every one therefore who shall confess Me before men, him will I confess before My Father Who is in heaven." There is a little preposition in the Greek New Testament which is omitted in translation, but our revisers have put it in the margin. What Jesus said was this, "Every one therefore who shall confess *in* Me before men, *in* Him will I also confess before My Father." But there is no such preposition in the other part of the statement—"But whosoever shall deny Me" —not in Me—"before men, him will I also deny,"—not in him—"before My Father Who is in heaven." Therein is revealed the difference between identification and separation. It is our work to confess *in* Christ, in the sphere of His life, to make Him the whole fact. "Who shall confess in Me before men, in him," says Jesus, "I will confess before My Father." That man stands before My Father in Me and I in him. Identification in confession on earth is identification in confession in heaven. Whenever we go forth and confess the truth in Christ, we are standing in Him, hidden and secure. While we are doing that, He is standing in us before the Throne confessing in us there, so that while men see Him in us, God sees us in Him.

Identification with Christ is a great responsibility as well as a great privilege. If we deny Him, then we are separate from Him, and He, in separation, denies us before His Father Who is in heaven.

There remain the last few words in which the relation of those in identification with Christ to the men of the world is stated. There are some who will refuse us; our coming will create variance, and foes, and a sword; but we are not to forget that in the presence of differences created by that variance and that sword and those foes, we must be worthy of Him. We must love Him more than husband, wife, father, mother, child. We must take up our cross and follow Him.

And then, by a sudden transition, the King speaks as though standing out in the far distance welcoming the workers. Mark the words, "He that findeth his life shall lose it; and he that loseth his life for My sake shall find it." Oh, to meet Him and to hear Him say, You lost your life for Me, find it!

MATTHEW XI. 1-19

HAVING charged and sent forth His disciples on their first work, the King went forward with His own work of teaching and preaching in enforcement of His claims.

His path was now beset with new difficulties, and the attitude of His enemies was marked by increasing opposition. In this chapter some of these things are vividly revealed. It is one of general survey in which different aspects of the obstacles confronting His work are brought before us in the revelation of the different attitudes of mind with which He had to deal, as He went forth upon His work. They are all typical. The same attitudes still confront His disciples as they go forward to service.

Let us first glance at this section in rough outline. In verses two to fifteen we have the story of John, in which the perplexity of the loyal-hearted is evident.

Then, at verse sixteen there begins the second section of the chapter, which is a very brief one, occupying four verses only. In this section we see the unreasonableness of His age.

In the third section, beginning at verse twenty and ending at verse twenty-four, we are brought face to face with the fact of the impenitence of the cities which He had visited. He names Chorazin, Bethsaida, and Capernaum.

At verse twenty-five begins the final passage in which we meet with quite another class of persons, which the King described as babes.

Four classes are thus revealed, and so four aspects of the opposition and difficulty which the King encountered. In each of these we see the perfection of His method. The loyal-hearted, who was perplexed, He corrected and vindicated. The unreasonable He committed to the judgment of time. The impenitent He cursed. The babes He called to Himself for rest.

First let us consider this story of John. A great many have attempted to defend John from what they seem to think a lapse in faith and confidence in the King Whose herald he was. In attempting to defend John from this supposed lapse of faith, it has been suggested that he sent his disciples because his disciples were wavering, and he knew that if they came into contact with Jesus, and had His answer, they would be re-assured. While there may be an element of truth in the suggestion, when John sent the question, there can be little doubt that he was strangely perplexed; it was a question not of disloyalty but of perplexity. Some have attempted to account for the question by saying that John, after the thrilling excitement of preaching to thousands, and being now in prison, was like Elijah under the juniper tree, disheartened. That however is hardly likely. John was too accustomed to loneliness to be disloyal because within prison walls. His hard and rugged life in the wilderness had probably made him quite independent of the soft raiment and luxury of kings' houses; and one cannot believe there was a tremor in his courage. His question was rather an evidence of the continuity of his courage. The thing that surprised him was that Jesus was not doing exactly what he thought He was going to do. He neither doubted nor faltered in his convictions about right, but he doubted and faltered as to the method of the Master. Let us therefore look at John and Jesus, and then at Jesus and John; that is to say, let us take first the question of John and the answer of Christ; and, secondly, Christ's vindication of John, after John's disciples had gone back with their answer.

In order to understand the question which John sent by his disciples, we must place the works of Jesus into contrast with what John had said of Him before He began His public ministry. John had been an almost fierce ascetic, thundering against the sin of his age. He had shaken off the dust of his feet against the cities, and had gone into the wilderness; and by that wonderful attraction of a man with a living message, he had drawn multitudes after him. There on the banks of the Jordan this rough, rugged, magnificent man, the final prophet of the Hebrew economy, had thundered against the sins of his time, had singled out from the crowds about him, the ring-leaders who were seducing the people from loyalty to God, and had called them a generation of vipers. Having denounced sin, he had spoken of the coming King in a wonderful description: " Whose fan is in His hand, and He will thoroughly cleanse His threshing-floor; and He will gather His wheat into the garner, but the chaff He will burn up with unquenchable fire." This was magnificent and majestic language, describing the King as a great and mighty reformer, breaking down abuse, sweeping out oppression, gathering precious things, and blasting evil things as with thunder-bolts. John in prison inquired about the King; and the prophetic fire was still burning within him, the passion for righteousness was still like a blaze in his heart. They told him that Jesus had gathered a handful of men, had gone up into the mountains, and had been talking to them; that He had healed a leper; that He seemed to be doing gentle, sweet, loving things. So far there had been no word of judgment. So far no woe had fallen from His lips. His was a mission of mercy, not of judgment; and John in prison was strangely perplexed. Abuses were everywhere, lightning was needed to blast them; and He was healing men. Men had turned their back upon the Divine government; they should have been dealt with in judgment; and He was preaching good news. John thought He would have smitten the oppressor to death; and He was singing the song of the Gospel. Out of the perplexity of his heart he sent his disciples hurriedly to Him, with the blunt and honest question, " Art Thou He that cometh, or look we for another ? "

Now carefully observe the Master's method with such perplexity of the loyal. Jesus said to his disciples, " Go and tell John the things which ye hear and see; the blind receive their sight, and the lame walk, the lepers are cleansed, and the deaf hear, the dead are raised up, and the poor have good tidings preached to them." If we are

surprised at the question of John we are more surprised at the answer of Jesus. But we miss the whole point if we do not notice that He linked the story of His works with a great prophetic word which John, who was of the very spirit of the prophets, would understand. When the answer came back in the words of Jesus to John, he must have found in it a new interpretation of the mission of the King. The last thing Jesus said was, " The poor have good tidings preached to them." This was a quotation from the great prophecy of Isaiah, and from that portion of it which He had already read in the Synagogue as He entered upon this very work that was causing John perplexity (Isaiah lxi. 1, 2). When Jesus read that in the Synagogue at His induction, He did not read the whole statement, but stopped before the last clause, " the day of vengeance of our God," ending with the words, " to proclaim the acceptable year of the Lord."

He it is Who proclaims the acceptable year of our Lord. He it is Who will proclaim the day of vengeance of our God. He has never proclaimed it yet. In the Bible there is only a comma between the two, and that comma indicates a measurement already of over nineteen hundred years. But the proclamation will be completed: " This Jesus, Who was received up from you into heaven, shall so come in like manner as ye beheld Him going into heaven." " He shall appear the second time apart from sin, to them that wait for Him, unto salvation." He Who came to usher in the day of the acceptable year of our Lord, must come to usher in the day of vengeance of our God. When John's disciples came back and told him what Jesus did, that He was making the blind to see, the lame to walk, raising the dead, and giving them life, he knew that He was fulfilling the ancient prophecy. He would turn back to it, and would see that the first part of the Messianic mission was the preaching of the acceptable year of our Lord; he would come to understand that he had not been wrong as the herald of the King, to speak of thunder and of judgment; but that he must understand the larger value of the

Messianic work, and know that, before the final judgment falls, there is a mission of tenderness and grace, and healing and wooing and blessing. In effect Jesus said, Go back and tell John to look again at the things that puzzle him, to look at them in the light of his own prophetic mission, in the light of the declared purpose of God concerning Me, of all that has been written concerning Me; tell him to look more carefully, and there will be light instead of darkness.

Are you troubled about Jesus? Then look more carefully and comprehensively at the very things that have troubled you, and you will find the mist merge to light, and a larger understanding will end in the solution of all your problems.

The King added another word, very tenderly, not rebuking him, but warning him, " And blessed is he, whosoever shall find no occasion of stumbling in Me." If you cannot perfectly understand My method, trust Me. If you are not able for the moment to see how I am going to accomplish that upon which your heart is set as a passion, do not be offended, do not stumble, do not halt, trust Me perfectly. That is always the word of the King to His followers.

Then Jesus turned to the crowd who had heard John's question, and who might have been inclined to say, John has evidently failed, he is afraid, he is trembling; and He said to them in effect, Let Me tell you the truth about John. What did you go out into the wilderness to see? A reed shaken by the wind? Do you imagine he is weak and trembling? And the question carried its own answer in the very tone and emphasis in which the Master asked it. No wind shook him. He dared guilty Herod, and told him the truth.

" But what went ye out to see? A man clothed in soft raiment?"—a man, weak, enervated, spoiled by luxury. And then with infinite and fine scorn, " Behold they that wear soft raiment are in kings' *houses*"—not in kings' *prisons*—that is the emphasis John might have had soft raiment if he would excuse the king's sin. Make no

mistake about him because he has sent Me this question. This was the King's defence of a loyal soul, and it is very beautiful.

" But wherefore went ye out? To see a prophet?" He had brought them back from wrong impressions to the earlier and the truer thought of John. " Yea, I say unto you, and much more than a prophet;" he was the herald of the King, commissioned, inspired, sent before His face. " This is he, of whom it is written,

Behold I send my messenger before thy face,
Who shall prepare thy way before thee."

He had prepared the way for Jesus, having fulfilled the prophetic word of Isaiah, " Prepare ye in the wilderness the way of Jehovah, make level in the desert a highway for our God." The throwing up of a highway is a rough, laborious process. Kings will pass along the highway presently, but there must be a great deal of work to prepare it—blasting with dynamite. That was the work of John; no reed, no soft man, no mere prophet was he, but the last of the prophets, the herald himself, flinging up the highway and preparing for the coming of the King.

And then the Master spoke perhaps the most wonderful word of all; " Verily I say unto you, Among them that are born of women there hath not arisen a greater than John the Baptist." The simplest exposition is that of changing the phrasing. Of natural men, never has there been a greater than John. It was Christ's tribute to his moral fibre, to his mental breadth, to his magnificent natural endowments. Born in the priestly line, he turned his back upon priestism to become the rough prophet of the wilderness; he was a statesman seeing national life and understanding the national sore; and he had rent the garments that hid the sore, and laid it bare in all its hideousness to the gaze of his age.

Then the King accounted for the fact that he was perplexed: " Yet he that is but little in the Kingdom of heaven is greater than he." This again is a passage which has been very much discussed. The only way to understand it is to take it in close connection with all the rest of the defence of Jesus. Our Lord meant to say, You have seen this man who naturally is greatest among men, asking a question in perplexity. Yes, there are things he cannot know, there are methods that he cannot understand, and presently the least soul brought into the Kingdom will have greater light than this man, with all his natural endowments, has had in the past. Presently the little child who comes into My Kingdom by the mystery of My mercy, might, and passion, will have more light than John, until he also comes to understand the sweetness and mercy and majesty by coming into this Kingdom of power. John was in the light that preceded the Kingdom, and the weakest inside knows more than John.

Upon this vindication of John the King based an appeal to the people. He said of the prophets, "for all the prophets and the law prophesied until John." Theirs was not the message of experience and realisation; and one five minutes of experience is worth long years of anticipation; one single half-hour in the Kingdom, by the mystery of the death of the King, has more of light, than gathered in all the centuries before His work was done. "The prophets and the law prophesied until John."

Now said Jesus, "The Kingdom of heaven suffereth violence, and men of violence take it by force;" because men cannot understand the method, they must enter in by the violence that tramples under foot all pride, and is content to trust the King.

Then followed the last word of Jesus to the people about John; "And if ye are willing to receive it, this is Elijah that is to come;" this is the reformer; follow him, obey him, and he will lead you by his thunder past Sinai until you find yourself in the presence of the dawning light and the new glory of the rule of the Kingdom of God.

And so we come to that brief paragraph in which the King complained of the unreasonableness of the age. Having answered John's questions, and vindicated him, He put John into contrast with his age—John, the rough, the violent, the magnificent, the strenuous. Of the age He said, "It is like unto children who sit in the market-places," and they "call unto their fellows and say, We piped unto you, and ye did not dance; we wailed, and ye did not mourn." Anyone who has children understands the figure perfectly. There come moments when nothing is right, and the only unanimity is that of complaint, of dissatisfaction. What is the meaning of it among children? First, an evil nature which they have inherited. Do not be angry with your bairns when they are discontented—they derive their nature from you. Then there is weariness which they have contracted. And again a little, strong, tender, shepherd-like discipline is lacking. All that was the matter with the age. Mark His application of His illustration. "We piped unto you, and ye did not dance." John came, and you all piped to John, you went out after him, you made him popular, you crowded to him, but he did not dance to you, he thundered at you. "We wailed, and ye did not mourn." The Son of Man is come, and you wail in His presence, but He has not lamented; He has been your friend, comforting, cheering, eating and drinking with you; and you say He is gluttonous. Oh, the unreasonableness of the age!

And what was the King's answer? "Wisdom is justified by her works." Some ancient manuscripts have the word "works" and others "children," so decision must be based on the context, and it would appear best to adopt the revised word "works," for this harmonises with the words of Jesus throughout this section. In every case He appealed to His works. Of these John in prison was to be told; and these were the evidences of His right, refusing to obey which, the cities were condemned. The works of John and Jesus were wise. They were both the methods of God. To the restless and unreasonable age the King declared that wisdom would yet be vindicated in John's ascetic strength, and in His own comradeship of tenderness.

The supreme value of this study is its revelation of the King as a worker.

The picture of His dealing with John shows us that honesty is always valued and patiently answered. Let us be true with the Lord; do not let us affect a confidence which our heart does not feel. Only, if the doubt be there, instead of turning our back upon Him and abandoning His cause, instead of turning to the philosophies of men for explanation of the method of God, let us go straight to Him and tell Him. Oh the comfort of being able to go into the Master's presence and tell Him that He is doing something that we cannot understand. He loves honesty, He would rather the Thomas who blurts out his unbelief, than the Judas who kisses Him. Thank God for John, who was honest, and more, thank God for Jesus, Who received the honest question and answered it so patiently and so perfectly. His answer to all such doubt, is a call to a larger vision of the facts creating the doubt.

MATTHEW XI. 20-24

WE now turn to the subject of the impenitence of the cities. There is something startling in the words with which this paragraph commences—"Then began He to upbraid." This spirit of upbraiding seems to be so foreign to Him, so unlike Him; and yet such an idea of Him reveals a very superficial understanding both of the cause and the meaning of His upbraiding. If we think it is foreign to His nature to upbraid, and to pronounce woe, because we think of Him as loving and gentle, we misunderstand love. Jesus is quite capable of being stern, severe. There is such a thing as the wrath of the Lamb, even though that description seems to contradict itself. If we are astonished, as we hear Him, in the midst of His teaching, upbraiding cities, it is because we do not understand love perfectly. Love is not always gentle, sometimes it is rough. Love is not always uttering sweet, smooth things. By the very necessity of its own nature there are moments when its speech is rugged, scorching, devastating. We have neither understood the Master, nor His essential love, if we really are surprised in the presence of such a section as this.

Three cities are here named by the Lord Himself—Chorazin, Bethsaida and Capernaum. We have no account of any visit to Chorazin, but it is perfectly evident that our Lord went through all these cities, and incidentally this whole passage shows us how much more Jesus did than we know. Chorazin was one of the cities in which most of His mighty works were done, and yet we have no account of His work there.

Then we pass to Bethsaida, and we find that the records refer to frequent visits by our Lord. We need to remember in passing, that from the city of Bethsaida, Peter, Andrew, and Philip had all followed Him, had obeyed Him, had repented in answer to His call, and set their faces towards the coming of the Kingdom of Heaven.

When we come to Capernaum we are almost irresistibly driven back to one of our earlier studies in the Gospel (chapter iv. 12-16). We have already seen that in the prophecy quoted there, interpreted from the Jewish standpoint, when they spoke of "the land of Zebulun, and the land of Naphtali, toward the sea, beyond the Jordan, Galilee of the Gentiles," their terms were those of reproach, because that whole district, more than any other, had become influenced by Gentile thinking. But when the King began His work, this public ministry of the Kingdom, "He came and dwelt in Capernaum." That is always His method. If there is a district neglected, abandoned, forsaken, there He comes and dwells. So we know of Capernaum that it was the adopted home of Jesus for a long period, during His public ministry, the centre from which He went forth upon His way. That fourth chapter goes on to say, "From that time began Jesus to preach, and to say, Repent ye, for the Kingdom of Heaven is at hand." When John preached that, he did so in the tone and with the emphasis of severity.

When he was cast into prison Jesus commenced His more public, set, and orderly ministry, with exactly the same message, and He delivered it in Capernaum. He came and dwelt there, and Capernaum then first heard the word of the King spoken with His own grace and tenderness, and ineffable sweetness, "Repent, for the Kingdom of Heaven is at hand."

But now we see Jesus looking out upon the cities where most of His mighty works had been done, and we hear Him beginning to upbraid. What was the cause of His upbraiding? "Because they repented not." This does not merely mean that Jesus was angry because they did not obey Him. That was true in a sense, but the reason of the anger lies deeper. It was not selfish resentment at being rejected; that was never present in the upbraiding of Christ; there was something infinitely deeper. We must go back to the initial word of Jesus— "Repent"—that is, Change your mind, for whenever a man changes his conception, his thinking is changed, and his conduct. The real creed of a man is the inspiration lying behind his conduct, and when Jesus began His ministry, and said to men, Repent, change your minds, He was doing a simple and yet a searching thing. He was asking men to change their ancient conception of things, in order that their conduct might be changed, in order that finally their character might be changed. That is always the order. First, the conception; then the external conduct based upon it; and, finally, the character resulting therefrom.

Christ's word was not only Repent. He indicated the direction of the change necessary; for a man may change his mind, and the new set of convictions may be as false as the old— "Repent, for the Kingdom of Heaven is at hand." The mind must be changed in the direction of submission to the Kingdom of Heaven. The root-wrong in all civic life then, and to-day, is godlessness; the fact that God is left out of account in its arrangements. So it was in these cities of the past, Chorazin, Bethsaida, Capernaum and the rest. He came to the city and He said, Change your mind toward the Kingdom of Heaven, the Kingdom of Heaven is at hand; it is here, embodied in the Person of its King. I am here to show you the Kingdom, to lead you into the Kingdom, to be your King within the Kingdom. Change your minds towards it. He had healed their diseases, and in the enforcement of His claims, He had been calling these cities to change their minds towards God, and towards the Kingdom of God.

He had shown the real meaning of the Kingdom of God. As we have seen, every miracle of Jesus was a revelation of what the Kingdom of God really means when it is perfectly set up. None of the miracles of Jesus was a violation of law; they were all reversions to law. Here was a man diseased; He healed him. He was not violating the law of the universe by doing so. Nay, verily, He was restoring the law broken by the presence of disease. All the way through, His mighty powers, operating in the realm of the physical, were revelations of what the Divine Kingship meant, and what the Kingdom of God really is. He had been to Chorazin, and to Bethsaida, He had dwelt in Capernaum, and in these three cities He had said, "Repent, for the Kingdom of Heaven is at hand." In these three cities, by mighty works, He had shown the meaning of the Kingdom; but they did not repent; and because they did not repent He began to upbraid them.

Now the second question that we ask is, What was the note of His upbraiding? The words "upbraid" and "woe" in this paragraph are mutually expository. We can only understand the upbraiding, as we hear Him say "Woe"! We can only understand what He meant when He said "Woe" as we catch the tone of His upbraiding! The meaning of upbraiding very literally is that He reproached them. Reproach may be perfectly pure, and inspired by love. It may, of course, be impure, and inspired by hatred, but that was impossible with Jesus. We take the word, then, in its simplest meaning. He reproached the cities. "Woe unto thee, Chorazin!" is not the thunder of some one highly angered, not the denunciation of some plague that is about to fall on the city; it is rather the wailing declaration of what must inevitably result from the city's own deliberate choice of action. "There is a wail in the woe," said one of the old puritan commentators, and in that sentence he comes to finest exposition of the meaning of the "woe." Jesus meant to say, You have refused to repent, you have deliberately chosen for yourselves the woes that are to come upon you, you have deliberately refused the light, and chosen the darkness; by refusing the life you have chosen the death. He was not pronouncing a judgment which He would inflict capriciously; He was announcing the result which they had deliberately chosen, and from which there could be no escape.

How have these woes been carried out? Remember they were woes pronounced upon cities. There is absolutely no trace of Chorazin to be found to-day. Men have never been able perfectly to agree about the site of Bethsaida. While Dr. Thomson argues for the probability of the site in Naphtali, a great weight of opinion is against his decision, and so we may broadly say Chorazin and Bethsaida, cities of nineteen centuries ago, rich and flourishing, in the midst of which the King came with light, and life, and love, have absolutely vanished as cities, because they repented not. The woe has wrought itself out by the working out of the law from which there is no escape, this simple law—whatever a man or city chooses, that is the destiny of the man or the city. I should like to lay emphasis upon this principle, in case some one should merely be interested in the exposition, and find no message for himself. This is the supremacy of Jesus, the sovereignty of Jesus, and the full majesty of Jesus, that, when He confronts a man or a city, then in the light of His coming that man or that city must make its choice. If the city shall return and repent, it shall be exalted to very heaven. If it will not hear Him, it must be thrust down into darkness. It is not His hand that thrusts it out; it is the city's own hand which slays itself when it rejects God's Kingdom.

This is still more markedly emphasised in the words which He addressed particularly to Capernaum, in which town He had dwelt. Notice the change from the Authorised, a change giving a more accurate rendering. Jesus did not say Capernaum was exalted to heaven. He asked a question, "Shalt thou be exalted unto heaven?" And He answered, I tell you no. Thou shalt be thrust down into Hades, into death, into darkness, into obliteration. Remember again, this was a civic word, the word concerning a city.

Observe the connection of this doom with the word He had spoken at the first, "Repent ye, for the Kingdom of Heaven is at hand." Capernaum had refused to repent. Then said Jesus to Capernaum, If you will not repent, do you suppose you will ever gain the benefits of the heavenly order? Do you suppose you can set up heaven's order, when you have rejected heaven's King? If you refuse to hear the voice of the King, will you be exalted unto heaven, with heaven's order, where love is the impulse, and light is the illumination, and love the energy? Do you hope to climb into the realisation of a perfect civic life when you refuse the King? Nay, verily; thou shalt go down into Hades. Capernaum desired the heavenly order, as all cities desire the heavenly order; yet, while the great ideal was seen, refused to repent. And in the prophetic words of Jesus—more than prophecy if prophecy be merely foretelling, but great prophecy if prophecy be foretelling with forth-telling of God's will—Capernaum has passed down as a city into Hades, into darkness, and into death, and into cessation. Why? Because she refused to repent at the call of the King.

From this upbraiding of Jesus, what is the teaching of value for us? First, that the greater the light the greater the responsibility. That leads us to touch upon a part of this section to which we have not yet referred—Jesus' comparisons. Look at them briefly in order that we may make other comparisons presently. He said, "It shall be more tolerable for Tyre and Sidon

in the day of judgment, than for you."
More tolerable for Tyre and Sidon than
for Chorazin and Bethsaida. Tyre and
Sidon were cities then existing. Then
when He came to Capernaum, the most
highly blessed of all the cities, He said,
"But I say unto you that it shall be
more tolerable for the land of Sodom
in the day of judgment, than for thee."
Sodom was a city that had long ceased
to exist. It had been blotted out of
existence for specific reasons hinted at
in the Old Testament history, clearly
declared in later prophecy. He took
the cities of Tyre and Sidon, and put
them into comparison with Chorazin
and Bethsaida; and the land of Sodom
into comparison with Capernaum.

Thus He revealed the truth that responsibility is always created by light.
Tyre and Sidon had not been visited
as Chorazin and Bethsaida had been.
Tyre and Sidon had perchance heard
the rumour of His work, but He had
not come into the midst of them. They
were two living cities when He spoke.
We hear His word and bow in the
presence of it. He declares that it will
be more tolerable for the cities of our
own day to which He has not come,
than for the cities to which He has
come if those cities refuse to repent.

When He speaks of Capernaum, we
have a yet more startling contrast. We
have but to read the history of the Old
Testament which is veiled and guarded
with an extreme delicacy, to know how
fearful were the conditions of life in
Sodom, how awful was the corruption
that held that wealthy city fast in its
grip. At least the Old Testament history reveals this much to us, that there
were not ten righteous men to be found
in the whole city, and therefore it was
swept out. Could anything be worse
than Sodom? Yes, Capernaum. Now
the possibility is that Capernaum never
descended to the beastliness of Sodom.
The probability is that the sins of
Sodom, judged by all human canons,
were far more terrible than the sins of
Capernaum; but Jesus Christ said in
effect, If Sodom had received My light,
if Sodom had heard My message, if
Sodom had seen My works, it would
have continued until this day. That is
to say, in the sight of God, sin is never

measured as it is in the sight of men.
We measure sin and call it vulgar, or
debased, or pardonable, or excusable,
according to some false measurements
of our own. God measures sin by the
light a man has had, or a city has had.
The city to which Jesus has come with
His message, in which He has manifested His mighty works, if it refuse
Him, and His ideals, if it will not
crown Him, is guilty of a more terrible
sin than the sin of the city which has
sunk to the lowest level of beastliness,
if it have never heard His message,
and never seen His work. This is
Christ's own estimate.

Let us, then, proceed further with
our comparison. We have compared,
following our Lord's word, Tyre and
Sidon with Chorazin and Bethsaida,
and Sodom with Capernaum. Now let
us compare Chorazin, Bethsaida, and
Capernaum with the cities of to-day,
simply indicating a line for solemn consideration. Our cities know Jesus
Christ far better than Chorazin, Bethsaida, or Capernaum; because when
Jesus Christ was in Chorazin, Bethsaida, and Capernaum, according to His
own estimate, He was straitened, limited. His mighty powers operating
very largely in the sphere of the physical, because He had not yet unlocked
the gate, had not scattered the fire, had
not yet Himself bent His head to the
great passion Baptism.

When Jesus came to Chorazin, Bethsaida, Capernaum, He was a Man
among men, a Teacher among teachers.
He was infinitely more, for His words
at once lifted Him above all other
teachers in His own age; and the purity of His life, its glorious beauty,
perfect tenderness, elevated Him above
all men in character. Nevertheless, as
men heard Him they had nothing to
base their conclusions upon save His
imperial presence and the essential and
inherent truth of the things He uttered.
We have a great deal more. We have
His resurrection from among the dead,
attested by witnesses, proved by the
miracles of the centuries. We have in
our midst to-day works that are far
more wonderful than any miracle He
ever performed in the physical realm.
Do we, as Christians, quite believe it?

Before Jesus went away He said, "Greater works than these shall he do, because I go unto the Father." There is a sense in which He did not value the miracles as credentials, but put them in a secondary place. He said, "Believe Me—or else believe Me for the very works' sake." "The works" constituted a secondary line of argument. Now He has been demonstrated in the centuries in His own Person by the resurrection, as that resurrection has been demonstrated in the life and progress of the living Church; and that Church by His living presence, His spiritual presence, is more wonderful and powerful than His bodily presence was, and He is still working miracles more marvellous, more wonderful, than any He wrought then.

Need we labour this point? If our cities have but eyes to see, in every quarter of the globe miracles are being wrought by Jesus Christ more wonderful than any He wrought while He was here—miracles of so renewing men in the inner facts of their life, that in the power of that renewal, they renew the externality of their lives.

This is the supreme miracle. The supreme miracle is not that the body shall be healed, but that the spirit shall be healed. The supreme miracle is that a man low sunk in the social scale, a beast, a plague to the city, may be touched by the Spirit of Jesus and be re-made, and become one who blesses the city wherever he goes. These miracles are on every hand.

What has this to do with us? Everything! If we are prepared to receive the King on His own terms, if we are prepared to obey His "repent," in the individual life, and if we are prepared to set our faces toward Him for the establishment of God's Kingdom, individually, then socially, and in all civic matters; then our cities may be lifted into the realisation of the blessedness of the Kingdom of Heaven. But if we turn our back upon the proof Jesus gives, if we turn our back upon the ministry He exercises, if we will not crown the King by obeying Him, then nothing can save the city. Its sorrows will put out its joy, its sighing will make its songs to cease, its sin will submerge it as sin has submerged the cities of the past.

Our duty, therefore, as Christians, is to preach the Evangel, to carry the great Gospel not narrowly but broadly, yet always with insistence upon the primal necessity of the yielding of the individual will to Christ, in order that the social relationships of the city may be influenced from that standpoint of regenerate humanity.

May God grant we may so live and serve as to help to bring our city into line with His law, and into obedience to His gracious will.

MATTHEW XI. 25-30

THERE can be no doubt that these last verses of chapter eleven tell the story of what happened immediately in connection with the events recorded in the previous verses. The King had upbraided the cities; He had pronounced woes upon them; He had declared that the measure of light creates the measure of responsibility; and with great severity, in every tone of which there vibrated the pity of His heart, He had pronounced the doom of the impenitent cities.

And now what followed? He turned from upbraiding the multitudes, and spoke to God. Having done that, He spoke again to the multitudes in proclamation and invitation.

It is important that we recognize this order and sequence. Pausing in His upbraiding, He lifted His heart to God: "I thank Thee, O Father, Lord of heaven and earth, that Thou didst hide these things from the wise and understanding, and didst reveal them unto babes, yea, Father, for so it was well-pleasing in Thy sight." Having thus spoken to God, He made a proclamation concerning Himself: "All things have been delivered unto Me of My Father: and no one knoweth the Son, save the Father; neither doth any know the Father, save the Son, and he to whomsoever the Son willeth to reveal Him." And then immediately, without a break, He said, " Come unto Me, all ye that labour and are heavy laden, and I will rest you." This more literal translation, "I will rest you," is very beautiful. Not as though rest were something apart from Himself. It was the mother love of God that spoke, " Come unto Me . . . and I will rest you. Take My yoke upon you and learn of Me: for I am meek and lowly in heart: and ye shall find rest unto your souls. For My yoke is easy and My burden is light."

First, then, He offered praise to God. Secondly, He made the proclamation concerning Himself; and wonderful are its terms. Then, turning to the multitudes, He called them to Himself in the light of the proclamation He had made, promising to lead them into relationship with the Father Whom He had worshipped, that they might find their rest.

Taking first of all His attitude toward His Father, we notice that the King worshipped in the presence of difficulty, that He offered praise in the face of discouragement. One supreme value of this chapter is its revelation of the fact of His restfulness even in the face of obstacles. John, loyal soul, whom He was so careful to defend, was wondering, perplexed by His methods; His own generation was petulant, unreasonable, complaining; and the cities that had seen the working of His power were rejecting Him. All these things He clearly understood, and yet He took the position of the worshipper. There was yet one other class of persons with whom He came in contact, the simple-hearted, who perhaps did not think deeply enough to be perplexed about anything; they were merely babes. The King saw more clearly than we do, and He said, "I praise Thee, O Father." That fact in itself comes as a ministry of inspiration and of love. Are you discouraged? Have you felt as though the people you are trying to reach are hopeless, always perplexed, always criticising, always impenitent? Pause then and worship! Make your difficulty the occasion of your thanksgiving. But this we shall

never do save as we live very near to Him.

Now let us look at the reason of His praise. That reason He distinctly stated. God had hidden the things He had come to make clear from the wise and understanding, and had revealed them to the untutored, the immature. He praised God for this method.

The first thing to be noticed is that the King rested in the absolute supremacy and will of His Father. He thanked God that this was so because it was God's will. Perhaps some of us must rest there very often, being unable to understand the reason of the will.

We may press this matter a little further and ask the question: was the fact that this was God's way the only reason for the thanksgiving? No, the Son knew that it was the best way, that it was the only way; this way of hiding these things from the wise and understanding, and the revealing of them to babes. Our Gospel is a Gospel for those who are fools and blind. That is not to say that the Gospel is not wise, that it lacks intelligence.

Who are the people from whom the Gospel is hidden according to Jesus? He called all people, but there are those whom He described as "the wise and the understanding" who do not come. "The wise" are, very literally, people who are gifted with practical skill, natural acumen, and ability to understand. The "prudent," in the Authorised, or "understanding," as it is in the Revised, are those who are able to put things together. Jesus says, Father, Thou hast hidden these things from the people who are naturally wise and have the power to put things together. We have heard a man say, "Oh, believe me, I know what two and two make." That is the man! Not that he does not know what two and two make; not that it is wrong to put two and two together; but that the putting of two and two together brings the man to the conclusion that when he has put two and two together he knows everything. It is the man of natural acumen who is able to put things together and come to logical conclusions; who imagines that he can express the things of the Spirit in the formulæ of the mind; from whom these things are hidden. The condition for acquiring knowledge is always conscious ignorance. The moment a man says he does not know, then at least he has fulfilled the first condition for acquiring knowledge. Some years ago a remarkable article appeared in *The Engineer* discussing the question whether the man of technical knowledge, or the man without it, was most likely to serve his age by the way of invention. In the course of that article the writer said: "There is not a portion of the framing of a bicycle that is not, in the eyes of any one carefully educated in the strength of materials, utterly wrong. If any one of our readers will take the trouble to work out the stresses in a bicycle weighing twenty-eight pounds, and carrying at ten miles an hour, a man weighing twelve stone, he will see that from first to last the whole machine is so completely impossible that nothing of the kind exists outside the land of dreams. Let us suppose that a law was passed under which no one was permitted to use a bicycle that was not pronounced to be quite safe by the Board of Trade; and let the Surveyors of the Board deal with the cycle precisely on the same lines as they deal with marine boilers, and see then what the Board of Trade machines would be like. Is it too much to say that, twenty years ago, any and every thoroughly trained engineer would have pronounced the modern light roadster a mechanical impossibility? Such men would know too much to attempt to produce anything of the kind. . . .

"Knowledge is too often assumed to have reached finality, when it has done nothing of the kind, and the belief is fostered and inculcated by those who write books, and treatises, and teach in various ways.

"Lastly, we would point out that it is not the possession of knowledge that stops progress; the mischief is done by the assumption that the knowledge is final."

That is the philosophy of our paragraph. There were men of Jesus' day who said; We know this is so, and that is so, and therefore this must be so; therefore He is wrong! They were

wise men, they were understanding men, they put two and two together, and they called it four; and they said this is final, there is nothing beyond, we know all to be known. And Jesus said, "I thank Thee, O Father, . . . that Thou didst hide these things from the wise and understanding;" that Thou hast not revealed these things to these men.

To what sort of people, then, does He reveal these things? To babes. And here the Greek word traced to its root means "not speaking," and in this use indicates the immature, which means that they are not indisposed to receive. Or again, to leave the figure of the infant, let the Master speak as He spoke on another occasion, and we see how His philosophy is always the same. "Except ye be converted"— turned back—"and become as little children" — believing that there is something you do not know, believing that the knowledge in your possession is not final—unless you get there, you cannot enter the Kingdom of God. "I thank Thee, O Father, Lord of heaven and earth, that Thou didst hide these things from the wise and understanding"—the men of acumen who put things together and imagine all God's truth can be expressed in the sequence of their reasoning—"and didst reveal them unto babes,"—who do not know anything, but who are dreaming towards truth, in whom is the spirit of romance, the spirit that soars.

What a blessed thing it is that God has always revealed these things to the simple-hearted and the simple-minded! One may have lost the priestism of ecclesiasticism, but there is a new priestism abroad to-day which says that we cannot interpret this Book unless we know original languages in all their ramifications. It is not true. The man who can put two and two together as to Semitic languages, and as to Greek dialect, may never see the flame of glory that any little child can see who takes up the Book and studies it with the simple heart of the babe.

Having uttered these words of worship, the King made the claim for Himself. His words are so clear and comprehensive, we need do little more than read them. The statement falls into three parts. First, the King claimed His own investiture with some peculiar authority. "All things." What things? We must go back to the previous verse, "I thank Thee, O Father, Lord of heaven and earth, that Thou didst hide *these things* from the wise and understanding, and didst reveal them unto babes." Revealed them, the things of truth, the things He had come to reveal, the things at which the unreasonable generation scoffed, the things the impenitent cities would not accept, the things of truth and righteousness and love. God has given Me, said the King, all these things. "All things have been delivered unto Me of My Father."

You may say, But does not this break down your argument? Would you speak of Jesus as a babe, as immature in any sense? We are speaking of Jesus in the realm of His humanity, as One Who did not depend upon His own human wisdom. He spoke always and only out of the infinite wisdom of His Father. We speak of Jesus as He spoke of Himself before these words were finished; said He, "I am meek and lowly in heart;" I am not petulant and unreasonable, I am not disobedient to light as it falls upon My soul. I am amongst the babes, and therefore all things are delivered unto Me. He was the great Mystic, the One Who, in all simplicity, waited for light, and recognized in all its infinite reaches, its relation to God and eternity. Speaking out of the realm of His perfect humanity He said, He hath committed all things unto Me; I come to bring the words of revelation. This is what Paul meant concerning Him in the Colossian Epistle when he wrote, "For it was the good pleasure of the Father that in Him should all the fulness dwell." Jesus thus stood in the midst of the men of His age and said to them, The things that wise men did not understand, the things that understanding men could not formulate and finally state, are committed to Me. I know them, not by deduction and logical sequence, but because God has committed them to Me, seeing that I am meek and lowly in heart.

Having thus claimed investiture, He went on to say, "No one knoweth the Son, save the Father." Here He was accounting for the fact that men had not understood Him. He thus declared the mystery of His own personality; no one perfectly understands Him, except the Father. This is a perpetual truth, and it may be said to this hour that no one knows the Son save the Father.

Let us carefully observe what now immediately follows. "Neither doth any know the Father, save the Son, and he to whomsoever the Son willeth to reveal Him. Come unto Me all ye that labour and are heavy laden, and I will give you rest."

Consider, then, this twofold fact. Jesus declared that no one can know the Son perfectly, except the Father; but He affirmed that the Father can be known through the Son. We have a far more correct knowledge of God at this hour than we have of Jesus. The great mysteries and the great problems, and the great perplexities, are still concerning the Person of Jesus. Grace operates by revealing the things that never were known through the instrument of a Person; but the things revealed are so mighty that the instrument of their revelation must remain a mystery. "No one knoweth the Son, save the Father, neither doth any know the Father save the Son, and he to whomsoever the Son willeth to reveal Him."

We make a great mistake when we commence to quote this passage at verse twenty-eight. We have no right to begin at "Come unto Me, all ye that labour." If we do so, we miss the music; we may indulge in a great deal of sentiment around this text, but all its strength, that upon which the soul of man takes hold for strength, is missed if we omit verse twenty-seven and fail to recognize the connection. This is no mere lullaby; it was no mere expression of sentimental pity when Jesus said, "Come unto Me." Reverently changing the actual wording it is as though He had said: Come unto Me and I will reveal the Father unto you; trust Me, and find God; accept My law of life by accepting Me, and so find rest; for My yoke, the yoke I wear, is easy; and My burden, the burden I bear, is light. Come to Me, be identified with Me, let Me become the window through which the light flashes, the door through which you pass to God. The trouble with men is that they do not know the Father, and seeing that they do not know the Father, they are hot, and restless, and feverish, and in agony. To all such He said, Come unto Me, I know the Father; I will bring you to Him, and when you find the Father you will find your rest. "Come unto Me, all ye that labour."

Notice finally that this call was uttered, not merely to the babes, but to all the multitude. "Come unto Me, *all* ye that labour and are heavy laden." It was His call to John when John was in difficulty about His method—Come to Me, and I will rest your perplexed spirit. It was His call to the unreasonable and unsatisfied age, to come to Him and be satisfied, by faith, and wait for the dawning light for full explanation. It was His call to the cities, rejecting, and rejected—Come to Me, and I will come back to you with healing and with blessing. It was His call to the babes—Come to Me, be obedient, and gain the light that leads you into the places of God's own wisdom. It was His call to all. They did not all obey as John did in his perplexity. When his disciples went back and set the works of Jesus in relation to the ancient prophecies, surely there came to John a quiet sense of rest. He found God anew in the dungeon, because in honest perplexity he had sent directly to Jesus. Perhaps some of the discontented children of the age found rest because they ceased their criticism and became babes. The cities would not come, and Chorazin, Bethsaida and Capernaum are names only, their very sites being blotted out. And the babes? Thank God they have been coming ever since, and as they come, they find God and rest.

Mark the conditions. "Come," that is the first. "Take My yoke," that is the second. "Learn of Me," that is the third. We must get to Him, we must submit to Him, we must obey Him. By these things we find our rest, a twofold rest some commentators say, but probably they are two manifestations of the same rest—the rest of finding the Father; the rest of obeying the Father.

Oh, there is rest for the storm-tossed soul in finding God! The cries of the old Bible are the cries of to-day. "As the hart panteth after the water brooks, so panteth my soul after Thee, O God!" "Oh that I knew where I might find Him!" And not in tones that ring through centuries only, but in the still small voice sounding in our hearts to-day, we hear the same sweet Saviour say, "Come unto Me." We have tried to find God, we have tried to encompass Him; but we have felt that such small atoms as we are, must be of small account; and it is almost impossible to be sure of God by these processes. But, when the Infinite Word, Whose tones fill eternity, Whose wisdom guides, and Whose power upholds all things, becomes flesh, a Man of men, human, warm, sweet, tender, we come to Him, and we find God. With one's head upon His bosom there comes to the fevered heart the rest of eternity, the peace that passeth all understanding.

How shall we perfect our rest? By obeying Him. When Jesus said, "Take My yoke upon you," He did not mean only the yoke He would give us, the burden He would impose upon us. He did mean that ultimately; but primarily He meant the yoke that He wore is easy, the burden that He bore is light. What burden did He carry? There was only one. The burden of doing God's will, the burden of obedience to the Divine command. "I do always the things that are pleasing to Him." "My meat is to do the will of Him that sent Me, and to accomplish His work." "We must work the works of Him that sent Me." That was the master-passion in the life of Jesus. He said, His burden was light. We hardly believe it. We say it is hard work to please God. In that view we are wrong. It is fearfully hard work to please our neighbours. It is impossible to please our friends. It is absurd to try and please ourselves. Then let the prayer of each one of us be; "Teach me to do Thy will, O my God." That is the easiest, the sublimest, the simplest law of life; and therein is rest. May we all find it.

MATTHEW XII. 1-21

THERE are three movements in chapter twelve, all of them dealing with the subject of the conflict between Jesus and the rulers. First, the conflict concerning the Sabbath, in verses one to twenty-one. Then, the conflict concerning His power, where He obtained it, and what its nature was; in verses twenty-two to thirty-seven. Finally, the conflict concerning a sign; they asked for some sign, and He refused it; in verses thirty-eight to fifty.

At the beginning of His ministry the rulers were not only interested in Jesus, they were attracted by Him, and admired Him. They invited Him to dinner. They propounded their questions to Him. This did not last long; and we saw in chapter nine that they really broke with Him when He claimed authority in the moral realm, and claimed the right to forgive sins. This was the first outward break; but the first waning of admiration of Jesus on the part of the rulers was born of the fact that He made Himself the friend of sinners, and so violated all their conceptions of righteousness and purity; their conceptions being that righteousness and purity consisted in external separation from sinners, and from their sin. Now we approach that period in His propaganda when hostility became evident, positive. It never ended until they folded their arms across their breasts satisfied because they had encompassed His death.

In these twenty-one verses the subject is the Sabbath; first, the Sabbath in the corn-fields, verses one to eight; secondly, the Sabbath in the synagogue, verses nine to twenty-one. In the first eight verses dealing with the Sabbath in the corn-fields, we have the King's claim of authority; in the second division, the Sabbath in the synagogue, we have the King's activity upon the basis of that authority.

Before proceeding to the examination of these two passages, it is well to specially notice that the Sabbath question was that which led the rulers to determine on the death of Jesus. They opposed and criticised Him before; they wanted to find some method of dealing with Him; but each of the Evangelists refers to this fact,—though in each Gospel it is stated in different setting, under different circumstances,—that it was because of our Lord's attitude toward the Sabbath that these men decided to kill Him. If this is established it reveals the importance of the Sabbath question, and forbids any superficial exposition of the verses we are studying. For instance, it has been very commonly said that the attitude of Jesus to the Sabbath was a protest against the Rabbinical view of the Sabbath. It has been generally said that when He defended His disciples for plucking ears of corn, and when He Himself healed on the Sabbath, He was setting the Sabbath free from false methods of observance. There is an element of truth in all this, but to leave the subject there is to miss the profoundest values of this wonderful section, in which the King, claiming authority for the Sabbath, and prosecuting His activity on the Sabbath, aroused the ire of the rulers so that they begin to plot to take His life. Probably these men would not have plotted to take the life of Jesus simply because He attempted to broaden men's views concerning the Sabbath. We must read more closely if we would find out what Jesus did both in the corn-fields, and in the synagogue. The Sabbath was the most sacred symbol of the real nature of Judaism; indeed the only symbol peculiar to Judaism. We think of other things in the Hebrew economy of the past; for instance their sacrifices, the rite of circumcision, the peculiarity of the Temple in which God was supposed to dwell. But all these things were found amongst heathen people in some form or other. Burnt sacrifices were found among all the Semitic peoples. Circumcision was a common rite among other peoples as well as Jews. Temples in which the gods were supposed to dwell were common things. But the Sabbath was peculiar to the Jew, the setting apart of one day upon which men were to give themselves wholly to, and exclusively to, the cultivation of the spiritual within them, in recognition of their perpetual and underlying relationship to the eternal things. The Sabbath as a physical blessing provided for men by God is as old as the human race, though not the peculiar quality of the Sabbath as the symbol of separation to God, the seal of God set upon all the phases of life. The Sabbath according to the Hebrew economy was not one day given to God, while men were permitted to keep six for themselves; it was rather the peculiar sign and symbol of the deepest things in the life of the people. Now both in the corn-fields, and in the synagogue, and on other occasions, Jesus said things about the Sabbath, and claimed relationship to the Sabbath, which the keen critics of His own day perfectly understood, and upon which they came to the decision that the only thing they could do with Him was to disprove the claim He made by killing Him. In no relationship or application of His teaching did Jesus make more remarkable claims for Himself than in the words He uttered about the Sabbath, and in our present study there are revealed both His claim, and the reason of their objection to that claim, in two movements.

Let us attempt to look at them with simplicity and naturalness, that we may see what Jesus really said, and understand the claim that He made in the matter of the Sabbath; and discover why it so stirred the hatred of these men.

First, the Sabbath in the corn-fields, the King's claim of authority. He was walking through the corn-fields on the Sabbath day with His disciples, prosecuting His work, journeying from one place to another to preach the Kingdom, to heal, to bless, to call men back again to God; and on the journey the disciples were hungry. There is a very wonderful teaching in that very fact; it is a revelation of the poverty of these men. And there is a very strange teaching in it, too. He, the King, was so poor in earthly things that He was not able to feed the men who followed Him. At the time they were hungry—to use the language of to-day—they

were doing missionary work, they were going somewhere to proclaim the evangel of the Kingdom. As these hungry men passed through the corn-fields they plucked the ears, and fed themselves with the corn. It was a perfectly simple and natural action of the disciples, and reveals very clearly their estimate of their Lord's heart. They did not for a moment imagine that He would rebuke them. They knew, as members of the Hebrew nation, that they were doing things that the Pharisees would object to, but they were with Him, and familiarity with Him, and a consciousness of His attitude towards the Sabbath, set them free to pluck the ears. to rub them, to eat, and so to satisfy their hunger. It is a revelation of the relationship existing between Christ and His disciples. There was no hesitation, no appeal, no fear. This action the Pharisees at once criticised. They *began* to pluck the ears of corn. They began, that is all. Criticism was dogging the footsteps of Jesus and waiting to blaze forth, and immediately the Pharisees raised their objection.

Again notice how the familiarity between Christ and His disciples is brought out in the fact that the Pharisees did not criticise the disciples; they criticised Christ, they put the responsibility for all the disciples were doing upon Him. The appeal which they made was an appeal to Him. " The Pharisees, when they saw it, said unto Him, Behold, Thy disciples do that which is not lawful to do upon the Sabbath." They knew right well that the disciples' action revealed the attitude of their Master, that either by express teaching, or evident example, He had set these men free from certain traditional obligations.

Now we come to that which is of supreme importance, our Lord's answer to His critics. First, His answer assumed responsibility for their action. There is not the faintest suggestion of defence of what they were doing, as though it were something apart from Him. He reminded them of what David did, and so identified Himself with the action of His disciples.

Moreover, He justified their action, and He did so by illustration. Not so much in the actual words He used as in the peculiar illustrations He selected, do we touch the deepest heart of this defence. He first reminded them of David, that is, He took as an illustration of the rectitude of His conduct the action of the one king of all their history who was after God's own heart notwithstanding all his failure. Solomon was the magnificent, but the name of Solomon never moved the heart of the true Hebrew as did the name of David. He passed back in their history until He came to the one king in whom the kingly ideal had been most perfectly realised, and He said, "David when he was hungry, and they that were with him . . . ate the shewbread, which it was not lawful for him to eat, neither for them that were with him, but only for the priests." David did the thing unlawful by their standards, unlawful by the technicalities of the law as well as by the tradition of the elders. Jesus would not have said unlawful if referring to tradition merely. Christ was always careful to distinguish between the law of Moses and tradition. And yet He said that David did this, and was guiltless.

Passing from David the king He took the other personality that bulks large in the Hebrew history, and spoke of the priest. He declared that priests profaned the Temple on the Sabbath day in the very act and attitude of their worship. The priest must break the Sabbath to do his manual work of the Temple on the Sabbath. And yet the priest was guiltless. Such is the clear inference.

We miss a great deal of the force of these things unless we keep our minds upon these Pharisees. They were the rulers, the teachers of the people; and Jesus said to them in effect, You are criticising My disciples for the breaking of the law; your criticism is not due to enlightenment, it is due to ignorance. Your objection to what you have seen is not due to your perfect understanding of the deep things of God; it is due to your blindness and misunderstanding of them. "If ye had known what this meaneth, I desire mercy, and not sacrifice, ye would not have condemned the guiltless." Hosea meant, that God looks for mercy and not sacrifice; and that if a man brings a sacrifice, and there is no mercy in his heart, his sacrifice becomes a blasphemy. If you knew, said Jesus to these men, what your own Scriptures meant. If you only understood that the hungry man must be fed Sabbath or no Sabbath! If you had known what all this meant, you would not have blamed the guiltless.

But we have yet to touch the deepest note. All that did not make the Pharisees angry enough to want to kill Him; but this did; "But I say unto you that One greater than the Temple is here." "For the Son of Man is Lord of the Sabbath." The Sabbath is a means of grace, the Sabbath is a Divine provision by which man can have help and strength and blessing, not something by which he is to be bound, and fastened, and burdened. The Sabbath is that through which God in infinite love would cheer the drooping heart of humanity; and it is the Son of Man, the Master of men, Who is the Lord and Master of the Sabbath. He will take the Sabbath and fulfil it according to the intention of God's heart, even though He violate all the traditions of the elders, even if He seem for the moment to be breaking the external commandment of the law. The King has claimed to have the perfect right to use the Sabbath as He would. The King distinctly declared that the priest was guiltless in what would have been his profanity, because he was ministering in the Temple; and then He said, "But I say unto you that One greater than the Temple is here." And if the priest in the Temple is freed from guilt, when he appears to break the Sabbath, how much more these men journeying with Me if they satisfy this hunger by plucking ears of corn! The vindication of what I do is in Myself. The vindication of what My disciples do is in the underlying purposes of My ministry. If you do not understand what that meaneth, "I desire mercy, and not sacrifice," I understand what it means, and as I prosecute the purposes of the infinite mercy amongst men, I am Lord and Master of the Sabbath.

So, to the listening ear of the rulers, this strange young Galilean peasant claimed a prerogative which is a prerogative of Deity. He spoke with the authority of the one and only God. He said what no other man ever dared to say. He laid that right hand of His upon the most sacred symbol of national life, that Sabbath which they were desecrating in spirit, and said: I am Master of it, and the vindication of what men do in fellowship with Me on the Sabbath is to be found in the fact of their fellowship with Me.

But to pass to the next section. Here the teaching is even more remarkably and beautifully brought out. We suddenly find ourselves in the synagogue. Again it was the Sabbath day. Jesus had come into the synagogue, and somewhere in the synagogue was a man with a withered hand. These two things are supreme; the presence of Christ, and the presence of the man with the withered hand. Have you ever noticed what unconscious compliments Christ's enemies paid Him? When Jesus came into the synagogue they immediately connected Him with the man with the withered hand, and asked Him if it was lawful to heal on the Sabbath. There was malice behind the question, for we are told they asked Him "that they might accuse Him." He had made an astounding claim about the Sabbath, and they were determined to deal with Him. They were trying to see if they could put Him into a difficult position in order to accuse Him.

He answered their question by asking another; "What man shall there be of you, that shall have one sheep, and if this fall into a pit upon the Sabbath day, will he not lay hold on it, and lift it out?" Again here is a small matter needing careful attention. He did not say, If a man *see* a sheep; but if he *have* one. He said, If your sheep fall into the pit you rescue it, and you rescue it because it is yours. "How much then is a man of more value than a sheep?" You own sheep and care for them and rescue them.

Now we have come into the new light and glory. Now the Son of Man is claiming not the Sabbath, but the man. Now the Son of Man is not only saying that He is Lord of the Sabbath, but

that He is Owner of man. That man belongs to Me. I am here to rescue him, and to set him free from the limitation of the evil that is in the world. You know full well, you men that criticise, that you would violate the Sabbath and be guiltless in saving your sheep, because it is yours. Understand, for evermore, that the supreme work of the Sabbath is that of reaching man and saving him.

All the emphasis of the argument here is upon the thought of ownership. Jesus Christ is not excusing what He is going to do upon the basis of authority. It is the work of necessity. I cannot help it; this is My man. That was the great cry of His heart.

There was another occasion when they criticised Him about the Sabbath, recorded in John's Gospel, which flashes its light upon this. When He passed through the porches at the Bethesda pool, He healed a man on the Sabbath, and they criticised Him then. He answered, " My Father worketh even until now, and I work." In other words He said; Man by his sin has broken God's Sabbath, and God is fulfilling the Sabbath intention of rest by working for the rescue of man. So Jesus said to the critics in the synagogue; That man is not at rest, look at his withered hand, he is restless and suffering and limited; and I Who am Lord of the Sabbath, Who made the golden splendour of the waving corn, have claimed authority over the Sabbath; and I am now exercising that Lordship by saving My man on the Sabbath, and so fulfilling the very deepest intention of the Sabbath. Yes, He said, it is lawful to do good on the Sabbath.

When Jesus had said these things the Pharisees determined to destroy Him, for He had claimed to be Lord of the Sabbath, and Owner of man; and to have the royal kingly right to do whatever was pleasing to His heart, impulsed by the tenderest love.

Then Jesus left the synagogue and multitudes of people flocked around Him. "Jesus . . . withdrew . . . and many followed Him; and He healed them all." Oh what virtue coming out of Him! Oh what a stream of life and health! It was still the Sabbath, "and He healed them all!"

He charged the people that they should not tell of this healing at the time, "that it might be fulfilled which was spoken by Isaiah the prophet." The prophet of the past saw that this supreme Servant, Whom he described, would overstep all the boundaries of mere prejudice, and nationality, and go out to those that lay farther away—the Gentiles. It is generally said that this passage from Isaiah teaches Christ's meekness, that if a man is bruised He will not break him, and that He will not put out the smoking flax, but that He will help it. But it really teaches Christ's restraint from judgment during His ministry of grace. He withdrew in order that He might not smite them for their hypocrisy; for a bruised reed is weakness weakened, and smoking flax has the element of destruction in itself, and Christ said of these enemies, they are bruised reeds, they are smoking flax, I cannot break or quench until I send forth judgment to victory, and then the bruised reed will be broken, and the smoking flax fanned into a flame for its own quenching.

This is not to deny that He is very gentle with weakness, but to recognize that it is not the teaching here.

It is the great King that we see, claiming the Sabbath, claiming the ownership of man, and restraining judgment which might have proceeded in fire against the blasphemers, in order that He may accomplish His work in His own way, and send forth the message of health to the Gentiles also. He restrained judgment because the day of His mercy was not perfected, and accomplished.

The outstanding matter of this study is that of the claims of Christ. Greater than the Temple, Lord of the Sabbath, Owner of man, Restrainer of judgment until He please. Let us kiss His sceptre anew, and bow the knee in the presence of His supernal majesty, and say, "All hail the power of Jesus' name."

MATTHEW XII. 22-37

IN this study we shall consider the second movement in the opposition of the rulers. We have already seen how the answers of Jesus to the different positions of the attack of the rulers varied; indeed there was a progress in His method. In the first, when their complaint was concerning His claim in respect of the Sabbath, Jesus stood on the defensive. In the second of these movements, the one which we are now to examine, He defended Himself against the charge they made, but He added to the defence words terrifically solemn as He warned these men concerning the peril which threatened them. In the last movement, which we have yet to consider, He denounced and condemned, refusing absolutely to give them evidence when they asked for it.

Let us first break up the section which we are to study into its component parts, and then consider them. In verses twenty-two and twenty-three we have the occasion of this outbreak of conflict.

"Then was brought unto Him one possessed with a devil, blind and dumb: and He healed him, insomuch that the dumb man spake and saw. And all the multitudes were amazed, and said, Can this be the Son of David?"

Then in verse twenty-four, brief and yet forceful, we have the account of the attack which the rulers made on Him, in the presence of this miracle which He had performed in their sight, and in the sight of the people.

All the remaining part of the paragraph is devoted to Christ's answer to the attack.

Let us look, then, first, at the occasion; secondly, at the attack; and principally and particularly, at Christ's answer.

The occasion was that of the healing of a demoniac. A man possessed with a demon was brought to Him, a man in whose physical life the demon had wrought sad havoc, a man who was both blind and dumb; and with a word of power, with no incantations, with none of the methods of the exorcists of that particular time, the man was healed; and the fact that the demon had been exorcised was made evident by the man seeing and speaking. It was one of the wonders that Jesus wrought habitually.

The effect produced by this particular miracle upon the crowd reveals the real meaning of the Pharisees' complaint and attack. When the crowds saw what Jesus did with this man, they are reported to have exclaimed, " Can this be the Son of David?" They did not say, "Is *not* this the Son of David?" If the question had been in that form it would have suggested a stronger conviction that Jesus was the Son of David than the question actually did suggest. It was the question of the perplexed crowd. They had been watching Him, and listening to Him, and beholding the wonders that He wrought, and at last in the presence of this wonderful miracle, wrought with absolute ease, simply by the uttering of a word, they cried out in perplexity, " Can this be the Son of David?" They meant to say, We cannot make up our minds. To insert a phrase for the sake of exposition it was as though they had said, " Is this, *after all,* the Son of David?"

When we hear the question, and see what it indicated, we know why the Pharisees said what they did. It was a perpetual fear among the Pharisees and rulers that they might lose their hold on the people. Upon occasion they said, " What do we?" . . . "The world is gone after Him." They saw very clearly that if His line of teaching was accepted, their power would be absolutely gone; and when they heard this wavering, hesitating question, " Can this be the Son of David?" they attempted to account for the wonder that had produced the question by this declaration : "This Man doth not cast out demons, but by Beelzebub the prince of the demons." What they said was either a lie and they knew it; or else it was the result of their degenerate moral nature, so that they were unable to distinguish between good and bad, between heaven and hell, between purity and pollution. Whichever alternative is chosen, this at least remains true, they

were attempting to turn the people from the Christ, by attributing the wonders that He wrought to diabolic influence.

The King's answer proceeded along two lines. First, that of refutation; and, secondly, that of declaration. He refuted their argument by appeal to logic. This was one of the rare occasions when Jesus by argument answered attacks upon Himself. As a rule, a man who criticised Him He let severely alone, or replied to his question briefly and finally. It would be a very profitable and interesting study to take the Gospels and collect the questions men asked, and the answers He gave. The wonder of the answers of Jesus is revealed in the fact that we hardly ever find that men asked Him two questions consecutively; and now, nineteen centuries later, no man can improve on any answer Jesus gave as to the philosophy revealed, the method adopted, or the purpose gained.

But here, so terrible was the thing the rulers had said that Jesus, first of all, refuted by argument what they said.

The charge made against Him was that He wrought His wonders by complicity with evil; that by Beelzebub, Satan, He cast Satan out. In His refutation, our Lord attacked and denied their suggestion; and then proceeded to state and defend the truth concerning His method; He affirmed that He wrought by the Spirit, and defended His affirmation.

He revealed in His answer, first, the folly of their suggestion; secondly, the inconsistency thereof; thirdly, the wilful rebellion that induced it; fourthly, the blindness which caused it; and, finally, their complicity with Satan as the secret of it. So that commencing by denying His own complicity with Satan logically, and in such a way that they could not reply, He ended by inferentially charging upon them complicity with Satan.

Let us trace these movements one by one. First He showed the folly of their suggestion in a simple and logical statement. He told them that by common knowledge a house divided against itself cannot stand, a " Kingdom divided against itself is brought to desolation." Therefore if He in complicity with

Satan were casting Satan out, then Satan was working for his own destruction.

He next revealed the inconsistency of their position, as He said, "If I by Beelzebub cast out demons, by whom do your sons cast them out? Therefore shall they be your judges." There was abundant evidence that there were exorcists abroad, men who in one way or another, were casting our evil spirits. Christ did not defend them or attack them, but simply referred to them in His argument with their fathers, the rulers of the people.

Mark the final words of the argument, "But if I by the Spirit of God cast out demons, then is the Kingdom of God come upon you." There was but one alternative to their suggestion; if not by Satan, then by the Spirit of God is Satan cast out; and in such action men were brought face to face with the Kingdom of God, not only as to its claim, but as to its power.

In a moment the deeper truth began to burn and flame before the eyes of these men as to Christ's intention. Not only was their charge false and inconsistent; it was of the nature of rebellion against the Kingdom of God. It was because they were living in rebellion against the Kingdom that they had attempted to attack Him.

Now follow a step further. He now took for granted that complicity with Beelzebub on His part could no longer be maintained; and that His claim that He cast out devils by the Spirit must be conceded. Taking these things for granted, mark the progress of His argument. "Or how can one enter into the house of the strong man, and spoil his goods, except he first bind the strong man?" In effect He thus said to them; You charge Me with casting out demons by the prince of demons; have you not eyes with which to see that when I cast out demons it is a proof that I have already laid My conquering hand upon the master of demons; that instead of working by his power I am working as the result of having overcome his power; that I have entered into the house of the strong man and bound him, and therefore am able to spoil his house? The binding of the

strong one was wrought out by the perfection of the Christ. Not merely by virtue of the death of Jesus, but by the virtue of His pure humanity did He bind the strong one, and so was able to spoil his house. As Man He overcame the enemy in personal temptation, bound him, and thereby made Himself able to spoil his house. God's children who have entered into His victory by the Cross, also know something of what it is to bind the strong one. His Cross is the force that sets us free to spoil the house of the strong one, and rescue other souls.

He said one other thing by way of refutation, "He that is not with Me is against Me, and he that gathereth not with Me scattereth." That was a statement containing principles of perpetual application. Carefully note its setting. "He" refers first to Satan, and in that verse, flaming with light, the two great personalities are brought into contact, the One the Gatherer, and the other the scatterer; and they are for ever against each other. The truth about Satan is not that the King was in complicity with him. The truth is that He was in antagonism to everything he did. He had cast the demon out of a man, and so had gathered him back into unified and balanced life; had gathered him back to His family, and to the family of God. It was Satan that had scattered, it was he that had spoiled.

Thus as the King commenced by showing the folly of saying that Satan was working with Him, He ended His refutation by declaring the absolute antagonism between them; He was the Gatherer; Satan was the scatterer. There are but two forces at work, the force that gathers and the force that scatters. And Jesus said in effect; Do not confuse the Person Who stands at the centre of the gathering force with the person who stands at the centre of the scattering force. A distinction must be maintained between good and evil in all logical thinking.

But the "he" of our Lord's statement has also personal application to every life. It is as though Jesus had said to these men, all life is centripetal or centrifugal. I am gathering. What are you doing? He meant to say that they were scattering; that it was not He Who was with Satan, but they.

Thus by one sweeping statement, true as God is true—and every man knows it is true in his deepest heart—that the Gatherer is against the scatterer, Jesus marked a clear line, dividing all He does from all the devil does, and that line is His dividing line between men. That line is the Judgment Throne. We are with Him or against Him; and we may know which by asking, Are we gathering or are we scattering?

We now reach those awe-inspiring words with which the paragraph closes. For searching solemnity they are unsurpassed in the records of the things Jesus said. We tremble as we read them. Jesus Christ opens here before the mind a sphere into which if a man ever enter, his case is absolutely hopeless. The One Who proclaimed, as the supreme meaning of His mission, that He had come to seek and to save the lost; the One Who declared that He was able and willing to save and remake men and women whom others had cast out as hopeless, is the One Who here declared that there is an attitude of the human soul which is hopeless. Such solemn words as these demand our careful attention for two reasons; first, in order that we may place no untrue emphasis on them; and, secondly, that we may by no means minimize their terrible meaning. We are in danger of making both these mistakes. We may read into them meanings which He never intended; or we explain away the most solemn words Jesus Christ ever uttered. The only way in which we can hope to understand, is by taking them in the simplest way possible.

The whole statement falls into three parts. The first is a solemn warning. The second is the chronicle of the appeal He made to His traducers. Then, finally, we have what seem to be the most awful words of all, because in them it would appear as though Jesus Christ Himself had become almost hopeless of the men to whom He spoke.

First, the warning. In order that there may be no undue emphasis put upon the solemn words, let us carefully

observe that they constituted a warning, and not a sentence. We are not warranted in believing that the Pharisees had committed the unpardonable sin, but that they had come near to its committal; so near that presently, in the final lament, Jesus, usually so full of hope for men, in one brief, wailing complaint makes it evident that they had almost crossed the boundary line. But, at the moment when these words were uttered, they had not crossed that awful boundary line, and the words were for warning, and not for sentence. Therefore we are not true to the context, when we say that the blasphemy against the Holy Ghost is that of attributing to the Son of Man complicity with Satan. That is blasphemy against the Son of Man, and He distinctly said that such may be forgiven.

What, then, is the nature of the warning? The Lord had said, "If by the Spirit I cast out demons, then is the Kingdom of God come upon you;" and in those words He evidently intended to teach that there are only these alternatives; exorcism of demons is either by Satan or by the Spirit of God. They said that He had wrought by Satan. In so doing they had denied that He wrought by the Spirit, which according to His interpretation meant that they were refusing the Kingdom of God. In the presence of the claims of that Kingdom, in the presence of the demonstration of the power of that Kingdom, they were refusing it. That, if it be ultimately and finally persisted in, is the sin against the Holy Ghost which has no forgiveness. The sin against the Holy Ghost is the ultimate refusal to believe on the testimony of the Spirit concerning Jesus Christ. The sin against the Holy Ghost is persistent, determined, and final rejection of the Spirit's demonstration of the meaning of the Kingdom, and of the power of the King.

In the final words of the King this statement is found; "Out of the abundance of the heart the mouth speaketh." Notice that principle. Speaking against the Holy Ghost does not consist in a theory advanced; nor in a sentence that drops thoughtlessly from the lips. When a man says I will not believe the testimony, he does so because in his heart he is refusing the King. That is the unpardonable sin. There is no sin under heaven that may not be put away by infinite mercy, through the Cross, except the sin which declines to receive the mercy, to receive the grace, because it declines to submit to the sceptre of the King.

These men were very near that sin. He declared that sin can be forgiven so far as it is a slight and insult to Him; but if men persist in refusal to obey, if they will have none of His grace, then they cannot be forgiven. The sin against the Holy Ghost is wilful, personal, final rejection of the Spirit's testimony, by words of the mouth which express the decision of the heart.

Then He made His appeal to them; "Either make the tree good, and its fruit good, or make the tree corrupt and its fruit corrupt." Say that you know the tree is corrupt because its fruit is corrupt; or dare to say that the tree is good, because its fruit is good. There is in these words the touch of a great pity, of a great desire to help these men. He appealed to them not to attribute good fruit to a corrupt tree. That is what they were doing. They said that the good result, of a man freed from demon possession, was wrought by Satan. He appealed to them to be consistent; to believe on Him for the very works' sake.

Then finally He uttered the most awe-inspiring words of all; "Ye offspring of vipers, how can ye, being evil, speak good things?" The severity of that consists in His evident pity for them. It seems as if even the hopeful spirit of Christ was almost hopeless about these men. He said, How can ye speak a true thing? How can ye say

the tree is good because its fruit is good? How can you tell the truth? You are the offspring of vipers; you are morally degenerate; you have lost your moral discrimination.

It is impossible to undertake a study like this, without feeling its searching force and power in one's own heart and life. The power of Christ is as evident to-day as ever. The works that He is doing in our time are far more wonderful than the works that He did in the days of His flesh. There are multitudes of witnesses who can tell of moral change in their lives, that cannot be produced in any other way than by His power; men who were mean and dastardly, and to-day are victorious and noble. On every hand evidences of His power abound, as mighty, and mightier, than any wrought in the material realm. They are the moral victories of Jesus to-day. J. Cotter Morrison, in his book, *The Service of Man,* in which he professes not to believe in Christ, says, "The Christian doctrine has the power of elevating and developing saintliness which has had no equal in any other creed or philosophy." How do we account for that? The answer to this question will depend upon what we are in ourselves. If in our heart there is simple honesty, there is but one answer —He Who flings out impurity is pure; He Who saves man from the power of passion is in Himself a Master of the tides of passion; He Who lifts a man from degradation is Himself noble and honest. To see these present-day miracles in the realm of morals, is to be compelled, unless the heart be utterly depraved, to crown Him Lord of all, kiss His sceptre, and bow in reverential worship in the presence of His glory.

MATTHEW XII. 38-45

IN this paragraph we have the last phase of this particular conflict of our Lord with the rulers. Concerning the Sabbath He had assumed the defensive attitude, claiming to be Lord of the Sabbath and Possessor of men. In the second phase of the controversy,

when His power was under discussion, He defended Himself against the charge they made of complicity with Satan, and then in some of the most solemn words that ever fell from His lips, warned them of the awful peril that threatened them when they made such a charge and thus revealed their inability to distinguish between good and bad.

The time-note "Then" with which this section begins shows us that this demand for a sign followed immediately upon the King's solemn words of warning. That is in itself significant and partly accounts for the answer they received. That answer was a positive and emphatic refusal to give them a sign such as they asked, followed by words of direct and searching denunciation and condemnation.

In Matthew's account of this event we have first the request of the Scribes and Pharisees; and secondly the careful and revealing answer of the King; both of which demand our very careful consideration in the light of the whole of the surroundings, and especially that process of controversy which we have been considering.

The tone and temper of these men is revealed in all that has gone before, and we must take time to consider this if we are to understand their request and the King's answer. If we glance back in the chapter to the fourteenth verse, we have at once a revelation of their underlying motive. Then Matthew tells us that after Jesus had answered their question as to the legality of healing a man on the Sabbath, by appeal to them, and by healing the man with the withered hand, "The Pharisees went out, and took counsel against Him, how they might destroy Him." That purpose was still in their heart when they accused Him of casting out demons by Beelzebub; and after His stern rebuke and solemn warning, it was the inspiration of this request. They were not honestly seeking for a sign, as men who really desired to know the truth about Him. The request was in itself malicious. They had come to definite conclusion as to what their line of action toward Him should be. They were set upon His destruction; and their request was inspired by their malice.

Its tone was that of satire, "Teacher, we would see a sign from Thee." This is self-evident in the light of the record of what they had already said concerning Him which we find in the twenty-fourth verse, "This man doth not cast out demons, but by Beelzebub the prince of the demons." If that statement did not express honest conviction, it certainly revealed their attitude toward Him personally, and out of such an attitude the request for a sign could not be honest. They were not really prepared to receive a sign. If they had been, the casting out of the demons was in itself sufficient to have proved His co-operation with the Spirit of God, as He had declared. Thus when a sufficient sign had been given they had refused it by attempting to account for it in the most terrible way. Yet these men, already hardened against convincing signs, asked for one; and the asking was satirical, the asking of men who were not prepared to accept as sufficient any sign He could give, because of their personal hatred of Him. That is exactly what He meant when He declared in words of the sternest, "Ye generation of vipers, how can ye, being evil, speak good things? for out of the abundance of the heart the mouth speaketh." Their use of the word "Teacher" was in itself an insult, as they refused to accept Him or His teaching. Their spirit was exactly that of the men who mocked at Isaiah, saying, "Whom will He teach knowledge?" (xxviii. 9). They despised and rejected the Teacher and were determined not to accept His teaching; yet they called Him "Teacher"! They came to Him with this request, while they were filled with wilful and wicked unbelief. They had seen many of His mighty works, but under the impulse of a deep and growing hatred they discounted them all; and their demand now was for a sensual and spectacular proof, such as He never gave, and such as, even had He given, they would no more have yielded to as proving the divinity of His mission than they had done in the case of the signs of His beneficent and mighty operations in the relief of human suffering both physical and mental.

The paragraph is occupied mainly with the King's answer. This answer is remarkable in every way, but the first matter which is impressive is that, refusing definitely and in so many words, to give them the sign they asked, He lifted the matter out of the then present surroundings, and spoke wholly of the future. For the purpose of careful consideration we may divide this answer into three parts. The first had to do with the Last Sign which would be given; and suggested another opportunity which would be created for that generation (39-40). The second dealt with the Last Judgment; and solemnly declared the nature of the verdict which would be found concerning the generation (41-42). The third described the Last State of the generation, and was of the nature of a sentence pronounced (43-45). Thus, in the presence of men who represented their generation, the King now spoke as One Whose testimony was rejected, and Whose signs had been ignored; and dealt with the future, foretelling an opportunity, a verdict, and a sentence.

While refusing a sign He promised a sign; and thus in the presence of their malicious hostility foretold the new opportunity which would be created for them by the carrying out to completeness of His divine work in the world. His purpose was that of saving and redeeming. Therefore He refused the sign they asked, which would have had no effect; and promised them the only sign that could by any means arrest and constrain them, that namely of His own Resurrection from the dead after their malice had encompassed that death. The giving of that sign would afford them a new and final opportunity.

The awful solemnity of the occasion is revealed in the words in which the King uttered His estimate of these men, and of the generation which they represented in their hostility to Him. That estimate is revealed in the two words which He employed, " evil," and " adulterous." The first described what they were in themselves. The second described their failure in relationship to God.

The word " evil " really means harmful, hurtful; and thus was two-edged as the King used it. It described the influence these men were exerting, and thus revealed their true character. In spite of all their external observances of religion they were essentially evil,

wicked of heart; and therefore in spite of all their teaching of the formulæ of religion and morality, they were exerting and influence that was hurtful; and thus the generation which they influenced was as evil as they were in themselves.

The word " adulterous " is a terribly searching one, and the more so in that here it is certain that the King used it, not in its material or physical sense, but in its spiritual significance. This was a method of use not unfamiliar to these men, in that they knew at least the letter of their own Sacred Scriptures. The figure implicated is that most sacred one of the Old Testament in which Jehovah speaks of His people as betrothed to Him; and the sin described is that most terrible sin of spiritual harlotry which Hosea had dealt with. The word, as the King used it, was a charge made against these men of disloyalty, infidelity to the sacred and holy covenant between them and Jehovah. They were adulterous, unfaithful to their vows. The one burning word was a condensation of the complaint of Hosea; " Jehovah hath a controversy with the inhabitants of the land, because there is no truth, nor goodness, nor knowledge of God in the land;" which was the prophet's interpretation of his figure of adultery and harlotry in the spiritual realm.

Such was the King's estimate of these men, and of the generation of which they were the spokesmen when they requested a sign. And in this hour of their malicious, satirical unbelief, He told them of the one full and final sign which would presently be given to them. That sign would in all essentials be similar to one with which they were perfectly familiar. They knew how Jonah had been a sign to Nineveh in its sin by virtue of the fact that he had appeared in the city a preacher of Jehovah, after he had been cast out to death. That is the only possible solution of the words of the King here, for in that is the only parallel between Jonah and Jesus. In every other way they stand in contrast. That throws some light upon the book of Jonah, but that is not now our subject.

Thus our Lord declared to these men

that His final sign would be that after their hatred had encompassed His death, He would return out of death, and the demonstration of the truth of His teaching, and the divinity of His mission would be found in that return. How all this was verified we know full well. To men in evil mood asking a sign, the King spoke of the only sign which would be sufficient for such demonstration, the sign which would be the last possible. They had refused every other sign possible. They must now wait for that.

From that foretelling of a last sign, the King passed to the uttering of His last verdict on these men and their generation. This He did illustratively by instituting two comparisons, and uttering a two-fold condemnation.

His first comparison was between the men of Nineveh and the men and generation with which He was personally dealing. The men of Nineveh were honest. They received the sign, heard the preaching and yielded to it in repentance. The men of His own generation would fail in that particular. The accuracy of the prediction we know. After the resurrection the truth was proclaimed with all the signs of pentecostal power following therefrom, and with what results we know.

His second comparison was between the Queen of the South and the generation. She had come from the ends of the earth in diligent determination to hear the wisdom of Solomon, while their diligence had been that of persistent determination to silence the speech of the King.

The condemnation which the King announced was the result of the comparisons He made. He claimed to be greater than Jonah under whose preaching Nineveh had repented, and greater than Solomon to receive whose teaching the Queen of the South had shown such diligence. The comparison has another application also. They were children of the Covenant, familiar with the Divine Economy, versed in the great prophetic Scriptures; while Nineveh was a city outside the Covenant, and without the advantages which Israel had possessed, and the Queen of the South was of another nation and peo-

ple, and so had not the privileges of the chosen and peculiar people.

Thus less enlightened people had obeyed less enlightening preaching and teaching; and in that fact the patent condemnation of those to whom He spoke, and who were to receive His final sign was declared.

The last part of the answer of the King was a very remarkable and inclusive summing up of the whole situation, and pronouncement of sentence. This takes the form of an illustration drawn from individual experience in the matter of demon possession; and if we examine that with care we shall be prepared for the application which the King made when He said, "Even so shall it be also unto this evil generation."

The illustration begins at the point of dispossession. An unclean spirit is cast out of a man. The Lord shows the activity of that spirit. It needs some medium through which to act; it is restless and dissatisfied, unable to find what it seeks, for lack of such material medium. That in itself is a most remarkable revelation throwing light on a dark subject. It does not, however, come within the purpose of the present consideration to follow it up. For us it leads up to the return of the evil spirit to the man, and to the discovery of what condition the man was in. That condition is described in the words, "Empty, swept, and garnished." The arresting word is the first, "*empty.*" The man was improved in certain ways, "swept and garnished;" but not possessed, empty! The result was that the improvements were of no avail. Seeing there was no indweller, possessing, holding, mastering, the unclean spirit re-entered, taking others with him, and all the improvement was swept away, and the last state of the man was worse than the first. To cast out the unclean is of no lasting value, unless there follow new possession by the clean.

That is in itself a wonderful revelation of what is necessary to the remaking of a man and of society; and the King applied it immediately to His generation, that is to the men with whom He was dealing and to those whom they represented.

Thus inferentially He claimed that His presence and mission had loosed the power of evil. All His casting out of demons, which they had criticised, had but illustrated this wider fact, that while He was among them, the whole underworld of evil was within His government, and for a period He had held it in check and given men and the age an opportunity for better things. At this point human responsibility began. It was not enough that men should be loosed from the powers of evil. They must be submitted to the good. He Who had cast out the evil spirits was Himself the King, able to possess the swept and garnished houses, so that they should be no longer empty, but held in possession by purity and power stronger than all the power of the enemy. This they had refused in their rejection of Him, and therefore the house though improved, " swept and garnished," would sink to a lower level as more and worse evil spirits took possession. It was a solemn but carefully explained sentence; every word of which was fulfilled so far as that generation was concerned; and every word of which is fulfilled in the case of all men who are brought into contact with the King.

In the course of this study we have incidentally noticed, and it should now be directly recognized, that the King treated the opposition of the rulers as being the expression of the dominant spirit of the age; and therefore while dealing with those men, He constantly addressed Himself to the " Generation." " An evil and adulterous *generation* " (39); "The men of Nineveh shall stand up in the judgment with this *generation* " (41) ; "The Queen of the South shall rise up in the judgment with this *generation* " (42). "This evil *generation* " (45). The lessons therefore are peculiarly applicable to an age, while having, of course, an immediate application to individuals.

Our generation lives in the light of the ultimate sign. The supreme vindication of the Christian Evangel, and demonstration of the Kingship of Jesus is that of the Resurrection; and that resurrection attested by the fact of the moral and spiritual changes wrought in the lives of countless multitudes of men and women. The Kingship of Christ is more than that of One Who casts out unclean spirits. It is that of One Who takes possession, and holds for purity against all opposing forces. This is proven, as we have said, in all those who have proved His power.

The teaching of His verdicts is that judgment will be according to opportunity. Therefore seeing that the Resurrection thus attested, proves Him the greatest Prophet, the greatest King, those who refuse His teaching and rebel against His rule will merit the severest condemnation.

The warning of His sentences is patent and pertinent. Christ's presence always loosens the bonds of evil. Men always are conscious of that, whether they confess it or yield to it or no! Sometimes in the sense of that possibility we sweep and garnish our houses! We are great on cleanliness and decoration! Let us beware! Such swept and garnished houses are attractive to demons. Unless they are possessed and held by the King through His Spirit, the last state may be worse than the first.

MATTHEW XII. 46-50

IN our last three studies we have been considering the opposition of the rulers to the King as it manifested itself along three lines of attack. The first was that of their criticism of His attitude toward the Sabbath; the second that of their attempt to account for His power; and the third that of their request for a sign.

His attitude toward the Sabbath He defended. His power, He declared to be that of co-operation with the Spirit of God, and solemnly warned these men of the peril they were running in refusing to recognize this fact. As to a sign, He refused what they asked in the material realm, and foretold the ultimate sign of His own resurrection.

We now come to a brief paragraph which at first does not seem to have any relation to this movement of opposition, giving as it does the account of the coming to Him, at this period, of His mother and His brethren.

As a matter of fact, the story is vitally and intimately related to all that has preceded it, and is the account of opposition of the most subtle and powerful kind, proceeding from an entirely different motive.

In the incident recorded, interpreted in the light of the words of the King called out thereby, we have a superlative revelation of the most subtle form which opposition to the work of the establishment of the Kingdom of God ever takes. In this story therefore we also find a revelation of the reason why the Master, in the prosecution of His work, did not depend upon purely human affection, or trust Himself to those who were united to Him merely by the ties of earthly relationship.

In order that we may understand the passage, we shall consider the significance of the coming of Mary, and the consequent meaning of the words of the King.

Matthew simply records the fact that while He was speaking to the multitudes, His mother and His brethren stood without, seeking to speak with Him. If we turn to Mark's account of the same incident, we have some explanation of the reason why they came to Him at this time. The multitudes were so eager to be near Him, and to hear Him, that He and the disciples had neither time nor room to eat bread; "and when His friends heard it, they went out to lay hold on Him; for they said, He is beside Himself" (Mark iii. 21).

It is evident that His mother and His brethren were not with Him at this time, but in all probability were in Nazareth, where the news reached them of His persistent and laborious toil, and of the fact that He was coming into conflict with the rulers of the people. The news filled them with alarm, and they came to the conclusion that He was beside Himself, and immediately started on their journey to Him, in order to take Him away, and

prevent His continuing this kind of work. Between the time when this rumour reached them and their arrival, His conflict with the rulers had continued concerning His power, and evidently concerning the sign also, although Mark does not chronicle that in the same connection.

At last His mother and His brethren arrived in Capernaum, where He probably then was (Mark iii. 31).

Thus Mary's journey from Nazareth to Capernaum was the result of her great love for Him, and was taken because she thought He had lost His reason, and she would fain save Him from the results of His own folly.

If that was the reason of the coming of Mary, we at once have a revelation which accounts for the attitude of the King when He was informed of her arrival. It is a clear and superlative illustration of the fact that the Kingdom of God cannot be established on natural lines. His mother was, as to all earthly relationship, His nearest of kin, and yet she was evidently entirely unable to understand His method. His foes had said that the works He wrought were the result of co-operation with Beelzebub. His lovers declared that He had lost His reason. This is a startling revelation of how near hatred and love may be in the conclusions at which they arrive, when neither is familiar with the deepest secret prompting the activity of those who are working in fellowship with God.

In the light of this consideration of the significance of the coming of Mary, we may now consider more particularly the meaning of the words of Jesus. In the question He asked, and the declaration He made, He gave fresh evidence of the fact that the supreme passion of His heart was that of the accomplishment of the will of God. Such accomplishment He made the standard of His judgment, and the gauge of His relationships. Every other interest, however near, or however sacred by all the laws of human interrelationship, He counted secondary, and without hesitation or tremor, broke with them completely when they threatened in any measure to interfere with that supreme matter.

This is not to say that He lost His affection for His brethren, or failed in love to His mother. In the last and awful hours of His intensest suffering, He still thought of her, and with tender solicitude entrusted her to the care of John. His brethren, moreover, according to the flesh, we find eventually numbered among His disciples. But in this hour, when unable to understand Him, they sought from the motive of a true affection to hinder Him in His work, He resolutely refused to yield to their desire, and by His words revealed the fact that He counted earthly relationships as nothing compared to those spiritual relationships which were born of a common loyalty to the will of God.

Thus we see the King Himself entering into the experience to which He referred when He declared that " a man's foes should be they of his own household;" and that He " came not to send peace, but a sword."

It is impossible thus carefully to consider the story of the mother and the brethren of Jesus without feeling that this was a phase of opposition more subtle than any which had preceded it. In so far as it is permitted us to interpret His experience by our own, we should certainly be inclined to say that it was easier to resist the definite hostility of those who were in open rebellion, than to stand firm against suggestions which came from those who loved Him, and who, according to the measure of their light, were acting in His interest. Nothing other than the clearest vision of the will of God, and the most perfect acquiescence therein, would be equal to victory in such an hour of crisis.

The words of Jesus on the positive side are full of beauty and of encouragement for all those who share His devotion to the accomplishment of the Divine will. Conscious of the mistake made by His mother and His brethren, He pointed to the disciples, and declared that they were His next of kin. It is a truth not easy to believe, and yet witness is borne to it in every department of life. The highest and closest comradeships are always the result of spiritual affinity. That is the basis of true marriage. It is moreover, the ground of all high fellowship, such as that of art, or music, or literature. Those who come into communion upon the basis of a common capacity for the higher things of the spiritual life, find closer kinship than those united by ties of blood where there is no such spiritual affinity. And supremely this is true of those who are one in their vision of the Kingdom of God, in their passion for its realisation, and in their devotion to the King Himself.

It is an amazing word when we think of the frailty of these disciples. Under the stress of all that lay before them, they were presently scattered like chaff before the wind; but notwithstanding all that, the history of the Christian Church has vindicated this gracious word of the King. When presently by the way of His resurrection, and the coming of the Spirit, the vision of these men was clarified, and their understanding of the true meaning of His mission was perfected, they were welded together with each other and with Him in a unity far mightier than that of flesh and blood relationship, and as they went forth to the fulfilment of His purposes in the world, like their Master they were enabled to count all the ties of human kinship as of no moment when in any measure they interfered with their loyalty to Him.

Such a meditation as this compels the inquiry as to how nearly those of us who profess to follow in His train are really related to the King. If we not only admire, but do the will of His Father, we are, according to His own most gracious words, related to Him as brethren, sisters, mother; that is, we are His next of kin.

As we have already inferred, in the case of the disciples who were gathered about Him, His words were prophetic rather than descriptive. In measure they were even then devoted to the will of God, but He knew how they, too, ere long would falter and fail. Nevertheless, they had made their choice, had left all to follow Him; and therefore it was possible that His power should operate in them, in order to their perfect conformity to that will. The sequel we know. That power won its victory eventually, and they became actually co-operative with Him in the carrying out of His purposes.

Through such next of kin in spiritual relationship and loyal devotion to the will of God, His Kingdom is set up.

The principle revealed in this story is one of very solemn present application. We prove our distance from Him when in the fellowship of Mary and His brethren in the days of their limited understanding, we attempt to dissuade those who are in closest fellowship with Him, from such sacrificial service as demonstrates their nearness to Him.

MATTHEW XIII.

THE thirteenth chapter of Matthew is necessarily full of interest to all students of the teaching of Jesus. In it we have a setting forth of truth concerning the progress of the Kingdom of heaven in this age. Any study of it, therefore, which is to be of real value, necessitates a careful consideration of its scope and method.

The chapter is a set discourse of Jesus, and not a collection of truths taken from the Saviour's teaching at different times, and set forth by Matthew as a consecutive discourse. Dean Alford's words on the subject may be quoted as giving one simple and yet sufficient reason for holding this view.

"The seven parables related in this chapter cannot be regarded as a collection made by the evangelist, as related to one subject, the Kingdom of Heaven and its development; they are clearly indicated by verse 53 to have been all spoken on *one and the same occasion,** and form indeed a complete and glorious whole in their inner and deeper sense.

The King was approaching the great crisis in His propaganda, when it would be necessary for Him to challenge His disciples as to the result of His mission, and their opinion concerning Him. In view of this, and in all probability in preparation for it, He uttered this parabolic discourse, which is in large measure illuminated by the experiences of His ministry, and which illuminated the future for them in the matter of their ministry.

Let us first briefly examine a group of Scriptures which forms the foundation of our present study.

* The italics are Dean Alford's.

Verses 1-3 A. We first see the King as He emerges from the house in which He had been holding communion with His disciples, and taking the seat of a teacher by the sea. Multitudes gathered about Him, and "He spake to them many things in parables."

Verses 10-16. In the midst of this discourse, indeed, after the first of the parables, His disciples approached Him and asked, "Why speakest Thou unto them in parables?" Then follows the answer which He gave to them, and which contains for us His own explanation of His method.

Verses 34, 35. At the close of the account of the parables addressed to the multitudes, Matthew carefully declares the fact that here He adopted the method of parable, and announces His reason for doing so.

Verse 53. The last verse (53) read in connection with the first three, reveals the boundaries of the discourse.

The question of the disciples, "Why speakest Thou unto them in parables?" is our question as we commence our study of this discourse. Perhaps we shall best be able to understand the answer as we look at the question in its context of time and circumstance. It is evident that at this point in His ministry Jesus commenced practically a new method. He had already made use in His teaching of the parable-method, but from now He employed it supremely. The disciples noticed the change, and therefore asked Him the question.

Perhaps the force of their question is to be discovered by placing the emphasis upon the words "unto them," for in answer, Jesus immediately said, "Unto you it is given to know the mysteries of the Kingdom of heaven,

inductive preaching

but to them it is not given." If this contrast between the multitudes and themselves were in their mind, and if it were a real one as the reply of Jesus made clear, it must still be remembered that before the discourse was finished, He addressed Himself to them also in parables. I draw attention to this, in order that we may at once understand that whatever was the reason of His adopting the parabolic method with the multitudes, it obtained also in some degree at that time in the case of His own disciples.

We are not left to any speculation as to the meaning of the method. The King answered their question, and His explanation of His own method must be accepted. It is, however, of such a nature as to demand a very careful consideration, or it may be entirely misinterpreted. I utter this word of warning because I am convinced that it often is sadly misinterpreted, and much of its most tender purpose lost thereby.

Let us first inquire into the meaning of the word parable. Literally, it is a throwing or placing of things side by side, with the suggestion of comparison. Something is placed by the side of something else, with the intention of explaining the one by the other. Such a method is that of the parable. The old and simple definition comes back to us—"A parable is an earthly story with a heavenly meaning;" that is to say, some familiar thing of earth is placed alongside of some mysterious thing of heaven, that our understanding of the one may help us to an understanding of the other. The method is that of taking some one set of facts, familiar and material, and making them explanatory of others, strange and spiritual. Invariably in the teaching of Jesus a parable was a picture of things seen, intended to reveal and explain things unseen, and a rapid glance over this chapter will show how the King made use of the things that were most common in the experience of those amongst whom He was teaching for this purpose. I do not suppose that if Jesus were teaching in our cities to-day He would use any of the comparisons He used then; He would rather draw attention to the commonest sights of

the city life, and use them as illustrations. All the parables of this chapter were facts under the actual observation, or within the immediate experience of the men He was teaching. Perhaps even then in the distance a sower may have been seen scattering his seed. The field sown with wheat and intermixed with darnel was one of the most familiar things to them from boyhood. The mustard tree, about which we know so little, they knew full well. The woman hiding the leaven in the meal was an everyday home picture. Treasure found in the field was not so common, but still not unknown; and so with the merchant seeking pearls. The fisherman with his net, and the householder of the final parable were perhaps the most familiar of all. *Note.*

In the use of the parable it is always necessary to emphasize the teaching of similarity and disparity. The similarity of principle is emphasised by the recognition of disparity. To forget the teaching of disparity is to fall into the blunder of fanciful interpretation.

The question naturally arises as to why Jesus adopted this parabolic method of teaching. What was His intention? Let me answer first by a simple statement based upon what we have already seen. The purpose of the parable is that of revelation by illustration, and the method is always intended to aid, and never to hinder understanding. I know of nothing more curious, and at the same time more pernicious, than a certain interpretation of the motive which the King had in His use of parables, and I feel that it is of the greatest importance that we should avoid it. I refer to the view that our Lord adopted the parabolic method with His hearers because He had abandoned them in anger, and that His purpose was to hide His truth so that they should not see it. This I most strenuously deny. Christ never adopted any method characterised by such subtlety and cruelty. He never professed to be teaching men while at the same time He was resolutely attempting to hide truth from them. To charge Him with doing so would be to charge Him with dishonesty. The parable is an aid, not a hindrance. It veils truth, not that men may not grasp it, but that it shall not escape them. There is a sense in which the sun is hidden by the piece of smoked glass which the boy holds before his eyes, and yet without such an instrument he could not look upon the sun at all. Essential light unveiled, blinds. Its veiling is the opportunity of vision.

It is not, however, for us to speculate, but to hear what the King Himself said in answer to the disciples' inquiry. Let us, however, hear all He says, not contenting ourselves with His first sentence, but giving attention to His whole explanation. In answer to the inquiry, "Why speakest Thou unto them in parables? He said unto them, Unto you it is given to know the mysteries of the Kingdom of heaven, but to them it is not given." If Jesus had said no more than this, I should have made the deduction which I maintain has often been falsely made. I should have understood Him to mean that He was compelled to use the method of the parable in speaking to these people because it was intended that they should not know the truths concealed. Having made such a deduction, I should have been sorely perplexed. The whole meaning of His mission was that of giving men to know the truth; why, then, should He use a method ordinarily employed for illumination, in order to obviate His first intention of revelation, and produce exactly opposite effects in His hearers?

But let us follow Him further, and the meaning of the first statement becomes apparent. "For whosoever hath, to him shall be given, and he shall have abundance: but whosoever hath not, from him shall be taken away even that which he hath." Note most carefully the contrast of which this is an explanation. "Unto you it is given . . . to them it is not given." Now the explanation. "Whosoever hath, to him shall be given." He declared that it was given to His disciples to know the mysteries. Why was this knowledge given to them? According to the Teacher's explanation it was because of something they already possessed. Bearing that in mind, turn to the con-

trasted position. "But whosoever hath not, from him shall be taken away even that which he hath." He declared it was not given to these men to know the mysteries. Why was that knowledge denied? According to His own explanation it was because of something they lacked. These men lacked that which the disciples possessed, the possession of which created in them a capacity for receiving the mysteries of the Kingdom. It was not therefore possible for them to grasp these mysteries, and even what understanding they did possess, they were in danger of losing.

What, then, did the disciples of Jesus possess which these men lacked? In order to answer that question let us take it in another form. What was the essential difference between the disciples and the rulers and multitudes standing around? Did it not lie here, that the disciples had received Jesus as King, and by reason of that action and their attitude towards Him had become able to receive the mysteries of His Kingdom?

The people, notwithstanding His ministry, had rejected Him up to this time, and therefore He could not give to them, nor could they have received, the mysteries of the Kingdom. To the men who had crowned Him, He belonged; and all the principles and privileges of the Kingdom they were able to appreciate and possess. The others had so far refused their allegiance and were therefore unable to see, or enter into, the Kingdom.

If we go further back for a moment, we may state the case thus. All these men among whom the ministry of Jesus had been exercised had preliminary knowledge of the ways of God as a result of the religion in which they had been born and trained. In fulfilment of the messages of their own Scriptures He had come. Certain of them had received Him, others of them had rejected Him. To those receiving Him were given the mysteries of the Kingdom. To those rejecting Him these messages could not be given, and they were in danger of losing the real value of all that they had gained through their early religious training. Now with these men to whom are denied the secrets of the Kingdom, because of their disloyalty to the King, Jesus adopts a new method. He will give them pictures to lure them toward the truth.

Follow Him still further, " Therefore speak I to them in parables; because seeing they see not, and hearing they hear not, neither do they understand. And unto them is fulfilled the prophecy of Isaiah, which saith,

" By hearing ye shall hear, and shall in
    no wise understand;
And seeing ye shall see, and shall in
    no wise perceive."

That prophecy of Isaiah Christ declared to be fulfilled in the case of the people to whom the mysteries of the Kingdom were " not given." They were the people that hearing, did not understand; seeing, could not see, nor perceive. Upon whom was the blame of their blindness and deafness to be laid? In answer to this inquiry, let us continue the quotation as Christ continued it.

" For this people's heart is waxed
    gross,
And their ears are dull of hearing,
And their eyes they have closed;
Lest haply they should perceive with
    their eyes,
And hear with their ears,
And understand with their heart,
And should turn again,
And I should heal them."

Now in this passage the heart of the whole subject is laid bare. Christ declared in effect that these people did not see the things that His disciples saw. They saw without seeing, they heard without hearing. And why? They had shut their eyes lest they should see, and they had stopped their ears lest they should hear. They had rejected the King, and without the King they had no key to the mysteries of the Kingdom.

Because of this dulness consequent upon disobedience, He now proceeded to address them in parables. Nowhere is the infinite pity of the heart of God, revealed in Jesus Christ, more beautifully seen than in the method.

We have all seen a skilful teacher arrest a class with a story. Here, then, is the great Teacher, talking in parables, not in order that these men might not see, nor hear, nor feel, but in order to constrain them to a willingness to see and hear and feel. Presently we shall see that Jesus had to use the same method with His disciples, and for the self-same reason. Their vision was not yet perfectly clear, for they had not yet absolutely surrendered everything to His Kingship. There were things, therefore, which He could only interpret to them in this way.

The parable is always the method of Infinite Love. It is the method adopted in grace to meet the need of near-sightedness. All that it suggests to us is ultimately interpreted and enlarged by more direct teaching.

Let us first examine the scheme of the discourse. In it we have the King's own view of His Kingdom, as to its history in the age which He initiated.

The Kingdom of God in its fundamental ideal and ultimate realisation is infinitely greater than any condition revealed in the process of these parables. In human history there had been already different phases of manifestation, and various degrees of realisation of that Kingdom amongst men. Beyond the particular age in which we live, there will be, according to the teaching of Scripture, manifestations more perfect and far more glorious than anything our eyes have yet seen. In these parables the King deals only with the manifestation and method of progress in this age of God's Kingdom.

The first parable is not introduced by any direct reference to the Kingdom. It is simply the story of the initial work of sowing. Then immediately Jesus proceeded in a series of other parables to refer to the issues of that work throughout the age. That the application of these parables is limited to the age He initiated is clearly manifest in the phrases with which the King introduces each parable, excepting the first and last. The second parable, that of the two sowings, is introduced by the words, " The Kingdom of heaven is likened unto," and the remaining ones by the words, " The Kingdom of heaven is like unto." The first phrase means " The Kingdom of heaven has *become* like unto," the expression suggesting the changing manifestations of the Kingdom in succeeding generations. The second phrase implies simply the manifestation of the Kingdom in the generation then present.

What this limit of application is, is made perfectly clear as the discourse proceeds. Twice does Jesus refer to the "end of the world" (vers. 39 and 49). In each case a far more correct and helpful translation is that suggested by the revisers in the margin, "the consummation of the age." Thus the pictures of the Kingdom are pictures of conditions obtaining between the moment in which Jesus spoke and the consummation of the age—meaning not the end of the world, in the sense of the dissolution of the material universe, but the completion of the period which began with His first advent, and which will be closed by His second.

A general survey of the discourse reveals three principal divisions. First (vers. 1-35), "Jesus went out of the house" and uttered four parables in the hearing of the multitudes. Second (vers. 36-50), Jesus "left the multitudes, and went into the house," and spoke to His disciples parables which were of a different nature from those already spoken to the crowd. Third (vers. 51-53), Jesus addressed Himself to His disciples concerning their responsibility during the age.

Of these parables the King Himself gave the explanation of two. In each case the explanation was to His own disciples.

The first explanation, that of the parable of the sower, was possibly given in the hearing of the multitude. The second explanation, that of the two sowings, was given to the disciples privately.

In preparation for a more detailed study of these parables, it is of great importance to state certain necessary canons of interpretation. Let me first name these, and then consider them a little more particularly.

> I. Simplicity of interpretation, for remembering the intention of the parable, the simplest interpretation is the most likely to be the true one.

II. Restriction in application of the pictures to the limits clearly marked by the King.

III. A consistent use of the figurative terms employed, both within the system and with the general use of Scripture, except where specifically otherwise stated.

With regard to the first canon, it is quite possible to examine these parables of Jesus, as it is possible to examine His miracles, with a desire to find hidden depths and hidden meanings. That there are such in all of them, I do not deny, for the simplest thing Jesus said was in itself of the essence of eternal truth, and may have a thousand applications. I hold, however, that in our study it is better to interpret them in the light of the multitudes to whom they were addressed. Seeing that He spoke, not to hide spiritual truth, but to reveal it, we may take it for granted that the sublimest meaning is also the simplest.

As regards the second, it must be remembered that we shall utterly miss the real value of this discourse if we attempt to make any of the parables include the whole fact of the establishment and administration of God's Kingdom. We must recognize from the beginning that they are pictures of one age, and remember that that age is not final.

Upon the third canon I desire to lay special emphasis. The figurative terms of these parables are used consistently within the system. That is to say that Jesus was true to His own figures, and used them in one sense only. Personally I believe that to be a principle, not merely in the teaching of Jesus, but throughout the whole of Scripture. So important do I hold this to be that I desire at once to gather out from the parables some of the figures which Jesus used, and which at first sight may appear to have different significations, but which, as a matter of fact, have always the same value and intention. We read of the sower, the seed, the birds, the soil, the sun, the thorns, the fruit, an enemy, reapers or servants, the harvest, a tree, leaven, meal, a woman, treasure, a man, a merchant, a pearl, a net, the seashore, fish; and although some of these illustrations are repeated in different parables, it will be seen, as we continue our study of them, that their significance never changes. The figure always stands for the same truth, in whatever parable it is found.

The sower is found in three parables, in the first, in that of the darnel, and in that of the mustard seed, and when we come to their particular interpretation we shall find that the sower in each represents the same Person, the Son of Man.

Again in the same connection, we find the figure of seed sown, and with the exception of the bad seed, which is distinctly so called and thus differentiated from the other, it has a uniform significance in all connections.

The figure of birds is used in the parable of the sower, and in that of the mustard seed. It is a mistake to interpret it as symbolic of evil in the first, and of good in the second. In both parables, birds are symbols of evil.

Again the soil appears in the parable of the sower, in that of the darnel, in that of the mustard seed, and in that of the treasure. It has always the same meaning, and this meaning is once given, "the field is the world."

Fruit is found in the parables of the sower and the darnel, and in each case must be interpreted according to the seed.

Reapers or servants are found in the parables of the darnel and the net, and in each case represent angels at the end of the age, acting with the King Himself.

The harvest is referred to in the parables of the darnel and of the net, and in both cases refers to the end of the age.

Then lastly we have illustrations which do not repeat in the discourse, but which are used in other parts of the Bible. Thorns are here, as everywhere, symbols of evil. A tree is here, as always, a symbol of great and widespread worldly power. As in every other case in Scripture, so here, leaven must be the type of evil. The meal here must be considered as the three measures, and thus its identification with the meal offering of the ancient economy is seen. Treasure is found in

one parable, and it can only be explained in conjunction with the parable of the pearl. Thus I maintain that in order to an understanding of these matchless parables of Jesus, we must recognize the perfect consistency of Jesus in His use of figures.

Let us now turn to a general survey of the main divisions and particular parables, and the teachings contained in each. The first four parables (one, and three) were spoken wholly to the crowds, and reveal the Kingdom from the human standpoint. The second four parables (three, and one) were spoken exclusively to the disciples, and represent the Kingdom from the Divine standpoint. First, the external fact of the Kingdom in the four parables for the crowd. Secondly, the internal secret of the Kingdom in four parables for the disciples.

Taking the first four we find running through them the same elements. In each one the Lord reveals the fact of antagonistic forces with continued conflict, and an issue in which failure apparently predominates, rather than success. In the first parable there is hindrance in the soil. In the second, there is opposition on the part of an enemy who by night sows counterfeit seed in the field. In the third, there is seen the counter-development of a worldly power affording shelter and protection to evil. In the last of the four there is revealed an alien principle which makes for disintegration and destruction.

Thus it is evident that these four parables do not give us the picture of an age in which there is to be a greater increase of goodness until final perfection is attained; but rather one characterised by conflict, and one in which it appears as though evil triumphed rather than good. In the parable of the sower the work of the King is revealed, that namely, of scattering seed to produce Kingdom results. The work of the enemy is manifested in his attempt to prevent Kingdom results by the injury of the seed through the soil on which it falls. In the parable of the two sowings the work of the King is manifest, and also the spoiling work of the enemy who sows the same field with darnel.

In the parable of the mustard seed which, contrary to all law, produces a great tree, we have a revelation of an unnatural growth, an abortion, something never intended, and therefore lacking the true elements of strength. In the leaven, as we have seen, we have the simplest symbol of corruption.

It is most important to remember that these parables give us pictures of the Kingdom as realised in the world, showing how far that realisation is attained in the present age. The subject of the Church is involved as the means to an end and as the measure of the realisation of the Kingdom. Our Lord was not for the moment dealing with its ultimate destination and calling in the ages to come.

Leaving the multitudes by the sea, the King gathered His disciples about Him in the house, and proceeded to utter to them parables which were not for the crowd. In them He revealed one activity, that of the King Himself. Here a great and glorious success is achieved in each case, and yet there is discrimination. There is first the finding of treasure in a field, and the purchase of the field to possess it. By no stretch of imagination can that purchase be made the picture of what any human being can ever do. He Who purchased the field of the world is not a rebellious subject, but the King Himself; and the treasure hidden is that latent possibility for the development of which the whole field must be purchased. So also in the next parable, notwithstanding all our exposition, and singing,

"I've found the pearl of greatest price!
    My heart doth sing for joy;
And sing I must, for Christ is mine!
    Christ shall my song employ,"

the pearl is not intended to represent Christ. It is perfectly true that to find Him is to find the chief treasure here, but that is not the teaching of this particular parable. When we find Him, He is God's free gift to us, but this merchant purchased the pearl, selling all that he had to do it. Finally, in the parable of the net no workers are recognized in the casting of the net into the sea. It is the act of God Himself. At the end of the age, when it is gathered in, there will be discrimination, and the measure of success is clearly shown.

We have, then, simply and rapidly in this study, looked merely at the broad outlines of teaching. The chief interest at this moment is the contrast between the parables spoken to the multitudes and those to the disciples. To the crowds He declared the facts concerning the Kingdom in this age, which would eventually become patent to outward observation. When He gathered His disciples about Him alone, He showed them the inside truth. While there may appear to be in the passing centuries failure, shortcoming, the leavening of everything that should be pure, yet through all such failure God is Himself gathering out His treasure and finding His pearl.

Finally we come to the last parable. It is interesting to remember that almost invariably we speak of the seven parables of the thirteenth chapter of Matthew. As a matter of fact there are eight. Seven of them reveal truth concerning the Kingdom. The eighth, which is as full of beauty and of importance as any, deals with the responsibility of those who know the truth. Having uttered the seven parables, He asked His disciples, " Have ye understood all these things?" One is almost surprised to read their answer. " They say unto Him, Yea." I do not suppose for a moment that they did understand all, but they saw some little way, had some gleam of light, had in all probability caught the general teaching of the discourse in both its private and more public aspects. The King knew that presently they would understand, that with the coming of the Spirit there would come perfect illumination; and with infinite patience He accepted their confession, and proceeded to lay upon them a charge of responsibility.

This general survey of the scheme of the King's teaching makes evident certain matters of present and pressing importance. We must have the Master's conception of our age if we are to do the best work in it for His glory. If our eyes are set upon some consummation which He did not expect, then what can we expect other than that we shall be heart-sick ere long? If, on the other hand, we accept His view and consecrate ourselves to its realisation, then we shall be able to bear "the burden and heat of the day," and do the work He has appointed.

MATTHEW XIII. 3-9 AND 18-23

THIS first parable is one of two which the King explained. He evidently considered it to be fundamental, for He said that if men were not able to understand this one, they could not understand the others. Let us, then, first look at the picture presented in the parable, secondly attend to Christ's explanation thereof, and finally deduce from such examination the instruction which is of present value.

The picture is a perfectly natural one, but the naturalness is eastern rather than western. Let us, then, attempt so far as is possible to watch the eastern sower at his work. Speaking of this particular parable, Dr. Thomson says, in *The Land and the Book*, describing what he actually saw:

" Behold a sower *went forth* to sow.' There is a nice and close adherence to actual life in this form of expression. These people have actually come forth all the way from Dahr-June to this place. The expression implies that the sower, in the days of our Saviour, lived in a hamlet or village, as all these farmers now do; that he did not sow near his own house, or in a garden fenced or walled, for such a field does not furnish all the basis of the parable. There are neither roads nor thorns nor stony places in such lots. He must go forth into the open country as these have done, where there are no fences; where the path passes through the cultivated land; where thorns grow in clumps all around; where the rocks peep out in places through the scanty soil; and where also, hard by, are patches extremely fertile. Now here we have the whole four within a dozen rods of us. Our horses are actually trampling down some seeds which have fallen by the wayside, and larks and sparrows are busy picking them up. That man, with his mattock, is digging about places where the rock is too near the surface for the plough, and much that is sown there will wither away, because it has no deepness of earth.

And not a few seeds have fallen among this *bellan*, and will be effectually choked by this most tangled of thorn bushes. But a large portion, after all, falls into really good ground, and four months hence will exhibit every variety of crop."

This brief paragraph describing what may be seen any day in Palestine shows us how simple, real, and direct was the picture to the men to whom Jesus talked. The points of interest in the parable are the sower, the seed, the soil, and the sequence. One man is sowing. He sows one kind of seed. That seed falls on different kinds of soil. A certain sequence or result follows, such as is dependent upon the nature of the soil. That is the simple and perfectly familiar picture presented by the parable to those who heard the King's words.

Keeping this picture in view, we turn our attention to the King's explanation. In doing so there are one or two preliminary matters specially to be noticed before attempting a close examination. First, Jesus makes no reference to the sower. He gives no explanation of who the sower is. The chief value of the parable is seen in the fact that He speaks of the seed, and of the relation which the seed bears to the soil. Listening to the parable we should certainly be inclined to think that the chief lessons were to be learnt from the nature of the soil. Indeed, already in epitomizing we have said that the sequence depends upon the soil. When, however, we turn to Christ's explanation, we find that such is not the case, but rather that the chief lessons of the parable are those concerning the nature of the seed. Without His explanation we should inevitably say that the harvest depends upon whether the nature of the soil be the open highway or the rocky places of the fields, or the thorny ground, or the fruitful ground. Jesus, however, lays no emphasis upon the soil, but all emphasis upon the condition of the seed which is cast into the soil. This is a most important distinction to be kept carefully in mind, or we shall continue to misinterpret all the parables. I am aware that this statement may seem at first to obscure the vision of truth, contradicting, as it does, popular conceptions of the teaching of this parable. Yet it is only as this guiding principle is observed, that we shall be able to discover the profoundest and most remarkable teaching.

Let us, then, carefully examine His explanation, following Him as He takes each of the four sowings separately.

"Hear then ye the parable of the sower. When any one heareth the word of the Kingdom, and understandeth it not, then cometh the evil one, and snatcheth away that which hath been sown in his heart. This is he that was sown by the way side." Notice most carefully here the actual words: "This is *he* that was sown by the way side." Not, this is *it*, but "this is *he*."

"And he that was sown upon the rocky places, this is he that heareth the word, and straightway with joy receiveth it." Again notice the words, "he that was sown," not *it*, but *he*.

"And he that was sown among the thorns, this is he that heareth the word." Once more, "*he* that was sown," not *it*.

"And he that was sown upon the good ground, this is he that heareth the word." Thus finally, "*he* that was sown," not *it*.

We have generally regarded the "sower" of this parable as a type first of our Lord Himself, and then of all those who preach the word, and the seed as the word sown in the hearts of men who respond to it in different ways according to their nature. This is a treatment of the parable which contradicts absolutely Christ's own explanation of it. In that explanation He declares, not that the sowing of the seed is the word cast into the heart of a man, but that it is the casting of a man into a certain age and generation. The sowing here referred to, then, to state the case broadly, is the sowing, not of truth, but of men, for in the next par-

able, where the Lord again takes up the figure of sowing, He distinctly says of the good seed, "These are the sons of the Kingdom." This truth is emphasised, too, in the first parable by the fact that, in every instance in His explanation, the King said, "he that was sown."

Take a broad survey of this. Remember the two studies we have already taken, and that our Lord is describing in these parables the condition of the Kingdom. It is not a question of the creation of the Church by the gathering of individual men to Himself, but rather of the establishment of the Kingdom. Here, then, is the method of His work during this age—the sowing of the sons of the Kingdom. Some of them are non-productive, some of them productive. Some of them bring forth fruit, fruit that is toward the Kingdom. They influence the age, creating in it the recognition of, and approximation to, the government of God. Others produce no such fruit. They are men who come into contact with the thought of the Kingdom and the ideals of the Kingdom, but who never produce the fruit of the Kingdom. The keyword of the explanation is "he that was sown."

There is, besides this, another sowing, that of the word in the heart. In Luke's account of our Lord's explanation (Luke viii. 11-15) he shows that side of the truth. There is no contradiction between the two things. The sowing of the word in the heart of a man is the introduction of the principle which makes him a fruitful seed in the age.

Let us examine our Lord's description of these seeds, "He that was sown by the way side." Who is he that was sown by the way side? "Any one who heareth the word of the Kingdom, and understandeth it not;" that is, one who listens to the word of the Kingdom, but to whom that word is but a jingle of empty sounds. Such are seeds planted by the way side. "The evil one . . . snatcheth away that which hath been sown in his heart." There is the recognition of the sowing of the word in the heart. If the word be snatched away out of a man's heart, he becomes a seed of the hard highway, and no issue results from his planting, no fruitfulness, no influence in his age, nothing that brings the Kingdom nearer. This is the first kind of seed.

Again, "he that was sown upon the rocky places,"—who is he? The man who hears the word, and rejoices in the word, "with joy receiveth it; yet hath he not root in himself." This is a man who goes farther than the first man; one who not only knows the sound of the word of the Kingdom, and is familiar with its letter, but who consents to its claim, and rejoices in it; and yet he never allows it to take grasp of his own life, to take root therein. "When tribulation and persecution ariseth because of the word, straightway he stumbleth;" because the word has not taken root in himself, he cannot influence the age for the Kingdom. That man becomes a nonproductive seed in the soil.

Again, "he that was sown among the thorns,"—who is he? He is the man who hears the word, but the "care of the age, and the deceitfulness of riches, choke the word, and he becometh unfruitful." This is a man who has within him the life-giving principle, but who becomes so occupied with the things of the age, with its methods and maxims, its cares and its pleasures, that they operate in his life as thorns, choking the vital principle, and preventing his having any effect upon the age in which he lives.

But finally, we have "he that was sown upon the good ground." Who is he? He is the man who hears the word, and "understandeth it, who beareth fruit, and bringeth forth." This is the man who hears the word of the Kingdom, who understands it, who obeys it, and therefore in his age produces fruit.

Let us re-state these truths. The seed which the King plants is men who have heard the word. One has heard and never understood. To him the word is a form, a jingle of empty sounds. Plant that man in the age and what is the result? With persecution and testing his witness fails. Yet another receives the same word of the Kingdom, but he is enamoured of his

age, desires to catch its spirit, and to adopt its method. What effect has he on the age? None. The age chokes him—under the press and crush of the material interests to which he has given himself, his influence dies. Here is another who hears, understands, obeys. The word produces fruit in his life. Plant that man, and what is the result? He produces fruit toward the Kingdom of God. His life is the life that prepares for the return of the King.

Now, let us take the parable and explanation, and deduce their simple and natural instruction. Here again, I ask you to notice the apparent difference between the incidence of the teaching in the parable, and the explanation. In the former, the whole issue seems to depend on the nature of the soil. In the latter, it is seen to depend on the seed. This distinction, however, is only apparent. It cannot be real, because when Jesus explained His own parable, He distinctly said that the nature of the seed was the important thing. So that the harvest depends, not upon the soil, but upon the seed sown. The soil responds or refuses to respond according to what that seed is in itself. We all feel how much more nearly this interpretation of the parable harmonises with experience than any other. If it be interpreted in the usual way, then there is no responsibility whatever upon the seed, neither can the soil be blamed for the lack of result due to its own natural hardness, for it cannot help being what it is. But when we come to our Lord's explanation we find how serious our responsibility is, for He teaches that the age will respond or fail to respond according to what we are in ourselves. The age will be hard, rocky, thorny, or fruitful according to the nature of the seed. What a man's influence in the age is going to be depends entirely upon whether the word of the Kingdom is in his heart or not, and further upon his response to the word which is in his heart. Take a man who has never received the word, and put him down in his age, and he cannot produce the influences of the Kingdom. We shall meet such a man in our next study, in the parable of the tares.

Let us now fix our attention upon the men who have heard the word. There has been the primary sowing, the mysterious impartation of the principle cf life which makes of them seeds equal to producing harvest. At this point our parable begins, and we have one sower, the Lord Himself; one soil the age; one seed. men who have acquaintance with the word of the Kingdom. Now, however, we see four results, all depending upon the nature of the seed. To the seed understanding not, the beaten way of the age is hard, and there is no harvest. The seed with no root in itself, the persecuting age destroys. The seed which is careful for the things of the age, the age absorbs and chokes. None of these three bring any harvest. To the seed that understands and obeys and responds in personal life, the age responds, and an abundant harvest is the result.

Members of the Church are here, they are the sons of the Kingdom. Jesus in effect says in this first parable, as in the second, that the harvest of the Kingdom will be produced by implanting in the age such souls as have received the word of the Kingdom. If they receive the word and do not respond to it, they bear no fruit, and do not lift the age toward the Kingdom. If they respond and obey, they will bring forth harvest, thirty, sixty, a hundredfold. Then the philosophy of the parable is that Jesus Christ works toward the realisation of the heavenly Kingdom on earth, by planting in the midst of its life such souls as have heard His word, have received it, and obeyed it. He influences the age through their presence, through their living, through all that they are in themselves.

This is one aspect of Church responsibility. Our inclusive responsibility is that of the evangelisation of the world, but that evangelisation has in it two values; first, the calling out of individual souls, and second, that these may for the time become as seeds planted in order to a greater harvest. In this purpose we see the larger issue of the Church's responsibility. Paul, in his letter to the Romans, says: "The whole creation groaneth and travaileth in pain

together until now," waiting "for the revealing of the sons of God." It may quite correctly be affirmed that the apostle is there speaking of the fact that presently, when the hidden sons of God are manifest with Christ in His advent glory, then will begin the final work of healing creation's pain. That will be the historic fulfilment of the principle, but the principle itself is at work to-day. Wherever creation groans, the only method of healing its wounds and assuaging its grief is that of planting the sons of God in the midst. Wherever such men and women have come to live, there is found, in a measure, the healing of creation's wounds, and the soothing of its pain. That is the great story of missionary enterprise. The sob of the women and children of the dark places of the earth is healed by the preaching of the word, but there would be no healing but for the living presence of those who practise the word they preach. Plant the son of the Kingdom in the midst of an age that is against the King, and he will exert an influence that tells for the Kingdom. Wherever sorrow is assuaged, wherever wounds are healed, wherever love becomes the law of life, wherever men are loosed from the power of sin, there the Kingdom of God is come. And such a harvest is the result of the living seeds flung from the hand of the living Sower upon the soil, which of itself produces no Kingdom result, but which laughs into the harvest of the Kingdom in sure response to the fruitful seed.

Finally, one word by way of application to our own hearts. The harvest the King is seeking is the harvest of the Kingdom. He sows the age with the sons of the Kingdom, and yet many of them are non-productive. We know His word. The question is, What effect are we producing upon our age? The answer depends upon the extent to which the word we know has affected our lives. How many there are who hear the words of the Kingdom, who have never yet understood them. They repeat them, they sing them, they love them perhaps, but there is no resulting harvest in the age in which they live. The harvest of the Kingdom is not found even in their own homes. There is no Kingdom influence exerted in their social circle. There is no compulsion toward the Kingdom produced by their lives in city or nation. Why not? Because they heard the words, but did not understand them. It is possible to recite all the words of the Kingdom by heart, and yet in home life, in social life, in civic life, in national life, to realise nothing.

Or, again, some have gone beyond that. They have not only heard the words, but they rejoice in them. They consent to the glory of the ideal. Yet as the word of the Kingdom sets up its imperial demand within, seeking to change the life, they hinder it. They do not allow it to take root, with the result that the age remains hard and cruel.

Some have gone yet farther. They have heard and obeyed the word up to a certain point, but have never in their deepest heart been delivered from the age itself. No man can exert an influence for God until that deliverance is absolutely his. You were a worker, such a worker that men felt your power; but in the matters of this life you have been "getting on." Oh, this devil of "getting on," when it kills a man's power for God in his age! The care of the age, the deceitfulness of riches, the successes of material life have destroyed the testimony of many for the Kingdom. When a man gives himself wholly to the age, to be great with its greatness, to be wise in its wisdom, he cuts the nerve of his testimony for God. The thorns of worldliness choke him, and the voice that was powerful is silenced, and the life that was productive is barren, and nothing is done for the Kingdom.

But, thank God, there are those who have heard the word, who understand the word, who obey the word, and through whose lives the Kingdom is influential. What is the issue? There is a harvest coming wherever they go, some thirty, some sixty, some a hundredfold. There are men and women whose names never appear in the newspapers, who never found any report of their work even in the manual of their Church, but who have lived in obedience to the word of the King. If angels wrote the epitaph of such at their passing, they would write, These are they who helped the coming of the Kingdom. No finer testimony to successful life could possibly be written.

As we pass out to individual work, teaching in the Sabbath School, speaking amid the needy men and women of the age, whatever it may be, never forget that whenever we win man, woman, or little child to the word of the Kingdom, we are planting another seed in the age, and preparing for the harvest which is yet to be. Every one of us who has heard the word, and who understands it, and obeys it, is part of the King's influence, and every soul we win is another seed planted for the final harvest of His Kingdom.

MATTHEW XIII. 24-30 AND 36-43

THIS is the second and last parable which the King Himself explained to His disciples. It is perfectly clear that this explanation was given to the disciples alone, and at their request. The form in which they preferred that request reveals the impression made upon them by the parable as the Lord spoke it. They did not say, "Explain unto us the parable *of the two sowings,*" or "the parable *of the enemy;*" but, "Explain unto us the parable *of the tares of the field.*" This shows that the emphasis of the King was laid on the matter of the tares.

In considering this parable we shall follow our method with the previous one, first, looking at the simple picture suggested, secondly, attending to the explanation of Jesus, and, thirdly, deducing from that explanation the instruction which it contains for ourselves.

There are three outstanding things in the picture presented. The first may be dismissed quite briefly, but it must not be omitted. "The Kingdom of heaven is likened unto a man that sowed good seed in his field." The picture set forth is that of a field, the property of the man who sows the good seed, and not of the one who sows darnel. The proprietor is at work in his own field.

In the next place we notice that there are two sowings. The sowing of the good seed by the owner with the special desire of gathering a definite harvest is perfectly natural. There is so far nothing out of the common, nothing which specially arrests attention. But now immediately there follows something which is out of place, something which we recognize as wrong, against which our simple sense of right makes protest. It is the sowing of the field with darnel. I make use of the word darnel, because tares as we know them do not bear the slightest resemblance to wheat, and do not therefore suggest to us the essential meaning of this parable. Darnel, on the other hand, is so much like wheat that in the first stages of its growth it is impossible to distinguish between them. Yet they are absolutely different. The farmers of Palestine are perfectly familiar with darnel to-day, and there are some of them who affirm that it is simply degenerate wheat—the effect of a particularly wet and heavy season upon the originally good wheat seed. This, however, is not the case. It may be that a wet season is one in which darnel will flourish while wheat fails; but there is no doubt whatever as to the essential difference between the two. This difference, however, is only manifested in development, and it is in this fact of similarity that the maliciousness of the enemy is discovered.

The third matter which arrests us as we look at the picture is the enemy. We know this man of the second sowing to be a trespasser, for, as we have seen, the field was the property of the one who sowed the good seed therein. He had no right whatever in the field. "While men slept," he came, with subtlety and stealth. In indicating thus the occasion of the enemy's opportunity, there may have been rebuke in the mind of the Master for the men who slept. Be that as it may, the method so far as the foe is concerned marks his wiliness, his cowardliness, his dastardly determination to harm. He was a trespasser, full of subtlety, animated by malice. There was no other motive in his action. He could gain nothing by sowing another's field with darnel, for it is not a saleable produce, and no profit can be made out of its growth. It is as worthless to the man who sows it as to the owner of the field. This sowing, then, was the result of pure malice—if I may bring into conjunction so fine an adjective and so fearful a substantive. It was an act prompted by hatred for the owner, and judging the offence as we should a similar one in our own country, there is no one of us, however tender of heart, who would not consent to its punishment. The absolute meanness of the action appals.

The method of the owner is perfectly natural and proper. "Let both grow together until the harvest." First, for the sake of the good, lest while attempting to uproot the evil some of the good may suffer; and secondly, in order to the full manifestation of the truth concerning the darnel. If these sowings are allowed to work themselves out to consummation, discrimination will be possible upon the basis of manifestation, and in that manifestation there will be vindication of the destinies of darnel and of wheat. The darnel will be bound in bundles for burning. The wheat will be gathered into the garner of the owner.

We recognize at once that in the picture we have the simplicity of a great sublimity, and now turn to our Lord's explanation, first, of the field; secondly, of the two sowings; thirdly, of the harvest. As to the field (verses 36-43), "He that soweth the good seed is the Son of Man, and the field is the world." The word used for world here is not that which He employs later when speaking of the harvest. The phrase, "the end of the *world*," should certainly be translated as in the previous parable,—the consummation or completion of the *age*, but the word used in this connection is *cosmos*, meaning the whole of the ordered universe, including the earth, its inhabitants, and all creation. One cannot help wondering why certain fathers of the Church and theologians of an earlier age insisted on teaching that the field is the Church and that the darnel simply signifies the coming into the Church of unworthy persons and ideals. There is, of course, an element of truth in this; but the King was perfectly clear in His statement, "the field is the world." Thus He claims proprietorship of the whole creation. The same thought underlies the apostle's teaching in that wonderful chapter in his letter to the Romans, when, dealing with the condition of creation in its sorrow and pain, he writes, "The whole creation groaneth and travaileth in pain together." That which is indicated by the phrase, "the whole creation," is that which was also in the mind of the King when He said, "the field is the world." There is infinite poetry in this. The whole creation, every form of life, every condition of being, every part of the great whole belongs to the Son of Man. The creation is His field, and if indeed there be mourning everywhere, if nature is "red in tooth and claw," if it be true that there is suffering throughout all the *cosmos* let us never forget that this field of the world is His, and it is waiting for the sowing of the good seed which is to produce the harvest of the Kingdom. Wherever in the midst of the suffering and sorrow and groaning of creation the Son of Man plants a son of the Kingdom, there He helps towards the healing of the wound, the drying of the tear, and the turning of the groaning into an anthem of praise. I do not know how this appeals to you, or how it may affect you. I can never tell the inexpressible comfort it is to me in all life and service. I never feel that I am engaged, even under the leadership of Christ, in attempting to wrest something from one to whom it belongs. Our toil and conflict are directed rather toward bringing back to the rightful owner that which belongs to Him. "The earth is Jehovah's, and the fulness thereof." A certain man "sowed good seed in his field." I find in these facts a conviction which sends me out upon the track of His feet to serve and to suffer, and to share the travail which makes His Kingdom come. Everything belongs to Him, mountains and valleys, continents and countries, beasts and birds, flowers

and fruits, and men of all kindreds and tribes and nations. The recognition of this fundamental fact is necessary to the interpretation of the parable. The great Kingdom of Jesus is far from its perfect order, but no other than He has any crown rights throughout the whole world.

Turn now to our Lord's explanation of the two sowings. First, the good seed, "these are the sons of the Kingdom;" secondly, we see that the sower of the good seed is the Son of Man; and finally, that the harvest He seeks is the Kingdom itself. Now turn to the other sowing. The sower of darnel is the devil. The very name which Christ uses for him here is suggestive—the adversary, the enemy, or to be perfectly literal, the traducer, the one who from the beginning and continually, traduces, libels, blasphemes God. Notice what this parable teaches about him. First of all, as we have seen, he has no right in the world. He is a trespasser. I once heard a Methodist local preacher say, "The devil is a squatter," and then proceed to explain that, "A squatter is a man who settles on land he has no right to, and works it for his own advantage." With that definition I am perfectly in agreement. It expresses the whole truth concerning the devil. When presently we shall know the mystery of this great personality, we shall perhaps find that he was the god of this world before he fell. It may be that this world was given to him in some past economy which ended in failure. The opening story of the Bible suggests this possibility. There was a certain economy which ended in darkness and void, and it may be that behind that catastrophe is the story of the devil. Be that as it may, we know from Scripture that he left—mark the words—left his "proper habitation;" that is, he wandered from the orbit in which the infinite wisdom of God had placed him, sacrificing all right to his principality. Again I am constrained to exclaim, Oh, the comfort of the certainty that the devil has no claim to the world! I think we have missed much in our thinking and work as Christian people, because we have been too ready to yield to him as his right everything upon which his hand rests. Our business is ever to say, Hands off in the name of the Proprietor: to declare at every point that the whole field belongs to the Son of Man, and wherever it is sown with the seed of evil it is done by an enemy, a marauder. In this parable the King has done what indeed He did in all His life and teaching—dragged the great foe from his hiding-place into clear daylight. To me it is as remarkable and valuable a fact that Jesus came to show the work of the devil as that He came to reveal God. Paul could say, "We are not ignorant of his devices," but he could not have said that until he had been brought into the light of the Christian revelation. It is when a man submits himself to Jesus Christ that he sees clearly, not God only, not himself only, but his enemy also It is one of the great advantages of coming into the light of Christ's teaching that man is enabled to see the devil for what he is, and is able therefore to place a true value on both his person and his purpose.

Then as to the seed. The seed is the sons of the evil—of the evil one. I prefer the word evil to stand in its abstract suggestiveness of not only the evil one, but of all the issue of his work. The seeds producing darnel are the sons of evil. As to the sowing, there is a phrase which we must not miss, "among the wheat." This does not necessarily mean that all who are not Christian people are to be described as darnel. The word "among" has behind it two Greek words. One of these words would suffice for ordinary expression, but the combination of the two lends intensity to the thought. The phrase occurs only four times in the New Testament, once used here, again by Mark in connection with the same teaching, again in the Corinthian letter in quite another realm of thought, and once more in Revelation, where it is said that the Lamb is "in the midst of the throne." It is the most intense way of saying "among." Herein is revealed the subtlety of the foe. He scattered his darnel *among* the wheat. The devil's method is that of mingling the counterfeit with the real. It is that of introducing into the Master's own

property that which is so like the good that at first you cannot tell the difference. That is the devil's mission of imitation. It is the heart of the parable.

What is to be the issue of the two sowings? Their time of operation is to be until "the end of the age," and until then the word of the King is, "Let both grow together until the harvest." Let these two sowings work themselves out to final manifestation, and then there will be separation.

No matter how closely together sons of the Kingdom and sons of evil are planted, in process of time the difference must be seen. The Kingdom heart will manifest a Kingdom life. The evil nature will produce an evil character. "Let them alone." The sons of the Kingdom will influence the age toward the Kingdom, and the King will gather His harvest as the result of their presence in the world. The sons of evil will produce a harvest of abomination which at last the reapers will bind and burn. The harvest of the sons of the Kingdom will be a harvest of sunlight upon the world. They shall "shine forth as the sun in the Kingdom of their Father." The harvest of the sons of evil will be one of evil, of things which offend and defile, and He by His reapers will at the last gather them out and cast them forth to burning.

Now, finally, what instruction are we to gather from this parable? First, that the method of the foe in this age of the Kingdom is that of imitation. This is the teaching of the parable of the darnel. The parable of the mustard seed reveals another quality, and of the leaven yet another; but here the enemy's method of imitation is revealed. He began in the days of the apostles. Ananias and Sapphira, Simon Magus with his following were darnel among the wheat. Later on, as the apostolic writings show, men crept in privily, came in unawares, men who were "not of us," who taught another doctrine and yet talked in the language of the Christian faith. It was perpetually the method of imitation. Leaving behind the apostolic times and passing through the centuries it is still to be found. The essential power of the sons of the Kingdom has been imitated by false power. Their true purity has been counterfeited by that false sanctity which insists upon external things, and knows nothing of cleanness of the heart. Even to-day the method is still apparent. In matters of doctrine men are taking the great phrases of the New Testament, and are interpreting them so as to contradict their simplest meaning. In matters of spirituality, some " holiness " movements have run riot, until they have become bestial, and an unholy traffic with matters occult masquerades as spiritual religion. Imitation is the devil's master-method.

The method of the King is still that of waiting for the development of the inner truth. No harm can come to the good seed because darnel is sown beside it, and in order that judgment upon the evil may be complete it must be permitted to work itself out to final manifestation. The two sowings will go forward to the end of the age, and difficulty is often caused through not recognizing this truth. One person tells me that the world is getting worse and worse, while another affirms that it is getting better and better. The pity is that the two quarrel, for they are both right. Evil has become more evil in every age. Devilry has become more devilish with the passing of the centuries. Evil to-day is far more diabolic than anything which existed before the coming of Christ. It is more cunning, more insidious, more cruel in its refinement.

On the other hand, goodness is being manifested on ever higher planes, and the Kingdom harvest is surely growing. Everywhere darnel is growing by the side of the wheat. What, then, is our duty toward the darnel? I am sometimes asked to take part in the uprooting of imitations, but the method of the King is other. He said, " Let it alone."

The King will not always let it alone. There is a day coming when this age shall end. Then there will be the burning of the darnel and the garnering of the wheat. The King will clear out of His field all the things which offend.

There are questions not discussed in this parable, and we must not therefore look for them here. It is taken for granted, for instance, that a man who is a son of evil may be changed into a son of the Kingdom. Thank God that it is possible. It is the stupendous miracle of Christianity that the son of evil, the darnel, can become changed into the son of the Kingdom, the wheat. This is one of the things impossible with men, but possible with God. Everywhere such men are to be found, and where they live and work, the Kingdom of heaven is growing. It is the comfort of the hour. Darnel is everywhere; but wheat is everywhere. Throughout the world the King has sown the sons of His Kingdom, and their presence everywhere is creating an influence and preparing for the consummation of the age.

MATTHEW XIII. 31, 32

WE now come to the first of the parables of which the King gave no distinct explanation. It is therefore important that we proceed with care. There are perils of interpretation which we must avoid, and principles of interpretation which we must observe. The perils to which I refer are two ;—first, popularity of opinion ; secondly, misinterpretation of history. Unless we guard against the first we shall constantly find ourselves mistaken as to the meaning of Scripture. The fact that in the judgment of a majority of expositors a passage has a certain meaning is not necessarily proof that that meaning

is correct. Popular interpretations of the Old Testament Scriptures resulted in the crucifixion of Jesus Christ.

We need also very carefully to guard against a misinterpretation of history which may drive us to misinterpretation of the parables. We may be inclined to say these parables mean certain things because of what has happened in the centuries : while yet as a matter of fact we do not correctly understand the history.

As to the principles of interpretation. First, we must expect to find in this parable harmony of teaching with the other parables. We must be suspicious of any interpretation of the one parable which contradicts that of any other. We may take it for granted that Christ is consistent in His teaching. Hence the value of the fact that the first two parables were explained by the King Himself. From these explanations we may proceed to an examination of all the rest. Once again, we must remember the consistency of our Lord's figures. He does not confuse them in His use. The sower of the different parables always represents the same person, and so throughout. When He has given us the explanation of a figure we may apply that explanation uniformly.

Let us now inquire into the meaning of our parable, remembering both the perils and principles of interpretation. It is generally believed that by it Jesus intended to teach the satisfactory growth of the Kingdom idea until it became dominant in human history, and an expositor of Holy Scripture, whom I personally value most highly, but from whom at this point I differ, expresses the popular interpretation as follows:

"The parables already considered might suggest that the Kingdom was destined to partial and shaded success. The first spoke of three parts of the seed as coming to nothing, and the second, of the fourth part as coming up amid tares. The listeners might say, 'Is this all?' Therefore in the next two, our Lord sets forth a brighter aspect of the future of the Kingdom, exhibiting in the former its growth from small beginnings to great magnitude, and in the second its transforming influence on the mass in which it is deposited."

Such a view admits in the first two parables what they most certainly suggest and teach; but it then declares that the next two contradict that teaching. I claim, therefore, that such interpretation, though popular, is incorrect. Take the history of the Kingdom during the past nineteen centuries. Is there any one who will care to affirm that it has been a complete success? Is it not true—if I may borrow this phrase again—that it has met only with "partial and shaded success"? Who will care to say that the Kingdom of God has ever been truly exhibited among

men? We talk very glibly about Christian nations; but there are no Christian nations. Of course, if we use the phrase in a limited sense we may by comparison be called Christian nations; but even so I fear that our Christianity, manifested nationally, is of a very poor type. The world has never seen the Kingdom of God set up in perfection yet; and notwithstanding the fact that nineteen centuries have passed away, the Kingdom idea of Jesus has met with but "partial and shaded success." Let no one misinterpret me, God is not failing. He is doing the work He intends to do, and beyond the little while of this age and the tiny span of our endeavour, He has other and mighty work to accomplish. Do not let us ever attempt to interpret the doings of God by the appearances of half an hour, or half a millennium. To make any parable teach the complete and final success of the Kingdom purpose in the present age is not only to misinterpret the other parables to make them square with this idea, but it is to misinterpret the actual facts of history. The general teaching of the parables is that throughout this age there will be difficulty, limitation, admixture, opposition. Separation between the conflicting elements is postponed to the consummation of the age, when perfect victory will follow.

Now, notice the figures in this parable which have appeared in previous ones. The seed—and we have already seen that in the thought of Jesus the seed is ever that of human lives in which the word has been realised. The sower—according to His own teaching the sower is Himself, the Son of Man. The soil—and as we have heard Him say, "the field is the world." The birds —and according to His interpretation already given, they are such as harm rather than help. These facts must be kept in mind as we proceed to examine this parable, first as to the picture presented, and then as to the lessons taught.

The picture presented is one of an unnatural development, and unintended issue. The mustard is well known in Palestine, and is not a tree, but a herb. As a tree it has been well described as a "garden shrub outdoing itself," and all attempts to make it symbolic of unqualified success are of the nature of special pleading. In connection with this parable I have been interested to notice how many expositors refer to a sentence in Dr. Thomson's *The Land and the Book.* He says:

"Is this wild mustard that is growing so luxuriantly and blossoming so fragrantly along our path? It is; and I have always found it here in the spring; and, a little later than this, the whole surface of the vale will be gilded over with its yellow flowers. *I have seen this plant on the rich plain of Akkar as tall as the horse and his rider.*"

It is this last sentence which is so constantly quoted in support of the idea that the mustard seed becomes a tree. Let us, however, read further from Dr. Thomson in this connection. He continues:

"It has occurred to me on former visits that the mustard tree of the parable probably grew at this spot, or possibly at Tabiga, near Capernaum, for the water in both is somewhat similar and so are the vegetable productions. To furnish an adequate basis for the parable, it is necessary to suppose that a variety of it was cultivated in the time of our Saviour, which grew to an enormous size, and shot forth large branches, so that the fowls of the air could lodge in the branches of it. It may have been perennial and have grown to a considerable tree, and there are traditions in the country of such so large that a man could climb into them; and after having seen red pepper bushes grow on year after year into tall shrubs, and the castor bean line the brooks about Damascus like the willows and poplars, I can readily credit the existence of mustard trees large enough to meet the demands of our Lord's parable."

Thus it is evident that Dr. Thomson, after careful observation, was convinced that it was possible for there to be, occasionally and exceptionally, a mustard tree large enough to correspond with the description of Jesus. What is the necessary and simple deduction? That if there be such a tree it is abnormal, unnatural, something which has escaped its original intention.

Again, so accurate a writer as Dr. Hamilton says:

"When this little seed is sown in the 'garden' or 'field' it shoots up, and soon overtops the pulse and other potherbs around it and becomes a 'great tree;' not meaning thereby an oak or a cedar, but a plant sufficiently tall and expansive for birds to find shelter in the branches."

These quotations serve to show the difficulty that the popular interpretation of this parable at once creates. A mustard seed cannot properly and normally produce a magnificent and far-spreading tree. It must be recognized that Jesus was describing something out of the ordinary, something unnatural. The mustard is a herb and not a tree, and if it so happen that the mustard plant, which is naturally small and unobtrusive, pass out of the stage of the yellow flowering herb of beauty to that of a great and mighty tree with branches, then both process and result are abnormal and unnatural. Dr. Carr says, "The mustard plant does not grow to a very great height, so that Luke's expression, 'waxed a great tree,' must not be pressed." But I cannot consent so to deal with Luke's expression. I must abide by the actual words, and doing so I learn from the lips of Jesus the fact of the perverted growth of the Kingdom in this age. The mustard seed was to become greater than all herbs, but when it becomes greater than its true species it is abnormal. It is not what the man who planted it intended it to be, and the fact that it affords lodgment in its branches for the birds of the heaven, proves its abnormality.

What, then, are the lessons which the parable teaches us? First, that in this age there will be an unnatural development of the Kingdom principle. The true line of development is suggested by the figure of the mustard seed which is that of lowliness, meekness, unobtrusiveness. What has been the actual development? From the mustard seed, the herb denoting humility, has arisen a great and lofty tree significant of pride, dominance, mastership. I recall a conversation I once had with Sir Hall Caine, soon after the publication of his book, *The Christian*. I strongly objected to what seemed to me to be a misinterpretation of the Christian ideal in that book, and I said to him, "Do you mean to tell the world that John Storm is a Christian?" His answer was a remarkable one. "By no means. I intend to teach the fact that we do not understand what Christ really taught." He then gave me two illustrations of what he meant. "I am prepared," he said, "to put the whole ethical teaching of Jesus into two phrases: first, 'He that is greatest among you shall be your servant,' and second, 'Lay not up for yourselves treasures upon the earth.'" I am not for the moment discussing the comprehensiveness of these two principles—I am simply quoting Sir Hall Caine. He then declared, what is perfectly patent to all of us, that our national greatness is such as has resulted from our violation of these two principles. We have sought power before service, and possession before sacrifice.

Turning from Sir Hall Caine's declaration of the nation's failure to realise the Kingdom, I ask if the Church of God has realized that Kingdom in its ideal of lowliness, of meekness, of service? In the days when Jesus was preaching the Kingdom His own immediate followers were constantly asking, Who is master among us? Who is the greatest among us? Who shall sit at the King's right hand in power? In the early Church the same spirit was manifest, men so craving for mastership, homage, power, that Peter was compelled to write to those who had oversight of the flock of God, charging them not to "lord it" over God's heritage.

In process of time Constantine espoused the cause of Christianity. With reference to this epoch one of the old expositors says that the mustard seed planted in Judea was but a small thing, but it suddenly sprang into a tree, great and magnificent, in that wonderful hour when Constantine became a Christian. That statement is, I believe, true, but was the development good or bad? Did it help Christianity or hinder it? I am of opinion that nothing so hindered the true Kingdom principle in the world, as Constantine's espousal of the cause of Christianity.

In the Papacy the same principle is manifest. The spirit of the Church which desires worldly power and worldly authority, is the very opposite of the spirit of lowliness and meekness and service. The small and lowly seed has become a great tree, and into its branches the fowls of the air have come to lodge. Greatness in external and material things is but a false greatness, and wherever the Church has risen to anything like worldly power it has become a refuge for the things that are unclean and polluting and life-destructive.

We must remind ourselves again that the Lord in these parables is not dealing with the true nature of the Kingdom, neither is He declaring the ultimate issue thereof. God's Kingdom will yet be set up on this earth, and the true principles of greatness revealed in His own humility and enunciated in His teaching will be the principles which obtain in the affairs of the world. Somewhere on in that dim distance— and measuring distances by our measures it sometimes looks a long way —he will be counted great who has girded himself with a towel to serve. Sometime, when God's great Kingdom comes, we shall not imagine that he is great who has mastered his fellow man; rather, he who has served him in lowly and loving unobtrusiveness. The ideal is already dawning. Men are beginning to see its glory. An influence is being exerted to-day among men which will come to harvest when the King Himself comes. Do not imagine that this parable teaches the ultimate failure of the Kingdom life and growth, but it does teach comparative failure, the result of misinterpretation and misapplication of the ideals of Jesus. Men have attempted by manipulation of material things to make of Christianity a great imperial power. The figure of the tree as denoting worldly greatness was used of Nebuchadnezzar and of Pharaoh, and in this sense our Lord made use of it. True to His prediction, the seed typifying the meekness and lowliness of the Kingdom ideal has developed along a false line which has resulted in a tree of worldly power affording shelter and protection to that which is evil and dishonouring.

What is the bearing of this study upon us? Surely first the recognition of the facts of the case in order that we may be aided thereby in our life and service. I pass by that application, however, that in a closing word I may make a personal one. In our individual life, and so far as possible in our Church capacity, we ought to attempt to realise the purpose of the King. We ought to be ready to turn from the false greatness which He disowns to the true greatness which He recognizes. In individual life, and also in the corporate life of the Church, we shall realise His purpose in proportion as we remember that in meekness and lowliness, in unceasing zeal and consecrated service, in perpetual outpouring of the life in sacrificial toil, in endless running on His errands of tender mercy we shall be most loyal to the King, and shall best give the world to see the infinite contrast between the material ideal of pomp and pageantry and pride, and the spiritual ideal of simplicity and sweetness and service.

Christ was under no delusion as to what would happen in this age. A sower sowing seed, and only a quarter of it responsive! A sower sowing seed, and an enemy sowing darnel! A sower sowing seed which transgresses the bounds of its own nature and becomes a tree sheltering evil things. It is for us to bow in the presence of His knowledge of the characteristics of the age which He was introducing; but it is ours, moreover, to give ourselves so fully to Him in consecration as to realise in the sphere of our own responsibility His ideals and His purposes, and so to move toward the consummation of the age, and the dawning of the one which lies beyond.

MATTHEW XIII. 33

THERE are two interpretations of this parable. The first and the most popular is that which treats leaven as the type of the Kingdom. The other claims that the whole picture is required to set forth what the King intended to teach concerning the Kingdom. That is to say, one method of interpretation lays emphasis upon the fact that the Lord said, " The Kingdom of heaven is like unto leaven." The other interpretation insists that to stop there is to miss the Master's meaning, and that it is necessary to read " The Kingdom of heaven is like unto leaven, which a woman took, and hid in three measures of meal." Either leaven alone is the type of the Kingdom, or all the facts of the picture—the meal, the woman, the leaven, the hiding, and the issue—are required in order to understand what the King intended to teach.

If the first interpretation of the parable, that leaven is the symbol of the Kingdom, be the correct one, we are necessarily driven to the conclusion that in this instance leaven must be the type of good, and that as a result of its working all things will be finally brought into subjection to the King. That is the view which seems to be held to-day by the great majority of expositors.

According to the second view leaven is not a type of good but of evil, as it is in every other case in Scripture. It is thus the type of a principle which affects for evil the Kingdom testimony of this particular age. The ultimate issue described, therefore, is not the conquest of the age by the principles of the Kingdom, but rather the intermixture with the Kingdom testimony of forces which enfeeble it.

If a view is not to be accepted because of its popularity, neither ought it to be rejected on that account. There are, however, other reasons which compel me to accept the second theory as the true one. I do so in the first place because the former view is out of harmony with the symbolic use of leaven in the Bible in other places. Those who hold the first view admit frankly that this is the only case in which leaven is used as a type of good. Uniformly, from its first mention to its last, with this one exception—if it be an exception—leaven is a type of evil. In its actual effect leaven ever produces disintegration and corruption, and in all other cases it is used in harmony with this fact, as a type of evil. I do not personally believe that in this one instance there is a departure from the general rule. But secondly, and this to me is a more convincing proof, I cannot accept the more popular interpretation, because it contradicts the teaching of all the other parables, not one of which suggests that the Kingdom influence in this age is to be victorious wholly and absolutely. Mixture is suggested from beginning to end. The sowing of the seed in the first parable results not in universal harvest of good, for three-quarters of the seed so sown is inoperative. In the second we have not merely the sowing of good seed, but the deliberate sowing of darnel, and the Master distinctly commanded that there was to be no separation until the consummation of the age. In the parable of the mustard seed, while its growing was a symbol of good, its false development revealed the intermixture of evil. If these first three parables teach that this age is not to be characterised by perfect victory for good, and if the leaven is a type of good, then all the teaching of the first three is contradicted by that of the fourth.

A further reason for my inability to accept the more general interpretation is that the history of the centuries and the experience of the present hour alike contradict that interpretation, and harmonise rather with the teaching of the earlier parables. There has been no complete mastery of evil by good in any part of the world in any age, nor even in the Church of God. The mixture of the two principles is manifest everywhere. Finally, I cannot believe that the teaching of the parable is according to popular interpretation, because it would be out of harmony with the other parables as to method. It is perpetually insisted that Jesus said, "The Kingdom of heaven is like unto leaven," and that therefore no one has any right to say that leaven is not typical of the Kingdom of heaven. But in the parable of the darnel we read, "The Kingdom of heaven is likened

unto a man," and here nobody suggests that the man in that parable is the type of the Kingdom of heaven. It is absolutely necessary to take the whole picture of the man sowing darnel in a field already sown with good seed in order to understand the teaching of the Lord. We have no more right to pause upon the word "leaven" in the fourth parable than upon the word "man" in the second. If the word "leaven" exhausts the Master's teaching at this point concerning the similitude which He is suggesting, then the word "man" exhausts His thought in the parable of the darnel concerning the similitude which He there sets up. The same test may be applied to other parables. In a subsequent one the King said, "The Kingdom of heaven is like unto a king," and if we are compelled to stop at the word "leaven" in this parable, we must do so at the word "king." It is evident, therefore, that to understand the teaching the whole picture must be kept in mind. That picture is one of three measures of meal, of a woman deliberately hiding the leaven in the meal, and of the working of that leaven until all the meal is under its influence.

Now let us examine the symbolism. In order to do so we inquire first, What is the essential thing in the picture? Then, What are those matters which affect the essential thing? As regards the first, we reply that the thing of primary importance is not the leaven, and not the woman, but the three measures of meal. The woman and the leaven are considered according to their relation to the meal, and the effect produced is regarded also in its relation to the meal, "Till it was all leavened." Therefore, the matter of supreme interest is the meal, and what happened to it. We proceed to inquire, then, what Jesus meant by using this figure. It has been correctly pointed out that it is both important and interesting to interpret any expression or thought in Scripture by the presence thereof in other parts of Scripture, and especially by its first occurrence. Following that principle of investigation, we find that the first occasion upon which the three measures of meal are mentioned in Scripture is as far back as the book of Genesis (xviii. 6). There we have an account of the entertainment of Jehovah by Abraham. In one of the great Theophanies of the Old Testament Jehovah manifested Himself as an Angel. Whether Abraham at the moment knew Who the visitor was, I am not prepared to affirm; but recognizing Him as supernatural he hastened to entertain Him. In order to this, Sarah took three measures of meal and prepared it. Passing on through the Bible I find the figure again in connection with the meal offering. For this there was fixed a minimum and a maximum amount. Gideon brought an offering, and Hannah also, and on each occasion three measures of meal are spoken of. In the book of Ezekiel, in connection with the final and perfect offerings, seven times over in one brief instruction the amount of the meal offering is three measures of meal. In the Divine economy the meal offering followed the burnt offering. The burnt offering signifies the devotion of the life to God. The meal offering was the result of cultivation, manufacture, preparation, and, therefore, so far as man was concerned, always signified dedication of his work to God. Remember, too, the meal offering was an offering of hospitality; part was retained by the worshipper and part was at the disposal of the priest. In the meal offering, then, we have a symbol of the perfect communion established between the worshipper and God upon the basis of the worshipper's service. From the simple rites of home life was taken that which was to be the perpetual symbol of dedication to God in service as the ground of perpetual communion with Him.

In the list of offerings it was most explicitly commanded that no leaven was to be mixed with the meal offering. Its presence would have been the symbol of intrusion of that which corrupted, into the fellowship of service. In our parable then, fellowship with God in service is seen to be marred during the present age by the introduction of a corrupting influence. The woman mixing the meal stands as the representative of authority and management in the matter of service to God. Turning

to the leaven, we repeat that it is in itself a corrupt thing, and can only exercise a corrupting influence. I know it may be objected that in our common life to-day it is used, as, for instance, in the making of bread. It is, however, by no means certain that this method is the best possible. Just as we are coming to understand that the intrusion into the physical life of man of alcohol is in itself a grave peril, it may be that presently we shall come to believe that the use of leaven is injurious physically. That I am not prepared to discuss; it is simply a passing suggestion. The fact that leaven is used in certain ways to-day does not for a moment affect the simple truth that if it have its perfect outworking the result is destruction. It is in itself corrupt, and is always an agent of corruption. When Sarah prepared the meal for the angel, she mixed no leaven with it. Leaven was distinctly forbidden in the meal offering, and when Paul used the figure of the leaven, whether in reference to the Levitical code, the Jewish custom, or the Master's use of it, it was always in the sense of evil. " Your glorying is not good. Know ye not that a little leaven leaveneth the whole lump? Purge out the old leaven, that ye may be a new lump, even as ye are unleavened. For our passover also hath been sacrificed, even Christ: wherefore let us keep the feast, not with old leaven, neither with the leaven of malice and wickedness, but with the unleavened bread of sincerity and truth."

In the parable, then, we see a woman, the type of authority and management, hiding leaven, the emblem of disintegration and corruption, in the meal, symbol of service and fellowship. Such is the principle of the parable. What, then, according to this interpretation, does it teach? It first recognizes that the Kingdom testimony in the present age must be based upon the fellowship of the people of God with Him in incorruptness; that the Church and the individual can only bear testimony which is influential for the Kingdom of God as they are entirely separated from all that of which leaven is the symbol. Underneath the oaks of Mamre, after participation in the symbolic meal, Abraham stood talking face to face with the One Whom he had entertained. There he pleaded for Sodom, and his right of approach, his right of appeal, his right of argument were based upon the fact of his personal separation from all the corrupting influences of the country into which he had been brought, the unleavened cakes which Sarah had prepared being the symbol of that separation. While Abraham thus interceded with Jehovah, Lot was in the midst of Sodom; a righteous man, according to the teaching of Peter in his epistle, and yet utterly without influence for good in the city. Lot could do nothing for Sodom. He could not lift it. He could not persuade it. He could not save it. If the city was nearly saved, it was not by the influence of Lot, but by the intercession of Abraham. Lot, though a good man in his personal attitude and in his deepest intention, had corrupted his testimony and lost his power by admitting the influences of Sodom into his heart. Abraham, on the other hand, living in separation from its sin, had maintained his power to pray for Sodom. Similarly in the teaching of the parable. The Kingdom testimony depends upon separation. It follows by necessary sequence that testimony for the King is weakened in the measure in which the Church in her management of her own affairs—the woman becoming the type of ecclesiastical government—is weakened by the intrusion of such motives and methods as are worldly.

The use of the word "leaven" in the New Testament is most remarkable. Its first occurrence, in the actual reading of the books rather than in the chronology of events, is in our text. Later on, as the King came to Cæsarea Philippi, and approached the crisis when the period of His propaganda merged into that of His Passion, He warned His disciples to "Beware of the leaven of the Pharisees and Sadducees." Mark tells us that He said, "Beware of the leaven of the Pharisees, and the leaven of Herod;" while Luke reports Him as saying, "Beware ye of the leaven of the Pharisees, which is hypocrisy."

Coming to the letter to the Corinthians, from which I have already quoted, Paul uses the figure in connection with the toleration in the Church of an incestuous person, and the lack of discipline which characterised that toleration. Yet again, in the Galatian epistle, in combating the influence of Judaizing teachers, Paul declared, "A little leaven leaveneth the whole lump." These references exhaust the use of the figure in the New Testament. Thus in the Old and New alike, leaven is the symbol of that against which the men of faith are to guard. From these references we may clearly see its evil nature. Christ distinctly affirmed that the leaven of the Pharisees was hypocrisy; that is, the acting of a part, professing to be something which one really is not, the uttering with the lips of certain formulæ of devotion while the heart is not subject to the King. The leaven of the Sadducees was that of rationalism. They denied angel, spirit, resurrection. The leaven of Herod was that of materialism, government by the manifestation of material splendour. He overawed his people by pageantry and display. Ignoring true greatness, he laid all emphasis upon external magnificence, and the result was the utter corruption of his empire.

According to Paul, leaven was the symbol of the toleration of evil inside the Church. He used it in connection with a man living in actual impurity, to whom had been given the shelter of her fellowship. Again, leaven was the type of formalism, and of return to such ritualistic practices as robbed religion of its spirit and life.

To summarize, the New Testament teaches that hypocrisy is leaven; rationalism is leaven; a material idea of government is leaven; toleration of evil within the borders of the Church is leaven; formalism is leaven. Any or all of these things serve to break up the life of the Church, and a weakened testimony results. They constitute a ferment, a disturbance, a disintegration. Wherever the Church has come under the influence of such evils, corruption has spread throughout, manifested in spoiled lives and feeble witness to the Kingdom of God.

If we turn from this interpretation of our parable to the facts of history, what do we find? Has it not been the case that the Church's power to speak authoritatively of the mystery of God, and to exhibit the benefits and enforce the claims of the Kingdom in the world, has been paralysed by the evil things of which the New Testament clearly teaches leaven to be the symbol? Is it not true that at the present moment the Church's power to bring the world under conviction concerning the Kingdom of God is feeble because of her complicity with evil things? She is still weakened by the leaven of hypocrisy, which is profession without possession: by the leaven of rationalism, which is denial of the supernatural: by the leaven of materialism, which is the adoption of the world's standpoints and principles, making the fact of Christ one of ostentation rather than one of purity and power. And is it not true that not least among the leavening influences at work is that weak toleration of evil, and false pity for the wrongdoer which allows him to stay within her borders, making her incapable of speaking with authority to those in rebellion against the Kingdom of God? Moreover, is it not true that formalism in a thousand different forms, expressing the widespread hankering after ritual, is a leavening force to-day, marring our testimony and spoiling our service of God which can only be effectual when based upon our own separation to Him?

In this connection I say, as I have said in dealing with former parables, that this is not a picture of the final fact concerning the Kingdom of God. It is a picture of the age which ends with the advent. "When the Son of Man cometh, shall He find faith on the earth?" The popular answer of theology is, Yes. Christ's answer is, No; and it is infinitely better in order to do our work as it ought to be done, that we should accept His estimate of our age. It may be objected that this outlook is pessimistic in the extreme. It would be, indeed, if this age were the final one; but it is not so, it is only initial. With the flaming of His advent feet will come the Kingdom administration of the King's own presence. For that the world is waiting, and that we, by consecration, are attempting to hasten.

Thus far we have considered the first four parables, those spoken to the disciples in the hearing of the multitudes. In them, two things are made perfectly clear. First, that the Kingdom influence is to be felt from beginning to end of the age. The Son of Man sows His good seed and waits for the harvest; and there is relationship with God on the part of His own in separation and service. We have also seen that throughout the age there is present and at work the principle of evil. Three-fourths of the good seed fails of harvest, and the enemy deliberately intermixes with the wheat the darnel. There is a false development even of the good into ostentatious display which is out of harmony with the true spirit of the King. The meal offering of fellowship in service is corrupted by the intrusion of the leaven of impurity.

There are other aspects of this age to which we now come in parables addressed only to those who were His own disciples.

MATTHEW XIII. 44

WE now turn to the second section of the parables, that is, to those which the King uttered to His disciples alone. Having left the multitudes, His disciples gathered about Him in the quietness of the house. There, first in answer to the request they preferred, He explained to them the parable of the darnel, and then proceeded to give them further instruction.

As we turn to the consideration of these parables we must still bear in mind that our Lord is dealing with the subject of the Kingdom in the age between His advents. The view-point now, however, is changed. There are distinct differences between the first four and the last four parables. In the first series the King was addressing Himself especially to men of sight, to those who would watch events, to those who, in all probability, would be intellectually interested in the progress or failure of the Kingdom He had preached; that is, to men who were not in the Kingdom, but who viewed it from the outside as interested spectators. He had therefore dealt with such aspects of the Kingdom as would be patent to all observers—the different results dependent upon the quality of the seed, the enemy's imitation, the unnatural development of the Kingdom principle into material power, the corruption of the Church's influence by the introduction of wrong methods. All these have been evident to those who have watched in every successive age.

Now, in the parables which remain, the King addresses Himself no longer to men of sight. He speaks from this moment exclusively to men of faith, to such as live not merely in the consciousness of things seen, but in the confidence of things unseen. Therefore, as in speaking to the men of sight He had dealt with the evident things of the Kingdom, so in speaking to men of faith He set forth the hidden things of the Kingdom. Having declared what the external manifestation of the Kingdom would be in this age, He proceeded to show to His own circle of disciples what God is accomplishing. The parables we are considering, therefore, will teach us the specific values of the Kingdom in this age, from the standpoint of the Divine purpose and economy. Let us, then, pause to glance in broad outline at these parables which we are about to consider.

The first one sets forth the relation of this age to the purpose of God for the whole world. The great sentence is, "He . . . buyeth that field." In the parable of the pearl we see the relation of this age to other spheres and other ages. It is the story of the gathering out from this age of all the precious treasure which is to belong to succeeding ages, and in them to have its mission. In the parable of the drag-net there is revealed the method of this age in the economy of God. Finally, the parable of the householder, bringing things new and old out of his treasure house, indicates the responsibility of the

disciples in this age, in view of the teaching of all the former parables.

In considering the first in order, the parable of the treasure, we shall follow our usual habit, and notice, first, the picture presented. In doing so, we must still bear in mind the principle insisted upon, of the consistency maintained in the use of the figures in these parables as throughout all the Bible. Bearing this in mind, we find two figures we have already met with, and which have had explanation. There are also two new figures at which we shall specially look. The figures already used are those of the field and the man. The field has appeared before, and we have seen the Son of Man sowing therein His good seed, and the enemy sowing his darnel. We have, moreover, seen the mustard seed planted in the field. What the field was in the earlier parables, it is also in this. We go back to our Lord's direct explanation—" The field is the world." The field, therefore, in which the treasure was discovered and hidden is the world. The second thing in this parable which we have met with before, is the man. In each case he has been the King Himself—the sower of the seed in the first parable, the man who sowed the good seed in the second, and again, the man sowing the mustard seed. The man, then, in this parable who finds the treasure and then hides it, is the Son of Man Himself. Of the new elements in the parable, the first is that of the treasure, hidden in the field, discovered, and hidden again. The second element, which is new, is that of purchase, and purchase at cost, " He goeth and selleth all that he hath, and buyeth that field." This presence of two old figures with the two new ones in our parable should help us in the study of it. On two points we are relieved of the necessity for speculation. Concerning the field and the man, we start with light already in our possession. I think, in the light of these things, we may now discuss the new figures, those of the treasure and of purchase.

It will immediately be seen that our interpretation of the parable will conflict with the popular conception of its meaning, which explains both the treasure in this parable and the pearl in the next as a type of salvation, or Christ. If that be so, then the man who found the treasure in one case, and the pearl in the other, is the sinner. Any such view contradicts the figurative language of the earlier parables, and is indeed nothing short of absurd. It may be said that this is a strong statement to make. I make it, nevertheless, without hesitation. If, indeed, the hidden treasure is salvation, and I am the man who finds, then I am able to purchase that which contains my salvation, and am saved by selling all I have. My own conception of my true position is that when I seek for salvation, my condition is bankrupt, and I can only obtain it as the free gift of God's grace. If the hymn which we have sometimes sung be true—

" I've found the pearl of greatest price !
  My heart doth sing for joy ;
And sing I must, for Christ is mine !
  Christ shall my song employ,"

then it is possible for me out of something I possess to purchase Jesus Christ. It surely needs no argument to prove that there is no warrant in Scripture, or indeed in the experience of men, for accepting such a view of the method of salvation.

Claiming, then, that the two figures referred to have their true explanation in the use made of them in the earlier parables, we affirm that the man who found the treasure is Christ, and that the field in which He hid the treasure is the world. We turn at once to the teaching of the parable concerning the treasure, and concerning its purchase.

If we think in all simplicity of the field as the world, there can be very little difficulty in discovering what the treasure is which the King finds therein. That hidden treasure is the latent possibility in the world of the realisation of the Kingship and government of God. The principles of that government, the order of that government, and the beauty of that government all constitute the treasure hidden in the world. The world is made for the display of the Kingdom and government of God. The being whom God placed in dominion is in rebellion against Him, and therefore the whole territory lies waste, failing to realise, and therefore failing to manifest, the breadth and beauty and beneficence of the Kingdom of God. Supposing, for the sake of argument, that this world is under observation by other worlds, does it reveal these things? It may be said that this is a piece of gratuitous imagination, but I submit that it is quite in order, for if we do not know that other worlds are observing ours, revelation has assured us that the " angels desire to look into these things," and it is impossible not to believe that the earth is the centre of observation in the universe of God. My question, then, is, supposing other worlds are watching this world, does the present condition of things exhibit the glory of the Divine government? There are some aspects, some places, and some matters, concerning which of course our answer would have to be, Yes. For eyes which are clear enough to see, every flower that decks the sod exhibits the glory of the Divine government; and the coming of seed-time and harvest, and the regular rotation of the seasons, attest the perfection of His rule. But in all the higher facts of life is there not everywhere manifest a condition of chaos? Taking men, not in any individual case, or even, perhaps, in the small circle of personal friendship, but in the broad outlook upon humanity as a whole, does the human race exhibit the glory of God's Kingship? Are there not in the world habitations of cruelty? Are there not places where darkness dwells and devilry obtains? Or if we come to the places upon which the light is falling, do we not find that what we call civilisation is endeavouring to make unrighteous profit out of the uncivilised? I imagine that were I a visitor from some other planet I should be inclined to say, Where is God? The earth is made for Him. It is His, and in every blade of grass there thrill the forces of His life, and every flower sings the song of His glory, but when I come to examine the men who should be supremely expressing the fact of God's government, I cannot discern the glory of the Kingdom. It is not yet clearly manifest. The world does not know it experimentally, and cannot therefore reveal what the Kingdom of God really means. We sing of it, and speak of it, and imagine that we see it in the light of morning, and the darkness of night. It has been the perpetual refrain of the song of prophets, seers, and psalmists; but experimentally the world has not found it. It is the supreme fact, and yet it is hidden.

But the man in the parable found it. The finding was not a discovery which startled him. He knew that the field contained the treasure, and he came deliberately to seek it. What does this parable suggest concerning the Kingdom? First, that the King knew this hidden fact of the government of God in the world. He, looking through the chaos, clearly saw the cosmos. He, looking at the sheep scattered and harried by wolves, saw through and beyond the vision to the still waters and quiet resting-places and the flock of God shepherded from all harm. He saw the Kingdom as it ought to be through the Kingdom as it was. He knew the hidden secret of the world. This is one of the fundamental truths necessary to the understanding of all Christ's love, and necessary, moreover, to any co-operation with Him in service. What is equal to the sustenance of the heart in strength in the midst of the travail and toil of Christian service? Simply a clear vision of the Divine possibility which lies behind all the dereliction, both in the case of the individual and of the world at large. It was this hidden treasure which this man knew of and brought to light. He knew that where ruin reigned, order might prevail. He saw that every man, and all society, yes, and every blade of grass, and every inch of earthly territory, were of God and through God, and could only realise their latent possibilities in relation to His Kingship. He discovered in the world the treasure, the Kingdom idea.

Jesus exhibited this in strange ways during His ministry. He declared it with unceasing iteration. His one message as He passed from place to place was that of the Kingdom of God. Flowers? God clothed them. Chil-

dren? God's angels guarded them. Men? God's Kingdom was their first concern. He saw that everything was in God and of God, and He set Himself to tell men that God is King. He revealed in the flashes of His simplest sentences, and in the glory of His set discourses, the truth concerning the unrealised values of the world. He came into the field in which His treasure was hidden. It existed though men did not know it. Every man was capable of God's government. All society was waiting for the recognition of the throne. The whole world needed the Divine administration. But all this was hidden from the eyes of men. Men were in rebellion, nature was in rebellion. Sin and sighing were everywhere. Or, to put the whole fact in the forceful language of the apostle, "The whole creation groaneth and travaileth in pain together until now." Behind the ruin He saw the possibility, and in teaching and doing He discovered this possibility to His age, and, to all subsequent ages. In His personal life He realised all that the psalmist declared concerning man (Psalm viii), He had dominion over fish and fowl, and over the beasts of the field. In the hour of His temptation He was "with the wild beasts." That is not a statement inspiring terror, but revealing a truth full of beauty. He was with them in comradeship, Master of them, because He was God's perfect Man.

If this Man came and discovered treasure, He also hid it. Here perhaps is the touch of greatest mystery in our parable. It affirms the hiding of the treasure discovered. What have we that is parallel to this in the case of Christ? If we think of His ministry and interpret our parable in the light of it, we shall find that this is exactly what He did. He Who called people to the Kingdom of God, because of their refusal, because of their rejection of Him as King, shut the door of the Kingdom against them. By solemn act He rejected the nation, pronounced eight woes over against His eight Beatitudes, announced the doom of Jerusalem, flung out the city from the place of government, and hid these things from the wise and prudent.

Then as Redeemer King, He prevented the manifestation of the glory of God in material magnificence and proceeded to the administration of the Kingdom in redemption and grace.

This parable does not cover all the ground. There are other things not dealt with here. It does, however, reveal what is the relationship of the Kingdom of God to this age. This is the age which rejects Christ. It is the age of the Church, which is the realisation of the Kingdom within its own borders. It exists to realise its principles, and reveal its beauties, and call men individually into relationship with it. But socially, and by act of Parliament, even the Church cannot establish the Kingdom of God. That will be done eventually, but only by the King Himself. Our hope for the world is in the coming of the King to rule with a rod of iron. I never quite understand why men tremble when they hear that He rules with a rod of iron. The rod of iron is not a terrible thing. It is that which is perfect in its straightness, inflexible in its rule. We thank God for One Who will rule with a rod of iron. The world has suffered so long from ruling by reeds which bend and break. It has been cursed for ages by india-rubber government.

The King purchased, not the treasure only, but the whole field.

Carefully notice the passion which lay behind the purchase—" In his joy." Notice, moreover, the price paid—" all that he had." Notice, finally, the purchase—" He . . . buyeth that field."

First, then, how came that joy of heart in the finding of the treasure? The question can only be answered by asking another. What was the treasure, the finding of which filled Him with joy? It was the certainty of the possibility of setting up the government of God. That was always the joy of Jesus. It is His personal word, " I delight to do Thy will, O my God." Concerning that thought we may get light from the great classic passage in the letter to the Hebrews. The writer had been speaking of the men of faith who had seen in the dim distance the city of God, of the men who had turned their backs upon the failure all about

them, and lifted their faces towards the light of God's great city. Having spoken of such he wrote: " Therefore let us also, seeing we are compassed about with so great a cloud of witnesses, lay aside every weight, and the sin which doth so easily beset us, and let us run with patience the race that is set before us, looking unto Jesus the Author and File-leader of faith, Who for the joy that was set before Him endured the Cross, despising shame, and hath sat down at the right hand of the throne of God." What was the joy? That of the certainty that after the passion should come the fulfilment of purpose—the building of the city of God, or, in other words, the realisation in the world of the Kingdom of God. For that joy He sold all that He had. The joy which constituted the strength of the Cross was the joy of leading back to God in reconciliation that which had wandered from Him. He came down into the world, and knew its possibility, knew its hidden treasure; but He knew that it was bound by chains of gold to the throne of God, and that its anthem could only be perfectly sung as it realised its fundamental relationship, and answered it in full surrender. He recognized that every man was capable of worship, and the whole social order capable of a perfect realisation, and the whole world capable of singing the anthem of God's praise. The joy of that certainty was the strength in which He " endured the cross, despising shame."

The man in the parable sold all that he had. The equivalent to that in the case of Jesus is: He " emptied Himself," and made Himself of no reputation. Who " endured the cross, despising shame." By this infinite sacrifice He purchased the whole field. The whole world is redeemed, waiting to be claimed. That sacrifice was necessary. Had Jesus Christ remained an ethical Teacher merely, He could not have set up God's Kingdom. There must be the intrusion into the ruin of a new regenerative dynamic. He must change the nature of the dog ere it can appreciate holy things. He must refashion and absolutely change the nature of the swine ere pearls will have any value. He bought the whole field at cost.

I should like to say one word in this connection concerning the word *bought* or *purchased*. Never read into this word as it represents the work of Jesus anything merely of a commercial nature. To do so is to bring oneself into inextricable confusion. We shall ask from whom He purchased the field. I have even heard it said that He purchased it from the devil. Never! He never granted the devil's right to it. He never paid to the devil any price for the possession of the world. Then I hear it said that He purchased it from God. He was God. There was never the slightest difference between Himself and God. He did not attempt to persuade God to any new line of action, or to any line of action out of harmony with His own nature. It is impossible to read into this merely a commercial explanation. There is a use of the word which is more in harmony with its intention here. A man finds himself beset by robbers, and, speaking afterwards of the peril, he declares that he determined to sell his life dearly. That is the true figurative use of the word. Or another man, who has rescued some precious thing at the cost of suffering, declares he has purchased it at great price. We know that in neither case is there the thought of purchase by commercial interchange, but that of securing the desired thing by strife and tears and pain. In that sense Christ purchased. We "were redeemed, not with corruptible things, with silver or gold "—that is commercialism—" but with precious blood . . . even the blood of Christ." That blood was not handed over to meet the devil's demand, nor even to persuade God. That outpouring of blood was the material interpretation of that passion of God, through which the world in which the treasure was hidden might be redeemed by passion, at the deepest heart of which is joy, and the expression of which is pain.

The man of faith will be conscious of all that the man of sight sees in this particular age. Yet the things of sight cannot make the man of faith hopeless, because he has heard the teaching of this parable.

It gives me Christ's estimate of possibility. Christ's purchase of the world makes Him possessor of the world, and that is the guarantee of His ultimate realisation of all upon which His heart is set. If in the one point of His hiding the treasure for a while there is an element of mystery, I am still perfectly sure of its infinite wisdom, and I know that presently, as a result, the manifestation will be more perfect and more glorious. Yet, finally, remember He does not hide from faith. To trust Him is to have revealed in the deepest life the glory of the Kingdom upon which His heart is set. He will kindle in the heart of the faithful the joy which made Him endure, and so equip them also for that suffering with Him which must eventuate in triumph with Him.

MATTHEW XIII. 45, 46

THE parable of the pearl, while most evidently kin to that of the hidden treasure, is in advance of it, and in some aspects different from it. Essentially there is nothing here which we have not already dealt with. The central and acting Person is again "a man." The search for, and the discovery of treasure dealt with in the last parable is also present. The thought of purchase at cost, to which we were introduced in the last parable, is also in this, "He went and sold all that he had, and bought it."

It is upon new emphases that our attention is principally centred when we come to a study of this parable. The man here is a merchant seeking treasure of a peculiar kind, "goodly pearls." In this quest he is rewarded, as he finds "one pearl of great price."

I need hardly stay to say that I do not accept the interpretation of the parable which regards the pearl of great price as the Saviour, and the merchant seeking and selling all to obtain the pearl, as the sinner. Such an interpretation, as we have already seen, contradicts the whole scheme of the teaching, and is out of harmony with all the facts of experience.

Let us first examine these new emphases of the pearl and the merchant, and then attempt to interpret the parable according to their suggestiveness.

While the actual wording of the parable introduces us first to the man who is a merchant seeking goodly pearls, I propose to commence examination by taking the pearl itself. "One pearl of great price." We invariably speak of this parable as the parable of the *pearl*. It is that which arrests our attention, and, I think, according to the Master's intention.

First remember, the pearl was not precious to the Hebrews. In the Old Testament there are some wonderful and graphic descriptions of precious stones, "stones of fire," as they are poetically called, but the pearl is not mentioned. It had no place on the breastplate of the high priest. When Job answered the criticism of Bildad the Shuhite in parable, he asks,

"But where shall wisdom be found?"

Then he proceeds to enumerate precious things which are not current coin in the market place where wisdom is to be sought, things with which wisdom cannot be bought.

"It cannot be valued with the gold of Ophir,
With the precious onyx, or the sapphire.
Gold and glass cannot equal it:
Neither shall it be exchanged for jewels of fine gold.
No mention shall be made of coral, or of crystal:
Yea, the price of wisdom is above rubies."

You will notice in the Authorised Version the word "pearl" occurs instead of "crystal." I think there can be no doubt that the revisers are right in substituting "crystal" for "pearl." The root of the Hebrew word suggests something frozen. It is certainly open to doubt as to what is really meant, but there can be very little question that the reference is not to pearl. Again,

instead of "Yea, the price of wisdom is above rubies," the margin reads, "The price of wisdom is above red coral," or "above pearls," a very questionable reading. Now it is a striking fact that only in these cases is the word pearl mentioned in our translations. Supposing, however, for the sake of argument, that the word pearl is the one intended, still remember it is quoted by the greatest of all the men of the East as not to be mentioned beside the worth of wisdom. Other stones are mentioned, even though dismissed, but he says, "No mention shall be made of coral or of pearl," thus signifying its contemptible value.

I have taken time to show this, because it is an interesting fact that the Hebrews did not count the pearl in the least precious. One can imagine, therefore, when Jesus used the figure how surprised a look would come upon the faces of the Hebrew disciples gathered round Him. He had spoken in previous parables of the treasure hidden in the field, and they understood it; but when He particularised, and used the words "pearl," "goodly pearls," the thought was startling from the Hebrew standpoint. These men were, of course, quite conversant with the fact that the pearl was held as a precious stone among the Gentiles. The study of the place of the pearl in Gentile usage is most interesting. From recent investigations made in Egypt, it has been discovered that the decoration of ancient kings consisted largely of gold, inset with jewels, and occasionally with pearls. When we come to Nineveh, we find that the pearl was in greater use. An increasing value was gradually set upon it, until in our day it is accounted as the most precious thing in the East. It is, however, of Gentile value. Thus Christ took as an emblem of the most precious thing that which was most valuable according to Gentile estimate, but something which was outside Hebrew figures of speech, because outside Hebrew conceptions of value.

Bearing that in mind, let us go a step further. There are certain facts about the pearl we shall do well to notice. First, the pearl is the direct product of a living organism. So far as I am aware there is no other precious stone of which that is true. In the next place, remember that the pearl is the result of injury done to the life that produces it.

" A pearl is found beneath the flowing tide,
And there is held a worse than worthless thing,
Spoiling the shell-built home where it doth cling—
Marring the life near which it must abide."

A grain of sand intruding, something that hinders and injures and harms, is the root principle of the pearl.

But that is not the pearl. What, then, is it? The pearl is the answer of the injured to the injury done. The pearl is the injuring element transmuted by processes of covering until the injurious thing is turned into a precious jewel. We all know the story of how in the shell of the oyster the pearl is formed. The intrusion of a grain of sand, or some other foreign substance; and then the covering of it with the nacre, or mother-of-pearl, layer after layer, exquisitely wrought, until at last the thing that hurt and harmed and injured has been made the basis upon which this whole pearl, a rare and beautiful jewel, is built up. So the pearl is the answer of the injured life to that which injures it.

Go one step further in considering this. What is the use of the pearl? It is to us wholly a thing of beauty, ornamental, decorative; but in eastern thought it is emblematic and symbolic. From the artistic standpoint merely, it is regarded carelessly, but in those eastern countries, where all the lights and shadows of imagination play so wonderful a part, and every rare thing is symbolic, the pearl is an ornament symbolising innocence and purity, and prized for its significance. The equivalent Greek word, *margarites,* means purity. It probably is derived from an old Sanscrit word also meaning purity, and this fact is very suggestive. The pearl is the answer of an injured life to the thing that injures, and the pearl

is the symbol of innocence. That which has worked an injury, that which was impure and harmful, has been so dealt with by the very life it has injured that it is transformed into a thing of glorious beauty, and stands for ever as a flashing illustration of essential purity. But the pearl is more than the symbol or emblem of purity. It stood for the triumph of purity over impurity, and the wearing of the pearl was not in its deepest significance the wearing of that which stood for innocence only, but for the mighty triumph of good over evil.

Turn for a moment to the other special emphasis, that of the merchant. He is here one who is seeking goodly pearls. Yet it is impossible to think of him as seeking goodly pearls merely for his own sake or adornment. He is a merchant seeking goodly pearls for others, and the easternness of the picture is apparent. Put yourself back into the eastern land, and watch the operation. His haste to purchase, his determination to purchase at any cost, is the eastern colouring of the picture, and shows that he has at length discovered a jewel so precious as to be worthy for the adornment of a king only; for in those eastern lands none but kings were allowed to wear the finest, and even in Persia to-day the discovery of any costly pearl means that it must find its way to the Shah. Here, then, is a merchant, finding a pearl which is worthy of the king's acceptance, and which may be for the adornment of one who alone has the right to wear it. There are other pearls, but this is of supreme value, for it manifests the most wonderful victory, contains within itself the most resplendent beauty, and is therefore the most perfect symbol of all that such a jewel may represent.

Turning from this examination of the special emphases of the pearl and the merchant, let us in the light of these things think for a moment of what this parable really means. At this point our Lord touches a mystery far deeper than any already declared. Here He speaks in the hearing of His disciples things they will only come to understand presently. This is what Paul speaks of as the definite and specific "mystery" of the Church.

In this parable Jesus shows that the chief, though not the final value of this Kingdom age is that during it there is to be gathered out and presented to God that which will be the finest, fairest, and most resplendent jewel that will ever flash upon His bosom in all the ages of eternity. I know full well how imperfect these words are, and yet I have no other in which to clothe the thoughts. Out of the mystery of sin, and out of the mystery of evil, and out of the mystery of this age in which the Kingdom values seem to be so fluctuating and uncertain, there is yet to be found and gathered the chief jewel of the Father's house, the most glorious thing for His possession, which shall reveal to the ages to come, and to unfallen intelligences, the grace and glory of God. Among the treasures of this age the Church of Jesus Christ is supreme. The finding of the Church, in this as in the previous parables, is not accidental. Its discovery includes discernment of it, the indication of it to others, and the obtaining of it. The merchant came, not seeking promiscuously, but bent on finding this very pearl. Remember, no figure can ever convey all the infinite fact, and looking at it in its infiniteness we see the limitations of the picture, and its inability to represent the whole truth. We see Christ discovering this precious pearl, bringing it to the light and then—mark very carefully the words made use of concerning Him here—"having found one pearl of great price, He went and sold all that He had, and bought it." May I change that, and read, very literally, "Having gone away, has sold all that He had, and bought it." This does not for a moment mean that He went away from the earth to buy it, but that He went away from Heaven to buy it. We are looking at the Kingdom from Heaven's standpoint, not from earth's. Earth has never seen the precious pearl, has no conception of it. The pearl has not yet found itself. The Church has never been seen by the eye of mortal man. We catch glimpses of its glory, but the Church itself has never been seen. But Christ has seen the Church

from eternity. He sees it through all the processes of its working; His love is set upon what it is, and what it will be; and He patiently awaits the accomplishment. This parable records the estimate placed upon the pearl in the sight of high Heaven. "Having gone away" from Heaven, "He sold all that He had, and bought it." It is a perfect picture of One Who, seeing a pearl of great price, surrenders place, possessions, and all, that He may purchase that pearl, and take it back with Him to the place which He left for its purchasing.

Turn with me once more to another Scripture, 1 Peter ii. 4 and 7. Here again while the figure of the pearl is not to be found, the great facts of which it is a figure are set forth perfectly. "Unto whom coming, a living Stone, rejected indeed of men, but with God elect, precious." Mark that word "precious." "The precious Stone," this is spoken of the Lord Himself. "Ye also, as living stones, are built up a spiritual house." I omit the rest, because it describes the issue, and I go to verse 7, which describes the process. "For you therefore which believe is the preciousness." What preciousness? His preciousness. The Christ of God is here described as being precious, and you may read all values into that word. In character, precious; in conduct, precious; in all the facts of His great personality, precious. All the things God values centre in Him. Rejected of men, but precious to God is He.

We come to Him, says the apostle, and are built up. "For you which believe is the preciousness;" that is to say, all that is precious in Him, is communicated to us who believe. That is the whole story of the development of Christian character. To the last, to the unending ages of eternity, I shall never have anything of myself of which to boast in the presence of God. I shall always boast in the values that have been made mine by communication—the values of the Christ character. Anything excellent in us is the Christ-life realised in us. He is precious, but unto you that "believe is the preciousness." That does not mean that you hold Him precious in your affection; but that the precious values in Him are communicated to you, and we who come to Him worthless and base, are changed into worth and preciousness because He communicates to us His own infinite value. Such is the story of the pearl. It is first of all base, a worthless thing, harming the life to which it comes. And here is a most remarkable and exquisite figure of what happens in the building of the Church of Jesus Christ. We " were no people "—I still quote from Peter, and he is quoting from Hosea—we " now are the people of God;" we " had not obtained mercy," we " now have obtained mercy." How has the change been wrought? We came to Him worthless, and it was in our approach to Him that He was wounded and harmed, injured and bruised. Yet the answer of the injured One to that which harmed, was that He made over to us in the mystery of His harming, all the virtues and glories of His own character. As the pearl is the outcome of a hurtful thing transformed into beauty and innocence by the communication of the life it hurt, so the Church of Jesus Christ in its entirety consists of such as wounded Him, and yet from that very wounding, and because of it, there has been, and is being communicated to them His virtue, His grace, His glory, His beauty. He Who for the moment in the parable is the merchant, is infinitely more than the merchant. He is not only the One Who sees the possibility of the precious Jewel, but He Who transmutes the unsightly thing into the thing of beauty, the impure thing into the thing of innocence; the One Who has lifted out of the troubled sea of human sorrow a people that shall flash in glory for ever upon the bosom of God, the chief medium through which He shall manifest His grace and His glory in all the ages to come.

This is the subject of the Ephesian epistle. The parable is silent about that final issue, because it is only dealing with this age, but we may follow the pearl in imagination until it flashes upon the bosom of some potentate. If we reverently inquire what becomes of the pearl that Jesus finds, we may turn to that epistle and there see its destination. Paul first of all prays that these Christians may know " the riches of the glory of His inheritance in the saints," a phrase rich and gracious and glorious in meaning. Notice carefully Paul did not pray that they might know what was the greatness of their inheritance in God, but what was the greatness of God's inheritance in them. The thought is not that the saints are made rich in God, but that God is enriched in the saints, that in them He gains something for His possession. I dare not say that if it were not the teaching of the whole epistle, and I dare hardly say it if it were but the suggestion of a verse. But mark the argument of the great Ephesian epistle, and see to what end it works out. In it Paul distinctly teaches us in what sense God gains in the Church. He tells us that the Church is to be the medium through which His grace, His goodness, His love are to be made known to the ages to come. The Church is to be that through which the unborn ages will know the grace of God and the love of God. A little further on in the same epistle, he tells us that the Church is to be the instrument through which angels, principalities, powers, the unfallen intelligences of other worlds, will learn the wisdom of God. This Church, redeemed, purchased, purified, glorified, is for ever more to be the instrument through which the grace of God and the wisdom of God will be made known to ages and to principalities and to powers, until we get to the close of the letter, and Paul with one flash of light says—and reading, think of the pearl of the parable—" Christ also loved the Church, and gave Himself up for it; that He might sanctify it, having cleansed it by the washing of water with the Word, that He might present the Church to Himself a glorious Church, not having spot or wrinkle, or any such thing; but that it should be holy and without blemish."

The pearl of great price is found in the midst of human wreckage, is gathered out of it, exalted, and made the medium through which in coming ages the infinite truth of God's grace and wisdom shall be revealed. Thus does God gain in the Church. He gains nothing of essential glory, but He gains a medium through which He may manifest that glory. He gains nothing of essential grace, but He gains a people, through whom His grace shall be revealed as could be in no other way. No angel can sing the story of God's grace as we whom His grace has transformed. Some of you remember that wonderful poem by Mrs. Barrett Browning, "The Seraphim." Imagination call it if you will, but it is high and holy imagination. She describes seraphim watching the processes of the Master's work on earth, watching with wonder as their Lord and King stoops to its dark places and suffers along its ways, until the meaning of His work breaking upon the intelligence of the angel-watchers, one turns to the other and says—

"Hereafter shall the blood-bought captives raise
The passion-song of blood."

And the other answering says—

"And we extend
Our holy vacant hands towards the throne,
Crying, 'We have no music.'"

And by comparison it is true. When the ransomed reach the land of light there will be some things of which they cannot sing more perfectly than the angels; but they will be able to sing of His love as angels never will. No angel can put into these words so much as I can put into them, "He loved *me* and gave Himself up for *me*." And when all earth's anthems have ceased, that will be the highest music of the eternities.

So in this age He is building this Church. He saw the pearl when yet but a possibility, injurious, useless, far off in the deep, dense darkness. He gathered the offending thing into His own life, and it wounded Him, harmed Him, and slew Him, but,

"He death by dying slew,
He hell in hell laid low,"

and as He transmutes the evil thing that harmed Him by the impartation of His own blameless character and holy life, He is building a glorious body for Himself, to which He ever shall be the Head, and which shall, in union with Himself, be God's chief adornment in the ages yet to come.

"He found the pearl of greatest price,
My heart doth sing for joy;
And sing I must, for I am His,
And He is mine for aye."

He has drawn and lifted me who harmed Him, and bestowed upon me His nature, His character, and His beauty, and presently He will present me, oh, matchless wonder, even me, "faultless before . . . glory!" Then, O blessed be God, He will send me forth to other worlds, to other ages, to other beings, to preach His Cross, that they, too, may know the glory of His grace.

This Church of the living God, the chosen and elect company who will become in their union with Christ the medium of manifestation, is the pearl the Merchant saw; and to give which to God He poured out all that He had. Our hearts may rest assured that in all the apparent failure of the Kingdom ideal in the age—not actual failure, for everything moves toward God's ultimate—the chief value, the chief glory, and the chief business, from Heaven's standpoint, is the gathering out of the Church, and its preparation for a high and holy vocation in the ages yet to come, for that Church is the redeemed Kingdom of God.

MATTHEW XIII. 47-50

WITH this parable the series revealing the process and condition of the Kingdom principle in the present age comes to conclusion.

In this study we are greatly aided by our Lord's partial interpretation. The picture is that of a great net cast out into the sea. This is not Ezekiel's picture of fishermen standing along the waters from En-gedi to En-eglaim, drawing out fish individually. This is not a picture of the work that the apostles were to do which Jesus described when He said, " I will make you fishers of men." This is quite a different method of fishing. A great net is taken out, let down into the sea, and left until after a while, those who placed it come back and haul it in, including within its meshes all kinds of fish. When filled it is drawn up upon the beach, and a process of selection and separation goes forward. The good are gathered into vessels. The bad are cast away.

Now our Lord does not explain all the parts of this parable. " So " indicates the beginning of His interpretation. " So shall it be in the end of the age." The Lord's interpretation has to do with the final fact depicted in the parable. The first is the casting out of the net. The second gives a glimpse of the intervening hours when the sea plays backwards and forwards through the net, and fishes of all kinds are enclosed. The last draws attention to the drawing in of the net at the moment of its fulness by skilful hands. All these suggestive facts are in the parable. But Jesus does not attempt any explanation concerning the net or the sea or the fishes. His explanation has to do with the final movement, the separation, the selection. " So shall it be in the end of the age," the consummation of the age: " the angels shall come forth, and sever the wicked from among the righteous, and shall cast them into the furnace of fire: there shall be the weeping and the gnashing of teeth."

We grasp at once, therefore, the true emphasis of this parable. It is intended above all to reveal the method of the completion of the age. My own conviction is that we are in danger of fanciful interpretation if we attempt in any detail to explain the other parts of the parable. Let us take that which our Lord explains, and only explain the former as His explanation of the final movement may make possible. The main value of the parable, broadly stated, lies in the fact of the separation which is to follow upon the drawing in of the net. This separation is to take place at the end of the age, and understanding that, we are saved from wrong conceptions, both as to the net and the fishermen, and such fish as are enclosed within the net.

Very popularly this parable is taken to illustrate the work of evangelism, but though that work is spoken of by our Lord under the symbol of fishing, it has no place in the teaching here.

Let us say at once that in some senses this parable is of no vital moment to us. In some senses it does not help us in our work; it is just a glimpse, a flash, of events transpiring at the end of the age. In another sense it is of great and immediate value, as I shall hope to show in conclusion. Here we are not looking first at the processes of the moment, but at the final process with its great meaning.

The process that is to bring to an end the age in which we live and work is a single process. It is that of severing the bad from among the good, of severing " the wicked from among the righteous." The picture our Lord used was altogether familiar, but He chose out of the picture a single fact, and let all the rest go. He pointed His disciples, who for the most part were fishermen, to what they had done many a night, flung the nets out, and left them; and then hauled them in, and sitting down on the beach rejected the bad and conserved the good. But only on one incident in the familiar picture does He lay any emphasis. Ignoring the conservation of the good, and all other processes, our Lord selects this one fact, the severance of the bad. " So shall it be in the end of the age."

What is this severance of the wicked for? That they may be destroyed, that they may be cast to the fire; and our Lord's words here are full of significance. He says, There, on that occasion, when angels gather out evil men and cast them to destruction, "there shall be the weeping and the gnashing of teeth." And when Christ uses such startling words, we may well ponder solemnly, and read into them nothing that is not there; and read out of them nothing that is evidently in them. "Weeping," lamentation; "gnashing of teeth," the grinding of the teeth, either in pain or rage, or in all probability, both.

What, then, can be the meaning of this net, and this gathering of it up, and this action of the angels regarding it? "Again, the Kingdom of heaven is like unto a net," and as I have said before, the whole picture is needed to show the process of the Kingdom in this age. Notice where the emphasis begins, "So shall it be." This net enclosing within itself a certain number is undoubtedly that of the Kingdom influence of which we have spoken, which is being exercised in the world through the presence in the world of Christ and His Church; and the net is let down into the sea of human life, and wherever it spreads, wherever the influence of the Church is exerted, this final work of the gathering out the bad will proceed. The fact of the Kingdom, as a consciousness, a sub-consciousness, a semi-consciousness, in human thinking has come wherever the Church has come, wherever the missionary has come, wherever the Gospel has come. Wherever the Gospel has been preached as a witness, there men have been brought consciously face to face with the fact of the Divine government, and it is of such that the number enclosed by the net is made up. At the close of the dispensation or age, when the net is gathered in, the great separation will take place.

There will come a moment when there will be, according to the teaching of Scripture, and this specific word of Jesus, the return to direct intervention in human affairs of angels. To-day their ministrations are unseen. They

are still all ministering spirits: but they minister specifically to the men of faith in the mystery of this little while. But as they have been visible in olden days—and if you deny the truth of it, you have to deny your Bible—so will they be visible again. The new era in the world's history will be ushered in by this strange and marvellous and overwhelming angel visitation, angel discrimination, and angel separation. Angel discrimination means Heaven's standards set up among the affairs of men. Angel separation means Heaven's might enforcing Heaven's standards.

One of the most interesting subjects in art is the history of angel painting. I am not proposing to discuss it at length. I am inclined to say that I think the great artists, the great masters as we still call them, who in my own opinion so sadly and absolutely failed to represent Christianity, were far more successful in depicting the truth concerning angels. Take one of the latest, that great picture, "Despised and Rejected of Men," by Sigismund Goetz. Everybody has seen it. Everybody has gazed upon the awful figure of the Christ and the crowding figures of the men and women about Him, but how many have noticed that majestic angel form in the background? To me that is the finest thing in all the picture. If this be true, that representation of towering majesty, that conception of angelic being such as is according to Scripture—and here you must not charge me with imagination—"a flame of fire," flashing in beauty and in glory —if that be true, then think of what it will mean for the world when angels come to sever the wicked from among the good. Do not be afraid of materialising spiritual things. In our great fear of spiritualising material things, do not let us run to the other extreme. Think what it would mean if angels could come upon our city to-day to lay an arrest upon all evil-doers, and extract them from the midst of the people. That is what will happen. This is the day of long-suffering patience. This is the day when the net lies out in the sea, and the waves lap it and rock it, and men wonder what is happening. This is the day when the great Merchant is gathering out the pearl, and preparing it for the mystery of unborn ages. When presently the day is ended, and its purpose in the economy of God accomplished, then this new age begins for the world itself, and angels, according to Jesus, are to initiate it by gathering out the wicked from among the good.

There the parable leaves us. In some senses we can go no further. And yet while our parable does not declare to us what the final issue will be, we may for purposes of understanding it, in all fairness refer to the King's previous and fuller statement which at the time we did not dwell upon at any great length. So that returning to the parable of the darnel and the wheat, we shall find something that helps us in interpretation of the present one. "The Son of Man shall send forth His angels, and they shall gather out of His Kingdom all things that cause stumbling, and them that do iniquity, and shall cast them into the furnace of fire: there shall be the weeping and the gnashing of teeth." The parable we are looking at goes no step beyond that. But this parable of the darnel does. "Then shall the righteous shine forth as the sun in the Kingdom of their Father."

What, then, is the meaning of the angel ministry which will consummate the age? First the cleansing of the Kingdom from things that cause stumbling, and from them that do iniquity. But what beyond it? "The righteous shall shine forth as the sun in the Kingdom of their Father.' I do not know when that hour will be. I have no idea when the King is coming. It may be immediately. It may not be for a thousand years. I do not know, and I do not attempt to discover. The fact is everything—"The Son of Man shall send forth His angels, and they shall gather out of His Kingdom all things that cause stumbling," everything that offends.

This parable is of the nature of a look ahead. In some senses we to-day have little to do with it, but in other senses it is a gracious source of strength, as it assures us of a sure process of judgment, and so gives us hope where otherwise there would be none. Take this parable, and study it in the light of all the rest. It will give you, oppressed with all the failure of the hour, to see that if man fails, God is not failing. The world, the scarred, seamed, sorrow-stricken earth, will be healed by a mercy that operates in judgment, by justice that operates in mercy.

MATTHEW XIII. 51, 52

THE parable of the householder is the completion of the octave. We have considered seven parables. This is the eighth and last. The others have set forth the truth concerning the history of the Kingdom of God in the present age. This parable teaches the responsibility of the disciples during the same period.

There are two statements which have been almost monotonously repeated in this series, but they need to be made again and again. These parables do not deal with the deepest facts concerning the Kingdom of God, neither are they parables which tell the whole story of that Kingdom. They have no application to the age which preceded the first advent of our Lord, neither

have they application to the age which shall succeed His second advent. They are simply His setting forth of truth concerning the process and history of the Kingdom during the period commencing with His first advent and ending with His second.

So these verses, with the brief parable which they contain, reveal the responsibility of such as have been made disciples of the Kingdom in an age when Kingdom principles are not wholly and absolutely victorious.

The parable follows a question and description, and must be considered in the light thereof. First the question, "Have ye understood all these things?" When they answered Yes, He said, "Therefore every scribe who hath been made a disciple to the Kingdom of heaven." These two sayings of Jesus, question and description, are mutually explanatory. To understand the things which He has taught is to be instructed to the Kingdom of heaven. To be a scribe instructed to the Kingdom of heaven is to have received His teaching, and to have understood it.

Let us examine this requirement. In the question, "Have ye understood all these things?" the emphasis is most certainly upon the word "understood." They had heard them all, they had been interested in them all. They had heard the first four parables spoken to the listening multitudes. They had heard His explanation of the first two of them. They had heard the three parables spoken to themselves privately within the house, and they had heard His explanation of the last of the three. They had heard everything, and their interest had been manifested in the questions they had asked.

Now He asks, "Have ye *understood* all these things?" and the word translated "understood" means quite literally to put together. That is, have you comprehended the main drift of this teaching? Have you put together these things so that you see what I have been attempting to teach you? Notice very carefully that our Lord says, "All these things." There has been a balance and proportion in the teaching. He has been moving steadily forward, unveiling different phases of Kingdom history and process during the period. Now He says, "Have ye understood all these things?" What He asks is whether they have recognized the system of His teaching, for this is what is necessary in order to fulfil responsibility in the age. When they answered Him, "Yea," upon the basis of that answer He proceeded to declare their responsibility. In doing so He first described their position in the words, "a scribe, made a disciple to the Kingdom of heaven."

Our Lord's use of the word "scribe" at this point necessitates an inquiry as to its real significance, for we know that the scribes of His day were bitterly opposed to Him. As a class the scribes began to exist in the time of Ezra. The word is used before the time of Ezra, and yet a careful examination will show that it was never used before that time in the sense in which it was used then, and subsequently. The scribes originally were chroniclers, and were closely associated with the military movements of the ancient people. But with the advent of Ezra the scribe filled a new office. He became, as in the case of Ezra himself, a reader and an expounder of the law of God. Ezra is the most conspicuous example of the true scribe, he who stood in the midst of the people and read the words of the law, indicating the meaning of them, not merely by elocutionary perfection, but by comment, annotation, exposition. That was the real office of the scribe. In the days of Jesus they were still the professed exponents of the law; but they then proceeded upon two principles, that first of oral tradition, and that secondly of the interpretation of the letter with an almost painful accuracy.

These two principles had become the means of obscuring rather than expounding the law. The scribes themselves declared that the oral tradition for which they stood was a fence around it. They had superadded to the actual law of God the traditions of the elders, and according to their own philosophy they had done this to maintain the law in stricter integrity. But their tradition had become a fence around the law in another sense than that intended, for, being a misinterpretation of the law, it had become that which shut men out from the law. In the days of Jesus, therefore, the scribes were in constant antagonism to Him Who ruthlessly swept aside all their traditions, and yet religiously lived within the sphere of the law.

Moreover, these scribes were men who had indulged in literal interpretation to such an extent as to absolutely change the meaning of the law. Devoid of any understanding of its deeper spirit, they had slavishly given themselves over to the letter.

Jesus now chose the word which had been used to define the office of the men who had led the opposition to Him in His kingly propaganda, and He said, "Every scribe who hath been made a disciple to the Kingdom of heaven," and by so doing, He suggested that His disciples were to take hold of the old idea and fulfil it. They were to become in their age the interpreters of the law of God. He said in effect, You are to become the new scribes, the interpreters of the Kingdom, those through whom the age will know the facts concerning the government of God.

In order to fulfilment of this responsibility there must be understanding of the King's teaching concerning the Kingdom in this age. A wrong conception of its true meaning and value may not interfere with our enthusiasm in its cause, or with our devotion to the King; but it will interfere with the intelligence of our service, and thus limit the sphere of its action. What, then, is the teaching of these parables in broad outline? That this age is one of conflict from beginning to end; that it is characterised to a large extent by human failure; that it is an age in which God accomplishes definite purposes; that, as to the heavenly side, it is an age from which a people is gathered out to serve God throughout the countless ages that are to come as the revealers of His grace and His love; that, as to the earthly value, it is an age that moves to a super-natural consummation. These truths must be understood. If we fail to perceive them, then our service may be sustained, but it will surely be defective. I pity from the depth of my heart the man who is labouring to-day in the hope that this age is to be consummated by the conversion of the world. I cannot personally understand where he gathers his comfort when he sees how heathendom is increasing proportionately with every decade as it passes, as he sees that even in so-called Christian countries, notwithstanding all the light that has come, and is still coming, notwithstanding all the undoubted progress that is being made, there is also along with the progress, retrogression; along with the increasing light, increasing darkness; side by side with a new sense of the Christ spirit in the age, an ever new revolt against that spirit. But I realise through the teaching of Jesus in these parables that this is an age of conflict, of conflict stern and necessary, when the enemy sows his darnel by the wheat, and that I have no right to attempt to uproot the darnel until the end of the age. Then as I understand this to be an age in which God is gathering out for Himself a people for heavenly service, and is preparing by all the processes of the years for that consummation, I can take up my day's work, and do it with full purpose of heart, knowing that the world's great hope is the advent of the King, with the rule of the rod of iron, when righteousness will be established.

Jesus declared that it is the scribe instructed to the Kingdom of heaven, according to the teaching which He had Himself given, who is to fulfil the responsibility which is then described.

Now let us turn to that responsibility. The picture is a very simple one, and yet again, wholly eastern. We pause and look at it in its separation from the teaching. It is the picture of a householder—an eastern householder, I pray you remember. You cannot interpret this parable by anything you know of the householder in this country, or in any western land. One must go back to the East. The word translated "householder" might be translated with a bluntness that perhaps is unfair, and yet perfectly accurate, as the house-despot. All our western mind is in revolt at the very use of the word, but despotism is not necessarily cruel; it may be gracious, tender, kind, beneficent. In the East the householder was one in absolute authority, a king, a shepherd, a father. And so the figure employed is that of a despot, apart from the undesirable significance of the term. In this word "householder," then, there is present the thought of loving yet absolute authority. Christ often used the word, and almost invariably concerning Himself.

Then pass to another word in the picture. "Which bringeth forth out of his *treasure*." Here we have the same word for "treasure" that occurred in the manifesto of the King. There are two distinct Greek words for treasure —each indicating a certain value. This is the word that indicates treasure laid horizontally. It is wealth, treasure laid up, possessed. The treasure possessed is that of the truth concerning the Kingdom.

Then take the next phrase, the householder brings forth out of his treasure "things new and old." "New" does not mean young. "Old" does not mean worn out. The phrase means things fresh and ancient, rather than things young and worn out.

Again, the householder *brings forth* out of his treasure things fresh, ancient. "Bringeth forth," literally, flinging forth, scattereth around. There is the thought of prodigality in giving, of great generosity and bountifulness.

The whole picture is one of an eastern householder, the master of a house, an authoritative ruler, lavishly scattering out of his wealth the things which are necessary for the supply and government of his household. Those who are gifted with imagination see the picture. It is full of colour. No neutral tints are in it. The eastern housemaster, house-despot, out of his treasure scattering upon his people, upon the children of his family, the sheep of his flock, the subjects of his kingdom, all that they need. It is the attitude of real kingship, and real fatherhood, and real shepherdhood.

Having looked at the picture thus we are filled with astonishment at it, for Jesus said that it represented the position His disciple is to occupy throughout all this period.

What, then, does it mean? First, that His disciples are the householders of this age. Moreover, in proportion as they bring out of their treasure-house, which is His treasure-house, things new and old, they are the rulers of the age.

I am increasingly impressed with the fact that some of the simplest things Jesus said are the most startling and sublime. At the end of the parables of the Kingdom, with stately and kingly dignity the King sweeps aside all the thrones of earth, and all the governments of men, and He says for purposes of God's great and only Kingdom throughout this age, the ruling authority is to be vested in the disciples who

are instructed to the Kingdom of heaven. Every scribe is to be like a householder. He had spoken of Himself as the great Householder. These disciples are now to represent Him, and take His place in the world, and what He has done they are to do. According to the suggestion of this wonderful, brief, final parable, the disciples of the Christ, instructed to the Kingdom, are the ruling class in the centuries as they come and go, until the King Himself appears again. They are to bring out of the treasure-house, out of the wealth that is theirs, "things new and old."

Let us consider a little more closely this expression, one of the most remarkable of the whole paragraph. "Things new and old." Not, if I understand the Lord aright, new things and old things; but "things new and old." The same things, new and old. Not one set of things that are new, and another set of things that are old. That would be opposition, antagonism, mutual destruction. Christ has said that no man puts new wine into old wine-skins. There you have the opposition of a new thing to an old thing, and that is destruction. That is not the thought here. "Things new and old." The principle is old, the application is new. The root is old, the blossom and the fruit are new, and the two are necessary to growth and development. Destroy the old root in your garden, and there will be no new blossoms in spring-time, nor fruit in autumn. But the absence of the new denies the life of the old. If there be no bud, no blossom, and no fruit, then I take it the tree is dead, and may be destroyed. "Things new and old"—old in their unseen and eternal principles; new in their seen and temporal practice. The interrelation is for evermore a test. The new thing which contradicts the old is always false. The old thing that has no fresh and new production is dead, and the sooner we are rid of it the better. "Things new and old," said Jesus. You are going to represent Me, the great Householder. You are to be the householder of this age. It was as though He had said, I depose kings and rulers and governors. They will sit upon their thrones, and pass their measures, and imagine they are manipulating the age. That is not so. You are to be the householders. You are to be the masters of the age, not with the mastery which is apparent always, but with the mastery which prepares for Me. You are to be My householders, and you are to do your work by bringing out of your treasure-house, out of this infinite wealth that is Mine, and which I make yours, " things new and old."

That is the perpetual responsibility of such as understand the way of His Kingdom. Surely Russell Lowell had this great thought in mind, subconsciously or not, when he wrote:

" New occasions teach new duties,
  Time makes ancient good uncouth;
They must upward still and onward,
  who would keep abreast of truth;
Lo before us gleam her camp fires!
  we ourselves must pilgrims be;
Launch our *Mayflower*, and steer
  boldly through the desperate winter sea,
Nor attempt the Future's portal with
  the Past's blood-rusted key."

That is a plea for the new; yes, but if you try the future's portal with any other key than the key that hangs upon the girdle of the King, you will never unlock it. If you forget that the new door can only be opened by the old principle, that door will never be opened. We are to come into every successive decade or century with things new and old, living messages to the age in which we live; living application of the truth which God has eternally enthroned. Because the Kingdom of God is old, ancient as God is ancient, it has ever new applications. Methods, manners, men may change; but this underlying principle of Divine government abideth, rooted in the nature of God, and active in redeeming grace, and it blossoms fresh in every generation among the sons of men.

Now, said Jesus to these disciples, Have you understood these things? Have you understood the underlying principle? Have you understood My teaching concerning the age in which you are to serve? Have you put My measurements upon this age? Do you understand what God is doing? Do you understand these things—the things of the Divine purpose, of the Divine programme, of the Divine plan? And upon the basis of the gleam of light that had come to them, upon the basis of the fact that if at least they did not perfectly understand, they yet belonged to Him Who held the key of knowledge as well as the key of power: upon that basis He said, Then go out into this age and be householders, bringing out of your treasure things new and old. Insist wherever you are upon the old and abiding, but make application of it to the new and the transient. " New and old."

That is the work of the people of the Kingdom of God in this age. The old for us is the Kingdom of God. Will not somebody give me another phrase? How shall I find another? There is no better, but we have taken these Bible phrases, and robbed them of their virtue by repetition. What is the Kingdom of God? The Kingship of God. The fact that He is King, and that amid the clash of devilish attack His throne has never trembled for a moment. That is the old, the Kingship of God. And what is the new? The application of that eternal verity to the age in which we live, to personal life, to social life, to national life. Our business, as we are disciples instructed to the Kingdom, is to make this application.

May I illustrate what I mean by a protest? I am often told to-day—told seriously—that what the Church of God needs in order to succeed is to catch the spirit of the age. I reply that the Church of God only succeeds in proportion as she corrects the spirit of the age. I am told that if I am to succeed in Christian work, I must adopt the methods of the world. Then, by God's help, I will be defeated. We are not in the world to borrow the world's maxims and spirit. The world would crucify Jesus as readily now as nineteen centuries ago. The Cross is no more popular in the world to-day than when men nailed Him to it on the green hill outside the city gate nineteen centuries ago. The Church of Christ is for evermore to stand for Him as King, and for that redeemed Kingdom which He represents; and as she does it, as the disciples instructed to the Kingdom bring forth things new and old from the treasure-house, that and only that will save individuals and society and the nation.

Do you not believe that here is great need for such bringing forth of things new and old? Do you not recognize in this hour in which we live, we need to emphasise supremely the Kingdom of God? This is a matter I am almost afraid to put into words lest I should be misunderstood. There are times when it seems to me that in our mis-interpretation of Jesus as gentle and pitiful and tolerant, we have imagined that all we have to do to make a man a Christian is to sing him some sweet, soft nothing, set to dance music. We need to get back to the sterner teach-ings of our Puritan fathers, or back to the rugged magnificence of the old He-brew prophets. If we are householders true to the great Master-Householder, we shall insist upon the Kingdom of God, and we shall never say to men, It does not matter, you are doing your best, you are struggling through. We shall say to men, You will be for ever lost, unless you submit to the throne. Yes, salvation is by the Cross, but the Cross is the place of the throne, and these old eternal truths are the things we need to recognize and preach.

We have been playing with the surf that beats upon the shore. We need to get down to the depths and pro-fundities of faith, the everlasting rock upon which our feet rest. Things old, not worn out, but ancient and honour-able things that are grey with the ma-jesty of the eternities. These are the things that we stand in the world for; and in proportion as we stand for these, and make application of them to per-sonal life, and social life, and national life, in that proportion we become for our absent and hidden King, Who presently is to be revealed in glory, the true householders.

Yet, brethren, what gracious gifts there are in our hands, what treasures we have for this age that none other has, if we but understand our position! Never must we forget the throne. But, thank God, it is also the throne of grace, and when we, in the name of God Almighty, have uttered our fiercest denunciation against the sin of the age, we can come to the man who is scorched with the lightning of denun-ciation, and bring him to the healing of the Cross, and the cleansing blood, and the power of the Spirit.

" We come, we come, the children of
　　salvation,
　　Treasures all countless in our hands
　　we bring."

We are to bring out of our treasure-house things new and old, and give them to the age. Then we need not be at all anxious about statistics. It does not matter whether one, or a hun-dred, or a thousand names are taken. The thing that matters is that we have brought out the old thing in its new meaning and new application. Pres-ently the King will come, and will sever the wicked from the good, and to the old and weary world will come at last its golden age.

MATTHEW XIII. 53-58

THE parabolic discourse completed, our Lord went on with His work, and in continuing our study of the par-ticular section dealing with the enforce-ment of His claims, we have two sub-divisions left. First of all the period marked by increasing opposition; then the brief story of how one man at least had seen Him and known Him—the confession of Peter at Cæsarea Philippi.

Looking at the section beginning with verse fifty-three of chapter thirteen, and running to verse twelve of chapter sixteen, we see the King going forward once more, and the opposition was more marked, more definite. He moved on in His propaganda in an atmosphere characterised by hatred and misunderstanding.

There are two ways in which this whole passage might be analysed;

around the opposition offered, or around the mistakes made concerning Jesus. To survey it from the second standpoint would be to find mistake after mistake chronicled. First, the mistake of the men of Nazareth, then the mistake of Herod, then the mistake of the multitudes who wanted to take Jesus by force and make Him the King, and then the mistake of the disciples, who saw Him moving over the water at midnight. Mistake followed mistake, because the people did not understand Him. This was the last period of the intensive public ministry. Not that the public ministry entirely closed now, for after Cæsarea Philippi our Lord appeared publicly, but He specially devoted Himself to His own disciples, instructing them concerning the Cross. Finally He appeared in Jerusalem for the official rejection of the Nation.

In this study we take the first of the sub-divisions, which deals with the opposition of His own people; not His own disciples, but the people of Nazareth. Having instructed His disciples in the mysteries of the Kingdom of God, that is to say having taught them what the Kingdom would be in that particular age, thus preparing them for future ministry, the King continued His work, and the first place to which He went was Nazareth. He set His face again toward the old and familiar scenes of His boyhood and His young manhood. This visit of Jesus to Nazareth is not the same as that which is recorded by Luke. This was much later. Here He was going back to Nazareth after prolonged ministry, and very near to the close of things.

The picture of this verse is one very full of beauty. Perhaps we can best interpret it to our own hearts by calling to mind what our own sensations have been, when, after years of life's strenuous battle, we have taken our way back to the scenes of childhood, of youth, to what we sometimes think of as the dull and dreary days of preparation for the more public service. That description would not be at all applicable in the case of our Lord, for the perpetual sunshine of His life was the consciousness that He was doing God's will; and whether at Nazareth, or on the public highways and byways, His one joy and delight was His Father's will. But He had taken His way back again to these scenes of early life; and one can imagine Him, as He went into the old familiar synagogue on the Sabbath day, the synagogue to which His mother had taken Him in the earlier days, where He had listened to the reading of the law, and sometimes to its exposition; the synagogue so closely associated with those days of childhood, boyhood, and youth. It is well sometimes to strip ourselves of the larger and truer ideas of the Christ, and try and look at Him on the purely human level. If we can do so here, we catch the beauty of this story. He had gone back again to the little town nestling on the hillside, far removed from the great crowds and activities, the great centres in the midst of which He had been busily occupied. He had left them for ever, when He began His ministry, and set His face to go to Capernaum, and to take up His residence there. He had made Capernaum the centre of His operations, but at last He had to say, " And thou, Capernaum, shalt thou be exalted unto heaven? thou shalt go down unto Hades." He had turned His back upon it for the last time, and He was now back again in Nazareth. Back home in the old synagogue, among the old familiar scenes, looking into the faces of the men who were boys when He was, and who had grown up to manhood with Him. And there in the synagogue He taught them. After the reading of the law He expounded it, told them its inner meaning. Oh, to have heard Him as, beginning at Moses, and on through the prophets, He taught those listening men ! He had gone back from the crowds to the quietness of Nazareth. Now let us see what happened. In order to do so we must look first at the men of Nazareth ; then at the King Himself.

The men of Nazareth. What was their first attitude as He came that day to the synagogue? They had heard the fame of Him : it had spread through all the region round about. The very next paragraph, with which chapter fourteen opens, makes it perfectly plain how far the fame of Jesus had spread, for we find that the report concerning Him had reached Herod, and the last place in which any man becomes famous is the royal palace. Everybody knows the rumour before it reaches the King. And so the people of Nazareth had heard of Him, and undoubtedly had been interested in Him. They knew about Him, so that when He returned to Nazareth, and went into the synagogue, their first attitude toward Him was one of perfect familiarity with Him. They were His people. "Is not this the carpenter's son? Is not His mother called Mary? and His brethren James, and Joseph, and Simon, and Judas? And His sisters, are they not all with us?" These were the things naturally in their minds when He entered. We know Him, we know all about Him, His people are all here with us. Mother, and brothers, and sisters. He is just one of us. We know His development; we watched Him grow up here as a Boy, and we loved Him in those old days. He grew "in wisdom and stature, and in favour with God and men." We know all about Him. We know His occupation. Did we not often come and watch as He began to use the trols of His craft by the side of Joseph? Did not He make the very yokes in which our oxen are ploughing? That was the first attitude, and it was a very dangerous attitude, and yet it was perfectly natural. He went into the synagogue, not as a stranger. There was very little curiosity in their midst as He entered, save curiosity arising out of the reports that had reached them. It is all so human; we understand it perfectly. The boy who grew up by your side went out. Other people were startled and surprised because he did something, and accomplished something. He comes back. His success is interesting; but you say, we know him. That was the attitude of Nazareth towards Him. It was very perilous, as we shall see, that first attitude of perfect familiarity.

What happened? He began to teach them. We can quite imagine the faces of those men in that synagogue, those strange, strong, Jewish faces, as they watched Him that day before they began to discuss Him. We can imagine the astonished surprise on their faces. They were listening, they had never heard things like that before; such exposition, such interpretation of their own Scriptures. As He talked about them, the old familiar words they had been reciting for years, flamed into light and glory. He merely repeated them; and as they listened they heard illustrations which proved that He was in possession of a knowledge which was quite foreign to them. There was no university in Nazareth. There was no school of the prophets in Nazareth. The great Rabbis never set up their seat in Nazareth, and He had been there all the time, through all the years; and yet interwoven with His matchless speech were allusions which they had always imagined, and rightly imagined within the limitation of their own life, could only be gained by the processes of learning, and the school. We are not told upon this occasion that He wrought any miracles. Indeed we are told, "He did not many mighty works there, because of their unbelief." The inference is that He did some; and perchance before He spoke they saw some wonder, or it may be that the report of wonders He had wrought had come to the place. They watched Him and listened to Him, and there was no escape from the conviction that He had wisdom, and there was no escape from the evidence that He had power. These things they could not deny. But, they said, This wisdom is not of human origin, for we watched Him as a baby, growing into boyhood; we watched Him as a boy growing into youth. He never went away to study in the schools, and yet He has the wisdom. And the power certainly comes from no human source! Look at His people, Mary, and His brothers and sisters, just ordinary people. He is one of the same kith and kin, but He has the power, He has the wisdom. And so the second attitude was one of astonishment.

Now we come to the final attitude of these men of Nazareth. "They were offended." Perhaps we are not warranted in reading that word exactly in that form. Literally, they were made to stumble. One of the old versions gets very near the heart of translation when it reads, "they were scandalised," for remember the *scandalon* was the rock of offence over which people stumbled. He had become a rock of offence, something over which men stumbled. At first they were perplexed, but perplexity is not offence and stumbling. There was more in it than that. In the presence of the mystery presented to their view, they stumbled by taking up a wrong attitude towards Him. There was only one logical sequence. What astonished these men was not to be accounted for, yet it existed. Therefore these things were supernatural things, beyond human ken and understanding, but to be received because of what they were, and because of what they testified concerning Him. A mystery, but yet a revelation. Here is the point where they fell and stumbled. They did not admit the sequence concerning Himself. They made their judgment blind. Wrapped up in that simplicity of personality with which we have become acquainted, was a sublimity of personality which even we have never yet fully discovered. There is only one attitude in the presence of such a phenomenon as that. While we cannot understand the mystery, at least we ought not to reject the Person simply on account of the fact that we cannot follow the working and explain the method. But there they failed. They were offended. The link was missing, they could not find it. Therefore they refused the wisdom and refused the works because they refused Him. "And He did not many mighty works there because of their unbelief." Such is the picture of the men of Nazareth.

Now let us look at the King Himself. If we have noticed their familiarity with Him, what shall we say of His familiarity with them? He also knew them; He had lived in their midst and observed them. He had seen them in the process of their growth, as they had seen Him in the process of His growth; and from the human side He was more familiar with these people than with any others. But He also knew them in their deepest life, as He knows the underlying secret in every life. "He needed not that any one should bear witness concerning man; for He Himself knew what was in man." And yet, notwithstanding this, He went back to them once more. He taught them, and wrought amongst them, and gave them new manifestations of Himself; things they never could have discovered, for they were not emblazoned upon His personality. He gave them manifestations of His power in great grace; but the final thing is this, "He did not many mighty works there because of their unbelief." The popular conception of a miracle or "mighty work" is that it is something which creates belief, and we should be inclined to say that was His opportunity for a miracle, just because they did not believe. But there is a matter to bear in mind perpetually. Jesus never wrought miracles to create belief. Not in a single instance in the New Testament can we find that a miracle was wrought to create belief or faith. They were all beneficent. Unbelief was the atmosphere in which He could not perform a miracle, and there was lacking at Nazareth the atmosphere in which it was possible for Him to work a miracle, a wonder, a mighty power. Belief is not merely intellectual conviction. They had intellectual conviction. They knew His wisdom, they knew His power; they were perfectly convinced of the wisdom of His speech, of the might of His work. Belief is the abandoning of the will to conviction, the handing over of the life to the thing concerning which we are convinced. If we say we believe in God the Father Almighty, and live all the week as though there were no God, we may have an intellectual conviction of His existence, but we do not believe in God. They believed intellectually certain things concerning Him, but as belief is the abandonment to conviction, when that abandonment is withheld there can be no progress, contact is not made.

Now let us go back with Him to the synagogue of His boyhood. There He was mighty in speech and mighty in deed. All wisdom and power were His. He spoke the words of wisdom and He worked the deeds of might. Those people heard the wisdom and recognized it; saw the deed and knew it, and then said, Whence did He get His wisdom and His might? The men of Nazareth went astray attempting to account for something half understood. Oh, that they had responded to the fact of wisdom, and to the fact of power, and believed in Him upon the basis of the evidences! He could then have wrought miracles amongst them, He could have done other things, and said other things, but their unbelief sterilised His power, and He could make no contact with them. At the first evidence of His wisdom and might which makes a demand upon us, let us answer it, yield to it, not merely intellectually but volitionally, and we shall see that the same wisdom can go further in its giving of light, that the same power can work more mightily. Refuse to answer it, and Christ Himself cannot make us understand Him, and Christ Himself cannot do more mighty works.

Nazareth is the symbol of many an individual life. The Christ comes, there is the flash of His wisdom, the thrill of His power; and then the man begins speculating and wondering, and ofttimes refuses light. Christ can go no further with that man. Christ Himself cannot make that man know Him; until he answer the first flash of light with obedience, the first thrill of power with abandonment. That is the great word here, the startling word, the tremendous word—"He did not many mighty works there because of their unbelief."

There are in this study lessons of personal relationship and lessons of co-operative fellowship.

As to the first, this story teaches us the unutterable folly of refusing to accept fact because it is astonishing. Yet there are thousands of people standing in that position to-day concerning Jesus Christ. It is utterly unscientific, not to say irreligious. Here is an astonishing thing. They say we cannot understand how this Man hath this wisdom. Has He the wisdom? Why, yes, we cannot escape it. Then in the name of God and common honesty, obey

the injunction and postpone the investigation. Oh, the unutterable folly of refusing to accept a fact because it is astonishing! If we had done that persistently in other realms, we should never have had our buildings lit with electricity, for no man understands electricity. There are certain laws we have discovered, and we are obeying the laws, and the light is illuminating our buildings, and the force is driving the machinery. We have harnessed the lightning, but we do not understand the lightning. These men of Nazareth came into the presence of an actual fact, and they saw wonders, and they were in danger of eternal perdition, because they tarried in the wonder.

That is a peculiar characteristic of our own age. We may not understand the Incarnation, and we never shall; we do not understand the Atonement, and we never shall; but is there any other teacher who spake as this Teacher spoke? Oh, no. We are bound to admit the wisdom. We may be puzzled. Let us postpone the problem, and obey. That was the blunder of the men of Nazareth. They saw the wonders, and their attitude remained the same as when on a former occasion they had tried to fling Him over the brow of the hill.

And immediately growing out of this there is the tremendous blunder of attempting to account for Christ by ordinary standards. There are men who say: Until we can account for Him we cannot submit to Him. If we could account for Him, we would not submit, because there are many people we can account for by ordinary standards, and we have never submitted to them. If we could once put the Christ of God into the formulæ of human interpretation, we should consider Him useless as Teacher, and Lord, and Saviour. It is because He towers above us, and impresses us, and baffles us, and eludes us; enwraps us with love, and thrills us with power; that we are Christians. We are Christians in the presence of the Infinite Mystery, infinitely more than in the presence of things that can be perfectly explained.

There is another peril, that of familiarity with Jesus. There is a terrible danger threatening those born in the atmosphere of Christianity. We may thank God for Christian parents and Christian home training. And yet, oh the peril of it! As a great preacher once said to a crowd of preachers, Whatever else you lose, pray God you may never lose the element of surprise when you see Jesus. Does He startle us? Does He astonish and surprise us? Let us be careful not to be familiar with the familiarity of the men of Nazareth. If they had not known Him so well, they might have known Him better, and that principle abides for ever true.

One thought as to the lessons of co-operative fellowship for workers. Let us remember concerning each other as with Him, faith fertilises, criticism sterilises. It is in the atmosphere of faith, and belief, and confidence, that the worker does his best. It is the critical, and the cynical, that kills.

And yet once more. Are we ever guilty of hindering Him by unbelief? He is the same to-day. If we are saying in our hearts we are not sure of Him, we shall have to end by saying, He did not many mighty works. It is when we come believing in Him that He touches our hearts with His fingers, and heaven's music is in our souls. He is to-day, as ever, the One Who answers faith. God help us to believe in Him with all our heart and soul. So shall we receive from Him new wisdom and new light in all the enterprises of life.

MATTHEW XIV. 1-22

IN this passage we are introduced to two other opposing forces; first, the opposition of the false king Herod, which was threatened; secondly, that of the multitudes, which did not seem to be opposition, but which Christ treated as hindrance rather than help.

To see this division of our paragraph is to understand the place of these narratives in the history of the King.

Let us, then, carefully notice its structure. First observe the connection between verses one and two, and verse thirteen. "At that season Herod the tetrarch heard the report concerning Jesus, and said unto his servants, This is John the Baptist; he is risen from the dead; and therefore do these powers work in him." "Now when Jesus heard it, He withdrew." That is the true connection. Verse thirteen should be read, as to the continuity of the story, in immediate connection with verses one and two. It was not when He heard the story of the death of John. That had taken place before, and is introduced here for a special purpose, as we shall see. It was when Jesus heard what Herod the tetrarch was saying concerning Him that "He withdrew from thence in a boat, to a desert place apart."

In verses three to twelve we have the story of the murder of John, told here because of the light it throws upon the character of Herod, and because it explains Herod's attitude at that time toward Jesus. Herod heard of the fame of Jesus, of the mighty works that were manifesting themselves wherever He went, and he said, "This is John the Baptist risen from the dead." We do not understand that opinion, until we have read the story that follows of how Herod had rid himself of John, and until we begin to enter into the feelings of Herod, and remember how a guilty conscience makes cowards of us all. It was the cry of a terror-stricken conscience, but it created his attitude toward the Christ. When, presently, he pulled himself together, he in all probability said: Of course it is not John the Baptist, but it is another who is saying similar things; I must be rid of him. Opposition threatened the King therefore from that quarter. When Jesus heard that His claim had reached the Herodian dwelling, and that Herod was at first afraid, He withdrew thus in a boat, and departed to a desert place, for Herod's case was utterly hopeless. It is at this act of Jesus, that we must look very carefully.

In John's Gospel we have an explanation of the action of Jesus, when He withdrew from the multitude. It was when He found they would take Him by force and make Him King, that He withdrew. Our King is seen therefore withdrawing Himself from the fear and opposition of the false king; and He is seen moreover withdrawing Himself from the desire of the multitude to crown Him under certain clearly defined conditions.

First, the attitude of Herod. The story of Herod is the most terrible in the whole of the New Testament. We will only touch upon certain points which are necessary to our understanding of his relation to our King. Herod was a tetrarch—that is, the ruler of a fourth part—who claimed the title of king. That sentence should be enough to give us an insight to one side of his character. He was not a king in the true sense of the word, but one who held rule under authority; and yet he was a man who was rebellious against the authority under which he held sway, and had, as far as possible, established for himself the full courtly life and régime. He was ambitious, aspiring, and rebellious politically. Think again of the man himself. It is an astonishing fact, and one revealing the condition of the age, that he was a descendant of Esau, reigning over a portion of the children of Jacob. He was a dissolute man, giving himself over to all excesses, yet he was a man troubled with a conscience, and perpetually refusing to obey its call. If we trace the story of Herod, we find there was a day when he heard John gladly. In all probability, setting aside for some brief hour the purple of his royalty, he found his way to the prophet to listen to him, and he had come very near the Kingdom which John had proclaimed. Even in that hour of drunken and shameless debauch, in which he ordered the murder of John, there are the evidences of the pain of his conscience. He did not desire to kill John; and yet he did so. It was an hour of drunken and shameless revelry, an hour in which the central attraction was something sprung upon a half-drunken crowd, the dancing of a shameless wanton. It was an

hour that becomes most tragic and awful, when we look carefully at this man Herod; an hour when he felt himself bound by the maudlin honour of an evil oath to violate every principle of right and truth. "For the sake of his oaths." Notice the plural in the Revised. He had repeated his oath more than once, as a drunken man will, the oath that had come out of his diabolic animalism, that had come under the false inspiration of drink.

When shall we be rid of the idea that because we have said a thing, it must be done? If we have taken an oath that violates righteousness, let us break it before the sun sinks. If under some stress we have sworn an oath, let us not think we save our conscience by keeping it; if the oath be evil, then we sear our conscience and spoil it, and wrong ourselves in the keeping of it.

The reports of Jesus reached this man. There came, through the crowds of men about him, the sycophants who had helped him in his baseness, news of some new Power working through the district, doing mighty deeds, speaking wondrous words; and the king, shaking in his purple, said, "This is John the Baptist, he is risen from the dead; and therefore do these powers work in him." There is hardly any doubt that Herod was of the sect of the Sadducees. It has been said he could not be a Sadducee, because he spoke of John's rising from the dead. But that is to forget that in a moment when conscience troubles, a man's false philosophy generally breaks down. Herod's Sadducean philosophy was forgotten as he said, "This is John the Baptist, he is risen from the dead." He was nearer accuracy than he knew, or would have acknowledged, perhaps five minutes after. You cannot murder truth, though you may silence the voice that utters it. It filled him with alarm, and the issue of it must inevitably be a new antagonism to Jesus Christ, for it is a remarkable fact that frenzy born of fear will do the most foolhardy things. Even if he really did believe that this was John the Baptist risen from the dead, that there was a re-incarnation of the prophet, under whom he had been almost persuaded; that would not hinder the man who had violated his conscience and refused the claim of truth, from attempting to lay unholy hands upon him.

That is a very graphic picture which Jesus once drew of a man who had passed the borderline, and was lost, and who said, "Father Abraham, have mercy on me—I have five brethren," send Lazarus to them. And the answer was startling and strange, Christ's own interpretation of Heaven's estimate, however we may account for it; "They have Moses and the prophets, let them hear them—if they hear not Moses and the prophets, neither will they be persuaded, if one rise from the dead." And if Herod would not listen to John, living, he would not listen to him risen from the dead. If Herod would not listen to John ere he murdered him, he would attempt to murder him again, though he came back from the dead. There was a frenzy in his soul as well as a terror; there was a determined opposition to that which he once rejected in the fear that paralysed him; and, "When Jesus heard it, He withdrew from thence in a boat."

This withdrawal of Christ was final. Herod never saw Jesus until Pilate sent Him to him, a few hours before His death. He had long wanted to see Him, and he had been intensely curious about Him; and it is an awful fact that he and Pilate were made friends over the death of Jesus. Herod never heard a single accent of the voice of Jesus. Though he cross-questioned Him, gathered his soldiers about Him, laughed at Him, mocked Him, made sport of Him, and put Him to shame, through the whole process Christ never opened His mouth. There are men for whom Christ has no word. But what a fearful revelation it is of Herod's condition! How far this man must have gone in his determined opposition to truth, before Jesus would be silenced! Upon the very cross, in the midst of all the mystery of His dying pain, a malefactor who demanded His attention, received His pity, and before His glazing eyes the dying Christ flung open the pearly gates of God's own Kingdom to let him in. Yet He had not a word for Herod.

Why did Jesus withdraw Himself? It was the attitude of the true King towards the false. He once sent Herod a message; "Go and say to that fox, Behold, I cast out demons and perform cures to-day and to-morrow, and the third day I am perfected. Nevertheless I must go on My way to-day and to-morrow, and the day following; for it cannot be that a prophet perish out of Jerusalem" (Luke xiii. 32, 33). Mark the pathetic majesty of this word of Jesus to Herod. It is reported that Herod would kill Thee, said the Pharisees, and with the only touch of contempt we ever find in the words of Jesus, He said, "Go and say to that fox," go tell him that he is helpless, there is no fear in My heart of him, he cannot kill Me until I have done My day's work. I have three days' work to do—this was figurative, poetic—two of them will be for works of wonder wrought in the sight of men, the third will be a day of mystery and darkness and passion, the perfecting day. So that when He withdrew, it was not for fear of Herod, but it was because the two days' work was not yet finished. The hour had not yet come for the third day's mystery and perfecting; and He passed with quiet dignity out of the reach of the man, left him to his terror, his fear, and his frenzy; abandoned him.

There are occasions when it seems as though men are rejecting Jesus; when as a matter of fact, He is rejecting them. He never rejects a man until the man rejects Him; but there is a moment when the line is crossed. We often speak of Jerusalem's rejection of Christ. Never forget that we have not told all the story until we remember that there came a day when He went back to Jerusalem officially, with Kingly dignity, and rejected it. There were tears in His voice, there was pain in His heart when He did it, for God's act of judgment is always a strange act. There was a day when He looked over Jerusalem and said, "O Jerusalem, Jerusalem—how often would I have gathered thy children together, even as a hen gathereth her own brood under her wings, and ye would not!"—*I would; ye would not;* —"Behold your house is left unto you desolate." If Jerusalem rejected Him, the final word, the higher word, the reigning word, the word that had the throne of God behind it, was the word that declared that He rejected it. So with Herod. The King turned His back upon the man who had his opportunity, and had flung it away.

Then the scene strangely changes. Christ, escaping to a desert place, there found the ubiquitous crowd waiting for Him. One never reads these stories without noticing how the multitudes flocked after Him. Then follows the story of the feeding, a beautiful story in itself, which we must pass over now so far as making any application of it to our own condition is concerned. He had fed the multitudes, and again He withdrew. In John's Gospel we find an explanation of Christ's withdrawal in this case. "When therefore the people saw the sign which He did, they said, This is of a truth the prophet that cometh into the world. Jesus therefore perceiving that they were about to come and take Him by force, to make Him King, withdrew again into the mountain Himself alone" (John vi. 14, 15). There Jesus is seen withdrawing from Kingship. He had just fed five thousand men, besides women and children; and they were gathering around Him, most likely consulting in crowds, and He saw the popular will and wish to compel Him to become their King. It was one of those tense moments when a man may do anything with a crowd. Jesus Christ might at that moment have been crowned King, He might have gathered that five thousand men about Him and led them up against Jerusalem, not to victory perhaps, but He might have roused them. It was an electric moment. They were determined to have Him for their King. It was His chance, His opportunity, even the disciples might have said. But what was the motive behind the popular acclaim? Their motive was that of the material benefit they found He was able to bestow. If this Man can feed us as He has done, with five loaves and two

fishes, let us crown Him; we can have perpetual spring-time, perpetual harvest, perpetual plenty. There will be no more sighing or material discomfort; let us crown Him. The motive was material.

And then mark the method; Let us take Him by force, and make Him King; which may mean, either let us compel Him to the Kingship, or let Him claim His Kingdom by force. What was Jesus' answer to this attitude? Refusal. He refused the motive, He refused the method. He would not be made King upon any such basis. It is well to remember to-day that Jesus Christ declines to be made King upon the basis of His ability to feed hungry men with material bread. If we will make Him King as He ought to be made King, He will take care of all the things that follow; but He will not begin there. We cannot make Jesus King of the social order, until we have made Him King of the spiritual fact at the centre of our being. He refused the method of force, He dismissed the multitude, first sending His disciples away. Perhaps there was a touch of sweet art and high policy in the sending of the disciples away, knowing they would side with the multitude. They were always attempting to force Him. There are some who believe that Judas's action in betraying Him, was an attempt to force Him to take up His Kingdom. After He was risen they came back with the same old question, "Dost Thou at this time restore the kingdom to Israel?" Art Thou not going to do something?

So He sent them away first, very tenderly and beautifully, over the lake out of the way of the crisis, for He alone was equal to it. Alone He dismissed the multitudes, and went to the mountain. We have no account of what He said or did in the mountain when He was alone. One feels one would have liked to go with Him. But it is only permitted for us reverently to see Him as He turned His back upon the false king Herod, and upon the false thinking of the multitudes to look into the face of Him from Whom He should receive the Kingdom, the One Whose Throne He was here to establish and defend, and bring men into relationship with, as He turned from the clamour of the crowd that fain would have crowned Him. The real meaning of this act of Jesus is to be gathered from a study of the discourse chronicled by John wherein, on the next day, coming back to the question, Jesus reopened the question of that feeding of the multitude, and rebuked them because they were still materialised, seeking Him not because they saw signs, not even because of the wonder of what He did, but because they ate of the loaves, and were filled. In that discourse, following His action of turning His back upon the crowds, is contained the rebuke of all material ideals, and His enforcement of the fact of the supremacy of the spiritual.

And now, in conclusion, let us take these two movements in our study, and ask, What have they to say to us? Very solemnly one looks back at Christ's attitude toward Herod, and remembers that Christ's victories over corrupt rule were gained by withdrawal from that rule. There are things which are self-destructive. To such He makes no appearance. To such He utters no word. He leaves all the false rule and authority to work out its own inevitable destruction. Herod's curiosity was for ever unsatisfied. Herod's opposition was always eluded. Herod's doom was sealed by his own choice; and all that Jesus did for the ensuring of his doom was, when he had chosen, to let him alone. Oh, is there not in that some voice for us also? Is there not in it more than the message to kings and those in authority? How often have we put Him away when He has come to us? Remember if He goes, He abides by our decision; and that is our unutterable undoing. He has nothing to do save to leave us alone.

But turn to the other side. What are we to learn from Christ's attitude to the crowd? That Christ fed the multitudes despite their sin and despite their folly. Christ did not even ask

that they should bring a recommendation from the synagogue, before He gave them a meal. He took them just as they were, the hungry crowd; and we cannot gather together five thousand men, beside women and children, without having a strange assortment. He never asked a question about character. He fed them because they were hungry, and a hungry man, if he is the worst in the city, touches the heart of God with pity, and it is for us to feed him. Jesus did not begin by saying to a man, If you will enter My Kingdom, I will feed you. He fed him. But then He will not let a man say, Now, because You have fed me I will come into Thy Kingdom. No, a man must begin somewhere else. I will feed you, I will care for you, My pity will manifest itself in benevolent activity toward you, even though you are going to crucify Me. But I will not be crowned King upon the basis of that feeding. He will not ascend the throne of our life on that basis. He does not begin in the accidentals but in the essential. He does not base His throne upon the shifting sand of a man's material needs; He must establish it upon the rock of a man's spiritual recognition and spiritual life. He begins in the realm of spirit, but having begun there He proceeds through all the life, and the man who crowns Him honestly in the depth of his spiritual nature, may rest assured that He will take under His care and guidance and provision all his material life, and all his mental life.

It may be He will make poorer instead of richer; one of the most beneficent things that could happen to some. To crown Christ in the spiritual, and to obey Him, is sometimes to have to disgorge in the material. Jesus Christ will only be crowned upon the basis of Deity, the spiritual in us finding essential Deity in Him and bowing to it. When we do that He comes to us as King, and when He comes, He comes to break oppression, to set the prisoner free. May God help us to crown Him there, and so to find His gifts extending through all our lives.

MATTHEW XIV. 22-36

THE picture at which we are now to look stands in remarkable contrast to three which have immediately preceded it. All the outstanding facts noticed in them are revealed by contrast more clearly in this story. The first picture ended with the words, "He did not many mighty works there because of their unbelief;" but in this picture we see Him working one of His mightiest works. In the second picture we saw Him hiding Himself from a man who was afraid of Him, imagining that He was an apparition; in this picture the disciples also said, "It is a ghost;" they also being filled with fear; but instead of hiding Himself from them, He came nearer, and said, "Be of good cheer; it is I; be not afraid." In the third case we saw that He declined to be crowned upon the conditions which men desired; but in this picture we see Him holding the reins, and swaying the sceptre, and manipulating all events. Here we see Him the crowned Lord, in the midst of His own Kingdom. It was a poor Kingdom, measured by all the standards of men, just a frail fisherman's rowing boat, in the midst of a storm-tossed sea; a boat that the men who knew it best were absolutely failing to manage. Nevertheless, that little boat in the midst of the sea, that handful of men, that One Lord and Master; constituted God's established Kingdom in the world at that moment. His own had refused Him at Nazareth. The reigning authority, Herod, was seeking to find Him, probably that he might deal with Him as he had dealt with John. The multitudes would have been glad to have Him if He would have come to the throne on the basis of feeding them without work. He had left Nazareth, He had turned His back on Herod, and He had declined the Kingdom; and here He was in the midst of His Kingdom in that little boat, in which all God's enterprises were embarked. If we had known it at the moment, and had stood on the seashore, and had looked, we should have been as much afraid about God's Kingdom in the world as we are sometimes still. We should have imagined that the next wave would have engulfed the little boat, as we sometimes still think the next wave will destroy God's programme and God's purpose. So it is well for us to look back at the actual picture of Christ's Kingdom at that moment; and then to see how far it has spread, and to observe it in contrast with other things, that we may learn lessons of permanent value for our own help.

Notice first, then, the contrast between this picture and the other three a little more fully. First, "He did not many mighty works *there* because of their unbelief." Why was it that *here* He could do such a mighty work? Because here faith reposed in Him. You say that it was frail faith, and faulty faith, and failing faith. Yes, but it was simple faith, and convinced faith. Faith may often falter, and yet never finally fail. Faith may often tremble, and yet still continue to be faith. Faith does not always mean the fully instructed intellect grasping the whole fact. The faith that saves is a personal confidence in Christ. And that is what these men on the boat possessed. He came from the loneliness of the mountain, and prayer, to men who believed in Him. And again we have a revelation of uttermost importance—that we sterilise the power of the Christ when we are merely critical in His presence, but we create an atmosphere in which He can do His mighty works, when our faith simply and quietly takes hold upon Him. It is the difference between the Nazareth picture, and the sea picture. In the one case, we see men who thought they knew all about Him and refused to accept the things that astonished them; and because of their criticism He could do nothing. But He came to these bewildered, blundering men who had come to Him, and stilled the sea, and hushed the wind and made His power manifest.

Now look again at the next contrast; and notice the difference between the case of His hiding and the case of His revelation. On both occasions men took Him for something supernatural, strange, or, to use that very expressive Scotch word, uncanny. In the one case we see a man who was afraid of the mystic, who expressed himself imperfectly, hardly believing what he said —for we cannot really think Herod believed it was John the Baptist; it was just an exclamation of a panic-stricken conscience;—from that man He hid Himself, because he had deliberately and positively shut his eyes in the presence of light, and stopped his ears in the presence of truth, and sold his soul to keep a false oath made to a dancing wanton.

But on the other hand we see men who, in spite of all their failure, in spite of all their faltering, in spite of all their shortcoming, were true to the light they had received, and to them He revealed Himself. At that very moment they were doing a difficult thing. He had sent them in a boat to the other side of the sea. Matthew tells the story with artless simplicity. "The boat was now in the midst of the sea, distressed by the waves; for the wind was contrary." Think of it for a moment, and what it reveals. What should we have done under like circumstances? The probability is that, being as these men were, accustomed to the storms on Galilee, well able to manage the boat, we should have turned the boat round and run with the wind, for all the difficulty came out of the fact that the wind was contrary. It is not easy to turn a boat against the wind, but even that is easier than continuing to proceed against the wind. Why did they not do that? Because He had said, Cross to the other side; and it was their loyalty to Him which kept them in the place of peril. He had pointed to the other shore, and those blundering, frail, faulty men; men so much like ourselves that we are bound to love them when we read of them, were at any rate true enough to what they knew, to keep the prow pointing to the shore He indicated for them. Consequently He came to them, and when their hearts were sick with fear in the presence of the apparition, with splendid cheerfulness He spoke out of the mystery and said, "Be of good cheer; It is I; be not afraid."

Finally notice the contrast between this story, and the story of His refusal to be crowned. We have dwelt at length with His refusal to be crowned as indicating the perpetual principle that He will never be crowned upon the basis of supplying material things. He will supply material things, but we must crown Him for other reasons. Now here were men over whom He exercised the sway of a great Kingship. Where is the contrast? First, they were obedient men. Nay, we may go further back, they were, first, surrendered men. They were the men who constituted His Kingdom up to that moment, not the crowds that He fed. They were obedient men; they had set the prow of their vessel in the direction He had indicated. They were distressed men, distressed by the waves and the contrary wind. As the story goes forward, we see them to be men strangely perplexed by His coming, by this apparition. And yet as we watch them a little longer, we see they were men who out of the midst of their perplexity, when suddenly light broke upon them, were venturesome. Peter was the spokesman again; just a little in front of the others in the matter; he said, "Lord, if it be Thou, bid me come unto Thee upon the waters." In the next place they were men who were liable to fail even in their venture of faith. Peter came and walked upon the water. Some men criticise Peter and say he had no right to do it, that it was presumption. Christ said, "Come," and He never invites us to do anything that is presumptuous. Some pictures represent Peter as leaving the boat and beginning to sink at once. No. "Peter . . . walked upon the waters to come to Jesus." He did the thing he wanted to do; he made the venture of faith, and achieved the victory of faith. And yet we see that he failed also. There was a moment when he took his eyes off his Lord and fixed them upon the surrounding circumstances, and he went down. To do that is always to sink.

And yet what is the last thing recorded? They worshipped Jesus. "And they that were in the boat worshipped Him, saying, Of a truth Thou art the Son of God." It was not a Kingdom of perfect souls, but it was a Kingdom of souls that had put their trust in Him, and over whom He was reigning in order to make them perfect; patiently leading them on, waiting for them, halting by them, attempting to lead them by rapid stages, for "He would have passed by them," says one of the Evangelists. He tried their faith, but when faith was unequal to the strain He turned to them and delivered them. It is a perfect picture of His Kingdom as it is to-day. These were the men who had crowned Him upon the basis of the essential truth He had presented to them, who had crowned Him upon the basis of the spiritual within them. And He delivered them in the hour of material difficulty.

Let us look at this story from another standpoint. If in its setting it is a revelation of essential truth concerning His Kingdom by a contrast with the other pictures, then it remains for evermore a picture of Jesus in relation to His Church. There may be many applications, but we will confine ourselves to one. Here we have the revelation of our Lord's relation to His people in the times of difficulty and trouble and peril, which come to them because of their loyalty to His supreme will. One would not wish to take this story away from any tempest-tossed soul whatever may be the nature of the tempest; and yet it would not appear that this message is to those who may be in sorrow or in difficulty or in the midst of tempest as the result of their own disobedience. It seems to exclude them from this story, but it does not exclude them from the Christ. Whatever difficulty we have found our way into—and we have found our way into more difficulties through disobedience than obedience—He is always there to help us out. Peter got into difficulty when he sank, through failure, and the Lord was there "immediately." It is one of those words which ought to be printed in gold, and hung up in view of all faltering souls—"IMMEDIATELY!"

He then said to him, "O thou of little faith, wherefore didst thou doubt?" One would rather have missed the touch of His hand, and have missed the rebuke. But if we fall as Peter fell, and sink, thank God for the quick hand of our Lord, which is always there.

But the essential values of this are for obedient souls in difficulty. First we see the perfect picture of the relationship of Christ to His people to-day. When this story opens He was on the mountain alone with God. It was one of those rare and beautiful and brief occasions in which He broke away from the pressure of the crowd and was alone with God. It was His place of rest, of joy, of quietness, of perfect peace. His disciples were on the sea, where He put them, in the place of peril. He was in the place of calm restfulness; they were in the place where the storm might sweep at any moment. Such is the contrast between the attitude of Jesus our Master now, and ourselves. He has reached the right hand of His Father. All of us are on the sea. There are some who know nothing of storms. Thank God for every sunshiny day, with blue sky and sea; but the storm may come. That is the first contrast, He in the place of rest, we in the place of toil; He in the place of perfect calm, we in the place where the hurricanes may sweep at any moment.

What next? The storm which came to Gennesaret was one of those hurricanes about which we know so little, sweeping down upon the men ere they knew it, tossing wave upon wave, the whole sky black with a sudden blackness, and they, in imminent peril of their lives. Where was their Lord? First, notice that He had never lost sight of them, though He was on the mountain and they were on the sea. So now, He will have even His rest and communion broken in upon if His own people are in trouble, and He will never rest perfectly in high heaven so long as His own are tempest-tossed upon the sea of the little while. He turned His back upon the mountain, and treading its slopes, and crossing the intervening space, He put His feet upon the waters, and mark this as He went to them, in overtaking them, He went in the way they had gone. He did not meet them as from the other side; He followed them. He went to them over the very waters that threatened to engulf them, easily Master of them all; through the very wind that was contrary to them, it seeming to open its doors as He came with easy, quiet majesty.

Is this not a revelation that should give us peace? The billows perhaps are breaking upon the frail craft of some soul, some child of God, and all the storm that is being experienced is because he is where God has put him. But he is in the path of obedience and he knows it; no one can rob him of that sweet consciousness and conviction. But Christ does not seem to be near; He seems to be away in the day of tempest, and trial, and storm. That soul says, I was in a storm once before, and He was on the vessel and I could wake Him, but He is not here to-day, this is different. Ah, but He knows, He is coming. It is too dark for you to see Him yet, but He is coming. He cannot leave you alone to perish. And mark this, He is coming over the very waves you are most afraid of. The very waves that threaten to buffet and break you to pieces are the pavement for His blessed feet. But you say, it is not the waves, it is the contrary wind; if I could only turn round and run with the wind. But He is coming through that wind, and as the waves become adamant at the touch of His feet, the wind loses its power to hinder, when the majesty of His presence confronts it.

But look again at our picture. The darkest part of the dark night to those men was not the darkness of the clouds, not the terror of the wind, not the threatening billows; the most terrible thing in all that night was the phantom. They forgot all about the storm as they peered over the side of the vessel at the strange phantom approaching them over the waters. They were for the most part rough-handed fishermen. They knew the use of the oar. The storm was more than usually severe; they could fight that, but they could not fight a ghost. The most terrible

troubles that come to us are the unexplained, and the unexplainable things. There are troubles very severe, but they are common to all men. We expect them, they must come presently. But once or twice in the course of a lifetime, there come to every man and woman days of great horror of darkness, that have no explanation. "Mine own familiar friend in whom I trusted; who did eat of my bread! hath lifted up his heel against me." That is an almost unsurpassed horror of darkness. It may be you have never known it, it may be you never will; God grant you never may. It was trouble inexplicable that came to them that night. As they strained in their looking out over the side of the ship at this strange apparition, this phantom of the night, suddenly it took voice and said, "Be of good cheer; it is I." That is a part of the story where exposition fails. We cannot explain it; it is so simple a story, we are so familiar with it.

But what is the spiritual value here for a tempest-tossed soul? That almost invariably to the soul that is really trusting and true, the darkest hour is the dawning of the clearest day; the direst sorrow of the heart is that out of which the chief joy of life comes; the most brutal bruising of the vintage is that out of which the finest wine comes forth. The phantom is the Master. The hours that some of us would be most loath to have undone in our past are the hours of our greatest sorrows. It was in them we found Him; it was in them we heard the infinite music saying, "Be of good cheer; it is I; be not afraid." We may do without that yesterday of sunshine, but not without that day before, of shadow. It was out of that He came close to us. We have all sorts of little proverbs, some of them very true, and some of them very foolish; but a proverb we make great use of is, "Man's extremity is God's opportunity." Quite true! But let us revise it thus—Man's extremity is man's opportunity for finding God. It is in the hour of greatest heart-ache that we find Him. Be still, sad heart, if it be possible; wait, rest in the Lord, and wait patiently for Him, and presently you will look back to the day of your unutterable agony, and you will say, For that day above all days His name be praised; out of that darkness came the light; out of that bitterness came the sweetness; out of that mysterious phantom chilling my heart and well-nigh stopping my pulses, came my Lord, warming my heart and making every fibre pulsate with new joy and new enthusiasm.

Let us take one thing more out of this story. Matthew says, They gladly received Him on board, and they crossed over. Mark says, He came on board, and they crossed over, they finished the journey. But John says something else, "They were willing to receive Him into the boat; and straightway the boat was at the land whither they were going." What are we to understand by that word of John? Are we to understand there was a miracle wrought there; that the ship in the midst of the sea finished the journey by the annihilation of time and space? In our eagerness to retain all

the miracles we need not be eager to read miracles into things that are not miracles. John the mystic, John the lover, John the man who talks most about fellowship says, When He came on board we were there directly. Did not John go as far as the rest? "Straightway!" Every youth and maiden who is in love understands that. A long journey may be covered in what seems but a few moments. "Straightway the boat was at the land whither they were going." The storms are about us yet, and He is trying our faith by being absent from us, or so it seems. We are never far from Him nor He from us. He is coming over the waters and through the wind. Presently in the company of the King, we shall be home, and we shall hear His voice more clearly and see His face perfectly. O that God may help us to be so true to Him that He may be able to correct all our faltering and failing! May we be in His Kingdom, and He our King.

MATTHEW XV. 1-20

IN the verses we are now to consider we are still face to face with the manifestation of opposition to the King. Indeed, prior to the dividing of the ways at Cæsarea Philippi, the account of which is found in the next chapter, opposition became more direct, more keen, more systematic.

These Pharisees and scribes constituted a very definite deputation from Jerusalem. They sought Him out with the set purpose of critical consultation, the nature of their question revealed their eagerness and anxiety to draw Him into controversy; their critical attitude was at once manifest. The first eleven verses tell us the story of their coming, and of how the Lord dealt with them. In the other nine verses we have the account of the conversation of the disciples with Jesus concerning what He had said to the Pharisees, and the way in which He had dealt with them.

In the second verse we have the Pharisees' question. At the close of the section we find that our Lord was

still dealing with that subject, though speaking to His disciples.

The fame of Jesus was spreading, and His influence was also spreading among the common people, that is among all the people who did not hold official positions. All sorts and conditions of men were attracted by Christ. Pharisees and publicans mingled oftentimes; the rulers and the ruled were side by side; rich and poor, learned and illiterate followed Him and listened to Him. The attractive power of Jesus Christ did not lie in the accidentals which appealed to a few; it was rather that of His essential humanity, which found an answer in all human life, notwithstanding the accidentals of birth and position and education. There was growing opposition, but at the same time there was growing attractiveness; and men were crowding after Him, and that, notwithstanding that He was saying things of increasing severity as time went on.

At last this deputation of Pharisees and scribes came from Jerusalem, and came with a definite problem. The point of their criticism does not appear upon the surface. They asked, " Why do Thy disciples transgress the tradition of the elders? for they wash not their hands when they eat bread." Behind this question there lay the essential difference between their religion, and that of Jesus Christ. It is as though they had said to Him, We are anxious to understand Your position, and the meaning of Your teaching; and we bring You a simple illustration of difference between Your disciples and ours. We are ready to enter into consultation. Is there any way of compromise between us? They did not at the first say how strong was their objection to the attitude of His disciples; that they considered that His disciples were doing wrong. They simply asked a question, Why do Thy disciples eat bread with unwashed hands?

Now, in order to understand Christ's answer, it is necessary to recognize that this was not a question as to cleanliness; it was purely a question of ritual. They were objecting to the fact that His disciples, in their comradeship with Christ, neglected certain ceremonial observances, which they, the Pharisees, held to be of supreme importance. The whole religious life of Hebraism at this time had become encumbered with ceremonial observances that followed men into all the details of their lives; and these were based upon the interpretation of men, who had added the traditions of the elders to the divinely revealed religion. This very question of washing before meals was the result of a tradition that Shibta, a demon, sat upon the hands of men as they slept during the hours of the night, and if any person should touch his food with unwashed hands, then that demon sat upon his food and made it dangerous. We are very much inclined to smile at this, but it was the actual teaching of certain of the Rabbis. The Rabbi Taanith, in consequence of this superstition, taught that, " Whosoever hath his abode in the land of Israel and eateth his common food with washed hands, and speaks the holy language, and recites his phylacteries morning and evening, he may rest assured that

he shall obtain eternal life." Gradually religion had degenerated into the observance of such outward ceremonies as these. Men who had taught these things came to Jesus Christ and asked Him, How is it that Your disciples neglect this washing of hands, this ritualistic ceremonial before meals, whereby men may be made sure of eternal life? Thus behind the local and illustrative question, there existed their concern that the disciples of Jesus had violated tradition; and what that meant may be gathered from other Rabbinical teachings. One of the Rabbis had declared; " The words of the elders are weightier than the words of the prophets." While yet another had said, " Some of the words of the law and the prophets are weighty, others are not weighty. All the words of tradition are weighty words." Thus the real condition of affairs was that these Pharisees and scribes, who had become the authoritative interpreters of the law of God, had super-added thereto the tradition of elders; indeed they had submerged the law of God beneath tradition; they had actually minimised the value of the law of God and the messages of the prophets in their exaltation of these traditions. They said in effect, The Scriptures of the Hebrew people are not enough, they must be interpreted; and interpretation in many cases had become contradiction. Out of the midst of their traditions they brought this one illustration of how the disciples of Jesus Christ were violating them.

Our Lord's answer to these men was twofold. First, He directly answered the Pharisees; and then He called the multitudes to Him, and uttered a very remarkable and solemn word of warning to them about the Pharisees.

He commenced His answer to the Pharisees with the words; " Why do ye *also?* "—Mark the " *also;*" there is tremendous force in it. There was not a single word in Christ's answer that denied that His disciples had violated tradition. So far from denying that they had violated tradition, He vindicated them for doing so. If He had for one single moment said anything, or said what He did say in such a form as to suggest that after all they had not violated tradition, there may have been some excuse for tradition. But He did not, and therefore the set teaching of this passage is against tradition.

He admitted their violation in the word "also;" they did not wash their hands, not merely by neglect, but of set purpose. They had swept out of their lives the very things upon which the Pharisees set value.

His whole question to these Pharisees was: "Why do ye also transgress the commandment of God, because of your tradition?" and in that answering inquiry we come to the very heart of the difference between the religion of the Pharisees and the religion of Jesus Christ. He charged them that by their very tradition they had transgressed the commandment of God. His question suggested the inference, that the supreme thing in every life is not human tradition, but God's commandment.

These men had brought an illustration of how His disciples violated tradition. He gave them one of how they, by tradition, violated the Divine Commandment. He said to them in effect; You have a tradition that if a man shall say over anything that he possesses, "Corban"—that is, it is devoted; or it is a gift to God; in the case of everything so protected, he shall not only not be compelled to minister to the need of his parents, but is forbidden to do so.

Thus the King showed by this supreme and remarkable contrast, how tradition violated the commandment of God to honour father and mother; in that they would allow some mystic word to be pronounced to save a man from obligation; and thus a man was taught by tradition, that he could be religious and true to God, a worshipper, and a man of high principle, while all the while he was violating God's first commandment with promise. Our Lord did not answer them by dealing first with their own illustration, but by providing another illustration to show how tradition may cause a man to break in upon his relationship to God.

Then by quotation from their own ancient prophecy, which He directly applied to them, He revealed the secret of their failure;—

" Ye hypocrites, well did Isaiah prophesy of you, saying,
This people honoureth Me with their lips,
But their heart is far from Me.
But in vain do they worship Me,
Teaching as their doctrines the precepts of men."

Christ's charge was that it is possible to honour God with the lip while the heart is far from Him.

Then He turned to the multitudes, and, calling them to Him, He rebuked the Pharisees. In the words He uttered to the multitudes we find His condemnation of external religion, and His affirmation of the importance of heart relationship.

Now He took up their own illustration, as He said; the things that enter a man as to his body never defile a man, but the things that come from the centre of a man's essential life are the things that defile. How revolutionary these words must have sounded in the hearing of the multitudes; how searching even to His own disciples; and how angry they must have made the Pharisees. What to eat, and what not to eat; what to wear, and what not to wear; what to do and what not to do; these were trivialities which had become supreme matters in the influence and the teaching of scribes and Pharisees. In correction the King declared; It is not the thing that a man touches in his physical life that pollutes him. Not that Jesus meant to say that there is no relationship between the physical and spiritual. We must not take a single text and base a false philosophy upon it, or we shall be violating the commandment of God as these men did. There is the closest relationship between spirit, mind, and body; and this is taught throughout the old and new economies. But when a man thinks he makes himself religious by observing rules which deal only with the physical, he has missed the heart and centre of religion; and therefore the King affirmed in the hearing of the multitudes, that it was not the physical thing that entered into the man that defiled him, but the things that came from his heart, the seat of intelligence, and emotion, and will the spiritual centre of a man. Christ said that from that spiritual centre spring all the forces that defile. So that a man may wash his hands not only before meals, but as the Pharisees did, between the courses, a man may be ceremonially clean by the observance of all the traditions of the elders, and yet his heart may be a veritable sink of iniquity, a flowing stream and a river, not polluting himself only, but also the life of family, friends, of the city and the nation. This was the King's protest against any religion that consists in the observance of externalities; and His affirmation of the fact that nothing makes life pure but inward purity which will influence all the externalities.

After this teaching the disciples came to Jesus, filled with concern. They said, Do you know that the Pharisees are offended? There is a very human touch in this; something that makes it very kin to our own age. They seemed to say, The deputation was from Jerusalem, a deputation of elders; they were men of light and learning, and You have offended these men? Perhaps there was a touch of reproach in their question. Observe what we may describe as the ruthlessness of Christ's answer. There is no pity in the word of Jesus for error, no matter by whomsoever the error may be taught. Men who were violating the commandment of God by insisting upon the tradition, men who were hiding that commandment underneath tradition had no place in His pity. Our Lord said, " Every plant which My heavenly Father planted not, shall be rooted up." He was not referring to the men, but to the system for which they stood; and in effect He said to His disciples, when they told Him the Pharisees were offended, that He had nothing to do with these Pharisees. He never descended to the level of dealing with men personally in order to hurt and harm them. The plant of traditional religion God had not planted, and it was His indication of His method with His disciples when He told them that the plants which were not of God's

planting must be rooted up Therefore He said, " Let them alone: they are blind guides." That explained what He had done. He had not attacked them; He was not dealing with them as individuals; but with the evil thing in their system and teaching. He came, the Truth, to correct error; He came, God's own great Vine of life, and light, and love, to destroy the false fungus growths upon religious thinking which were sapping the very life of men and ruining them. When Peter came and inquired the meaning of the parable, showing how they were astonished at the radical thing Jesus had said, He repeated what He had already said as to the sources of defilement.

Now let us notice the teaching of this section for ourselves. First, in His dealing with the tradition of the scribes and Pharisees, Christ revealed the perpetual conflict between divine and human religion. Human religion is conditioned in externalities, and therefore fails to touch essential life. Divine religion begins in essential life, and from that centre governs the last externality. There is perpetual difference. It is manifest all through the New Testament, and when we come to the teaching of the Epistles we find it specially emphasised. If we take the Galatian Epistle, the charter of Christian liberty, it sets at nought the idea that any man may be made spiritual by fleshly observance; and insists upon the necessity for spiritual relationship, if there is to be spiritual purity. The difference between human and divine religion is always seen in this respect. In all heathen religions, religion and morality are divorced. This is the supreme test of religion. Is our religion a thing of the heart, a communion between our inner life and God, a force that drives us to the watch-tower in the morning to catch the gleam of the glory of the pathway of His feet, a passion that sends us back to Him with shame and disgust when we have sinned? That is the true religion. If Jesus in all the virtue of His life and love sits sentinel in our heart we shall guard our lips, and be careful as to what we eat or drink; but it is not the things that enter in, but the things that come out of the centre which defile the man. That is the perpetual test. Christ's estimate concerning tradition must be ours also. Wherever tradition violates the commandment of God, it is to be violated. And every plant which God has not planted must be rooted up.

Tradition still binds us very largely. We have super-added very much in our Christian life to the simplicity of Jesus Christ. Man is naturally, unless he be very careful, the slave of tradition. In certain parts of Wales people will not lay the bodies of their loved ones to final resting-places save as they are enswathed in flannel, because in a certain reign a law was passed that this should be done for the purpose of giving a new impetus to the flannel industry. There was a reason for the practice once; but the reason has become a tradition, and these people would think they were irreligious if they violated the tradition. What tradition binds us? Are we bound by a tradition that it is a good thing to read our Bible every morning? Break through it if there is nothing more in such reading than the observance of a tradition. If we are simply the slaves of tradition, even though the tradition may have had its foundation in a reason, the tradition becomes a barrier that shuts us out from God. There are some persons, for instance, who are so harmed by the traditions of public worship that all the warmth, and soul, and force of public worship fails to touch them. There are people to whom the tradition of Church relationship has no other value than that of the lightning-conductor to a building. It serves to catch the electric force and carry it off, so that it never touches the building. Our King desires to bring every man from the bondage of everything, into living touch with God. Everything that separates between us and God, though it be the most reli-

gious and sanctified thing by old associations, we had better sweep it away. The very sacred Supper of the Lord may become such a tradition as to shut us out of communion with Jesus Christ. The very ceremony of sacred and reverent worship may become a door that bars us from communion; the very conventionalities of our respectability may become the traditions that exclude us from God.

There must be personal and direct heart relationship with God. Let us therefore be very much afraid of any system of religion that declares that anything more is needed for the cultivation of religious life than the commandment of God. Any interpretation of men becomes at last a tradition. Any exposition which is human, when you lift it into a necessity becomes a curse. There is a place for exposition, there is a place for interpretation, there is a place for teaching; but the interpretation and the exposition, and the teaching, must never be made essential. The essential thing is the commandment of God, and lest our interpretations, and expositions, and traditions, should violate that commandment, let us guard our souls, and let us see to it that we stand first in relationship with God. In true religion there is no room for anything between the spirit of a man and the flaming Spirit of God, and whether the thing between be priest, or sacrament, or ceremony, or observance, it must be swept out,

" Nothing between, Lord, nothing
    between,"

is the cry of the true worshipper, and when that cry is answered, then there is religion which will immediately affect all the externalities. Let us be very much afraid of externalities, lest they seduce us from spiritual worship. Let us very jealously cultivate spiritual worship that it may affect and govern all the externalities of life.

MATTHEW XV. 21-39

THE key to the understanding of this paragraph in its relationship to the progress of the King's enforcement of His claims, is to be found in the opening statement; "And Jesus went out thence, and withdrew into the parts of Tyre and Sidon." A similar statement has occurred before in this Gospel three times at least; and now again we read that He withdrew; but here a break is indicated, and a marked contrast is manifested in the things before His withdrawal and those which followed. Perhaps we may summarize the whole matter by saying that He withdrew from the infidelity of traditional religion, to the faith which lives outside the covenant. He had been exercising His ministry amongst His own people, and, as we have seen, there had been an increase of confidence; men had gathered to Him, and had been helped, healed, and blessed by Him. On the other hand, there had been a clearly defined growth of opposition, which, so far, had culminated in the coming of the deputation of Pharisees and scribes, who raised in illustration the whole question of His method. Now turning His back upon them, and the whole ideal for which they stood, He broke more definitely with His own people than ever before, and went to Tyre and Sidon. The story following gives us the picture of His ministry among people other than His own. The Canaanitish woman, the multitudes that gathered to Him at Decapolis, and the multitudes that He fed, were people outside the Hebrew covenant of flesh relationship. He passed over the border, crossed the line of geographical limitation, and first dealt with the woman who was a daughter of the outcast people. He then exercised the power of His Kingdom among people who were all outside the covenant, and who came into living relationship with Him upon one single principle, as we shall see. Finally, in a great beneficent flow of His tenderness, He fed the multitudes outside the border of Israel, as but recently He had fed the multitudes

within that border. Such is the character of the passage we are now to consider.

First, let us look still more carefully at this contrast of place, and people, and condition. To the King the journey to Tyre and Sidon was one of set purpose, and for specific reason. He must have been supremely conscious of all the blindness that had happened to Israel, of the darkness that had settled upon God's own people, and to Him, may we not say, it was a journey in which the song of the larger purpose was in His heart.

The story of Tyre and Sidon—the region long under the curse of God—lay in the background. Not long before, when warning the cities inside the geographical boundary—Chorazin, Bethsaida, and Capernaum—He held Tyre and Sidon up, as an illustration, to a people who had received the light, saying Tyre and Sidon would have repented in sackcloth and ashes had they had the same light. Having dealt with the Syrophenician woman, He left the immediate neighbourhood of the cities, and came to the sea of Galilee. Mark distinctly tells us that He came into Decapolis, so that it is evident that He remained in Gentile territory and among Gentile people.

Let us look, then, at the new people by whom He was surrounded. Beginning with that Canaanitish woman, we recognize that she was a direct descendant of people who were outcasts in the divine economy, people who had been swept out on account of their awful and disastrous failure in the past, because the love of God needed to make way for purer people to fulfil His purpose in succeeding generations. We learn from Mark that she was a Syrophenician woman, and a Greek. The word Greek does not refer to nationality. She was not a Greek by birth, but one of the Semitic peoples, and yet not within the covenant. She was a Greek by religion, and Greek, as Mark used the word, meant heathen. It has been said that this was the first heathen convert to Christianity. She was undoubtedly a worshipper of Asherah or Astarte, that strange system, false and degraded on the one side, high and beautiful on the other. There were elect souls who saw the higher ideal, and who walked in the glimmering light. It may be this woman in the worship of Astarte had realised the highest ideal possible to her of religion. But presently, she turned from Astarte the goddess of nature, because she was unable therein to find the answer to her deepest need.

The new people also were foreign, using the word foreign as the Hebrew would have used it. In the last part of our chapter, at verse thirty-seven, we read, "And they all ate, and were filled; and they took up that which remained over of the broken pieces, seven baskets full." In the fourteenth chapter and the twentieth verse, we read, "And they all ate, and were filled; and they took up that which remained over of the broken pieces twelve baskets full." In chapter sixteen, verses nine and ten, the margin of the Revised Version draws attention to a suggestive fact when it says, "Basket in verses nine and ten represent different Greek words." Jesus, in referring to the two miracles, said; "Do ye not yet perceive, neither remember the five loaves of the five thousand"—that was the first miracle in the midst of the Hebrew people—"and how many *baskets* ye took up? Neither the seven loaves of the four thousand,"—that was the second miracle among these people outside the covenant—"and how many *baskets* ye took up?" He used two entirely different words in referring to the baskets. The word He used of the first miracle was the same as we have in the account of the first miracle, and the word He used of the second miracle was the same as in the account of the second miracle. There was carefulness and discrimination in this choice of words. If we trace this through the Gospels, we shall find that the four Evangelists give the account of the first miracle, and they all use the first word. Only two of them give the account of the second miracle, and they both use the second word. The difference is that the first

word translated *basket* refers to a receptacle that was peculiarly Hebrew, a small basket in which the travelling Hebrew carried his food. The second word *basket* refers to a much larger receptacle, platted and woven, the basket carried by the Gentile merchantman on his journey. With all accuracy we may describe the difference by saying that the one was the basket of the Jews, and the other the basket of the Gentiles. All this strengthens the view that the feeding of the four thousand was the feeding, not of the people of the same economy, but of people outside. We see the King halting with the child of the cursed race. We see Him healing people outside the covenant in Decapolis. We see Him feeding four thousand people outside the covenant.

Now mark the new condition to which Jesus had come. He had turned His back upon the critical unbelief of the rulers of His own people; and He found Himself in the atmosphere of faith; and this fact drew forth from Him a remarkable commendation. He had warned the people against the Pharisees, the rulers of religion in their own age, but to a woman outside the covenant, an idolater, a worshipper of Astarte, He said, "O woman, great is thy faith: be it done unto thee even as thou wilt."

This faith was manifested not only by the woman, but also by the multitudes. We see Him returning from the city and going to Decapolis and climbing the mountain, and we watch them thronging up after Him. What a sight it must have been, these people crowding, hurrying, jostling after Him, carrying sick, blind, maimed, lame! The Greek word suggests a great rush, and hurry. They flung them at His feet as fast as they could bear them to Him, and as fast as they came He healed them. What wonderful reticence there is in these Gospel narratives! Whole crowds of miracles are packed into a passing sentence; "He healed them." What made these people bring these sick folk? Faith. Not faith as a theoretical conviction, not faith as a creed recited, such as the Pharisees had, but faith in a Person,

200

faith in His ability. With all reverence we may say that day in Decapolis was a great day for Jesus. He found one woman, and He said, " Great is thy faith." He found great multitudes of people in the midst of idolatry, who nevertheless when the light shone, answered it, and carried their sick to Him for healing.

Finally notice, however, that the feeding of the four thousand was not the answer to faith. It was the overplus of His tenderness. Let us not try to add dignity to it by robbing it of its simplicity. He knew that if the multitudes went back as they were they would be hungry and faint; and He fed them. It was the King, unable to hold His bounty in check when hungering men and women, although outside the covenant, were in need.

The great truth taught by all this is that the benefits of the Kingdom are granted to simple faith. Look at this woman. In the background was her religion; in the foreground was her need. The worship of Astarte, perhaps, had sufficed for her till then. But when the dark day came, and the demon entered her child, and she cried and wailed to the goddess Astarte, there was no answer. And so as this woman came to Jesus Christ we see her religious background fading away, because it could not help her. In the foreground there was her anguish. Mark how she came; how faith operated. She came first of all against prejudice, for the prejudice of the Gentile was as great against the Jew as that of the Jew against the Gentile. Here the prejudice was on both sides, and yet this woman, driven by her need, came to seek Him.

She persevered against silence. Sometimes we question the meaning of Christ's strange attitude towards this woman. In Mark's Gospel we read, when He came into this region " He entered into a house, and would have no man know it." He went into the house for rest. How did the woman get to Him? Mark says, " He could not be hid." Why not? She was outside, and her need drew Him forth. He could not remain in hiding or in rest while that woman was outside in trouble. And when He came out of the house she proffered her request, first calling Him Son of David; and He was silent. And the disciples came to Jesus, and said to Him, " Send her away: for she crieth after us." We might misunderstand that request if it were not for Christ's reply to her, which shows that they meant, Give her what she wants and let her go. They were not unkind; they did not mean, Refuse her, send her away. Christ's answer was, " I was not sent but unto the lost sheep of the house of Israel." That was His reason for not giving her what she sought. She still pleaded; and dropped the title distinctive of Hebraism—" Son of David." She put the whole of her need into the one word, " Lord, help me." Then He turned towards her and spoke, and at the first moment His speech seemed almost more unkind than His silence. " It is not meet to take the children's bread and cast it to the dogs." Here again occurs a word we need to examine. There are two distinct words for dogs, and they mark two entirely different ideas. We all know how profound was the hatred of the Hebrew to the low, marauding, fierce, half-scavenger, half-wolf dog of that country. But then it is also true that dogs were found in Jewish households; they were the little dogs, the playthings of the children; and the word Christ used here was that for the little dogs. Probably there was a great welling of pity and tenderness in the voice of Jesus as He said to her, " It is not meet to take the children's bread and cast it to the little dogs." Now, on the basis of that distinction, let us see what she said—" Yea, Lord, for even *the little dogs* eat of the crumbs that fall from their masters' tables."—Notice carefully the placing of the apostrophe. " Masters " is plural. It is as if she said, It is true I am outside the covenant; *they* are masters, they have been for centuries. If you say you cannot take the bread of the children and give it to the little dogs under the table, the playthings of the children, it is quite true; but even the little dogs have the crumbs. It is not surprising that Jesus looked at her and said, " O woman, great is thy faith: be it done unto thee even as thou wilt." Against prejudice she came, against silence she persevered, against exclusion she proceeded, against rebuff she won. That is what He found outside the covenant. Her appeal was based on faith. When she said, " Son of David," it was the hope of faith. When she said, " Lord, help me," it was the appeal of faith. When she said, " True, Lord, yet the little dogs eat of the crumbs," it was what an old Puritan commentator called " the wit of faith," using the word wit in the true old Saxon sense, the tact of faith.

Turn for a moment from the woman, and glance at the multitudes. We have exactly the same truth—the Kingdom benefits given in answer to faith. The bringing of the unfit to Jesus was a venture of faith, in all likelihood the outcome of this woman's victory, for faith is always propagative, and some one else will believe because we have believed. Let faith in Christ be manifested in some victory we gain, and there is nothing in the wide world more propagative of faith in other people. As we see these people crowd up the mountain sides carrying all the incompetents of the neighbourhood, what does it mean? That one woman's faith, which had won a victory, had created faith in Jesus in the whole district and neighbourhood, and amongst all the people. And what did He do? He answered them all as they came. Oh the glory of the King! All the difficulties were in Jerusalem among those men who were always washing their hands! Christ has no difficulty with the man who is polluted with sin, when that man sighs his soul to Him in faith. But He has a good deal of difficulty with the traditional ritualist. It is the man who comes with the great burden, who in faith commits his need to the King, that feels all the virtue of His healing pass into his life. There was no difficulty with these people when they believed.

When these people obtained their blessings " They glorified the God of Israel." These were not of Israel after the flesh. They were outside, they were people of Decapolis. They were the condemned Gentiles, but they glorified the God of Israel. Why? Because one Man, Jesus of Israel, of Judah's Kingly tribe, had fulfilled toward them the Divine intention. When God made the nation He said, to the Founder, " I will bless thee and make thy name great; and be thou a blessing." This Man, living in the covenant relationship under God's blessing, was made a blessing; and through Him the rivers of God's life were flowing, not merely inside the geographical boundary in which He lived as a Jew, but out to Tyre and Sidon, to Decapolis, to a Canaanitish woman, to the multitudes of men and women outside the covenant! Thus the Divine ideal for Israel was realised in this King, and outsiders were made of Israel in spirit by faith.

Finally, notice how the movement of the latter half of this chapter is the demonstration of the strength of faith. Perhaps He took His disciples there, that they might see the thing He had not been able to show them in the midst of His own people with their traditionalism and ritualism; that *they* might see faith working free and untrammelled; and as He took them there He revealed to them the force of faith in contrast with the barrenness of ritualism.

In His dealing with the woman there was not half the severity we sometimes imagine. In His every action there was a gleam of light. First, He came out of the house and was silent; but she could not forget that because she was outside claiming Him, He had come forth. This was the inspiration of her firmer faith. Then when she cried, and He was silent, let us remember that silence is not refusal; indeed, we have heard that silence gives consent! In His silence there was still the gleam of hope. When He answered the disciples she heard Him say, " I was not sent but unto the lost sheep of the house of Israel." In that there was a suggestion of hope; she may have said within herself, Then perhaps He will do something, after all; If He is after lost sheep, perhaps He will come outside the one fold and touch me. Then she cried, " *Lord, help me.*" That cry was born of the gleam of hope when He said "*lost sheep;*" and when He turned to her it was not with the tone of severity, as we have already seen. Christ never spoke severely except to Pharisees. He was leading her on, increasing her faith. He knew the strength of her faith, and He wanted to bring it out into all its strength. He could have said to the woman, "great is thy faith" at the beginning, but He led her through the process of sifting until it flamed into the sight of men. The strength of faith as developed by Jesus, seems to be the special value of this story.

And then, finally, notice the King's pure pity as He fed the multitude. That feeding was not an answer to faith. The crowd did not ask Him to feed them. The disciples did not seem to believe that He was called upon to feed them. They had seen Him feed the multitudes in Judea; but that was within the covenant, and the geographically correct place. But there was pity in His heart and power there; and though among people who might never see the spiritual life, still He fed them, lest they should faint by the way.

Behold the King. Behold Him with the woman, all strength and tenderness, merging from the process of apparent severity to the triumph of a great beneficence. Behold Him with the incapable people as they are brought to Him, the breadth and plenteousness of His power operating on their behalf. Behold Him with the hungry; in simple and exquisite sympathy, He fed them.

Let us learn from this meditation what is the law of relation to this King which brings men into the place of blessing. It is faith which is persistent; faith which is amenable to law, answering every word He says! "Lord, increase our faith."

In our relation to Jesus Christ as His messengers and workers, let us look for faith in unexpected places. Let us not keep out of Tyre and Sidon because there are no good people there. There is a freshness of faith everywhere waiting to surprise us if we will only venture to cross the line.

MATTHEW XVI. 1-12

WE are now approaching the end of the second division of the book of Matthew, which deals with the King's propaganda. We have heard His Enunciation of Laws; we have seen His Exhibition of Benefits; and we are now approaching the end of the section dealing with His Enforcement of Claims.

In this paragraph we see the last coming of the rulers to Him, before He broke with them, and the nation, and the crowds; and devoted Himself to His own disciples, and to that sacred ministry which led up to, and culminated in, the Passion. In this paragraph, therefore, we have His last reply to the rulers during their period of probation. After Cæsarea Philippi, His relation to these men was that of judge, and His message that of denunciation. He never dealt with them again, save, directly or indirectly, to emphasise the doom that had fallen upon the nation that had rejected Him.

In this paragraph we have also the final proof of how little His disciples had understood His methods; for when He said to them after the Pharisees had left, "Beware of the leaven of the Pharisees," they were so dull of apprehension, that they imagined He was talking to them about a certain kind of leaven, for the Pharisees were very punctilious about leaven. They did use certain kinds under certain circumstances, but they were particular not to use any contaminated by Gentile use. They thought that He was afraid that they would have some of the Pharisees' bread in which was leaven. He said to them, "O ye of little faith, why reason ye among yourselves, because ye have no bread. Do *ye* not yet perceive?" It is in some senses a pathetic picture of Jesus Christ which this paragraph presents to us. By the rulers of His people His laws were rejected, His benefits contemned, His claims ignored. By His own, that little group of disciples He had gathered about Him, His spiritual meanings were entirely missed. It is the story of the failure of His times to know Him. It is the story of the failure of His own disciples to appreciate Him. The revelation that this paragraph gives us is the revelation of the absolute inability of man, unaided, to understand the highest and best things of God. We must be very careful that we do not speak of His failure. There is a danger, there is a peril, there is quite a tendency to imagine that He experimented and tried one method after another, and that when one failed He tried a new one. That is not the story. It is rather the story of consecutive links in one great chain. The master hand forged them all. He failed at no point, but by His patient persistence toward victory, He brought into view the failure of man. Thank God there is another chapter, the story of the Passion. Had there been nothing but Propaganda it would have been disastrous in its failure, but because there was a Passion, the Propaganda presently became powerful, and all the great harvest of that patient, suffering, lonely ministry was garnered.

Let us, then, look first of all at the King and the rulers, as they are revealed to us in the first four verses; and then at the disciples and the King, as they are revealed to us in verses five to twelve.

In looking at the King and the rulers, the first matter that attracts our attention is the coalition of criticism. "And the Pharisees and Sadducees came, and trying Him, asked Him to show them a sign from heaven." Some of us have read that so constantly, and have been so accustomed to put all these men in the same list—Pharisees, Sadducees, scribes—that we think of them as all alike. So they were in one particular, and yet it must have been a startling thing to those who knew them to see these men together at all, and together on a matter of religious principle, and on a mission to a religious teacher.

Who were the Pharisees? They were the ritualists of their day; or, to use the word that more correctly reveals them, they were the traditionalists of their day. They believed in God, they believed in the work of the Holy Spirit, not exactly as we understand it to-day, but in the fact of the Spirit's operation. They believed in the essential purity and holiness of God. They believed in the fundamental things. They believed in angels; they believed in resurrection; they held all the spiritual verities; but they hid them from the people whom they were supposed to teach and lead. They hid the spiritualities underneath the grave-clothes of ritualism and tradition. They heaped upon men's shoulders burdens too heavy to be borne, and as Jesus once said, did "not move them with their finger."

Who were the Sadducees? The rationalists of their day. They did not believe in spirits, they did not believe in angels, they did not believe in resurrection. They denied all the supernatural elements in religion. They made religion a mere ethical code. They declared that a man ought to be true to certain high and noble principles without any aid from an unseen world.

The Pharisee had no dealings with the Sadducee; the Sadducee looked with supreme contempt on the Pharisee. The Sadducee would speak of the Pharisee as the man of fanaticism, as being out of date, not level with his times; that he was still enslaved, not merely by the tradition that characterised his teaching, but by these very obsolete ideas concerning angels, and demons, and resurrection, and spirits. The Sadducee was the cultured man of the age, and nearly all the wealthy families of the time were Sadducees. The high priest himself, strange and marvellous mockery, in the midst of Hebraism was a Sadducee. It was the correct thing of the hour to be a Sadducee! They had left Jesus alone up to this point. That kind of man always professes to hold in contempt a man who believes in the spiritual and the supernatural.

These were the men who came with one purpose to ask a question, and to puzzle Jesus Christ—the Pharisees and the Sadducees. Men absolutely divided as between themselves were united on this occasion. Some of the old writers got right to the heart of this Scripture in ways that are somewhat rough. Trapp, referring to this passage, says, "Dogs, though they fight never so fierce, and mutually inter-tear one another, yet if a hare run by, give over, and run after her." That is the whole story of the coalition between Pharisees and Sadducees in their coming to Christ. The Pharisees found Him irreligious because He swept away their tradition. The Sadducees counted Him irrational because He insisted upon the spiritual.

Now, what was it they wanted? One is inclined to think that the Pharisees framed the request in view of the fact that the Sadducees were with them. They came and asked Him for "a sign from heaven." The emphasis is to be put on the words *from heaven*. The Pharisees taught that demons and false gods could give signs on earth. The feeding of five thousand or four thousand might be done by some false deity or demon: and it was a part of their teaching that signs from heaven were the final proofs of the working of God; and if the sun might be made to stand still, if fire might fall from heaven, if there might come to them some miraculous portent on the sky; then they would believe. Jesus had been working miracles on earth—healing sick, feeding men. As miracles they had the peculiar quality that they had touched the things of earth, and these men would be more impressed by a thunderbolt than by the healing of a man; by some vivid illumination of the sky in an impossible hour on a dark night, than by the fact that Jesus had gathered the hungry crowd of men and women together and fed them. These men were always seeking the spectacular, and Jesus religiously declined to satisfy their curiosity. He could have given them signs from heaven. "Thinkest thou," He said in the hour of His extremity, "that I cannot beseech My Father, and He shall even now send Me more than twelve legions of angels?" One sigh lifted to hea-

ven, and all the armies of heaven would have been let loose through the ambient air!

They asked Him this question "trying Him," which means to say that they did not at all believe that He could give a sign from heaven. What they wanted to do was to lead Him out into a realm where they thought that a sign of His power could not be manifested. Perhaps in their request there was a revelation of the fact that they still believed what they had suggested so long ago, that He wrought miracles by Beelzebub.

Mark the effect of this coalition. The Pharisees would say, This thing can be, there can be signs out of heaven, but He cannot produce them; therefore let us ask Him to do it. The Sadducees would say, There could be no sign out of heaven, so you are safe in asking Him to do it. We have two opposing ideas, but united in their opposition to Him. And so in a common hostility to Him, a common desire to see His defeat, these men came to Him.

Now mark our Lord's answer, "He answered and said unto them, When it is evening, ye say, It will be fair weather." Notice the italics here, "*it will be*." These words have been inserted to help us. We should be better without them. "When it is evening, ye say, Fair weather; for the heaven is red. And in the morning"—again miss the *it will be*—"Foul weather today, for the heaven is red and lowering. Ye know how to discern the face of the heaven: but ye cannot the signs of the times." The more we ponder His method with those men, and the matchless marvel of His wisdom with them, the more we are driven into the place of adoration, when we see the calm, quiet, satirical dignity of the whole movement; for we cannot read the story of Jesus and His teaching without finding a vein of satire, but which was never cruel and brutal. It was the satire of the summer lightning that clears the atmosphere; but it could become a thunderbolt that smote to death if men persisted in hypocritical criticism.

Jesus Christ did not say these men

were wrong. They came to criticise Him, but they went away criticised; they came to measure Him, but they went away measured. He knew the measure of their incapacity as well as the measure of their ability. They were equal to watching precedents and sequences in the realm of the external, but they were not equal to watching precedents and sequences in the realm of the spiritual. Said Jesus, You ask Me for a sign out of heaven. The air is full of signs. All about you are the voices of the eternal and infinite speaking to you, but you are blind concerning the things of God.

And He said much more than this. He accounted for their blindness in His use of the words—"An evil and adulterous generation." That was their measurement, that lay behind their inability, and was the reason for it. "Evil," that described them as wicked in themselves and as exerting an influence which was harmful. When Jesus used the word "adulterous" He did so in the spiritual realm, in the sense in which the old prophets had used it, as revealing the failure in relation between God and His people. "I will betroth thee unto Me for ever," was the great love-message of God to His people. The most scathing indictment brought by the prophets against the people was that they had played the harlot. Jesus employed the prophetic message of the past and flung it red-hot upon them. He said, How can you interpret religion when you are evil in yourselves, and adulterous in your relationship to God, unfaithful to the covenant with God? And now you come and ask for a sign, such a sign as will satisfy your debased and depraved nature, a sign in the realm which you think you understand. "There shall no sign be given unto it, but the sign of Jonah." That was but a repetition of what our Lord had said to them on another occasion at greater length. The sign of Jonah was not a sign given to Israel but to Nineveh. It was the sign of a man coming into Nineveh who had been flung out to death, and of that man's preaching in Nineveh. Jesus had amplified the illustration before, when He had said:

"For as Jonah was three days and three nights in the belly of the whale; so shall the Son of Man be three days and three nights in the heart of the earth." The man who had been in the heart of the fish, flung out to death, came back and preached; and the Lord told these men that the last time they would have this sign, which condemned their whole system, both of traditionalism and rationalism, would be when the voice that had been attempting to interpret the spiritualities to them, and which they would silence in death, would again be heard; and their traditional blunders would perish while His message would live on. He told the Sadducees, who held in contempt the whole story of the supernatural, that the Man whom they attempted to trap in His conversation, would come back to deny their rationalism by the fact of resurrection. That was their sign. They must wait for it.

"And He left them, and departed." In these words we have a revelation of the hopelessness of their condition, and an account of the act of the saddened and rejected King.

Now let us turn to observe the King and His own. They crossed over and they came to the other side, and when they got there Jesus said to them, "Take heed and beware of the leaven of the Pharisees and Sadducees;" take heed of that which is in itself corrupt, and which produces corruption; of that which is in itself disintegrating, and which, communicated to other things, will carry on that process of disintegration. "Take heed," that is, discern it, know it, be acquainted with it; literally—stare at it! And then "Beware"—literally, hold yourself against it. These were Christ's two words concerning the leaven of the Pharisees—the influence of traditionalism; and the leaven of the Sadducees—the influence of rationalism. Thus the King was guarding the religion of His own disciples, the religion for which He Himself stood, against His most insidious enemies for all time, for He knew the things that would most harm Christianity would be these two things—the addition of tradition, and the subtraction of the supernatural. These repeat themselves in every successive century. There are no men now wearing phylacteries, but there are a great many Pharisees who are saying, You must do this, which God has not commanded, or else you are not doing what God has commanded. Let us protest against that. Also against the naturalism of the Sadducees which brings Christianity to the level of a cult, a system of ethics, of an ideal. Let us still believe in the virgin birth; let us still believe in the actual resurrection of the body of Jesus; and that at the right hand of the Majesty on high, is the Man of Nazareth, the great Mystery of spiritual Omnipresence, and yet a physical form, existing in oneness with God.

But how came the disciples to misinterpret Him? They said, He is warning us against them because we forgot to take bread. Perhaps their misinterpretation was due first to preoccupation of mind. They were worrying about loaves. He reminded them they had seen Him feed four thousand before, and five thousand a little earlier—" O ye of little faith, why reason ye among yourselves?"; do you not remember what I have done? Preoccupation with loaves was due to lack of faith. We cannot quite understand the lack of faith when we remember that they had seen Him twice over, quite recently, feed the multitudes; when we consider that—

" 'Twas springtime when He blessed the bread,
'Twas harvest when He brake."

If they had seen Him feed five thousand with five loaves, surely they need not have been afraid so long as He was present. Somehow they forgot. Let the failure of these men utter its warning to us. Let us not imagine that victory in the past means that faith will never tremble again. The disciples saw the tongues of fire only once; then they had to work the spiritual fact out in their lives. Do not let us think too much about loaves. God help us to keep our mind upon the Master. Lack of faith, which means preoccupation with loaves, issues in spiritual blindness.

What did He do with them? He chided them for their lack of faith. He revealed to them that He was more occupied with the sustenance of the spiritual than the material. And it is written that at last they understood Him. He Who turned His back in satirical scorn upon the Pharisees and Sadducees who had come for no other purpose than to tempt Him, was very patient with the blundering disciples and waited for them. Oh He is a wonderful Master! He will say it again if we do not understand it the first time. If you are a Pharisee or a Sadducee with your animosity, and your criticism, and your cleverness, He will laugh at you in high heaven, and He will turn His back upon you. But if you are a weak, trembling, foolish, frail child, thinking about loaves when you ought to be thinking about spiritual things, He will say it again. Oh it is these *second things* that reveal His patience!

Thus ends, as to its apparent failure, the King's enforcement of His claims. His laws have been enunciated and rejected; His benefits have been exhibited and contemned; His claims have been enforced and refused. Nothing is clearer than the absolute necessity for more than propaganda in this very apparent failure of Jesus. To end here is to end at failure. Take the Gospel of Matthew and take out the last part, the story of the *via dolorosa* and the Passion, and the Resurrection, and Christ was a failure. But thank God the Passion is also here, and the victory is won. If He had ended here He would have been a failure, not as the Revealer of ideals, for His ideals are high and noble; not as the Teacher of an ethic, for His ethic is unmatched; but as a Helper of souls, as One able to take hold of the incompetent and make him competent. If that were the end, then our Lord was but a great Experimenter. The failure of such methods was due to man's incapacity, until touched with the new light and life to see the Kingdom and to enter in. He had said so at the beginning, " Except one be born anew, he cannot see the Kingdom of God." The failure was evident to His own mind from the very beginning; but it must be revealed; and on the way to the Passion He explained it.

This explains a great deal that perplexes us. We often think God is slow in the interests of His eternal throne and universe; but things that lie hidden in human life must be wrought out into manifestation; and that accounts for the slowness of the centuries. But, as to Propaganda He added Passion, so to Passion He will add His Perfect Victory.

MATTHEW XVI. 13-20

THIS is one of the most remarkable passages in the whole of this Gospel of the King. Here we are at the centre of our story; here we find light which flashes backward and forward, illuminating the path we have already travelled, and casting its light upon what remains to us of the study of this book.

The central matters of the paragraph are evidently those of the confession of Peter, and the answer of Christ to that confession. All the surrounding statements we may therefore treat first by way of introduction.

There is certainly some significance in the place where Peter's confession was made, and where our Lord uttered His first words concerning the Church. Cæsarea Philippi was situated at the northern extremity of Jewish territory. It was a district which had been peculiarly and terribly associated with idol worship. To this day there are remains of temples and altars which were raised in connection with idolatry.

There was also a political and religious significance in the place. It was in this vicinity that Herod the Great had raised a temple of white marble to Cæsar Augustus, a temple recognising the element of worship in the attitude of the Roman Empire to the Emperor.

The place in the ministry of our Lord is of supreme interest. The King was practically already rejected, in spirit if not outwardly and openly. The King was about to proceed to that new work, by which His Kingship would be established, and His Kingdom ensured.

Having gathered His disciples into this remarkable locality, He said to them, " Who do men say that the Son of man is? " The term, " the Son of man," is personal, and not generic here. It was perhaps sometimes used in a generic sense, but not by our Lord; and in this instance the disciples did not so understand it, or they would never have answered, " Elijah," " John the Baptist," " Jeremiah or one of the prophets." They understood it as a personal question. In effect Jesus said to these men, What is the result of My work so far? What do men say about Me? He did not need information; He was perfectly familiar with the general attitude towards Himself; but in order to prepare the way for the new movement, to lead these men forward, He gathered them quietly about Him at Cæsarea Philippi, and said to them, if we may reverently change the phrasing; Now let us see what all My work so far amounts to. What is the result of My preaching and teaching and working of miracles, and your preaching and teaching? " Who do men say that the Son of man is? "

Their reply was one that shows the measure in which He had succeeded; that there had come to His age a remarkable conviction concerning Him. But it also shows that the men of the age had not appreciated Him, and that the measure of their understanding was distinctly limited. These disciples at Cæsarea Philippi told Him only the best things they had heard about Him. Although they had heard men say, He is beside Himself, He hath a devil; they said, " Some say John the Baptist; some, Elijah; and others, Jeremiah, or one of the prophets."

Taking that answer very broadly, and accepting their testimony, as a correct estimate of the best which the age had discovered about Jesus; it is evident that there was widespread conviction that there was something supernatural about Him. Men had come so far as to decide that they could not account for Him in any ordinary way; they could not place Him in any school of the prophets of their own day. They listened to other men, and detected the accent of Hillel, or the accent of Gamaliel, or of some other teacher.

They could not do so with Jesus. They said, It is John the Baptist come again; or the prophecy that Elijah should come again is being fulfilled; or Jeremiah has returned with his thunder and his tears; or one of the prophets of the past has returned. They ranked Him amongst the prophets, the men of vision, the men who declared God's word to their age. They could not account for Him in any other way.

If we remember the differences between John, and Elijah, and Jeremiah, and the other prophets, it is evident that these differing opinions constitute a revelation of the variety of the message and mission of Jesus. They said, We cannot quite place Him. We can hear something of the lamentations of Jeremiah; we have seen a good deal of the fire of Mount Carmel flashing from His eyes; we have also heard the tones of the sweet lullaby of Zephaniah's final love-song. We do not know where to place Him; He has notes which remind us of them all. His own age had come so far as that, but it had not discovered the deepest truth concerning Him.

Then He narrowed the inquiry. Instead of the wider sweep, He turned to the smaller circle, to those who had been with Him, and still were with Him. He said, You have been with Me, you have walked this highway between Jerusalem and Jericho with Me, you have seen the healing and heard the teaching, and watched the opposition, and seen how I have dealt with it. The age has come so far and no farther; the age has lived in the twilight; have you found the light? "Who say ye that I am?" That leads us to the heart of our passage, to Peter's confession.

Nineteen centuries have passed, and the phrasing of this wonderful passage has been the familiar language of the Church of God for all that time; and we have often robbed it of its glory by attempting to add to its meaning. We have twisted it and contorted it, to establish some philosophy of our own, to bolster up some preconceived notion, until we are in danger of missing its music.

The simplest way in which to hear this confession is to attempt to lift ourselves out of our present position, and to put ourselves back into the midst of that first little group of disciples, and to listen as they listened to Peter's confession and our Lord's answer thereto. Peter looked at Him and said, "Thou art the Christ, the Son of the living God."

Let us take the first part of Peter's confession in all its simplicity; and hear only what Peter undoubtedly desired to express, the Hebrew thought, "Thou art the Messiah." If we say to-day, Jesus of Nazareth is the Christ, we have a larger conception of the meaning of the title Christ than Peter had. The very word Christ has taken on a more spacious, radiant, and mystic meaning. Peter was a Hebrew, a child of the Hebrew race. He was born in its midst, and had been nurtured upon its thinking. Every fibre of his personality was affected by its conceptions, and it was as a Hebrew that he said to that Man Who styled Himself "The Son of man," "Thou are the Christ," the Messiah. That is, Thou art the Fulfiller of all the expectations of the Hebrew people, the One by Whom our hopes are to be realised, the One in Whom the economy culminates, the One from Whom there is to break the dawn of a new day and a new era. The Hebrew seers, psalmists, and prophets, had all looked for the coming of One. All through their literature we see the ideal merging into a personality. If we read Isaiah with any carefulness, we see how through the national ideal there gradually emerges into view a Person, and that Person is at once Servant and King; oppressed, broken, afflicted; and triumphant, crowned, victorious. All the men of vision of the Hebrew economy had looked for One Who should fulfil their expectations, realise their hopes. The Hebrew prophets were perpetually speaking of the day of God. Their eyes were always looking forward, and as some of them climbed higher than others on the great mountain peaks, they saw farther along the distances, and, with wonderful accuracy, they described that Person. They waited for Him and watched for Him. He was to break oppression, to establish righteousness, to baptize the nations with the river of God, and wherever the river came there would be life.

At last a son of the nation, a fisherman only, standing in the neighbourhood of the ruins of the ancient temples of idolatry, looking into the face of this Man, Whom he had heard teaching and preaching for nearly three years, said to Him, " Thou art the Messiah," the One for Whom we have all been waiting, for Whom we have all been looking; and he added to that, " The Son of the living God."

We must read the question and answer carefully, if we would find the values. Jesus first said, " Who do men say that the Son of man is?" When He spoke to the disciples He said, " Who say ye that I am?" Thus He identified Himself with the Son of man. Peter said, " Thou," the Son of man, " art the Christ, the Son of the living God." The description, " the Son of the living God," is correlative to Christ's description, " the Son of man." I am the Son of man, said Jesus in effect, Who am I? " Thou art the Messiah, the Son of the living God," said Peter. So as the title, " the Christ," answered the question " Who;" the description, " the Son of the living God," stood in correlation to " the Son of man."

Peter's confession was a very definite one, and yet one that recognized his consciousness of the mystic element in this Man, beyond the things the age had seen. The age had caught the comprehensiveness of the prophetic note. The age had recognized more—the supernaturalness of this Teacher. Peter, recognizing all this, defined it, and went beyond the age, and said; " Thou art the Messiah;" more than John the forerunner, more than Elijah the foreteller, more than Jeremiah the watcher and the one who waited; Thou art the One toward Whom they all looked. There is manifested in all Thy doing, and in all Thy teaching, something that differentiates Thee from all other teachers and men. Son of man, but Son of the living God, the Messiah. United to us in that Thou art our Messiah, yet distanced from us by the mystic gleaming of Thy glory, the fair brightness of Thy Person as it falls upon our lives.

In the King's answer to this great confession let us notice first, His Beatitude;

" Blessed art thou, Simon Bar-Jonah: for flesh and blood hath not revealed it unto thee, but My Father Who is in heaven";

Secondly, His great announcement;

" I also say unto thee, that thou art Peter, and upon this rock I will build My Church; and the gates of Hades shall not prevail against it. I will give unto thee the keys of the kingdom of heaven: and whatsoever thou shalt bind on earth shall be bound in heaven: and whatsoever thou shalt loose on earth shall be loosed in heaven";

Finally, the warning note, strange and peculiar at first seeming, yet necessary when carefully considered;

" Then charged He the disciples that they should tell no man that He was the Christ."

First, the Beatitude. Jesus did not pronounce a reward upon Peter, for the discovery he had made, when He said, " Blessed art thou, Simon Bar-Jonah." On the contrary, He was rather describing the condition into which Peter had come by the gain of this new knowledge which he had confessed. Such confession, that He was the Christ, and the Son of the living God, was in itself the result of Divine illumination. Not in the confession, but in the consciousness out of which the confession was born, was Peter blessed. Probably he spoke for the rest as well as for himself, but one man at least had made contact with the purposes and power of God. He said, " Thou art the Christ, the Son of the living God." Jesus said, " Blessed art thou, Simon Bar-Jonah." That is the key to the situation. That is the discovery upon which the human soul is remade. That is the discovery upon which human society is to be remade. That is the discovery upon which the city of God is to be built, and the everlasting Kingdom established.

How did Peter learn this fact? Let the Lord continue, "Flesh and blood hath not revealed it unto thee, but My Father Who is in heaven." He took hold of a common colloquialism of His times and used it. The man in the street would say, Flesh and blood cannot endure this; flesh and blood cannot see through this. Christ said, That confession you have made is not something that another man told you; you have not discovered it; My Father hath revealed it unto thee.

How did the Father reveal that to Peter? Men have tried to account for it in various ways, and all the while the flaming truth is in front of them —Through Christ Himself. What Jesus said in effect was this—There is My victory as Revealer. I have come to reveal the Father, and I have been successful, for here is one man who finds in Me the expression of the Father, and knows My relation to the Father, not by the wit or wisdom of man, but by My own revelation of the Father. One soul at least had seen God in Him, and heard God through Him. He had followed and listened, and had come over the mountains, and through the driving mists, until at last it had flamed upon his consciousness that there was God, in His Son, the long-looked-for Messiah, and he confessed it. He had found God, he had touched the eternal principles, he had come into contact with the purposes and plan and power of God. That was the beginning of the new era; the first movement of which, as Christians, we are the continuation.

Then our Lord went farther. He said, "Thou art Peter." That is when he really obtained his name; he had never possessed it properly before. In the Gospel of John, in the first chapter, we read, "He findeth first his own brother Simon, and saith unto him, We have found the Messiah (which is, being interpreted, Christ). He brought him unto Jesus." Andrew brought his brother Simon. Jesus looked upon him, and said, "Thou art Simon the son of John: thou shalt be called Cephas (which is by interpretation, Peter)."

Now at Cæsarea Philippi He said, "Thou art Peter"—I told you what you would be when first My eyes rested upon you. I knew your human setting and pedigree; but I said to you, You shall be rock, a man of strength. He had led the man on and on, and at last He brought him to Cæsarea Philippi, and said, Now do you know Me, Simon? Simon said, "Thou art the Christ, the Son of the living God." Jesus said, "Blessed art thou;" not by the discovery of thy flesh-and-blood nature, which is represented by the symbol of Simon Bar-Jonah, hath it been revealed unto thee; but through My speech and life thou hast come to the light. Now thou art *Petros*, rock.

Then what? "Upon this rock"— not *Petros,* a piece of rock, a fragment of the rock nature, but *Petra,* the essential rock—"Upon this rock I will build My Church." Thou art the rock nature, and thou shalt be built upon the rock foundation.

"Upon this rock." Remember, He was talking to Hebrews. If we trace the figurative use of the word rock through the Hebrew Scriptures, we find that it is never used symbolically of man, but always of God. So here at Cæsarea Philippi. It is not upon Peter that the Church is built. Jesus did not trifle with figures of speech. He took up their old Hebrew illustration—rock, always the symbol of Deity—and said, Upon God Himself I will build My Church. My Kingdom shall consist of those who are built into God, "partakers of the Divine nature."

Mark the intention carefully by taking Peter's final words first—"The living God." Then the word immediately preceding—"the Son of the living God;" and then the first word—"Thou art Messiah." Jesus said; On that, I will build My Church, on Jehovah God, manifest in time in His Son, administering the affairs of the world through that Son as Messiah. Peter had found the foundation, had touched Jehovah, and by touching Him had become *petros.*

As to the structure to be erected on this foundation our Lord said, "I will build My Church." Our word Church does not correctly express the idea.

The word ecclesia was a very familiar word in our Lord's time, and it had a Hebrew and a Greek use. The Hebrews spoke of the ecclesia. They had two words very much alike in their intention, and yet separated in use—synagogue, and ecclesia. They marked the facts in which the Hebrew people were different from other nations. Synagogue meant the assembling together of God's people in worship. Jesus did not say, My synagogue, He said, My *ecclesia*. The Hebrew use of the word *ecclesia* marked the Hebrew people as a selected people, as a Theocracy. That was the great thought in the word, a God-governed people, not governed by policy or by human kings. That was the underlying thought in the Hebrew mind. *Ecclesia* was also in common use in Greek cities at the time. In one of the later chapters of the book of Acts we find that the whole *ecclesia* came together to discuss their affairs. It does not mean the Church of God. It was the town meeting, an assemblage of free men. No slave could be a member of the *ecclesia*. Jesus stood in the midst of these Hebrew and Greek ideas, and said, "My *ecclesia;*" My people, My Theocracy; and My assembly for the purpose of authority and government in the affairs of the world. "My Church."

Of that Church Christ said, "I will build." There was no unveiling here of the method, save as it is illuminated by the happening at the moment, when this one man was brought into relationship with Jesus Christ. We must wait for the teaching of the Spirit in the epistles perfectly to comprehend the meaning of the Master. The thought was afterwards elaborated in the teaching of Peter and of Paul. When Peter himself, later on, wrote about the building of the Church, he spoke of living stones, built on a living Stone. He introduced the thought of life. He lifted the figure out of its natural realm, and infused into it a new quantity and a new element, something which differentiated it from the figure itself, so that by the disparity we learn quite as much as by the actual symbolism. For illumination as to the process of the building we turn to that wonderful

fourth chapter of the letter to the Ephesians, with its unveiling of the Church in the process of its erection; "There is one body, and one Spirit, even as also ye were called in one hope of your calling." That is the whole fact of the Church. One Body, Christ the Head and all believers the members; One Spirit, the common life of Christ shared by the members. That is the catholic Church.

From that the Apostle proceeded to show how men come into that Body, and share that life, "One Lord," the object of faith presented to the mind; "one faith," fastening upon the Lordship, and yielding to it; "one baptism," that of the Holy Spirit, whereby the believer is made a member of the Lord. Through the illustration of Paul's phrasing we go back to Cæsarea Philippi, and watch the process. "One Lord," Jesus; "one faith," the faith which says, "Thou are the Messiah, the Son of the living God;" "one baptism" of the Spirit, that whereby Peter was at Pentecost made a partaker of the nature of his Lord, and a member of the body of Christ, a living stone in the great building. Then the Apostle completed his statement, "One God and Father of us all, Who is over all, and through all, and in all."

This is the Master's method of building His Church, but it will never be seen in all its perfect glory until the morning of the second Advent, when, gathered into perfect unity with Jesus, all the scaffolding removed, it will be manifested in its splendid beauty and glory.

Because Jesus said, "I will build," we are sure of the impregnability of the Church, that nothing can destroy it, that all the forces of darkness can never finally prevent the completion of His Church. No rite or ceremony of man can admit us to that Church. Its strength lies in the fact that He builds it stone for stone, fitting each into its proper place, taking only such as by living faith participate in His own nature, and therefore are ready to be built into His great Church.

We know from that declaration also that the Church will be glorious in beauty. If we are inclined to say that we have not seen very much of its beauty yet, we must remember that we have never seen its corporate beauty. We have, all of us, thank God, had some glimpses of the glory of the Church in its individual members. We have seen and known Christly souls who have not only caught the Spirit of Christ, but who so share the life of Christ, that His beauty, His compassion, and His tenderness are all manifested in their lives. Think for one prophetic moment, in which we forecast the future, of what it will be when that whole glorious company is gathered out and completed, and He presents His Church to God, a glorious thing, not having spot or wrinkle or any such thing. The beauty of His Church will consist, first of all, in the diversity of individual lives, all types and temperaments gathered into one great harmony; and the beauty will consist finally in the unity of the manifestation of the glories of Christ. In the letter to the Ephesians the Apostle urges us to "to keep the unity of the spirit in the bond of peace," and, as the argument proceeds, we see that we are to "grow up in all things into Him, Who is the Head, even Christ." If we take that passage as indicating the necessity and importance of individual development, we must not imagine that to be its only meaning, or that it exhausts the passage; "Till we all attain unto the unity of the faith, and of the knowledge of the Son of God, unto a full-grown man, unto the measure of the stature of the fulness of Christ." Individually we can never come to that. It will take the whole Church to realise the measure of the stature of the fulness of Christ."

The Colossian epistle, which is the twin epistle of the Ephesian one, throws light upon this, "It was the good pleasure of the Father that in Him should all the fulness dwell . . . in Him dwelleth all the fulness of the Godhead bodily." The fulness of God is the fulness of Christ; and the fulness of Christ is the fulness of the Church. That is the radiant splendour of the Church, that when He has completed His building upon the Rock foundation; then His ransomed and redeemed Church will be a medium through which all the glory of God, realised in Himself, shall flash in resplendent glory through ages that are yet unborn.

Christ then went on to speak of two present activities or influences of the Church. First, "The gates of Hades shall not prevail against it." That is a description of the aggressive mission, or the destructive powers of the Church. This word of Jesus needs careful consideration. In common with many of the utterances of our Lord, we have been in danger of dealing with it superficially. First, notice that there is a difference between the inclusive statement, "I will build My Church," and the next word, "The gates of Hades shall not prevail against it." The first word declares His construction of the instrument. The second word declares partially what the function of the instrument shall be; "The gates of Hades shall not prevail against it." This cannot refer to the strength of the Church against attack. Careless reading would give us to think that Jesus meant, I build My Church, and though all Hades come up against it, it cannot overcome it. The figure the Lord uses does not admit that interpretation. An attacking force never carries its city gates up when it goes to fight. It is not a figure of the defensive strength of the Church.

Neither does it mean that the Church shall be able to capture Hades. The Church does not desire to possess Hades. We must look more closely, or we miss the meaning of this great word. It is the figure of escape. It is a declaration of the fact that the Church will be able to make a way of escape from a beleaguered city, which is in harmony with the perpetual outlook upon death in the life of the Christian. Death in the New Testament is never getting into harbour; it is getting out of the harbour on to the boundless sea. Tennyson caught the New Testament idea when he sang,

"I hope to see my Pilot face to face
When I have crossed the bar."

That crossing is outward, not inward. It is a false figure of speech that imagines that in the case of the Christian, death is running into harbour with rent cordage and tattered sails. When Paul speaks of death he speaks of his departure, unloosing, the cutting of the cord that binds him, the liberating of the ship from the restraint of the harbour to the boundless sea for which it was made. Here the idea is the same. The Church is seen in a beleagured city; and Jesus says, The Church will take the gates of the city and escape into the larger life that lies beyond.

But that is not the deepest thing of all. What is death in the economy of Jesus? The last enemy. What are the enemies that precede death? First, sin, or rebellion, for sin in its genesis is rebellion against God's government. Next, sorrow, in its widest sense, as including all lack and limitation. Then the final enemy—death. There they stand, the three great enemies of the race; sin, sorrow, death. The Christian man sings an anthem when he looks at death, " O death, where is thy victory? O death, where is thy sting?" How can he thus sing in the face of death, the last enemy, that has held the race enthralled so long? " The sting of death is sin; and the power of sin is the law; but thanks be to God, Who giveth us the victory through our Lord Jesus Christ." Victory begins over sin; it proceeds over sorrow; it ends over death. Jesus Christ says, My Church which I build shall be a great aggressive force. Jesus was always merging the two figures of battle and building. He is the Builder, Who needs builders that He can depend upon. He is the King going forth to conquest, Who needs soldiers He can depend upon. For the moment He speaks as the great Commander leading His Church as an aggressive force, and as the great Commander He sees, not merely the battle, but all the issues of the campaign. The whole field was in the vision of Jesus, as He stood at Cæsarea Philippi. He Himself was about to enter into conflict with sin; to enter into conflict with sorrow, wiping tears away, healing wounds; mastering death; and all His people coming after Him, must be people in conflict with sin and sorrow, and finally in conflict with death.

Jesus here saw the whole field stretched out before Him, and with the tone of assured victory in His voice, He did not stay to enumerate the battles and the foes, but passed to the last, and said, " The gates of Hades shall not prevail against it." My Church shall be an aggressive force moving ever on, overcoming foe after foe, until, presently, when they come to the gates of the beleagured city, they shall find their way through them and into the life that lies beyond.

In the view of Jesus the world itself is seen as a beleagured city held in death's power. In the midst of the world, not outside it, He Himself is working, building; and His Church in the beleaguered city is to be a force intended to wage war against things that harm, and open the way out into life for the beleagured peoples. The war is within, not without. The Church wins its victory over sin by His blood; wins its victory over sorrow by His sympathy manifest in the presence of sorrow; wins its victory over death by breaking down the fear of death in trusting hearts, and, as the individual soldiers come down to the end, they find that the gates are captured, and they march through, not passing through swollen rivers as we sometimes sing, but dryshod into the land that lies beyond, without a thread of the garments wetted even by the dews that rise from the river. " The gates of Hades shall not prevail against it."

If the Church has not been victorious in the conflict with sin and sorrow and death, it is due to the unfaithfulness of the Church. Let us not blame the Master and Leader. Did we but realise all His preciousness, that the security and energy of His life is at our disposal by the Spirit, we should be perpetually victorious, and the Church of God would not only be, " Fair as the moon, Clear as the sun," but " Terrible as an army with banners." If we are defeated in the fight it is because, like the Israelites, we have some Achan in the camp with a wedge of gold or Babylonish garment; and that complicity with the things that are against God, weakens us in our conflict.

But further, the King said; "I will give unto thee the keys of the Kingdom of heaven." What are these keys? He was speaking to Hebrews, and the phrase, "the keys" was perfectly familiar to them. They were the insignia of the office of the scribe, the teacher of the law of God. The key was the sign, not of priestly office, but of the office of the scribe. The keys committed to Peter were not the keys of the Church, but the keys of the Kingdom. When Jesus spoke to Peter upon this occasion He spoke to him as a scribe. In chapter thirteen we have the parables of the Kingdom, and they end with the words, "Therefore," because ye have understood, "every scribe who hath been made a disciple to the Kingdom of heaven is like unto a man that is a householder, who bringeth forth out of his treasure things new and old." The parting of the ways had come at Cæsarea Philippi. Because Peter had answered, "Thou art the Messiah," he had become a scribe instructed in the Kingdom of heaven. Now, said Christ, I will give you the keys of the Kingdom of heaven. You are My scribe. The keys of the Kingdom were given to the illuminated, to those who understood the principle of the Kingdom, the laws of the Kingdom, the method of the Kingdom. When Jesus said to Peter, "I will give unto thee the keys of the Kingdom," He spoke to him as representative man, He spoke to him as the first man who had gained the vision of illumination, "Blessed art thou, Simon Bar-Jonah: for flesh and blood hath not revealed it unto thee, but My Father Who is in heaven;" thou shalt have the keys of the Kingdom.

To-day these keys belong to every one who proclaims that Kingdom. They are the warrant for the preacher. They do not constitute a warrant for priesthood, but for the scribe instructed in the Kingdom, preaching, teaching the Kingdom, unlocking its meaning, explaining its law. So that Christ said not merely; My Church is to be an aggressive force; but My Church is to be a constructive force in the midst

of the age, teaching the Kingdom and holding the keys of the Kingdom; not to lock, or shut out, or exclude, but to interpret and administer.

In close connection follow the words; "Whatsoever thou shalt bind on earth shall be bound in heaven: and whatsoever thou shalt loose on earth shall be loosed in heaven." In these words He committed to His Church the final authority in human life. These phrases were perfectly familiar to the Jew, we find them in the literature of the time. They said, Shammai binds this, but Hillel looses; which simply meant, Shammai makes this obligatory, but Hillel leaves it optional. Binding simply meant an authoritative declaration concerning what must be done, or what must not be done. Loosing meant permission given to men to do or not to do. It was purely and simply a Hebrew method of describing ethical authority. Jesus said, In the history of the world, My Church shall not merely be an aggressive force to which Hades' gates shall yield; My Church shall hold the keys of interpretation of the Divine Will; My Church shall erect the moral standards for the world. Whatever My Church shall bind, shall be bound; whatever it shall loose, shall be loosed. In the twenty-third chapter of Matthew Jesus is reported to have said, speaking of the scribes and Pharisees, "They bind heavy burdens," using the word in the same sense as that in which He used it of His Church. The Church is to be the standard of ethics. All the binding and loosing of the Church is to be based upon His authority, and that is what He meant when He said, "Come unto Me, all ye that labour and are heavy laden, and I will give you rest. Take My yoke upon you, and learn of Me; for I am meek and lowly in heart: and ye shall find rest unto your souls. For My yoke is easy, and My *burden* is light." In that word of Jesus is discovered the central authority; it is the will of God. Consequently the Church is to be, not merely an aggressive force, conquering His enemies, and opening a way out of all prisons; but it is also to interpret to the world the moral standards of life, and to teach men the will of God.

Every high ideal that obtains to-day in civilised countries has been learnt from the Church of God. The final ethic of the world was born with Jesus. Everything that is high, and noble, and uplifting, in the thinking and legislation of the nations, has come out of His heart by the interpretation of His Church.

If we had been true to Him the world would have learnt more rapidly; but the measure in which it has learnt is the measure in which the Church has been the interpreter of the ethic of God.

In conclusion let us glance at the warning that He addressed to these men. It seems a very strange thing that He said; "Then charged He the disciples that they should tell no man that He was the Christ." If we connect the word "*they*" of verse twenty with the "*My Father*" of verse seventeen, we shall better understand the meaning of that charge. Jesus said to Peter, "Blessed art thou, Simon Bar-Jonah: for flesh and blood hath not revealed it unto thee, but *My Father* Who is in heaven." Then He charged them "that *they* should tell no man He was the Christ." That is to say, it is not in the power of the Church to reveal the truth about Christ to the soul of a man; that must be the work of God. The work of the Church is not that of preaching a theory, even though it be a correct theory, of the Person of Christ; the work of the Church is that of preaching the Kingdom of God, the evangel of salvation, by bringing men into personal contact with Christ.

We can do what was done when Peter was led to Jesus, we can say to men, "Come and see." But they must look for themselves, they must have God's revelation in their own soul. If men attempt to depend for their Christianity upon another's theory of the Christ, they will be lost. If a man for himself listen, and watch, and wait, until there is personal revelation, there will come to him the light of the Father's own manifestation. So shall he be changed into a living stone, be built upon the Rock, become a member of His Church.

All this was teaching in advance, so far as these men were concerned. They did not understand Him perfectly. He had to begin now to show them how He could put His radiant, virtuous, victorious life at their disposal through dying; and when He did so, they were afraid. Never did they understand Him until the Spirit came, and, in answer to their faith, baptized them into living union with their Lord. They received their final explanation of Christ, His Cross, and His Church, by the baptism of the Holy Spirit; and so must we.

MATTHEW XVI. 21-28

THE words with which this paragraph opens indicate a new beginning in the mission of the King. "From that time *began* Jesus to show unto His disciples that He must go unto Jerusalem, and suffer many things . . . and be killed, and the third day be raised up." We are not necessarily to understand that He at once said all these things exactly in this form. He then *began* to tell them these things. This declaration is Matthew's summary, and constitutes the key to the final section of the Gospel. The ministry of Jesus was no longer mainly a ministry to the multitudes, but a ministry to His own. He devoted himself largely to preparing them for the experience of His Passion. Presently He went up to Jerusalem in solemn and Kingly glory in order to denounce and reject the whole Hebrew nation. Finally we see Him passing through the Passion experiences to complete triumph.

From here, then, to the end, we see the King; first, unveiling His Cross to His own disciples; secondly, authoritatively and officially casting off the Hebrew nation; thirdly, giving His disciples the programme of the coming economy; and, finally, passing to His Passion, and His triumph.

At the commencement of this division dealing with the Passion of the

King, we have this section; and there is a sense in which everything that follows is mirrored in this scene. It is, as it were, a preface to the rest. In it we see all the principles operating discovered to the end of the story.

These, moreover, are the principles of action from then until now, and throughout the whole of this age. The understanding of these is absolutely necessary to us at all times as we face our work for our Lord and Master.

The first matter of importance is that of the antagonism revealed. Christ began to talk of His Cross, and Peter at once objected. For a moment, very reverently, let us forget the persons, Christ and Peter, and see the antagonistic principles. The contrast is made plain in the words, " *The things of God —the things of men.*" "From that time began Jesus to show unto His disciples, that He must go unto Jerusalem, and suffer many things of the elders and chief priests and scribes, and be killed, and the third day be raised up. And Peter took Him, and began to rebuke Him, saying, Be it far from Thee, Lord: this shall never be unto Thee." Jesus began to say that He must suffer; Peter began to object and to say, "Be it far from Thee, Lord." The things of God are Christ's estimate of necessity and of method. The Son of Man "must go unto Jerusalem, and suffer . . . and be killed . . . and be raised up." The things of men are revealed in Peter's thought, Lord, not that; pity Thyself, have mercy upon Thyself; that be far from Thee; anything but that. The things of God; the method of the Cross that merges into the victory of resurrection. The things of men; the method of self-seeking that shuns the Cross, and ends in ultimate destruction.

Let us look at these things of God more carefully. "From that time began Jesus to show unto His disciples that He *must* go unto Jerusalem." Jerusalem was the place of danger and peril. The line of policy was to miss Jerusalem. The line of expediency, from human standards, was that, wherever else He went, He should not go to Jerusalem. And He began by saying The Son of Man "must go unto

Jerusalem." The emphasis of that "must" continues throughout the statement. "He *must* suffer many things," and "*must* be killed," and "*must* be raised again the third day." If we thus repeat the "must" before each of these declarations we notice that there is a value in the "must" which may be interpreted along the line of human experience and passion, and that there is a value in the "must" which defies any such interpretation. There is a sense in which the "must" was the "must" of human surroundings. "He must suffer and be killed," because that was the natural outcome of all that He had been saying and doing. It had been made perfectly evident in the period of the propaganda that men would not have Him, that they would reject Him. They were declining His ethic, refusing His ideal, laughing at Him, and attempting to get rid of Him; and He said to His disciples, There is only one issue to all this; I am compelled to go to Jerusalem, I must suffer, I must be killed. It was heroism, if we only look at it from the low level of human standpoint. Why must He? These men would not have made Him suffer, and would not have killed Him if He would have accommodated the standard of His teaching to their ideals. But in the mind of the King there was the "must" of a tremendous conviction, and an absolute loyalty to that conviction. It was as though Jesus said, I cannot lower My standard, I cannot deny My ideal, I cannot unsay My manifesto. I have not been uttering theories which I have learned in schools, and which can be abandoned upon occasion. I have talked out of the fibre of My personality. I must. And the "must" means that men who have shown their hostility will carry it out to consummation, and I shall suffer and die.

But that is not the deepest note. His last word was not of suffering. He did not end with dying. There was another *must.* He must be "raised again." That was not the language merely of an obedient man. It was not the language of a man who said; Well, I have done my best and I am prepared to die for it. It was the language of One Who knew that He held in His own hands the issue of all the way through which He was going; I am Master of the suffering, Master of the killing. I must be raised again. That was the must of the Divine procedure. I *must* go unto Jerusalem; and the immediate result will be that I shall suffer and be killed; but beyond that will operate the divine power; I must be raised up.

That "must" was older than the circumstances. That "must" came thundering in music out of eternity. When Jesus set His face toward Jerusalem, saying, I must go, and I must suffer, and I must be killed, and I must be raised up again, the force propelling Him was not merely the force of human devotion to an ideal, it was the force of His own ageless life; the Divine and eternal counsels of God were operating in Him and through Him, and driving Him along that pathway. That is what Peter, who misunderstood Him for a little while, came to understand presently. When we turn to the Acts of the Apostles and listen to Peter preaching for the first time in the power of Pentecost, the man who had shunned the Cross because he did not understand it, said, "Him"—that is, Jesus—"being delivered up by the determinate counsel and foreknowledge of God, ye by the hand of lawless men did crucify and slay." Thus he put the "must" back upon its true basis. He came at last to know that when Jesus said "must," He spoke with the authority of the eternal counsel of God, and was acting under the impulse of the things that are ageless and abiding; that He knew all the movements of eternity; that he saw through the mists of the moment all that lay beyond; past the bloody baptism of His Passion to the radiant morning of His crowning. These are " *the things of God.*"

But what are "the things of men"? First, the things of men are characterised by their lack. Peter did not see the ultimate, did not feel the original. He lived in the small conceptions of the immediate. That is always faulty and a failure. No man can live this hour unless he feels behind him the infinite movement of the ages gone, and before him the infinite pull of the ages unborn. If we live in the power of the things unseen we march to certain victory. Peter, in his letter, subsequently referred to those who see only the things which are near, having forgotten the cleansing. Near-sightedness! Peter was suffering from it at this point. He did not hear the music of the past; did not see the light of the future; his was the limited outlook, and therefore the present was misunderstood. And this was the attitude of all the disciples. They feared the present, and that because of the enthronement of self. They were still living for self, they were still considering self. Jesus Christ was so absolutely void of self-centred life that it did not matter to Him what suffering He endured if the great and ultimate victory should be achieved. We read, "For the joy that is set before Him," He "endured the Cross." Not the joy of His own victory but of God's victory. It was His joy to know that God, through the processes of His suffering, would win His victory and triumph. Peter saw only the things of men; present darkness, present pain, and present suffering. When he said to Jesus, "Be it far from Thee," he was speaking in affection, but it was near-sighted affection. When we stand in the presence of a soul suffering in the will of God, and employ such words as these, are we not asserting our own inability to bear that very pain, and is not that a refined form of the assertion of self-love within us? A self-centred man is self-circumferenced; a God-centred man is a God-circumferenced man, and to be God-circumferenced is to take in past eternity and coming eternity. Peter, being self-centred, was self-circumferenced, and being self-circumferenced lived in the dust of an hour, and saw only the pain of a process, and none of the glory of the ultimate issue.

But these are antagonistic ideals, they are mutually destructive. The things of God are a stumbling-block to the man who is minding the things of men. Christ placed before Peter the methods of His work, told him of the

Cross, and it was a stumbling-block. That is what Paul said in writing to the Corinthians, "The Cross . . . unto Jews a stumbling-block." A man minding the things of men always finds the Cross a stumbling-block.

But it is equally true that the things of men are a stumbling-block to him who minds the things of God. There is a very remarkable scene here. Peter took Him aside, just a little way from all the rest, and began to rebuke Him. We must not soften that word. Indeed, if we would have the real meaning of it, we must make it a little harsher. He chided Him, he was angry with Him. He said, What is coming to Your Kingdom if You die? How are You going to do the things You hope to do? Then Jesus turned. Probably He turned from him; He turned His back upon him, and His face to the other disciples; and said, "Get thee behind Me, Satan: thou art a stumbling-block unto Me." The man who loves Jesus, but who shuns God's method, is a stumbling-block to Him. A little while before Jesus had said, "Thou art Peter, and upon this rock I will build My Church." Now He said: Thou art a skandalon, a rock of offence, a rock still, but a rock in the way; a rock lying across My pathway to hinder Me. He turned His back upon him because the "must" of eternity was upon His Spirit. Thus with sternness and severity He rebuked the man who, minding the things of men had ventured to rebuke Him, a Man Who was minding the things of God.

How often the very stones of Christ's Church have become stones of stumbling in His way? When does a man become a scandal to the Church? When he obtrudes his view of method as against God's view of method; when he tries to build God's Kingdom without God's Cross, and without God's suffering; when he ventures to say in answer to the "must" of God spoken from the lips of Jesus, Not that way, that is a mistake, but by some easier method; when he attempts to make the method of His victory easy. Every suggestion of this age which leads us to imagine that we may bring His Kingdom in by softness and by sweetness, without blood and suffering, and agony, is a scandal, a stumbling-block.

In view of that mistake of Peter our Lord restated the terms of His discipleship, "If any man would come after Me." They all wanted to, they all loved Him, they all had affection for Him. He said, If this is so, if any man desires to come after me let him first "Deny himself;" and secondly, "Take up his Cross." Let us consider those conditions carefully. Denying of self is far more than self-denial in our usual sense of that term. Perhaps we may best illustrate it by declaring that we have no right to make any sacrifice for Jesus Christ which He does not appoint. When a man takes on him some effort of sacrifice, simply because he thinks sacrifice is the right thing, and does not wait for orders, he is as surely a skandalon to his Lord as when he does not deny himself and take up his cross at the command of the Master. The true disciple chooses neither song nor dirge, neither sunshine nor shadow; has no choice but to know his Master's will and to do it. If He appoint for us the blue waters of the lake and all the sunshine of the summer, then let us rejoice therein, and not vex our souls because we know no suffering and pain. If He appoint a *via dolorosa* and a sunless sky, then God make us willing to take the way, because the way is His appointment. We must be in His will if we are to co-operate with Him.

The programme of the disciple is expressed in these words, "Follow Me." That is, make the "must" of My life the "must" of your life. I must. Does not that mean suffering? It may, or it may not. Suffering is not the deepest thing in the "must." The deepest thing is this; I must co-operate with the purpose of God, whatsoever it may be. I must co-operate with Him towards that resurrection that means ransom and redemption. On the way there may be the suffering and the killing—there surely will be some measure of it—but the suffering and the killing are not the deepest things. The deepest thing is that we get into touch with God and do His

219

will; and whether it be laughter or crying, sorrowing or sighing, the secret of life is to follow Him on the pathway of loyalty to the Divine will.

He explained this in gracious terms when He said, " Whosoever would save his life shall lose it; and whosoever shall lose his life for My sake shall find it." This is the commonplace philosophy of true life. It is always so. Find any man who is always saving his life, and he will lose it. The way to lose our physical life is always to be saving it. The way to lose our mental life is to be careful that it never feels the storms and bruises of passion. The way to lose our spiritual life is to be so perpetually anxious to get into heaven that we never move into line with God in His work for the building of His Kingdom here on earth.

Then the King made His appeal in two questions: " What shall a man be profited, if he shall gain the whole world, and forfeit his life? or what shall a man give in exchange for his life? For the Son of Man shall come in the glory."

The Judge will be the Lord, Whose Cross you will not share to-day. To whom will you appeal from His verdict? The last throne is His throne, and at the final assize He presides.

If you save your life to-day, how will you buy it back, for the Man for Whom you will not suffer is the Man coming to reign in His glory?

The final appeal, therefore, is that we fall into line with His progress, and with the things of God; because He is also to come in the glory of His Father; and the glory of His Father is the outworking in history of the things of God upon which His heart and mind were set in the days of His flesh. And that means, first of all, a facing of the Cross.

The antagonism abides. We need not go far to find it; we can find it in our own heart. We hear in our own heart the searching and tremendous voice saying, " I must." We hear also in our own heart something that says; Not that, let me escape that, let that be far from me. To which are we going to yield? Let us in imagination hurry back to the rocky places of Cæsarea Philippi and ask ourselves, Which " must " shall master us? Are we going with Him in the will of God, enwrapped by the forces of eternity, to suffer and to triumph; or are we going to stand alone, saving our own miserable lives, and so lose them? May God help us to decision.

MATTHEW XVII. 1-13

THIS paragraph tells the story of the Transfiguration of our Lord. We need to give careful attention to the place of the Transfiguration in the scheme of our Lord's work as King. The question of first importance for us now is; What did this Transfiguration of the King mean to the three disciples who were permitted to witness it; and, subsequently, to those who, through them, heard the story? It is hardly overstating the case to declare that the glory of the Mount of Transfiguration rests upon Peter's two epistles. It was there, " On the Holy Mount," as he termed it, that he heard the voice and saw the glory, the meanings of which to him at the moment, were hidden, but the value of which came to him in subsequent years, so

that when he looked back through Resurrection, and the mystery of the Cross, to the mountain, he spoke of it as the " Holy Mount," and constructed his first letter around the twofold impression which that Mount made upon him—the impression which he describes as that of the Coming, and the Power, or more accurately, the Presence and Power of Jesus Christ.

In order to answer this question as to what the Transfiguration meant to these men, there are certain matters as to its setting which we must take time to notice.

First of all it is necessary to take the final verse of the previous chapter, which we have not yet considered, but which is intimately related to all that has preceded it. The King was talking to that group of men, so afraid of the Cross, of whom Peter had been the spokesman, when He said, "Verily I say unto you, There are some of them that stand here, who shall in no wise taste of death, till they see the Son of Man coming in His Kingdom."

There are many interpretations of the meaning of these words. There are those who believe that He meant to say that, in the age of Gospel preaching, and in the victories which should follow such preaching, man would live to see the vindication of His claim, and would live to see the coming of His Kingdom; and there is certainly an element of truth in that view.

There are those who say His reference to His coming was a reference to the destruction of Jerusalem; and here again we certainly have part of the truth. There is a sense in which there is no doubt He was present at that judgment of the city, as He is present, and presiding over, all the events of human history. It may be that there was some more special sense in which He came at that destruction, but surely none of us is prepared to say that He came into His Kingdom in the hour in which Jerusalem—"beautiful in elevation, the joy of the whole earth," over which He had wept tears of sincere pity, even though He had pronounced its doom—was swept away. As a matter of fact He had come into His Kingdom before then.

There is yet another interpretation of the meaning of these words. It is that His reference was to that which immediately follows in the chronicle, the unveiling of the established Kingdom in microcosm in the Transfiguration scene upon the sacred Mount. While that is also true, I do not think it exhausts the meaning. When He said, "Some of them that stand here," He was not distinguishing between certain of His disciples and others of them; but between His disciples and outsiders. From Mark we learn that by this time He was speaking to the multitudes He had called, as well as to His disciples (Mark viii. 34). His disciples saw Him come into His Kingdom, or as Mark puts it, "the Kingdom of God come with power," through the Cross interpreted by the Resurrection. (See Rom. i. 4.) Of this they had the final indisputable proof when power came to them at Pentecost. "The Kingdom of the Son of His Love," began at the Ascension of our Lord. Since then He has been reigning. If this be recognized we may turn to the immediate revelation of His Kingship as found in the Transfiguration.

Let us observe the setting a little carefully. Jesus took three representative men to the Mount, and was transfigured before them. They were dazed and overwhelmed. Peter said, "It is good for us to be *here;* if Thou wilt, I will make three tabernacles; one for Thee, and one for Moses, and one for Elijah." He was immediately rebuked by the encompassing quiet, and by the voice which said, "This is My Beloved Son in Whom I am well pleased: *hear ye Him.*" And the whole scene passed.

Now carefully notice these words; "And as they were coming down from the mountain, Jesus commanded them, saying, Tell the vision to no man until the Son of Man be risen from the dead." "And His disciples asked Him, saying, Why then say the scribes that Elijah must first come?" There does not at first seem to be any connection whatever between His charge, "Tell the vision to no man, until the Son of Man be risen from the dead," and their question. But there is a very intimate connection between their question and the promise He made to them at Cæsarea Philippi, that they should see His Kingdom. That question was their expression of the wonder that filled their hearts as they walked back down the mountain side, after all that they had seen. The glory had all vanished. There He was, walking by their side, the same Jesus Who had taken them up to the Mount, and there broke upon them the consciousness of the fact that they had seen the Son of Man in His Kingdom. Then they remembered the teaching of their own Scriptures, that before the Messianic Kingdom would be set up, there must come a Forerunner, and resuming the old conversation, they said, "Why then say the scribes that Elijah must first come?" If this strange glory upon the mountain that blinded us reveals the coming of the Son of Man in His Kingdom, how is it that Elijah has not come? Mark His answer. "Elijah indeed cometh, and shall restore all things." Then He added, "Elijah is come already, and they knew him not, but did unto him whatsoever they would." Then it was made clear to them that He was referring to John the Baptist. Thus He declared that by the coming of John the Baptist the promise of Elijah had been fulfilled, and that what they had seen was the *prophetic vision* of the Son of Man in the Kingdom. No doubt when He said, "Till they see the Son of Man coming in His Kingdom," He referred to what was about to take place not on the Mount when they should behold Him in His glory, but in all that was to follow His descent from the Mount.

Let us now consider, first, the natural place of the Transfiguration in the mission of Jesus; secondly, the Transfiguration as an unveiling of the coming Kingdom; and, finally, the message of the Transfiguration to us.

In considering the natural place of the Transfiguration in the mission of the King, we must see the place of the Transfiguration in the history of the Person of Jesus. On that Transfiguration Mount the human life of Christ reached its crowning glory. This is very largely, and very often overlooked. We may state the process of the human life of Jesus in three words; innocence, holiness, perfected glory. Innocence, the primal condition of human nature, not only not having sinned, but being without sin. There are no innocent children born to-day in the full sense in which the childhood of Jesus was innocent. He was absolutely sinless in nature; but it was necessary to the perfecting of that nature that He should face temptation. Human nature is never perfect until it has chosen for itself the right, as against the wrong which comes by allurement from without. A holy man is infinitely greater than an innocent man. A holy man is not merely a man in whose nature there is no sin. A holy man is a man who has looked into its face and said *no*. "He hath been in all points

tempted like as we are, yet without sin." He was victorious over every form of temptation that the enemy brought to bear upon Him. When He came to the Mount of Transfiguration, what the disciples saw was not the glory of Deity, not the glory of heaven shining upon Him; it was the outshining of the glory of humanity which had passed from innocence, through holiness, to absolute and final perfection. He was metamorphosed before them, and the glory they saw was the glory of perfected humanity. Just as there is a gulf that seems to be impassable between the newly born body of an infant child and the mature strength of a full-grown man, so there is an even more impassable gulf between that full-grown strength of a mature man and the complete realisation in that man of the fuller meaning of his own spiritual life, as it masters the body, flames through it, and flashes into beauty, as matter and spirit merge into a common radiance of loveliness. We know nothing of that because there is sin in us; but in Christ we see God's ideal Man, absolutely sinless, innocent, growing up to be holy; and at last, with all the temptations of life and of service overcome, there came a moment when, without death, He was metamorphosed, and ready for passing into a spiritual existence, carrying with Him His material body, changed, so that it was ready for life in the heaven of God. The Transfiguration was not the proof of Deity; it was the proof of absolute, essential, and victorious humanity. It was a revelation of what He is going to restore to us, if we trust Him; but we shall never reach our transfiguration but through His death and life. That is what the second advent means, that is what the changing of the bodies of our humiliation that they may be conformed to the body of His glory means. There is no hope for anything of that kind to any man who does not know Christ as his Saviour. This is the meaning of the Transfiguration in its relation to the Person of Jesus.

Now notice that the perfection of the Person was necessary for the perfect King. We have seen the King, His Person, His propaganda, and now we are coming to His Passion. But before we come to the Passion we must have the perfection of the Person.

That final perfection of humanity was reached in the fact of Transfiguration. But that perfection does not bring Him to the Throne. He cannot so come into His Kingdom. The Kingdom of God does not come with power so. Presently from that Mount of Transfiguration we shall go down the mountain side with the King, and along the rough and rugged road to the Cross. He descended out of heaven, the Son of God, and became incarnate, and in human life He won. Now for the second time He set His face towards the ways of men; and He Who came at first to share their life, from the Transfiguration Mount passed down to share their death. He talked in the glory of the mountain with Moses and Elijah, of His decease, His exodus; and presently He set His face towards it, and for the second time turned His back upon heaven, in order that, as perfected Man, He might share in the mystery of human death, and so perfect many sons for glory.

If that be the place occupied by the Transfiguration in the mission of Jesus, let us observe how in that glory those men had unveiled before them the order of the coming Kingdom. The Kingdom had not yet come. It was coming, and these men saw its order. In the flashing glory of that night scene they saw what it would be like. The Kingdom was revealed to them in that hour upon the mountain. What they saw, corroborated all He had said to them in that Cæsarea Philippi conversation eight days before.

They saw Him in the glory of His perfected humanity, and they heard His converse concerning the exodus He should accomplish. When, dazed and mystified, they suggested the perpetuation of the glory as there seen, the voice from heaven recalled them to obedience to what the Son said. The last thing He had said to them was that He must go to the Cross. Thus, though they did not apprehend the meaning then, they came afterwards to the understanding of the fact that the Perfect Son could only bring the Kingdom with Power by the way of His Cross.

As the vision passed, "they saw no Man save Jesus only." Then, mystified while yet illumined, they followed Him in His descent from the mountain—humbling Himself—and on to Death—and through Death to Resurrection—and through Resurrection to Ascension and Coronation—and so they saw "The Son of man coming in His Kingdom," "The Kingdom of God come with Power."

MATTHEW XVII. 14-27

IN this section we see the perfect King in the midst of His imperfect Kingdom. He was on His way to that mighty work through which alone He could come into possession of the Kingdom, and as we accompany Him we see the difficulties confronting Him, and observe His methods in the presence of such difficulties.

To-day the King has come into His Kingdom. He is appointed and anointed as God's King. The Kingdom is not yet perfected, but His Kingship is established. The antagonism still continues; the conflict is as severe as ever, if it be subtler. The terms of discipleship are not changed. There can be no fellowship with Christ in the perfecting of His Kingdom save by the way of the Cross. Nevertheless the light of coming victory still flashes upon the way.

This paragraph naturally divides itself into two parts. We have first, in verses fourteen to twenty-one, the account of the coming of the King from the mountain into the consciousness of the age in which He lived, the age which continues until now. In this picture we see Him coming down from the Mount, where, in radiant glory, He had been revealed as the prepared King; and now all about Him were the facts and forces of the age. In verses twenty-two to twenty-seven, we have the picture of the King and His disciples. We see Jesus gathering to Him His own disciples, and talking to them in view of the age in which their ministry was to be exercised.

Let us first consider our Lord's characterisation of the age as it is found in the twenty-seventh verse; " O faithless and perverse generation, how long shall I be with you?" In these words we have a revelation of our Lord's consciousness of the condition of affairs in the midst of which He found Himself. There was no thunder in the words, but rather the wail of a great sorrow; "O faithless and perverse generation, how long shall I be with you? how long shall I bear with you?" His use of the word "generation" shows that He was speaking of a far wider circle than that of His disciples. He was referring to the whole condition of things in the midst of which He found Himself. And more. These words of Jesus Christ, spoken in local circumstances, come reverberating through the centuries, with perpetual application. If Jesus stood in our cities to-day He would say, "O faithless and perverse generation." "Faithless," that is, lacking faith; a generation that cannot be provoked to faith. "How long shall I be with you?" In other words, Jesus said, For three years I have exercised My ministry amongst you, healing and blessing as I have gone, teaching the underlying principles of God's Kingdom. How long do you need persuading to faith? How many evidences do you want before you rise into an attitude of confidence? What proofs are sufficient to provoke you to believe?

Moreover, the age was not only " faithless;" it was " perverse;" which does not mean merely that it was rebellious, but that it was a generation twisted, and contorted; a generation in which things were out of the regular; a generation distorted in its thinking, in its feeling, in its action; a generation unable to think straightly, to feel thoroughly, to act with rectitude; a generation in which everything was wrong.

The use of the two words, " faithless and perverse," indicates a sequence. A generation that loses its faith, becomes distorted, out of shape.

A people who live exclusively upon the basis of the things seen, form untrue estimates; their thinking is distorted. their feeling is out of the straight, their activity is iniquity, which simply means crookedness. That was Christ's estimate of His own age. And the lament of the Lord's wail is this, " How long shall I be with you? how long shall I bear with you?" What do you need to provoke you to faith, in order that out of your faith may come the straightening of all your life in thought, and feeling, and action? So our Lord's conception of human conditions is revealed in this lament over His age.

What gave rise to this cry of the King as He came down from the mountain into the valley?

Let us now look at the immediate things. We see first a father with his boy, and the picture is yet again a microcosm in which the whole fact is revealed in one single case. This father brought his boy to Jesus, and he said, " Lord, have mercy on my son; for he is a lunatic, and suffereth grievously." The Authorised Version is preferable here. The Revised " epileptic " is simply a medical explanation of the signs following. The Greek word is lunatic. He may have been epileptic, but let us leave it as it is without attempting to account for the condition. The deepest tragedy of the story is found in the words; " I brought him to Thy disciples, and they could not cure him." Luke chronicles something here which Matthew has omitted, the fact that the man used a very remarkable expression when he came to Jesus. He said, " Have mercy . . . for he is mine only child," that is my only begotten son, exactly the same word which is used of Jesus in another connection.

In a moment we see the vision; two personalities confronting each other, the Only begotten Son of the Father, and the only begotten son of man. The son of man was demon-possessed, and nothing in the age was equal to setting him free. It was the age of culture, of refinement, of learning, of religion; and in the midst of the Hebrew people all the forces of light and learning were at work, but there was nothing that would touch that boy. At last they brought him to the disciples of Jesus, but they were not able to deal with him. That is the picture of the age. The King, ready for His Kingdom, passed down the mountain into the valley, and found Himself confronted by that helpless boy, by that helpless father, by that helpless age, by those helpless disciples. Then there broke out of His heart the great wail, " O faithless and perverse generation, how long shall I be with you? how long shall I bear with you? "

That is a true picture of the condition of things to-day. We may take every one of these points, and find them being fulfilled in this particular age. We still have the demon-possessed sons of men. We still have the absolute helplessness of the most modern philosophy to set them free from the demons that possess them. And alas, the Church is sometimes as helpless as the rest! Many Christian people are unable to cast out demons in this age; and it seems as though the Lord continues until now saying, " How long shall I bear with you? " What more do you need to provoke you to that living faith which lies at the back of all endeavour that is uplifting and ennobling?

But now let us observe the action of the King. He said to the father, " Bring him hither to Me." Oh the majesty of that word of Jesus! What confidence He had in His own ability! The boy was brought to Him, past the incompetent teachers of the age, past the feeble and faltering disciples, and it was but a few moments before He gave the boy back to his father, healed.

When the gracious deed was done, the disciples came to the Lord, or the Lord gathered the disciples about Him, and they said, " Why could not we cast it out? " Would that the Church would give time to ask that question. Then the Lord would say the same thing that He said to these men, " Because of your little faith." If these men had been discussing the question in an annual religious assembly they would probably have come to a very different conclusion. They would have decided that they were unable to cast

out the demon because of the difficulties of the surroundings, because of the criticism with which the air was filled; for undoubtedly they were in the presence of men who were always watching them keenly. Or perhaps they would have accounted for it by the fact that this was a very peculiar case, one far more subtle and complex than any they had touched before. But Jesus said, " Because of your little faith." Perhaps this unbelief began at Cæsarea Philippi, there at the parting of the ways, when Peter being the spokesman of the rest, had said, in the presence of the Cross; " That be far from Thee ! "

From that time they had been afraid; they had been at a little distance from Him; they had held back; there had crept into their heart insidiously, unconsciously, questioning about Himself. They were not quite so sure of Him as they had been. They had thought that His method was to be purely educational, or that His method was to be a method of policy; but this rough and vulgar Cross, with blood, and shame, and suffering, had filled them with doubt. Then these men who were afraid, and who were discounting their Lord—it may have been almost unconsciously, but quite positively—came face to face with a demon-possessed boy, and they could not cast him out because of their unbelief. Lack of faith in the imperial and Divine Person of Jesus is paralysis in the presence of the world's need, and the world's agony. We may reduce our thinking about Jesus to the level upon which we attempt to get rid of the supernatural mysteries that surround His birth and His being, but when we do so we inevitably paralyse our power to deal with demon-possessed men and women. Degrade Christ in thought by a hair's-breadth, and our faith is weakened. Be afraid of Him, afraid to press after Him, even though the pathway be rough, afraid lest He be mistaken in His estimates and thinking; and, in that moment, we have lost power to deal with demon-possessed children.

In the last half of the paragraph we have our Lord's teaching of the disciples. He repeated the very thing they had questioned and had feared. He took them back to the point where their faith in Him had weakened and faltered. " While they abode in Galilee, Jesus said unto them, The Son of Man shall be delivered up into the hands of men ; and they shall kill Him, and the third day He shall be raised up. And they were exceeding sorry." How long that quiet time and that teaching lasted we do not know. It is certain that for a time He stayed in Galilee, and taught His disciples, insisting upon the necessity for the Cross and the issue of Resurrection. Now mark the impression He produced— " And they were exceeding sorry." That sorrow was a proof of their lack of sympathy with Him. That sounds a strange and contradictory thing to say. We always thought sorrow was sympathy, and sympathy was sorrow. In this case sorrow was lack of sympathy. To the minds of the disciples there was a perpetual veiling of victory by suffering. During the months after Cæsarea Philippi, Jesus was perpetually talking about His Cross, and He never did so without declaring His Resurrection. He said He would fall into the hands of men, and they would kill Him, and the third day He would be raised up again, and " they were exceeding sorry." Sorry that He should be raised up? That is unthinkable ; and the only way to account for their sorrow is to recognize that they were so confused with the thought of the Cross, that they never heard the declaration of Resurrection, or else interpreted His story of Resurrection as Martha did when He said to her about her brother, " Thy brother shall rise again," and she said, " I know that he shall rise again in the resurrection at the last day." And perhaps these men, too, thought that when He talked of rising on the third day it was figurative. These men were unable to look through the Cross to the Resurrection. After this miracle at the foot of the mountain, they were still in the same condition, unbelieving.

There is a strange and beautiful story closely related to this. " And when they were come to Capernaum, they that received the half shekel came to Peter, and said, Doth not your

Teacher pay the half shekel ? " The negative form of the question shows that it was a question of criticism, a question of men who thought they had some occasion of complaint against Jesus. Peter replied to their inquiry by saying, Yes. And when they came into the house, Jesus, knowing what had happened outside, anticipated him, by asking him a question. The half shekel was not a Roman tax, but a Temple tax for every man, whether rich or poor ; it was the redemption money. Under the Divine economy it had a proper place and significance ; but gradually, by the tradition of men, it had become an annual payment exacted by the authorities. And they came to Peter and asked him if his Master paid it. And he said, Yes. Christ said to him, " What thinkest thou, Simon ? The kings of the earth, from whom do they receive toll or tribute ? from their sons, or from strangers ? " And the answer was correct. " From strangers." Then said Jesus, " Therefore the sons are free." He was reminding Peter of Cæsarea Philippi. There Peter had said, " Thou art the Christ, the Son of the living God." Now Christ said to him, This half shekel is the payment of the subjects of the King, and you have said that I am the Son. When you confessed that, you did not quite understand the dignity and glory of the fact, for now you say that I pay this half shekel. You must have recognized that there is no claim on Me to pay it, if you had understood your own declaration, and the revelation of the Mount. It is for you to pay this because you are the strangers, the subjects, the people under the rule of the King. I am the Son.

" But, lest we cause them to stumble ;" lest we put a stumbling-block in the way of these men that they may not understand, you and I will pay this together. " Go thou to the sea, cast a hook." That is the only occasion in the New Testament where that mode of fishing is referred to. " Cast a hook." Only one fish is needed. And he did it, and found a shekel. Not half a shekel-piece, for Peter and Jesus were together in this matter. " Thou shalt find a shekel; that take, and give unto them for Me and thee." Thus the King brought Himself to the place of submission in order that others might not be caused to stumble. He put Himself into fellowship with Peter. Peter, you must all pay the shekel, but I will pay it with you. You must take this place of submission; I take it side by side with you. In the commonplace of life I am with you, just as I was in the glory of the Mount, where all My Kingliness was manifested; just as I will be with you in the midst of the need of the age.

And so it would seem that our Lord was leading Peter and the rest back to the faith in Him which they lacked, and from lack of which some of their number, left in the valley, had been unable to cope with the difficulty which presented itself.

The first application of this story, as ever, is a simple one. We cannot exhaust the value of any of these stories in the day in which they happened, or in the circumstances in the midst of which we find ourselves in imagination. We must see Jesus standing in the age. He is standing in this age now. Still He is saying, " O faith-less and perverse generation." Still He is saying, " Bring him to Me." But we cannot do it if we have lost Him in any measure, if our confidence in Him is not all that it was, and all that it ought to be. If we place Him among other sons of men, one among many of the teachers of the nations, of the leaders of men, then we can no more take a demon-possessed boy to Him than to Buddha, or to Confucius, or to Mahomet. It is only when He is to us mystery of all mysteries the greatest; the " altogether Lovely " as well as the Living One, not less than the portraiture of the New Testament, but incomparably greater, because John was right when he wrote, " There are also many other things which Jesus did, the which if they should be written every one, I suppose that even the world itself would not contain the books that should be written." It is only when that vision of the Christ fills our souls, and that conception of Him is the rock-foundation of our confidence, that we can hope to cast out demons in His name. In the midst of a great deal that troubles the heart, if we have that Christ, we can look up in His face and say, " Lord, I believe; help Thou mine unbelief."

MATTHEW XVIII. 1-14

THE main purport of the King, in the period covered by this last division of Matthew, was not that of presenting His Kingdom to the outside world as He had done before, nor that of demonstrating His power to the outside world; it was rather that of gathering His disciples about Himself, and instructing them carefully, in view of His coming Passion. His public ministry continued. The multitudes came to Him with need, and He always turned to them graciously. He never refused to respond to the approach of the multitude even though He was devoting Himself to this training of His own.

This chapter records instructions which our Lord gave to these disciples in view of the work that lay before them.

It falls into two parts; the Master's instruction, first concerning greatness, and secondly concerning forgiveness. The first part was His answer to their question—" Who then is greatest in the Kingdom of heaven? " Then He merged His teaching concerning greatness, into His teaching concerning forgiveness, the attitude of His people towards wrongdoing. Our present study is concerned with the first of these teachings, that concerning greatness.

Now, in order that we may understand our Lord's teaching, let us consider it; first, by the examination of its method; secondly, and principally, by the consideration of the teaching itself. Our Lord made His answer clear and definite, precise and immediate; but He recognized that in the question asked there were many other matters involved, and He dealt with them, leading these men a great deal farther than they expected He would lead them, when they asked their question.

We will first notice the method of this section, and the method of our Lord's answer to His disciples' question. "In that hour came the disciples unto Jesus, saying, Who then is greatest in the Kingdom of heaven?" What did this question mean? First let us notice the little word, "*then*." In the Authorised Version this word does not occur, but it is of great importance. It is perfectly evident that the word *then* has no time-value here. They were not thinking of that time, or time past, nor of time to come. The "then" is an indication of the fact that these people were thinking about our Lord's teaching, and they were greatly puzzled by all the new things He was saying to them about the Kingdom. It is the *then* of contrast between their ideas and His ideas. They had looked for the Kingdom, with its gradations from King, through officers of State, down to the common level of the people; the ordinary human ideal of a kingdom, which is so utterly and absolutely false. They had looked for a King and a Kingdom upon the pattern of material purposes and ideals. They had expected Him presently to assert Himself in the midst of the age in which He lived, to break the power of Rome, and to re-establish the throne of David in Jerusalem; to appoint Peter in all probability as Prime Minister—that was the natural order of things—and the other apostles to all the other offices of State. He had said to them, Your King is going to Jerusalem to suffer, to be murdered, and to rise again. They said, "Who *then* is greatest?" All the hopes of Himself that they had been cherishing, had turned into dust, and they stood in the midst of the wreckage of their own ideals, and hopes, and aspirations. They may not have been personally seeking for office, although there evidently was a consciousness that they had lost the chance of office. This is a greater question than it appears, for as a matter of fact the actual word is, "Who then is the greater of them in the Kingdom?" What they really asked was, What is the condition of greatness in Thy Kingdom? They said in effect; Greatness in our kingdom is manifested by some high office, dignity issues in notoriety. If you rob us of our ideals, what is Thy ideal of greatness? In consequence of His strange prediction of the Cross they were completely baffled and perplexed.

Let us now consider Christ's answer, observing carefully His method.

We have first of all the action; "He called to Him a little child, and set him in the midst of them." We miss all the poetry of this if we do not see the actual scene in Galilee. Behold the King! We should never have taken Him for the King if we had been tourists through that district, and passed by while He was talking to those men. There was no beauty that material eyes, seeing, should desire Him. He wore a plain seamless robe woven from the top throughout; a home-made garment. But home-made garments are very beautiful when love's fingers have made them; and love made that robe for Jesus. It was perfectly evident that He was a Man of the people, a carpenter. Round about Him we see these men, for the most part young fishermen. They were men of infinite capacity, men capable of splendid daring yet frail, fickle, feeble, and often faint-hearted. These men asked this Man this question, a perfectly proper and pertinent question. In all likelihood some Hebrew lad was playing near, and Christ called him, and he came, and Jesus put him in the midst of these men. That is the first fact of His answer.

Then, after this action, came the answer direct. There was a kindly satire about the speech of Jesus, but His satire never wounded men. He said, You want to know what is the law of greatness. You must get down there, to the level of that boy, before you get in at all; "Except ye turn, and become as little children, ye shall in no wise enter into the Kingdom of heaven." But if you be as little as the child, "the same is the greatest." He meant first that everybody is great inside; there are no little souls inside the Kingdom. Thus He swept away any incipient desire for caste, and class, and gradation, that lurked in their question. He had said on another occasion, "Among them that are born of women there hath not arisen a greater than John the Baptist: yet he that is but little in the Kingdom of heaven is greater than he." Christ had a majestic conception of His own Kingdom. That was His answer direct.

Now notice that He proceeded from that point to bring out of His answer involved truths, and to apply them. First, He applied practical tests to these men. "And whoso shall receive one such little child in My name receiveth Me: but whoso shall cause one of these little ones that believe on Me to stumble, it is profitable for him that a great millstone should be hanged about his neck, and that he should be sunk in the depth of the sea." There seems at first sight to be a lack of continuity in these words, but as a matter of fact there is a most intimate connection. If we are like the child we shall receive the child. A man to be successful in the Sunday school or the day-school, must have the child-heart. Only those who lack the child-heart themselves could cause the child to stumble. Of such the King declared, "It is profitable for him that a great millstone should be hanged about his neck, and that he should be sunk in the depth of the sea." The thick millstone, not the millstone at which the two women ground, but the great upper millstone that had to be turned by a beast of burden. They knew what He meant. Put that round about his neck, and drown him in the depth of the sea. "It is profitable for him;" he will make more in the economy of God out of such drowning, than out of being a stumbling-block in the way of a child.

Then followed His resulting warning. "Woe unto the world. . . . Woe to that man through whom the occasion cometh!" Here was a curious change of application. He was talking about offences coming to some one else, and then He said, "If thy hand or thy foot causeth thee to stumble, cut it off, and cast it from thee," by which He meant to say that the man who causes the stumbling-block becomes a stumbling-block to himself, and if we destroy a

child we destroy ourselves. So He solemnly warned them.

Then He gave them the final instruction, beginning thus, "Despise not one of these little ones."

Now let us more particularly examine this, in order that we may have the teaching of it for ourselves. What was this that Jesus said and did when He took the child and set it in their midst? He gave us the type of character in His Kingdom, and of such as may enter that Kingdom. No man has ever entered the Kingdom of God who has not taken up this place, and come to the level of a little child, which is the level of imperfection, of simplicity, of submissiveness.

It is the level of imperfection. Perhaps that is where most men stumble. The little child is the emblem of imperfection, waiting for correction and instruction, in order to development. No man can enter the Kingdom except upon this level. Jesus Christ did not say, in order to enter My Kingdom you must be perfect. When we have entered He will say as one of the severest things, "Ye shall be perfect, as your Father . . . is perfect." But the condition for entrance is imperfection. That does not mean that the condition for coming in is hopeless imperfection. A little child is not for evermore troubling about imperfection. The child subconsciously knows it, and in the knowledge of its imperfection yields itself to instruction, and correction, if it have a true child nature.

It is the level of simplicity. In the child we have all the things that are elemental. Complexity is not yet. All the powers of its being express themselves freely, readily, naturally; there is no guile.

But the final thing is that the child is plastic, submissive. It was a Roman Catholic Prelate who said, Give me the children until they are seven, I care not what you do after. It is perfectly true. A little child is always plastic. There may be a good deal of inherited sin in the child, but give the child its opportunity, it is submissive, and yields to the touch of our hand. All this is for us, and it is fearfully solemn and searching for any who have children in the home, or who teach them in the schools. The little children will bear our impress to the end of their lives, and through eternity.

What, then, did He say to these men who wanted to know what was the condition of greatness in His Kingdom? " Except ye turn and become as little children." He was stating a general principle, that a man must turn back to that. Mark the recognition that when the child leaves childhood, and enters upon its youth and manhood, these very things pass and fail; and therefore He said, You must get back again to that condition of imperfection, and simplicity and submissiveness; if you will humble yourself to that, then you will realise the ideal of greatness.

But now, following along this line of application, let us look at the practical tests. The child-heart receives the child, and the being who has lost the child-heart will offend the child. Now while our Lord makes these statements and they become tests, they are not tests only; they are words of terrific meaning and importance, words full of comfort and encouragement. Do you know what it is to receive a little child? Do you know what it is to take a child into your heart and life in Christian sympathy? In the moment you of the child-heart receive a little child, you receive to yourself the Christ Himself. " Whoso shall receive one such little child in My name, receiveth Me." Offend that little child and you offend Him. By comparison " it is profitable for him that a great millstone should be hanged about his neck, and that he should be sunk in the depth of the sea." He was teaching His disciples by that which is dear to God's heart, a child; and He was teaching them that they could test their own spirit by their relation to the child.

And then it seems as though the eyes of the Master, from that moment, looked on down the centuries—" Woe unto the world "—and the first woe of that verse, by its setting, is evidently not the woe of a curse, but the woe of a great lamentation—" Woe unto the world because of occasions of stumbling! for it must needs be that the occasions come; but woe to that man

through whom the occasion cometh!" The second woe is the same, but it has taken on the nature of a curse. First Christ's pity for the world, and then Christ's pronouncement of punishment upon men by whom the offences come. He traced the woes of the world to those from whom they proceed, such as cause stumbling and offence; and gathering up the world's sorrow, He fastened it upon the head of the man that causes it. In it we see the infinite equity and justice of Christ. That is His attitude to-day. Woe to the city where the offences come! That is a lamentation. But woe to the men from whom they come! That is a fiery word, burning with anger. Thus He gathered up into the economy of His ultimate dealings with men, all the woes of the race, and fixed them upon the men that have been the cause of them. The spirit that receives a child and will not offend it, is the spirit that will not put a stumbling-block in the way of the world. The man who offends a child is the man who wounds the world. Let there be no softening of these words of Jesus. He talks about the age-abiding fire, the Gehenna of fire, always burning, where refuse is flung. That is the place for the man who lacks the child-heart. He will be treated in the economy of God as outside the city, fit only for the rubbish heap. So there rings through this great speech of Jesus His tenderness and His thunder.

What is the ultimate instruction? He came back again to the child. Maybe he looked once again on the boy who stood there wondering at the words which, perhaps, he did not understand at all—more occupied with the loveliness of the face of the One Who was uttering them—and He said, " See that ye despise not one of these little ones." He gave them three reasons. First of all, " In heaven their angels do always behold the face of My Father Who is in heaven." The children have angels who behold the face of the Father, and who minister to them, and Jesus said to these men who were going to be in His Kingdom, and who wanted to know about greatness; Do not forget that the angels do not despise the children.

They watch them and guard them, and stand in heaven's Court for them. The angels are all ministering spirits, sent forth to do service for the sake of them that shall inherit salvation. And if you have wandered from the tender Fatherhood of God, your angel is still following you, and if, without sound or sigh, you turn back again to God, all the angels will join in the joy of that angel who announces your turning, because he has watched you so long. The little ones have angels waiting.

But that is not the highest reason for not despising them. He moved on to a higher level. In the Revised Version verse eleven is omitted, but the truth is not omitted. Our revisers felt it was out of place here, and ought to be omitted—"The Son of Man has come to seek and to save that which was lost." Even though we miss that, the next statement is the same thing; "How think ye? If any man have a hundred sheep, and one of them be gone astray, doth He not leave the ninety and nine, and go unto the mountains, and seek that which goeth astray? And if so be that He find it . . . he rejoiceth over it more than over the ninety and nine which have not gone astray." So if we ask, What about the inherited sin of the child? The Shepherd came to seek such. He was still talking about a child, so that another reason we are not to despise a child, is the fact that He has come to find the little child.

Once again, there is yet a mightier reason than the reason of angel ministry, and the reason of the Son's interest and mission; "Even so"—as angels are interested, as the Son is interested—"Even so, it is not the will of My Father . . . that one of these little ones should perish." If you despise a little child, then you are against the angels, you are against the Son of God, you are against the Eternal Father.

Oh the false measurements of greatness! A man is sometimes thought great because of his notoriety. It is often a more unpleasant word but a truer word than popularity. Men sometimes measure greatness by a man's power to manage other men and reign over them. But there is another word for that—tyranny. What is Christ's standard? Begin with the last thing and move backwards. Despise not a child, offend not a child, receive a child. What is the condition for all that? Be like a child, and when you become like a child, you become great.

To despise a child is to be out of harmony with the angels, the Son, and the Father. To offend a child is to make it profitable not to be. To receive a child is to entertain Jesus Christ. To be like a child is to be great.

As we listen to the King talking to His disciples and to us, we see how close heaven and hell are to each other! In the words of His lips He illuminates for us the infinite spaces, and we see the glories of God's own heaven; and in another moment, He lights for us the lurid depths of the underworld, and of judgment and punishment! May God give us the heart of a child! May God help us to put upon our own ambition the measurement of the little child.

MATTHEW XVIII. 15-35

IN this whole paragraph we have practically one discourse of our Lord to His own disciples. There are two great subjects with which He dealt. The first is that of greatness; the second, that of forgiveness. In our last section we considered the King's teaching concerning greatness. Here we have another side of the same truth, that namely, of the attitude of the subjects of the King towards a man who offends. The theme therefore is that of forgiveness. We should hardly relate these two things, greatness and forgiveness; and yet they are intimately related, for the final proof of greatness is ability to forgive. This is true of God, and therefore it must be true of men.

In words that seem to scorch us, He

warned His disciples not to offend. But, supposing that some man has offended, has been a stumbling-block to some one else, what shall we do with him? We cannot study this teaching of Jesus without being startled at the way in which the thunder merges into the love-song, and the lightning into the sunlight. This Teacher, so severe, so terrible, Who makes one tremble lest one should offend, when a man has offended, summons us by the compassion of God's heart, to go after him, to bring him back. That is the whole story of the relationship between greatness and forgiveness. We put them far apart in these days, and speak of the man who forgives as a weak man. But Christ shows the greatness of the man who forgives.

This passage divides itself quite naturally into two parts. We have in verses fifteen to twenty the King's definite instruction concerning forgiveness, commencing with the words, "If thy brother sin against thee." The words "against thee" are open to question. In some manuscripts they are not found; while in others they are. In the margin of the Revision it is written, "Some ancient authorities omit *against thee.*" Nothing dogmatic can be said as to whether these words ought to be retained or not, and yet the whole context suggests that the word of Christ here had a wider application than that of dealing with sin against us personally. Our responsibility against our sinning brother is not created by the fact that he has wronged us, but by the fact that he has sinned and harmed himself.

Then in verses twenty-one to thirty-five we have an account of how the disciples misunderstood Him; and of the King's correction.

Now let us, first of all, look at the King's instructions. Before looking at some of the things particularly, let us observe the spirit and purpose of them. The underlying purpose of Jesus concerning the sinning brother is expressed in the words, "Thou hast gained thy brother." In considering our Lord's use of the word "gained" here, it is very interesting to trace it through the New Testament. It is a commercial word, a word of the market place. It is a word which is used to characterise the processes by which a man accumulates wealth. The use of the word in this connection, so far as the sinning brother is concerned, recognizes loss. A man who has sinned is in certain senses lost; when he is restored he is gained, and the gain is interpreted by the context.

We are personally to attempt to gain our brother, because we have lost him as a brother through his sin. If he will not hear us, we are to take two or three with us, because by persisting in sin, his friends have lost him, he is lost to comradeship. If he will not hear them we are to go to the Church, because the Church has lost him; by his sin. The Church is to take the matter to heaven, because heaven has lost him by his sin. It is the great tragedy of a man lost which colours all this instruction; and the purpose that is to be in our heart when we deal with a sinning brother, is that of gaining him.

This word "gain" suggests, not merely the effect on the one lost, but the value it creates for those who seek him. When presently we have done with the shadows and the mists of the little while, we shall understand in the light of the undying ages that if we have gained one man we shall be richer than if we have piled up all the wealth of the world, and never won a human soul. What a blessed thing to gain a man, to possess him for oneself, for the fellowship of friends, for the enterprises of the Church, for the programme of high heaven.

But now how is this to be done? Our Lord was very careful in His revelation of the method. We are to begin by personal effort. "If thy brother sin against thee, go, show him his fault between thee and him alone." This is not gentle permission. It is definite instruction. Any Church of Jesus Christ is weak in the proportion in which its members allow false pity or sentiment to prevent their being faithful to this great work of attempting to show an erring brother his fault, in order that he may be restored. Jesus said, "If thy brother sin, go, show him his fault," declare it unto him. Charge him with it. By no means in the spirit of jealousy or judgment, but bring him to realise it as a fault, as sin. It is not enough to convince him that we count it as sin. Our business is to bring the man to see that he has sinned. And if an erring brother shall say to us when we go to him, I know it in the depths of my soul, then we begin the ministry of restoration. There may be a great many things necessary with regard to the man's relationship to the Kingdom and the Church, but so far as his relationship to us is concerned, we have gained him when he confesses his sin. Out of such conviction contrition comes, and out of such contrition, the face is set back again towards God, and right, and purity. That is the first method.

But supposing he will not hear, then the Lord says, our responsibility is not over, for the interest is a larger one than personal, in any man who has sinned. There is the interest of the comradeship. And so we must take with us one or two; and we are still going on the same business; to show him his fault, in order to bring him to contrition and return.

But supposing this man will neither hear us nor those whom we take with us, does not realise his sin, will not confess his sin, or is rebellious in his sin, continuing therein, what then? Then we are to tell it to the Church. Here we must be very careful to notice what our Lord really meant, for He clearly declared the alternative that is before the Church, when, lastly, the case is brought to it. The one side of the alternative is, that he will hear the Church. If the Church can restore this man, when one has failed, when two or three have failed, to contrition and conviction and consciousness of sin, then the Church has gained the man. But if he will not, what then? The other side of the alternative on the part of the Church is that then the man is to be as a Gentile and a publican.

Now before we examine that, let us notice what follows, because what follows explains the meaning of this power of the Church, " Verily, I say

unto you what things soever ye shall bind on earth shall be bound in heaven; and what things soever ye shall loose on earth shall be loosed in heaven. Again I say unto you, that if two of you shall agree on earth as touching anything that they shall ask, it shall be done for them of My Father which is in heaven. For where two or three are gathered together in My name there am I in the midst of them."

These are some of the most remarkable things that our Lord said about His Church. They have much wider application than the application Jesus made of them at this point. We are perfectly justified in lifting them out of their setting, and using them over a wider area of thought. But sometimes the danger is that we take these great words of Jesus and use them in the wider application, and so lose the immediate first-hand application which He Himself made of them. All these great words have to do with the Church's attitude towards the sinning man, to which we will return.

Yet they have to do with a much wider area which we cannot altogether pass over now. For some of us this is the whole ground of truth concerning the constitution and power of the Christian Church. " Where two or three are gathered together, there am I in the midst." That is the charter of the Church. How spacious, and gracious, and wonderful it is! First of all it breaks down all idea of a localised meeting-place with God. We have gained a temple everywhere by the loss of the temple in a locality. Mark the magnificence of it. It is not the temple that makes the place of worship, but the gathering " in My name." There are worshipping souls in the great cathedrals, but they are not all there. On the mountain height, in some shepherd hut, far away from church, chapel, or conventicle, two shepherds are gathered in the name of Jesus. There is the Church. " Where two or three are gathered together, there am I in the midst." May God deliver us from putting limits upon His " where." All that is necessary, is that two or three should be gathered in His name.

Again, "If two of you shall agree on earth as touching anything that they shall ask, it shall be done for them of My Father Who is in heaven." That is the authority for collective praying. And yet once more, "What things soever ye shall bind on earth, shall be bound in heaven." That is the Church's ethical authority in the world. The Church teaches the standard of morality, and what the Church says is binding, is binding; and what the Church says is not, is not. But that is only true when we link it with what follows —the Church gathering in the name of Christ.

So the great passage is the charter of Church authority, of Church method, of Church foundation. The Church authority—she binds and looses—in the old ethical sense of the words in which the scribes perpetually made use of them. The Church is the authority in the world, which sets up the moral standards; and it has always been so, for the last nineteen centuries; the true standards obtaining in the common consciousness of this hour are those which the Church has established. How does the Church gain this authority? By asking the Father, seeking from Him the light. But upon what basis does the Church gather to ask the Father for the light which shall make her message authoritative? "Where two or three are gathered together in My name, there am I in the midst." These are some of the wider applications of this teaching.

Now mark this fact, that Jesus used these tremendous truths in this matter of how we should deal with our brother who has sinned. If the Church has consulted the will of God concerning him, because the Church has gathered in the name of Jesus, then her decision is binding, authoritative, final. Heaven ratifies it. The Church, consisting of only two or three units, or of tens, scores, hundreds, gathered waiting before God in the name and nature of God's Son, her conclusions are binding conclusions, and Heaven seals them. The Church, so gathered, is to deal with the case of this man, and if this man will not hear her, will not accept her ruling, will not be submissive to

her authority, what then is she to do? If he will hear, she will fold him to her bosom; if this sinning man, who has offended, and ought to have had a millstone about his neck, is won back by the individual, or the two or three, or the Church, then mother Church is to fold him, and as the father kissed repeatedly the home-coming boy, mother Church, Bride of the Son of God, is to receive him, and smother him with her kisses. God give us hearts like that!

But if not, what then? Then the pity of the Church is to be more than false pity for the individual, and the holiness of the assembly is to be of greater importance than the sheltering of a man that has done wrong, and is unrepentant. "Let him be unto thee as the Gentile and the publican." It is a terrific sentence. It is first, that the Church must put that man outside her fellowship, that the Church must exercise her authority on the side of Heaven's unsullied purity.

But is that all? If we have so read it, we have misread it. We may take these words of Jesus Christ and make them blasphemous by the very tone in which we read them. There is a hymn we often sing,

"Lord, speak to me, that I may speak
In living echoes of Thy *tone*."

He never put the tone of thunder and denunciation into those words. He never put into them the tone of an unholy and unchristian excommunication. That is what we have too often done. What did He say? This man you have been after, and could not gain, this man that two or three of you saw and could not gain, this man that the Church would fain have folded to her motherly bosom, and could not gain, "Let him be unto thee as the Gentile and the publican." You must put him outside the fellowship, and you must put him outside the shadow of the Church. He must not have the shelter of the Church for impurity. But the moment he is there, he is the man I came to win, he is the man for whom I came to die. "The Son of Man is come to seek and to save that which was lost." You must keep him from the privilege and the shelter of the

Church, in order to bring him to consciousness, first of his need, and then of My exceeding grace and free forgiveness.

Now let us glance at the misunderstanding of the disciples, because we are in succession to them, and are liable to make the same mistakes. Peter said, "Lord, how oft shall my brother sin against me, and I forgive him? until seven times?" Observe Peter's magnanimity and Peter's meanness; and whether you count it magnanimity or meanness will depend upon that with which you put his proposition into contrast. Now there is no doubt whatever that when Peter came to Jesus with that question, and that suggested answer, How oft shall I forgive my brother, "until seven times?" he thought he had climbed to the seventh heaven of greatness; he thought he had uttered the last word of magnanimity, "Until seven times?" The teaching of all the scribes and Rabbis was, forgive once, forgive twice, but the third offence merits no forgiveness. We find it scattered throughout all the Rabbinical teaching. Peter had been told that he was one of the new scribes, and so he borrowed the language of the scribes to show how graciously he went beyond it. The scribes had said thrice, Peter said, I know more than those men; I am prepared to go beyond that; "seven times." It was magnanimity by the side of the teaching of the scribes. How some things perpetuate themselves through the centuries. There are some things that never die until submerged in the life of God. The proverb of to-day says, "The third time pays for all." The world at its best forgives a man twice, and damns him at the third time. Peter said, Master, I am beyond that, "until seven times." John Wesley makes a very caustic comment on this story. He said, "If this be Christianity, where do Christians live?"

Now note the Master's answer. May there not have been a smile of love or pity for the meanness of this concep-tion of His own Spirit? "I say not unto thee, Until seven times; but, Until seventy times seven."

Then He gave a parabolic illustration, which is a picture fair and wonderful. It was a picture for Peter. How much did this man owe the king? Ten thousand talents. Translate it into the coinage of England, and it was at least two million pounds; or of the United States, roughly ten million dollars. This man had involved the whole State, and he owed the king at least ten thousand talents, and the king loosed him from all his bondage, and set him free. And then he went out and found a fellow servant who owed him a hundred pence. Let us take a penny as the Roman denarius, and say this man owed him less than five pounds, or twenty-five dollars. I owed the king two millions sterling, and he let me go; and I got my brother by the throat for five pounds! What did Christ mean? You have been forgiven a debt immeasurable. You have no right to exact a hundred pence from a man who, if you will give him three months, will pay you.

Mark carefully Christ's last word, "So shall also My heavenly Father do unto you, if ye forgive not every one his brother from your hearts." The arrest of the man that had been released, and his imprisonment, not for the debt which he had been forgiven, but for the brutality against his brother conveys its own teaching.

The two sections of this chapter as they reveal the two sides of the one attitude toward the subjects of the King, are very remarkable. Absolute absence of pity towards sin in oneself which may cause a brother to offend; and unceasing pity toward a sinning brother with never-failing attempts to gain him. To fail in the first is to make the millstone a profitable investment; and to fail in the second is to be dealt with in severe and dire punishment by God Himself, for the one thing God will not forgive is an unforgiving heart.

MATTHEW XIX. 1-22

THIS paragraph constitutes one of the interludes which characterise the third section of the Gospel according to Matthew. In it Christ is seen turning to the multitudes, from His more immediate work of instructing His own disciples. The King, rejected already by the rulers, and growingly the cause of perplexity to the multitudes, yet responded to all who came, acording to their needs.

There are four classes represented here. The multitudes who came to Him in need, bringing their sick with them; those who came in the critical spirit, attempting to entrap Him in His talk; those who came impulsed by natural affection, bringing their children with them; and one who came with a profound inquiry and a sincere desire for help.

And there are four subjects dealt with by the King. He invaded four different spheres, and revealed His power in each. The physical, as He healed disease; the ethical, as He answered the criticism of the critics; the social, as He rebuked the disciples, and gathered the children in His arms; the spiritual, as He flashed light upon the pathway of this man who came to Him; and through all the story we, who are following the pathway of the King with loving interest and adoring hearts, are impressed by the ease with which He dealt with the varying conditions.

The first is a brief story, contained within the first two verses. The occasion was that of His departure from Galilee. His life there was closed, His work was done, His message was delivered, His power was made manifest. He went into the borders of Judea beyond Jordan. His face was set toward Jerusalem. He had said that it could not be that a prophet perish out of his own country. He had said to them over and over again since Cæsarea Philippi, "I must go up to Jerusalem and suffer . . . and be killed . . . and be raised." The *must* of His Passion was upon His heart and soul. As He came into the coasts of Judea

He found Himself again surrounded by great multitudes of people; and although details are not given, it is perfectly evident that the people came bringing their sick folk with them. We simply read, "He healed them there." In that sentence is the revelation of a mighty compassion, and an equally mighty ability. There are no details, yet do not let us miss the grandeur of the scene, the pathos of it, the greatness of it, the tenderness of it, the glory of it. We see the King. The years of His earthly life were drawing to a close. He had enunciated His ethic, exhibited the benefits of His rule, enforced His claims; and He knew full well what the verdict of the people would be; "Crucify Him, crucify Him," "we will not that this Man reign over us." He had told the disciples this, and He was now setting His face towards that final fact of the Cross. Nevertheless when these people crowded around Him with their sick folk, all the compassion of His heart responded, and He put forth His might to heal.

In the next section we have, first, the question of the Pharisees, and the Master's answer; then the objection which they raised to His answer, and His reply to that objection; and finally, the surprised comment of His disciples, and His answer to them.

First, the question and the answer. We at once see that the question was of the hour, something which was then debatable. They said, "Is it lawful for a man to put away his wife for every cause?" There was something behind that question, a division of opinion amongst the rulers; two schools of thought were involved. The whole dispute arose out of the teaching in Deuteronomy (xxiv. 1). "When a man taketh a wife, and marrieth her, then it shall be, if she find no favour in his eyes, because he hath found some unseemly thing in her, that he shall write her a bill of divorcement, and give it in her hand, and send her out of his house." Now there was a difference of opinion between two masters, Hillel and Shammai, as to what Moses meant by these words. Hillel had been the mightiest influence in Judaism for long years as a teacher, and had been dead about twenty years when Christ was teaching. He had maintained that in that word Moses allowed divorce upon the ground of what we to-day should speak of as incompatibility of temperament. Shammai held that there was only one cause for divorce. The two schools had many bitter disputations as to which was right; and that dispute was in the background of this question to Jesus.

By way of answer, Christ first revealed the true foundation of the marriage relation; "Have ye not read, that He Who made them from the beginning made them male and female, and said, For this cause shall a man leave his father and mother, and shall cleave to his wife: and the two shall become one flesh?" That was in itself a full and final answer. The method of the King here is to be carefully observed. In the presence of a surface difficulty, He appealed to the foundation of eternal principle. He ignored Hillel and Shammai; He passed Moses; and sweeping back through interpreters and lawgivers to the divine arrangement, He said, "From the beginning." This method of our Lord is in itself a revelation of the final law of life. The things that Moses said were transitory, having application only to certain times and places. If we are in doubt or difficulty we are not to appeal to teachers who are interpreters; to a lawgiver who was the lawgiver of an age, and whose ethical code has been superseded by a higher; we are rather to make our appeal to divine intention.

Having thus appealed to the age-abiding principle, He made application thereof; "For this cause shall a man leave his father and mother, and shall cleave to his wife; and the two shall become one flesh." Thus He revealed in a sublime statement the awful sanctity of marriage. The marriage relationship is to supersede, because of its sacredness, the most sacred relationship that can exist apart from it, that of the child to father and mother. Christ made no allowances for the difficulties

by which these men were surrounded, and by which we are surrounded, these declarations of incompatibility and dissimilarity. Christ lifted the subject to the pure altitudes of the divine intention as to the sanctity of the marriage relation.

Then He came down to the level of their disputes, "What therefore God hath joined together, let not man put asunder." Mark the marvellous meaning of this. To express the thought of Jesus in other words, it is as though He had said; According to the divine intention a man leaves father and mother, and cleaves to his wife, in the high sanctity of the marriage relationship. If that ideal of the marriage relationship has been realised, then let no man break in upon it, "what God hath joined together, let not man put asunder." Jesus did not mean to say that every man and woman living together in civil relationship is married in the sight of heaven; but He did mean to say where this ideal lies at the basis of the marriage relationship "let not man put asunder." A marriage according to eternal principles, and according to the sanctity of this ideal, is consummated by God.

Then they brought their objection, and the objection was stated in the terms of their own dispute—"Why then did Moses command to give a bill of divorcement, and to put her away?" What they meant to say was, For what reason did Moses command it; what were the grounds of his permission? Jesus replied in effect that when Moses gave that permission, he accommodated himself to the need of the hour; there was in the permission, contravention of the divine intention, but it was made necessary by the hardness of men's hearts, by the fact that they had lost the simplicity and tenderness that made is impossible for them to realise the high ideal. The permission of Moses to a hardened people is not to be taken as the final standard of ethics in the Kingdom of God.

Then He proceeded to utter words which, if read by Christian people, answer all these difficulties for the present hour, "I say unto you, whosoever shall put away his wife, except for fornication, and shall marry another, committeth adultery; and he that marrieth her when she is put away committeth adultery." To that nothing need be added! No man, believing on Christ, and taking Christ's pure name on his lips, can say that upon the basis of dissimilarity, or upon the basis of incompatibility of temperament, there may be divorce. Oh the tragedy may be a lifelong tragedy, but for the sake of the strength of society, and for the sake of family life, we must accept the standard of Christ. It is a solemn and a searching word; it makes indissoluble the bond once made, save for the one, and only sin. If there be suffering, that is not the fault of Christ, or of God; it is the result of the violation of the ideal of the marriage relationship; and the penalty must remain until the end of time.

Having thus dealt with the Pharisees, the disciples in amazement said; "If the case of a man is so with his wife, it is not expedient to marry." This was not so much complaint as a recognition of the high ideal which was set up by Christ. They said in effect, The ideal is too high for the present life; had not men who are going to be true to God, better live the celibate life?

Christ's answer to them is important for all time. He did not contradict their view, but said; "Not all men can receive this saying." To what saying did He refer? Not His own, but theirs. Thus Christ declared that the celibate life is not for all. It may be for some. All men cannot receive it; which does not necessarily mean that they are weak, but that they are not called to it, for it is only given to some. He named three classes of men who can observe the celibate life; some are born to celibacy; some are made celibates—a class with which we have nothing to do, the reference being local and obsolete—and some choose celibacy for the sake of the Kingdom of God. Christ did not condemn such; He spoke of them with respect and honour; but He would not allow His disciples to condemn the men who did not observe the celibate life. It is not given to all. Thus He forbade His disciples to build upon His underlying principle a rule or

set of rules to be observed by all men. That was the perpetual method of Christ. We cannot build rules upon His principles; we must deal individually with the underlying principle. Here is a man to whom it is not given, he is not called to the life of celibacy, and we must not apply any rule to him. Here is another man who is called, and for some purpose that we cannot understand, he devotes himself to celibacy for the sake of the Kingdom of God. That man is to be honoured; but he is not to despise a man who does not devote himself to celibacy. This is the perpetual method of Christianity; every man must find his own rule out of the principle. We cannot make rules for our fellow men.

Christ recognized two things in this wonderful passage. He recognized first of all the absolute sacredness and sanctity of the marriage relationship; and safeguarded it from every attempt to break it down and undervalue it with words of burning fire; and He recognized with fine taste and beautiful sympathy, that there may be those who will devote themselves to the celibate life for the Kingdom of God, and declared that they are to be held in absolute esteem. When the Christian Church preached the doctrine of celibacy for its ministry, they erected a rule upon a principle, with disastrous results, as we know full well. Nevertheless there have been men devoted to celibacy in the ministry of the Roman Church, pure, strong, high, noble sons of God; but again and again, because men have tried to bind their lives by rules never intended for them, they have violated the very principle upon which they attempted to work, and that is always so. To be governed by Jesus Christ is to be governed by Him directly and immediately, and by principles which one must apply to one's own life, always declining to allow others to make rules.

The last two paragraphs are very familiar. We have first the exquisite story of the children. Both Matthew and Mark put this incident of the bringing of the children immediately after the words of Jesus about the marriage relationship. May we not have some light on the action of the disciples when they attempted to forbid the bringing of children, from what was in their mind concerning celibate life? Did they not recognize that their Master was living the celibate life? And may it not be that after all, notwithstanding His correction of the falseness of attempting to erect a rule upon a principle, there was in their mind an underlying thought that celibacy was the purer and higher and nobler life; and therefore the children must be kept away from Him? If so, how powerfully and finally Christ corrected their false philosophy!

The bringing of the children to Him was an act of parental solicitude, the last sign of confidence in Him. They brought their children to Him. It is wonderful how this lives! There are many parents to-day, who have no personal relationship to Jesus, but who want their children to be His. In the men who want their children to be right with God, there lives a conviction about Him, which makes the sin of rejecting Jesus Christ yet more heinous.

But observe the disciples' mistake. It was based upon a wrong estimate of their Lord; it may have been a wrong estimate of His dignity; it may have been a wrong estimate of the quality of His purity. It was also due to a wrong conception of the child. One of the old Puritan Fathers has a very graphic description of what happened. Perhaps he was right. He imagines the disciples talking to these parents about the absurdity of the idea that so great a Teacher, Who had answered the politicians, could have any interest in a little child. But be that as it may, it is evident that they did not know their Lord, and they did not know a little child, from their attempt to keep a little child away from Him. If we read the story in the light of the other Evangelists, we see that Christ's attitude towards His disciples in connection with the children was one of anger. We have it distinctly declared by Mark that He was moved with indignation. There are only two or three occasions where we read that Christ was angry at all. This is one of them. He was angry with the men who so misunderstood Him, as to think He was not willing to welcome a child. His attitude towards the child was that of welcome and blessing, on the simple, warm, everyday terms of pure human affection. He blessed them, yes, and not with two fingers outstretched to touch them; He took them in His arms and blessed them; it was a great warm loving embrace. Thank God that is the place of all the babes, in the very arms of this great Christ.

The last picture is that of the rich young ruler. In studying it, let us notice the seeker and his search. A clean, upright, honest man, of fine natural temperament was searching for the one thing of supreme importance—age-abiding life. In observing the Master's method with Him, notice first the young ruler's arresting question concerning goodness, which indicated the fact that he was already on the track, in that he connected life with goodness; "What good thing shall I do, that I may have eternal life?" The question moreover revealed the fact that in his thought of the Teacher as good, he had come nearer the mark than he himself knew. Then Christ flashed upon him external light, the light of the Second Table of the Decalogue with all its requirements concerning the relation of man to man. And the young man stood erect, and said, "All these things have I observed: what lack I yet?" Then the Master, instead of flashing upon him external light, sent light right through the darkened cells of his inner life, and revealed the fact that he was a self-centred man, never having found his true King, never having kissed the sceptre, or bent to control. He found that the power of the things that ministered to selfish desire was greater than the call within him after goodness. "He went away sorrowful; for he was one that had great possessions." Perhaps that was not the end of the young man, but it is the end of the story. One of two things happened. Either there was a day when he turned back again to Christ and the Cross, and found life; or he found a tomb for his soul in the very things he refused to give up, when Christ called him so to do.

Now let all the others pass out of sight. The King fills the vision, as He deals with disability in forceful ease; establishes the ethical standard of marriage for all time; gathers all little children into His arms and into His love; and flashes upon the soul such brilliant light that whether that soul walk henceforth towards death or life, the pathway is perfectly clear.

In the presence of such a King; because of what He is, we say,

" True hearted, whole-hearted, faithful and loyal,
King of our lives, by Thy grace we will be."

MATTHEW XIX. 23–XX. 16

THE main values of this section are indicated in the words of Jesus recorded in verses twenty-six and thirty of chapter nineteen, taken in conjunction with those found in verse sixteen of chapter twenty, " With men this is impossible; but with God all things are possible . . but many shall be last that are first; and first that are last. . . . So the last shall be first, and the first last." These verses bring into immediate prominence our Master's deductions from His teaching; but the section cannot be intelligently understood save as we remember its relation to that which has preceded it.

In this section the King turned again from the crowd to His own disciples. The paragraph begins, " And Jesus said unti His disciples," and it is directly connected with the case of the young ruler. All that our Lord said to His disciples concerning riches and the Kingdom of God; and all that He said in answer to a question which Peter propounded, grew out of the coming of the young ruler, and our Lord's dealing with him. The teaching goes far beyond the case of the young ruler, and far beyond all similar cases; but it begins there; and we certainly shall not understand our Lord's attitude when He spoke of riches, neither shall we understand His parable, if we forget these two preliminary matters; first, that He was talking to His own disciples; and secondly, that He was speaking to them in the light of what had happened with regard to the young ruler, and of the attitude of their minds resulting from His attitude toward the young ruler.

We may, then, divide our study into two parts; the first, a comparatively brief, and yet a most important one, Christ's comment on the case of the rich young ruler, and the resulting conversation. Then secondly; Christ having settled the difficulty suggested by the disciples, Peter raised a new question, " We have left all, and followed Thee; what then shall we have? " and Christ answered him.

First, Christ's comment on the case of the rich young ruler and the resulting conversation. We may read an entirely false meaning into the words of Christ concerning the rich young ruler unless we are careful to catch the Master's tone. Although the fact is not recorded here, one of the other Evangelists makes the very interesting declaration that when the rich young ruler had said to Jesus, in answer to His presentation of the twofold table of the Decalogue as the standard of measurement, Master, all these things have I observed from my youth, " Jesus, looking upon him, loved him."

Now with that love in His heart, Christ turned to His own disciples and said, " It is hard for a rich man to enter into the Kingdom of heaven." That was a severe word, but there were tears in it, there was pity in it, there was love in it. We shall do no violence to this text if we change it slightly, and read—It is very difficult for a rich man to enter into the Kingdom of heaven. And when He repeated the same thing with a new emphasis, there was still the same tone and the same spirit, the tone and spirit of regret, and sorrow, and love, " And again I say unto you, It is easier for a camel to go through a needle's eye, than for a rich man to enter into the Kingdom of God."

Why is it difficult for a rich man to enter into the Kingdom of heaven?

Here again we need not indulge in speculation. Let us go back to the King's own wonderful Manifesto—the Sermon on the Mount. In His first sentence He set the door open, and revealed how men may enter into all the blessedness which He described. " Blessed are the poor in spirit; for theirs is the Kingdom of heaven." Now over against that fundamental assertion put those tender, regretful words of Jesus, It is hard work for a rich man to enter in. Why? Because wealth means power, and power is far more likely to create pride than to create poverty of spirit. It is very difficult for a wealthy man to be poor in spirit; not impossible in the economy of God; but very, very difficult. Jesus had seen the going away of that rich young ruler, and the cry of His heart was full of sorrow, for He loved him.

It is more than hard, it is practically impossible. " It is easier for a camel to go through a needle's eye." Possibly by the " needle's eye," our Lord referred to the small gate of a city, through which no camel could pass except by being unloaded, and bending in order to gain entrance. It is a figure intended to teach the impossibility, so far as the man himself is concerned. It is impossible for any man who is possessed of wealth which gives him power, to become poor in spirit, and learn the lesson of an absolute submission in his own strength.

Now notice the disciples' question. When Jesus had said this thing, and said it with a sob and a regret in His voice, the disciples were astonished exceedingly, saying, " Who then can be saved?" Here we may wrong the disciples if we are not careful. The usual, and popular, and yet superficial interpretation of this is, that they meant to say, If a rich man cannot be saved,who can? that they were each looking to the time when rich and influential men would come into the Kingdom the more easily because of their wealth. But probably that would be to charge them with baser materialism than that of which they were really guilty. One would rather believe that when Christ said that, they saw very deeply into the heart of His meaning, and saw that He intended to teach that absolute poverty of spirit, freedom from the desire to possess for selfish purposes, lay at the wicket-gate of the Kingdom; and that they said in effect, in one of those confessions of the heart that men suddenly make oftentimes, and hardly know they are making them. There is not one of us that would not be rich if we could; and if the desire to possess wealth, and the determination to do it if we were able, prevents us coming into the Kingdom, who can be saved? These disciples were in all likelihood more honest than we often are. They recognized that if they could have possessed the young man's wealth, they would; and they recognized that Jesus Christ in His statement of difficulty was not dealing with a class after all—He never did deal with a class—but that He was getting down to the common facts of human nature and human peril; and they said, Who then can be saved?

Now carefully notice our Lord's answer, which is an answer to the whole question, and not to a part of it. The question is this—If a rich man cannot be saved, who then can be saved? Who then, in view of these terms and these requirements, can be saved at all; what hope is there of any man's salvation? Christ's answer was to the question concerning the salvation of man; and not merely to that concerning the salvation of a rich man—" With men this is impossible;" no man can be saved out of his own will, by his own determination, whether he be rich or poor, bond or free, " But with God all things are possible."

This word of Christ was not simply His declaration that a rich man cannot be saved by the power of men; but that with God he can be saved. In a moment He had risen from that first ground of viewing the wealthy class; into the larger ground of recognizing the underlying humanity of all men.

One other thought as to emphasis here. Our Lord did not say, to men this thing is impossible, to God all things are possible. There is a very peculiar value in the preposition which He used. *With* men impossible, *with*

God possible. If a man co-operates with men, makes their maxims his, makes their methods his, salvation is impossible. So long as a man lives upon the plane of humanity alone, and loses his touch with God, and recognition of Him, he cannot be saved. The material level of life will have material ideals, a material goal, and material failure. But *with* God; that is the man who has linked his life to God will find it possible, be he wealthy or be he poor, to enter the Kingdom and be saved. So the whole theme of human salvation lies by suggestion within this statement of Jesus.

Now let us consider Peter's comment and the answering instruction of our Lord. Peter's question went back undoubtedly to the case of the rich young ruler, and we are simply compelled to understand it thus, and to put a resulting emphasis upon the passage. "Then answered Peter and said unto Him, Lo *we* have felt all, and followed Thee; what then shall we have?" Jesus had said to the ruler, "If thou wouldest be perfect, go, sell that thou hast, and give to the poor, and thou shalt have treasure in heaven; and come, follow Me." Peter said, We have done it; what is the treasure we are to have? The subject of the possibility of human salvation had gone out of Peter's mind. The Lord had settled that, and now we have a new subject. Peter was, in his deepest thinking, putting himself and others into contrast with the young ruler. It is as though he said, A young man came to Thee, O Master, with great wealth. You told him what to do, and You promised him treasure in heaven, and he has turned his back upon Thee, he has not been obedient. But, Master, we have been obedient, we have left all to follow Thee; what treasure are we to have?

Now mark the answer of Jesus, and let His answer rebuke any tendency in our soul to be angry with Peter on account of his question, for the Lord was not angry with him. The answer of Jesus moved within two distinct realms; first, a definite answer to his question about reward; and secondly, a warning against what is revealed in his asking the question.

He said to him in effect, You have asked Me what you shall have, I will tell you, "Verily"—mark the word of authority—"I say unto you, that ye who have followed Me, in the regeneration when the Son of man shall sit on the throne of His glory"—not Ye that have followed Me in the regeneration, but "Ye who have followed Me, in the regeneration when the Son of man shall sit on the throne of His glory"—placing the comma as in the Revision—shall occupy twelve thrones under My control and My government; judging, not condemning, but overseeing, administering on My behalf the affairs of the Kingdom to be set up in the world. He took one long glance ahead over the centuries to the day which He described as "the regeneration." These men were to share in His authority in His Kingdom—which is that of regeneration. That was His first answer to them. But His answer was broader. Not only ye, but all others who shall suffer loss, and those people who in the coming days shall leave "houses, or brethren, or sisters, or father, or mother, or children, or lands, for My name's sake, shall receive a hundredfold, and shall inherit eternal life." So that our Lord did not rebuke Peter's question, but answered it. It is as though He said to them, Is it true you have left all to follow Me? If you want to know what you shall have, here is My answer, as to you particularly, the twelve first messengers of My love. My Kingdom is the day of regeneration and restoration, and when I have won the victory, you shall be administrators sitting upon thrones, and judging; and all who suffer loss, turning the back upon property, and friends, and love, and relations, shall enter into great possessions. I did not speak idly to the young ruler; whoever sacrifices for Me shall win a hundredfold.

But now notice the word of warning. "But," said Jesus, "many shall be last that are first; and first that are last." Then followed the parable, and it ended with these words, "*So* the last shall be first, and the first last." Notice carefully these two statements, and the relation of the parable to them. Christ warned His disciples by saying to them; "Many shall be last that are first; and first that are last." Then He illustrated the meaning of His words by a parable, which was a parable to His own disciples. We must not take this parable and make it of general application. John Ruskin, in his book, *Unto This Last*, has absolutely missed the meaning of it. There is an application of it to the social order which will be realised when that order becomes Christian. But within the Christian Church it is a parable concerning precedence in the matters of reward. It is a parable directed against Peter's implication of superiority over the young ruler. "Lo, we have left all and followed Thee; what then shall we have?" We are the first of Thy disciples. That man has turned his back, and even though he comes back presently at the eleventh hour, we are first; "What shall we have?" There are many first that shall be last, there are last that shall be first. So our Lord would teach these men the truth concerning precedence in His Kingdom, and He would correct their implication of superiority.

The figure of the householder was here used by Jesus of Himself. He had used it upon one occasion of His own disciples, in chapter thirteen. He used it in several parables of Himself. The whole application of the parable is to service, and the reward of service for men in the Kingdom. There is no question here about salvation, no question about entering the Kingdom. There is no thought about equal payment for unequal work. If we attempt to base upon this parable the teaching that if a man lives and loiters through ten hours, and comes in at the eleventh, he is on equal rights with the man who has worked from the beginning, we are absolutely unfair to the other parables of Jesus. If we build upon this parable a doctrine of social order, we must also include the parables of the talents and the pounds, for all three are needed to have a perfect picture of social service. This parable is intended to teach one simple truth, that a man's reward will be, not according to the length of his service, not ac-

cording to the notoriety of his service, but according to his fidelity to the opportunity which is given him. The men at the beginning of the day entered into a covenant and an agreement. The Master of the vineyard went out later in the day, saw others standing idle, and sent them in. When He said, "Why stand ye here all the day idle?" their answer was, "Because no man hath hired us." That is why they had not been at work before, they had not had their opportunity. When He created opportunity by sending them in, then in that last hour they were true to the only opportunity they had, and therefore their reward was as great as the reward of the men that had been at work twelve hours. It is as though He said to Peter, to revert to our illustration, If that young man comes now, though he has been long delaying, his reward will be as great as yours, if he is faithful.

Yes, but why did not the Lord give him the opportunity before? That is not in the parable. If we take the other parables we find in that of the pounds, that He gave to every man a pound. That teaches that there is an opportunity for every man. If we want the doctrine of opportunity we find it there, not here. It is absolutely unfair to read into any parable something for which the parable was not used. He first corrected the false standards of comparison, such as length of notoriety of service; and then revealed the true standard of reward—that of fidelity to opportunity. Here is a man to whom is given the opportunity to speak to thousands upon thousands of people the great word of God. It is a great opportunity. But here is a woman living away off upon the mountain, who never saw a city in her life, but has wrought with God in the training of two or three children. When that man and woman stand for final reward, they will each have their penny if they have been faithful. This is so in all Christian service.

So in conclusion we have no right to take this parable and use it in application to the social questions of unregenerate men. It is impossible to do so without violating the sense of justice. Christianity has no pity for those who, being unfit remain so, in spite of the opportunity for fitness which He creates. It is a false message to the age which says that Christianity will take hold of the unfit man and nurse him and take care of him, when by response to her evangel he can be made fit. If his unfitness is the unfitness of a physical limitation for which he is not to blame, Christianity will take hold of him, and love him. But if the unfitness is a moral disease which Jesus Christ can correct, then Christianity is sterner than Hebraism in refusing to feed him or help him until he have taken advantage of the dynamic of Jesus Christ. The one plain meaning of this parable is that those highly privileged will not receive wage according to privilege, but according to fidelity. Or again, those whose privilege is less, will not receive less wage if they are true to the opportunity which comes to them.

Consequently the great word to each one of us is a word that warns us against being proud of anything we have done in the past, and imagining that by virtue of a greater opportunity we are entering into a greater reward. It is a word that drives us back to the whole day, or the one hour of opportunity, in order that we may fill it to the full with consecrated toil, and so enter into the reward which He gives to faithfulness.

MATTHEW XX. 17-34

THE words, "The Son of Man came not to be ministered unto, but to minister, and to give His life a ransom for many" (xx. 28), may be said to constitute the central statement of the whole paragraph. The great truth therein declared, explains the mind of the Master as revealed in this story; the perplexity of the disciples; and the Master's attitude toward need, as revealed in the crowds which followed Him.

This section is most interesting, as it brings before us the different classes of people by which the King was surrounded in the last days. Again we may describe it as a microcosm, showing us the whole condition of affairs in those last days. We have watched Him as He devoted Himself almost exclusively to His own disciples, and yet manifested a perpetual readiness to turn to the multitudes as they came to Him in their need, and with their question, and continually maintained His attitude of defence against the attacks of His foes. Now in this paragraph we see first the Lord Himself— and there is a wonderful revelation of the working of His mind at this point. We see next the group of disciples, the first circle immediately around Him, and we learn what they were thinking. We see beyond them, a great multitude following Him, curious, interested, and expectant.

We shall divide the paragraph into three sections for our study. First, that revealing the mind of the King (verses 17-19). Secondly, that revealing the mind of the Kingdom, as it was established in the hearts of those who were yielded to the King (verses 20-28). Finally, that revealing the multitudes (verses 29-34).

First, then, as to the revelation of the mind of the King. It is first manifest that He had a clear understanding of what lay before Him at the hands of lawless men. Mark the minuteness of His description. There is not a *perhaps in it*, or a *peradventure*, or a *maybe;* not a single word that will allow us to imagine that Jesus was speculating as to the future. He said, "We go up to Jerusalem; and the Son of man shall be delivered unto the chief priests and scribes; and they shall condemn Him to death and shall deliver Him unto the Gentiles to mock, and to scourge, and to crucify." There is the utmost accuracy in the details, and a calm, quiet knowledge of the actual things that were before Him. The roads to Jerusalem were thronged with multitudes who were going to the feasts. Many of them would be near Him because of their interest in Him.

He took His disciples apart from these crowds—perhaps turning off the highroad into some bypath for a little, or making it evident that He desired to be alone—and calmly told them in brief words of the facts to which He was moving in Jerusalem.

In the second place there was evidently in the mind of the King a clear vision of the fact that what lay before Him was within the determinate counsel of God, for He ended the declaration of coming suffering with these words, "And the third day He shall be raised up." From that wonderful day at Cæsarea Philippi after the confession of Peter, when Jesus began to talk about His Cross, He never mentioned His Cross to His disciples upon any one occasion without also declaring the fact of His coming resurrection.

Not only the clear vision of the darkness, and the clear vision of the light beyond; not only a certain knowledge of all the suffering and the pain, and an equally certain knowledge of the ultimate triumph over these things in resurrection; but, and because of this dual certainty in His mind, there was manifested a quiet and dignified co-operation with the "determinate counsel" of God as He set His face towards Jerusalem, saying quietly and calmly to His disciples, "Behold we go up to Jerusalem." There was never a thought of turning aside; undeterred by what He knew most certainly of coming pain, He set His face toward the suffering deliberately, compelled toward Jerusalem by no other than His perpetual devotion to the will of God, and His perpetual determination to co-operate with that will, to its ultimate purpose.

Then notice the action consequent upon that consciousness. He took the disciples apart, and He told them in detail the things He knew. It has been said our Lord was attempting to draw these men into sympathy with Him; that He wanted them to come into a closer comradeship with Him, in order to His own comfort. The probability is that He was not thinking of Himself for a moment, that He was still a self-emptied soul; and that He was rather getting them ready for the pathways of pain that lay before them. He did not

lean upon human sympathy as He faced the lonely sufferings of the Cross. The only strength He knew was the strength of His unbroken fellowship and communion with God. He was storing their minds with things which at the moment they could not possibly understand, for these men never knew Him while He was still amongst them. They loved Him, they saw enough in Him to draw out their affections after Him. They saw enough to make them believe in Him in some unintelligent sense, but they never understood Him. In the Paschal discourses, which John has preserved for us, He said to them in effect, The things I am saying to-day, you will understand in the days to come, when the Comforter has come and opened your minds. It is better for you that I go away, for if I do not go away, the Comforter cannot come, but when He comes He will guide you into the truth. And in the first four-and-twenty hours after the baptism of the Spirit, on the day of Pentecost, they were more familiar with the truth concerning Jesus than they had ever been during the whole period of His ministry in their midst. Nineteen centuries have passed away, and now by the illumination of that Spirit of God, Who has withdrawn the signs which were material, the tongues of fire, but Who abides in all spiritual power, we can walk with Him on the pathway of suffering in a more intimate fellowship than those men could.

But let us consider the mind of the Kingdom. Taking the story of the coming of these two men with their mother, let us notice the revelation of mind which it affords. First, in the mind of those who constituted the Kingdom, there was evident present faith in Him. They still believed in His coming into His Kingdom. As to what they meant by the Kingdom does not at all matter for the moment. They were not perfectly clear concerning His Kingdom; their ideas were largely material ideas, yet not wholly; but they did not see all the spiritual height and depth and spaciousness. What made those two men persuade their mother to come and ask that they should sit one on His right hand and the other on His left? They would never have preferred the request if they had not believed that He was coming into a Kingdom. Then mark the anger of the ten, and remember that their anger and criticism was because of their belief in the King, and because they wanted the positions of importance themselves. The twelve believed that He was coming into a Kingdom. Yet they were strangely perplexed since Cæsarea Philippi. He was always making them uncomfortable by talking of a Cross, and they could not believe that by death life could begin, that through defeat a crown could come. Perhaps they said within their hearts; He is tired, weary, and oppressed; He thinks He is going to be defeated, but we do not. He is going to build His Kingdom. Perhaps in this request, a repeated one, there was a desire on their part to comfort Him. He said; I am going to Jerusalem to be mocked, and scourged, and crucified. They replied; Nay, Lord, who art Thou going to appoint in Thy Kingdom, who will sit on Thy right hand and on Thy left? One's admiration for the faith of these men grows, the more we study the records. They came to Him, and asked things which evidenced their faith in Him. No man asks to sit on the right hand and left of a man who is going to the gallows. They still believed that He was a King, and that He was about to establish His Kingdom.

Again, we see not merely their faith in Him, but their devotion to Him. When, in infinite patience and great gentleness, and as it always seems, with a touch of loving satire, He said, "Are ye able to drink the cup that I am about to drink?" they said, "We are able." Again they meant well; they thought they were able, and they were willing, so far as they could, to go with Him. They were just as magnificent, devoted, and honest-hearted as Peter was when he contradicted his Lord's estimate of himself, "If all shall be offended in Thee, I will never be offended." It was a mistake, a blunder to put his opinion against his Lord's, a mistake also to put himself into comparison with his own brethren, to their disadvantage. But it was devotion.

And these men meant it when they said, "We are able." Had He not called them sons of thunder?

Ah, but they were not able! A few short weeks at most, days in all probability, and He would see the sons of thunder flying with the crowd of frightened disciples. The failure revealed then, is the failure of the self-centred life. Faith in Christ, devotion to Christ, and yet self-seeking. "Command that these my two sons may sit, one on Thy right hand, and one on Thy left hand, in Thy Kingdom." They wanted the places of power.

He never spoke of Cross and Resurrection but that some of His disciples broke in and asked Him who was the greatest man, or who was to have the place of power in His Kingdom. If we read on to the last Supper and the institution of the Christian feast, when He said that awful and tragic thing that no man can read without trembling, "One of you shall betray Me," then we also read, "There arose also a contention among them, which of them was accounted to be greatest." Their devotion was sincere, and yet there was the desire to get out of this Kingdom something for themselves.

Let us go back to Cæsarea Philippi once more in memory, and see the shadow of it all. As long as Jesus talked to Peter about building the Church, and giving him keys, Peter was contented. But when He mentioned the Cross, he drew back. The King had set His face towards Jerusalem, and the next thing was the Cross, the thing for which He was almost eager, the thing concerning which He continued to speak to these men. But they were anxious about the keys, and the seats of power, and precedence. How these things have continued!

What did the King do with these disciples? Observe first, His patience in that He did not say one single angry word. Probably if we had been doing what He was doing, we should have been angry. When they said, Grant that we may sit, one on Thy right hand, and the other on Thy left, He looked back at them with ineffable tenderness, and said, "Ye know not what ye ask. Are ye able to drink of the cup that I am about to drink?" And when they said, "We are able," He did not even then tell them that it was impossible. No, He allowed them to come into fellowship, and He told them they should do so; "My cup indeed ye shall drink;" You also shall come to death and sorrow. You shall follow Me presently, and shall consent to the very thing from which you shrink. One, swift sudden death by the sword; one, long wearisome exile in Patmos. They drank of His cup. They did not drink of its fulness. They never knew its unutterable fulness, but they drank in some measure; but lo, they found it to be the red wine of life as they drank. He pressed that sacramental cup of sorrow to His lips alone, and then allowed men to share in the sorrow. But as for Him, so also for all who share that cup, it became full of blessing, the cup of salvation, not in any narrow sense, but in the broadest, and deepest, and highest sense. When the shadows were about His soul, and there was no sympathy, He said I will admit you even to this.

His correction is discovered in the words, "But to sit on My right hand, and on My left hand, is not Mine to give, but *it is for them.*" These four words are in italics in the Authorised and the Revised, and they are put in by the translators, not so much by way of translation as interpretation. If we leave them out, the wording is somewhat awkward. If we include them it is as if Jesus said, It is not Mine to give the places of power and precedence in My Kingdom, but they shall be given by My Father, to those for whom it is prepared. If we miss the words out, He said, It is not Mine to give these places, except to those for whom it is prepared.

He did not for a moment say He had not power to give the places. He had the power; but He could only give the places, the precedence, the power, to those for whom it was prepared. That is to say, He corrected the thinking of the disciples by telling them that when they came, asking Him to give to them capriciously, or in arbitrary fashion, places of power, it was not His purpose so to do. That is the kind of

thing that still goes on in the world, although we are moving slowly toward the great ideals of the Christ in this respect. We are beginning to put men into power upon the basis of their moral fitness for power; to erect monuments to men upon the basis of character. Christ said, Not upon the basis of favour will men get into office in My Kingdom; they will be put into office according to fitness, and that within the will of God. When God prepares an office for a man, He prepares the man for the office; and there is perfect fitness. And the King said, So shall I appoint in My Kingdom. There was no anger in it, He was correcting them, and He ended by giving them the one supreme example, His own, of what brings a man to the place of power in His Kingdom. He said, among the Gentiles this is the method, this exercise of lordship, but not so among those of My Kingdom, "Not so shall it be among you: but whosoever would become great among you shall be your minister; and whosoever would be first among you, shall be your servant: even as *the Son of man came not to be ministered unto, but to minister.*"

We see the light flashing back upon their request. They wanted the positions of power, not to do good to others, but that they might be ministered to. No, He said, "The Son of man came not to be ministered unto, but to minister, and to give His life a ransom for many." He had told them that He was going to Jerusalem to suffer, to rise. They had broken in with this request about place and power. He took them back to the original word—The Son of man came to give His life a ransom, by the pathway of that suffering. Do not argue about your place of power, but get ready for any place your King may give you by following the Son of man, in giving your life for the ransom of others. By sacrifice a man fits himself for power. By self-abnegation, by the actual denial of self and readiness to serve does a man climb to the throne of power; and he only retains his throne of power as he retains his badge of service.

Then we have one passing glimpse of the multitudes. They took their way through Jericho, on that last journey to Jerusalem, and as they went forth from Jericho, the multitudes looked at them, curious, expectant, wondering what He was going to do, following Him along the highway, sharing the disciples' idea of the Kingdom. Now let us listen to the blind men. They were in need, and they made a venture. We do not know whether it was a venture of faith. Perhaps it was. If not, it was a venture of hope, as they said, "Lord, have mercy on us, Thou Son of David."

Mark the crowd's estimate of Him. The crowd silenced these men, in all probability because they thought He was too dignified to turn to beggars. But, "They cried out the more." It was their one chance, He was passing by. Now let us leave the multitude, and the men, and look at the King. He halted the whole movement, and stood still and called for these two men, and they were brought to Him. We shall fail to understand this if we forget that which we have been considering. He was going to Jerusalem to suffer. He had a little group round about Him, who did not understand Him at all. The multitudes were after Him, the curious, crushing mob; but He halted the whole movement to help these two men. He would wait till they came. And then the old word recurs, surging in music, beating in beauty, He was "moved with compassion," He "touched their eyes; and straightway they received their sight, and followed Him." The first thing they saw was this wonderful King, and they followed Him in the way. Mark the relation of the last scene to the foregoing sections, how by this action the King corrected the false idea of the Kingdom, the false idea of dignity, the false idea of the right to place and power, as He revealed Himself as a King Who had compassion enough to halt the movement toward the mystery of the Cross, for the sake of two men that needed help; that He would turn aside from that pathway, which according to His own showing was a pathway toward His crowning, to heal them.

One can only say again, Let us behold our King. Let us press more closely to Him, and, in order that we may be more kingly after the measure and manner of His life, let us follow Him, even by the way of the Cross; knowing this, that for evermore the light of resurrection life and power lies just beyond the place of the pain and the suffering.

MATTHEW XXI. 1-17

WITH this chapter we reach the second section of the final division of the Gospel. The first section revealed the King as specially devoting Himself to His own disciples in view of His coming Cross. In this section, which occupies three chapters, we really begin the study of the last week in the life of our Lord. The time covered was brief, but filled with solemnity. The King is seen deliberately passing back to Jerusalem for the express purpose of definitely and officially rejecting the Hebrew nation. It is the story of the rejection of the Hebrew nation by the King, not that of the rejection of the King by the nation.

In this paragraph the subject is that of the coming of the King to Jerusalem. In the first seven verses we have an account of His preparation for entering the city. In verses eight to eleven we have an account of the actual entry. In verses twelve to seventeen we have the story of the first act of the King in the city, His executive cleansing of the Temple of God.

First, let us observe carefully this story of the preparations; how He acted when they drew nigh to Jerusalem. There are three very simple and yet important points to be noticed. First, He acted deliberately and with evident intention. His going into Jerusalem as He did, was not a result of accident. He rode in by His own will and upon His own initiative. This action of Jesus was an extraordinary one for Him: He had always seemed to avoid anything which would provoke enthusiasm; but upon this occasion He definitely did so. There have not been wanting those who have questioned the authenticity of the narrative, because it seems to be out of harmony with that unobtrusiveness of spirit, which fulfilled the prophetic word concerning Him, "He will not cry, nor lift up His voice, nor cause it to be heard in the street."

It is our business to interpret these actions of Jesus by the King Himself; and to remember that, if for a moment He departed from the ordinary course of the exercise of His ministry, there must have been some reason for it; and it is good for us to seek that reason. He did not yield Himself to the popular clamour, but He evoked the popular clamour, and that of set and deliberate purpose.

It is evident also that He acted with knowledge. This is manifested in the detailed instructions. If we read the story quite naturally and simply, we cannot escape from this view. He knew where they would find the colt. He knew the frame of mind in which the people would be, to whom He sent them. This is another of the simple and yet complex stories, which we must change in some way if we are to think of Jesus as a man within the limitations of other men. As He hastened His disciples down and across the ravine to prepare for His coming, He choosing to travel round with the rest of the people along the highway, there was manifest an accurate knowledge which none of them shared, "Go into the village that is over against you, and straightway ye shall find"—and He told them exactly what they would find—"And if any one say aught unto you, ye shall say, The Lord hath need of them: and straightway he will send them."

And finally He acted with unquestioned authority. A great deal has been written about the fact that Jesus said, "If any one say aught unto you ye shall say, The Lord hath need of them: and straightway he will send them." There are those who have interpreted the word Lord there as referring simply to the local association between Jesus and His disciples. It is

more in harmony with the facts of the incident to say that He used the word as indicating His universal authority, His Chief Proprietorship of all things —the Lord hath need of them. Matthew's interpretation of what our Lord said warrants us in this conclusion. Referring not merely to the sending of the colt, but to everything that happened afterwards, Matthew wrote; "This is come to pass, that it might be fulfilled which was spoken through the prophet, saying,

"Tell ye the daughter of Zion,
Behold, thy King cometh unto thee,
Meek, and riding upon an ass,
And upon a colt the foal of an ass."

That quotation is from the ninth chapter of Zechariah. It occurs in that portion of the prophecy of Zechariah which is called, "The burden of the word of Jehovah upon the land of Hadrach and Damascus." If we pass on to the twelfth chapter we read, "The burden of the word of Jehovah concerning Israel." These are the beginnings of two consecutive messages, and yet two separate ones. "The burden of the word of Jehovah upon the land of Hadrach," occupies chapters nine to eleven, and consists of the message of the prophet concerning an anointed King Who would be rejected. If we take the next burden, "The burden of the word of Jehovah concerning Israel," chapters twelve to fourteen, we find that the message is that of the rejected King enthroned. Out of the prophecy then which deals with the rejection of the anointed King, Matthew quoted; and he affirmed that this sending for the colt, this riding into Jerusalem, this cleansing of the Temple, all was in fulfilment of the prophecy of Zechariah, and of that part of it which foretold the rejection of the anointed King. So that according to Matthew, we see this action of Jesus set in relation to the ancient prophecies; and we see how He Who inspired the prophecy, Himself came to fulfil it; He Who fore-arranged all things, and gave men visions of things to come, moved into human history with set purpose, and fulfilled the things according to His own interpretation by the spirit of prophecy in the past. That is the value of the quotation.

Now that quotation emphasised two things according to Matthew's interpretation of the ancient prophecy; first, the coming of the King, "Behold, thy King cometh unto thee;" and, secondly, the meekness of the King,

"Meek, and riding upon an ass,
And upon a colt the foal of an ass."

Two things were intended by the coming of Jesus to Jerusalem in this way. The first was that of official kingly entry. That is one reason why He provoked this demonstration, riding into Jerusalem in such a way as to attract attention. He had often passed into Jerusalem quietly. Men had often crowded to Him. He had spoken kingly words and phrases, and had exerted kingly power in benefits conferred; and men had listened, criticising, admiring, rejecting, believing. But here, once, and once only, He went in such a way as to manifest the fact of His Kingship to the crowds of Jerusalem, "Behold, thy King cometh." And yet Jesus went in this way to exhibit not merely His Kingliness, but His meekness. And if Jerusalem, in that last hour of her dying day, had known Him, there would have been not judgment, but mercy. He never closes the door in the face of a sinner. He waits only until the sinner closes that door for himself. Thus they found the colt, and brought it to Him. His own disciples yielded Him homage as they spread their garments on the colt, and He accepted the homage as He sat thereon.

And so we pass to the second stage of the story, that which records the actual entry. Notice the things material, and the things essential in this story.

The things material. If it were possible for us to imagine ourselves back in Jerusalem, not among the Galilean crowds coming up with Jesus, but among the dwellers in Jerusalem; if we could imagine that we were Romans in Jerusalem on the day of that triumphal entry, we should find ourselves saying; Who is this that is coming?

If we asked the multitudes they would say, Jesus of Nazareth. That would mean nothing to us, for Nazareth was obscure; or if we knew anything of it our attitude would be one of contempt. The Central Figure in the strange procession was riding upon a beast of burden. Kings never ride upon beasts of burden. There was a race of swift asses in those eastern countries, the peculiar animals of Kings, but the word describing this one is the word showing that it was a beast of burden picked up by the wayside. Who were those people all about Him? An unorganised mob. What were the signs of loyalty and rejoicing? Old clothes and broken trees. Imagine how a Roman, familiar with imperial Rome—having perhaps seen one of those triumphal entries, when some emperor or general returned from war, was led in triumph through the streets of the city, that imperial city on the seven hills—would have looked upon this scene. What the Romans really thought of it all we can gather by noticing their attitude toward the movement. Pilate's attitude was one of absolute indifference from the beginning. All the gathering of this mob of Galileans around some man that they thought was a prophet, did not affect Rome. Rome could afford to ignore it. She said; There are no arms amongst them, there is not a scowl upon a face, they are all full of laughter and song; it is perfectly harmless; it is amusing; they think it is a triumphal entry; they are shouting about a King; let them shout. Remember, that notwithstanding all our popular interpretation of the text, when presently Pilate said, "I find no crime in Him," he did not mean that He was sinless; but that He was not guilty of sedition; He had not plotted against Rome.

If we look back upon the triumphal entry from the standpoint of earthly kingship it was indeed characterised by weakness and poverty. A beast of burden, an obscure man, a shouting mob, mainly of Galilee. Metropolitan Jerusalem despised them. We know the current contemptuous phraseology of Jerusalem concerning Galilee— "Galilee of the Gentiles."

But let us look again, " Behold, thy King." Nineteen centuries vindicate the truth of the prophetic message. He was a King; royal without trappings. His garment was a home-made garment. Presently they would cast lots for it, perhaps because it was pre-eminently comfortable, woven from the top throughout without a seam, which simply means woven by the deft fingers of some loving woman. A King in a home-made garment! His steed was a beast of burden not yet broken to harness, " Whereon no man ever yet sat." His courtiers were fisher-folk, His cavalcade a mob of Galileans. And yet no pageant that ever passed through the streets of imperial Rome has so impressed the centuries as that. The triumphal entries of Roman emperors are almost forgotten, but of that entry of Jesus to Jerusalem, every detail recorded is known by the common people everywhere.

As they moved into the city, " All the city was stirred." The Greek word translated *stirred* is the one from which we obtain our word *seismic*. There was an earthquake, not materially, but mentally. His coming made an earthquake, it shook the metropolis to its very centre. The wildest excitement prevailed. A man, a mob of shouting Galileans, old clothes, and palm branches; and the city was stirred to its very centre. That was His intention; He would attract the attention of Jerusalem to the fact of His coming. He was compelling Jerusalem to recognize Him at least for an hour, at least till it should have heard His voice again, and have seen His authority once more. As she would not listen, He would stir her as by an earthquake, and attract her to Himself, if only to pronounce that final doom upon her.

But now we come to the last part of this paragraph. This was the second time Jesus had cleansed the Temple. He did so at the commencement of His ministry. John tells the story of that. But now again at the close of that public ministry, the King, Who had thus come deliberately to attract men and to make them see and hear Him once again, Who had come in all the symbolism of Kingship, a symbolism suggestive of meekness and poverty in material things, went immediately and directly to the Temple of God. How many things He passed on the way which needed attention. His eyes must have seen many things out of harmony with the Kingdom of heaven, contrary to the will of God His Father. There were many things waiting for the activity of the social reformer, but He passed the whole of them and went to the Temple. Do not misinterpret this. It does not mean that He had nothing to do with the social conditions through which He rode, but He knew the best way to touch them. " Judgment " must " begin at the House of God." That is the meaning of His passing through to the centre, of His going to the Temple. As long as the Temple was wrong the city was bound to be wrong. Presently there will be a City Without a Temple. As the Seer in Patmos said, " I saw no Temple therein." Why not? Because the whole city will have become a Temple. All the streets will be courts in which men worship, and all the civic authorities will be ministers of the Most High. So long as the Temple at the heart of the city is wrong, the city cannot be saved. The King came to the city Jerusalem, beautiful for elevation. How He loved it! At the end of this section we shall hear the tears in His voice as He said; " Oh, Jerusalem, Jerusalem . . . how often would I have gathered thy children, and ye would not ! " The ancient King-Psalmist never loved Jerusalem as He loved Jerusalem; and He went to the city, the centre of the nation, and He went to the Temple, the centre of the city.

Now what did He do? We love the tender pictures of Jesus, but we need such as these also. He " cast out," He " overthrew." There is more than gentleness in that. There is more than sentiment in that. He " cast out all them that sold and bought in the Temple." There was a magnificence in His roughness. He " overthrew the tables of the money-changers, and the seats of them that sold doves." Why did He do these things? Notice very carefully His own words; " It is written, My house shall be called a house of prayer, but ye make it a den of robbers." Two quotations from the Old Testament prophecies are brought together here—Isaiah, chapter fifty-six, verse seven, and Jeremiah, chapter seven, verse eleven. Let them be read in connection with their context.

The King, having come to the city, and come to the Temple, cast out and overthrew; and He vindicated His action by quotation from the ancient writings of Scripture, one descriptive of what the house should be—a house of prayer; the other descriptive of what the house had become—a den of robbers. Taking a word from Isaiah, the prophet of vision and hope; and capturing a word from Jeremiah, the prophet of vision and of tears, He put them together. The house ought to be a house of prayer. They had made it a den of robbers. Those were great moments for Jerusalem. Oh if Jerusalem had but known! There, at the centre of the city, not because He did not love the city, but because He did love it, He stood in the Temple and said in effect, If the city is ever to be seasoned with salt, the Temple must be right:

" Let the priests themselves believe
And put salvation on."

Then for one brief moment, so brief a moment that if we are not careful we miss it in our reading—we find the Temple made beautiful indeed; " the blind and the lame came to Him in the Temple, and He healed them." That was one brief moment of restoration. For one brief moment the house was no longer a den of robbers, it was a house of prayer. What a picture! The Temple was not tidy. There were overturned tables, and money scattered everywhere, the débris of a great reconstruction. But there were the blind and the lame; and the face that a moment before had flamed with indignation was soft with the radiance of a great pity. That is one of the greatest pictures in the Gospel according to Matthew. He casts out, but He takes in; He overthrows, but He builds up.

Let us go back to Isaiah. In that fifty-sixth chapter we read, " My house shall be called a house of prayer for all peoples." That is what the King quoted. He stayed His quotation there; but what follows? " The Lord Jehovah Who gathereth the outcasts of Israel, saith, Yet will I gather others to Him, besides His own that are gathered." He did not quote that, but He did it! He rebuked them for the desecration of the house. He cast out, and He overthrew; and then He gathered the outcasts of Israel; and He gathered others besides His own. We know there is a wider significance. We know that this was one of the greatest prophetic words of Isaiah; but there was the first fulfilment of it.

Thank God for that vision of the King. We could not live in the midst of all the iniquity that prevails if we did not believe in a King Who can overthrow and cast out. And thank God, that before the rearrangement of details, before we have put the house in order; with the tables still upset, the money scattered, and the men of affairs driven forth, He gathers the outcasts, and heals them.

We know the rest of the story—priests; and as surely as we hear the word, we know that mischief is brewing. They heard of the wonderful things, and they heard children singing, and were moved with indignation! Think of it! They saw the wonderful things that He did, and they heard the bairns singing, and they were angry. We do not want to know anything more about them; that is their condemnation. These children were practically proclaiming the Messiah. Dost thou hear it? they asked. " Yea," said Jesus, I do hear it, and " Did ye never read, Out of the mouths of babes and sucklings Thou hast perfected praise?" It was an uproarious day in Jerusalem. The Galileans had been shouting, and Jerusalem had been shaken. He had turned out money-changers, and the crash and the flash of it all was about Him. Then the children sang, and He said, That is perfected praise. God help us, what a King He is!

MATTHEW XXI. 18-22

THE last verse of our previous study declared that after the priests' objection to the singing of the children, " He left them, and went forth out of the city to Bethany, and lodged there." These verses contain the story of His coming from Bethany, after a night spent there, back to Jerusalem, and of what happened on the way. This story has created difficulty in the minds of many, and it is well to notice at once, and to recognize the fact, that it is peculiar, in that it is the only record we have of the performance by Christ of a miracle of judgment. There are other occasions when, by exercise of His power judgment was manifested, but on such occasions there was also always deliverance wrought. According to the story of the Evangelists, in the country of the Gadarenes He destroyed an unholy traffic in swine, but He did it in connection with His freeing two men from demon possession. But this is the story of Christ coming to a fig-tree, and pronouncing upon it a doom, and of how the disciples saw it wither away. Mark tells us the story with a little more detail than Matthew, and we gather that their question was asked not there and then, but on the morning after.

its important and permanent values. '

Let us consider first of all the difficulties; and then look at the story as to

It has been said that this act of Christ was an act of injustice, because, according to Mark, it was not the season of figs. The story has also been objected to because it has been said that Christ manifested a spirit of anger, that, being hungry, and finding no fruit, He immediately cursed the tree, and that such manifestation of anger is out of harmony with the character of Christ. That same thing has also been stated, not as a reflection upon the character of Christ, but as being out of harmony with His method, in that He did not come to destroy life, but to save it, that He did not come to execute judgment, but to show mercy.

Let us look at these three objections. First, what are the facts concerning

this fig-tree? The usual time of figs was June, and there is no doubt whatever that this was what would answer to our month of April. But there was a " first ripe fig before the summer." The phrase occurs in the prophecy of Isaiah, the twenty-eight chapter, and there is an intimate association between the prophecy of Isaiah and this particular miracle. The phrase referred to was undoubtedly used by Isaiah as a figure of speech, and yet of course it was one that was familiar to the men of his time, and indicated a fact concerning a certain kind of fig-tree to be found in Palestine. There were those that constantly produced what the prophet called " the first ripe fig before the summer," and one of the peculiarities of that tree was that the fruit appeared before the foliage. The presence of foliage on the tree before summer ought to have indicated the fact that fruit was there, too. If this explanation is accepted we have a perfectly natural understanding of the equity of His dealing with this tree, so that there was no injustice in the sentence He pronounced upon it. This miracle was also a parable, as all His miracles were; and this tree was not faithful in fulfilling its true function: it was putting forth a manifestation which was not true to its inner life.

There is not in this parable any sign of personal vindictiveness. Notice, the effect produced upon the men who beheld what happened, was not one of wonder that He should act as He did in the presence of the tree, but rather at the speed with which His fiat was carried out; and surely we have the right to interpret the attitude of Jesus, and the method of His action, and the spirit manifested, by the effect produced upon the men who were there, rather than by the effect produced upon others, centuries after, who did not see or hear what He said, and how He said it. The disciples were evidently in agreement with what He had done.

Then, finally, the objection—and this is perhaps the most serious of them— that this is not in harmony with the methods of Jesus as revealed in the Gospel stories. When He entered into the synagogue at the commencement of His public ministry, and read from the prophecy of Isaiah the great Scriptures which indicated the meaning of His mission, He ended abruptly in the midst of His reading. He read from that portion of the prophecy of Isaiah where it is written, "The Spirit of the Lord is upon Me;" but He did not read the latter part; He paused with the words, "The acceptable year of the Lord." He was then commencing His ministry, and in the prophecy of Isaiah, as we have it by translation, there is but a comma between that phrase, "The year of Jehovah's favour," and the phrase, "The day of vengeance of our God." So that we need to remember that in the counsel of God, as revealed in the ancient prophetic writing, the Servant of God came not only for the "year of Jehovah's favour," but also for "the day of vengeance of our God." That day of vengeance had not yet dawned. But so far as the Hebrew nation was concerned, the "acceptable year of the Lord" had ended; and the King had now come up to Jerusalem for the specific purpose of pronouncing its doom. We immediately find Him in conflict with the rulers in the Temple. In a series of parables He revealed the doom, and the reason of it. He gathered His disciples together, and most marvellously predicted the overthrow of Jerusalem by aliens; and cursed it with an eightfold woe. All this has no application to personal salvation, but only to national accountability. Also in Matthew another of the prophecies of Isaiah is quoted. "A bruised reed shall He not break, and smoking flax shall He not quench," and it is an interesting thing, we almost invariably end our quotation there. And yet the quotation ends, "Till He send forth judgment unto victory." When He sends forth judgment unto victory, He will break the bruised reed, and quench the smoking flax.

One other illustration of the method of Jesus. We remember His own parable of the fig-tree. The parable of words was borrowed, as to its thought, from the song of Isaiah, "Let me sing for my well-beloved a song of my beloved touching his vineyard." That parable declared that a certain man had a vineyard, and a fig-tree planted within it. The plea of the intercessor was that he might have opportunity to provoke it to fruit-bearing, and the final word was, "If it bear fruit thenceforth, well; but if not, thou shalt cut it down." The intercessor was at one with the proprietor; and the last method of the intercessor was a method of judgment and destruction for that which did not yield to his ministry. Jerusalem had had its opportunity. The King was coming up to pronounce judgment upon it, to be at one with the Proprietor in flinging it out as a nation for testimony, and reducing it to ashes in the economy of God. On the way, this method of His work, never seen before, flamed out, as He no longer acted in pity, but in judgment; no longer in mercy, but for the destruction of something which in itself was a failure.

Let us now look at the immediate and permanent values of this miracle of judgment. Carefully notice the opening words of this section; "Now in the morning as He returned to the city, He hungered." Why did He hunger? During the last week in the life of our Lord, He never stayed in Jerusalem for the night. Speaking merely on the level of the human, He dare not. Men were waiting to arrest Him. The first night that He did stay in the neighbourhood of Jerusalem, on the mount of Olives, He was arrested. So that during those days, in which He was officially denouncing Jerusalem by parable and by woe, He went out every night to Bethany. Now Bethany calls to mind at once certain associations. Bethany was the home of Lazarus, and Martha, and Mary, and it is a most strange thing to read at the beginning of this paragraph that, coming back from Bethany in the early morning, He was hungry. It is inconceivable that He had spent the night in the home of Martha and Mary, and Lazarus. It may be only speculation, but perchance it was out of tender regard for them, knowing He was being fol-towed, knowing very likely that Lazarus's life would be in danger on His account. In all probability He had spent the night in some long lone vigil on the hill-side, in a quiet and secluded place, and when the morning came, and He turned His face back toward Jerusalem, He was hungry. Through the stress and strain of the spiritual conflict there had been no sense of hunger; and suddenly, He hungered. And what had been His spiritual experience through that night, and during the whole of that period? One of intense spiritual hunger. The song of Isaiah and the parable of Luke both come back to mind. In that great song of Isaiah, God's desire after the fruitfulness of His people is pathetically and magnificently declared, " What could have been done more to My vineyard, that I have not done in it? Wherefore, when I looked that it should bring forth grapes, brought it forth wild grapes? " Jehovah in the person of Jesus of Nazareth had been in Jerusalem, looking for judgment and finding oppression, looking for righteousness and finding a cry. Or, to take His own parable, He Who was at once Proprietor and Intercessor in a strange and wonderful unity of purpose, had been there, attempting by the ministry of His teaching and the ministry of His doing, to provoke Jerusalem to fruitbearing, and the men and rulers of His time to being what God intended they should be; and they had refused Him. We can enter in some measure into the intense and overwhelming hunger of the heart of the Christ. " Who hath believed our message? and to whom hath the arm of Jehovah been revealed? " was infinitely more than the cry of Isaiah. We know how it was fulfilled in this King, and probably during that night He had been filled with spiritual hunger. The material hunger was caused by the spiritual. That is to say, the spiritual hunger had made Him for the moment careless as to food, careless for the sustenance of the body, and when morning came, and He set His face toward Jerusalem for all the awful ministry to be exercised there, the spiritual hunger was expressed through the material.

Now notice what happened. With all naturalness, walking back to Jerusalem with a little group of men, strangely perplexed around Him, we have this *strange act*. Let us go back again to the prophecy of Isaiah, the twenty-eighth chapter. It is the chapter in which the prophet declares that at last God deals in judgment with people who refuse the ministry of His servant. That is the peculiar message of the chapter in which the prophet describes the taunts of the men who opposed Him, " Precept upon precept, precept upon precept; line upon line, line upon line: here a little, there a little." And he answered them, Yes, so God has spoken to you, because He has been bound so to speak. And at last the prophet uttered this word, in verse twenty-one, " For Jehovah will rise up as in Mount Perazim, He will be wroth as in the valley of Gibeon, that He may do His work, His strange work, and bring to pass His act, *His strange act.*" If men will not listen to the wooing, patient, halting speech of grace, halting because men can only hear line upon line, precept upon precept; then at last God will be driven to judgment, and He will be compelled to do that which is strange to Him, His strange work, His strange act.

Now on His way to the national rejection, conscious of material hunger, He stood in the presence of the fig-tree with leaves that ought to have been the sign of the early ripe fruit before summer. There was no fruit, and the condition was symbolic. He understood His relation to the ancient prophecies and that the prophet of old had foretold His coming there. There at the parting of the ways stood the fig-tree, symbolic of the new condition of the people to whom He had been sent, with a fine exterior of promise, but with no fruit. Then the wail of God sounded in His heart, " Wherefore, when I looked that it should bring forth grapes, brought it forth wild grapes? " —and the word of God thundered through His soul, " Cut it down; why doth it also cumber the ground? " In the presence of the symbol He acted in answer to material hunger, but in order to express the spiritual hunger,

255

and the absolute necessity that was thrust upon Him for carrying out the intention and the purpose of God.

When His disciples wondered, He gave them no answer to the astonishment in the way in which they expected; but by saying a thing which seemed to have very little connection, He declared to those men that if they had faith, not only this fig-tree, but mountains should be removed. Let us try to enter into the very mind of Christ and see what was passing therein.

Why was it necessary for Him to denounce this nation, and cast it out? Because of its lack of faith. The whole economy of God in connection with the Hebrew nation was that of revealing to the nations of the world the fact that the one master-principle of life for men was that of faith in Himself. The whole nation was founded upon faith. "By faith Abraham."—And because the people had failed in their faith, and had garbed themselves in the works of a mere external ritualism, they must be flung out. They had lost their contact with infinite power because they had lost their faith. And so, in the presence of the miracle, Jesus did not account for His power at all, did not draw attention to Himself at all, but said to this little group of men round about Him, "If ye have faith, and doubt not, ye shall not only do what is done to the fig-tree," but you will be able to fling all obstacles out of the way of God's progress. He gave no explanation of the meaning of this miracle of judgment; but calling His own disciples, the little group of men to whom He was about to give the responsibility of expressing the will of God in the world, which responsibility was being taken away from the Hebrew people, He called them back to the fundamental principle, for having forgotten which, the Hebrew people were to be cast out from testimony and to be rejected, while He pronounced upon them the woes that negatived the Beatitudes with which He had opened His ministry.

There are permanent lessons here which we do well to understand. First of all, we have a revelation of the absolute oneness of Christ with God. His ministry of mercy merges into that of judgment when men refuse to submit themselves to His mercy. Of course, this is to recognize and to abide by the truth of man's responsibility. The next two parables are both parables of the vineyard—the ancient figure of Isaiah—directed against the rulers, and then against the people; and through all Christ recognized human responsibility. Jesus Christ is one with God in underlying purpose as He deals with men. He seeks to provoke men to fruit-bearing for the satisfaction of God. He comes seeking righteousness; He does more, He comes to make it possible for men to live the life of judgment and of righteousness. But if man refuses, then Jesus Christ is absolutely one with God and as in the parable of the fig-tree, so in the miracle of the fig-tree, the ministry of Jesus is intended not to be a ministry of pity merely, but a ministry that provokes us to the realisation of God's underlying purpose for us. To imagine that He simply came to plead for pity upon men who fail, is false to the whole of the New Testament teaching. He came to reveal sin to be what it is, active, wilful, definite, positive rebellion against God; and He came to deal with men, so that their will should be turned in the direction of the will of God, that men should be made to fulfil the divine intention. Of course the application in this story is national, but we may apply it also in individual life; and if a man shall, in spite of all the ministry of grace, and mercy, and power, still refuse and fail to trust Him; then, as surely as Jesus blasted the fig-tree on the way between Bethany and Jerusalem, He will blast the life of that man.

There is the other side of the application; and it also is of permanent value. The power in which His own are to cast obstacles out of God's highway is to be that of faith in Him. He was emerging along the great highway of the Divine purpose, and if we miss that view, we miss the whole point of our story. When we see Him as the great Servant of God, that His every act was a link in the chain of the Divine continuity of purpose and of power, when we understand that His casting out of Jerusalem was by the act, and power, and will of God, then we understand what He meant when He said to His disciples, If you have faith, you will not only be able to wither away one fig-tree, but all the mountains; you will be able to speak to them with faith, and they shall be removed.

The Hebrew people had become God's greatest hindrance instead of God's greatest help; and officially and positively He flung the nation away, declaring in detail how that judgment should fall within a generation. Within one generation the Roman legions had swept through the city, and it was flung down until no stone was left upon another. He was thus flinging a mountain of difficulty out of the way of God, that He might move forward according to the purpose of His heart, in blessing to others. So men of faith, operating through faith, are able to take hold of the power of God for the accomplishment of the purpose of God, that purpose being the setting up of His Kingdom. God operates through faithful men, but men can do nothing toward removing mountains of difficulty without God. So that when Christ tells us we are to have faith, it is not merely an individual thought, it is not merely in order that a soul may

be saved; it is that, but it is in order that we may be workers together with Him, in order that we may fling the mountains of difficulty away, and make the high places smooth, and fling up the valleys to levelness.

God through the centuries has been moving ever onward, and He has always moved onward through human agency, but He has never been able to move onward through human agency save where man has operated upon the rock foundation of faith in Himself. Let us remember as we go forward we are the servants of a Christ Who waits in infinite and long-continued patience, but Who, at last, if the fig-tree bear no fruit, will Himself wither it with a word, and fling it away; but He does it in order that in the place which it occupied in the vineyard of God some other may be placed for the fulfilment of His ultimate purpose.

And so the miracle becomes a flaming teaching, filling the heart with fear in the presence of the Lord, making one recognize that if He be the Lamb of God which beareth sin in the mystery of an infinite meekness, there is such a thing as the wrath of the Lamb, against which none can stand. If we fail to answer the ministry of His love, we must be blasted by the ministry of His judgment.

MATTHEW XXI. 23-44

WE now commence the section in which we see the King in Jerusalem, and in the Temple, the Centre of opposition. The hostility of the priests and rulers is more than ever manifest. First, they challenged Him as to His authority, and He answered them in parables. They were angry, for they saw that His two parables were intended to apply to them, and they commenced with more earnestness than before to plot against His life. He answered their anger with a third parable, a parable of judgment. Then they endeavoured to entangle Him in His talk, bringing to Him questions.

In this section we see the forces that had always been against Him manifesting themselves in clear succession; and they are the forces which are against Him still. They are, first unbelief, as represented in the rulers who asked Him concerning His authority; secondly worldliness, as represented in the men who asked Him questions concerning the tribute money; thirdly rationalism, as represented in the men who asked Him questions about the resurrection; and, finally intellectual dishonesty, as represented in the man who asked Him a question which was merely that of casuistry.

Let us consider first, the challenge of unbelief; and the King's answer. The challenge was expressed in the words: " By what authority doest Thou these things? and who gave Thee this authority?" Let us remember the occasion upon which the question was put. Think of the surroundings. We have studied the story of our Lord's entry into Jerusalem, and the fact of the cleansing of the Temple. We now see the Christ, having returned from the quiet, lonely vigil near Bethany, coming into the Temple which He had cleansed. Remember these events all took place within two or three days. He had driven out the money-changers, overturned the tables of the traffickers in the courts of the House of God, and for one brief moment restored the Temple to its original purpose.

He had now returned to the cleansed Temple, and was teaching. He had come with quiet assumption of authority. We cannot understand these men's questions at this point unless we see this,—the Man Who had dared to cleanse the Temple, had now returned to it in order to teach, and the people —Jerusalem was very full at this time —were crowding upon Him. That was the occasion.

never far away, sometimes on the While He was so teaching, the chief priests and the elders came to Him. That appears a simple statement, but it was no mere casual coming of the chief priests and elders. They were fringe of the crowd, sometimes nearer, these rulers, the members of the official council, members of the Sanhedrim. But this was not an occasion when some member of the Sanhedrim, having heard Him teaching, asked Him some casual question. This was an official visit of the chief priests and the elders of the people, the representatives of the ruling powers of Jerusalem in matters of religion, the men of authority, the men whose authority had perhaps never been questioned for long years until Jesus came. He did not commence by questioning their authority. As a matter of fact, He told His disciples that they were to do all that the Pharisees told them as they sat on Moses' seat. He had never called in question the fact that these men had authority; but He had so taught as to make the people call in question their authority; for as we have already seen, they

"were astonished at His teaching; for He taught them as one having authority, and not as their scribes."

Now this was His last visit to Jerusalem, and the men of authority, who had been put into contrast with Him by the people, and not by Himself, came to Him, and interrupted Him in His teaching. They had the technical right to do this within the Temple Courts, according to their own understanding of their own position, and according to the popular estimate of that position.

They now asked Him two questions. First, "By what authority doest Thou these things?" "*In* what authority," as the word is more accurately; that is, What is the note of Your authority? Is Your authority a political authority, a social authority, or a spiritual authority? What do You claim? That was the first question, and that was the deepest. But that which really troubled them was revealed in their second question, "Who gave Thee this authority?" His presence there was without their sanction. He had asked no permission from the elders or priests to find His way into the Temple Courts and to teach. Such was their challenge, and it was made in order that they might encompass His arrest, and end His mission.

Now let us carefully notice the King's answer. This story, in common with many others, has suffered from a very superficial interpretation. We need to understand the spirit of it. First, He declared to them that He was quite willing to tell them, if they were ready to receive His answer. "I also will ask you one question, which if ye tell Me, I likewise will tell you by what authority I do these things." It was not that He declined to declare His authority. It was not that He resented their interference, and was not prepared to answer; but that it was quite useless for Him to tell them His authority; they were not prepared to believe Him. He was perfectly prepared to declare what was the nature of His authority, and whence He obtained His authority, to men who were ready to receive it.

What was His test? "The baptism

of John, whence was it? from heaven or from men?" He said, in effect, You are challenging Me as to whether I have any right to come into the House of God, and assume authority in the House of God. Am I a Teacher answering the authority of God, or am I here as a man craving the popular acclaim of the people? I will ask you one question, "The baptism of John, was it from heaven or from men?" Before He could reveal to them what they asked, He took them back to the last revelation which they had received; for readiness to receive a new revelation always depends upon the attitude to the previous one. That is always the principle of God's dealing with men. Thus we see that there was more in Christ's question, than appears upon the surface. Supposing these men had admitted that the baptism of John was from heaven, then their question concerning Christ was immediately answered, because John had been His herald. John discontinued his ministry when Jesus began. John had said, "He must decrease, but I must increase." If they had accepted that testimony as from heaven they would not have asked Him this question about His authority. They knew full well what John's testimony to Him had been. Thus there was an intimate connection between His question and their answer. The prime meaning of Jesus' question was this; What did you do with the last light that fell upon your pathway? If you tell Me that, I shall know whether you are ready to receive more light or not!

How did they reply? Their difficulty was twofold. "If we shall say, From heaven"—and that is what we ought to say—then He will ask us why we do not obey Him. "If we shall say, From men"—and that is what we would prefer saying—"we fear the multitude." The people had come to the common conclusion that John was a prophet, and they dare not say that he was not. Therefore "they answered: We know not."

To catch its significance we must interpret that particular answer of these men in the light of what Jesus said to them immediately afterwards—

"Neither tell I you." He ignored, and treated as untrue, what they declared, when they said they knew not. They withheld an honest answer; He withheld the answer which they asked. Theirs was the answer of blindness and of dishonesty. Of blindness, for they had seen the issue of John's ministry. They had seen an ethical revival resulting from the emotional revival. They had seen harlots and publicans pressing into the Kingdom of God, which meant obeying God, yielding to His demands, giving up the things John denounced, turning to the way of righteousness; and yet they dared to look in the face of Jesus, and say, "We know not." It was wilful blindness, and it was absolute dishonesty; and as such our Lord treated it. Then said He, "Neither tell I you."

And why not? Because it was quite useless. If they were blind in the presence of the evidences of the Divinity of the mission of John, then they would also be blind, as they were, in the presence of the evidences of the Divinity of the mission of Jesus. If they were dishonest in dealing with the former light, they would be dishonest whatever He declared to them.

And not only because reply was useless, but because reply was needless. "By what authority," said these men, "doest Thou these things?" and in the use of that word they revealed their subconscious conviction. They did not say, By what authority sayest Thou these things? They knew perfectly well that wherever He had come with His ethic, He had also provided a dynamic, and by obedience men had been changed. His answer therefore declared that the things concerning the authority of which they had questioned Him, were themselves the evidences of the authority.

Then immediately, not allowing them to escape, He continued; "But what think ye?" And then He gave them two parables, in which He condemned first of all their methods, in the parable of the two sons; and, secondly, their motives, in the parable of the vineyard, the husbandmen, and the one son who was cast out.

In considering the blasting of the

fig-tree we turned to the song of Isaiah, that great song of the vineyard. Now observe that both these parables are parables of the vineyard. Christ spoke as in the particular region which the prophet had described; as the Servant of God. The song of the well-beloved concerning His vineyard, was the song of the vineyard neglected. The fences were to be broken down, and destruction was to come thereto; and He was in Jerusalem for the specific purpose of pronouncing doom upon that very vineyard of the Lord of hosts, because of its failure. Thus when He was dealing with the rulers, His two parables returned to the figure of Isaiah, the figure of the vineyard. The second one is most evidently an accommodation of the Song of Isaiah, in order to apply its truth to the rulers of His day, who had failed.

Let us take the first, and notice what our Lord did. He stated the case by employing the figure of two sons. The father said to the first of them, " Son, go work to-day in the vineyard," and he said, " I will not," and then he repented—and the word "repent" here is not to change the mind, but to be filled with sorrow—he realised the mistake, and he went into the vineyard. To the next son he said the same thing, and he replied—and it is a somewhat curious and yet remarkable reply—"I sir." We read it, " I go, sir," but the word " go " is not in the Greek. He simply said, " I sir." The phrase is idiomatic and suggests that this son put himself into contrast with the other one, who said he would not go, as though he said, You may depend on *me* sir! That is the graphic force of the word here. And he went not. Now said Christ to these men: Which was the true son which did the will of his father? He compelled them to find the verdict. He made them the jury of their own actions. They found the verdict. " They say, The first;" the man who said, I will not go, but repenting, went, is the man who does the will of God; rather than the man who declared, I am ready to go, but went not.

Then notice carefully the application. He put into contrast two classes of people—the publicans and the har-

lots, the rebellious people who said, We will not do the will of God; and those very men who were the rulers. He said in effect; You have given a verdict against yourselves. The publicans and harlots had said, We will not; and then repenting, went. The rulers had said, We go, and had not done so.

For the purpose of this contrast He had taken them back to John's ministry. They had heard him, and professing obedience had been disobedient. The publicans and harlots had heard him, and they who had said, We will not go, had repented, and entered into the Kingdom of God. There is no question as to what Christ thought of those men; He knew perfectly well that they were sure John's ministry was from heaven. John came in the way of righteousness, and they knew that they, the exponents of the ethic of Judaism, could not quarrel with the great ethic he declared; they knew it was the way of righteousness; and yet when he pronounced the way of righteousness they did not obey; they who affirmed their loyalty to God, would not obey the ethic through John. And it was not merely true that the publicans and harlots believed and obeyed, and they did not; the truth was that they refused to believe, even though they saw the signs of the publicans and harlots entering into the way of righteousness. They not only refused to be persuaded by John himself, but when they saw the effect of John's preaching, that those men and women whom they despised, and would not help, were helped, and lifted, and healed, they still refused.

The parable was indeed a white light, and a fierce fire; and the King standing there in the Temple, challenged as to His authority, instead of answering the quibble, assumed the throne of judgment, and welcomed into the Kingdom of God harlots and publicans who set their faces toward the Kingdom, and flung out the men who had professed to be the exponents of His Kingdom, who nevertheless had been disobedient to His command.

If in this first parable He had condemned their methods, He now probed more deeply into their lives, and dealt with their motives. And once more the figure is Isaiah's figure. The proprietor's perfect provision was in order to the production of fruit. " Hear another parable : There was a man that was a householder, who planted a vineyard, and set a hedge about it, and digged a winepress in it, and built a tower." He made every provision necessary in order that He might gather fruit from His vineyard. To borrow the word of Isaiah, " He looked for justice, but, behold, oppression; for righteousness, but, behold, a cry." What did He look for? For judgment, for righteousness. Thus Jesus reminded them of this song of their own prophet. He then declared that the proprietor let this vineyard " out to husbandmen." He said, " he went into another country," which was a figurative way of saying that God made the priests and rulers and elders responsible for the vineyard; and the failure of the vineyard was to be charged back upon them.

That was the perpetual message of the prophets; " Woe to the false shepherds." And so also when Christ saw the multitudes and was moved with compassion it was because they were as sheep without a shepherd. This parable is not for the crowd, but it is for the shepherds. The priests and the elders were in front of Him; the men who ought to have taken care of the vineyard of the Lord of hosts, and so cultivated it that it would have brought forth fruit for which God looked; judgment which is justice, and righteousness. They were responsible. But what had these husbandmen done? The messengers came to receive the fruit. They beat them, bruised them, flinging them out, because instead of husbanding the vineyard for the proprietor, they had been cultivating it for themselves. And at last, said the King, He sent His own Son. Now, said the husbandmen, is the opportunity, that for which we have been waiting. We have gathered the fruit for our own self-enrichment, now we will possess the whole husbandry; let us kill Him, and the inheritance shall be ours. Said Jesus, What shall be done with these men?

He had made them find the verdict; He now made them pass the sentence. He Who compelled them to be the jury, finding the verdict in the case of their own wrong, now compelled them to be the judge, passing sentence upon their own iniquity. And they were quite vehement about it, and their very vehemence is the evidence of the tremendous force with which Jesus spoke the words, that searching intensity that stirred the conscience, and compelled attention, and made the chief priests forget their quarrel with Him and speak out the truth. He found the deepest in them, and appealed to that deepest in them which they were resolutely setting themselves to stifle, in order to crucify Him. He compelled them to tell the truth. What shall be done to these men? Oh, they said, " He will miserably destroy those miserable men, and will let out the vineyard unto other husbandmen, who shall render Him the fruits in their seasons."

There was no need for Christ to say anything more. They saw He spoke concerning them. They knew perfectly well that they had come to arrest Him, and challenge His authority in the Temple; and yet with quiet and match-less authority He had gathered them to the judgment throne of the unending ages, and made them say they were miserable sinners who deserved punishment at the hands of an angry God. They made their own confession.

This was the condemnation of their motive. They had been exercising authority in ethical and religious matters, but never for the sake of the glory of God, but for the sake of the maintenance of their own official position. They said, We will take this vineyard of Jehovah of hosts; it is our great opportunity to maintain our own position; we will farm it, and work it for ourselves. We are not anxious that God should find judgment and righteousness, we are anxious that we should find dignity and office. That is the dastardly sin of false authority in every age, that it cares for its own robing and dignity, and for the enslaving of the people to its own rule, and not for judgment and righteousness and truth for which God is seeking.

Thus our King brought these rulers to His judgment throne, and then flung back upon them their own sentence, " I say unto you, The Kingdom of God shall be taken away from you, and shall be given to a nation bringing forth the fruits thereof." You are here to arrest Me, you are here to encompass My death, you are the builders, you are here to take this Stone that lies in your way, a stumbling-block, and fling it out! " Did ye never read in the Scriptures,

" The stone which the builders rejected, The same was made the head of the corner :

This was from the Lord, And it is marvellous in our eyes? "

A stone of stumbling, and a rock of offence. Fall on it—and there is a touch of mercy even here—and you will be broken, but the broken man can be healed. But let it fall on you, and you will be ground to dust, and there is no healing then.

The supreme interest in this paragraph is the revelation of Jesus. He is the Master of all ages, and His judgments are the judgments of the ages. His is the voice of eternity, and He so deals with men as to compel them to acquiesce in the justice and righteousness of His verdicts and sentence.

MATTHEW XXI. 45–XXII. 14

IN our previous study we found the solemn words of the King in which He declared the Hebrew nation to be rejected :—" Therefore say I unto you, The Kingdom of God shall be taken away from you, and shall be given to a nation bringing forth the fruits thereof." There is the most intimate connection between that declaration and the parable which we have now to study.

There is a difference between this parable and those already considered which we must notice at the outset. In the former two the King was dealing with the rulers' responsibility concerning the Kingdom of God in the world. In this it is no longer responsibility, but privilege which is under consideration. The figure changes from that of a vineyard into which labourers are sent, to that of a marriage feast to which guests are bidden; and if we interpret the figures from the Eastern view point, we at once see the contrast. On the one hand, we have toil and service; and on the other, rejoicing, and gladness, and merriment.

Then notice that running through all these parables there is an identity, not declared, but most evidently claimed, between Christ and His Father. Whatever we may think of the meaning of these parables, it is quite evident, as

Matthew tells us, that the chief priests and the Pharisees knew that He was applying them to themselves. It is quite evident that our Lord intended to teach the proprietorship of God, the fact that these men owed allegiance to Him. Moreover, by the second parable it was perfectly evident that He intended to teach that He had come as the Sent of the Father; they having refused the messengers, He had come with the final message as the Son. In the three parables there is a growing movement. In the first He showed what the attitude of these rulers had been toward God. They had said, I go, and had failed to go; the attitude of disobedience and disloyalty. In the second He showed what their attitude would be toward Himself, " This is the heir; come, let us kill Him, and take His inheritance;" His inheritance of rule and authority and influence shall be ours. In the third parable He revealed to them what their attitude would be toward His messengers, those who are sent to bid them to the privileges. So long as He was dealing with their attitude to the Father, and to Himself, the parables moved in the realm of responsibility. When He began to deal with their attitude toward His messengers, His parable moved in the realm of privilege.

There are three distinct movements in the particular parable we have now to consider, indicated by the three invitations sent out. The King was very near the end of His ministry, and was in Jerusalem for the specific purpose of casting out from privilege and responsibility the people that had refused His Kingship. Thus all His parables become more intensely suggestive, and need examination in the light of that fact. To take this parable, and to preach the Gospel from it, is to strain its meaning. There is not a word here concerning the preaching of the Gospel.

Remembering that our Lord was in Jerusalem definitely for the purpose of dealing with the rulers and the nation, notice how these three invitations exactly cover the fact of His ministry in the world, concerning the Kingdom of God. In the first invitation He was referring to the call already given by Himself and His disciples in their journeyings throughout that whole district. By the second invitation He was referring to the work which His disciples would do from that moment until, the nation rejecting the message for the second time, God would send His armies and destroy their city, a definite prophecy of the destruction of Jerusalem. We have therefore in the second movement, a reference to the call to the Kingdom, from the point of His rejection, until, rejecting not merely Jesus, but the ministry of the Holy Spirit, Jerusalem was destroyed. That took place a generation afterwards. Thirdly, we have in the parable a movement which follows that. After the destruction of Jerusalem the messengers would be sent forth into the highways; that is, beyond the places of covenant, beyond the people of privilege, beyond those who were originally bidden; and they were to go forth with the same message. But the difference is that, instead of bringing to the marriage feast the bidden ones, they were to bring bad and good together, in order that the house might be filled, in order that the ideal might be realised. In that third invitation, then, we have a picture of the call which His messengers were to utter after the destruction of Jerusalem until

this time. It is a reference to work which we have to do.

Turn, then, to the first of these invitations, " The Kingdom of heaven is likened unto a certain king, who made a marriage feast for his son." What is the Kingdom of heaven? Exactly what this Gospel has revealed. In order to understand the phrase here, we must first, behold the King; secondly, listen to the laws which are in His Manifesto; thirdly, observe the facts of His Kingship as revealed in His authority in the realms of the material, mental, and moral. If we would know the claims of the Kingdom, let us listen to the King as He demanded of men that they should submit and obey, and yield to Him their allegiance. If it were possible for us to lift out of this Gospel the great ideal which Jesus presented; if it were possible for us to forget these particular men that crowded about Him; and if it were possible for us to forget popular interpretations of the meaning of the Gospel; and if we could appreciate the ideal of the Kingdom, apart from the refusal, and apart from the local circumstances, what would it be? God absolutely enthroned. It is the Kingdom of God. Under His enthronement character is the supreme thing. Individualism consists of the realisation of character that harmonises with the character of God. People of character, harmonising with the Kingdom of God, living in mutual interrelationship, would constitute a great theocracy of souls loyal to the Throne of God, and serving each other, and thus bearing testimony to those outside, concerning the graciousness and goodness of the government of God. That was the ideal that filled the heart and mind of Jesus. When He taught us to pray the prayer, Thy Kingdom come on earth, He saw the ideal conditions of life in the world. It is not a prayer that anything may come in Heaven; it is a prayer that things may be here as they are there. Wherever we take the words of Jesus, and apply them simply, we see that to have been His ideal. " Thou shalt love the Lord thy God with all thy heart, . . . and . . . thy neighbour as thyself. On these two commandments the whole law hangeth, and the prophets."

Now said the Master, the Kingdom of heaven is likened unto a marriage feast. As our Lord, in dealing with responsibility, chose the figure of the Old Testament, the vineyard, so here, in dealing with the privileges of His Kingship, He employed the prophetic figure; "I will betroth thee unto Me for ever." That was the word of God to the people whom He had chosen to represent Him in the world. And yet Hosea uttered those awful prophecies of his! He charged Israel with having broken the relationship between herself and God, between husband and betrothed. Spiritual adultery and harlotry, said Hosea, is the sin of the chosen people. That figure of the Old Testament, Christ now employed, and said, God has made a marriage feast for His Son, a day of gladness and rejoicing. But this is Christ's picture of the Kingdom of God as to its righteousness and peace and joy. "The Kingdom of God is . . . righteousness and peace and joy in the Holy Spirit."

The first call to the Kingdom went out "to them that were bidden," to those who were under authority, to those who ought to have heard, and understood, and answered. With what result? They would not come. Jesus and His twelve disciples had through that whole neighbourhood, for about three years, preached that Kingdom, preached its principles, preached its privileges, preached its responsibilities, and the people would have none of it. They had, as His previous parables revealed, declined the responsibilities, and so they had rejected the privileges. They would not come to the marriage feast. That was His first charge against them.

Then He told them that there was another invitation. First, the figurative description of the King's preparation; "Again He sent forth other servants, saying, Tell them that are bidden, Behold, I have made ready my dinner : my oxen and my fatlings are killed, and all things are ready : come to the marriage feast." Very quaint, and very beautiful, and very solemn, are some of the Puritan writings upon

that passage. They draw attention to the fact that the way in which the King spread the great feast, whereby men should come into the Kingdom realisation, was a costly way. When Jesus uttered those words, and said, "All things are ready," He knew at what infinite cost God was preparing for the possibility of the realising of that great Kingdom which He had preached, and which men had rejected. This declaration that all things are ready so far as God is concerned, was a new call to men to come into the privileges of the Kingdom.

How did they respond? There were two classes, the indifferent, and the rebellious. The indifferent turned every one to his own farm; and there is a special emphasis there. "His *own* farm." Christ had preached the Kingdom, God's Kingdom, in which men should seek, not their own, but His and each other's good; a Kingdom in which the first passion of the individual life should be the glory of God; and the necessary sequence of that passion the good of other men; but they would not come. They went back to the self-centred life that sought for personal enrichment and comfort, without regard to the Kingdom of God, or the good of their fellow men. Others were definitely rebellious. They treated the messengers ill, they beat and flung them out, and killed them. And all that actually happened in those days succeeding the ministry of Jesus. In the Acts of the Apostles we find the story. We must not forget that in those early days of Christian preaching, they preached the Kingdom of God, not nebulously as we do, as though the Kingdom of God only meant that a man should submit to God; but socially, as we do not, realising that they came, not merely for the saving of their own soul, but for His glory, and for the realisation of the ideal national communal life.

But they killed the messengers and at last the King was wroth, and He sent His own armies. He Who girded Cyrus long before, led and guided the Roman armies, sweeping the city out, burning and destroying it, and irrevocably scattering to the winds His

264

people who would not have His Kingdom because His Kingdom interfered with their own self-centred interest.

Then said Christ in this parable, "The wedding is ready, but they that were bidden were not worthy. Go ye therefore unto the partings of the highways," go and gather in the bad and the good; which does not mean that He was inviting into His Kingdom a promiscuous crowd both bad and good, but that no longer was the invitation to be confined to a people of a certain order. Our Lord was not minimising the importance of character, as we see by the final reference to the man without a wedding garment. This is one of the cases where one is bound to confess that no translation can quite accurately carry the sense of the method by which Jesus said that the King addressed that man; "He saith unto him, Friend, how camest thou in hither not having a wedding garment?" The word *not* in verse eleven is a different word from the *not* in verse twelve, and it is impossible to translate the different meaning by any equivalent in our language. Dr. Vincent stated the matter in the simplest form when he said, In the Greek language the first *not* was always used when referring to a matter of fact, while the second was always used in reference to a matter of thought. By that he means, and this is certainly the intention of the passage, there came in a man *not* having a wedding garment; that is the fact. But when the king looked at him and said, "How camest thou in hither *not having*," that is, *deliberately* not having, with determination not having, it is the *not* of thought—you did not mean to have a wedding garment, you have dared to come without a wedding garment. And so by that Jesus revealed to us that, even though the bad and good were to be called into the Kingdom, the question of character did matter.

Let us now go back to that statement in the previous chapter, not so much now for its application to the Hebrew people as for its principle. "The Kingdom of God shall be taken away from you, and shall be given to a nation bringing forth the fruits

thereof." How does this apply to us as to responsibility? What is the fruit of the Kingdom of God? The fruit of the Kingdom of God is the Kingdom of heaven. They are intimately related. The greatest word of all is the Kingdom of God, which means the Kingship of God, which means the Kingship of God recognized and obeyed; and the Kingdom of God in some senses includes the whole universe over which He governs. Hell itself is in that Kingdom. The Kingdom of God, if we understand the phrase in all its breadth, and length, and height, and depth of meaning, describes His ultimate and final and present authority everywhere. The immanence of God, and the transcendence of God, are not contradictory ideas, but mutually expository ideas; and whether it be far or near, near or far, God is, and rules, and governs all. He has created in the great mystery of His universe, beings with will, and to certain of these people, in a fallen world, and in the mid.t of a fallen race, He has committed the Kingdom of God; He has made them responsible to reveal it, to let other men see what it means. If we can find a community realising the Kingdom of God in its own life, that is the Kingdom of heaven; it is the fruit of the Kingdom of God. There was a time, a little time in the history of the Hebrew people when they realised it, when they were a theocracy purely and simply; no King interfering but the one King Jehovah; all their life centred about Him. That was the Kingdom of heaven. There were a few fleeting months in Florence when the world saw the coming of the Kingdom of God in power and judgment, when in answer to the preaching of Savonarola people woke, and broke the chain of Lorenzo de Medici. There was a moment in our English history when we had a glimpse of the Kingdom of God—it was never a perfect glimpse—when men called Ironsides held sword and Bible, and tramped to the music of the declarations of Holy Writ. We had one gleam when Oliver Cromwell saved us all from the evil of a decadent age. They were never lasting. They could not last because, even though there was a gleam of the glory of the Kingdom, the conditions were not established by the methods of the King. The Kingdom of heaven is realisation in actual human life of the fact of the Kingship of God. The King coming up to Jerusalem, said to the people who had been made the depository of the holy and sacred truth, "The Kingdom of God shall be taken away from you, and shall be given to a nation bringing forth the fruits thereof;" that is, to a people who will exhibit all that is meant by the Kingdom of God. And what was the nation to whom it was given? The Church.

Peter, to whom our Lord first spoke concerning the Church, said in his letter, "Ye are an elect race, a royal priesthood, a holy nation, a people for God's own possession." That does not exhaust the Divine intention. It will never be exhausted until the whole world realises the Kingdom of God. From then until now the world is only able to know the meaning of the Kingdom of God as it sees it realised in the Church of Jesus Christ. But the Church has failed to reveal the Kingdom of God in all its earthly meaning and glory as the Hebrew people did. That is why we are being broken up, and scattered abroad; that is why our work has become largely individualistic. There have been some attempts; some stately and magnificent, and yet terrible; some full of marvellous power, yet always failing; and some grotesque. One of the greatest attempts to realise it has been that of the Roman Catholic Church; that great and massive structure, boastfully one o'er all the face of the earth. But Rome has failed because she has allowed the Christian ideal to be paganised, and thus has ruined the testimony to the Kingdom of God. The movement of the Plymouth Brethren was a great one. They had the vision of a great ideal, but their testimony is a ruined and spoiled testimony, because they became Romanised with a popery more severe than that of Rome, a popery that tracked a man from village to village if perchance he did not quite agree with some view of truth, until he was ostracised and hounded almost out of existence. More recently another attempt at the manifestation was seen in Dowieism. But Dowie's ministry was that of taking his community, and putting it into a city by itself. Jesus Christ would have His people scattered, for His salt must live next door to the corruption; His light must shine in the darkness. Outside the borders of the Church, there are men to-day who are seeing at least the Divine intention though they have not discovered the Divine dynamic; and perhaps, presently, we shall be surprised to see God moving toward a realisation through people we thought could not be used for it, and all because His Church has not been true to Him in this matter.

What is our responsibility? What shall we do? Attempt to re-unite Christendom? In the name of God, no. There is no time to waste; life is all too brief. What shall we do? At least we ought, wherever there is a Christian fellowship, to realise the Kingdom of God within it. Every Church ought to find out how, in that local fellowship, there may be at least a centre of light, a revelation to the men outside, of the love, and the light, and the life, which come to men inside the Kingdom of God. It is not enough that in our personal life we reveal to the world what Christ can do for us. The world is waiting to see, not merely what Christ can do for a man, but what Christ can do for the community of souls who, having come to Him individually, are now living within His Kingdom. And if He has committed to us the Kingdom, and we do not bring forth the fruits of it, so surely as He cast His Hebrew people away from service—not from salvation, but from service—so surely will God move outside the churches and do His work beyond it in ways that will astonish us. This is the message of His Kingship, and unless we realise what He means, and obey Him, we also will be cast away from service, and from helping to fulfil His great ideals in the world.

MATTHEW XXII. 15-46

THE King is still seen in the Temple. In this section we have a radiant display of His wisdom. All that we read concerning the Pharisees and Sadducees is background, and serves to throw up into clear relief the matchless wisdom of the King.

The Pharisees now gathered themselves together for a new attack by the most despicable of methods; they descended to the meanness of attempting to lay traps for Him, to bring such problems to Him, or questions, or difficulties, as would involve Him in complications with regard to His own teaching, His own claim; or, far more to their satisfaction, which might involve Him in conflict with the civil authorities. The Sadducees somewhat flippantly suggested a problem to Him, and when He had muzzled them—using that word quite accurately, it is the word in the New Testament—a lawyer, perhaps sincerely, so far as his question was concerned, and yet with unbelief in his heart, asked Him a question. Finally, the King propounded a question, which flashed its light upon all their questions, and upon them.

Examining this series of pictures, we have four groups, and four happenings. The coming of the Pharisees; then that of the Sadducees; then that of the lawyer; and finally Christ's question.

Examining them one after the other, taking picture by picture, these are the things which impress the mind; first, that these men did not know Him; and, secondly, that they did not understand the very problems which they themselves suggested to Him. By contrast to that, one cannot read these four stories, or look at these four pictures, without seeing how perfectly He knew them, and how absolutely He was Master of all the problems which they suggested to Him.

There came to Him first the Pharisees and Herodians. This was a coalition. The Pharisees and Herodians represented opposing political views, and their question was distinctly a political one. They came together in order to entrap Him in His talk; and

the very fact that this was a coalition created the subtlety of their approach, and the difficulty of Christ.

How little they knew Him! They attempted to fling about Him the mist of their flattery. Reading the story carefully we find that these men had come to challenge His authority as evidently as the official deputation from the Sanhedrim, the leading Pharisees, had come on a previous occasion. These men were not leading Pharisees, but disciples of the Pharisees; that is to say, the leaders, having been answered, were in the background; but they sent up some young men, some of their disciples, with a new method of attack; not with the official dignity that challenged authority, but with the civil manner that suggested a belief in Christ's integrity.

How little they knew Him, and how very surprised they must have been when, before attempting to answer their question, He looked back into their faces and said, "Why make ye trial of Me, ye hypocrites?" They thought that He might be moved or at least mystified by flattery. Praise is a graver peril than blame to a strong soul. Blame a man, challenge him, and if he stands upon a bed-rock of certainty and conviction, he will win; but it is a trying moment when a man is told that he is quite perfect and upright, and knows the way of God. Jesus ruthlessly tore the veil away, as He said, "ye hypocrites."

What was their problem? Its blindness is self-evident, but it was a very subtle one. The question was of the simplest, "Is it lawful?" There is no meaning in this, save as we remember that they understood that He had made Messianic claims. They were not referring to Roman law, but Hebrew law, Messianic law. "Is it lawful to give tribute unto Cæsar, or not?" The subtlety of the question lay in the dilemma into which they intended to put Him. If He had said, Yes, it is lawful, then, according to their idea, He would have abandoned His claim to be Messiah and Deliverer; for the

Messiah could never consent that the Hebrew people should put their neck under a yoke. If, on the other hand, He had said, It is not lawful, then they would have been able to report Him to Rome, and have Him arrested.

Mark the answer. He said to these men, " Shew Me the tribute money." In that very request, and in the fact that He proffered that request to them, we see His method. If the King had Himself produced a penny, or asked one of His own followers for the denarius, the silver Roman coin with the Hebrew inscription, intended for the specific purpose of paying tribute—it was the amount and coin for that purpose—He still might have said all He said, but His declaration would have lost something of weight. The penny was immediately produced, perhaps handed to Him; and then He looked into their faces, and said, " Whose is this image and superscription?" Without a moment's hesitation, they replied: " Cæsar's."

That settled it; the penny was theirs, and the image Cæsar's. They were using Cæsar's coinage. Let them be honest enough to pay Cæsar his due; but let them not forget that there is a higher law than the law of Cæsar; let them " Render unto God the things that are God's."

The second part of the answer led them into the inner secret of how they were to fulfil the first part. " Render therefore unto Cæsar the things that are Cæsar's;" but while you do it, in the doing of it, " render to God the things that are God's." When you pay tribute—and you must pay tribute—do not forget that the final Throne to which you owe allegiance, is the Divine Throne.

What is the principle? The King recognized man's place in the State, and his obligation to the State; and declared that if men be in the State, it is their business to pay tribute to the State. He does not take men out of the State, and put them as separate from it; but He does say, that the deepest and the final thing in the life of men who are supposed to represent the Kingdom of God in the world, is the Kingdom of God. Such men are to be in the State, recognizing its responsibilities, fulfilling their obligations, but all the while they are to act under the one master-passion and principle of loyalty to the Throne of God.

This was a political problem, and in it we see the King's relation to politics for all time. He reveals the principles which bind the State to the Throne of God. He declares that the Throne of God is final and supreme; and a man in the State is to pay his tribute, and do his duty to the State; but always under the guidance and inspiration of his loyalty to the Throne of God. No man can interfere with what any other man does in that respect. We have no business to tell each other what we ought to do. It is by individual loyalty, and not by an association or resolution of crowds that we affect the State. The Church affects the State toward God in no other way than by the individual conscience; and its absolute freedom to God.

Next there came to Him the Sadducees, the rationalists in religion. The Sadducee denied angel and spirit and resurrection; that is to say, he attempted to be religious without any reference to what people speak of as supernatural things. They came to Christ and first of all quoted to Him the Mosaic command, that if a man die, his brother should take his wife, and raise up seed. Then they gave Him an illustration, a grotesque illustration. We can almost see the self-satisfied air with which they said: " In the resurrection therefore, whose wife shall she be of the seven? for they all had her." And yet notice when our Lord answered these men there was an utter absence of the severity which characterised His answer to the Pharisees. He did not speak to them as hypocrites, and it may be that if their illustration was grotesque, and their method was flippant, they were yet stating an actual difficulty in their thinking. First of all He answered their illustration by declaring to them that they were ignorant of the Scriptures. But further, He answered their philosophy by declaring that they were ignorant of the power of God.

He answered their illustration. They

were ignorant of their Scriptures, and in one quiet dignified sentence He declared to them, "In the resurrection they neither marry, nor are given in marriage, but are as angels in heaven;" you are imagining a condition of affairs that cannot, and will not exist. In a moment their illustration was swept on one side as being not applicable to their argument or their philosophy.

But He did not so leave them. "But," said He, "as touching the resurrection of the dead." By that phrase He touched the underlying philosophy that had made the difficulty and suggested the illustration. Not ruthlessly, not with the severity which characterised His answer to the Pharisees, but quite as surely, He stripped them of all disguises. He said to them in effect, Your difficulty is this difficulty concerning resurrection. Your difficulty is the difficulty concerning the supernatural in religion. You are rationalists concerning resurrection; "Have ye not read that which was spoken unto you by God, saying "—do not miss the apparently trivial things in reading your New Testament, they said, "*Moses* said;" He said, "spoken unto you *by God* "—"I am the God of Abraham, and the God of Isaac, and the God of Jacob? God is not the God of the dead, but of the living."

This answer of Jesus was a most remarkable one. He went beneath the surface to the underlying fact of God. "God is not the God of the dead." The difficulty as to the bodily resurrection of a man is no difficulty at all when the question concerning God is settled. When a man understands the truth that the Bible reveals concerning God, the difficulties that the Bible presents concerning man, and what we call the supernatural, melt into thin air. He said to these rationalists in effect, You are building your view of the impossibility of resurrection upon a misconception of God. Ye neither know the Scriptures, nor the power of God; which does not merely mean God's power to do this one thing, but God's essential power, the truth concerning God. God is the God of the living. In that great word of Jesus we have a declaration of the immortality of the soul. He is not the God of the dead. These men are not dead. Christ did not say a word about a bodily resurrection, but He affirmed that these men were alive. He declared that the God, Who is the God of Abraham, and the God of Isaac, and the God of Jacob, is the God of the living; and what He said, indicates the fact that through all ages He is their God, and that they are living still. If we once recognize the truth of the immortality of the soul, the question of the bodily resurrection is very simple. Just as in the mysteries of the original economy of God a man who is a spirit and not a body, is clothed in a body by certain processes, some little of which we understand; so that selfsame man, that spirit, can presently be clothed in a body again, and it will not be the body that was, but a new body, yet in some mystery beyond our comprehension fashioned out of the old body. An actual resurrection is in this way conceivable when we believe in God, as to His power, and His relation to all souls who put their trust in Him.

So, not answering their difficulty concerning bodily resurrection, but by declaring the true philosophy of God, new to them, He corrected their rationalistic speculations. This was a rationalistic problem, and the King's answer was clear, as it revealed the fact that the degradation of human thinking about man, is due to a degraded conception of God,

The third questioner was a lawyer, a Pharisee lawyer. He came, as we have seen, with a sincere question. "Which is the great commandment in the law?" This does not mean, Name one of the commandments which is greater than the rest. The particular word translated "which" is qualitative; and therefore the meaning of the lawyer was, What is the principle which makes any commandment great? In that day men were teaching the relative importance of the commandments. There was a school of interpretation which taught that the third commandment in the Decalogue was the supreme commandment, and that all the rest were minor ones; and so this particular question grew out of the differences of opinion concerning which commandments were greatest, and they asked Christ to decide what was the real principle by which they might test the greatness of a commandment.

When He gave the answer He did not name one of the commandments in the Decalogue, but went outside them. Both of the passages that He gave are to be found in the Pentateuch. The one is in the book of Deuteronomy, and the other is in Leviticus. First, "Thou shalt love the Lord thy God with all thy heart, and with all thy soul, and with all thy mind. This is the great and first commandment." The man had asked the Master to tell him the principle of greatness in a commandment. "This is the great;" and it is great because first, great because fundamental, great because underlying all the others. "This is *the* great and first commandment." The article is emphatic. "And *a* second" —not *the* second—"*a* second," a something coming out of the first, related to the first, not standing even in distinction from it. Then He declared: "On these two commandments the whole law hangeth, and the prophets." The principle of greatness is the recognition of the fundamental law which includes the whole. This is great and first, and these two are the strength of all the rest.

This was a problem of conduct. It was the King's revelation of His understanding of the meaning of law. What is law? Relation to God, expressed toward the neighbour. "Thou shalt love the Lord thy God." The second is like it, kin to it, belonging to it, the outward expression of it, "Thou shalt love thy neighbour as thyself." John afterwards wrote about love, and unfolded this great philosophy of Jesus Christ, teaching us that if a man say he love his brother, and leave him hungry, he is a liar. Thou shalt love the Lord thy God, and thou shalt love thy neighbour as thyself. The principle in law is love.

Notice the words introducing the last picture, "Now while the Pharisees were gathered together." That is, when the Pharisees had done, when He had muzzled the Sadducees, when the lawyer had gone. Probably that had been a concerted movement and these men had come one after another by arrangement. The Pharisees were still there, and for a moment Jesus arrested them, and asked them two questions.

The first was startling, "What think ye of Christ?" Let us understand that. He was not saying to them directly, What do you think of Me? If we change the word Christ to Messiah, we find the meaning. What is your opinion, your conception of Messiah? He asked their opinion of Messiah in one particular only: Whose Son is He? Their answer was ready and accurate, "David's." That He did not deny. He asked the question in order to receive that answer. He knew that would be the answer. It was the only answer possible. It was true, absolutely true, according to all prophecy, according to the inspired expectation of the nation.

Then He asked His second question: "How then doth David in the Spirit call Him Lord?" Christ was quoting from Psalm cx. He said three things about that psalm. He said David wrote it. We are told to-day that he did not. He said in the second place he wrote it by the Spirit. We are told it is not inspired. He said in the third place He wrote it about the Messiah. We are told it is not Messianic. Let us stand with Christ, and maintain that David wrote Psalm cx. by the inspiration of the Spirit, and concerning Messiah.

What He asked these men was; If Messiah was David's Lord, how was He also his Son? They were silent. The silence is a revelation. This question of Christ was a revealing question. Their conception of Messiah was a wrong conception. Moreover, the bearing of His question on all their questions is a very interesting one. They came to Him about their politics, they expected a Messiah who would lead an army, and break the yoke and set them free; but He said, You do not know your Messiah. You think of Him as coming in David's line, but He is more than David's Son, He is David's Lord. Account for that, and if you do, you will have all your political problems solved. He comes for the interpreta-iton of a spiritual Kingdom, which is not to be powerless, but which is to be an inward dynamic, correcting all things from the centre.

In the next place, if the Messiah is David's Lord, His dominion is an ever-lasting dominion, and the doctrine of resurrection is not a difficult one. If the Ruler that was to come, of Whom David sang in the Psalm long ago, is his Lord, Son of God as well as Son of David, then all your difficulty about those who have passed on, as to whether there is to be resurrection, is solved.

And once again, your wrong concep-tion of your Messiah has meant the materialisation of your ideals concern-ing greatness in law. Realise that when Messiah comes, He will be, not merely son of David, but David's Lord, and you will understand the abiding authority and supremacy in law.

Take that word of Christ and ex-amine it more carefully. We have only touched upon the outlying truths, at-tempting to reveal the structure of the argument in all its delicacy of applica-tion. Here is His problem, Who is Messiah? David's Son? Then why does David call Him Lord? If He is only David's Son, He cannot be David's Lord. The inferential claim of Christ is that He is David's Lord, as well as his son, descended through the flesh from David, yet before David. If you cut out the first part of your Gospel, the story of a virgin birth, you must cut out this also, for they are inti-mately related. As in the beginning we saw Him coming through the line of the flesh, yet not by the act of the flesh; so here we find Him claiming that His Messiahship is based, not merely upon His Davidic descent, but upon His absolute supremacy and Lord-ship, as David had long ago foreseen.

MATTHEW XXIII. 1-12

THIS passage constitutes a brief parenthesis in the special work which the King was doing at this time. It gives the account of words spoken to the multitudes and to His disciples, between His conflict with the rulers which ended in their discomfiture; and His pronouncing of woes upon them, and doom upon the people who had rejected Him.

The passage is a very interesting one in that it reveals a remarkable contrast between the false and the true in re-ligion. The King addressed Himself to the multitudes and to His disciples, and it is by no means difficult to see that part of the address was intended for the disciples, and that part was in-tended for the multitudes. He first spoke to the multitudes. Having done so in general terms of warning, He ad-dressed Himself specifically to His own disciples. This contrast between the false and true in religion is made by the comparison between the false rulers with whom He had been in conflict, and the true spiritual teachers, His own disciples, whom He was commissioning

to go forth to exercise a religious au-thority as they should interpret the meaning of His own message.

At the close of the thirteenth chap-ter of our Gospel, after the King had spoken the great parables of the King-dom, part of them to the multitudes and part of them to His own disciples, He ended that parabolic instruction by declaring that a scribe instructed to the Kingdom of heaven must bring forth out of His treasure-house things new and old; and by that statement He ap-propriated the word scribe for His own disciples. In that statement He enun-ciated His rejection of the official scribe of the period, but also indicated the fact that His disciples constituted the new order of scribes for the days to come. In this passage, He first warned the multitude against the false teachers, the scribes and the Pharisees, that sit on Moses' seat; and turning from that warning He charged His own disciples as to what their attitude and relationship to men should be, when He said to them, Ye shall not be called Rabbi, you shall call no man father, you shall not be called masters or guides. The false teachers are exposed in the words our Lord addressed to the multitudes contained in verses two to seven; and as He exposed the false rulers, He revealed what false religion is. The true position of spiritual teachers is revealed in His charge to His own disciples, to be found in verses eight to twelve; and in that charge He also revealed the essence of true religion.

First, then, we have His revelation of the essential failure of the rulers. Christ's conflict had never been with the people, it had been with the rulers. All His anger wherever it was manifest, wherever it flamed and flashed, was directed against false shepherds, men who, standing between the people and God, had misinterpreted the way and will of God; and we find in this passage a very remarkable and carefully expressed estimate of that which was wrong in the rulers; against which, Christ, with all the dignity of His Kingship, with the force of His personality, cast Himself.

Notice in the first place His recognition of the position occupied by these men; He said: "The scribes and the Pharisees sit on Moses' seat." There is a fine discrimination in the statement, which perhaps we are apt to lose sight of in the reading. We can only express what Christ said by using another tense, and using the verb in a slightly different form. Said He, The scribes and Pharisees have seated themselves on Moses' seat. That is not to say that Christ was saying their position was a false one, although there was a remarkably fine indication of the fact that they were never appointed by God. He was not saying their position was out of harmony with the thought and purpose and intention of God, because immediately afterwards He said to the people, " all things therefore whatsoever they bid you, these do and observe." He recognized that a certain authority belonged to scribes and Pharisees. Bearing these two things in mind we must be careful to see what He really meant. First of all He said that they had seated themselves on Moses' seat. This was not a reference

merely to the men of His own age. This was His definition of the position occupied by the whole order of the scribes. In all likelihood the order was instituted in the days of Ezra; and the scribe was the interpreter of the law, the man who taught the people its meaning. Now there was nothing wrong in such a position, and yet Christ was very careful to indicate in the way He stated the case, that they were self-appointed teachers. They seated *themselves* on Moses' seat. The expression, "Moses' seat," demands our attention. It is peculiarly the word that indicates authority. The Greek word here is Cathedrâ. These people sat on Moses' seat, the seat of the teachers, of authority, the seat from which they spoke in interpretation of the law with final authority. Their position was authoritative so far. It is impossible, however, to imagine that Christ meant here that men were to obey all the things that the Pharisees were telling them to do. We must not omit the "therefore" from the text, because He Himself resolutely broke the traditions of the elders, treated with disdain the thousand and one things which they had superadded to the Mosaic economy, ignored their multitudinous technicalities, sat down with unwashen hands to eat as a protest against the externality of their religious ideals. So that He certainly did not mean to say that everything the scribes and Pharisees said to men, they were to do. We shall understand Him by putting emphasis on the "*therefore.*" They have seated themselves on Moses' chair, therefore, that is, in so far as their interpretation is indeed true to the Mosaic economy, you must obey them; so far as they fulfil the function of the position they have taken, they have authority, and their teaching is binding upon men.

But having said so much, our Lord proceeded to show the failure of these men. There is no need for exposition, for the statement is so clear. "They say, and do not." "They bind heavy burdens and grievous to be borne, and lay them on men's shoulders; but they themselves will not move them with their finger;" which does not mean they put burdens on men's shoulders, and then would not help men to bear the burden; but that they put burdens on men's shoulders which they would not carry themselves even with the finger. That is to say, they were not true to their own ethical teaching.

The King then proceeded to show the supreme motive of these men. They wore the phylactery. Christ did not say it was wrong to wear it. Tradition has it, and perchance tradition is accurate, that He Himself wore phylacteries. They wore phylacteries, and were careful to wear them conspicuously. They widened the borders of the garment, broadening the cases in which the phylacteries rested, in order to attract the notice of men, in order that men might see the phylacteries. There we have the underlying reason of all the failure of the scribes and Pharisees, "to be seen of men." It was a ruthless unveiling of the false in religion. The false in religion is that which is punctilious and particular in all the matters of external observance, and this in answer to the underlying desire to be notorious religiously, in the view of men. In the Manifesto He had said that men prayed at the corners of the streets. He did not say it was wrong to pray at the corners of the streets, but He said these men prayed at the corners of the street to be seen of men, and with a fine scorn for them He added, " Verily I say unto you, They have received their reward." That is, they pray to be seen of men, and they are seen of men, and they get out of their praying all they want. So here again, coming to the end of the conflict, with the rulers standing around Him, listening to Him, He denounced the same evil.

We miss very much of these stories if we allow the local setting to fade from our mind. Christ was in the Temple, multitudes were with Him, His disciples were there; and there all around were the men who had been questioning Him, and He had silenced and defeated them. With these men as object lessons, the broadened borders of their garments visible, the enlarged receptacle for the phylactery patent, He said, All this to be seen of men!

All their interpretation of law had as its inspiration, the desire to create for themselves a position of authority, of pre-eminence. They loved the salutation in the market-places, they loved the recognition of the crowd, and in order to gain these things, they sat in the Mosaic seat, and interpreted the law.

Now the false in religion stands revealed in Christ's contemplation of these men, not only in the case of the men themselves, but in the case of the people who are under the influence of such men. The false in religion in the case of the people is due to failure to discriminate between the human and the divine; and consists of submission to unauthorised authority. This always issues in degradation. Obedience to anything other than the highest, issues sooner or later in bondage to the lowest. Here was the peril of the age; nay more than the peril; here was the reason of its doom, when presently it was uttered by the lips of the gentle Servant of God.

Immediately turning from His warning, He addressed Himself to His own disciples, and He said to them, " But be not ye called Rabbi;" you are not to claim to have in your teaching any final authority; you are not to call any man your Father; there is to be no claim on your part of spiritual-life relation to any human being; you shall not be called Master, or Guide; you have no right to direct the conduct of any other individual soul. This was His threefold charge to His own disciples. How largely we have lost sight of these things!

In that threefold negation the King recognized the essential element in religion. The deepest fact in religion is suggested by the central of the three things, and we will take that first. You shall call no man Father. It is a superficial treatment to imagine that Jesus meant, we are not to give other men the title of father; it is not the title that matters; it is the thing the title indicates that matters. " Call no man your father." This is our Lord's forbidding of the recognition of any man's power to impart by ceremony or in any other way, spiritual life to his fellow man. The father is the one who begets, the one from whom life comes. That is the essential and deepest fact in fatherhood in our common use of the word. So undoubtedly the word means in this connection. The essential thing in religion is life. The false knew nothing of life in the soul, the false spent its time in making burdens, and binding them *on* men. There is the difference between false and true religion. False religion is *on*, true religion is *in*. That is Isaiah's teaching, in that fine chapter in which he satirises idolatry. The man goes to the forest, he cuts down a tree, makes an image, and he carries it. That is false religion. But Isaiah goes on to say Jehovah hath carried us. That is true religion. And the difference between the two is Life. That is the central word. Now said Jesus Christ, "Call no man your father on the earth," you shall never recognize any man who claims to be able, by sacramentarian grace or any other thing, to communicate life to your soul. The life of God in the soul of a man must come by the begetting of God.

The other two words reveal the other essentials in true religion. First, Authority. Every man feels his need of it. It is of the very essence of religion. When we have life, our life needs authority, the ultimate and the binding fact, that which commands us. The whole story of religion, false and true, in its conflict in the world, gathers around this question of authority. The Roman Church claims authority, and pity us who are not within the pale of that Church, because they say we have no authority. Let us dismiss all the differences and recognize the need. The soul of man needs authority, needs the voice that speaks to it with authority, needs the word that is binding upon it.

And more, the soul needs direction, not merely that direction of truth, which is authoritative and binding and final, but the perpetual application of truth to the incidents of everyday life, to the commonplaces and the crises as they come. We are always needing in the religious life some one to say to us, This is the way, walk ye in it; the

relating of truth to conduct at every point in the life. Religion is life first; secondly it is the authority to which man yields allegiance; finally it is the perpetual guidance which he follows. These are the things that Christ recognizes.

Here we have revealed the standard of truth, and here we have revealed to us the fact of what the real essence of religion is. First, it is the life of God in the soul of a man. And that life can only come to us by His imparting. It was He Who said to an honest and sincere inquirer upon the housetop, in the loneliness of the night, You must be born anew, you need life. "As Moses lifted up the serpent in the wilderness, even so must the Son of man be lifted up: that whosoever believeth may in Him have eternal life." This is how you will obtain life —by My lifting up. We can only understand what Christ meant as we track Him through, and hear when He uses the phrase again, "And I, if I be lifted up from the earth, will draw all men unto Myself." And that there may be no doubt as to His meaning the Spirit interprets it for us, "This He said, signifying by what manner of death He should die." So the King offers men life which is the fundamental necessity of religion, through the mystery of His own dying.

And then He stands for evermore as the final authority. Remember that His authority is not the authority of the interpretation of truth. His authority is the authority of essential truth. He said not, I teach, I declare, I explain truth, but, "I am the truth." If we can bring the soul of man face to face with the Christ, not with any human interpretation of Him, but to the actual Christ of the New Testament, that man immediately knows that he stands in the presence of essential and eternal truth. The one and final authority in religion, is the authority of Christ, and the authority of Christ as revealed to us in the Scriptures of truth.

Finally, the immediate guidance of Christ, for He is near to every one of us, and in every moment waiting to

" Direct, control, suggest, each day."

He sweeps away the intermediation of the man who claims authority, the intermediation of the man who claims to be able by any process to communicate life to the soul of a man, the intermediation of the man who dares to interfere in the conduct of another soul as between that soul and God. We see at once how religion has been falsified wherever its vital principles have been interfered with. We speak with awe and profound respect, of the saints of the great Roman Church, and we see at once how that Church recognizes this threefold conception of religion. There is the reason of its long-continued strength. It recognizes that man needs authority, that man needs Life, that man needs guidance, and in the threefold office of its ministry it professes to meet those needs. In the priestly office it claims to communicate life through sacramentarian processes. In the teaching office it claims to speak infallibly to man and answer his cry for authority. In the office of the confessional it claims to investigate and guide men, and so to meet their need at that point. Its appalling heresy consists in the fact that it takes hold of the essentials of religion and attempts to continue them by cutting their nerve, and denying what Christ said concerning them.

Our protest, in the name of spiritual religion, is for evermore to be made against all such blasphemous misuse of sacred things. First against all that intermediates between the soul and God as Life Giver; we can only receive life directly from Him; neither through official priesthood nor sacramentarian arrangement can life touch the soul; the Supper of the Lord is the Eucharist, beautiful word indeed; the sacrament of thanksgiving; but the Table of the Lord is not the place where we receive life; it is the place where we give back our song in praise to God; but no man is richer in life by sitting there.

So also with baptism. There is no sacramentarian grace in it. No infant was ever made an inheritor of the Kingdom of heaven in baptism. No adult was ever made a member of the Church by baptism. These things may be valuable external symbols of internal truths, but there is no communication of life to the soul thereby, or kind or measure. The soul can only have life by His begetting, by its actual contact with God.

So also in matters of guidance. Let us make our perpetual, our constant, our vehement protest, against any human interference in matters of conduct. Remember here that priestism is a very insidious thing. It reappears in strange new forms with the passing of years, and there are some people, most pronounced in their objection to Roman Catholicism, who themselves are practising it in their interference with others. Away with priestism! Let us take our orders from Him alone.

But do not let us forget that this conception of religion is more than a negative responsibility; it reveals a positive duty, that of actual submission to Christ's authority if we deal with authority as something which is to illuminate our intelligence, and not command our will, it is a peril and a poison. But if we remit our soul to the Christ for His commanding word, and when we hear that commanding word obey it, then are we fulfilling our positive duty.

This fact that One is our Father, lays upon us the positive duty of the practice of fellowship with God. If indeed His life be in our soul, then our life in all its externality is to be ordered by the fact of the impulse of that indwelling life. We are to have fellowship with Him, not merely on the morning of the first day of the week in assembling for worship, but in all the acts and attitudes of everyday life. We are to remember that the only constraining force to which one must yield oneself is the force of the life of God in the soul.

Finally, if indeed we are determined that we will suffer no interference in matters of conduct, we must be equally determined that we will remit every matter of conduct to the arbitration of the Christ. We have no right to have anything in our business that we have not asked His will concerning. We have no right to have anything in our recreation that we are not quite sure He approves. We have no right to have anything in our attitudes towards civic, or national, or world-wide interests, that we have not held up in the light of His present and immediate interpretation.

This is religion. It is the bringing of the individual soul into direct relationship with God; the answer of the soul to the lonely authority of Christ; and the testing of the life in the presence of Christ, and by His will and His will alone. May God lead us into these deepest things of religion.

MATTHEW XXIII. 13-39

THIS passage contains the most terrible words which ever fell from the lips of the King. At the commencement of His ministry, in enunciating the laws of the Kingdom to His own disciples, He declared that their righteousness must exceed the righteousness of the scribes and Pharisees, and now as we follow these woes through, we discover that He was elaborating that comparison, showing how the righteousness of these men had failed, how it had come short. His sentence was but a ratification of the definite choices which these men had made.

Here, as everywhere, we may do strange violence to the very spirit of the King by missing His tone, and failing to discover the pity which is evident throughout the whole of these strange and undoubtedly terrible words. The final impression of the reading of this passage is that of the severity of Jesus, and His unbending loyalty to righteousness. But while that is true, it is impossible to read this carefully without discovering that the method was the method of tears, that from beginning to end there was evidence of sorrow; that there is a wail running throughout the whole of this discourse, as well as the thunder of denunciation. It is only as we catch these two tones that we shall understand all the meaning of this passage.

The severity of Jesus is discovered in the words He made use of; in the repetition of the word "hypocrites," in the use of the words "fools and blind," in the one terrible sentence that appals as we read it, in which He called them "serpents" and "offspring of vipers," in that most fearful illustration suggested by His use of the term the "judgment of Gehenna." All these are terms which indicate the severity of Christ. We cannot cancel these terms, they are as surely here as anything else in the passage.

And yet not to discover the other tone is to miss much. There were tears in His voice; there was sorrow in His heart. These things are not merely manifest in the last lamentation, "Oh Jerusalem, Jerusalem," but in all the woes. We do violence to the spirit of the Christ, and to the genius of the whole passage, if we put into the reading of the word "woe" nothing but thunder. It was a wail of compassion as well as a message of strong and severe denunciation. Yet even this compassion was denunciatory, for in every case He declared that the woe was unto these men.

We have in this passage; first, the King's judicial verdict, His findings concerning the people to whom He was addressing Himself; and, secondly, His judicial sentence.

In the Manifesto, the King had said to His disciples; "For I say unto you, Except your righteousness shall exceed the righteousness of the scribes and Pharisees, ye shall in no wise enter into the Kingdom of heaven" (chap. v. 20). Those words were spoken in the first section of the Manifesto. Immediately following we read, "Ye have heard that it was said to them of old time, Thou shalt not kill: and whosoever shall kill shall be in danger of the judgment:" He took up the law under which these people had been living, and so far from abrogating it, emphasised its binding nature by interpreting its inner meaning. But He indicated the failure of the scribes and Pharisees by this declaration of requirement. This comparison between that righteousness of which He had come to teach men the necessity, and that of the Pharisees must be interpreted in the light of the Beatitudes, those words in which Jesus revealed the character which is necessary in His Kingdom. We go back to that because we are now at the end of the Master's ministry. That is how He opened it. We have now come to the passage in which He closed it; and the verdict which He found, as addressing the scribes and Pharisees directly, in the presence of the multitudes, is an elaboration of the suggestion He made at the beginning. They stood before Him, in character the direct opposite of that which He described at the beginning of His ministry.

While not desiring unduly to press the comparison between the Beatitudes and the woes, this at least is true, that if we get the view of the whole character revealed in those Beatitudes, and then the view of the whole character revealed in the woes, the contrast is patent; they stand in direct opposition to each other.

Let· us place the Beatitudes side by side with the woes, and we shall see how the King said in effect; I came to bring you face to face with God's ideal of righteousness; you have rejected the "blessed" with which I opened My ministry; there is nothing for it, therefore, but that I should utter the "woe" that must inevitably result from the rejection of the blessing.

The first blessing pronounced was upon poverty of spirit, "Blessed are the poor in spirit." And the resulting blessing from that attitude was possession; "theirs is the Kingdom of heaven." Now mark the first woe of Jesus. "Woe unto you, scribes and Pharisees, hypocrites! because ye shut the Kingdom of heaven against men." Poverty of spirit results in possession of the Kingdom. Pride of spirit results in the closing of the door against such as would strive to enter in, by men who refuse to enter in themselves.

"Blessed are they that mourn, for they shall be comforted." "Woe unto you, scribes and Pharisees, hypocrites! for ye compass sea and land to make

one proselyte; and when he is become so, ye make him twofold more a son of hell than yourselves." In the first place penitence, the mourning which issues in the comfort of God. In the next place the things which are against the Kingdom of God, they attempt to make a man proselyte, for which Jesus says in fine scorn, "Ye compass sea and land." And the issue, "Ye make him twofold more a son of hell than yourselves." The expression, "the son of Gehenna," does not indicate the evil character that results, but rather the pain, and unrest, and misery that result. We remember upon another occasion our Lord, referring in figurative and symbolic language to punishment, spoke of Gehenna as the place "where their worm dieth not." And so over against the comfort that comes to mourning and repentant souls, there is the pain and unrest and remorse that come to such as persist in the attitude of rebellion.

"Blessed are the meek, for they shall inherit the earth." Over against meekness we have the woe against the blind guides, the exposure of the subtle casuistry which characterised the age in which Christ lived, which is the very essence of iniquity, the very opposite of meekness, the final expression of that pride of heart which is in revolt against God and issues in profanation.

"Blessed are they that hunger and thirst after righteousness: for they shall be filled." That is followed by the woe against men who were tithing mint, anise, and cummin, and were leaving undone weightier matters. This is a contrast between spiritual health and spiritual disease. On the one hand is the healthy hunger after righteousness; and on the other hand the fastidiousness of disease, which is particular about the small external things of no matter, and feels no hunger after righteousness; the neglect of the weighty matters of law, which attempts to atone for itself by all the minutiæ of the tithing of small things. Christ was careful to say that these things also should be attended to, but that the weightier things should not be neglected.

"Blessed are the merciful: for they

shall obtain mercy." The next woe was that upon such as veil internal vice by external profession. We do not touch the heart of it until we read these words, "full from extortion and excess," two things that stand exactly opposite to the merciful spirit.

"Blessed are the pure in heart: for they shall see God." Standing opposite to that is the woe that describes these men. Mark it carefully, outwardly beautiful, but inwardly full of dead men's bones and uncleanness! The contrast is striking between purity of heart, and the uncleanness of the inner life.

And, finally over against the blessing pronounced upon the peacemakers who are the sons of God is the woe against men who "build the sepulchres of the prophets" while yet they are the sons —mark the contrast—of the men who slay the prophets.

If in this contrast we do not find every woe set in direct contrast to every blessing, we at least discover that the character which our Lord described in that sevenfold Beatitude of the Manifesto, is in absolute opposition to the character which He described in this sevenfold woe of the final denunciation. We might continue the contrast further, for in the fifth chapter there is the added and double Beatitude upon persons who suffer for righteousness' sake; and when we turn over to the twenty-third chapter we find Him saying to these men, referring to the ministry which should follow His own crucifixion, "I send unto you prophets, and wise men, and scribes; some of them shall ye kill and . . . scourge, and persecute." At the beginning of the ministry in the Manifesto, He said to the disciples gathered about Him who would enter into the suffering as they proclaimed that Manifesto, "Blessed are ye when men shall . . . persecute you." At the close of it He drew attention to the fact that the men of opposite character would be the men who would inflict the suffering, afflicting and scourging and crucifying those who should stand for righteousness.

Our Lord in uttering these severe words revealed first of all their absolute justice. If we agree with the blessing of the character upon which He commenced His ministry, we must of necessity agree with the woe upon the character revealed in the men whom He denounced. He had spoken the words of abiding truth and righteousness, and every woe is but the other side of every blessing. The blessing was upon character, the woe was upon character; and the character upon which the blessing rested, was the exact opposite of the character upon which His final woe was pronounced.

The judicial sentence was a declaration of sequence. "Wherefore ye witness to yourselves, that ye are the sons of them that slew the prophets. Fill ye up then the measure of your fathers." One sometimes feels as though that word can hardly be understood by the Western mind. It is peculiarly Eastern. We Westerners have broken away more and more from the consciousness of relationship to our fathers. These men were perpetually boasting of their relationship to Abraham. They said one day, "Our father is Abraham." He said, You make your boast in your fathers, in your relationship to the past, you refuse to stand on the plane of isolated responsibility, "fill ye up then the measure of your fathers," be true to the thing you boast, and do not now by the garnishing of the tombs of the prophets attempt to dissociate yourselves from the sins of your fathers. You are still of their spirit, you are still rejecting the right, as they rejected the right, you are still persecuting and will continue to do so. We cannot believe that Jesus Christ was pronouncing sentence save as He was indicating the sequence. He was showing them what they would do, He was showing them what the issue of it would be; for mark what immediately follows the words, "Fill ye up then the measure of your fathers," "Ye serpents, ye offspring of vipers, how shall ye escape the judgment of Gehenna?"

When John the Baptist opened his ministry as the herald of the King, when these selfsame men came to him, he said with a touch of irony and scorn, " Who warned you to flee from the wrath to come?" Now at the close of His ministry Jesus took up the word and used it differently, with no irony, but with the terrible revelation of a necessary sequence, How can ye escape? " Fill up the measure of your fathers," you are the sons of the men who slew the prophets, you also have refused the righteousness of God. Carry this out to the end, and what then? There at the beginning are the Beatitudes, the words indicating the Master's purpose and intention for His people, accompanied by the conditions of righteousness upon which happiness must depend. Here He was talking to the men who had refused the conditions, and He asked, " How shall ye escape the judgment of Gehenna?" Thus our Lord declared that the judgment of hell is the inevitable issue of refusal to submit to the truth of which the inward conscience has been convinced, for that is the meaning of His word hypocrites; hypocrites are men who play the part that is not true in the externalities of righteousness, while within they are evil. And there is a deeper significance, they are men who remain evil in their inner life, in spite of profound conviction. It was His declaration of sequence, His declaration that hell is the inevitable harvest of a man's own sowing.

He then proceeded in the terms of His great lamentation to show that this is the result of their own deliberate choice, " How often would I have gathered thy children together, even as a hen gathereth her chickens under her wings, and ye would not! " That is the very heart of sin—" Ye would not;" the human will set up against the will of God. The human will set up against the will which had interpreted righteousness, and had expressed to men God's desire for human happiness and blessedness. " Blessed " is the word which revealed the purpose of the King. " I would have gathered you." Incidentally we have here another of those illustrations of the startling claims of Christ. Mark the magnificence of it. He personified the nation in the city, as the prophets of the past had so often done. " Oh Jerusalem,

Jerusalem, that killeth the prophets, and stoneth them that are sent unto her! how often would I "—the Galilean peasant, Jesus of Nazareth. " How often would I have gathered thy children together, even as a hen gathereth her chickens under her wings." His claim was that had they but come to Him, He could have gathered the whole of them from the impending judgment of evil. It is an exquisite figure; simple, but more than simple. It is the coming out in the simplicity of truth, of all the great underlying fact of the Motherhood of God as well as that of His Fatherhood. He said, " I would have gathered." Just that one Man, just a Galilean carpenter? A thousand times no; infinitely more, God incarnate! In these last words, standing there as the One Who had uttered the Manifesto, and the One presently to be rejected and cast out, He was gathering up all the brooding tenderness of the old revelation of God, and expressing it in that sobbing word of lamentation, " I would." His purpose was not to pronounce a curse but to bring a blessing; not to wail in woe over failure, but to sing over men. We remember the mother-figure of Zephaniah, " Jehovah thy God is in the midst of thee, a mighty One Who will save: He will rejoice over thee with joy, He will be silent in His love, He will joy over thee with singing." This was His purpose, " I would;" and this was their sin, " Ye would not."

Then He pronounced the sentence. " Behold, your house is left unto you desolate." Some of the ancient manuscripts omit that word " desolate," but the concensus of opinion is in favour of its retention. Probably He was referring to the Temple as the centre of their life, the place to which they had looked from long distances and to which He came at the commencement of His ministry, cleansing it and saying, " It is written, Make not My Father's house a house of merchandise." He came and cleansed the Temple again and said, " My house shall be called a house of prayer." Now He said, " Your house is left unto you:" to you hypocrites, blind, fools, men in whom there is uncleanness, men who have rejected the throne of God, the righteousness of God, the mercy of God, and the will of God.

And yet once again, notice most carefully His claim. " Your house is left unto you desolate. For I say unto you, Ye shall not see Me henceforth." The desolateness of the house is created by the absence of the Master of the house. And in the next chapter He said, " There shall not be left here one stone upon another, that shall not be thrown down." " Desolate."

But look at the King. His sorrow we have spoken of, His judgment we have heard pronounced. What is this last word? " For I say unto you, Ye shall not see Me henceforth, till ye shall say, Blessed is He that cometh in the name of the Lord." Who shall interpret that? It is interesting to see how many interpretations there are, and how eager and anxious some are to adapt the word of Jesus, so that it can fit their own philosophy. We do know what He meant as to local application, and local fulfilment of that Scripture; but we need to see, that even here, as He pronounced the final judgment upon a nation, a city; even as He spoke of their house being left desolate, hope was in His heart; and looking forward, He saw some hour in which they should say, " Blessed is He that cometh in the name of the Lord."

After that survey of this passage let us notice two things. First, that its study has meant an almost terrific revelation of the appalling issue of dishonesty. The word hypocrisy is the revealing one. The action of these men had been wilfully wicked. Even their external cleanness was proof of their consciousness of the beauty of holiness, and their inward pollution was of choice. " Ye would not." At last that attitude must work out to its own issue.

In the words of Jesus, men become the sons of Gehenna, they pass to the judgment of Gehenna. This has nothing at all to do with the men who have never heard the message. This has nothing whatever to do with the men who have never confronted this Christ of God, this King of kings. It has everything to do with us. Standing in the presence of this Teacher and Lord, remember and know assuredly that any hypocrisy must issue in the harvest of hell. There is nothing else for it. If we who heard the " blessed " will not obey the condition, then we take our own way of set purpose toward the " woe," and there can be no escape.

Behold the King! What a solemn revelation we have of Him here. How gracious and yet how just. In these words there is a revelation of His passion for righteousness, and also of His compassion for the worst and most degraded. His passion for righteousness never destroys His compassion for the worst. His compassion for the worst never destroys His passion for righteousness. It is well that our hearts should be warned by these solemn woes. The work of the King is not the work of excusing a man who persists in unrighteousness, and presently admitting him to the presence of God and the heaven of light. Naught that defileth can ever enter there, and the man who, in spite of all His ministry of infinite grace, persists in disobedience, passes to the judgment of Gehenna; there can be no escape. The deepest and profoundest passion of the King, is the passion for the Kingship of God and righteousness, and if He must pronounce a doom it will be with tears, but it will be pronounced. So let us ever bring ourselves to His judgment, and as we yield to that, pray for that which He will supply, grace to obey.

MATTHEW XXIV. AND XXV.

AS the King passed out from the Temple, His disciples showed Him its buildings. Why did they draw His special attention to the buildings of the Temple at this point? How often they had been there together, how often they had walked with Him the streets of Jerusalem, how often they had passed through the courts of the Temple, how often they had listened to His teaching, but they drew His special attention to the buildings now. There can be little doubt that we must link this fact with what He had just said, " Oh Jerusalem, Jerusalem . . . how often would I have gathered thy children together, and ye would not! behold, your house is left unto you desolate." There was nothing that indicated desolation in the material aspect of affairs at that moment in Jerusalem. The Jews had never been more strongly attached to their Temple. Of course the ancient glory of Solomon's Temple had passed and had never been replaced in some respects; but in other ways, the Temple existing was even finer than that existing in Solomon's time. As Jesus passed out of that Temple, His disciples came to Him to draw His attention to it, to its beauty, to its strength, to its solidity, in all likelihood to contradict the possibility of what He had said. It was as though they had said, Master, do you mean to say this house is ever to be desolate? Behold its beauty, we want Thee to examine it. He immediately answered; "See ye not all these things? Verily, I say unto you, There shall not be left here one stone upon another, that shall not be thrown down." That was a definite and positive prophecy, fulfilled quite literally, a little more than a generation later. Nothing seemed so unlikely when our Lord said it. The Hebrew people were then on excellent terms with their Roman Governors. There had been rebellions, there had been difficulties; but these things had been largely settled to all appearance. The perpetual principle of Roman government was never to interfere with the religion of a people unless the people made that religion the cause of disaffection. Everything seemed at the moment to be hopeful and prosperous.

The King passed on through the Temple to the Mount of Olives, and as He sat on the Mount of Olives the disciples came to Him, and said, " Tell us, when shall these things be? and what shall be the sign of Thy coming, and of the consummation of the age? "

We are very much in danger of taking this question out of its setting, and considering it as a later day question, and not understanding what these

men really meant by it. We must put the question into relationship with what they had asked Christ to behold, and what Christ had said concerning the destruction of the Temple. That is where it began. It led to much larger things in His answer, but so far as the men who asked the question were concerned, that is where it began.

In the form in which these men asked their question, it is evident that they considered that the destruction of the Temple would be associated with His presence, and with the consummation of the age. In the parables of the Kingdom in the thirteenth chapter, there is an unfortunate translation, which has been perpetuated in the Revised Version, in the phrase, " The end of the world." Not that this is necessarily inaccurate; but our interpretation of it is inaccurate. We have spoken of it as though it meant the break up of the material universe. We have had graphic pictures of a day of Judgment, when things are all burnt to a cinder, and pass away. Nothing of the kind is intended by this phrase, which would be better rendered, the consummation of the age. And just as in the thirteenth chapter when our Lord spoke of the end of the world according to our translations, He really referred to the ending of one particular age, so also in His reply to His disciples on this occasion. Evidently in their mind they associated three things; the destruction of the Temple, the presence of Jesus, and the ending of the age. What they meant by the age, who shall say? Possibly they did not mean by the age exactly what Christ meant by it, but they had some conception of a purpose of God, which was working out toward a consummation. They were looking for the setting up of a material Kingdom on the earth.

We shall never understand this prophecy of Jesus, if we do not get back into the spirit of these men. We must know what their question meant. Volume after volume has been written on the subject, and almost invariably we start by tabulating these questions in the light of our interpretation of the answer. That may be quite legitimate.

but it is well to begin with the question as it was asked.

Jesus had been strangely puzzling these men for months. Ever since Cæsarea Philippi, they had been quite out of harmony with Him; they did not understand what He was doing. They had followed Him with intense eagerness until He came to Cæsarea Philippi; and then He began to talk about a Cross, and they had never been able to understand Him since. They had watched Him come up to Jerusalem, had seen His conflict with the rulers, had heard His scathing denunciation and His parabolic inquisition, and, finally, His actual sentence and doom; and they had heard Him say, that the beautiful house was to be left desolate, and they said, Master, come and look at these buildings. "Verily, I say unto you," was His answer to them, "There shall not be left here one stone upon another, that shall not be thrown down." Then they were silent. It was a silent walk out of the city, and down the hill, and up the other side of Olivet. Then on Olivet they looked at Him as He was looking toward the city, and they gathered to Him, and they said, Master, "tell us, when shall these things be? and what shall be the sign of Thy presence, and of the end of the age?" Such was their question.

What did they mean by "these things," by "Thy coming," by "the consummation of the age?" One cannot believe that these men meant; When shall be Thy second advent? All that they were thinking of could only come by the way of the second advent, but they had no conception of it. The second advent must be prepared for fundamentally by the Cross and the Resurrection; and they had no apprehension of the Resurrection. He had told them again and again that He must suffer, and that He would rise again, but they had never grasped the truth of Resurrection, or consented to the necessity for the Cross. They were in revolt against the idea of the Cross, and blind to the fact of the Resurrection. So that if we take this question not in the way our Lord answered it, but in the way they asked it, we see

that they evidently thought that presently, in some way or other He would pass out of sight, perhaps would escape from this pronounced hostility of the rulers. And yet they had heard Him say, that the very scene before them was to be one of devastation and desolation; and they said, "Tell us, when shall these things be? and what shall be the sign of Thy coming, and of the consummation of the age?" If these things are to be, if this Temple is to be destroyed, if Thou art coming in judgment, how art Thou coming in judgment? when art Thou coming in judgment? Their question simply meant, When art Thou going to do these things?

To this question Christ gave the longest answer He ever gave to any question recorded in the New Testament. His answer occupies all that remains of chapter twenty-four, and all that lies within chapter twenty-five; and constitutes what we speak of as the prophecy on Olivet. Here Christ became a prophet in the predictive sense of the word. A prophet is a forth-teller of the Divine Will. He had been that, through all His ministry, but one element of prophecy, not the most important, but a most evident one, is the predictive element. Here Christ became a prophet in that sense. He had done this before, incidentally words had fallen from His lips which pointed to the future; but here, in quietness, speaking to His own disciples on Olivet in answer to their question, He spoke of things that were then wholly to come. How important a study this is, and how careful we need to be in proceeding with it.

In attempting to see the general outline of the prophecy we at once see that the question of these men was one which indicated their desire to look into the future, and Christ did not altogether rebuke that desire. He did warn them of the danger that beset investigation, yet He answered that desire so far as it was proper that it should be answered to inquiring and investigating minds. In our Lord's answer, we find, first, a warning; "And Jesus answered and said unto them, Take heed that no man lead you astray." This is not to be passed over lightly. When Christ adopted the predictive element in prophecy He warned His disciples lest they should be led astray. Whenever we speak of future things we are dealing with a matter full of importance, yet so full of peril that there have been all kinds of fanciful interpretations, all wandering from the clear declarations of Scripture, in order to fit in with some preconceived notions of future things, until we find in the Church of God to-day, vast numbers of God's own children, saints without a doubt, who have altogether given up any attention to what the Bible has to say concerning things to come. Christ knew this danger. These men came to Him in the supreme moment when the shadows were upon Him, and when the great strain was before Him, and they asked Him, Tell us something about the future? And His first word was, " Take heed that no man lead you astray." As we read these two chapters, we need that that warning should fall upon our spirits. " Take heed." We cannot read these things carelessly.

In the next place notice, in the reading of these chapters, the very evident and indeed most careful discrimination on the part of our Lord between the parts of their question, must be observed. Their question was one, as they asked it, and expressed in His hearing all the puzzling emotion of their minds. When they said to Him, " Tell us, when shall these things be? what shall be the sign of Thy presence, and of the end of the age? " they thought of these things as closely connected. One of the first things that we discover in the reading of the prophecy which followed is that Christ corrected the false impression. They said, " These things . . . the sign of Thy presence . . . and of the end of the age." He spoke of "these things," that is, the destruction of Jerusalem, which He had foretold; and then of the coming of the Son of Man, and of the consummation. He said, " Ye shall hear of wars and rumours of wars: see that ye be not troubled: for these things must needs come to pass; but the end is not yet;" the wars and the

rumours of wars, leading up to the destruction of Jerusalem, must come to pass, they were at hand; but He said, " The end is not yet."

Then notice how He separated His coming from "these things." He had been warning them against false Christs, those who should come in His name and declare, " Lo, here is the Christ," and in reference to that He said, " For as the lightning cometh forth from the east, and is seen even unto the west; so shall be the coming of the Son of man," which simply means that the coming of the Son of Man shall be clearly manifest. There shall be no need of prophets to announce the fact that He has come, or invite men to visit Him.

He continued by declaring that the coming of the Son of Man would be followed by the mourning of the tribes of the earth, and the gathering together of His elect, that is, of all Israel. He finally told them, that " of that day and hour knoweth no one, not even the angels of heaven, neither the Son, but the Father only." Thus He took the truth about the coming of the Son of Man, and removed it from the region of the destruction of the Temple.

It may be said that there are other senses in which He was spiritually present at the destruction of Jerusalem, and there is no doubt that that is so. Nevertheless, He separated His coming at the end of the age from the destruction of Jerusalem with great care, rather than associated it therewith.

He also declared, that these things of judgment and terror and tribulation and destruction, would be completed in connection with the destruction of Jerusalem. This principle of discrimination on the part of the King ran through all this prophecy. He corrected the false impression of His disciples. He discovered to them the fact that the things of immediate judgment, and the presence of the Son of Man, and the consummation of the age, were separate.

If this principle of discrimination be discovered we find that for general teaching this great prophecy of our Lord falls into three parts, and the three parts are not chronologically divided. He first showed them what the future had in store for Israel after the flesh. He then showed them what the future had in store for His Church, that is, Israel after the Spirit. He then showed them what the future had in store for the Gentile nations; and the divisions are most clearly marked. In verses five to thirty-five, the prophetic utterance concerned the excommunicated nation.

Beginning at verse thirty-six, "But of that day and hour knoweth no one," and running right on to the thirtieth verse of the twenty-fifth chapter, He was dealing with the responsibility of His Church as the spiritual Israel of God in the parables that teach the Church's position between the destruction of Jerusalem, and the ultimate gathering together of the elect at the coming of the Son of Man.

Finally in chapter twenty-five, verses thirty-one to forty-six, the King was looking on to the judgment of the nations. All this is in harmony with the teaching of the Old Testament and with the teaching of the whole Bible, in which it is evident that God deals with men, never by an election which is to the exclusion of any who will turn to Him, but by an election which is to service, in order that through the elect the light may flash, the message be delivered, and the ultimate purpose of God be realised.

Our last thought must be of the King Himself, and of the position He here occupied, quite alone on Olivet. Yes, the disciples were with Him; but are we ever quite so much alone as when people are around us who think they understand us, and do not? They did not understand Him; He was alone. The rulers had rejected Him, and while He sat on Olivet with His disciples they were planning and plotting for His life, and He knew it. His face was resolutely set towards the Cross, for He saw more than the Cross, He saw His victory, and God's victory. And yet for the moment He was alone. At that moment He knew the attitude of His enemies. They thought they were plotting in secret, but all was naked and open to His eyes.

He knew also the frailty of His friends, and how those men, eagerly inquiring for some glimpses into the future would presently, to the last man of them, turn their back upon Him. His Cross was just ahead, and yet behold Him on Olivet. Whether we understand all this prediction or not, let us come reverently into His presence. Here sat the King, despised and rejected, "a Man of sorrows and acquainted with grief." And yet He was looking through all the shadow to the light, looking beyond all the difficulties to the accomplishment. It is the King upon Whom our eyes are resting, Who, quite quietly, looking through all the darkness and difficulties in the future, saw His own crowning and His own vindication.

If He could so talk under the shadow of the Cross, then we can only be convinced again, as we ever must be convinced when we listen to Jesus only, that He is the Son of God as well as the Son of Man; Christ, in all the mystic meaning of that word which the New Testament writers perpetually convey.

A man whose claims were false, a man who had simply been deceived by the clamour of his own disciples, would break down in the presence of approaching death, when his disciples were about to leave him, and he knew it. But our King is seen intimately acquainted with the fact that all the powers of the world were against Him, that His own friends were so frail that they would forsake Him, and yet He quietly indicated the processes of the coming centuries. And if any one question His accuracy about the more distant things, at least let them remember that they do so while admitting that the things He said about immediate desolation and the actual destruction of the city were carried out to the very letter, within a little more than a generation from the moment in which He spoke.

And so again it is the King we see, in all His dignity, and to that King let us anew yield ourselves, and listen attentively that we may know how to serve the King, for it is certain that we can only serve Him, as we hear Him and understand His teaching.

MATTHEW XXIV. 1-44

SOME preliminary words are necessary before we attempt a brief survey of the long passage before us. This is a difficult part of our Gospel, where interpretation should be reverent, and where there should be a perpetual recognition of the fact that interpreters have differed, and still are differing. If that is recognized we may go forward.

Our attitude toward this prophecy of Christ must be largely determined by our attitude toward the prophecies of the Old Testament. That may be a somewhat startling thing to say, and yet our conception of the prophecies of the Old Testament, naturally, even though subconsciously, will affect our attitude toward this prophecy of Christ.

The standpoint from which we approach all the ancient prophecies, and consequently this prophecy of our Lord, is that all the things which the ancient prophets said concerning Israel which have not yet been fulfilled, will be fulfilled. This being so, it is also of supreme importance that we should clearly recognize that our Lord did finally reject the earthly people, and clearly declared that their responsibility for bringing forth the fruits of the Kingdom of God should be transferred to another nation.

Therefore we are to look for fulfilment, not in the rejected nation, but in the newly appointed nation, in which all of God's essential purposes are to be fulfilled, and through which His programme is to be carried out.

The present section is in some senses not of immediate interest to us, as it has a very small application to ourselves. Yet a clearer apprehension of it is of value in appreciating the next section, which reveals our present position and responsibility.

In the forty-fifth verse we read, "Who then is the faithful and wise servant, whom his lord hath set over his household, to give them their food in due season?" and that question takes us a good way back in our Gospel in order to explanation. At the close of chapter thirteen, when our Lord had been uttering the parables of the Kingdom, His last parable was the parable of the householder, and the householder's responsibility concerning the truths of the Kingdom which He had committed to His disciples. He spoke there of the disciples' new position as scribes instructed to the Kingdom, as that of the householder who brings "forth from his treasure things new and old." Now, in the midst of this great prophecy on Olivet, our Lord asked the question, "Who then is the faithful and wise servant?" and from that moment the prophecy which had been dealing with the earthly people passed to a revelation of the present responsibility of His own disciples and of the Christian Church, the spiritual Israel. From that question, at verse forty-five, through chapter twenty-five, to verse thirty, we have a section of the prophecy which deals with the Church's responsibility, the parable of the virgins and the parable of the talents. At verse thirty-one, we begin a third and final section of the great prophecy, "But when the Son of man shall come."

Our Lord first distinctly and carefully warned these men who asked the question with a warning that is of perpetual application and value. "Jesus answered and said unto them, Take heed that no man lead you astray. For many shall come in My name, saying, I am the Christ, and shall lead many astray." The fact that Jesus uttered this warning is in itself most significant. They had asked Him a question in a realm full of mystery, full of difficulty, in which it was very difficult indeed for them to follow His teaching, and He knew it; and He knew full well how in this very realm of the method of the interpretation of the ways of God in the future, there would be room for false Christs and false teaching; and so He first solemnly warned men.

Then He commenced to utter His prophecy as to the earthly people, Israel. He first spoke of things immediately at hand. "And ye shall hear of wars and rumours of wars: see that ye be not troubled: for these things must needs come to pass; but the end is not yet." Nothing can be clearer than that. He distinctly told these men standing round about Him, that they were on the eve of consternation and difficulty, but they were not to be troubled because, said He, "the end is not yet." Read that in the light of their question, "When shall these things be? and what shall be the sign of Thy coming, and of the end of the world?"

Through the discourses which followed, He was very careful to show that the end lay far away. But He clearly outlined the course of events then close at hand, that is happening within a generation.

Everything predicted from verse six to verse twenty-two was fulfilled to the letter in connection with the Fall of Jerusalem within a generation.

Having revealed these things, and shown that the destruction of the Temple was imminent, but that the "end" was not then, He told them what would be the manner of His coming. From beginning to end of the prophecy He emphasised the fact that none knew, nor could know, *when,* that coming would be, but the fact of it was certain.

Thus we come to those final words in verse forty-four, "Therefore be ye also ready: for in an hour that ye think not the Son of man cometh."

The day of vengeance for the world at large is yet to come, and toward that day our Lord was looking when in the final discourses on Olivet He talked of days yet to come, when the Son of man shall be manifested. To-day He is still the Servant Who does not cry, or lift up His voice. But He has another method, illustrated in the figure of the smoking flax and the bruised reed. Smoking flax is that which has the element of destruction within itself; the bruised reed is weakness weakened; and if we take the ancient prophecy, and look at that passage, we find it is a description, not of a penitent soul seeking mercy, but of a rebellious soul as it appears in the sight of God. Beyond the method of the gentle Servant Who does not cry or lift up His voice, is the method of the King Who quenches the smoking flax and breaks the bruised reed, and proceeds by judgment to ultimate victory. Our Lord here in quiet calmness on Olivet's slopes, with His own disciples and none other about Him, was looking on to the final movements. Beyond the method of His patience is the method of His power. Beyond these quiet years in which He suffers men and bears with them, and woos them and stands patiently waiting to deal with them in mercy, lies another day in which with fire and flame and flashing glory, by vengeance He will cast out all evil. The day will come when He will exercise the powers which are to-day restrained, held in check in the economy of infinite grace. As to the earthly people, the day of vengeance came with the destruction of Jerusalem. As to the world at large, it is yet to come.

MATTHEW XXIV. 45–XXV. 30

IN this second part of the Olivet prophecy of Jesus there are certain marked differences from the first, and from the third.

In this section, commencing with this question, "Who then is the faithful and wise servant?" and ending with the thirtieth verse of the next chapter, our Lord does not once refer to Himself as the Son of man. In the Authorised Version, in the thirteenth verse of the twenty-fifth chapter the expression does occur: "Watch therefore, for ye know neither the day nor the hour wherein the Son of man cometh," but the Revisers have omitted the last phrase, and there is no question that the omission is warranted. The title, "Son of man," was the one by which our Lord most often described Himself in the days of His earthly ministry. Indeed it may be said that He never called Himself the Son of God, save when it was necessary so to do in answer to criticism, or inquiry, or investigation of the deepest truth concerning

Himself. The title, "Son of man," was one which indicated His relation to the purpose of establishing the heavenly Kingdom on earth. It cannot be too often repeated that this was the purpose included in the mission of Christ. This is not for a moment to deny the fact that He came to seek and to save lost men individually in the deepest and profoundest evangelical sense of that word; so to change men, that when this probationary life is over, they shall enter into the home, and the joy, and the rest of the Divine presence. But if we think of the mission of Jesus as one simply of saving men here, in order that they may be ready for the life beyond, we have most strangely misread all that He ever said, and all He ever did, and taught men to pray for. The prayer taught in the Manifesto clearly sets forth the passion of the heart of Christ for the earth, as therein He taught His disciples to pray that the Kingdom might come, and the will of God be done, on earth as in heaven.

It is very significant that this title, "the Son of man," drops out of use in the writings of the New Testament. It is never found in the epistles. He is not therein referred to in this way at all. It is equally suggestive that it comes into sight again when we reach the Book of Revelation, the Book which, whatever present application it may have, surely does set forth in pictorial form the movements by which Babylon is to be destroyed, and the Kingdom of God is to be ultimately and finally established. There the title, "Son of man," reappears. In this particular prophecy the title appears in the first part; and again immediately at the thirty-first verse of the twenty-fifth chapter, when the third section is reached—"When the Son of man shall come in His glory."

Then again in this section there are no references to prophets, no references to the Temple, and no references to the Sabbath day; no references indeed, to any of those sacred signs and symbols of the old economy, which had indicated the truth concerning the government of God in the world.

The time of the employment of these means passed for ever away with the beginning of the age of His redeeming reign.

To turn from this negative survey to a more positive one; this passage consists of three parables, indicating the responsibilities resting upon His own, during a period in which He, as to bodily presence, would be absent from them. In these three parables there are marked similarities, and distinct differences.

Let us first observe the similarities between the three. In every parable there is an absent lord. In the first the lord of the household, who has committed certain duties to his servants, is absent. In the second, the bridegroom is waited for, but is absent. In the third, the lord is the owner of goods, and he has given talents to his servants, but is himself absent.

In the next place, there is the relation to him of those from whom he is absent. In the first they represented his authority; in the second their very waiting attested the fact of their belief in his return; in the third they prosecuted His commerce, with his goods; the talents which he gave to them are all his goods; not their ability, not their capacity, for a talent does not stand for quality, but for quantity in this parable.

Then again, it is evident in each of these parables that the responsibility of these servants is always to their lord, and to him alone. The servant of the household is responsible to none save the absent lord. The waiting virgins are only responsible to him. So also those to whom he gave the talents are responsible to him only.

Now let us notice the differences between the parables. These may not be so obvious, but they are very certain. The first parable is communal. It is the picture of His household in itself, while He is away. The, second is personal. It is a picture of individual souls in relation to Himself—the wise and the foolish. The last is imperial. It is a picture of the responsibility of those whom He has left behind for the carrying out of His enterprises in the world. The parable of the household, and of the two examples of servants set over it; the faithful and wise, and the wicked—is a parable wholly pertaining to the Church of God, as a household over which He is Lord and Master. The parable of the virgins, if we take the parable of the virgins as a whole, is one that indicates the true attitude of individual souls to Him in the days of His absence. The last is a parable which teaches the responsibility of His servants in His absence concerning His enterprises,—His goods, of which He gives them talents, that is measurements, quantities, that they with these may trade.

There is much of detail in this section, but we will take it as a whole, that the cumulative message of the three parables to Christian people may not be missed. Prophetic literature has lost its power to appeal to us, partly because we have been prone to trifle over details, instead of gathering up the great messages of Christ to His people. Therefore, in the broadest outline let us look at these parables, that we may catch the spirit of the messages, and understand the one great message to the Church of God in this age which lies between His ascension and His coming again.

In the parable of the household, the word itself is suggestive. Jesus said: "Who then is the faithful and wise servant, whom his lord hath set over his *household?*" The Greek word here translated household is only once again used. In Revelation we read that "the leaves of the tree were for the *healing* of the nations." What relation can there be between *healing* and *household?* This question can only be answered by an understanding of what this word household really signifies. It is the word from which we derive our word therapeutic, and the basal idea of it is healing. The word household refers to all such in the house as serve.

That first word, "Who then is the faithful and wise *servant?*" is the word bond-slave; but the word household comes from another term for servant, which is other than the word bond-slave. It is a word that signifies a loving service, a purpose of healing in service. This is a case of metonymy, where one word is put for another,

which the other suggests, as when we say a man keeps a good table, when we refer really to his food. This word in the parable, then, suggests the picture of a great house, and one Lord; and of all those in the house under His control, as thinking of His interests, while serving under His command. He used the word that indicated the love principle in service, the tender healing ministry that only grows out of love. Thus in a word, flaming and flashing with meaning, we discover our Lord's conception of His Church, during the time of His absence. His household all serve, but all serve by love, and the ministry is a healing ministry.

Now let us very carefully notice His word; "Who then is the faithful and wise servant, whom his lord hath set over his household?" This word must be interpreted by the consistent teaching of the Lord, that service is the condition of greatness. The servant is "set over." Why "set over"? Because he is a servant. This is not a picture of the priesthood, or of the ministry according to many modern conceptions of these. There is no sense in which any priesthood or ministry is set over the Church of God, save by their ministry. "Whosoever would be first among you, shall be servant of all." Here is Christ's picture of one servant set over the rest, because he serves all the rest. It is not a picture of any man in the household, it is not a picture of one in official authority; it is the picture of each one in the exercise of the ministry of healing and of love.

Now, in the parable we see two attitudes. First that of the faithful and wise servant. His attitude is simply that of bringing forth meat in due season, and feeding the rest; the attitude of caring for all the other members of the household during the Lord's absence, for the sake of the absent Lord. But there is another servant here, and Jesus speaks of him as "that evil servant." He says, "My lord tarrieth," He is not returning yet; and with that sense of the Master's absence, he turns to evil courses within the household, beating his fellow servants, instead of feeding and caring for them; turning aside to the companionship of drunken men, instead of standing in the place of loyalty to the absent Lord.

In the parable we have two results. When the lord returns, the servant who has been loyal to the service of his fellow servants, for the sake of his absent lord, is promoted and put into the place of a new authority; while the evil servant is cut asunder and cast out.

We must not attempt to carry these parables farther than they go. This is a picture first of all of a household, and the relation of all within it to the absent Lord. To gather it up we may state it thus. We shall prove our loyalty in the Church of God to the absent Lord, by the measure in which we serve one another; and we shall prove our disloyalty by the measure in which we beat and slay our brethren.

In the next parable there is a common hope, that of the coming of the bridegroom; but there are two attitudes. First the foolish. This is that of expectation—they "went forth to meet the bridegroom;" but of carelessness—"they took no oil with them." The details we pass over, and come to the end in order to see what this really means. To these the bridegroom says, "I know you not." There is nothing more. We must not confuse this with another parable in which men claimed a right to entrance upon a basis of work done. This is not a story of service, but of personal relationship. Apparent expectation, for they went to meet him! But no true expectation, for they took no oil with them. When presently they came to the door, according to the figurative and poetic language of the parable, and asked admission, there could be but one answer. It was the answer of a perfect justice, and a perfect knowledge, "I know you not."

Look upon the wise. Definite expectation; they "went forth to meet the bridegroom." So far apparently there was no difference. They all set their faces toward His coming; they all spoke as though they were interested in him; they all spoke as though

they desired to meet him. But these took oil. They said, The vigil may be long, he may not come so soon as may have been expected, and there must be provision for the waiting. These went into the marriage feast. This is a picture not of a particular section of Christendom, but of individual souls in their relation to Him. There is nothing here about a household, or any responsibility; this has to do with an attitude to Christ. The wise virgins are such as have no eyes, no thought, no care for anything except the Bridegroom, and the hour of His approach.

The last parable is concerned with enterprise; He "delivered unto them his goods." Mark His method. As we have already seen, the word talent here indicates quantity rather than quality. In our language we use the word as though it signified some special capacity or ability. But that is not the meaning of the parable, for mark this well, "unto one he gave five talents, to another two, to another one; to each according to his several ability." Ability is thus evidently something entirely separate from the talents. The talents were given according to the ability. In ability the question of measurement does not come in. That is a question of fitness. Out of His goods, His property, He gave to this man the amount of goods which he was able to make use of. And if we take up all the Pauline writings about gifts in the Church, we find this philosophy —He gives according to each man's ability; the gift of tongues, the gift of healing, the gift of prayer, the gift of prophesying, the gift of help; all are given according to ability. The principle revealed here is that the Lord and Master, Christ, never sets a man to preach who has not natural ability for preaching. We may do that sort of thing, but He never does. He never puts a man down to the oversight of the business enterprises of His Church, who lacks business enterprise. If we turn to the Ephesian letter, we find all these parables there. We find there first of all the household, "endeavouring to keep the unity of the Spirit in the bond of peace." We find loyalty, personal loyalty to the absent Lord.

"Put away . . . the old man . . . put on the new man." Walk as before Him. We find the business of the King prosecuted, "Buying up the opportunities, because the days are evil."

Now observe the different use of the talents. Fidelity; five produced five; two produced two. Infidelity; the one hidden by the man who attempted to silence his own conscience by traducing his absent Lord.

Mark the issues. The reward in the case of the man with five talents committed to him, and in the case of the man with two, are exactly the same. To each of these men Jesus said; "Well done, good and faithful servant, thou hast been faithful over a few things, I will set thee over many things." The reward of service is apportioned according to fidelity to opportunity.

In the case of the unfaithful servant; first his life was exposed; secondly, his talent was recalled; thirdly and finally, he himself was cast out.

With those broad, rough outlines of the three parables upon our mind, let us notice what they teach concerning the threefold responsibility of the Church.

Within her own borders the Church is to be a great household of mutual ministry. Is it possible to say a thing like that without having the heart saddened? The faithful servant is the one who cares for and feeds the other servants. The evil servant is the one who illtreats and beats his fellow servants.

In her own personal life the Church is to maintain an attitude of loyalty, of love to the Lord Christ. Her loyalty is to be tested by that very love; and her love is to be tested by her loyalty in the small things. How many of us have set our faces toward the East, and sing the song of His coming? But what is our attitude toward it? If we merely sing of it, and in our heart there are other loves, other desires, other aspirations, so that we neglect whatever may be typified by the oil; if we neglect attention to the details, the waiting of loyalty, then we are failing. But if indeed the lamps be trimmed and burning, and the oil be carried, then there is meaning in the song, and love for our Lord is demonstrated and proven.

The Church is responsible for the Master's work. He has committed to us His goods. There are many figures of the Christian life, but this is one which combines the commercial and imperial ideas. "His goods;" the things which He would have us represent to the age He has committed to us, the things of His Kingdom. All the light of the thirteenth chapter of Matthew flashes here; all the truth which culminated in that eighth and final parable in which our Lord said a scribe instructed to the Kingdom of heaven brings forth things new and old out of his treasures. What are the things? The goods of the absent Lord. His revelation of God and of man; His provision for man's great need; His perpetual call; His mediation; His dynamic for paralysed souls. We all have some of them committed to us; talents, five, two, one, according to our ability, and His choice; and these talents become our deposit. The mind reverts to the Pauline word, "I know Him Whom I have believed, and I am persuaded that He is able to guard." What? "That which I have committed unto Him." That is by no means necessarily the apostolic meaning. What, then? Hear Paul's own word, "*my deposit*," which may mean that which He had committed to Paul, and I think that the context proves that is what he did mean. That charge which He has given to us; that charge which made Paul say, I am debtor, I have something committed to me from the absent Master, with which I am to trade for Him; He is able to guard.

The Church has committed to her the goods of the absent Lord. What is she doing with them?

Notice, finally, in each case that the Church's responsibility is defined by her relation to her Lord. True to the absent Lord, the household is at peace. Waiting for the absent Lord, the lamps are burning, and individual character is what it should be. Working for the absent Lord, His goods are increased, and the five gain five, and the two, two.

So that whether it be the Church as a household, whether it be the Church in her individual membership, whether it be the Church as the great army carrying out His enterprise, everything depends upon her relationship to Him.

Thus we may turn the lessons of these parables back upon our own hearts, as each inquires, Oh soul of mine, what is thy relationship to thy Lord? If I am true to Him, I shall spend no time beating my fellow servants! If I am true to Him I shall be more careful that I have oil for the long vigil, than about anything else. If I am true to Him I dare not hide His talent, but must trade with it, that I may have wherewith to greet Him when He comes.

MATTHEW XXV. 31-46

THIS is the third and last section of the Olivet prophecy. In order to its interpretation we must first remind ourselves of its relation to the two previous sections, and of its relation to the whole message of the Gospel in which it is found. Then, moreover, we must be careful not to read into this section of the prophecy things which it does not contain; for while it has often been interpreted as though it were a description of the final judgment, it really has nothing whatever to do with the final judgment, that is with the Great White Throne.

When these things are seen we shall be able to understand the true meaning of this remarkable passage, and to examine the process which it so graphically describes.

Along these lines, therefore, we shall proceed, first examining the section in its relation to its context; secondly, attempting to see the events which the Lord refers to, in their place in His whole economy; and finally examining the process which it describes.

First, then, the relation of this section of the Olivet prophecy to its context. Jesus had come forth from the Temple, and we must bear in mind that in the Temple He had been dealing with those who were opposed to Him, whose opposition culminated in His own rejection and casting out. Coming from the Temple, He uttered that distinct prophecy of the destruction of Jerusalem and of that Temple. Then, presently, when they asked Him the question, "Tell us, when shall these things be, and what shall be the sign of Thy coming, and of the end of the age?" in replying, our Lord uttered the Olivet prophecy. Christ was standing in the midst of circumstances which were all against Him, from the standpoint of human observation. To all human seeming He was defeated. The opposition which had characterised the attitude of the rulers toward Him was succeeding, and in a very few hours their work would be complete, and they would have put Him away. Yet He stood in the midst of a group of loyal disciples. This was the first night He stayed near Jerusalem. As we have seen, He had been going down to Bethany, not staying in Jerusalem, and the very night that He did stay in the neighbourhood, He was arrested. He was on the verge of the final defeat, and yet He stood among that little group of men, the Master of Empire, quietly and with dignity surveying all the centuries, and telling these men in language which their finite minds could not perfectly comprehend, in language about which, until this day, we have not been able to say the last word, telling them the process, and the issue. There was not a shadow across the imperial brightness of His thinking; there was not a tremor in the accents of His voice. The King was looking through darkness to light, through defeat to the ultimate victory.

This third section of the prophecy He commenced with the words, "When the Son of man shall come in His glory," and then proceeded to describe what would happen at that coming among the nations.

But now let us set the whole prophecy in relation to the Gospel according to Matthew.

This Gospel is the Gospel of the King, and the theme is that of the Kingdom, the Kingdom not as a state into which men pass by death, but as a condition to be established on the earth. First of all in our Gospel the *King* was presented to our view. Then we had a great section describing His propaganda; He enunciated laws, He exhibited benefits, He enforced claims. Whether we study the laws, or consider the benefits, or listen to the claims, they all have to do with the earth. The laws of the Manifesto are not for life in heaven when a man has escaped this earth. The benefits existing are not benefits conferred upon the heavenly inhabitants; they are benefits for time and earth. The claims, as He enforces them, are claims of present Kingship, and present authority. Christ taught His disciples to pray, "Our Father Who art in heaven, Hallowed be Thy name. Thy Kingdom come. Thy will be done. Where? "As in heaven, so on earth." The passion of Jesus was for the setting up on earth of a divine order.

Do not misunderstand this. He has other work. He also takes all the ages and all the universe of God into the compass of His mind and His purpose. It reaches to the uttermost bound of the universe of God, and includes all the unborn ages. But for this earth Christ had a purpose, and for this world He had a passion, and all through the Gospel of Matthew He is seen dealing with this. When we come to this third section, we find, the rejection by men of God's King for the world. But if man rejects the King, God enthrones Him. Presently we see Him coming back from the dead, and standing on the slopes of Olivet with His disciples, we hear Him utter the commission according to Matthew. "All authority"—it is the word of the King—"hath been given unto Me in heaven and on earth." In the heaven, which is the pattern; on the earth, where the pattern is to be realised. "Go ye therefore, and disciple all the nations." Not make disciples of the nations. There is absolutely no warrant for such translation; there is no substantive in the verse—"Disciple the nations, baptizing them into the name of the Father, and of the Son, and of the Holy Ghost . . .

and lo, I am with you always, even unto the end of the world." There is not a word there about gathering out the Church, or electing a people for eternal purposes, or the salvation of the individual soul. Such truths are to be found in other places, but here the commission is, "Disciple the nations," that is, prepare them, influence them. The figures of the Manifesto are first salt, aseptic, preventing the spread of corruption; and then light, flashing upon the darkness. So the disciples were to be a presence in the world affecting the national life of the world. The King, Who had enunciated His laws, exhibited His benefits, enforced His claims, and been rejected, and was about to be cast out, stood in the midst of the little company of men who had crowned Him, and He said to them, This advent is not the last thing, this dying is not the end, this refusal to receive Me is not the consummation; the rough and bloody Cross which will be raised in a few hours is not the end; "When the Son of man shall come in His glory, and all the angels with Him, then shall He sit on the throne of His glory." The King was looking through the darkness of the accomplishing Passion to the light of the accomplished Purpose, and He described in this section, not the final judgment, not the last assize, not the great day, but the initial movement when He shall be manifested again.

Now let us look at the events as described. Notice first the matters which must be excluded, if we are to understand this prophecy. This is not the Great Assize, not the Great White Throne. The Son of man is not seen here as Judge, but as King. When we come to the wonderful language of Revelation we read, "And I saw a great White Throne, and Him that sat upon it, from Whose face the earth and the heaven fled away; and there was found no place for them. And I saw the dead, the great and the small, standing before the throne; and books were opened; and another book was opened, which is the book of life." There is not a single hint of this kind of thing here. The great Throne is not set; earth and heaven are not fled away, there is no resurrection of the dead; these are not dead people raised that are seen in front of the King.

What are the facts? The first is that the Son of man is on the Throne, which is a regal rather than a judicial throne. He speaks of Himself through all the processes as the King. "Then shall the King say . . . I was hungry, and ye gave Me to eat; I was thirsty, and ye gave Me drink." This is the word of the King, Whose person we saw in the first chapters, Whose propaganda we followed through the central chapters, to Whose passion we are now coming. It is the King, the Son of man on the Throne of His glory, in contrast to the Throne of His grace, which was the Cross. It is Christ's declaration that beyond all the things of the moment, which seemed to spell out defeat for Him, the Son of man will be manifested as occupying the throne.

The next fact is that of the Son of man manifested as holding the reins of earthly government. He shall gather about Him all the nations. The Son of man is the Administrator of the affairs of the earthly Kingdom, and this is His picture of the initial process in the consummation of that administration—the gathering of the nations, the separating between them, the finding of a verdict, and the passing of a sentence.

Now let us examine the process, and first we observe the centre of order, the Son of man upon His throne. This is the hope of the world.

We notice next the first exercise of His authority—the gathering of the nations. This does not at all necessarily mean that all the nations of the world are to be gathered to one geographical situation; it is the exercise of actual power on the part of Jesus, the gathering up of the nations into one great whole, Himself being the centre and reigning King. This is to be brought about by an actual advent. We cannot spiritualise these things without losing them. Having gathered the nations around His Throne He separates them, putting on the one hand those who are described figur-atively as sheep, and on the other those who are described figuratively as goats. This is the national separation. He first gathers the nations into one, so breaking all our present divisions and separations. But then He makes a new separation. It is a separation upon the basis of character—sheep and goats, to adhere to these words which are symbolic. In that hour the distinction between Englishmen, Frenchmen, Germans, and others, will be secondary. He will compel their attention to Him, demand their subjection, and having gained it, He will separate amongst them. What an hour of separation that will be in the history of the world; while all the lines of division which are so patent to-day, and in which some of us boast, will end, and end for ever. If a man sees God, he sees Christ's separation and Christ's division even now; he believes that fundamentally "He hath made of one every nation of men." The first process of the King will be thus to gather together, and then to institute a new separation, not between tribes and families and nationalities as in the past, but between those whom He designates sheep and goats.

Then He proceeds to explain the difference between the two, by the verdicts He finds, and the sentences He passes. The sentence of those on His right hand will be: "Come, ye blessed of My Father, inherit the kingdom prepared for you from the foundation of the world." That has nothing to do with heaven. That is earth. The King is seen establishing the earthly kingdom, and He calls righteous people to inherit it. It is the Kingdom of God. The King will say in effect; Go back to God's Divine intention. Enter into this world as God intended it should be when He made it. From the foundation of the world that Divine purpose was that humanity should constitute a theocracy, that God Himself should govern, and that men should owe and own allegiance to no one but Himself. When Christ comes He is going to set up that order.

Then He made very clear the basis upon which He will separate, and the reason upon which He will admit to this Kingdom. He said; "I was hungry and ye gave Me to eat." What did He mean? He told His disciples that the very people He would invite into His Kingdom would ask that question; What dost Thou mean? Wast Thou hungry, O Thou that sittest upon the Throne. When saw we Thee hungry? What was His answer? "Inasmuch as ye did it unto one of these My brethren, even these least, ye did it unto Me." What did our Lord mean when He spoke of His brethren? In the twelfth chapter of this Gospel we read, "While He was yet speaking to the multitudes, behold, His mother and His brethren stood without, seeking to speak to Him. And one said unto Him, Behold, Thy mother and Thy brethren stand without, seeking to speak to Thee. But He answered and said unto him that told Him, Who is My mother? and who are My brethren? And He stretched forth His hand towards His disciples, and said, Behold, My mother and My brethren! For whosoever shall do the will of My Father Who is in heaven, he is My brother, and sister, and mother." Now Christ was talking to this selfsame handful of men, telling them of the process when He comes and sets up His Kingdom; and He told them that He will say to those whom He gathers from the nations, "Inasmuch as ye did it unto one of these my brethren, even these least, ye did it unto Me." That is to say, nations will be admitted to the inheritance of the Kingdom upon the basis of their attitude toward Christ as revealed in their attitude toward His people during the preliminary period. Let us keep the perspective in view. The last commission given to these, His brethren, was to disciple the nations. Among the nations there are those who hear, obey, follow, receive, are at least sympathetic toward,—and in the measure in which the disciples of Jesus create that attitude, they are preparing for the establishment of His Kingdom in the world. And there before His throne He will receive all men of character whose attitude toward Himself has been defined by their attitude toward the brethren, not after the

flesh, but by that closer affinity of loyalty to the will of God.

Then He will turn to those upon the left, and reveal the righteousness of their exclusion from the order which He has come to set up; "Depart from Me, ye cursed, into the eternal fire, which is prepared for the devil and his angels," that is, into association with those who have destroyed the earthly order. They will not be admitted when the King commences His sifting operation, into the benefits of the Kingdom. Any of those who have been against the ideals and the character of the Kingdom, as they have been represented, will not be admitted.

This is the picture of a crisis initiating a new order and ending of a previous one. This is national judgment. The thought of personal retribution is not before us here, or of personal reward; it is that rather of Christ's sifting among the nations as He prepares for the setting up of the Kingdom. Exactly the same process goes forward. "I was hungry." Why, we never saw Thee, Lord of glory, hungry! "Inasmuch as ye did it not unto one of these least." I have sent through all these centuries into your countries and among your peoples, My brethren, souls living in the will of God, My witnesses; and I have sent them not merely that men may be saved, but that you may see the ideal of God's government in the world. You would not receive them, you have neglected them, and in neglecting them you have neglected Me. Therefore you cannot enter into the Kingdom. "These shall go away into age-abiding punishment; but the righteous into age-abiding life." The terms are co-equal in value, and whatever one means the other means. Only remember that here Christ is not dealing with the subject of the soul's destiny either in heaven or in hell. They are terms that have to do wholly with the setting up of the Kingdom here in this world, and those methods by which He will assume the reins of government, excluding some and including others.

Now to summarize. This section of the prophecy describes in broad outline, and as to underlying principle, how the King, to quote His own words as they appear in the parables of the Kingdom in the thirteenth chapter, "will gather out of His Kingdom all things that cause stumbling, and them that do iniquity;" and thus prepare for that new era in which "the righteous shine forth as the sun in the Kingdom of their Father."

Before turning to the application of this to ourselves as to personal responsibility, let us be clear as to the solemnity of these words. It does not minimise the solemnity of the words, to deny that this story has anything to do with the Great Assize, or the Great White Throne, or the settlement of the eternal destiny, and to accept the picture as a simple prophetic portrayal of what will happen in connection with the second advent.

When looking at anything in perspective down a long distance, it is always difficult to dissociate the far from the near. When studying the Old Testament prophets we find constantly that the prophet described as he saw things coming, and yet he seemed to bring together things which we have found far apart. One prophecy only in instance of it—"To proclaim the year of Jehovah's favour, and the day of vengeance of our God." As the ancient prophet uttered it seems as though the two things were close together, but when Jesus came He said, "To proclaim the acceptable year of the Lord," and He shut the book, and nineteen centuries have gone and the final day of vengeance has not begun yet. We must allow for perspective. There may be an order, a development, a programme, but it would not appear that any one has found it out accurately. But quite simply this is Christ's picture. He is the King. Men have

said, We will not have Him, they will drive the nails and break His heart, and fling Him out. And He said to the little group around Him, "The Son of man shall come in His glory . . . then shall He sit on the throne of His glory." And when He comes there will not be merely pity, but power; not merely mercy, but might; not merely the gathering-in tenderness of such as need His help, but the flinging out in stern severity of all that which is against the eternal principles of right. In the words of the Christ, He will "Gather out of His Kingdom all things that cause stumbling, and them that do iniquity." What for? In order that "the righteous" may "shine forth as the sun in the Kingdom of their Father;" not in heaven, but here on the earth.

Finally this picture flashes its light back upon our last study and reveals anew to us our responsibility. Within the household we are to be obedient to the absent Lord. As individuals we are to be ever waiting for His coming. As His representatives we are to be prosecuting His commerce in the world, trading with the Master's goods, gathering men one by one to the living Christ for personal salvation; living and witnessing by life so as to create an atmosphere, an influence, a testimony which shall be the opportunity for men everywhere to see and know something of the Kingdom, and so to prepare the way for His coming, that when He comes He may enter into an inheritance which we have created for Him, far wider than that of the individual souls gathered, an inheritance of an influence created, and a test made by which nations shall be admitted to, or excluded from, the Kingdom as He shall establish it.

MATTHEW XXVI. 1-30

THE last three chapters of this Gospel admit us to the final things in the mission of the King. If ever it is fitting that we should put off our shoes because the ground is holy, it is so as we read these stories. Here the Passion of God, and the passions of men

come into conflict and communion. It is apparently a strange contradiction, and yet it is a truth which stands revealed in the story that we are now to study, the last story. Jesus had demonstrated His authority and His power in the realms material, mental, and moral, as the one and only King commanding our loyalty by His inherent royalty. And now we are to see Him moving through those scenes which so perplexed and puzzled His early disciples, moving through defeat —not to defeat; moving through darkness, through pain, through all the things that men most fear and dread and attempt to escape, yet never losing His dignity, never losing that imperial magnificence which has been so manifest in the earlier movements of the book.

In the section which we are now to study, perhaps not observed upon the surface, but most evidently set forth when the section is carefully considered, the supreme fact is the authority and power of the King. To briefly summarise what seems to be the content and message and portion of this passage, it is this. " No man taketh My life from Me. . . . I lay it down of Myself." We see here the King hemmed in, surrounded; and yet arranging for the hemming-in, manipulating by the strange and mystic might and majesty that overwhelms us as we look, all the forces that seem to be against Him, compelling them to act at His divine command, in His way, for the fulfilment of His own purpose.

May the Spirit of God, Who searcheth all things, yea the deep things of God, baptize us into solemn awe, and enlighten our minds and hearts, as we approach this last section of the Gospel.

The whole section falls into three parts. The first chronicles for us the preliminary things, and that is the section at which we are now to look. Let us divide it into three parts. We have first of all the King's approach to His passion. He tells His disciples that, after two days, He will be crucified. While He is telling His disciples this, the Sanhedrim is meeting somewhere else, plotting to take Him.

Then follows that exquisite and matchless story of the Supper at Bethany, chronolgcially out of place here, of which fact there is internal evidence. The story opens by Christ's declaration, " After two days." The

story in the Gospel of John begins, " Six days before the Passover," so that quite evidently the story recorded happened four days before Christ told His disciples definitely that in two days He would be crucified. It is here out of chronological order, but it is given in explanation of how things came to pass according to the word of Jesus.

Finally, we have the story of the Passover Feast, and the institution of the new memorial feast. Everything ends with the declaration that they went out after the singing of a hymn, to the Mount of Olives.

Before considering these separately, let us notice their inter-relation. First we have the declared determination of Christ, the word of Jesus to His disciples. He said to them, " Ye know that after two days the Passover cometh and the Son of man is delivered up to be crucified." Then we have the record of the determination of the rulers. There is a point of oneness; and there is a point of difference. The Sanhedrim was an official religious court, and it was gathered together in its official capacity in the court of the high priest; it was a gathering together of the whole movement of opposition. " They took counsel together that they might take Jesus by subtlety and kill Him. But they said, " Not during the feast, lest a tumult arise among the people." He said, " After two days the Passover cometh, and the Son of man is delivered up to be crucified." They said, " Not during the feast;" He said, Crucified during the feast. The determination of the rulers, and the determination of Christ, agreed as to His death, differed as to the time.

Now Matthew turns aside from the sequence of events in order to tell how it came about that He was right, and not they, as to the time. Four days before, Mary had found her way to His feet, and had anointed Him. Matthew tells us the story of that anointing, and of how Judas went out from that gathering at Bethany to the priests. Thus probably four days before Christ said He would be crucified, Judas had covenanted with them, had received from them the thirty pieces of silver, and for four days he had carried them about with him, for four days he had watched his opportunity. The counsel of the priests had said not till after the feast be over, and Judas was charged, no doubt, by the rulers not to precipitate matters, but quietly to wait until the Passover was over and the crowds had gone. Then Christ compelled Judas to act at once. Having said, "One of you shall betray Me," and having indicated the one, John tells us that He said to him, "What thou doest do quickly." Judas, acting under that compulsion, finding that he was discovered, without any repentance in his soul, hastened to the priests, hastened and obtained a company of men, and, not according to the will of the rulers, but before they intended, he had precipitated the arrest and trial of Christ in the midst of the Passover feast.

Thus we see the King deliberately moving towards the end of His set purpose, but not allowing the rulers to choose the hour, or the method; by His own quiet and deliberate act putting the right hand of His supreme authority upon all their counsels, and bringing it to effect His purpose; dragging their crafty subtlety from the lurking-places of their deceit into the clear light, as He drove Judas out to do his dastardly work, at the hour of God's appointing, rather than at the hour of the rulers' choice. Such is the relation of this part of the story to the movement of preparation.

Now let us look at things a little more carefully.

Look first at the two forces moving toward the death of Jesus. After the Crucifixion, and after the Resurrection, and after Pentecost, Peter stood up and began to preach in the power of the outpouring of the Spirit, and as he looked out upon those masses of people before him, and saw amongst them rulers, He said, "Jesus of Nazareth, a Man approved of God unto you by mighty works and wonders and signs, which God did by Him in the midst of you, even as ye yourselves know; Him, being delivered up by the determinate counsel and foreknowledge of God. ye by the hand of lawless men did crucify and slay." Mark the two

things that Peter recognized. "Delivered up by the determinate counsel and foreknowledge of God." That is one side of the story. And the other, "Crucified by the hands of lawless men." Here is the historic fact in Christ's approach to the Cross. Here in a mystery which almost overwhelms us, we see God and sin combining towards one goal.

Look at the King. He was moving towards His Cross. One might almost say leisurely, for notice, "When Jesus had finished all these words, He said." His was the leisure that had in it no unrest, no haste, no friction. "When He had finished all these words." How often they had tried to arrest Him. How constantly He had said, "My hour is not yet come." "Go and say to that fox, Behold, I cast out demons and perform cures to-day and to-morrow, and the third day I am perfected;" when I am ready I shall be perfected. "When He had finished all these words." His teaching was not complete until He had said the last word, until He had not merely enunciated the ethic given at the commencement of His ministry, until He had not merely uttered the glorious and prophetic instructions to His own, but until He had also uttered the mysterious and marvellous prophecy on Olivet. "When He had finished, He said"—and no hand could arrest Him until He was ready. That man has never read these stories thoroughly who says that Jesus Christ was a victim of circumstances and men. He was the Master of circumstances and of men.

Thus we see this Galilean, this Man, lacking in all the things that men count great, moving in the midst of circumstances that seem to hem Him in, and master Him, and beat Him; and yet as we look at Him, His hand is upon them all, and with quiet leisure and definite intention, and intelligent purpose, unafraid, and unsurprised, He moved towards His Cross.

There in the court of the high-priests was the Sanhedrim. They were also moving towards the Cross. It was the final gathering, and they were attempting to encompass His death officially. It was a crafty gathering.

They saw He must die, but they were not quite sure of time and place. The only thing to avoid is the feast. "Not during the feast."

Thus grace and sin were moving toward the same sad end; grace in the person of God's King planning for the Cross; sin in the person of the rulers plotting for the Cross. As we look back upon those two scenes, of the Christ in the midst of His disciples, of the rulers at the palace, they were as far apart as heaven and hell, as love and malice, as right and wrong, as clear open action, and crafty devilish deceit. Yet both were moving toward the one end. As we read the story again, and the two pictures become impressed upon our mental vision, we see the Lord high and lifted up, His train filling the Temple, and we learn anew the meaning of the old Psalmist's declaration,

" Surely the wrath of man shall praise Thee:
The residue of wrath shalt Thou gird upon Thee."

This was no human Teacher to be bruised and beaten at man's choice. It was the King, with His hand upon circumstances, governing the Sanhedrim, letting them work out their own nefarious designs, and yet so high seated over all, that presently He took the spear of their uttermost malice, and bathed it in the blood of God's uttermost grace. So He approached His Cross.

Then let us look at this picture of the Supper at Bethany—the action of Mary and the action of Judas. We will not now go into the details of these stories, all the touches of exquisite beauty in the action of Mary; and all the lines of red and flaming fire that frighten us when we come to Judas. But with the general impression of these two things upon our minds, let us notice carefully how the instruments were the instruments of grace and of sin. Mary was the instrument of grace. Judas was the instrument of sin. In the story we see shining about the Master a great light, and deepening over Him a great darkness. There is the light of Mary's love.

There is the darkness of Judas' treachery. These two people were also moving toward His Cross, she with a love that went beyond death, anointing Him for burial; he with a hate that merred all things in death, arranging for His death. The contrast is vivid. This woman got nearer to the inner heart of Jesus than any human being prior to Pentecost. When she brought that alabaster cruse and poured some ointment on His head and some on His feet, the whole company of the disciples, and not Judas only, murmured, they all said, Why this waste? What a revelation of apostolic incompetence was that question. Quite kindly one may say, and yet with tremendous conviction, one would rather be in succession to Mary than the whole crowd of apostles. Mary saw into His soul; not that she perfectly knew all the meaning; but she saw in His eyes the shadow of the coming suffering and the Cross. A mutual sympathy was there, hers for Him and His for her. Maybe Mary looked at Him sitting there in Simon's house, and she thought in her soul, there is a shadow in His soul, the end is near; I wonder if I can do anything to let Him know that at least I have touched the fringe of His garment of sackcloth. Love is always prodigal. Love overlaps all the bounds of prudence, and gets the most precious thing in the house and pours it out. It was a sacrament of sympathy, but it will not be a perfect picture unless He knows. Sympathy must be answered by sympathy. Love like this must have the answer of love. He said, "In that she poured this ointment upon My body she did it to prepare Me for burial. Verily I say unto you, Wheresoever this Gospel shall be preached in the whole world, that also which this woman hath done shall be spoken of for a memorial of her." That is the only time Christ ever suggested the raising of a memorial to any one, and the memorial He suggested was not a memorial of marble or of gold, not of a temple upon which old Time will act until it crumbles its magnificence to the dust. It was a memorial of a fragrance; and earth is sweeter, and heaven richer, for Mary's love and Christ's acceptance of it. There was no tremor in His voice, " She did it to prepare Me for burial." He was arranging, manipulating, mastering evil; and He gathered up the sweet and precious fragrance of a devoted love. It was dear to Him and precious, and He said, It shall be her memorial. Thank God for that light in the darkness. Thank God there was one heart came somewhere near to Him, one frail woman, despised as sentimental by the apostles, who poured upon Him an ointment that makes heaven finer for its rich and rare aroma.

And then the darkness is revealed in Judas' lack of sympathy. He had no sympathy for Mary, because he had no sympathy for Jesus. Observe his selfishness and his act of baseness. No comment is necessary; in such brief words we leave it.

Finally we come to the Passover. Here we see the perfecting and passing of the old economy, and the beginning of the new. The Passover was observed, the feast of deliverance from slavery, the feast of the exodus, the feast of hope. Men had kept it fitfully through the long centuries, regularly at first, and then occasionally through the age of decadence. The King sat down to keep it as one of that nation and people. That was its last keeping in the economy of God, because all that it had foreshadowed was fulfilled as He sat at the board, and all that to which it had pointed found the ultimate fulfilment in Him. He completed that of which the exodus had been but the preparation. The final exodus came by the way of that Cross to which He was going.

Then, still sitting there in the midst of the feast of a past and failing dispensation, at a board where there was still the unfermented wine of the Passover feast, and where there was still the unleavened cake fragments remaining, He instituted a new feast. He took bread, some of that which was there, and broke it, and said, " Take, eat; this is My body." He took the cup and said, " Drink ye all of it; for this is My blood of the covenant, which is poured out for many unto remission of sins." Jesus was at the Passover board, and He took the Passover bread, and the cup of the old economy of anticipation; but as His hands touched that Passover bread, He made all things new; as His hand took hold upon the Passover cup, He made it flush with the new glory of a new dawn, and a new age, and a new dispensation. In the simplicity of this picture we see the establishment of the Christian feast.

There are three things we need to remember concerning it. It is a commemoration. Christ said, " This do in remembrance of Me." It is more than a commemoration, it is a communion, in which, through all the coming age, bands of His disciples shall sit down and take bread and fruit of the vine, and in the sacred material act enter into an actual and spiritual communion with Him. It is more, it is a covenant, declaring that those who sit at the board are made one with Him in all the enterprises of His heart. The old Passover feast was the feast of the exodus, and was a feast of hope. The new is the feast of the exodus, but the exodus that He has accomplished, which no longer fills the heart with hope, but with the certainty of an already achieved victory. When men and women gather through the ages around that board, it is to remember Him, it is to commune with Him, it is to pledge themselves in loyalty to Him. Never let us forget that. Away behind ecclesiastical Rome is pagan Rome, and there among the ruins of pagan Rome we still see upon the fresco the Roman soldier taking his sacramentum. This is our Sacramentum, our oath of allegiance to live and fight and die for this King.

Thus symbolically He led His disciples through the shadows of darkness into the sunlight of a new morning. How simple it was; at the end of the Passover feast. He touched the old bread and it broke into infinite sustenance for the world; He put His hand upon the old cup, and out of it came the red wine of the Kingdom of God. When we sit in simple symbolism around the table let us never forget that He is there, the King Himself.

"And when they had sung a hymn they went out into the Mount of Olives." There is no doubt whatever that they sang the great Hallel. And if we turn back to Psalms 113-118 we find exactly what they sang. They sang the first two of those hymns, Psalms 113 and 114, at the commencement of Passover; the psalms which tell of Jehovah the high and the humbled One, a song of the exodus, how He led them out of Egypt into Canaan. Think of Jesus sitting at that last Passover Supper, singing those two Psalms before the Passover, and see how exquisitely they fit and perfectly fall in with all those thoughts that are in our mind. Then Psalm 115 begins,

"Not unto us, O Jehovah, not unto us. But unto Thy name give glory."

That speaks of Passion for the glory of God.

Psalm 116 is the story of a passing through death to life and service.

Psalm 117 is the psalm of universal praise following upon that passing through death to life and service.

Psalm 118 has as refrain,

"His lovingkindness endureth for ever,"

That was the last note of the song.

And when they had sung that hymn they went out to the Mount of Olives. Thus the King came to the darkness of the Cross singing of the enduring lovingkindness of God.

MATTHEW XXVI. 31-56

WITH reverent reticence we have now to follow the King through Gethsemane. We cannot attempt to interpret the sorrows of Christ as they are suggested to us by this narrative; from beginning to end of the meditation we shall but walk around the margin, stand on the outside of the darkness, and come to know in a very faint and far-off way all that is revealed in this story of Agony.

Let us notice, however, that in this passage there are again three subdivisions, and let us make Christ the centre of all our meditation. The disciples are here; we shall see them incidentally; we are bound to do that; but let us fix our reverent thought upon the Lord Himself as He is seen in this matchless picture.

First we stand in the vestibule of that inner shrine and sanctuary of sorrow to which the Lord came under the shade of the Olive trees in Gethsemane. Standing there, we see Christ preparing His disciples for what was then immediately to follow.

Then, in the central section of the passage, we pass to the inner sanctuary of sorrow, and there Christ is seen alone. The disciples are there also, but their presence but emphasises the fact of His absolute and desolate loneliness.

Then finally, we have a picture of Christ triumphant.

We come first to the vestibule of the sanctuary. It was night. The moon was at the full, as we know by the feast that was being observed. There had been that strange and wonderful gathering in the upper room, the passing of the old feast and the institution of the new. They had sung a hymn, the Hallel Psalms, and the song was in their minds as they had gone forth from the upper room, along the streets and out by the road, until they came to the slopes of Olivet and found their way into *the enclosed place*. Such is the meaning of the word Gethsemane. How strangely they had been perturbed, and perplexed, and puzzled by the things He had said. They had asked Him, "Whither goest Thou?" and He had answered them in what seemed to be emphatic terms, of going to the Father, but He had failed to give them any geographical description of His goings. Now He was going and they were accompanying Him. Suddenly the silence of that walk toward Gethsemane was broken by Christ Himself. Turning to this group of men He said, "All ye shall be offended in Me this night: for it is written, I will smite the shepherd, and the sheep of the flock shall be scattered abroad."

His first words told them of the darkness which was just ahead. Maybe they were hoping that He had done with the strange and troublous things since Judas had left the company. But now He looked at the eleven that remained, and said, You will all be scandalized in me this night, made to stumble in Me; I shall be the object over which you will fall; you will all be offended in Me, for it is written, I will smite the shepherd, and the sheep of the flock shall be scattered abroad. He knew the darkness far better than they, and He told them of the worst thing that was coming to them, that the whole of them would be offended. Yet it was not the voice of a fatalist, but of One Who told them whither they were inevitably moving, of One conscious of a pre-arranged programme. These men were familiar with the Old Testament Scriptures; they knew full well the great prophecy of Zechariah from which the quotation was made. And He said, This is the night of that smiting and scattering. No accident is happening to-night; this is part of a divine plan and movement. How constantly He said, "It is written," or, the Scriptures have foretold. And so, while the shadows were deepening about them, He told them of the deeper darkness, and of the fact that they were going into a darkness so profound as to scandalize, and drive them away.

But that was not all. He was preparing them by giving them to know before they should be offended, that He knew they would be offended. Christ was always making it easy for these men to get back presently; and when He told them the worst that was in them, and they did not believe Him; though they all personally declared they would not be offended, He did not argue; but He left something in the heart, and mind, and memory, which, returning presently, would make it easier for them. It is a great thing to be able to say within one's own soul, Well, my friend knew and warned me, I will go back to Him. Christ was telling them the worst. But not only the worst. Mark the next words well, words flashing with light, "But after

I am raised up, I will go before you into Galilee."

Christ was on the way to Gethsemane with this little group of men, frightened souls, not knowing what was going to happen next, wondering what He meant, sadly disappointed He had not forced things to an issue and set up a Kingdom; brokenhearted because they thought He was going to be murdered; and He said, "All ye shall be offended in Me this night. . . . but after I am raised up I will go before you into Galilee." Your scattering is not the last thing, there will be a gathering; My defeat is not the end, there will be a raising up; this darkness is not finality, there is light beyond it.

Peter's answer was the protestation of love and of ignorance; "If all shall be offended in Thee, I will never be offended." Jesus said unto him, "Verily I say unto thee, that this night,"—and then to emphasise the immediateness of it—"before the cock crow, thou shalt deny Me thrice." And Peter replied, "Even if I must die with Thee, yet will I not deny Thee."

The King Himself was quiet and calm, full of tenderness for these frail men. He had no rebuke for them, but a solemn warning of what was coming, so definite and positive, that there could be no mistake. The one thing He was impressing upon them was His knowledge. Peter said in effect; If I do not know myself, who does know me? The one thing a man does not know is himself, and that is what we find out when we see Christ with His disciples. Peter meant it, "I will never be offended in Thee;" he was absolutely sincere; but he did not know himself, he did not know his weakness or his power, he did not know the forces coming against him, he did not know how dark the darkness could be, or how terrible the temptation might become. He was perfectly honest. But Christ knew him, Christ knew that beneath all that wonderful devotion which was so precious to His heart, in the very strength of his nature lay his weakness, the passionate man, impulsive, fiery, like a thunderstorm; He knew under stress of great temptation that he could and would deny. The King was calm and tender toward His disciples. They, while loving Him, were nevertheless perplexed and blundering.

Then we pass into Gethsemane. The presence of the disciples throughout this section but serves to intensify the realisation of His loneliness. Notice how He passed to loneliness with them. He took eleven of them from the upper room, and having come to the garden, eight of them were left either outside its gate or perhaps just inside. Three of them were taken yet a little further with Him; they were the boanergic men, Peter, James, and John. They were the men who had been with Him on the Mount of Transfiguration. They were the men who had been with Him in the house of Jairus when He raised the maiden. They were the men who for some reason or other He perpetually took a little nearer to Him than the rest. It is almost uniformly held that they were an elect inner circle, and that He trusted them more, and could say more to them. One cannot be at all convinced of that. Perchance they were the weakest three of the twelve, and therefore it was necessary for Him to keep them near to Himself. Perhaps the man who never has a vision is stronger than the man who gets his vision. Presently, in the light of our Lord's revelation of Himself in the Father's home, we may find that the people who always seemed to be left at the gate and never had a flaming vision, and no high ecstatic experience, but who have quietly pursued the line of commonplace devotion, are stronger than the others. It is recorded that a long time ago a nun was dreaming that she saw three other nuns at prayer, and she imagined that as they were at prayer she saw the Master Himself coming, passing by them. The first of them He brushed by almost rudely without a glance or touch. To the second He spoke some brief word as He passed, but with the third He lingered, and laid a caressing hand upon her head, and with His face all wreathed in smiles, whispered some word of infinite love in her ear. And in her dream the nun thought to herself, How the Master loves that last woman; the second must have grieved

Him somehow; and with the first He must be very angry. Then in her dream she thought the Master turned to her and said, O woman of the world, how wrongly hast thou judged. The faith and trust and obedience of this first woman is so perfect that I can train her for higher service than the others can ever attain. The last one needs all my attention or she would never follow at all. Perhaps Peter, James, and John were of that sort. He took these three men, yet they were unable to go with Him all the way. He asked them to watch, and then going still a little further He prayed.

Next let us notice the terms that are used here about our Lord. He "began to be sorrowful and sore troubled." We have seen that word "began" twice before in this book of Matthew about Jesus. In chapter four, He began to preach. In chapter sixteen, He began to tell His disciples that He must suffer. Now He began to be sorrowful and sore troubled. This word, "sore troubled," is a strange word. Nothing can be definitely said as to its derivation. It may have come from two words. Most probably it has come from one that means "away from home," He began to be sorrowful and away from home. It means more than that, of course; but that is the root idea, that of desolating loneliness. He began to enter into that consciousness of His absolute isolation. When He began His ministry the crowds were with Him. They had left Him long ago. When He began His ministry the rulers were interested, they now were plotting for His death, and He knew it. He had gathered about Him a band of disciples, a large company, more than twelve; but there came a day when He tried to teach them spiritual things concerning bread that comes out of heaven, and from that time many of His disciples went back and walked no more with Him. But at least there are twelve. No, one of them is now out somewhere, bringing the mob. But at least there are eleven? No, eight of them were left at the gate. But at least there are three? No, they will all be asleep in half an hour. He began to be sorrowful and away from home. And then He spoke of it. How seldom He spoke of His sorrow! But He said to these men, "My soul is exceeding sorrowful." And here we have another word that arrests the attention. He "began to be *sorrowful*" is one word. Then "He said My soul is *exceeding sorrowful*." That is the same word with a prefix which gives emphasis to it. It means, My soul is the centre of surging sorrows, and He said to them, "Abide ye here, and watch with Me." It was His last appeal to humanity, His last appeal to His disciples.

Then we go a step further with Him. We can do nothing more with this threefold prayer than notice three of the simplest things about it. Three times He prayed. First, He said, "My Father, if it be possible, let this cup pass away from Me: nevertheless, not as I will, but as Thou wilt." The second time He did not ask that if it be possible the cup should pass, but He consented to the impossibility, "My Father, if this cannot pass away, except I drink it, Thy will be done." The third time He said the same thing.

Mark the first prayer most carefully. In the presence of it, one is inclined to think that there was a shrinking there had never been before, yet it is not a prayer that the cup may pass, it is a prayer that God's will may be done. Notice first of all, His recognition of His abiding relation to God, "My Father." We hardly dare venture to try and illustrate from our own experience because there is a gulf between His sorrow and ours that never can be bridged. And yet, seeing it is the Man Christ we are looking at, may we not venture to say, It is in the moment of overwhelming agony that the soul is tempted to doubt God's love and goodness. But with all the surging sea of sorrow surrounding Him, and His intense loneliness filling His heart, His sense of relation was unbroken; as yet there was no obscuring of the face of God. And then the request. First the condition, "If it be possible let this cup pass away." And the final prayer, "Nevertheless, not as I will but as Thou wilt."

Again He speaks. The relation is unchanged, "My Father"—and there is a recognition of the impossibility of the passing of the cup—"if this cannot pass," and the same great prayer ascends, "Thy will be done."

The final attitude was that of the repetition and ratification of abandonment to the will of God. What did Christ pray for in the garden? That God's will might be done. What is the meaning of this shrinking? The last shadow of temptation. To go back in the story of His ministry to the things we have already seen; long ago in the wilderness, the enemy, in open guise, unveiled before the eyes of the Christ, the kingdoms of the world and said, If Thou givest me one moment's homage I will make them over to Thee. This was a suggestion that He might gain the kingdoms without the passion. That was the first temptation. It was in open guise in the wilderness, and with quiet, calm dignity and absence of perturbation, the answer was, "Thou shalt worship the Lord Thy God, and Him only shalt thou serve." That was at the beginning of public ministry.

Then at Cæsarea Philippi the same temptation, no longer voiced by the enemy in open guise, but voiced by the devil disguised in an apostle, "He began to show unto His disciples, that He must go unto Jerusalem, and suffer —and be killed, and . . . be raised up." And the apostle said, Not that, Lord, "Be it far from Thee." And eight days after, or thereabouts, with the glory of the mount flashing upon Jesus, the same apostle had made as great a blunder when he said, "It is good for us to be here," which meant, Not the Cross, but the mountain of glory, Lord. Get the Kingdom, but miss the Cross. He refused the temptation with greater severity in the case of the apostle when the devil was in disguise, than in the case of the devil when he was in open vision. "Get thee behind Me, Satan: thou art a stumbling-block unto Me: for thou mindest not the things of God, but the things of men."

Now in Gethsemane the devil is not there in open guise; the apostle is asleep; but the shadow of it all is upon the soul of Christ, "If it be possible, let this cup pass away from Me." To go back outside the garden for a moment. He had said to these men, You will all be offended in Me this night; but after I am raised up I will go before you into Galilee. That is to say, I am going through the passion, but I am coming to the Kingdom. I must set up this Kingdom. The will of God must be done. I must leave you, but you who will be scattered will also be gathered. Now, alone, the last disciple away, He looked again toward the light beyond. The darkness was around Him, and the cup, this mystery of a sorrow that we cannot understand, this cup, this sacrament of infinite sorrow, was presented to Him. The shadow of the passion was upon Him, and with it came the shadow of a great temptation; "If it be possible, let this cup pass away from Me." If that had been all; if He had halted! But He did not halt! Quick, sharp, immediate, resolute, followed the words; "Nevertheless not as I will, but as Thou wilt." In that moment He took the cup, took it finally, took it alone, took it as He had taken it against the devil's temptation, and the apostle's suggestion, took it in the desolating loneliness, because it was the will of His Father. All this is but an unveiling, that we may see something that is too great for human explanation. It is the unveiling of the passion and agony of God Himself in the presence of human sorrow. We cannot read this story without feeling somehow or other that it is too difficult to see. It does seem as though at least there was a breach, a difference, between this Man and God. Yet there never was a difference, never a shadow of a difference. Jesus was never more God Incarnate than when He was in Gethsemane; and at the back of all we see that which we can never fathom—God's heart broken in the presence of human sin.

At last He came to His disciples and He said, "Sleep on now, and take your rest; behold, the hour is at hand, and the Son of man is betrayed into the hands of sinners." "Arise, let us be going." These two verses have caused some difficulty. A great many of the old expositors declare that when He spoke to them of taking their rest He spoke satirically. That is impossible. Satire had its place in His method, it had often played like summer lightning, clearing the atmosphere. But this was no satire. Then what did He mean? We must put a break between verses forty-five and forty-six. He came back to them, His own triumph won, and they were still drowsy, and opened their eyes as He came perchance, and He quietly said to them, There is a little time left, sleep on now. And they went back to sleep and He watched over them. He kept the lone vigil over those sleeping men until presently He saw the flash of the torches, for Judas was coming, and then He put His hand upon them and said, "Arise, let us be going." What passed through His soul in those hours we do not know. Nothing but love for those men, those drowsy men whom He had to rebuke was in His heart. He knew that presently out of the darkness He would win the inspiration that should make them selfless in their toil for Him, flames of fire carrying on His victory. O that vigil and that awaking!

Lastly observe the Master's victory. He said to Judas, What you do, do quickly; to Peter, Put thy sword up; I have no need of it. Twelve legions of angels I could have, but I will not. Why not? For very love of humanity.

So we see Him coming out of the garden and men attempting to hold Him. Hold Him fast said Judas, as if the puny hands of soldiers could have held Him. But He was held fast. What held Him? "He loved me, and gave Himself up for me." That is the whole story. May God help us to say it each for ourselves.

MATTHEW XXVI. 57-75

THE supreme impression made upon our minds by our last study was that of the triumph of the King, as we saw Him emerging from the garden, Master of all the forces that had gathered about Him in the lone hour of the night.

Now we are to see the King passing through the hands of men, while still in the hands of God. First His judges;—and one is almost inclined to say, God forgive us for calling them judges; those men who sought His death by the violation of justice. Then Peter, His own, a representative man here as everywhere. Then the traitor Judas. And finally Pilate the vacillating, time-serving slave of expedience. Our contemplation of the King flings all these men up into clear relief, and we see them for what they really are. Then, presently, He passed again into that unutterable loneliness on the margin of which we may be able to stand, and listen to the sighing wind, and the beating surf, but we shall never be able to fathom it, or understand it perfectly. Throughout the whole movement we shall see the same attitude of authority and dignity. He was never beaten, never defeated.

In the passage before us there are two things which arrest our attention. The first is to be found in verses fifty-seven to sixty-eight, omitting verse fifty-eight because it has to do with Peter. The second section we find in verse fifty-eight, and verses sixty-nine to seventy-five. In the first, we have brought before us the vision of the King rejected of men, but chosen of God. In the second, we see the King denied by His own, but saving them.

In the first section let us fix our attention first upon the King Himself. Very little is said about Him. It is announced that they had taken Him, led Him away to the house of Caiaphas, where the scribes and elders were gathered together. The next thing that we read about Him immediately is that He "held His peace." The final thing is that in answer to the priest's administering to Him a judicial oath, He made a double claim for Himself, first, that He was the Messiah, the Son of God; and, secondly, that He would ascend to the place of power, and finally come again and manifest Himself. So that two things impress us as we look at the King, first His silence; and, secondly, His speech on oath.

First His silence. Notice it carefully; He was silent when the witnesses, quite correctly called false witnesses by Matthew, bore testimony against Him. He was silent because He knew full well the purpose of the lie, and that correction was useless. They were men with the one set purpose of putting Him to death. When a court proceeds upon such lines as that, there is no hope. How many witnesses they brought we do not know, quite a number evidently, and the stories they told were so flimsy, and foolish, and futile, that even the high priest made no use of them; until at last two were found who could represent something that He was reported to have said, upon which the high priest thought he could fasten. Even they lied ignorantly or wilfully. They declared that He had said, I will destroy this temple and build it again in three days. No such word had ever passed His lips. He had said, "Destroy this temple," not "I will destroy." He had never affirmed His ability to destroy. He is not the Destroyer. His words had been a supposition of their power to destroy. They were men blinded by their rationalism, having no vision beyond the immediate, no conception beyond that which was absolutely and wholly material; and they had twisted His supposition into an affirmation.

We next observe His silence in the presence of the priest. When the priest asked Him purely in his personal capacity, "Answerest Thou nothing?" and as attempting to enforce Him to incriminate Himself, He was silent, no word passed His lips.

But that which is the most surprising and arresting in this scene, is

Christ's claim on oath. Notice very carefully how the high priest spoke to Him; "I adjure Thee by the living God."—That was the legal form of administering the oath. That which follows is not part of the legal form, but declares what would be the issue of His answer on oath. He did not say, I adjure Thee in order that Thou tell us; but I place Thee on oath in order that we may hear from Thee on oath, whether or not Thou art the Son of God, the Christ. It is the exact phrasing with which the Hebrew was familiar at the time. It was a careful question, and it was a question revealing the true attitude of the priest toward Jesus. It was a question revealing first of all the high priest's conception of the Messianic hope and office as it existed among his people. It was a question revealing the high priest's familiarity with the ancient Scriptures, and his perfect understanding of that Messianic hope which burned at the centre of the national life. The hope of the people concerning the Messiah was that He should be the Son of God, and the anointed One for the accomplishment of a Divine purpose.

But the high priest's question revealed more. It revealed quite clearly the fact that he understood that Jesus had been making this very claim. He gathered up into his question the result made upon the mind of the high priest and all the rulers, of the teaching and preaching of Jesus. The question would only be asked of a Man Who made claims which amounted to this. And without staying to go back over the whole of our Gospel, or even to gather incidents, if we think what Christ had been doing we shall recognize that it did amount to this. He had claimed over and over again, Messianic power and office; He had claimed to be the Son of God; and therefore the high priest in effect said to Him, The hope of the Hebrew people is Messiah; Messiah is to be the Son of God; Thou hast been so speaking and teaching as to lead men to think that Thou art the Messiah, the Son of God. Let us have no more uncertainty, I place Thee, on oath; tell

us plainly is this Thy claim? He did not believe Jesus, and he did not believe that He was trifling. He felt it was necessary to put Him on oath, in order that He might be compelled thus definitely to make His claim.

It is necessary to emphasise this because that emphasis lends tremendous force to Christ's answer. If we once clearly see that the high priest was definitely leading Him to open confession, then immediately we see the meaning of His answer. It was a double answer. He first immediately answered the high priest's question, and then added to it something other, more startling than the suggestion the high priest had made. With regard to the question, Jesus said, "Thou hast said." This was an affirmation as direct, simple, and profound, as the question of the high priest.

Thus we see the King, hemmed in by His foes, standing at the illegal tribunal, silent while witnesses lie, silent while the priest asked Him why He did not answer; but when challenged on oath answering immediately, affirming that He was exactly what the high priest suggested, the Christ, the Son of God.

And now, with this in mind let us carefully observe the next word which has caused some difficulty in the minds of expositors. "*Nevertheless* I say unto you, Henceforth ye shall see the Son of man sitting at the right hand of Power, and coming on the clouds of heaven."

Efforts have been made to change the word "nevertheless," and to say it must be translated in some other way. Let us look at this simply but carefully. "Thou hast said." That was His answering affirmation on oath. One suggests we must change the next word "nevertheless" and read instead "*Moreover.*" Another suggests that we substitute the word "*But.*" None of these changes is necessary unless we lose our sense of the scene. But there is no real escape from it, the word means "Nevertheless," and we have no business to change it. Watch the scene for a moment. Look carefully into the face of the high priest and elders about Him. Endeavouring to entrap Him, the high priest had put Him upon oath. Christ absolutely, definitely, clearly, positively, without ambiguity or circumvention, on oath affirmed His Messiahship. In a moment we see upon the face of the high priest the infinite scorn and incredulity with which he heard the answer. If we see that, we shall understand the "Nevertheless." Nevertheless, that is, in spite of thine unbelief, thou shalt see!

So that here Christ, in answer to the high priest's charge, declared on oath that He was the Christ, the Son of God; and secondly in answer to his scorn and incredulity He laid claim to triumph even in the hour of defeat. This was His last magnificent claim to the high priest of the Hebrew nation.

In the second Psalm we find the Hebrew conception of Messianic hope crystalized. There is no doubt whatever that the Hebrew expositors, and teachers, treated that psalm as Messianic; it is the psalm that tells that the Son is anointed, and set upon the throne of power, that He shall ask for the heathen, and possess them, and for the uttermost part of the earth, and they shall be granted to Him. The high priest had used the thought crystalized in that psalm, and had said, Are you that Person, You, Galilean peasant, Nazarene? Do you claim to be the Person described in our ancient Scripture, the Son Who is anointed to such a place of power, the very Son of God ruling? And Christ said, Yes! The high priest was astonished, incredulous. And then Christ said, "Nevertheless," and immediately quoted from the book of Daniel, which was as surely Messianic to Hebrew thinking as was the great psalm. In the book of Daniel the place of vision is heaven. The coming in the clouds there, is a coming from earth to heaven. When Daniel wrote, "I beheld till thrones were placed," it was the uppermost spaces into which he was looking, the infinite, and the spiritual. Then followed Daniel's vision of the Ancient of Days; "I saw in the night visions, and, behold, there came with the clouds of heaven one like unto a Son of man."

He came from the earth, to the Ancient of Days; and the One Who came was "Like unto a Son of man. He came even to the Ancient of Days, and they brought Him near before Him. And there was given Him dominion, and glory, and a kingdom, that all the peoples, nations, and languages should serve Him."

Now let us return to our scene. Jesus said, You have asked Me if I am the Son of God, the Messiah. I am. You do not believe it. Then let Me remind you of another of your Messianic predictions that speaks of the Son of man coming to the Ancient of Days for crowning and dominion and power. I am that Son of man. You do not believe the spiritual claim; you shall have it wrought out into your sight. I stand here in the midst of you, beaten and baffled as it seems. You have encompassed My death by lying, treachery, meanness. You have suborned false witnesses, to whom I have given no answer; and now you ask Me on oath to make declaration, and your face indicates incredulity as I make My declaration. Nevertheless, henceforth, from this hour of mock injustice, from henceforth the Son of man of Daniel's vision, shall ascend to the place of power, and you shall see it.

And did they see it? They nailed Him to the Cross; they bartered His life away; they flung Him out; and one can imagine that after He was dead, buried in Joseph of Arimathæa's grave, they said, Now He is done with! Within four days they began to find out that He was not done with; they had to reckon with Him as on the throne of empire; and in a very little while we find them gathering a little group of fishermen with perturbation in their hearts and terror in their souls, saying to them, "We strictly charged you not to teach in this name; and behold, ye have filled Jerusalem with your teaching, and intend to bring this Man's blood upon us." What does that mean? It means that the Son of man had ascended to the throne, and received dominion from the Ancient of Days, and all the things that they had tried to encompass were nothing to

Him. So that either He was all that He laid claim to be, or Caiaphas was right when He charged Him with blasphemy. We have no middle course to-day any more than they had; He is a liar, or incarnate Truth; an impostor, or God the Son, raised to the place of eternal Empire.

We have looked at the King; now let us look at the things seen incidentally. Is there anything in human history that compares with this for a travesty of justice; it was a lie in the name of truth, wickedness in the name of religion. This was not a Roman court, but a Hebrew court, and by the laws of the Hebrew people it was illegal for the Sanhedrim to meet in the night to try a case such as this, but they arraigned Him in the night. It was illegal for the Sanhedrim to pass sentence on the day that the prisoner was arrested, but they did it in this case in a few hours.

Mark the travesty of justice in the witnesses. "The chief priests and the whole council sought false witness against Jesus, that they might put Him to death; and they found it not, though many false witnesses came." After Christ's great claim we see the high priest rising, and we hear the clamour of his angry voice, "What further need have we of witnesses," and then he rent his garments, and in the doing of it violated the law under which he served as a priest. We have but to turn to Leviticus and we find it distinctly ordered that the high priest shall not rend his garments in the hour of sorrow or anguish. It was but a little thing, but it was symbolic of the whole attitude; they were trampling upon law, violating justice to encompass the death of this Man. The verdict of the council was shouted out in hot anger, and was followed by brutality to the prisoner as they buffeted Him. That is human nature, and that is human nature as it is to-day, but for the grace of God.

The story of Peter is a very familiar one. We may first of all say that, making allowance for his failure, all allowance for the awfulness of his denial, we must not forget that we must account for Peter by one word, and

that word is love. He loved his Lord throughout all the process. Truly love works through faith. Love needs faith as its central element, and Peter's faith in Jesus never failed, his love never failed. Christ had said to him a little before, "Satan asked to have you, that he might sift you as wheat, but I made supplication for thee, that thy faith fail not." His courage failed, his hope failed, his faith that Jesus would accomplish the thing Peter thought He was going to accomplish, failed; but His faith in Jesus never failed, his faith in the Person never failed, he believed in Him all through. And so as we trace the story it is one of love, blundering love, foolish love, but it is love.

Let us notice three things about Peter. Love at a distance and curious, "He followed Him afar" to see what the end would be. Secondly, love challenged and cowardly, until he denied. But finally, love remembering and contrite, "He went out, and wept bitterly." Love at a distance, and curious. That was Peter's failure. Love challenged, and cowardly. That was the devil's sifting. Love remembering, and contrite. That was Christ's victory.

First, love at a distance and curious. We need not lay any undue stress upon this, but it is certainly interesting to read the first Psalm when we read about Peter. As we read this Psalm we think about Christ.

"Blessed is the man that walketh not
    in the counsel of the wicked.
Nor standeth in the way of sinners,
Nor sitteth in the seat of scoffers."

But negatively Peter is there also. There is the process; we can hardly say progress, for it is a downward movement. Walking, standing, sitting; that is exactly what Peter did. Walking, "He followed Him afar off." Standing, he went "into the court" and stood among these people. Sitting, he "sat with the officers" by the fire that the enemies of Christ had built. He was following afar. But why did Peter come there at all? And if he could speak he would say because I loved Him, I wanted to see the end.

I was disappointed, He was doing nothing of what I thought He would do. Ah yes, but love merely curious, that walks with sinners and stands with sinners, and sits to gain its warmth by the fire that sinners have built, is in peril. That was Peter's failure.

Then mark that love was challenged. One maid spoke to him, " Thou also." Why the also? John was there somewhere, Judas was lurking somewhere. " Thou also wast with Jesus the Galilean;" " Of a truth thou also art one of them." He tried to evade denial the first time. " I know not what thou sayest." We know and understand that. Challenged, we do not deny, but we evade! That also is a lie. Then another maid did not speak to him, but spoke to the whole company and said, " This man also was with Jesus of Nazareth." Then it was that he put himself on oath, for that is the meaning of swearing here. He took his oath that he did not know Him. Then the whole of them spoke to him presently, saying, Really you are one, your very speech betrays you, you have the Galilean accent, you cannot escape that way! Then he added curses to the oath. That was Satan's sifting. Long ago Jesus had said, Satan will sift you! Someone has quaintly said Peter shut the door to all the upper things and opened it to all the downward things. Peter was finding himself out. Never a man that loves Jesus Christ but that he comes into circumstances

sooner or later that will reveal what is in him. He is brought into them in order that he may be delivered from the things that are in him.

And then the last thing. It is so full of light and colour even in the darkness. The whole thing is so dramatic if we could but see it. He had just uttered that last protestation and had cursed; and outside in the darkness was heard the crowing of the cock; and he remembered. One cannot read it without forgetting Peter, and thinking of Christ. Christ had said to him, "before the cock crow thou shalt deny Me thrice." It was such a simple thing, such a childish thing, that does not seem to have anything in it. But He will employ the chirping of a sparrow to win a soul to God. He will press into the business of restoring a wandering one, the crowing of a cock in the dawning of the morning. He remembered, and we need not follow him out, as he went weeping; the evangelist with a fine delicacy leaves him a brokenhearted man, because he had denied his Lord.

So we see hate murdering the King, and love denying the King; and it seems as though the King says to us two things. First, come, see if there ever was sorrow like Mine! But perhaps the final thing He said was, From henceforth the Son of man is on the throne of power! Let us trust Him and follow Him, even though it be through darkness.

MATTHEW XXVII. 1-26

THE first two verses of this chapter link its narrative to that of the preceding one. We have considered the first trial scene, that travesty of justice; the gathering of the Sanhedrim in the night, which was in itself illegal according to their own law. That is revealed in the action which Matthew so briefly chronicles in these two first verses; " Now, when morning was come, all the chief priests and the elders of the people took counsel against Jesus to put Him to death." That is they met in the morning and

took counsel as to how they should carry out the decision of the night, in order to be technically within the law. Their decision was that they would so act as to compel the Roman power to be the instrument of their own base decision; so they "bound Him, and led Him away, and delivered Him up to Pilate the governor."

The outstanding figures in the section are those of the King Himself, Judas and Pilate.

First of all our eyes are fixed upon the King. Standing in the presence of Pilate, He made His claim to be the King of the Jews. On solemn oath, in the presence of the Sanhedrim in the night, He claimed to be the Son of God, the Messiah. Now once again before Pilate the question was asked, not with the same formality, but it was the question of the judge directly spoken to the prisoner; "Art Thou the King of the Jews?" And again quietly, with little formality, and yet as clearly as in the night, He answered the inquiry of the Procurator. "Thou sayest." That is to say, What thou sayest is so, I am the King of the Jews. Then immediately Pilate turned aside from his true line of action as a dispassionate judge, and reminded the Prisoner of the clamour of these priests. And Christ answered nothing. Christ's sense of true judicial procedure was far finer than Pilate's. He would answer His judge, but He had no answer for clamour, no answer for those men who were there for the set purpose of encompassing His death. The foregone conclusion of His opponents made Him silent.

Let us now look at the two men here coming into contact with Christ. In each case we see the most disastrous failure.

This is the final picture of Judas. What are the things that are impressed upon our mind as we look at him? First, a too late repentance; secondly, a too late restitution, the flinging back of the thirty pieces of silver; and finally, an appalling retribution coming upon him by his own hand. Judas appears in this trial scene as one of the band of Christ's own disciples, one of the inner circle. In following this Gospel, we have seen vast multitudes crowding about Him, the rulers and those in authority deeply interested in Him. We have also seen how they gradually fell away, the rulers first, and then the multitudes, until He slowly and solemnly proceeded to the place He occupied in the awful hour of His passion, absolutely alone so far as human friendship was concerned. Judas had been His companion along the highway of His public ministry. He had sat at the table with Him, and had heard those intimate and private

conversations. He had been one of the inner circle of souls, loyal to Him, at least by confession and profession. This man was the traitor in the camp, the betrayer of our Lord from the inner circle to the outer circle; as in turn, they of His own nationality became His betrayers to that yet wider circle of Roman power. So by a process of betrayal from the inner circle outward, our Lord was handed over; by a member of His own disciples to the foes plotting for His own life; and by the members of His own nation to the nation without, which cared nothing for Him, but wholly for themselves.

Many brilliant and interesting attempts have been made to redeem Judas from obloquy, but let us be content to abide by his own conception of what he had done—"I have sinned." Not, I have blundered, or have been mistaken, or foolish, or wrong; not, I have attempted to hurry this Messiah to declare Himself, but, "I have sinned." As we look at Judas in that terrible picture, we see a man filled with terror, the terror of a lost soul; the sense of sin, and the dread of its issue. Not regret, not the sense of sin with desire to escape it, but the sense of sin with desire to escape the issue of it. That is not the repentance that brings a man to God. If a man simply repents of sin, by attempting to escape its issue, he knows nothing of repentance in the true sense of the word. Repentance which would be glad to bear the fire of hell if it would purge from sin, is the repentance that works salvation.

His restitution was also too late. It was a dramatic scene. The priests were moving across the courtyard, from the place where they had met in the palace of the high priest to the palace of the Procurator. Just over the wall were the Temple courts; and suddenly this man confronted the procession of priests, with Jesus in the midst, and cried to them, "I have sinned in that I betrayed innocent blood." Mark the brutality of the answer, "What is that to us? See thou to it;" you made your bargain, abide by it! Then, realising the whole meaning of the situation, Judas took those thirty pieces of silver—he had not spent one of them, what he got he did not gain, a man never does when he is selling Christ—and flung them over into the Temple enclosure. An awful revelation of the illumination of a soul too late! Then he hurried away and hanged himself. Thus the one traitor in the inner circle of Christ's Kingdom, became his own executioner.

If we would know the difference between true repentance and false, let us go back to the story of Peter, and put the statement there into comparison with the statement here. Peter had basely denied Him; but mark the ending of the two stories. Of Peter it is written, " He went out and wept bitterly." Of Judas it is written, " He went away and hanged himself." In the one case, we have the man repentant, sorry for the actual sin, and turning from it, desiring to escape from the wrong done. In the other case we have a man, desiring to escape the consequences of his sin, by his own act plunging himself into them.

Now let us look at the high priests, and if it be possible, calmly. They gathered up those thirty pieces of silver. Notice their religious conscience. In the midst of the greatest travesty of justice that the world has ever seen, themselves the inspirers and instigators of the foul deed, the darkest sin ever committed, they said—" It is not lawful to put them into the treasury." What shall we do with them? We will endeavour to cleanse this money which has been cast into the Temple courts by putting it to charitable uses! We will buy the potter's field, and we will make it the place to bury strangers in. How often men attempt to cleanse money by putting it to charitable uses. Mark the irony of the whole situation, how the people named the thing correctly, even when the priests tried to hide it. The priests said, A field to bury strangers in. The people said, The field of blood! Thus, all unintentionally, they sent down through all the years the right naming of the thing they had done, " The field of blood."

The story of Pilate is a story of conscience; and there are these distinct movements in the process; first

conscience startled; then conscience struggling; then conscience compromising; and, finally, conscience drugged, silenced! The final revelation of the study is that the man who governs his life simply by conscience, is likely to ruin his life.

His conscience was startled by the very presence of Jesus. There would seem to be no other explanation. Pilate was a man never popular, even among his own friends; hard, cold, dispassionate, used to scenes of blood; a man who in all likelihood had risen from the rank of a slave, not immediately, but by succession. The man who rises, without the grace of God, always becomes the greatest despot, when he is given power. But when the priests came to him, bearing that Prisoner, he was a startled man. No such prisoner had stood before him up to that moment. Pilate embodied Roman authority; but here was a Prisoner at the bar, Who immediately became the Judge, while the judge became the prisoner. Pilate felt the influence of His stately and quiet affirmation of Kingship. " Art Thou the King of the Jews? " which meant to say, Thou art claiming to be the King of the Jews; it is an absurd position; settle it at once by saying that Thou art not! But instead of a denial, there was an affirmation. Pilate expected the Prisoner would wish to escape; he found the Prisoner had no desire to escape. Pilate himself would have given anything to escape. His conscience was aroused.

Then we see a man struggling with his conscience. His arguments for Jesus as against the priests, and that last suggestion supposed to be by himself a master-stroke of cleverness, prove this. It was his custom to release a notable prisoner. Barabbas was a man guilty of robbery and murder, and yet a man making claims to free his people. Barabbas means son of the father; and is a title rather than a name. Some of the ancient manuscripts give the name as Jesus Barabbas. In all probability he had set up Messianic claims, on the low level of a material fight and robbery. Pilate saw the difference, and thought that surely these religious men, if driven to choice, would be bound to accept Jesus. So little did Pilate know of priestism! Which will you have, Jesus which is called Christ, or Barabbas?

Then there occurred an interval, in which the priests persuaded the people to ask for Barabbas; and, as John tells us, in the loneliness of an inner chamber, face to face with Christ, Pilate asked, "What is truth?"

The hidden interview over, the people were ready to answer; and Pilate came with his question, "Which of the two will ye that I release unto you?" They replied, "Barabbas." Then, perplexed, struggling with his conscience, Pilate said, "What then shall I do unto Jesus Who is called Christ?" Again the answer came, quick and ready, priest-inspired, "Let Him be crucified." And again Pilate asked, "Why, what evil hath He done?" We see how now his conscience was struggling between obedience and expedience; struggling as to whether it would obey the deep conviction concerning the Man in front of him or listen to the clamour of these men, and secure his own position. He knew the subtlety of the priests, he knew full well if he handed Jesus over to freedom, they would complain against him at Rome, that he had committed high treason against Cæsar.

Then followed the washing of his hands in water. Judas, a frenzied soul, went back and faced the high priests and said, "I have betrayed innocent blood." Now Pilate said, "I am innocent of the blood of this righteous Man; see ye to it."

What next? Conscience drugged. "Then . . . Jesus he scourged and delivered to be crucified."

Now once more we look back; and this story of Judas teaches us that there is an unpardonable sin. There are many passages in the New Testament that speak of it, always with awful solemnity. What is it? Rejection of the Saviour. If Judas, instead of confessing his sin to the high priest, had confessed it to Christ, he would have been pardoned there and then; if, instead of allowing an awful fear resulting from sin to drive him to self-destruction, he had flung himself upon the tender compassion of Jesus he would have been forgiven even then. The unpardonable sin, and the only one for which Christ has no word, no look, no help, is the sin of deliberately, and wilfully, and finally, rejecting Him, as Saviour.

As we look at Judas, we learn also that whatever price we put upon Christ we are likely to get for Him. Is is an awful truth. We can sell Christ for our own price! The devil will take care of that! F. Beard, of Chicago, in one of his wonderful cartoons, has a picture that would shock the sensibilities of some. It is that of a man in his inner office, leaning on his desk, writing, and looking over his ledgers and books. Outside the door of that office stands the Christ, knocking, but the door is locked and there is no entrance for Him. Standing by the man is the devil—not the devil of the Middle Ages, with horns and hoofs, but the cultured, refined, and insidious devil of the nineteenth century, who woos and wins with gold. And what is he doing? He is giving this man all that he asks, in order to keep Christ out. It is graphic, awful, and true! That is the devil's mission, to give men anything, in order to keep Christ out.

But there is a difference between getting and gaining. The things a man gets when he sells Christ are not current in the eternities; and at the last, his soul passing out into the darkness, as did that of Judas, he will fling back the getting of years into the Temple, having lost Christ and the thirty pieces of silver.

We see the King in Pilate's hall arraigned. But Pilate was arraigned. Nineteen centuries have gone and the world knows it now. Not the high priests are jailors. He is the Jailor; He holds them in His right hand, and their eternal destinies depend upon Him. Not the Roman Procurator was judge. He was a prisoner, and his question was more than he knew, "What shall I do with Jesus?" In that moment when Pilate released Barabbas, and gave Jesus to the Cross, the Roman kingdom was doomed in the economy of God. Presently the followers of the Christ found their way to Rome. A halting man, feeble in bodily appearance, came into Rome as a prisoner, and receiving into his own hired house all that came to him, he taught them the things concerning Jesus, Whom their Governor had given to the Cross. Thus Rome was shaken at the centre; and its pagan power was broken by the coming of the King Pilate had flung out.

MATTHEW XXVII. 27-56

THESE verses tell the story of the Passion and Passing of the King. To say that, is to recognize the difficulty of exposition, and to fill the soul with that awe and reverence without which all such attempts would be sacrilegious. There are matters here too profound for words, things that cannot be fully apprehended by our finite minds. Here, as never before in the reading of this Gospel, we see the King in a loneliness and a dignity which defy explanation. The story is full of contradictions, and yet wonderfully complete. If we read it as a passage out of merely human history, it would be a story of an ignominious and overwhelming defeat. It is not too late to read it in that way. Nineteen centuries have revealed the fact that the rough and bloody Roman gibbet was the throne of imperial monarchy, and spiritual empire.

As we come to the story, we have the great advantage of all the gathered light of the experience of the Church, and the experience of the world, and we see these things as it would have been utterly impossible for men to see them at the time. The seeing of these things in the gathered light of the centuries, creates this difference, among others, between the men who looked upon them then, and ourselves. They imagined that they perfectly understood all that was happening. We know that we do not even now understand all that happened. Had that been an ordinary death, then all that these men said in the presence of it was true; but that is a supposition which cannot be entertained in view of the effect which has been produced in individual, social, national, and worldwide life, as the issue of that Cross. There have been other details sublimely heroic; but to speak of this merely as heroic, is almost to insult it. There have been other deaths tragic and dreadful, and while this is more tragic than any other, to speak of it as a tragedy merely, would savour of irreverence.

One is quite powerless in the presence of this story. Here exposition has to end, save as perchance it may reverently touch upon some of the outer things. To the inner heart of the mystery exposition cannot penetrate. It is well in that connection to notice the remarkable reticence of Matthew. Other evangelists tell us more than he tells us, and yet they are all reverently reticent in the presence of the Cross. Much more might have been written of that scene in the palace, when Pilate, having handed Jesus over in answer to the clamour of the mob inspired by the priests, the whole band of Jews gathered about Him; but there is a dignity and reverent reticence in the story of Matthew. That reticence is more marked as we proceed. He does not describe the crucifixion at all. There is a change in this connection in the Revised Version, full of significance. The Authorised makes it appear that Matthew declares that they crucified Him, for it reads there "they crucified Him," as though drawing attention to the act itself as being performed. The Revised reads, "when they were come unto the place called Golgotha, that is to say, The place of a skull, they gave Him wine to drink, mingled with gall: and when He had tasted it, He would not drink. And *when they had crucified Him,* they parted His garments among them, casting lots: and they sat and watched Him there." He does not describe it, but refers to it as a fact accomplished. We need in the reading of that to remember that between verses thirty-four and thirty-five the crucifixion took place. It would seem that Matthew, when writing the story of the King, turned away as though he would say to those who would read, I cannot even look upon that. Let us observe the same attitude. The longer one lives and contemplates this central mystery of our faith, the less one can peer into it on the material side, and the less one can attempt to explain it in the profundity of its spiritual meaning.

Let us, then, reverently meditate on this paragraph, in three ways. First, the attitude of God as revealed; secondly, the attitude of the King; finally, the attitude of humanity.

The attitude of God in the presence of this Passing and Passion of the King. One may be inclined to say that the passage says hardly anything about God. And that indeed is the first matter which arrests attention, the apparent non-interference of God. That becomes most remarkable as we remember previous matters in this Gospel, how at the close of the years of privacy God broke the silence and spoke, "This is My beloved Son, in Whom I am well pleased;" how on the Mount of Transfiguration when His humanity had wrought itself out to an absolute perfection and was ready for glory, and yet turned again to the earthly way, and the way of sorrow, God said to the disciples who were fearful in their obedience and their following, "This is My beloved Son, in Whom I am well pleased: hear ye Him." Think of the relation existing between the King and God as we have seen it flashing out every now and then in the course of the ministry and teaching of Jesus. Remember how He said, "No one knoweth the Son, save the Father." Then turn to this picture in which we see this One,—Who was perfect in His life, Who pleased God in His teaching so that God had broken the silence of heaven to set the seal of His approval upon Him,—now in the midst of a brutal band of soldiers who were making sport of Him, and there was no interference. That is the mystery of all mysteries. We talk of the problem of pain; there it is focussed. We talk of the problem of evil, there it is concrete: that God could leave Him alone in that hour of human persecution. All this is most apparent at

Golgotha. When the King was hanging upon the Cross and the interpreters of religion, the priests, misinterpreted God, there was a great silence. God's non-interference is the first thing that impresses one, as the story is read.

But that is not all the story. It was not wholly non-interference. There is one touch full of beauty; "From the sixth hour there was darkness over all the land until the ninth hour." That seems to have been the act of God. It would seem that in infinite tenderness God wrapped the land in darkness in the hour of His Son's supreme suffering. About those three hours we know nothing, save the words that escaped the lips of the Sufferer Himself. Here we approach that which is perhaps the matter most difficult of interpretation. There came a moment when the voice was heard amid the darkness, and it said, "My God, My God, why hast Thou forsaken Me?" The men about the Cross were quite familiar with the words. They were not strange words. They were quoted from the Psalter, from the Worship-book of the Hebrew people. They had often chanted the psalm in solemn monotone and recited it in many an hour of heart anguish. But there are values in it far deeper and more profound than the Psalmist knew when he wrote the song. When he wrote it, it was the expression of sorrow such as he was then passing through. But it has become for evermore full of meaning to us, because Christ uttered these words upon the Cross. There is great value in recognizing the fact that it was a human cry, and that Jesus quoted it. And the value is all the greater if we remember that all that follows in that twenty-second Psalm is an exposition of what it is to be God-forsaken. The Psalmist was not looking at the Cross on the green hill, he had no vision of it; he was writing of his own heart's agony; and here this One, this King upon the Cross, stretched back through the centuries and took hold of the most awful wail of agony that ever escaped the human heart, and quoted it as His own experience. He was of our humanity, born of the virgin, throughout the whole of His public ministry He had spoken in human terms, and yet with an unequivocal Divine authority. When we look at this Cross and listen to His words thereon, we must be very careful that we do not divide between the Deity and the humanity of Jesus. If He was God manifest in the days of His teaching, He was God manifest on the Cross; God coming into identification with the issue of the sin of man. "My God, My God, why hast Thou forsaken Me?" It was first of all the cry of a soul at the uttermost of sin, having lost the vision of God. It was the cry of a soul at the uttermost of sorrow, conscious of its lack of God. All sorrow is lack. All grief is consciousness of lack. And the final lack is God. When the soul becomes conscious of the lack of God, that is the uttermost sorrow. Moreover, it was the soul in the presence of mystery, in the presence of silence, with no voice, with no answer. Here, then, because this Man was God incarnate, because from beginning to end every word that fell from His lips was a word of God, this also is the word of God. In that moment He expressed in human speech the fact that the pains and penalties of the human sin were His. That is as far as we can see into the Atonement. That is the heart of it, and the centre of it, and the soul of it, and the marvel of it, and the mystery of it! If we make this Man upon the Cross a Man merely, then the presentation is out of harmony with the rest of the Gospel story, and out of harmony with the deepest of human experience concerning Him. But when we say that this Man upon the Cross was still the unveiled God, then all the physical bruising, terrible as it was, so that eyes can hardly bear to look on it, is but a material shadow of the suffering of the Divine heart in the presence of sin, by which suffering He dealt with sin and bore it, as the Lamb slain from the foundation of the world. We see the Man among the soldiers, we see them press the crown of thorns upon His brow; they are thorn-crowning God!

Whence came the thorns? Let us go back to the beginning of Bible human history, and we find it was said; "Cursed is the ground for thy sake: in toil shalt thou eat of it all the days of thy life, thorns also, and thistles shall it bring forth to thee." In Pilate's judgment hall, we see the soldiers with rough hands plaiting a rude crown of thorns; and there is a suggestiveness which arrests the soul. They were pressing back into the brow of God incarnate, the very curse that followed sin. And what was He doing? We speak of the non-interference of God; it was His non-interference with Himself, for it was His determination to work out the mystery of His pain in the shedding of blood in order to cleanse the very sin of the men who crushed the thorns upon His brow.

But where was God when the last word had been spoken and the King had yielded up His Spirit? And again the answer was not the answer of speech, but the answer of an act. "And behold, the veil of the Temple was rent in two from the top to the bottom." That was a great symbolic act, indicating the fact that symbolism was for ever over. The veil of the Temple was that which excluded men from God. Think of that holy of holies in the Temple in Jerusalem, of its darkness! No light was ever there! There had been light in olden days when the glory of the Shekinah shone between the overshadowing wings of the cherubim; but that had long since passed away. Men were outside, not permitted to enter. But when our King died, the veil was rent, and that meant first that light broke through where all had been darkness, and secondly that the God Who had been a mystery became a Revelation, shining out upon all human history; and it meant also that excluded men were admitted. What happened when the veil was rent? All the world was brought inside; and all souls were made priests, who come through the name and merit of the Priest Who that day had died. And so if we see first the non-interference of God; we see also the triumph of God by identification with men; and we see that triumph manifested, in the rending of that veil.

Now let us reverently look at the King Himself. We begin exactly where we began before. Mark these words for a moment as the very words of the King Himself, "My God, My God, why hast Thou forsaken Me?" Notice that they indicate His identification with God in the experience of that issue. No one can read this story consecutively from the beginning of the Gospel until this point and imagine that in the Cross there was some kind of conflict as between Christ and God. There was nothing to mar the perfect harmony between God and Christ in that Cross. He was neither persuading God to love us, nor overcoming reluctance in the heart of God to save us. He was co-operating with the work of God in the revelation of the love that makes man know what the heart of God really is. As we listen to the voice of the King, we detect the perfect harmony, and realise how here, as everywhere, the first recorded words of Jesus were still true, "Knew ye not that I must be about My Father's business?" This also was His business, and the King was in perfect accord with the law and purposes of God.

He cried with a loud voice. Matthew does not tell us what He said, but that having spoken, He yielded up His Spirit; very literally, He sent His Spirit away. This was a phrase in common use to describe death. In the Cross of Christ, it was justified. We have seen as we have traced the story, how, in the last days of the King's Passion, as He was approaching the Cross, He compelled circumstances to His own will, and the same fact is revealed here. That was the King's triumph. He triumphed, not merely by resurrection, and not alone in that He compelled the hour of His dying to fall in with the counsels of God and with the symbolism of the ancient system, but in that, at the moment when He had passed through all, "He yielded up His Spirit."

As we look at the attitude of humanity we need do no more than indicate certain lines of thought. It is a very interesting study, that of the people who gathered about the Cross of Jesus. We see humanity materialised, in the soldiers. They began by making sport of Him in the palace. Then they manifested a touch of rough

pity as they offered Him the wine and the gall. This was succeeded by an awful indifference, as, having done their work of crucifixion, in the sight of the Cross they gambled for His garments; and "they watched Him." To what depths humanity falls when its ideals are materialised! To these men there was no beauty that they should desire Him, because they were blind to all high and spiritual things.

But there is a worse picture than that. It is that of religion in the presence of the Cross. The most devilish thing in human history is religion when it becomes false. The higher and the nobler a thing, the lower and the more ignoble it becomes when it is false. Begin on the lowest level of illustration. A lost woman is a greater tragedy than a lost man. All reformers and all workers know that it is most difficult to lift and reclaim a woman. And why is this? Because her nature is finer, nearer the spiritual. One is appalled by the ignorance of the priests, far more than horrified by their brutality. "He saved others, Himself He cannot save." Now had these men had any spiritual understanding at all, they would have known that this was not true of Jesus merely, but has always been true of humanity. In order to save any one to the highest degree, from the lowest plane, the saviour must be willing not to save himself. It is only by the giving of our life away that we can hope to save another life. The whole of life is built upon that great principle, and yet here were interpreters of moral and spiritual things, flinging this as a gibe and a taunt into the face of the dying Christ Himself, "He saved others, Himself He cannot save."

Then observe their misinterpretation of God, "He trusteth on God; let Him deliver Him now, if He desireth Him; for He said, I am the Son of God." How ignorant they were of God!

All the things they said to Him were true, but not as they meant them. These final taunts of the priests constitute a great revelation of the heart of atonement.

There is one other group at which we will glance, that of the women

Reverently, though perplexed; loyal, though disappointed; standing afar off and waiting; were the women who had ministered to Him. We leave them there, that sorrow-stricken company. We shall meet them again; and we shall find that some of them stayed and watched His burial. No apostles did. Some of them watched through the darkness of the night for the break of day. No apostle did. As we look back at that scene, we thank God for the women who waited!

Look finally at that Cross. It is the throne. See how it divides to the right and the left. It divided the soldiers. One of their number looked, and looked, the captain of the band, the centurion, and the truth broke upon him, and he said, "Truly this was the Son of God." It divided the thieves; the dying Christ had no word for one but the imperial word of entrance to light for the other. It divided attitudes of mind; priests and women; priests laughing and mocking in their ignorance of spiritual things; women waiting and worshipping in their ignorance of what He was doing.

So to-day we are judged by that Cross, and when we pass our verdict upon it, the verdict we pass upon it is, if we could but hear and understand it, its verdict upon us. Ever since that hour, that has been His throne for present administration. Presently He will change it for the throne of glory, and the throne of empire. To that throne of the Cross He brings us now; and according to what we do with it, He will do with us, when He sits on the throne of His glory.

MATTHEW XXVII. 57–XXVIII.

MAN'S last and worst was done. The King was dead! From the moment of His dying, none but tender hands touched Him, and from the moment of His burial none but loving eyes saw Him.

Night is past; day is breaking! A new glory is on the whole creation. Long years, as men count time, must intervene ere the groaning cease, and the sob is hushed; but the deepest pain is past in His pain, and the wound of humanity is staunched at its very centre in His wounds.

Strange glories broke with the dawning of the first day of the new week. The King's followers, discouraged and scattered by the Cross, were gathered together again; a new affection manifested itself, and a new heroism possessed them. For a brief while, He tarried among them, and meeting them in Galilee, with the majesty of an authority, such as man had never known, He uttered His great commission, and declared His abiding presence among His own disciples.

Reverently then, and with meaning such as mortals never knew, there pass our lips in His presence, the presence of the risen King, words often uttered before, but never with such confidence and such courage, "Long live the King!" And in answer, we presently hear His own words spoken to a lonely man on an island of the sea, "I am alive for evermore."

In this final study, then, we see the end of the beginning, and the beginning of the end. In order to dismiss the question of difficulty, or of harmony as between the Gospel narratives, let us still remember that Matthew wrote from the one standpoint, that of presenting the King of Israel; and therefore from the appearances after the resurrection, and from the different facts concerning Resurrection, he selected only those which are necessary for setting forth this one truth of the Kingship of Christ in its last manifestation in the earthly mission of Jesus, and in the ultimate intention and purpose of God.

Our study falls into three parts, First, the King resting; secondly, the King risen; finally, the King reigning.

The King resting. For a little while He is out of our sight. Our attention therefore is fixed first upon the King's lovers, and then upon the King's foes, and upon how they acted after the death of the King.

His lovers are represented by Joseph

317

and the Marys. We are immediately arrested by the fact that the light of Resurrection had not yet broken upon the hearts of His disciples. Nevertheless, while as yet they had no understanding of the spiritual meaning of His mission, while as yet they were only simple souls who had learned to love Him, but had not come to understand Him; a secret disciple, and those avowedly His, were brought into a sacred and beautiful union in their ministry of love. Not only is it true that secret and avowedly open disciples are brought together; it is also true that among these lovers of Jesus, fulfilling their last tender offices of love in the presence of His dead body, were those who represented the highest in the land, and those who represented the simple and lowly. Joseph of Arimathæa was a member of the Sanhedrim, and Luke tells us that he was the minority in the hour of the trial (Luke xxiii. 51). He was the man who did not give his consent to the decision of the illegal gathering of these people at night, or to their decision to hand Jesus over to death. His had been a hidden loyalty, and yet a true one, and now in the presence of the ultimate catastrophe, in the presence of the death of his Lord, the secret disciple became the most courageous of them all; he begged the body of Jesus the Crucified, the One of Whom they had been so eager to rid themselves. The secret discipleship flamed out into a great courage when Jesus was dead. He took his way to the Roman governor, and asked for the privilege of taking that body and laying it to rest; and for resting place he gave Him his own tomb. What did he feel that day as he laid Christ to rest? Probably there was no hope in his heart, but there was love there. Perhaps he felt He had been wrong, as all the other disciples felt they had been wrong, in placing their confidence in the ability of Jesus to do the great things He said He was going to do. But he had not lost faith in Christ; for there is a distinct difference between faith in Christ's ability to do things, and faith in Christ for what He is in Himself.

Then there were the Marys; Mary of Magdala, and the other Mary. Nothing is said of them save this, that they were sitting over against the sepulchre. If we arrange these stories chronologically, we find that these women watched even after Joseph of Arimathæa had gone, that they watched and waited through all that first night. Augustine said, "Oh that men in all time would learn the lesson of the Marys, and when they can do none other for the Christ, watch!"

It is a tragic picture, this of His lovers; but it is a beautiful picture. Hopeless, disappointed, bereaved, heartbroken; but the love He had created in those hearts for Himself could not be quenched, even by His dying; could not be overcome, even though they were disappointed; could not be extinguished, even though the light of hope had gone out, and over the sea of their sorrow there was no sighing wind that told of the dawn.

His foes are next seen; the priests, with the Pharisees, and Pilate. Priests and Pharisees were filled with a nameless and superstitious fear, "We remember that that deceiver said, while He was yet alive, After three days I rise again. Command therefore that the sepulchre be made sure until the third day." Side by side with this superstitious fear, a great and continued contempt for Him was revealed in the words "that deceiver." It is wonderful how men may set themselves in such resolute antagonism to a truth, that at last they are persuaded that their antagonism is the truth, and the truth itself a lie. These men had listened in the early days of our Lord's ministry with profound interest to Him, had been impressed by Him, impressed by the scholarly note in His preaching, "How knoweth this Man letters, having never learned?" impressed by the loftiness and beauty of His ethical ideal, impressed by His marvellous unveiling of the glory of God; yet because they were not able to account for Him, and were jealous of the power He exerted, they fought against Him until at last, when He was dead, they could only speak of Him as "that deceiver."

Pilate responded to their request by saying; "Ye have a guard: go, make it as sure as ye can." With what emphasis shall we read that word? Was his the emphasis of doubt? Was there still in his heart the hatred of the priests which was manifest during the trial? Was there a sarcasm in the word, born of the consciousness that they were helpless in the presence of that dead Man? Or was there a lurking suspicion of fear? Was he coming into sympathy with those priests in their desire to stamp out the Name? We do not know. Most probably it was the language of weary indifference as though he had said, Let me be done with this thing; take the guard and get away, and do anything you like.

Whatever our interpretation may be, this we do know, that in the day of his vacillation he had chosen expedience rather than obedience, had sought to save himself, as his Prisoner had not done; and so had lost himself, while his Prisoner was saving Himself, and His Kingdom.

The King risen. The account of the earthquake, and the coming of the angel is interpolated to explain the presence of the angel who spoke to the women as they returned from their Sabbath observances. Chronologically, therefore, these events stand first in the story, and we will so look at them. The risen King and the angel; the risen King and the women; the risen King and His enemies.

The risen King and the angel. When the King was coming angels announced the fact; and now an angel came again. He did not come to roll away the stone, in order that Christ might come forth from the grave; but to roll away the stone, in order to show that Christ had left the grave. He had risen ere the angel came, He had left behind Him the linen cloths without displacing them, and the grave without the rolling away of the stone. He had emerged into that new, mysterious, and yet actual bodily life, which so baffles all our explanation as we read the story in the Gospel of John. He had departed without flame or flash of glory upon which the eye of sense might look. He had left His grave behind Him, not through a door opened by disciple fingers, or angel fingers, but without the opening of a door. So the Christ had risen, unseen by friend or foe in the mysterious and majestic act; and the angel mission was to show men, not the exit or exodus of the Christ from the grave, but the empty grave.

The effect of the angel's coming to the foes of Christ, was that of their absolute discomfiture. They became as dead men in the presence of the blinding glory of the angel visitor; but to the friends of Christ it was a strange and tender comfort. He said to the women, "Fear not ye; for I know that ye seek Jesus." But the place where they laid Him could not hold Him. Their coming was the coming of love and fear, as we have already seen. Their coming was the agony of a mistaken intention, they brought "spices that they might come and anoint Him." They thought of Him only as dead. How strange that seems, in the light of the fact that, as the evangelists record, He never spoke of His Cross in those last days, but that He also foretold His Resurrection. They seem never to have heard Him, or never to have understood Him. They were so blinded by the blood of the tragedy, that they never saw the light shining beyond. They loved Him with a great love; though He had failed, they loved Him, and would minister to Him dead. With what surprise they found the angel there, and listened to the message! First their fear was assuaged, "Fear not ye: for I know that ye seek Jesus Who hath been crucified." They were seeking Him in the wrong way; but they were seeking Him. Their knowledge was not perfect, but their love was strong, and that is ever the supreme thing. Then came the announcement, the great fact was declared, "He is not here, He is risen," and that was accompanied by a gentle touch of rebuke, in the words, "as He said."

The last words the angel spoke indicated the real meaning of His presence there: "Come, see the place where the Lord lay." The value of the actual bodily Resurrection of Jesus, both to the disciples and to disciples for all ages, was its demonstration that He had accomplished all He said He would accomplish, that His great announcements concerning Himself were not the dreamings of a disordered imagination, were not the hopes of a helpless, powerless man. When He came out from the grave in bodily Resurrection, all He had said was verified, and all He had done began to be explained. The ministry, of teaching, and of wonder working, the patient love of the three years, began to take a new colour, and tone, and emphasis, as they looked at the empty grave and saw that the King Whom they loved was dead, and Whose body they would have embalmed, was beyond their reach; that He had broken the bands of death, and without the aid or assistance or intervention of disciples or of angels, had left the tomb, and left it for ever.

The risen King and the women. His first appearance was to them, that is to love at its finest, and fullest, and strongest. They were mistaken. In all probability when the angel gave them their commission, and had started to tell the disciples that Jesus would meet them in Galilee they dropped their spices. He knew the business upon which they had come to the sepulchre, and He appeared to them in spite of their mistake, in spite of the fact that they had come to embalm Him dead. We are anxious that people should hold the absolute truth concerning Him; He is anxious that souls should love Him! We turn away from fellowship with those who do not hold all we hold to be true concerning Him, forgetting that we as well as they, they as well as we, may be incorrect or partial only, in our present conclusions concerning Him; He will give Himself first to love, even when love is so blind and foolish, that it desires to embalm Him dead, never having believed the great words concerning Resurrection.

He said to them—" All hail! " This was the ordinary salutation of the marketplace, the highway, and the home. There is a glory in that fact. There is, as He says it, a Kingly tone in it, a majestic touch, that appeals to us; yet in the artlessness of it, in the simplicity of it, in the ordinariness of it, is the revelation of the perfect ease with which He had passed through the old life into the new, and the unveiling of the fact that He had brought into the new resurrection life all the old human tendernesses and natural human sympathies.

They were conscious of the change, and in a moment they were at His feet. Quickly He called them back from that attitude of adoring worship, and exultation, and sent them to their new work; " Go tell My brethren that they depart into Galilee."

Thus the risen Christ met His disciples, appearing first to love, which we do well to remember. When we meet Him let us know that He will speak to us in the ordinary and everyday language of our own life. While He values our adoring worship, He will always lift us from the attitude of prostration, and will send us about His business. To lie at His feet is a sacred and blessed thing; but to remain there is to miss the meaning of His Resurrection. It is a greater thing to tell some soul out of personal knowledge and conviction that Christ is risen, and that therefore there is hope for all men.

The risen King and His enemies. This story is told in one brief paragraph. Their last weapon was a lie, and their last craft was folly. There we leave them, in order to follow Him.

The King reigning. Our attention is first directed to the disciples. They kept the appointment with Him, in Galilee. They yielded wholly to Him, for they worshipped Him. Yet they were imperfect, for " some doubted." Nevertheless everything He subsequently said was addressed to the whole of them, to the men who doubted as well as to those who worshipped.

The King was standing upon a mountain; the eleven men were round Him, and perhaps the five hundred brethren were round Him also. How He loved the mountains! It was upon a mountain that He uttered the ethic of His Kingdom; that He came to the perfecting of His Manhood in transfiguration glory; that He uttered His great prophecies, so imperfectly understood even unto this hour; that He wept over the doomed city He was to reject.

Again He gathered His disciples to a mountain. There He uttered three things; His claim, His commands, and His final declaration.

His claim; "All authority hath been given unto Me in heaven and on earth." These were the phrases of the prayer He taught them when He uttered the Manifesto of His Kingdom, "Our Father Who art in the heavens, Hallowed be Thy name. Thy Kingdom come. Thy will be done, *as in heaven, so on earth.*" Now He claimed that His place in the economy of God is that of all authority in heaven and on earth.

His command; "Go ye therefore; and disciple the nations." He did not say, make disciples of, there is no substantive in the command except *nations.* This command includes a far larger enterprise than that of bringing individual souls to Himself. It is a command to influence all the nations toward His standards and His ideals. Disciple the nations, teach the nations. Then He spoke of the individual work. "Baptizing them;" that is the work of bringing individual souls into relationship with God, in the name of the Father and of the Son and of the Spirit. "Teaching them;" that is the work of insisting on the ethic of the Kingdom. It is a great and gracious and spacious commission. Observe its relationship to His claim. He is put in the supreme place of the economy. All authority hath been given unto Me. Therefore His Church is to go forth to bring the whole world into recognition of the place of authority in which God has put Him, and into agreement therewith by submission.

His final word; "I am with you always, even unto the end of the world." Many years ago I was sitting by the side of an aged saint of God, an old woman of eighty-five. I had been reading this chapter to her, and when I finished I looked at her and said, That is a great promise. She looked up and said sharply, with the light of sanctified humour in her eyes; That is not a promise at all, that is a fact. Oh if the Church of God could remember that *fact!*

There is no story of ascension here; the last matter is that the King takes the Divine name by which Israel had known Him, "I am," and puts it into living association with His disciples as they go forward on His business; "*I am with you.*" The ideal of ancient Israel is to be fulfilled in the Church, Emmanuel, God with us. "All the days," days of sunshine, and of shadow; days of strength and days of weakness; days of battle, and days of victory; the longest day and the shortest day.

Have we really crowned this King? If we are only interested in Him, we sadly fail. On His head are many diadems. He is waiting for the crown of our manhood, our womanhood. He cannot rest in us, until He have our love and our loyalty. If we reply, Yes, He is our King, then are we obeying Him in His final command; "Go ye therefore and disciple the nations"? Are we helping to make our own nation like Him? Are we winning individual souls to Him? Is the highest passion of our life to weave another garland wherewith to deck His brow, to place another gem in His diadem? If not; then to see such a King and not to obey Him is to add to our condemnation! But to see Him, and know Him, and crown Him; and to suffer with Him as we serve, is life indeed.

Printed in the United States of America